MW00439538

THE JESUS THE JEWS NEVER KNEW

The Jesus The Jews Never Knew

Sepher Toldoth Yeshu
and the
Quest of the Historical Jesus
In Jewish Sources

Frank R. Zindler

2003
American Atheist Press
Cranford, New Jersey

American Atheist Press
P. O. Box 5733
Parsippany, New Jersey 07054-6733

www.atheists.org

Copyright © 2003 American Atheist Press
All rights reserved
Published March 2003
Printed in the United States of America

ISBN (paper): 1-57884-916-0

Library of Congress Cataloging-in-Publication Data

Zindler, Frank R.
  The Jesus the Jews never new : Sepher Toldoth Yeshu and the quest of the historical Jesus in Jewish sources / Frank R. Zindler.
    p. cm.
  Includes bibliographical references and index.
    ISBN 1-57884-916-0 (pbk.)
    1. Jesus Christ—Jewish interpretations—History—To 1500 2. Christianity—Controversial literature. 3. Jesus Christ—Historicity. 4. Rabbinical literature—History and criticism. 5. Toledot Yeshu. 6. Jesus Christ—Biography. I. Title.

  BM620.Z56 2003
  232.9'06—dc21

                                                    2003041834

About Frank R. Zindler

Formerly a professor of biology and geology and chairman of the Division of Science at Fulton-Montgomery Community College (SUNY-Johnstown), Frank R. Zindler for many years has been employed as a linguist, senior editor, and analyst of biochemical literature by a major scientific publishing society in Ohio. A veteran of more than four hundred radio and television talk-shows, he has debated many creationists, theologians, and purveyors of the preternatural in defense of Atheism, naturalism, and evolutionary science. Since the brutal murder in 1995 of Robin Murray-O'Hair, the editor at that time of American Atheist Press, Zindler has succeeded her in the role of managing editor.

In Anguished Memory

of

Madalyn Murray O'Hair
Jon Garth Murray
Robin Murray-O'Hair

Liberators of the Human Mind

If we travel to the very sepulchre of Christ, we have only to discover that he was never there: history seeks evidence of his existence as a man, but finds no more trace of it, than of the shadow that flitted across the wall. The star of Bethlehem shone not upon her path, and the order of the universe was suspended without her observance. She asks with the Magi of the east, "where is he that is born King of the Jews," and like them, finds no solution of her inquiry, but the guidance that guides as well to one place as another; descriptions that apply to Esculapius, as well as to Jesus; prophecies, without evidence that they were ever prophesied; miracles, which those who are said to have seen, are said also to have denied that they saw; narratives without authorities, facts without dates, and records without names.

—Robert Taylor, Oakham Gaol, February 19, 1829

CONTENTS

PART III *Sepher Toldoth Yeshu*

ILLUSTRATIONS

PREFACE

After American Atheist Press sold out its last copies of Foote and Wheeler's *The Jewish Life of Christ: Being the Sepher Toldoth Jeshu*, orders for the title continued unabated, it fell to my lot as editor of AAP to prepare a reprint of the little book. Originally published in London in 1885 by the Progressive Publishing Company, nearly a century later Dr. Madalyn Murray O'Hair had brought out an American Atheist Press edition of the booklet (in 1982) and had supplied a foreword relating the study of the *Toldoth Yeshu* ('The Genealogy of Jesus') to Atheist interests. Rereading the *Toldoth* for the first time in nearly twenty years, I was dismayed to discover enormous numbers of typographical and capitalization errors, as well as poorly reproduced Hebrew words. (In fact, on one page there was a space in a line where Hebrew text should have been inserted but had been overlooked!) Worse yet, a crucial part of the text – the part dealing with Bar Panther's seduction of Miriam (Mary) – was reprinted in Latin, with no English translation for modern readers no longer plagued by Victorian prudishness – or blasphemy laws. (Foote had been imprisoned twelve months for blasphemy and couldn't risk publishing such inflammatory material in the Queen's English.) It was instantly obvious that reprinting this Atheist classic would not be a simple task.

American Atheists stalwart Josh Karpf volunteered to prepare a corrected copy of the text in electronic format, and momentarily the burden was off my shoulders. But my mind kept coming back to the book during the entire period that Josh was working on it. Something seemed incomplete about the book. It seemed to be a piece of literature put forth without a context – gratuitously set before Atheist readers who could only speculate as to the true nature and significance of the work.

When Josh sent the edited text back to me along with numerous criticisms and suggestions, I realized that AAP could not simply reissue the booklet by itself. It had to be supplemented with other material. But with what, and to what purpose?

It occurred to me that readers of the book all too easily could draw the erroneous conclusion that the work derived from a single medieval manuscript and might even be an anti-Semitic fraud – despite the preface, introduction, and notes attesting to ancient authors' knowledge of the core of *Toldoth* material. It seemed advisable to add a second version of the antigospel – doubling the size of the book so readers could better perceive it in the context of an evolving literary tradition rather than as an isolated polemic effusion. (Although including several further versions representing highly variant traditions of the *Toldoth* would have been even more useful, this did not prove to be practicable given the constraints of time.)

The *Toldoth Yeshu* translation published by Foote and Wheeler in 1885 had been based on a book published by Johannes Wagenseil in 1681 [*Tela Ignea Satanae. Hoc est: Arcani et horribiles Judæorum adversus Christum Deum et Christianam Religionem Libri ANEKΔΟΤΟΥ*]. For a second version of the *Toldoth* story, I decided to publish a translation of the so-called Strassburg Manuscript, which had been printed in Hebrew and German in 1902 by Samuel Krauss [*Das Leben Jesu nach jüdischen Quellen*] and translated into English and published by G. R. S. Mead in 1903 [*Did Jesus Live 100 B.C.? An Enquiry into the Talmud Jesus Stories, the Toldoth Jeschu, and Some Curious Statements of Epiphanius – Being a Contribution to the Study of Christian Origins*].

After scouring the scholarly literature on the *Toldoth* in order to annotate Mead's English text, I realized that the two-part book would still be something of a puzzle to readers needing a broader frame of reference in which to assess the value – or lack thereof – of the *Toldoth Yeshu*. It became obvious that a rather detailed introductory essay would be needed to provide a context for evaluation. But just what sort of frame of reference was needed?

For most Atheist readers, the major question evoked by any ancient witness's mention of Jesus was a fundamental one: How does this affect conclusions about the historicity (or non-historicity) of Jesus of Nazareth? Since for many years I have argued that Jesus was not a historical figure, but have never published very much about alleged Semitic religious testimonies to his historicity, it seemed desirable to discuss the *Toldoth* data with respect to the basic question, Did the ancient Jews know Jesus?

This having been decided, I was surprised by the realization that the book I would be offering to the public would not be simply a new edition of the *Toldoth Yeshu*. What I had imagined would be a short foreword to the *Toldoth Yeshu* turned out to be the focal point of the book – with the *Toldoth* texts themselves relegated to the status of evidentiary appendices. Seldom has there been a better example of a tail wagging a dog!

The result of all this editorial convolution is the present *The Jesus The Jews Never Knew: Sepher Toldoth Yeshu and the Quest of the Historical Jesus in Jewish Sources*. Although most of my research perforce has had to deal with rather old scholarly works, I have tried to incorporate the findings and opinions of modern scholarship as well.

Since so much of this book is not of my own writing, it is – alas – a hodgepodge with regard to style and spelling. But I could hardly abolish the King James diction of Foote and Wheeler's text, nor could I change source-document spellings of the name *Yeshu* ('Jesus'). Spelled *Jeschu* in the German literature and *Jeshu* in the English literature dependent thereon, *Yeshu* spelled with *j* for the Hebrew semivowel *y* occurs in titles as well as texts, and so has become petrified bibliographically in card catalogs all over the world. The Germanic spellings of this word had to be retained for bibliographic accuracy, if nothing else. I am confident, however, that readers will adjust to this inconsistency of spelling and will be no more annoyed than when seeing the Israelite god referred to variously as *Yahweh, Jahweh*, or *Jehovah* in the same text. Changing fashions in the transliteration of Hebrew and Aramaic words is another problem I have been unable to deal with consistently – except that in quoted material I have always reproduced the spelling conventions of the authors quoted. Thus, readers will encounter both *Sepher* and *Sefer* ('book'), *Toldoth, Toldot*, and I think even *Tol^edot* ('generations'), and many similar variations.

One last explanation – if not apology – is in order concerning my inclusion of an entire chapter on Balaam. Highly educated though most of my readers might be, I would guess that only a small fraction of them (especially the Atheists) had ever heard the story of Balaam and his talking ass before picking up this book. Certainly, most readers will have expected this book to deal only with the historical Jesus problem. (I too expected that when I embarked on this project.) Upon reaching that chapter, some may feel exasperated at having to slog through so much material about a character whom I show many pages earlier has nothing whatsoever to do with Jesus. By adding a full chapter on Balaam, I might fairly be accused of flogging a dead ass.

However, at the time that the awful realization sank in that I would have to write a book – not just an introductory chapter – I resolved to be as exhaustively complete as possible. I wanted to deal with *every* datum ever alleged to be an allusion to Jesus in early Jewish sources. Any less thorough approach would leave me myself in a condition of not knowing for sure if any early Jewish sources did or did not know of Jesus of Nazareth. So I have dealt with each character in turn who has ever been alleged to be a code for Jesus.

When I began work on Balaam, however, I discovered that the literature about him is vast. It turns out that early rabbis and other Jewish authors were thousands of times more interested in Balaam than in Jesus. Very soon, I felt like Brer Rabbit boxing Tar Baby. Every time I hit him with a blow I thought should finish him off, he stuck to me all the harder. Only when I had written everything about Balaam that even remotely relates to the theme of this book could I be free of him. Readers who find themselves unenchanted by this legendary enchanter may wish to skip over the lengthy excursus about him between chapters 6 and 7.

But Balaam was not the only surprise with which I have had to deal in my effort to place this book before my readers. After the book was essentially finished and I was attending to what I thought were minor cleanup tasks, I happened upon photocopies of several articles I had obtained a year earlier when beginning this project. Buried amidst the general clutter of my office, they had gone unread and unnoticed during the entire period of my research and writing. What a shock they gave me when I glanced through them!

The first article, by Louis Ginzberg of the Jewish Theological Seminary of America, was titled "Some Observations on the Attitude of the Synagogue towards the Apocalyptic-Eschatological Writings" and had been published in 1922 in the *Journal of Biblical Literature*. In it Ginzberg came to the same conclusions that I reach in part 2 of this book, *viz.*, there are no nicknames by which Jesus is discussed in the Talmuds. For the most part, however, he did not present all his evidence for his conclusion and I considered it a good omen that I, probably using different lines of reasoning and data selection, had independently come to the same conclusion.

While the first article merely presented me with a pleasant surprise, the second article had an effect on me that can only be described as stunning. Written in 1938 by Jacob Z. Lauterbach of Cincinnati's Hebrew Union College and published posthumously in 1951, the lengthy article was entitled "Jesus in the Talmud." It could fairly be described as a précis of part 2 of my book – to

which had been added some material that I too had explored but
had decided was not relevant enough to include in this book.
Lauterbach even allowed for the fact that Jesus might not have
been historical!

Only the cliché about being hit by a ton of bricks can describe
how I felt after reading through Lauterbach's monograph. I had
spent a full year of sometimes painfully difficult intellectual
exploration – producing a text that advanced at a glacial pace,
"inch by inch, line by line" – only to find that all the things I
thought were my unique discoveries had been committed to paper
cogently, clearly, and convincingly a year before I was born. The
birthing of this book has been painful.

Consequently, I cannot present *The Jesus the Jews Never
Knew* to readers as a novelty in the literal sense. However, since
in twenty-first century America the notion that Jesus never lived
has the *appearance* of novelty, I commend my work to the public
with the hope that what I have written will nevertheless excite
wonder and stimulate critical thought. Finally, I am consoled by
the fact that although my professional education has been in
geology and neurophysiology, I have managed to reach the same
conclusions in a year as did one of the giants among humanities
scholars after a lifetime of study. It is immensely reassuring to
find that scientific procedures and modes of thought can be
applied successfully in the humanities. That may prove to be the
most important discovery I have made.

ACKNOWLEDGMENTS

Gratitude is expressed to Josh Karpf for his hard work in
purging this book of so many errors and for his valuable advice.
Errors remaining in this complex publication are in spite of him,
not because of him. A number of stylistic indelicacies have been
removed at his suggestion. For those that remain, I alone am to
blame. To John Sikos go thanks for his production of a usable,
analytical index. Thanks to him, readers will not find an entry
Jesus followed by an unbroken string of two hundred page numbers. To my wife Ann goes the credit for the cover art and for the
immense effort expended in solving endless problems in typeset-
ting and page layout on her trusty Macintosh.

INTRODUCTION

We can be quite certain that the miracle-working Jesus described in the New Testament never existed. Even if we disregard the fact that from a scientific point of view his magic-mongering can be ruled out *a priori*, if he really had "cleansed" all those lepers, given sight to the congenitally blind, catered a large mob with a bit of fish bait and pigeon snacks, restored locomotion to the halt and the lame, turned water to wine at a wedding in Gentile territory, walked on water, wreaked financial havoc in a foreign country by destroying two thousand pigs that were the livelihood for who knows how many hogranchers, and withered a fig tree with his invective-laden breath, at least *someone* would have recorded it at the time and would have been motivated enough by the shock of such events to broadcast the news and see to it that the reports were passed on to posterity. While many such miracles were indeed reported in antiquity, none are attributed to "Jesus of Nazareth" – nor could they have been, since the existence of a place called Nazareth* is unattested until well after the second century of the common era. Rather, such miracles are attributed to a variety of gods and heroes and had become oft-retold tales already by the time our alleged messiah is supposed to have lived.

---

*It is often claimed in biblical archaeology references that the present-day city of Nazareth was inhabited during the first centuries BCE and CE. All such claims are based uncritically upon the unscientific work of Franciscan monks who excavated Christian tourist sites from the 1890s to the middle of the twentieth century. Most of the blame for the disinformation surrounding Nazareth archaeology must go to Fr. Bellarmino Bagatti [1905–90][In-1] and his predecessor Fr. Prosper Viaud, who perhaps permanently destroyed the stratification of the Nazareth site and made it impossible for real scientists ever to unscramble the evidence. At any rate, neither the Franciscans nor anyone else has ever found the remains of any buildings that could be ascribed to the centuries straddling the turn of the era – when Jesus is said to have lived there and was driven out of a synagogue near the crest of the Nazareth hill [Luke 4:28–30]. Of course, no first-century synagogue has ever been discovered at "Nazareth" – on top of the hill or anywhere else at the site. The first

If the prodigies that the synoptic gospels associate with the death of Christ had really occurred, it is unthinkable that the whole world would not have noted. If there really had been a "darkness at noon" [Matt 27:45, Mark 15:33, Luke 23:44] covering *the whole earth*† around the time of the Passover death of Jesus – a time when an eclipse of the sun is astronomically impossible – certainly the Chinese, Indian, and Babylonian astronomers and astrologers would have recorded it and reported it. In fact, even the author of the Gospel of John could not have failed to mention it!

Apologists sometimes cite the obscure writers Thallus and Phlegon as having reported this very "darkness at noon." However, virtually nothing is known of these characters – not even when approximately they lived. Furthermore, their original texts are reported as claims of a solar eclipse – thus ruling out the reported event as a candidate for the miracle of Matthew 27:45. Most assuredly, if Thallus and Phlegon had

---

mention of Nazareth outside the New Testament (it is unknown to the Hebrew Bible, the Talmud, Josephus, and all pre-Christian historians and geographers) *might* be on a fragment of a stone tablet unearthed at Caesarea on the Mediterranean coast of Palestine.[In-2] The Hebrew word interpreted as 'Nazareth' (נצרת) is actually broken on the right-hand margin, and it is not absolutely certain that the broken letter on the right is a *nun* (נ), although that is highly likely. Nevertheless, even if the word is indeed *Nazareth*, it is no evidence whatsoever of a place by that name existing in the centuries around the turn of the era. The stone slab bearing the inscription was derived from a synagogue built at the end of the third or beginning of the fourth century CE.[In-3] By that time it is entirely possible that the Nazareth site was inhabited. In fact, it might have been founded as early as 135 CE, by Jews who had been expelled from Jerusalem after the collapse of the Bar Kozeba (Kochba) revolt.

†Rendering the Greek ὅλην τὴν γῆν as "all the earth," as in the King James Version translation of Luke 23:44. It can be argued, however, that the Greek should be rendered "all the land" – as does the KJV for Matthew 27:45 and Mark 15:33 – implying that only the Land of Judaea was blacked out. Unfortunately for orthodox apologists, there were lots of astronomically capable Greeks and Romans in that country who would have reported the astronomical anomaly. While the prodigy might then not have been reported in China or India, it certainly would have reverberated within the bounds of the Roman Empire.

really published a credible report of this prodigy, it is impossible that Christian scribes would not have preserved the actual works of these authors; they would not have settled for mere hearsay.

But hearsay is all we have. Thallus is mentioned only in Julius Africanus, and Julius Africanus survives only in the form of quotations in Eusebius and other Church Fathers! Phlegon also is mentioned by Africanus, as well as by Origen.

All the surviving scraps of Africanus [c200–245 CE] can be found in a single chapter of one volume of *The Ante-Nicene Fathers*! In a fragment from his *Chronography* surviving only in the works of Georgius Syncellus, Africanus mentions Thallus and Phlegon with regard to the "darkness at noon." Africanus is trying to explain the problem of the worldwide darkness that supposedly attended the crucifixion:

> On the whole world there pressed a most fearful darkness; and the rocks were rent by an earthquake, and many places in Judea and other districts were thrown down. This darkness Thallus, in the third book of his *History,* calls, as appears to me without reason, an eclipse of the sun. For the Hebrews celebrate the Passover on the 14th day according to the moon, and the passion of our Saviour falls on the day before the Passover; but an eclipse of the sun takes place only when the moon comes under the sun. And it cannot happen at any other time but in the interval between the first day of the new moon and the last of the old, that is, at their junction: how then should an eclipse be supposed to happen when the moon is almost diametrically opposite the sun? Let that opinion pass however; let it carry the majority with it; and let this portent of the world be deemed an eclipse of the sun, like others a portent only to the eye. Phlegon records that, in the time of Tiberius Caesar, at full moon, there was a full eclipse of the sun from the sixth hour to the ninth — manifestly that one of which we speak. But what has an eclipse in common with an earthquake, the rending rocks, and the resurrection of the dead, and so great a perturbation throughout the universe? Surely no such event as this is recorded for a long period. But it was a darkness induced by God, because the Lord happened then to suffer. And calculation makes out that the period of 70 weeks, as noted in Daniel, is completed at this time.[In-4]

We may note that Africanus seems not to know of any other secular authorities who attest to a universal darkness at the time in question, other than these two obviously ignorant authors. Of what value are "historians" who think an eclipse of the sun is possible at the time of the Passover? Nevertheless, Africanus – whose knowledge of geography is so poor that in his *Epistle to Aristides* he states that Nazareth is a town in Judaea – is desperate to prove that the world turned dark at the time of the crucifixion, and so he has to quote these obviously incompetent 'authorities.' Notice that there is no clue as to when Thallus and Phlegon might have lived. They could have been contemporaries of Africanus, for all we know here.

Origen ("Born of Horus": 185–254 CE), in his *Against Celsus*, mentions Phlegon, but not Thallus. In Book 2 of *Against Celsus,* Origen refers to Phlegon three times – twice with regard to the prodigies attending the crucifixion:

Chap. 33....And with regard to the eclipse in the time of Tiberius Caesar, in whose reign Jesus appears to have been crucified, and the great earthquakes which then took place, Phlegon too, *I think,* has written in the thirteenth or fourteenth book of his Chronicles. [*Interestingly, Africanus seems not to have noticed Phlegon's mention of the earthquake.*]

Chap. 59. He [Celsus] imagines also that both the earthquake and the darkness were an invention; but regarding these, we have in the preceding pages made our defence, according to our ability, adducing the testimony of Phlegon, who relates that these events took place at the time when our Saviour suffered. [In-5] [*emphasis added*]

Phlegon clearly is being cited from memory here, and Origen might have his facts scrambled. The second citation adds no new knowledge of Phlegon's teachings. There is no clue in any of these passages as to when Phlegon lived. He could have been a contemporary of Origen or only a bit older. Certainly, there is no reason to suppose that Phlegon is a contemporary witness to any historical Jesus. He may have been an anti-Christian polemicist who simply took the Christian story and criticized it. It is clear that none of these "witnesses" is early enough to have witnessed an historical Jesus. They tell only of the growing Christian movement and its opposition.

If, at the time of Jesus' "yielding up the ghost," the veil of the temple in Jerusalem had really been "rent in twain from the top to the bottom," surely the contemporary Jewish theologian and writer Philo Judaeus [c20 BCE–c50 CE] would have recorded it, and the Jewish historian Flavius Josephus [37 CE–c95 CE] would have learned of the fact from his father Matthias [b. 10th year of the reign of Archelaus (r. 4 BCE–6 CE)], who was of the priestly caste and a contemporary of our alleged wonder-worker.*

Finally, if all those graves that were supposed to have opened up at the time of the unrecorded crucifixion (a Friday) had in fact stayed open – with their cadaverous contents exposed all the while over a Passover weekend until Sunday morning – certainly it would have drawn the attention of many people who could read and write. Moreover, if, at the start of the workweek, all those saintly corpses came back to life as reported in Matthew 23:51b–53† and marched into town to report for duty, accounts of the macabre event could not have been suppressed. The Matthean story would have been superfluous, and the silence of Mark, Luke, and John concerning this miracle would not seem so odd. (Of course, the fact of so many people ultimately coming to be issued second death certificates might itself have become a story overshadowing the tale of Jesus – imagine how many biographies would have been written about how so-and-so died *the second time!* – thus necessitating the Matthean report after all, to correct the less sensational Jesus stories told in Mark, Luke, and John.)

Thus, the gospel Jesus could not have existed.

Apologists not easily being daunted, those of a more liberal stripe might readily agree with what I have just written but argue that nevertheless there was *someone* behind the gospel stories – someone who, though not possessed of magical powers, had so powerful a personality that he spawned the gospel legends in the minds of his (unknown) followers and their converts. While the gospels cannot be taken literally, such might argue, they are at least evidence of *somebody* extraordinary. But these apologists miss the irony of Jesus being an extraordinary and memorable character, while simultaneously being so obscure that no secular record of him survives. (It is ironic also that despite being a well-known public figure and rabble-rouser, Jesus nevertheless is so colorless and forgettable that the authorities have to bribe Judas to point him out!)

---

*Not surprisingly, Josephus is made to testify of the rending of the temple veil, the massacre of the innocents of Bethlehem, and the raising of Lazarus in the medieval Old Russian translation.[In-6]

†Matthew 23:51b–53— "...and the earth did quake, and the rocks rent; And the graves were opened; and many bodies of the saints which slept arose, And came out of the graves *after his resurrection,* and went into the holy city, and appeared unto many."

Believers in a mortal, mundane Jesus underlying the gospel tales are usually sophisticated enough to understand that the gospels themselves cannot be adequate proof of their hypothesis, and they realize that extrabiblical evidence is needed. Otherwise, the hero of the gospels is indistinguishable from a fictional character conceived in mediocrity.

Unfortunately for the believers in an historical Jesus, there are no secular Gentile accounts early enough to be evidence of *Christ* as distinguishable from *Christianity*. Publius Cornelius Tacitus [c55 CE–c120 CE] – even if his wild story of Nero's persecution of Christians and his mention of a "Christus" who was put to death under sentence of "the procurator Pontius Pilatus" are not Christian interpolations* – could not have obtained his misinformation in official Roman records. Had he in fact consulted official records, he would have found that the Roman ruler during the first half of the first century was called a *prefect* (Lat. *præfectus*), not a *procurator*. According to the Pilate inscription recovered from Caesarea, Pilate bore the title *eparchos* (ἔπαρχος), the Greek equivalent of *præfectus*. (The equivalent of *procurator* is *epitropos* (ἐπίτροπος) in Greek)[In-7] Quite certainly, Tacitus could not have been consulting official records concerning the execution of Jesus. Moreover, he would not have found *Christus* used as a personal name in official Roman records, since the word is the Greco-Latin equivalent of the title *Messiah*. We can be quite sure that Tacitus never saw an official document reading something like "We executed the Messiah last Friday." At most, assuming his 'testimony' not to be a forgery, Tacitus is attesting to the existence of Christians at the time in question and is retailing hearsay derived from them. Everything he 'knows' can be found in the Apostles' Creed. He is no more a witness to the historicity of Jesus than he is to the historicity of Jupiter, Venus, Isis, or Mithra – of whose devotees he knew far more than he knew about Christians.

---

*John E. Remsburg, in his book *The Christ: A Critical Review and Analysis of the Evidences of His Existence* [In-8] lists fourteen reasons for considering the Tacitus passage [*Annals*, Book 15, sec. 44] to be spurious:

    1. It is not quoted by the Christian fathers.
    2. Tertullian was familiar with the writings of Tacitus, and his arguments demanded the citation of this evidence had it existed. [*In chapter 5 of his* Apology, *after claiming that the*

emperor Tiberius [d. 37 CE] had been a Christian, Tertullian writes, "Consult your histories; you will there find that Nero was the first who assailed with the imperial sword the Christian sect, making progress then especially at Rome." In chapter 21, after asserting that Pilate also had become a Christian, he says that "His disciples also… after suffering greatly themselves from the persecutions of the Jews… at last by Nero's cruel sword sowed the seed of Christian blood at Rome." There is no hint that this man's balloon-like imagination had ever been inflated by Tacitus' tale of Christians being burned as night-lights in Nero's garden. It is even possible that Tertullian's Latin remarks later would become a stimulus prompting a forger of refined Latinity to compose the romance now found in the Annals *of Tacitus.]*

3. Clement of Alexandria, at the beginning of the third century, made a compilation of all the recognitions of Christ and Christianity that had been made by pagan writers up to his time. The writings of Tacitus furnished no recognition of them.

4. Origen, in his controversy with Celsus, would undoubtedly have used it had it existed.

5. The ecclesiastical historian Eusebius, in the fourth century, cites all the evidences of Christianity obtainable from Jewish and Pagan sources, but makes no mention of Tacitus.

6. It is not quoted by any Christian writer prior to the fifteenth century.

7. At this time but one copy of the "Annals" existed, and this copy, it is claimed, was made in the eighth century—600 years after the time of Tacitus.

8. As this single copy was in the possession of a Christian, the insertion of a forgery was easy.

9. Its severe criticisms of Christianity do not necessarily disprove its Christian origin. No ancient witness was more desirable than Tacitus, but his introduction at so late a period would make rejection certain unless Christian forgery could be made to appear improbable.

10. It is admitted by Christian writers that the works of Tacitus have not been preserved with any considerable degree of fidelity. In the writings ascribed to him are believed to be some of the writings of Quintillian.

11 The blood-curdling story about the frightful orgies of Nero reads like some Christian romance of the dark ages, and not like Tacitus.

12. In fact, this story, in nearly the same words, omitting the reference to Christ, is to be found in the writings of Sulpicius Severus, a Christian of the fifth century. *[It is entirely possible that the story found in Sulpicius Severus' Chronicles 2:29 – itself*

apparently modeled upon the story of Galerius' burning of Nicomedia in 303 CE – served as the stimulus for a Renaissance forger to add the story to Tacitus' Annals.]

13. Suetonius, while mercilessly condemning the reign of Nero, says that in his public entertainments he took particular care that no human lives should be sacrificed, "not even those of condemned criminals." [*In his* Lives of the Cæsars [Book 6 §6] *he notes that "Punishment was inflicted on the Christians, a class of men given to a new and mischievous superstition." The Latin* affligo supplicium *used here can sometimes mean capital punishment but is not specific for it. The fact that Suetonius shortly before this passage asserted that Nero avoided killing people in his public entertainments argues against the translation of this Latin expression in the meaning of capital punishment.*]

14. At the time that the conflagration occurred, Tacitus himself declares that Nero was not in Rome, but at Antium.

To these arguments a fifteenth point could be added: Tacitus himself when dealing with this same period in his earlier work [*Histories,* 5.9.2] gives no hint of this outrage. To the contrary, he says that in Palestine at this time "all was quiet."[In-9]

Chapters 11–16 of the *Annals* all derive from a single manuscript, the so-called Second Medicean Manuscript, which now is preserved in the Laurentian Library. It has been dated to the eleventh century, but there being no radiocarbon dates to substantiate this, it might very well prove to be a fifteenth-century forgery. The circumstances surrounding the discovery of this and other manuscripts of Tacitus' works are extremely murky – at least as they were described by Georg Voigt in his 1895 treatise *Die Wiederbelebung Des Classischen Altertums* (*The Revival of Classical Antiquity*).[In-10] Indeed, so suspect was the situation in which the sole surviving manuscripts of Tacitus' historical works were recovered, several writers of the nineteenth century were able to argue that the *Annals* in their entirety were counterfeit! In 1878, a certain Londoner named Ross published *Tacitus and Bracciolini: The Annals Forged in the XVth Century* – according to which Poggio Bracciolini forged the whole shebang between 1422 and 1429. Then, in 1890, P. Hochart's *De l'Authenticité des Annales et des Histoires de Tacite* argued for the same Italian scholar as the forger.

It is perhaps relevant to the question of the authenticity of the *Histories* and *Annals* – the works that serve as the defining standard for Tacitean Latinity and style – to note that the supposedly quintessence of Tacitus' style is not to be found in the

If Tacitus can be of no use as evidence of any historical Jesus, still less can Pliny the Younger [c62 CE–c113 CE] or Suetonius [c69 CE–c140 CE] be enlisted in that cause. They are so late that their "witness" is of no utility at all. And so, the only hope for apologists of a historical Jesus is to find evidence of their putative person in Jewish sources.

Unfortunately for scholars on both sides of the historicity question, the number of historically relevant Jewish materials that have survived to modern times is lamentably small. With the destruction of the Jerusalem Temple of Yahweh in 70 CE and the removal of all Jews from Jerusalem in 135 CE, it cannot be doubted that many records and documents were lost. Then, with the accession of Christianity to political power in the fourth century, the endless censorings, forgeries, and bookburnings that marked the triumphal "progress" of that *superstitio* pretty much emptied the cupboard of potentially useful information.

Apart from the writings of Philo of Alexandria and the Dead Sea Scrolls, almost no Jewish materials contemporary with our would-be messiah survive. The writings of the Jewish historian Josephus, which are roughly contemporary with the fabrication of our canonical gospels, therefore have received the most attention from apologists seeking evidence of historicity in Jewish sources. A chapter of this book is devoted to the Josephus data. As for the Dead Sea Scrolls, no mention of Jesus whatsoever can be found. Not surprisingly, many authors have made sensational claims that the so-called "Righteous Teacher" of the Scrolls texts was actually Jesus, and "the Man of Sin" was none other than St. Paul. Examination of such claims, however, is beyond the scope of this little book and, in my opinion, is not justifiable by the quality of the claims.

Distant seconds as potential sources of historical information concerning Jesus are the Mishnah (completed around the year 200 CE), the Tosefta (completed somewhat after the Mishnah), and the two Talmuds – the Jerusalem (Palestinian) and the Babylonian – which elaborate upon the Mishnah and were

works concerning which there is little or no question of authenticity. The *Dialogus de Oratoribus* and the *Agricola* resemble the styles of Cicero and Sallust more than what is taken to be the style of Tacitus himself! It is amusing to contemplate the possibility that one of the greatest models of Classical Latin Style might actually be a model of Renaissance Latin Style.

completed in written form around the years 395 and 500 CE, respectively. In even more remote third position for evidentiary purposes is the so-called *Sepher Toldoth Yeshu* (ספר תולדות ישו) – the 'Book of the Genealogy of Jesus,' which has been the main stimulus for creation of the present work.

In the pages that follow, all of the above-mentioned Jewish sources are examined within the frame of reference of the Jesus historicity question. Appendix A comprises a new edition of the 1982 American Atheist Press reprint of the 1885 *The Jewish Life Of Christ: Being the Sepher Toldoth Jeshu,* by G. W. Foote and J. M. Wheeler, with an introduction by Madalyn Murray O'Hair. Appendix B is a reprint of another version of the *Toldoth* story – a version first published in English in 1903 by the London Theosophical Publishing Society, in G. R. S. Mead's *Did Jesus Live 100 B.C.?* – to which I have added considerable commentary of my own.

PART I

EARLY SOURCES

CHAPTER I

Philo Judaeus and Others
Who Never Knew Jesus

Despite nearly two millennia of Christian propaganda, we still do not really know where Christianity began, nor do we have convincing evidence to support the thesis that the religion stems from the career of a single person or began at any specific point in time. Proof that Christian origins differ qualitatively from those of Hinduism, say, or, from those of the hoary religion of Egypt, is utterly absent. According to the traditional myth of origin, the new religion began in Jerusalem after the crucifixion of a failed messiah. There exists, however, absolutely no extrabiblical evidence sufficient to prove that claim. No eyewitness accounts whatsoever survive from the Jewish homeland concerning any figure that credibly can be equated to the gospel Jesus. Such circumstantial evidence as we have would seem to make it just as likely – if not more likely – that Christianity began in Egypt (Alexandria) or Rome, or Syria (Antioch), or even in Greece or Asia Minor. Whatever the truth might have been, it is significant that *no* eyewitness accounts of the career of "Jesus of Nazareth" have survived from *any* of these areas – despite the fact that there were plenty of writers in existence at the time (or shortly thereafter) Jesus is supposed to have lived. If ever there had been a historical Jesus, this is embarrassingly hard to explain. If Christianity is simply the result of an evolutionary development that progressively incorporated elements from multiple religious communities throughout the Roman Empire, however, this all makes a lot of sense. In fact, the observed lack of eyewitness reports can be seen as predicted by the evolutionary model. Christianity seems to be the product of religious evolution, not revolution.

John E. Remsburg, in his *The Christ: A Critical Review and Analysis of the Evidences of His Existence*,[1-1] lists some writers who would likely have commented on "The Christ" if they had heard any whisper of his affairs:

Josephus	Arrian
Philo Judaeus	Petronius
Seneca	Dion Pruseus
Pliny the Elder	Paterculus
Suetonius	Appian
Juvenal	Theon of Smyrna
Martial	Phlegon
Persius	Pomponius Mela
Plutarch	Quintius Curtius
Justus of Tiberias	Lucian
Apollonius	Pausanias
Pliny the Younger	Valerius Flaccus
Tacitus	Florus Lucius
Quintilian	Favorinus
Lucanus	Phaedrus
Epictetus	Damis
Silius Italicus	Aulus Gellius
Statius	Columella
Ptolemy	Dio Chrysostom
Valerius Maximus	Appion of Alexandria

While it is true that four of the names in the above list have been claimed in fact to mention Jesus, two of the witnesses (Josephus and Tacitus) almost certainly have been altered by Christian hands, and two more (Suetonius and Pliny the Younger) are too late to be evidence of Christ as distinguished from Christianity – even if they should prove not to be Christian interpolations. The lengthy list would be even more impressive if it were true that the texts of Josephus and Tacitus *were* authentic. For if the hullabaloo surrounding Jesus and his associates were loud enough to draw the attention of these Roman writers (Josephus, though Jewish, became a Roman citizen and had strong ties in Rome), it is inexplicable that the noise had not been heard by all the other Greco-Roman authors listed above.

1.1. Justus of Tiberias

If the traditional view of Christian origins be true, it is even more difficult to account for the silence of Jewish authors closer to the setting of the gospel stories. One of these is the historian Justus of Tiberias, the great rival of Josephus. Although Tiberias, the city for which he is named, is mentioned only in the Gospel of

John [6:23], and Jesus is never said to have visited there, it was right in the midst of Jesus' alleged Galilean activities, and it is hard to understand why he is never represented as having had *some* contact with the place. (A similar puzzle is presented by Sepphoris, the Roman capital of Galilee, just five miles away from modern Nazareth. If the scenes and sites of the gospel stories were created to serve symbolic rather than historical purposes, this all is understandable. If the gospels were histories, they could not have failed to have mentioned Tiberias and Sepphoris.) Although the writings of Justus of Tiberias have been lost (their loss is very hard to account for if they had ever mentioned Jesus or his disciples), we can be quite confident that this critically positioned historian knew nothing at all of any Jesus of Nazareth – or of Nazareth itself, for that matter. This is because his writings *did* survive up until at least the ninth or tenth centuries CE.

Around the year 891 CE, Photius, the patriarch of Constantinople [858–67 and 878–86], wrote a monumental review of several hundred important books he had read. Usually referred to in English as *The Library*, it also is known as the *Myriobiblon* or *Bibliotheca* – Greek titles given to it by editors in the centuries after its composition. It so happens that among the books reviewed by Photius was *The Chronicles of the Kings of the Jews*, by Justus of Tiberias. Obviously disappointed by the work, Photius sadly recorded that "of the advent of Christ, of the things that befell him one way or another, or of the miracles that he performed, [Justus] makes absolutely no mention" [*Codex 33, my translation*].[1-2] The crucially positioned historian clearly had never heard of Jesus, his disciples, St. Paul, nor any of the earth-shattering New Testament events that are supposed to have happened on his turf.

It is likely that the last remaining copies of Justus and many other books reviewed by Photius were destroyed in the mass bookburnings and general conflagrations attending the capture and sack of Constantinople by the Fourth Crusade in 1204 CE.

1.2. Philo Judaeus

Philo of Alexandria, also known as Philo Judaeus ('Philo the Jew'), is another Jewish author who could not have failed to have noticed Jesus had he been a real person. So necessarily is this the case, three 'Fathers of the Church' (Eusebius, Jerome, and

Photius) sought to incorporate him into Christian history in one way or another, as we shall see presently.

Born in Alexandria around 20 BCE, Philo lived there until his death around the year 50 CE. Little specifically is known about his life, but it is known that he made at least one pilgrimage to the temple in Jerusalem, visited the Syrian city of Ascalon, and took part in an embassy to the emperor Gaius (Caligula) in an attempt to dissuade him from erecting his statue in the temple at Jerusalem. Despite his living in Egypt, more than 300 miles away from Jerusalem, he was well informed of what was happening in the Jewish homeland – and *vice versa*. After his death, the Jewish historian Josephus mentioned Philo's embassy to Caligula [*Jewish Antiquities* 18:8:1] and wrote about members of Philo's family [*Jewish Antiquities* 18:8:1, 19:5:1; *Jewish War* 2:15:1, 5:5:3]. Philo's brother, Alexander, was a wealthy Roman official in Egypt who loaned money to Herod Agrippa I and paid to have the gates of the temple in Jerusalem plated with silver and gold. Philo's two nephews, Marcus and Tiberius Alexander, were also involved in Roman affairs. Marcus married Bernice, the daughter of Herod Agrippa I (Bernice is mentioned in Acts 25:13, 23; 26:30). Tiberius Alexander – after renouncing Judaism – held the office of procurator of Judaea (46–48 CE) and was a prefect in Egypt (66–70 CE).

The fact that Philo's niece-in-law Bernice is mentioned in the canonical Acts of the Apostles is of great import for evaluating the significance of Philo's silence regarding Jesus and Christianity – and for understanding why it was so important for the Church Fathers to claim the Alexandrian Jew as a witness to their god-man.

According to the account in the twenty-fifth and twenty-sixth chapters of Acts, Bernice and her brother, King Herod Agrippa II, actually met St. Paul when they went to greet Porcius Festus, the Roman procurator. Not only is it alleged that she heard all about Paul's legal problems, she also heard the names *Jesus the Nazarene* [26:9] and *Christ*, [26:23] and even the probably anachronistic term *Christian* – when her brother, upon hearing Paul's sermon recounting his conversion after seeing lights and hearing voices, exclaims "...almost thou persuadest me to be a Christian" [Acts 26:28].

For any of the Church Fathers who knew that Bernice was the niece-in-law of Philo, it would seem obvious that the latter should have heard all about Paul, Jesus, and Christians from his nephew's wife – or from his nephew, if he was still alive at the time of the meeting. This being the case, Philo's silence concerning Jesus must have been intolerable and some connections between Philo and Christianity had to be manufactured.

Before exploring how and why these connections were made, it is of interest to examine the story in Acts more critically. It is generally accepted that the speeches in Acts are not authentic, but have been invented 'in character' by the unknown author of the book – as was the custom of virtually all ancient authors. The dialogues too are composed to express what the author feels must or should have been said. The story of the conversion of Saul/Paul preached to Bernice and Agrippa II [Acts 26:12–18], although not to be found in any of the letters attributed to Paul himself, is found in two contradictory other versions – in Acts 9:2–19 and 22:5–16.* (The entire story of Saul's conversion and change of name to Paul appears to be a fabrication of the author of Acts.

---

*The most glaring contradiction in these two accounts concerns who saw and heard what:

Acts 9:3. And as he journeyed, he came near Damascus: and suddenly there shined round about him a light from heaven: 4And he fell to the earth, and heard a voice saying unto him, Saul, Saul, why persecutest thou me? ... 7And the men which journeyed with him stood speechless, **hearing a voice, but seeing no man.**

Acts 22:6. And it came to pass, that, as I made my journey, and was come nigh unto Damascus about noon, suddenly there shone from heaven a great light round about me. 7And I fell unto the ground, and heard a voice saying unto me, Saul, Saul, why persecutest thou me? ... 9And they that were with me **saw indeed the light,** and were afraid; **but they heard not the voice** of him that spake to me.

[In order to hide this glaring contradiction from biblical inerrantist readers, the fundamentalist New International Version renders the Greek οὐκ ἤκουσαν as "did not understand" instead of "did not hear" – even though it is a form of the same verb (ἀκούω) used in 9:7 (ἀκούοντες)]

The speech presented in Acts 26 makes no comment at all about who saw or heard what, and also makes no mention of the blindness that allegedly afflicted Saul for some time after the seizure-like experience. Incompatibly, the speech before Bernice and Agrippa II represents Paul as being immediately told by Jesus – as soon as he has introduced himself – to get up and start ministering. The clear implication is that Paul was able to see what he was doing.

There is no hint in the so-called Pauline Epistles that Paul ever was called Saul.) It is not to be supposed that real history is to be found in these chapters of Acts.

It is interesting that Bernice is represented in the story in such a way that any non-historian reader would naturally suppose that Bernice was Agrippa's wife or consort, rather than his sister – with whom he may have had an incestuous relationship. It is as though the writer had no real knowledge of what had happened but had created a historical setting for his hero Saul/Paul with fragments of historical data. Once he had chosen a time frame, he inserted characters he had reason to believe existed at the time.

That the author of Acts did not have precise data with which to invent his story is clear from the general language that at times he was forced to use. Thus Festus (as elsewhere Felix) is referred to [Acts 26:30] as a *governor* (ἡγεμὼν), whereas his actual title was *procurator* (ἐπίτροπος). It is the sort of thing one expects from a mediocre historical novelist, but not from a real historian.

1.2. A. Eusebius' Account of Philo

Philo was an enormously prolific writer. Despite the fact that much of his work has been lost, a modern edition of his surviving works fills nearly 900 two-column pages with eight-point text. Philo wrote about everything – making his total omission of any mention of Jesus and his cohorts a particularly glaring deficiency and embarrassment. Moreover, it is quite likely that the unknown author of the Gospel of John had used Philo's developed concept of the *Logos* ('Word') in his prologue, which begins: "In the beginning was the Word (ὁ λόγος), and the Word was with God, and the Word was God."

New Testament authors and early Christian theologians were even more in debt to Philo for his concept of *pneuma* (πνεῦμα). Originally meaning 'breath' or 'breeze,' in Philo *pneuma* has developed into a supernatural power that can flow from Yahweh directly into the human soul, an agent that can fill a person with higher awareness; it is the vehicle of inspiration – the "spirit of prophecy." Being in effect the breath of Yahweh, the *pneuma* is actually the *hagion pneuma* (ἅγιον πνεῦμα) – the Holy Spirit or Holy Ghost, which soon was incorporated into the Christian Trinity. Without Philo, the Christian Trinity could not have been invented.

Among the writings of Philo that drew the attention of the Church Fathers was his essay "On the Contemplative Life, or Suppliants" (*De Vita Contemplativa*). In this he described a monastic order, called the Therapeutae, which was so similar to Orthodox Christianity that Eusebius of Caesarea [c260–339 CE] concluded that the Therapeutae were in fact Christians, and that Philo was one also – and actually had dealings with St. Peter in Rome! Because I think the Therapeutæ may actually be one of the several groups from which Christianity evolved, and because I think Eusebius' account is intrinsically of interest, I shall quote at length from the 1890 edition of *The Church History of Eusebius*, edited by Philip Schaff and Henry Wace.[1-3]

The Church History of Eusebius, Book 2

Chap. 16. And they say that this Mark was the first that was sent to Egypt, and that he proclaimed the Gospel which he had written, and first established churches in Alexandria. And the multitude of believers, both men and women, that were collected there at the very outset, and lived lives of the most philosophical and excessive asceticism, was so great, that Philo thought it worth while to describe their pursuits, their meetings, their entertainments, and their whole manner of life.

Chap. 17. It is also said that Philo in the reign of Claudius* became acquainted at Rome with Peter, who was then preaching there. Nor is this indeed improbable, for the work of which we have spoken, and which was composed by him some years later, clearly contains those rules of the Church which are even to this day observed among us. And since he describes as accurately as possible the life of our ascetics, it is clear that he not only knew, but that he also approved, while he venerated and extolled, the apostolic men of his time, who were as it seems of the Hebrew race, and hence observed, after the manner of the Jews, the most of the customs of the ancients.

In the work to which he gave the title "On a Contemplative Life" or "On Suppliants," after affirming in the first place that he will add to those things which he is about to relate nothing

---

*This is the first known indication of the tradition that Philo [d. 50 CE] had gone to Rome a second time, in the reign of Claudius [25 Jan. 41 CE–12 Oct. 54 CE]. According to Philo's own account, he went to Rome to see Gaius Caligula [r. Mar. 16, 37 CE–Jan. 24, 41 CE], when anti-Semitic strife had occurred in Alexandria and Caligula was about to desecrate the temple in Jerusalem. There is no evidence to support this second trip to Rome.

contrary to truth or of his own invention, he says that these men were called Therapeutæ and the women that were with them Therapeutrides. He then adds the reasons for such a name, explaining it from the fact that they applied remedies and healed the souls of those who came to them, by relieving them like physicians, of evil passions, or from the fact that they served and worshipped the Deity in purity and sincerity. Whether Philo himself gave them this name, employing an epithet well suited to their mode of life, or whether the first of them really called themselves so in the beginning, since the name of Christians was not yet everywhere known, we need not discuss here.

He bears witness, however, that first of all they renounce their property. When they begin the philosophical mode of life, he says, they give up their goods to their relatives, and then, renouncing all the cares of life, they go forth beyond the walls and dwell in lonely fields and gardens, knowing well that intercourse with people of a different character is unprofitable and harmful. They did this at that time, as seems probable, under the influence of a spirited and ardent faith, practicing in emulation the prophets' mode of life. For in the Acts of the Apostles, a work universally acknowledged as authentic, it is recorded that all the companions of the apostles sold their possessions and their property and distributed to all according to the necessity of each one, so that no one among them was in want. "For as many as were possessors of lands or houses," as the account says, "sold them and brought the prices of the things that were sold, and laid them at the apostles' feet, so that distribution was made unto every man according as he had need."

Philo bears witness to facts very much like those here described and then adds the following account: "Everywhere in the world is this race found.* For it was fitting that both Greek and Barbarian should share in what is perfectly good. But the race particularly abounds in Egypt, in each of its so-called nomes, and especially about Alexandria. The best men from every quarter emigrate, as if to a colony of the Therapeutæ's fatherland, to a certain very suitable spot which lies above the lake Maria [*Mareotis*] upon a low hill excellently situated on account of its security and the mildness of the atmosphere."

And then a little further on, after describing the kind of houses which they had, he speaks as follows concerning their churches, which were scattered about here and there: "In each

---

*It has been hypothesized that these colonies of Therapeutae, scattered throughout the Eastern Mediterranean world, became the "churches" with which the New Testament involves St. Paul in his peregrinations and epistolary activities.

house* there is a sacred apartment which is called a sanctuary and monastery, where, quite alone, they perform the mysteries of the religious life. They bring nothing into it, neither drink nor food, nor any of the other things which contribute to the necessities of the body, but only the laws, and the inspired oracles of the prophets, and hymns and such other things as augment and make perfect their knowledge and piety."

And after some other matters he says: "The whole interval, from morning to evening, is for them a time of exercise. For they read the holy Scriptures, and explain the philosophy of their fathers in an allegorical manner, regarding the written words as symbols of hidden truth which is communicated in obscure figures. They have also writings of ancient men, who were the founders of their sect, and who left many monuments of the allegorical method. These they use as models, and imitate their principles."

These things seem to have been stated by a man who had heard them expounding their sacred writings. But it is highly probable that the works of the ancients, which he says they had, were the Gospels and the writings of the apostles, and probably some expositions of the ancient prophets, such as are contained in the Epistle to the Hebrews, and in many others of Paul's Epistles. Then again he writes as follows concerning the new psalms which they composed: "So that they not only spend their time in meditation, but they also compose songs and hymns to God in every variety of metre and melody, though they divide them, of course, into measures of more than common solemnity."

The same book contains an account of many other things, but it seemed necessary to select those facts which exhibit the characteristics of the ecclesiastical mode of life. But if any one thinks that what has been said is not peculiar to the Gospel polity, but that it can be applied to others besides those mentioned, let him be convinced by the subsequent words of the same author, in which, if he is unprejudiced, he will find undisputed testimony on this subject.

Philo's words are as follows: "Having laid down temperance as a sort of foundation in the soul, they build upon it the other virtues. None of them may take food or drink before sunset, since they regard philosophizing as a work worthy of the light, but attention to the wants of the body as proper only in the darkness, and therefore assign the day to the former, but to the latter a

---

*Robert Taylor, in his *Diegesis*, translates this "In each *parish* there is a sacred edifice which is called the temple, and a *monastery*, in which the monks perform the mysteries of the sublime life..."[1-4] [*emphasis original*].

small portion of the night. But some, in whom a great desire for knowledge dwells, forget to take food for three days; and some are so delighted and feast so luxuriously upon wisdom, which furnishes doctrines richly and without stint, that they abstain even twice as long as this, and are accustomed, after six days, scarcely to take necessary food." These statements of Philo we regard as referring clearly and indisputably to those of our communion.

But if after these things any one still obstinately persists in denying the reference, let him renounce his incredulity and be convinced by yet more striking examples, which are to be found nowhere else than in the evangelical religion of the Christians. For they say that there were women also with those of whom we are speaking, and that the most of them were aged virgins* who had preserved their chastity, not out of necessity, as some of the priestesses among the Greeks, but rather by their own choice, through zeal and a desire for wisdom. And that in their earnest desire to live with it as their companion they paid no attention to the pleasures of the body, seeking not mortal but immortal progeny, which only the pious soul is able to bear of itself.

Then after a little he adds still more emphatically: "They expound the Sacred Scriptures figuratively by means of allegories.† For the whole law seems to these men to resemble a living organism, of which the spoken words constitute the body, while the hidden sense stored up within the words constitutes the soul. This hidden meaning has first been particularly studied

---

*Eusebius seems not to have realized that at the time Philo wrote this (well before his death in 50 CE) Christianity could not have been in existence long enough for virgins to have grown old in the church. Of course, if Christianity did not begin with the death of a single person in 33 CE, but rather evolved out of long-existing groups such as the Therapeutae, it could well have been the case that the group described by Philo were monastic proto-Christians. So great is the similarity between the community described by Philo and what is known of primitive Christianity, many writers after Eusebius have been convinced that the Therapeutae *were* Christians. Because this would be an anachronism in the context of the traditional myth of Christian origins, some nineteenth-century authors denied the piece to be a work of Philo. Thus Lucius, in his *Die Therapeuten und ihre Stellung in der Geschichte des Askese* (*The Therapeutæ and Their Place in the History of Asceticism*, Strassburg, 1879) argued that *De Vita Contemplativa* was the apologetic work of a Christian of the second half of the third century, written to promote the monastic system. However, it is quite generally accepted that the work is authentic Philo – leaving us with the ineluctable conclusion that either Christianity was anticipated in the most minute detail by the Therapeutae, or that Christianity existed before the time of Christ.

†"Which things are an allegory."—Gal 4:24

by this sect, which sees, revealed as in a mirror of names, the sur-passing beauties of the thoughts."*
   Why is it necessary to add to these things their meetings and the respective occupations of the men and of the women dur-ing those meetings, and the practices which are even to the pres-ent day habitually observed by us, especially such as we are accustomed to observe at the feast of the Saviour's passion, with fasting and night watching and study of the divine Word? These things the above-mentioned author has related in his own work, indicating a mode of life which has been preserved to the present time by us alone, recording especially the vigils kept in connec-tion with the great festival, and the exercises performed during those vigils, and the hymns customarily recited by us, and describing how, while one sings regularly in time, the others lis-ten in silence, and join in chanting only the close of the hymns; and how, on the days referred to, they sleep on the ground on beds of straw, and to use his own words, "taste no wine at all, nor any flesh, but water is their only drink, and the relish with their bread is salt and hyssop."
   In addition to this Philo describes the order of dignities which exists among those who carry on the services of the church, mentioning the diaconate†, and the office of bishop, which takes the precedence over all the others. But whosoever desires a more accurate knowledge of these matters may get it from the history already cited. But that Philo, when he wrote

---

*This difficult passage is rendered somewhat differently by Robert Taylor: "For the whole divine revelation, to these men seems to resemble an animal, and that the words spoken are the body, but the soul is the invisible sense involved in the words: which it is their religion itself which first began to exhibit distinctively, as in a glass, putting the beautiful results of the things understood under the indecencies of the names."[1-5]

†In Philo, the deacons are young men who serve at table (διακονοῦντες), and he tells of a president (πρόεδρος) who leads in the exposition of scripture, which Eusebius interprets as the dignity of a bishop (ἐπισκοπῆς προεδρίαν). Although obscure and lowly officials in modern churches, deacons appear to have been quite important during the formative period of Christianity. Burton Mack, in his *A Myth of Innocence: Mark and Christian Origins*[1-6] argued con-vincingly that early Christian meetings resembled a fraternal supper club more than a church service, and that table-waiters (deacons) constituted a sig-nificant rank in those early sodalities. A relic of this primitive understanding of deacons as table waiters appears to have been preserved in the pericope of the "Appointment of the Seven," in the sixth chapter of Acts: "So the Twelve called the whole body of disciples together and said, 'It would be a grave mis-take for us to neglect the word of God in order to wait at table'." (διακονεῖν τραπέζαις) [NEB, Acts 6:2].

these things, had in view the first heralds of the Gospel and the customs handed down from the beginning by the apostles, is clear to every one.

Chap. 18. [*This chapter is a catalogue of the works of Philo known to Eusebius. It adds, however, one more pseudobiographical datum concerning Philo.*]

After these was composed by him the work *On the contemplative life*, or *On suppliants*, from which we have drawn the facts concerning the life of the apostolic men; and still further, the *Interpretation of the Hebrew names in the law and in the prophets* are said to be the result of his industry. And he is said to have read in the presence of the whole Roman Senate during the reign of Claudius the work which he had written, when he came to Rome under Caius [*Caligula*], concerning Caius' hatred of the gods, and to which, with ironical reference to its character, he had given the title *On the Virtues*. And his discourses were so much admired as to be deemed worthy of a place in the libraries.

1.2. B. St. Jerome's Account of Philo

Born in 347 or 348 CE, less than a decade after the death of Eusebius, Jerome came to be a master in the composition of Latin prose. Mastering Greek and Hebrew as well, he achieved his greatest fame for his translation of the Christian and Jewish scriptures into Latin. Eventually, the Old Latin Bible was superseded by his Vulgate Bible. Jerome eventually read Eusebius' account of Philo and embellished it in his *On Illustrious Men (De Viris Illustribus)*. His first mention of Philo is in Book 8, a brief pseudobiography of St. Mark the Evangelist. After retailing the legend that Mark composed his gospel at Rome and then took it to Alexandria, Jerome has him found a church there. If this had been true, of necessity Philo would have come into contact with St. Mark and his church. Jerome writes:

> Philo, then, most eloquent of the Jews, seeing the first church at Alexandria still following Jewish customs, wrote a book on their manner of life as something creditable to his nation, and, as Luke says that "the believers at Jerusalem had all things in common," so he recorded what he saw was done at Alexandria, under the learned Mark.[1-7] [*Thomas P. Halton translation*]

Book 11 of *On Illustrious Men* is devoted to "Philo the Jew." His embellishment of Eusebius continues – appearing to make Philo an acquaintance of St. Mark as well as of St. Peter:

Philo the Jew, born in Alexandria of a priestly stock, and for that reason included by us among ecclesiastical writers, because, writing a book on the first church in Alexandria of Mark the evangelist, he engaged in praise of us Christians, recalling that they existed, not just there, but in many provinces, and calling their dwellings monasteries.

From this it is apparent that the first church of believers in Christ was such as the monks now imitate and emulate, so that nothing is held in private by anyone, not one among them is rich, not one poor, their patrimonies are divided among the needy, they spend their time in prayer and the psalms, in doctrine and continence, just as Luke describes how believers lived at the beginning in Jerusalem.

They say that Philo came at great risk to Rome in the reign of Gaius, to whom he had been sent as an ambassador of his people, and that he came a second time in the reign of Claudius and spoke with the apostle Peter in the same city [of Rome] and that he became his friend and that for this reason he embellished with his praises the followers of Mark, a disciple of Peter, at Alexandria.[1-8]

Jerome then lists the works of Philo surviving in his day. Readers will note how the probability of the second trip to Rome is put into the same class as Philo's well established first trip, by having "they say" govern both the first and second trips. Thus has history been manufactured to document the historicity of St. Mark and St. Peter – men whom we must otherwise adjudge to be sheerest legends, for want of credible proof of their physical reality.

1.2. C. Philo in Photius

Photius [c810–c893 CE], the Patriarch of Constantinople whom we have already encountered in our discussion of Justus of Tiberias, also deals with Philo, devoting three codices of *The Library* to the Alexandrian sage. Codex 103, however, is only two lines long – noting simply that "Philo the Jew's *Allegories of the Sacred Laws* was read, and *On the Political Life*." Codex 104 notes that he read Philo's accounts of the Essenes and the Therapeutae

– apparently confusing which group Philo styled as "practical philosophers" (the Essenes) and which he depicted as "theoretical philosophers" (the Therapeutae).

It is in Codex 105 that he brings the legend of Philo's relationship to Christianity to its fullest development. After mentioning that he had read Philo's *Gaius Denounced* and *Flaccus Denounced*, he writes:

> He [Philo] lived in the reign of Gaius Cæsar, to whom he went, by his own account, as envoy on behalf of his nation when Agrippa was king of Judæa. Various writings of his are known, essays on moral questions and interpretations of the Old Testament, mostly straining to see allegory in the text. From him, I suspect, all allegorical reading of the scriptures began to find its way into the church.
>
> A story circulates that he was converted to Christianity and later left the church in grief and anger. But they say that earlier, in the days of Claudius, he had been to Rome and met Peter, the leader of the apostles. He was on good terms with Peter, and so thought it right to make favourable mention of the pupils of Mark the evangelist (Mark was a pupil of Peter). According to the report, he said that Mark's pupils had studied with Jews. He calls their dwellings monasteries and proclaims their ascetic achievements, dedicated to fasting, prayer, and absolute poverty.
>
> He descended from a family of priests and came from Alexandria. His skill as a writer provoked such admiration among the hellenists that they said 'Either Plato is philonising or Philon is platonising.'[1-9] [*N. G. Wilson translation*]

1.2. D. The Loud Silence of Philo

Beginning the conclusion of this chapter as we began the chapter itself, with arguments from John E. Remsburg's *The Christ*,[1-10] we may summarize and paraphrase his points regarding the silence of Philo:

1. Philo was born before the beginning of the Christian era and lived until long after the reputed death of Christ.

2. He wrote an account of the Jews covering the entire time that Christ is said to have existed on earth.

3. He was living in or near Jerusalem when Christ's miraculous birth and the Herodian massacre of babies are supposed to have occurred.

4. He could not have failed to learn of Christ's triumphal entry into Jerusalem.

5. He could not have failed to learn of the crucifixion with its attendant earthquake, supernatural darkness, and the resurrection of the dead that took place when Christ himself rose from the dead and, in the alleged presence of many witnesses, ascended into heaven.

6. He was oblivious of many events which, if they had actually occurred, would have astounded him and filled the world with amazement.

7. Despite the fact that it was Philo who developed the doctrine of the Logos, or Word, when that Word incarnate dwelt in Philo's nearby homeland and, in the presence of multitudes, demonstrated divine powers, "Philo saw it not."

Notwithstanding the efforts of Eusebius, Jerome, Photius, and perhaps other apologists to enlist Philo into the ranks of witnesses of their Christ and his first minions, Philo tells us neither of Jesus the man nor of Christ the god. But, as developer of the key Christian concepts of the Logos and the Holy Ghost (or Holy Spirit) and as ethnographer of the Therapeutae, he has much to teach us about the origins of the Christian religion. Concerning Jesus of Nazareth, however, he bears no witness.

It is altogether possible – if not probable – that Robert Taylor's assessment of the multinational therapeutic sect as the rootstock from which the lowly branching shrub of Christianity sprang is correct. I will let him conclude this chapter with his summary of the importance of Philo's Therapeutae in understanding the origins of a Christianity without a corporeal Christ.

Here then have we, in the cities of Egypt, and in the deserts of Thebais, the whole already established system of ecclesiastical polity, its hierarchy of bishops, its subordinate clergy, the self-same sacred scriptures, the selfsame allegorical method of interpreting those scriptures, so convenient to admit of the evasion or amendment from time to time, of any defects that criticism might discover in them; the same doctrines, rites, ceremonies, festivals, discipline, psalms, repeated in alternate verses by the minister and the congregation, epistles and gospels – in a word, the *every-thing*, and every iota of Christianity, previously existing from time immemorial, and certainly known to have been in existence, and as such, recorded and detailed by an historian of unquestioned veracity, living and writing at least fifty years

before the earliest date that Christian historians have assigned
to any Christian document whatever.

Here we see through the thin veil that would hide the truth
from our eyes, in the admissions that Christians have been constrained to make, that the Therapeutæ were certainly the *first*
converts to the faith of Christ; and that the many circumstances
of doctrine and discipline, that they had in common with the
Christians, had previously *prepared* and *predisposed* them to
receive the gospel. We find that the faith of Christ actually originated with them, and they were in previous possession, and that
those who, by a chronological error, or willful misrepresentation,
are called the first Christians, were not the converters of the
Therapeutæ, but were themselves their converts.

This accounts for a phenomenon that everywhere meets us,
and which were otherwise utterly unaccountable: that the religion of one who had expressly admonished his disciples, that his
kingdom was not of this world, and which purports to have been
first preached by unambitious and illiterate fishermen, should in
the very first and earliest documents of it that can be produced,
present us with all the full ripe arrogance of an already established hierarchy; bishops disputing for their prerogatives, and
throne-enseated prelates demanding and receiving more than
the honours of temporal sovereignty, from their cringing vassals,
and denouncing worse than inflictions of temporal punishment
against the heretics who should presume to resist their decrees,
or dispute their authority.

We find the episcopal form of government, even before the
end of the first century, fully established; and if not the very
Galilean fishermen themselves, at least those who are called the
apostolic fathers, and who are supposed to have received their
authority and doctrine immediately from them, established in all
the pride, pomp, and magnificence of sovereign pontiffs, and
lords of the lives and fortunes, as well as of the faith of their
flocks; and everywhere inculcating, as the first axiom of all
morality and virtue, that there was no sin so great, as that of
resistance to the authority of a bishop.

"Since the time of Tertullian and Irenæus, it has been a fact,
as well as a maxim, *Nulla ecclesia sine episcopo* – no church without a bishop."—*Gibbon*.

We find Ignatius, Bishop of Antioch, even while the Apostles,
or John, at least, is supposed to have been living, venturing to
stake his soul for theirs, and himself the expiatory offering, for
those who should duly obey their bishop.

Dionysius, Bishop of Alexandria, the very seat and centre of
the Therapeutan doctrine, in his epistles to Novatius, maintains

that schismatics, or those who should venture to follow any opinions unsanctioned by the bishop, were "renegadoes, apostates, malignants, parricides, anti-christs, blasphemers, the devil's priests, villainous, and perfidious, were without hope, had no right to the promises, could not be saved, were no more Christians than the devil, could not go to heaven, the hottest part of hell their portion, their preaching poisonous, their baptism pestiferous, their persons accursed, &c. &c., and much more, to the same heavenly-tempered purport."

Such a state of things, such sentiments and language, and the like thereof, invariably found as it is in the very earliest documents of Christianity that can be adduced, and attested by the corroboration of independent historical evidence, is utterly incongruous, wholly irreconcilable and out of keeping with any possibility of the existence of the circumstances under which the Christian revelation is generally supposed to have made its appearance on earth.[1-11]

CHAPTER 2

Faking Flavius

2.1. Forgery as a Christian Commonplace

Joseph Wheless, in his monumental Atheist classic *Forgery in Christianity: A Documented Record of the Foundations of the Christian Religion*, defines forgery as follows:

> Forgery, in legal and moral sense, is the utterance or publication, with intent to deceive or defraud or to gain some advantage, of a false document, put out by one person in the name of and as the genuine work of another, who did not execute it, or the subsequent alteration of a genuine document by one who did not execute the original. This species of falsification extends alike to all classes of writings, promissory notes, the coin or currency of the realm, to any legal or private document, or to a book. All are counterfeit or forged if not authentic and untampered.[2-1]

In the foreword to his book, Wheless declares his intent to prove "from unimpeachable texts and historical records, and by authoritative clerical confessions, beyond the possibility of denial, evasion, or refutation," the following seven theses:

1. That the Bible, in its every Book, and in the strictest legal and moral sense, is a huge forgery.
2. That every Book of the New Testament is a forgery of the Christian Church; and every significant passage in those Books, on which the fabric of the Church and its principal Dogmas are founded, is a further and conscious later forgery, wrought with definite fraudulent intent.
3. Especially, and specifically, that the "famous Petrine text"–"Upon this Rock I will build my church"–the cornerstone of the gigantic fabric of imposture,–and the other, "Go, teach all nations,"–were never uttered by the Jew Jesus, but are palpable and easily-proven late Church forgeries.

4. That the Christian Church, from its inception in the first little Jewish-Christian religious societies until it reached the apex of its temporal glory and moral degradation, was a vast and tireless Forgery-mill.

5. That the Church was founded upon, and through the Dark Ages of Faith has battened on–(yet languishes decadently upon)–monumental and petty forgeries and pious frauds, possible only because of its own shameless mendacity and through the crass ignorance and superstition of the sodden masses of its deluded votaries, purposely kept in that base condition for purposes of ecclesiastical graft and aggrandizement through conscious and most unconscionable imposture.

6. That every conceivable form of religious lie, fraud and imposture has ever been the work of Priests; and through all the history of the Christian Church, as through all human history, has been–and, so far as they have not been shamed out of it by skeptical ridicule and exposure, yet is, the age-long stock in trade and sole means of existence of the priests and ministers of all the religions.

7. That the clerical mind, which "reasons in chains," is, from its vicious and vacuous "education," and the special selfish interests of the priestly class, incapable either of the perception or the utterance of truth, in matters where the interests of priestcraft are concerned.[2-2]

Even the most hardened Christian apologist would have to be shaken if he or she could be courageous enough to study all four hundred pages of Wheless' book – for long before reaching the end it becomes shockingly clear that mendacity has been both the bricks and the mortar with which the edifice of Christianity has been built. The bricks are the ancient fables, lies, falsehoods, and fantasies that in time became petrified into oracles, epistles, gospels, dogmas, and creeds that could be manipulated as structural units. The mortar of Christianity is the deception, prevarication, fraud, bogus relics, and subliminal seduction perpetrated to hold those units together – protecting them from immediate collapse when Free Inquiry hammers its theses upon the Church's door.

This history of fraud is of great relevance to our examination of the writings of the first-century Jewish historian Flavius Josephus, which we shall show were repeatedly interpolated – doctored up, in plain English – by Christian hands. Since one of the major players in the history of the Greek text of Josephus' writings was the Christian bishop of Caesarea, Eusebius Pamphili [c264–340 CE], it is well to note at the outset that his honesty has often been called into question and the veracity of many of his claims has long been disputed. But, then, what can one expect from an author who, in his treatise *Præparatio Evangelica* ('Evangelical Preparation') scandalously titles the thirty-second chapter of the twelfth book "How it may be Lawful and Fitting to use Falsehood as a Medicine, and for the Benefit of those who Want to be Deceived"?* While it may seem a gratuitous insult to Christian believers, it is necessary to state plainly my working hypothesis when examining the work of Eusebius and many other Church Fathers: Whenever one encounters material that is suspect on historical, philological, scientific, or other grounds, the default interpretation should be that fraud is involved. As in the *Code Napoléon*, the author is to be considered guilty until proven innocent. This rather un-American rule of thumb is necessitated by the pandemic of priestly pettifoggery which has infected the Christian churches since earliest times and has been transmitted in one mutant form or another right up to the present. (The argumentational techniques and "evidences" created by so-called scientific creationists and Intelligent Design theorists leap easily to mind as modern examples of this thimblerig tradition.)

While it is true that one of the greatest of the Church Fathers, St. Augustine of Hippo [354–430 CE], wrote two books against lying,[†] he nevertheless approved of the dishonest practice of *suppressio veri*, suppression or concealment of truth for the sake of Christian edification. In chapter 17 of his *On Lying* he says that "It is lawful, then, either to him that discourses, disputes, and preaches of things eternal, or to him that narrates or speaks of things temporal pertaining to edification of religion or piety, to conceal at fitting times whatever seems fit to be concealed, but to tell a lie is never lawful, therefore neither to conceal by telling a lie."[2-3] (This is a rule that has been followed in modern times by some Franciscan 'archaeologists,' especially one who concealed awkward finds from his excavation at so-called Capernaum.)

---

*The free translation of Edward Gibbon [*Vindication*, p. 76]. The actual Greek heading reads: "λγ′ OTI MH XPHN EK TΩN OΥ KATA ΛOΓON ΠAP′ HMIN BIOΥNTΩN TO ΠAN EΘNOΣ ΔIABAΛΛEΣΘAI."

†*De Mendacio* ('On Lying') and *Contra Mendacium* ('Against Lying').

As it turns out, however, St. Augustine could not follow his own rule with regard to lying, for he tells us that "I was already bishop of Hippo, when I went into Ethiopia with some servants of Christ there to preach the Gospel. In this country we saw many men and women without heads, who had two great eyes in their breasts; and in countries still more southly, we saw people who had but one eye in their foreheads."* Even though it is hard to understand why Augustine would have told such a whopper, a lie it is beyond dispute.

Lest it be thought that this exposé of mendacity amongst the Church Fathers be a libel concocted by modern skeptics, no less a personage than Cardinal John Henry Newman [1801–90], in his *Apologia Pro Vita Sua*,†[2-6] confirmed the utility of prevarication and deception in the service of religion: "The Greek Fathers thought that, when there was a *justa causa*, an untruth need not be a lie... Now, as to the 'just cause,'... the Greek Fathers make them such as these—self-defense, charity, zeal for God's honour, and the like."

With the realization that *everything* surviving from early Christianity – as well as anything that has passed through its hands – is automatically suspect, we proceed to investigate what the Church has preserved or manufactured of the works of the first-century Jewish historian Flavius Josephus.

---

*Joseph Wheless, in his *Forgery in Christianity*[2-4] quotes this as being from "Sermon 37" of St. Augustine. Robert Taylor's *Diegesis*[2-5] identifies it as being from "his 33rd Sermon addressed to his reverend brethren." I have been unable to locate this passage in any Latin edition of Augustine's works published during the last 150 years. Thus has the Roman Church protected its reputation.

†The only book in which I was able to find this damaging passage was *Newman's Apologia Pro Vita Sua: The Two Versions of 1864 & 1865 Preceded by Newman's and Kingsley's Pamphlets* (With an introduction by Wilfrid Ward). The quotation is from the appendix, note G. Not surprisingly, this note seems not to have been reprinted in any editions of the *Apologia* produced during the last half of the twentieth century.

Figure 1. Presumed bust of Flavius Josephus in the Ny Carlsberg Glyptotek at Copenhagen.

[From Robert Eisler, *ΙΗΣΟΥΣ ΒΑΣΙΛΕΥΣ ΟΥ ΒΑΣΙΛΕΥΣΑΣ*, Heidelberg, 1929]

Figure 2. Representation of M. Mettius Epaphroditus, the publisher of the works of Josephus, in the Villa Altieri at Rome.
[From Robert Eisler, *ΙΗΣΟΥΣ ΒΑΣΙΛΕΥΣ ΟΥ ΒΑΣΙΛΕΥΣΑΣ*, Heidelberg, 1929]

2.2. Tampering with the Texts of Flavius Josephus

Although Josephus [37–c95 CE] was born too late to have been an eyewitness of the lives of Jesus or John the Baptist, nevertheless he was a contemporary of the evangelists who wrote of those characters. He should have heard of St. Paul and the ruckus allegedly raised by him and the other apostles as they set out to save the world from its real and imagined sins. Furthermore, he should have heard from his priest-caste father Matthias [b. 6 CE] about the religious ferment supposedly stirred up by the doings of Jesus. He should have known of Herod's slaughter of the innocents after the birth of Christ – and he should have written about all these things in his histories.

Although we cannot be sure that all of the writings of Josephus have survived until modern times (the Jews generally considered him to have been a renegade and traitor and seem not to have been as motivated as were the Christians to preserve and transmit his writings to posterity), we do have his autobiography, *The Life of Flavius Josephus*, his treatise *The Antiquities of the Jews* in twenty books, his treatise *The Wars of the Jews* (also called *The Jewish War*) in seven books, and his polemic *Against Apion* in two books. Although some or all of his works were first written in Aramaic and then translated into Greek, they have survived only in Greek – although secondary translations into Latin, Armenian, and Semitic languages are known. (Greek was, after all, the first language of Christianity.)

In the manuscripts that are extant, Josephus is made to bear witness not only to Jesus the Messiah, but also to John the Baptist and James the Just, a.k.a. James, the Brother of the Lord, a.k.a. James, the Brother of Jesus. As the question of the historicity of Jesus is closely related to that of the other two characters, we shall discuss the circumstances surrounding the appearance of all of them in the Josephus manuscripts.

2.2. A. Known Forgeries

That Christians tampered with the text of Josephus as much as they altered the text of the Septuagint (the Greek version of the so-called Old Testament) is evident if one compares extant manuscripts with each other and with manuscripts existing in the past that have not survived but whose contents can be inferred from early translations and from the writings of the Church Fathers. Thus, a version of the so-called *Testimonium Flavianum*, the infamous interpolation which we find in Greek manuscripts of the *Antiquities of the Jews*, is found interpolated into the Old Russian version of *The Wars Of The Jews*. The early Church Father Origen [185–254 CE] had a Greek manuscript that referred to James in a way unknown in any surviving manuscripts.* St. John Chrysostom [c347–407 CE], when composing his *Homilies on St. John*,[2-8] appears to have had a manuscript of Josephus that attributed the fall of Jerusalem and destruction of the temple to the death of John the Baptist – a passage lacking in all surviving manuscripts and differing from the interpolated manuscript cited by Origen, which attributed these disasters to the death of James the Just, the "Brother of the Lord." Finally, Photius [c810-893 CE], the patriarch of Constantinople, almost certainly had a manuscript of Josephus' *Antiquities* that did not mention Jesus at all.

---

*In his *Commentary on Matthew*, §17, Origen informs us, "And James is he whom Paul says in the Epistle to the Galatians that he saw, 'But other of the Apostles saw I none, save James the Lord's brother.' And to so great a reputation among the people for righteousness did this James rise, that Flavius Josephus, who wrote the *Antiquities of the Jews* in twenty books, when wishing to exhibit the cause why the people suffered so great misfortunes that even the temple was razed to the ground, said, that these things happened to them in accordance with the wrath of God **in consequence of the things which they had dared to do against James the brother of Jesus who is called Christ.** And the wonderful thing is, that, though he did not accept Jesus as Christ, he yet gave testimony that the righteousness of James was so great; and he says that the people thought that they had suffered these things because of James."[2-7]

Robert Eisenman, in his mammoth treatise *James the Brother of Jesus: The Key to Unlocking the Secrets of Early Christianity and the Dead Sea Scrolls*,[2-9] says that Origen "railed against traditions he knew giving James more prominence than he was prepared to accord him, namely those connecting James' death to the fall of Jerusalem. The normal scriptural view and popular theology to this day connects Jesus' death not James' to the destruction of the Temple. ... Though Origen was later accused of heresy, his view of the tradition connecting the fall of Jerusalem to the death of James, which he credited to

2.2. B. Silence in the *Wars*

Before examining the *Testimonium* in detail, it is worth noting that the original absence of any mention of Jesus, James, or
John the Baptist from the *Wars of the Jews* – written perhaps
twenty years earlier than the *Antiquities* – is itself of great significance. If Josephus actually had known of these characters,
why didn't he mention them in his first book covering the appropriate place and period? (Remember, Josephus, being born in 37 CE
could not have had direct knowledge of John or Jesus, but his
priestly father could not have failed to know of them if they were
real people living at the times Christian tradition assigns to

Josephus, is probably not a little connected with its disappearance
from these materials as they have come down to us."

I cannot agree with this strained explanation of why no present-
day manuscripts of Josephus contain the passage attributed by
Origen to Josephus' *Antiquities*. First of all, at least in the passage
quoted above, Origen certainly is not *railing* against the tradition. To
the contrary, he says it was a "wonderful thing" that although
Josephus "did not accept Jesus as Christ" (*i.e.*, as the Messiah), nevertheless he testified to the righteousness of James. Secondly, even
supposing the passage was an authentic expression of the pen of
Josephus, it is hard to believe Origen's successors would have
expunged the passage because of its perceived misplaced emphasis.
The natural Christian thing to do would have been to alter the passage by interpolation of whatever material the defenders of the faith
deemed necessary. While text material can be lost because of scribal
errors, it is rare for material to be deleted deliberately.

Quite clearly, the reason we do not have any manuscripts of
Josephus' *Antiquities* that attribute the fall of Jerusalem to the martyrdom of James is simply that the story had been interpolated into
the family of manuscripts – now entirely extinct – to which Origen's
copy of Josephus belonged, but it had not made its way into any of the
other manuscript families that have survived to the present. In
exactly the same way, a variant *Testimonium Flavianum* found its
way into the *Jewish War* manuscript family from which the Old
Russian version is descended, but no other surviving manuscript
family was thus contaminated. This is why we do not have the
Testimonium Flavianum in Greek manuscripts of both the *Wars of
the Jews* and the *Antiquities of the Jews* – except for the blatant forgery shown in Figure 5.

them.) If the passages in the *Antiquities* that mention these three characters be authentic, why did Josephus wait until the time at which the last of the canonical gospels were being composed to name them?*

Even if we accepted the argument that, despite heavy Christian redaction and interpolation, Josephus did in fact mention these three characters (perhaps negatively), it still would be of little value in establishing their historicity. The *Antiquities* being written in the nineties of the first century – a time when everyone agrees that Christianity should have been a detectable phenomenon *in some part of the Roman Empire* – it is more parsimonious to suppose its author would have been reacting to Christian propaganda rather than historical records or his father's memories. If he had had legitimate sources of information, he would have used them in his earlier book. If he didn't have legitimate sources (such as his father or official records), he would have had to wait twenty more years until Christian missionaries had become a great enough annoyance to warrant notice.

---

*Earl Doherty, in his relentlessly logical book *The Jesus Puzzle: Did Christianity Begin with a Mythical Christ?*, states the case succinctly:

In the section on Pilate in the earlier *Jewish War*, written in the 70s, Josephus outlines the same two incidents with which he began chapter 3 of Book 18 in the *Antiquities of the Jews*, incidents which caused tumult in Judea during the governorship of Pilate. In the *Antiquities*, these descriptions are immediately followed by the Testimonium about Jesus. In *Jewish War* (2.9/169–177) no mention of Jesus is included.

One is further intrigued by a similar situation in Tacitus. While the later *Annals* contains the passage about Jesus as a man who had "undergone the death penalty in the reign of Tiberius by sentence of the procurator Pontius Pilate," an earlier work in which Tacitus summarizes the reign of Tiberius contains no mention of either Jesus or Christians. In the *Histories* (5.9.2) Tacitus merely says that in Palestine at this time, "all was quiet."

A coincidence? If the silence on Jesus in the earlier works of both Tacitus and Josephus casts doubt on the authenticity of their later references, then we have truly lost every clear non-Christian reference to Jesus as a human being before the latter half of the second century.[2-10]

2.3. The *Testimonium Flavianum*

Probably the most notorious of all Christian forgeries (after
that of the so-called 'Donation of Constantine,' in which the
Emperor Constantine is made to donate Italy to the Pope of
Rome) is the interpolation that was first made in Book 18, chapter 3, of Josephus' *Antiquities of the Jews*. (A later variant of the
interpolation was inserted into a manuscript of *Wars of the Jews*,
from which the Old Russian version was derived.) I shall quote it
in context in the 1867 English translation of William Whiston.
Paragraph 1 (not quoted) describes the tumult in Jerusalem and
Caesarea resulting from Pilate's importation of "images" – the
Roman ensigns – to spite the Second Commandment (according
to Jewish and Protestant reckoning, but omited by Catholics)
which prohibits 'graven images.' Paragraph 2 tells of the massacre of Jews reacting to Pilate's financing an aqueduct with temple funds. Paragraph 3 is the *Testimonium Flavianum*.
Paragraphs 4 and 5 describe "another sad calamity" that "put the
Jews into disorder."

2. But Pilate undertook to bring a current of water to
Jerusalem, and did it with the sacred money, and derived the origin of the stream from the distance of two hundred furlongs [*25
miles*]. However, the Jews were not pleased with what had been
done about this water; and many ten thousands of the people got
together, and made a clamour against him, and insisted that he
should leave off that design. Some of them also used reproaches,
and abused the man, as crowds of such people usually do. So he
habited a great number of his soldiers in their habit, who carried
daggers under their garments, and sent them to a place where
they might surround them. So he bade the Jews himself go away;
but they boldly casting reproaches upon him, he gave the soldiers
that signal which had been beforehand agreed on; who laid upon
them much greater blows than Pilate had commanded them, and
equally punished those that were tumultuous, and those that
were not, nor did they spare them in the least; and since the people were unarmed, and were caught by men prepared for what
they were about, there were a great number of them slain by this
means, and others of them ran away wounded; and thus an end
was put to this sedition.

3. Now, there was about this time, Jesus, a wise man, if it be lawful to call him a man, for he was a doer of wonderful works,–a teacher of such men as receive the truth with pleasure. He drew over to him both many of the Jews, and many of the Gentiles. He was [the] Christ [Messiah]; and when Pilate, at the suggestion of the principal men amongst us, had condemned him to the cross, those that loved him at the first did not forsake him, for he appeared to them alive again the third day, as the divine prophets had foretold these and ten thousand other wonderful things concerning him; and the tribe of Christians, so named from him, are not extinct at this day.

4. About the same time also another sad calamity put the Jews into disorder; and certain shameful practices happened about the temple of Isis that was at Rome. I will now first take notice of the wicked attempt about the temple of Isis, and will then give an account of the Jewish affairs... [Here follows an entertaining account of the seduction of the virtuous matron Paulina in the Temple of Isis by Decius Mundus, who pretended to be the god Anubis.] I now return to the relation of what happened about this time to the Jews at Rome, as I formerly told you I would.

5. There was a man who was a Jew, but had been driven away from his own country by an accusation laid against him for transgressing their laws, and by the fear he was under of punishment for the same; but in all respects a wicked man:– he then living at Rome, professed to instruct men in the wisdom of the laws of Moses. He procured also three other men, entirely of the same character with himself, to be his partners. These men persuaded Fulvia, a woman of great dignity, and one that had embraced the Jewish religion, to send purple and gold to the temple at Jerusalem; and, when they had gotten them, they employed them for their own uses, and spent the money themselves; on which account it was that they at first required it of her. Whereupon Tiberius, who had been informed of the thing by Saturninus, the husband of Fulvia, who desired inquiry might be made about it, ordered all the Jews to be banished out of Rome; at which time the consuls enlisted four thousand men out of them, and sent them to the island Sardinia; but punished a greater number of them, who were unwilling to become soldiers on account of keeping the laws of their forefathers. Thus were these Jews banished out of the city by the wickedness of four men.[2-11]

It is immediately apparent that paragraph 3 could not have been written by a man who remained a Jew all his life. According to Origen,[2-12] Josephus "did not accept Jesus as Christ," *i.e.*, he did not accept Jesus as the Messiah. Clearly, he could not have written that "He was [the] Christ." Furthermore, it doesn't take a rocket scientist to understand that if Josephus really had recounted as factual that "when Pilate, ... had condemned him to the cross, those that loved him at the first did not forsake him, for he appeared to them alive again the third day, as the divine prophets had foretold these and ten thousand other wonderful things concerning him," the Jewish historian would perforce have converted to Christianity and his writings would be overflowing with the "ten thousand other wonderful things." To the contrary, however, all Josephus had to say about Jesus is here in the *Testimonium* plus a fleeting, disputable mention in Book 20, chapter 9, of "the brother of Jesus, who was called Christ, whose name was James"[2-13]

Not quite so immediately apparent, but nevertheless quite glaring when pointed out, is the fact that paragraph 3 abruptly intrudes into the narrative of events that caused turmoil among the Jews. In the *Testimonium* as it stands above, there is not even a hint that the Jews were thrown into turmoil by the "ten thousand other wonderful things" concerning Jesus. The completely upbeat comment that the Christians "are not extinct at this day" is in jarring contrast to the first sentence of paragraph 4 which cites "another sad calamity" that "put the Jews into disorder." If one omit paragraph 3, paragraph 4 follows naturally and perfectly from paragraph 2.

Lest it be thought that paragraph 3 is just a random wandering by Josephus from his theme of things that put the Jews into disorder, it is clear that our author was extremely self-conscious of his theme in this part of his book. Faced with the dilemma of history providing two comment-worthy events after the incident of Pilate and the aqueduct – of which only one pertained to his theme – Josephus explains his momentary digression from his plan: "I will now first take notice of the wicked attempt about the temple of Isis, and will then give an account of the Jewish affairs." No such notice is given to explain his alleged digression into Jesus appearing alive again on the third day.

Beyond all doubt, the *Testimonium Flavianum* is a Christian interpolation into the text of Josephus. It does not fit into the structure of the narrative and its content could not possibly have been written by a Jew. Furthermore, if we can trust the *Annals* of Tacitus [*Ann*. ii 85], the editor of Volume 9 of the Loeb Classical Library edition of the *Jewish Antiquities* has pointed out in a footnote to paragraph 4 that "about the same time" – the time when the Isis temple escapade occurred – should have been 19 CE, not *c*30 CE, which is the time when Jesus is supposed to have been executed.

2.4. Loud Arguments from Silence Concerning the *Testimonium*

While 'argumentation from silence' (*argumentum e silentio*) is always fraught with danger, with proper caution it nevertheless can be useful in evaluating opinions reached by independent lines of evidence and reasoning. In the present case, it is noteworthy that *none* of the early Church Fathers – who collected all the evidence they could find pertaining to the imagined founder of their religion – seems to know about the *Testimonium*. John E. Remsburg sums up the situation well in his *The Christ*:

> The early Christian fathers were not acquainted with it [*the Testimonium*]. Justin Martyr [*c*100–165 CE], Tertullian [*c*160–*c*225 CE], Clement of Alexandria [*c*150–*c*215 CE], and Origen [*c*185–254 CE] all would have quoted this passage had it existed in their time. The failure of even one of these fathers to notice it would be sufficient to throw doubt upon its genuineness; the failure of all of them to notice it proves conclusively that it is spurious, that it was not in existence during the second and third centuries. [*The* Testimonium *was also unknown to Irenæus (late second century), Cyprian (mid-third century) and Arnobius (late third century).*]
>
> As this passage first appeared in the writings of the ecclesiastical historian, Eusebius, as this author openly advocated the use of fraud and deception in furthering the interests of the church, as he is known to have mutilated and perverted the text of Josephus in other instances, and as the manner of its presentation is calculated to excite suspicion, the forgery has generally been charged to him. In his "Evangelical Demonstration," written early in the fourth century, after citing all the known evidences of Christianity, he thus introduces the Jewish historian: "Certainly the attestations I have already produced concerning our Savior may be sufficient. However, it

may not be amiss if, over and above, we make use of Josephus the Jew for a further witness" (Book 3, p. 124).

> Chrysostom [*c347-407* CE, *Archbishop of Constantinople 398-404*] and Photius [*c810–893* CE] both reject this passage. Chrysostom, a reader of Josephus, who preached and wrote in the latter part of the fourth century, in his defense of Christianity, needed this evidence, but was too honest or too wise to use it. Photius, who made a revision [*a book review*] of Josephus, writing five hundred years after the time of Eusebius, ignores the passage, and admits that Josephus has made no mention of Christ.[2-14]

Remsburg exaggerates slightly in his claim that Chrysostom and Photius *reject* this passage. Nowhere does either one of these Church Fathers betray knowledge of the *Testimonium* at all. It is clear that in the copies of Josephus available to them *even after the time of Eusebius* there was no attestation of Jesus for them to employ or reject. If Eusebius was in fact the forger, only manuscripts belonging to the manuscript family founded by him would contain the *Testimonium*. Chrysostom and Photius, then, must have had manuscripts descending from manuscripts that had never passed through the forgery mill at Caesarea.

2.4. A. St. John Chrysostom

As indicated by Remsburg, although Chrysostom is quite familiar with Josephus and cites him a number of times, he is quite unaware of the *Testimonium Flavianum* or any likely variant thereof. A comprehensive examination of his citations of Josephus will show how necessary it would have been to mention the *Testimonium* if his copy of Josephus contained it.

Chrysostom first refers to Josephus in Homily 76 of his *Homilies on the Gospel of St. Matthew*. Preaching on the text of Matthew 24:16–18 ("Then let them which be in Judaea flee into the mountains," *etc.*), supposedly dealing with the coming destruction of Jerusalem, Chrysostom refers his audience to Josephus' description of the siege of Jerusalem and tells them that Jerusalem was destroyed because of the crucifixion of Jesus:

> And let not any man suppose this [*the horror of the coming destruction*] to have been spoken hyperbolically; but let him

study the writings of Josephus, and learn the truth of the sayings. For neither can any one say, that the man being a believer, in order to establish Christ's words, hath exaggerated the tragical history. For indeed he was both a Jew, and a determined Jew, and very zealous, and among them that lived after Christ's coming.

What then saith this man? That those terrors surpassed all tragedy, and that no such had ever overtaken the nation. For so great was the famine, that the very mothers fought about the devouring of their children, and that there were wars about this; and he saith that many when they were dead had their bellies ripped up.

I should therefore be glad to inquire of the Jews. Whence came there thus upon them wrath from God intolerable, and more sore than all that had befallen aforetime, not in Judæa only, but in any part of the world? Is it not quite clear, that it was for the deed of the cross, and for this rejection? 2-15

The next mention of Josephus is to be found in Homily 5 of Chrysostom's *Homilies on the Acts of the Apostles*, expounding upon Acts 2:14 and the meteorological accompaniments to the taking of Jerusalem:

Then he [*St. Peter*] goes on with the prophecy, which has in it also something terrible. "And I will show wonders in heaven above, and signs" [*"in the earth beneath"*]. (v. 19) In these words he speaks both of the judgment to come, and of the taking of Jerusalem. "Blood and fire, and vapor of smoke." Observe how he describes the capture. "The sun shall be turned into darkness, and the moon into blood." (v. 20) This results from the internal affection of the sufferers. It is said, indeed, that many such phenomena actually did occur in the sky, as Josephus attests. At the same time the Apostle strikes fear into them, by reminding them of the darkness which had lately occurred, and leading them to expect things to come. 2-16

There is no knowledge of the *Testimonium* here, despite the appeal to Josephus for a weather report.

It is in Homily 8, dealing with 1 Thessalonians 4:15–17, that we find Chrysostom next appealing to the authority of Josephus – in the context of the Second Coming and the Last Judgment!

I have something that I wish, beloved, to relate to thee... There was once a famine, it says, and the king was walking upon the wall; then a woman came to him and uttered these words: "O king, this woman said to me, Let us roast thy son to-day and eat him—tomorrow mine. And we roasted and ate, and now she does not give me hers." (From 2 Kings vi. 28) What can be more dreadful than this calamity? Again, in another place the Prophet says, "The hands of the pitiful women have sodden their own children." (Lam. iv. 10) The Jews then suffered such punishment, and shall we not much rather suffer?

Would you also hear other calamities of theirs? Read over Josephus, and you will learn that whole tragedy, if perchance we may persuade you from these things, that there is a hell. [2-17]

Once more we see that Chrysostom knows his Josephus well but knows nothing of the *Testimonium Flavianum*.

Our final citation of Josephus by Chrysostom is of considerable interest with regard to understanding the interpolation history of the text of Josephus. It is in Homily 13, on the subject of John the Baptist, that we last hear of Josephus from St. John Chrysostom:

What then is it which is set before us to-day? "John [*the Baptist*] are witness of Him, and cried, saying, This was He of whom I spake, He that cometh after me is preferred before me, for He was before me." The Evangelist is very full in making frequent mention of John, and often bearing about his testimony. And this he does not without a reason, but very wisely; for all the Jews held the man in great admiration, (even Josephus imputes the war to his death; and shows, that, on his account, what once was the mother city is now no city at all, and continues the words of his encomium to great length) and therefore desiring by his means to make the Jews ashamed, he continually reminds them of the testimony of the forerunner.[2-18]

Now there is no extant manuscript of Josephus in which the Jewish revolt and the destruction of Jerusalem are described as the consequence of executing the Baptist. Although the passage bears resemblance to an earlier interpolation [*Antiquities* 18:5:2] attributing the defeat of the troops of Herod the tetrarch by Aretas to the death of the Baptist, we have here, without doubt, *another* example of a Christian interpolation in the text of Josephus, forged some time before the end of the fourth century. Chrysostom knew his Josephus well and reported everything of relevance to Christianity. Although his copy of Josephus contained an otherwise unattested forgery pertaining to John the Baptist, it did *not* contain the now ubiquitous forgery known as the *Testimonium Flavianum*.

2.4. B. The Patriarch Photius

Our pursuit of church fathers who were ignorant of the *Testimonium Flavianum* – because their manuscripts of Josephus did not contain the counterfeit – takes us now to late in the first millennium, when Photius [c810–c893], the patriarch of Constantinople, at the behest of his brother Tarasios, wrote a colossal review of several hundred books written during antiquity and the Byzantine period. Entitled *The Library* (*Bibliotheca* or *Myriobiblon*), the treatise dealt with the works of Josephus in four different chapters ('codices') – if one counts Codex 48, which was actually written by Hippolytus but falsely attributed to Josephus.

Codex 47 reviews the part of Josephus' *Wars of the Jews* dealing with the suffering of the Jews during the siege and destruction of Jerusalem. There is no mention of Josephus (or anybody else) attributing the destruction of Jerusalem to the death of either James the Just or John the Baptist, arguing in favor of the hypothesis that his manuscript did not contain the interpolations inferred to have been present in the manuscripts used by Origen and Chrysostom. Of course, there also is no mention of Jesus.

Codex 76 contains Photius' first review of Josephus' *Antiquities of the Jews*. Although Photius reviews the sections of the *Antiquities* in which one would expect the *Testimonium* to have been found, he betrays no knowledge of any Christian connections being present in his manuscript. Since Photius was highly motivated to report ancient attestations to the beginnings of Christianity, his silence here argues strongly that neither the *Testimonium* nor any variant thereof was present in the manuscript he read. This also argues against the notion that the *Testimonium* was created to supplant an originally hostile comment in the authentic text of Josephus. Had a negative notice of a false messiah been present in the text read by Photius, it is inconceivable he could have restrained himself from comment thereon.

Codex 238 is devoted to a second review of *Antiquities of the Jews*. There is no mention of the *Testimonium* here either. Nevertheless, instead of accepting this as evidence that Photius' manuscript did not contain the disputed passage, René Henry,[2-19] the first scholar to translate the entirety of the *Bibliotheca* into a modern language, appears to share an opinion expressed by some other scholars that Photius would have said something if the *Testimonium* or something similar had *not* been in his text! We have already seen in chapter 1 that when Photius reviewed the histories of Justus of Tiberias, he noted disgustedly that "of the advent of Christ, of the things that befell him one way or another, or of the miracles that he performed, [*Justus*] makes absolutely no mention" [Codex 33].

The argument that Photius would have said something if the *Testimonium* had not been present seems also to suggest that he would *not* have reported the "evidence" even if the text had in fact contained it! This is so contrary to the psychology of Christian apologists of all times and all places that it hardly bears answering. However, the pages of Codex 238 contain data that not only refute this argument but give us deeper insight into *honest* ways in which spurious passages can become incorporated into manuscripts.

Although Codex 238 most definitely does not mention the *Testimonium*, Photius *does* report that "It is during his [*Herod's*] reign likewise that Christ our God is born from the womb of the Virgin for the salvation of our race," and that "in his insane anger against him [*Jesus*], Herod did not injure the Master but did bring about the murder of many small children." From the wording it is relatively clear that the sentence quoted was not actually in the main text of Josephus. Most likely, it was a *scholion* (a marginal note) written in the margin of the manuscript by someone who had the manuscript before Photius. In all innocence, we may suppose, Photius read the note and incorporated it into his report as an explanatory enhancement. With a bit more editorial reworking – whether honest or dishonest would not matter – we would have a manuscript of Josephus citing the virgin birth of Christ! (It is significant, I think, that an actual Greek manuscript of Josephus *is* known which contains a scholion pinpointing Herod's "slaughter of the innocents.")[2-20]

Evidence that Photius reported all Christianity-related data found in his text is the fact that in Codex 238[2-21] he *does* report the disputed passage about John the Baptist in Book 18, chapter 2, of *Antiquities*: "[*Herod*] was the one who put to death John the Precursor out of fear, Josephus says, that he might arouse the people against him since everyone was following the instructions of John due to his extraordinary virtue. It is during his reign also that the Passion of the Savior occurred."[2-22] It is quite clear that the Baptist story *was* present in the manuscript read by Photius. The "Passion of the Savior" sentence most likely was an interlinear gloss inserted by someone who read the manuscript before Photius.

St. Peter also puts in an appearance in Codex 238. It is very possible that Photius' copy of Josephus contained yet another Christian interpolation, although he might be just making an editorial comment when discussing "Agrippa the Great": "This Agrippa, to distinguish him from his son, is called Agrippa the Great. He ruled the Jews, says Josephus, by currying their favor. It was in order to please them, it would seem, that he put to the sword James the brother of John and attempted to kill Peter, the chief of the Apostles, but his scheme came to naught" [*cf.* Acts 12:1-18]. [2-23]

It just wouldn't be right to find St. Peter in Josephus without a mention of St. Paul, and so Photius dredges him up too: "It was under this Agrippa that St. Paul gave the speech before Festus" [*cf.* Acts 25 & 26].[2-24] Here again, Photius either has incorporated a scholion into the text or we have his own annotation of our historian. It is relatively clear that St. Paul was not mentioned in the main text of his copy of Josephus.

Finally, we discover that Photius' manuscript of Josephus' *Antiquities* also contains the disputed passage about James the Just[2-25] – which we shall discuss in more detail in chapter 3. For the moment we shall simply note that Photius' reading of James' title differs from that of the received text [*Antiquities* 20:9:1] in a very important way. Whereas the received text has "the brother of Jesus, who was called Christ, whose name was James," Photius' text reads simply, "James, the brother of the Lord." Why I think this is highly important will be explained later.

2.4. C. An Ancient Table of Contents

It is nothing short of a miracle that the Greek manuscripts of Josephus have been transmitted down to the present with a table of contents attached. Datable without question to before the fifth century of the common era, according to H. St. J. Thackeray, the first translator and editor of Josephus' *Antiquities* for the Loeb Classical Library bilingual edition, the chapter headings "are ostensibly written by a Jew," and "though it is improbable that these more elaborate chapter headings are the production of his [*Josephus'*] pen, they may well be not far removed from him in date."[2-26]

Despite the fine detail displayed by this ancient index, there is no indication of the *Testimonium Flavianum* at the requisite place. Nor is there notice of the death of James the Just or John the Baptist in the Greek manuscripts. Perhaps to be expected, a fifth- or sixth-century Latin (Christian) version of the table of contents adds "Concerning John the Baptist" at the point where surviving manuscripts have the disputed story.[2-27] All in all, the evidence of this ancient epitome provides dazzling confirmation for the thesis that Josephus knew nothing of Jesus, James, or John.

2.5. Evolution of the *Testimonium Flavianum*

2.5. A. Attempts to Trace the *Testimonium* to Josephan Text

So important is it to Christians to have any evidence whatsoever supporting the historicity of their Messiah, it has become fashionable to agree that the *Testimonium* in its present form is indeed a Christian interpolation – but an interpolation that simply modified an authentic mention of Jesus made by Josephus. A typical exponent of such apologetics is John P. Meier of the Catholic University of America. In an article entitled "Jesus in Josephus: A Modest Proposal,"[2-28] Meier argues that if one merely delete the most egregiously Christian sentences and phrases from the *Testimonium* one is left with a paragraph that matches Josephus' vocabulary and style – in Meier's opinion, a paragraph written by Josephus. The article is replete with an appendix statistically comparing the language of the *Testimonium* to the rest of Josephus' works and – for no understandable reason – to the Greek New Testament. Not surprisingly, Meier concludes that what he identifies as the Josephan core of the *Testimonium* matches Josephus' normal usage and differs from that of the New Testament. Since no one, to my knowledge, has ever suggested that any New Testament author was the forger of the *Testimonium*, it is hard to understand why Professor Meier would suppose his statistics prove anything at all.

In fairness, I must note that he himself admits as much: "One final caution: Word statistics are used here simply to indicate whether a word occurs fairly frequently either in Josephus or in the NT. The statistics should not be used simplistically to contrast the two bodies of material taken as a whole." That being the case, one must then ask, "Why bother with the show of statistics if it can't demonstrate that which is to be proved?" As we shall see, there do in fact appear to be several layers of interpolation comprising the present text of the *Testimonium*, and we have no reason to suppose that all the interpolators were incapable of faking Josephus' style. About the only value of Meier's statistics would be to show the unlikelihood of Abelard Reuchlin's hypothesis that Josephus (allegedly a pseudonym of Arius Calpurnius Piso) wrote the first 15 chapters of Acts along with the gospels of Matthew, Mark, and Luke (the last, however, with help from Pliny the Younger)![2-29] Reckoning more precisely, the value of Meier's statistics might be $1,416.19 – the amount of the prize offered by the Abelard Reuchlin Foundation to anyone able to disprove the hypothesis of Josephus/Piso as a New Testament author.

After pruning away what he considers to be the only Christian interpolations, Meier offers the following as *bona fide* Josephus:

> At this time there appeared Jesus, a wise man. For he was a doer of startling deeds, a teacher of people who receive the truth with pleasure. And he gained a following both among many Jews and among many of Greek origin. And when [*or better: although*] Pilate, because of an accusation made by the leading men among us, condemned him to the cross, those who had loved him previously did not cease to do so. And up until this very day the tribe of Christians (named after him) has not died out.

For obvious reasons, Professor Meier does not follow the above with the next authentic sentence of Josephus: "About the same time also, another sad calamity put the Jews into disorder...."

Apologists here risk impalement on the horns of a terrible dilemma. The more they pare down the *Testimonium* to phraseology that plausibly could have been used by Josephus, the less it can qualify as a calamity that put the Jews into disorder. On the other hand – or horn – is the fact that the more they reconstruct the text to make it describe a disordering calamity, the less plausibly could it be attributed to Josephus. There is no escaping the fact that *anything* placed between paragraphs 2 and 4 of chapter 3 of Josephus' *Antiquities* Book 18 would have to be a forgery.

It is sometimes suggested that a passage such as that reconstructed above would have been "neutral," and thus not something a Christian interpolator would have written. But although the reconstruction is free of Christian extravagances, it is far from neutral. Jesus is "a wise man" and it is implicit that he taught "truth." As Earl Doherty notes in his book *The Jesus Puzzle*,

> There is so much in this "neutral" account that Christians could have 'put a spin on' in defense of themselves and Jesus, so much that could have provided succor, support and even ammunition for what the Christian apologists were attempting to do in their writing. Origen alone spent a quarter of a million words contending against Celsus, a pagan who had written a book against Christian beliefs some half a century earlier. Origen draws on all manner of proofs and witnesses to the arguments he makes, including referring to Josephus. In Book I, chapters 46, 67, and 68 of *Contra Celsum*, Origen reports that Celsus had disparaged the miracles of Jesus, accusing Jesus of having learned his wonder-working tricks from the Egyptians. Origen counters this by claiming that Jesus' deeds were superior to anything contained in the Greek myths, and that Jesus performed his miracles in order to win people over to his commendable ethical teachings, something no Egyptian trickster could emulate. An appeal here to the declaration by Josephus, a respected Jewish historian, that Jesus had been a "wise man" who performed "wonderful works," would have served to place Jesus and his miracles in the favorable light in which Origen is trying to cast them.[2-30]

2.5. B. The Evidence of Translations and Text History

Even many scholars who hold the *Testimonium* to be a fraud do not suppose the interpolation sprang forth fully formed as it now stands from the hand of the forger whose quill first prized apart the story of Pilate's aqueduct from the story of the temple of Isis. Almost everyone accepts the fact that the first material inserted into the text of Josephus' *Antiquities* differed – probably significantly – from the received text quoted previously. A significant advance in understanding the evolutionary history of the *Testimonium* came in 1971 when the Jewish scholar Shlomo Pines published *An Arabic Version of the Testimonium Flavianum and its Implications.*[2-31] In a linguistic *tour de force*, Pines traced the translation and citation history of the *Testimonium* and demonstrated beyond reasonable doubt that an earlier form of the piece was not as outrageously Christian as the received text. Perhaps for diplomatic reasons, he did not offer his opinion on the authenticity of the earlier form, and so some polemicists have cited Pines' text as a vindication of the view that Josephus had at least *some* knowledge of Jesus. (As we shall see, Pines' text cannot pass the "another sad calamity" test with any higher score than does Meier's.)

2.5. B. a. Agapius of Manbij

Pines' monograph drew attention to a long-known tenth-century Arabic historical work, the *Kitāb al-'Unwān**of Agapius, the Melkite bishop of Manbij (Hierapolis). In his (apparently indirect) quotation from Josephus, Agapius supplies what would appear to be the earliest form of the forgery. Readers will note that it is much more realistic as an attempt to produce what a Jewish historian could actually have written. Pines translates the relevant part of the text as follows:

---

*In transliterating Arabic, Hebrew, and other Semitic languages several special characters are required for sounds that either are not found in English or are not recognized as separate sounds having their own alphabetic characters. The character | ' | is used to represent the glottal stop – the brief constriction of the throat that occurs when one pronounces a vowel at the beginning of an isolated word, but which is often absent when the word is preceded by *an*. Thus, we have *'apple*, pronounced with a glottal stop, but *'an apple* which, when smoothly pronounced, lacks the glottal stop before the second *a*. In Semitic languages, the glottal stop is given a symbol of its own and has the honor of being the first letter of the alphabet – *alef* – although in Arabic it carries a special diacritical mark called *hamza* to make it clear that the glottal stop is actually pronounced. Modern Arabic and ancient Hebrew have another special sound, a deep-throated, laryngeal glide,

Similarly Josephus the Hebrew. For he says in the treatises that he has written on the governance of the Jews: "At this time there was a wise man who was called Jesus. His conduct was good, and [he] was known to be virtuous. And many people from among the Jews and the other nations became his disciples. Pilate condemned him to be crucified and to die. But those who had become his disciples did not abandon his discipleship. They reported that he had appeared to them three days after his crucifixion, and that he was alive; accordingly, he was perhaps the Messiah, concerning whom the prophets have recounted wonders." This is what is said by Josephus and his companions of our Lord the Messiah, may he be glorified.[2-32]

Before investigating the apparent evolutionary history of this version of the *Testimonium*, it is perhaps necessary to note that although this is much more realistic a forgery than the received text of the *Testimonium* published in all editions of Josephus, it nevertheless could not have been written by Josephus. Despite the dubitable "he was perhaps the Messiah" and ascription of the implied resurrection to a report by the disciples, it is still much too positive in its description of Jesus and would suffer as much from Earl Doherty's criticism (above) as do attempted "neutral" reconstructions.

It is curious indeed that "Josephus" gives no rationale for Pilate's condemnation of this "virtuous" man whose "conduct was good." Had Josephus actually written this passage, it is inconceivable that he would not have at least hinted at the charges leveled against our alleged wonder-worker. But alas, Josephus is

---

which is lacking in English but is considered to be a separate letter of the alphabet – *ayin* – and is transliterated with the special character | ‘ |. The difference between *alef* | ’ | and *ayin* | ‘ | can be illustrated by two rather undignified examples. A string of alefs (glottal stops) is pronounced when one imitates the sound of a machine-gun: ’aa!-’aa!-’aa!-’aa!-’aa! The *ayin*, however, is the dipping glide one makes when imitating the sound of an automobile engine being started up when it's ten below zero: aah ‘aah ‘aah ‘aah ‘aah. Ancient Hebrew, like most Semitic languages, had three gradations of aitch. The lightest of them, transliterated as *h*, was identical to the aitch of English. The harshest of them, usually transliterated as *kh*, was like the *ch* in the German name *Bach*. The middle aitch, transliterated as *ch* or with the special character *ḥ*, was pretty much like the sound one makes when breathing heavily on bifocals to fog them for cleaning.

silent as to the practical reason for the execution. But then, he could not, after all, have given the gospel reason why Jesus "suffered under Pontius Pilate" – for blasphemy – for the simple reason that a Roman official would not have taken jurisdiction over a trivial religious squabble among the Jews. Josephus would have had to say that his countrymen – not Pilate – stoned the bloke to death for blasphemy. Nor could Josephus have given the gospel reason for the blasphemy charge, *viz.*, that Jesus had called himself a "Son of God" – for the simple reason that that was a common expression potentially referring to *all* men and was not at all blasphemous.

Shlomo Pines considers it likely that Origen's text of Josephus' *Antiquities* contained a passage similar to the one quoted from Agapius that had prompted Origen to state clearly that Josephus did not believe in Jesus as the Christ (*i.e.*, the Messiah). On the face of it, there is nothing impossible about this supposition. After all, we know that Origen's text of Josephus had already been interpolated by Christians in other places in regard to the Jews attributing the fall of Jerusalem to the death of James, the brother of Jesus. Why not another interpolation dealing with Jesus himself? However, this idea is implausible because Origen would have made apologetic use of even the anemic Agapius version had it been available.

It is hard to say when the Agapius version first appeared. Even though the text we have dates only from the tenth century, it is clear that it represents a very early version of the interpolation. It could have existed already by the time of Origen [185–254], even if Origen himself is not likely to have seen it. From then, evolution must have occurred quickly, producing essentially the received version by the time of Eusebius [c260–c340]. (It has been common among Atheist writers on this subject for nearly two centuries to attribute the fraud to Eusebius himself. I shall consider this possibility subsequently.)

2.5. B. b. Michael the Syrian [1126–1199], Patriarch of Antioch [r. 1166–1199]

Although the *Chronicle of Michael the Syrian* dates to nearly three centuries later than Agapius, he too reports a version of the *Testimonium* that is more primitive than the received text, but more "evolved" than that preserved by Agapius. Shlomo Pines renders his version as follows:

> The writer Josephus also says in his work on the institutions of the Jews: In these times there was a wise man named Jesus, if it is fitting for us to call him a man. For he was a worker of glorious deeds and a teacher of truth. Many from among the Jews and the nations became his disciples. He was thought to be the Messiah [or Perhaps he was the Messiah]. But not according to the testimony of the principal [men] of [our] nation. Because of this, Pilate condemned him to the cross, and he died. For those who had loved him did not cease to love him. He appeared to them alive after three days. For the prophets of God had spoken with regard to him of such marvelous things [as these]. And the people of the Christians, named after him, has not disappeared till [this] day. [2-33]

Although Michael still retains the dubitative language concerning the possible Messianic identity of Jesus, it now sports the obviously fraudulent phrase "if it is fitting for us to call him a man." It also asserts baldly that Jesus came back to life three days after "he died." (It is curious that the received text of the *Testimonium* no longer mentions Jesus' death, even though it is implied by his restoration to life three days after the crucifixion.)

St. Jerome [c340–420] made a Latin translation of the *Testimonium* in chapter 13 of his *De Viris Illustribus* [*On Illustrious Men*], in his discussion of Josephus. It too is in one respect less developed than the received text with respect to the Messianic identity of Jesus:

> He [*Josephus*] wrote about the Lord in this way: "At about this time there was a wise man, Jesus, if it is proper to call him a man. He was the doer of marvelous deeds and teacher of those who receive truth willingly. He had many followers both among the Jews and the Gentiles, and he was believed to be the Christ [*Messiah*]. When, because of the envy of our principal men, Pilate had condemned him to the cross, those who at the first had come to love him persevered in faith. Living, he appeared to them on the third day. These and countless other marvels about him the prophecies of the prophets had foretold. And up until today the tribe of Christians, named after him, has not disappeared [*my translation*].[2-34]

Although Jerome lived a generation later than Eusebius, his Latin version of the *Testimonium* is more primitive than the received Greek text preserved in the latter's *Historia Ecclesiastica* and in most manuscripts of Josephus. It will be noted that Jerome retains the dubitative "he was believed to be the Christ," making it clear that the Greek text Jerome owned did not ascribe the belief in Jesus' messiahship to Josephus himself. It is a minor miracle that a Latin text disagreeing with so sacrosanct a text as the received Greek text of the *Testimonium* has survived to the present. It is not at all a miracle, however, that the Greek translation of *De Viris Illustribus* has eliminated all differences and reads exactly the same as the received text![2-35]

2.5. B. c. Did Eusebius Do It?

As I have noted previously, it has long been believed by Atheist scholars and others that Eusebius was the forger of the *Testimonium*, since no quotation or reference to it is to be found in any author's works surviving from before his time. Nevertheless, it is unlikely that Eusebius created the entire text *ex nihilo*. We know that Josephus had been interpolated in some places (perhaps by Baptists and followers of James the Just) already by the time of Origen, and it is possible that the germs of the *Testimonium* had already begun to infect certain Christian-copied versions of *Antiquities of the Jews*. It is more likely that Eusebius simply "improved" the wording of the available manuscripts.

Is there any way to decide what the truth is in this matter? The answer to this question is a qualified 'yes.' If all the examples of the *Testimonium* found in Eusebius' writings are identical, it could indicate equally well either that Eusebius received the passage entire from a previous counterfeiter and reproduced it faithfully throughout his career, or that he invented it to his satisfaction early in his writing career and never thereafter changed it. On the other hand, if the *Testimonium* can be seen to change during Eusebius' career, it becomes fairly obvious that he had at least some hand in the creation of the interpolation as we now have it. Of course, such evidence could not tell the difference between the case where Eusebius made up the whole *Testimonium* early in his career (and merely 'improved' if from time to time thereafter) and the case where he simply doctored up the fabrication of a predecessor.

Eusebius actually quotes or refers to the *Testimonium* in three different works. The best known, of course, is found in his *Historia Ecclesiastica* [I, xi, 7-8], the Greek text of which is almost identical to the received Greek text of Josephus' *Antiquities*. The Syriac translation of this passage (from the fourth to the beginning of the fifth century) is very similar, although the Syriac has "For those who had loved him did not cease to love him" instead of the received text's "those who first had loved him did not cease." We have already seen that Jerome's Latin version differs from the received text of Eusebius by having "He was believed to be the Christ," instead of "He was the Christ."

According to Shlomo Pines, there exists a Latin manuscript of the *Testimonium* written before the eighth century that contains no equivalent of the "if indeed one ought to call him a man" that is so obviously inauthentic for Josephus. However, it is not clear if this represents a copy of Josephus himself or of Eusebius' quotation of the *Testimonium*.

Eusebius also quoted the *Testimonium* in his book *Theophania*, the Greek of which is lost and survives only in a Syriac translation. The *Theophania* dates from the late period of Eusebius' writing career,[2-36] and it is probably significant that its version of the *Testimonium* – judging from Hugo Gressmann's German translation of the Syriac[2-37] – does not seem to vary in any significant way from the received text in the *Historia Ecclesiastica*. If Eusebius was reworking the text of his church history through a series of editions – and polishing the *Testimonium* in the process – it is only natural that one of his last works should reflect the final form of his fabrication. It would appear that the *Theophania* was never as high-profile a work as Eusebius' *Historia Ecclesiastica*. In fact, the Greek text of it was allowed to suffer extinction. It is highly likely that its text was not monitored by apologists and censors to be brought into line with whatever was the current reading of the *Testimonium*. And so, the Syriac version of the *Theophania* would seem to indicate that the received version was in fact the final version Eusebius himself quoted. It is unlikely, therefore, that the received version grew into its present form as a result of 'editing' of Eusebius' writings after his death.

The fact that at least Jerome's Latin version of Eusebius' *Historia Ecclesiastica* differs from the received text in one important point ("He was believed to be the Christ," not "He was the Christ") would seem to indicate that Jerome possessed an earlier edition of Eusebius' history, and that at least one change in the text had occurred between that edition and Eusebius' final edition. Thus, at least in a small way, the charge that Eusebius was the forger of the *Testimonium* is true. How many editions his history went through during his lifetime and how many other changes he made we cannot judge giving the scant evidence surviving from antiquity. While Eusebius almost certainly had a hand in bringing the *Testimonium* to its present form, it seems unlikely that he was responsible for its *de novo* creation. It is my guess that Eusebius began his work with a text essentially identical to that surviving in Agapius' Arabic version and doctored it in stages until it became the received text. Who first forged the interpolation (and when he forged it), however, we probably shall never know. In any case, we must keep in mind that the first forger may have been a Jewish Christian with an agenda very different from that of the churches of Rome or Constantinople.

2.5. B. d. Further Evolution of the *Testimonium*: The Old Russian Version of the *Wars of the Jews*

It must have puzzled ancient readers to read about Jesus and Pilate in Josephus' late work, the *Antiquities of the Jews*, but find Jesus missing from the discussion of Pilate in the *Wars of the Jews*, a work preceding the *Antiquities* by perhaps some twenty years. Why would the Jewish historian omit mention of the Messiah in the book dealing most closely with the period in which Jesus should have lived, but find occasion to mention him twice in a book dealing with all of history, commencing with the creation of the world?

The gap must have been an embarrassment as well as a puzzle. Josephus *should* have mentioned Jesus in his first book. Eventually, the void was filled. Perhaps because the void was so well-known in the major cities of the Roman Empire, it could not easily be filled in without causing a scandal. Nevertheless, sometime before the thirteenth century, in Constantinople or its environs, a mutant form of the *Testimonium* found its way into the Greek text of the *Wars* – accompanied by forged Christian material totaling more than all the interpolations in the *Antiquities* combined. Probably not long after finding its way into the Greek text, it was

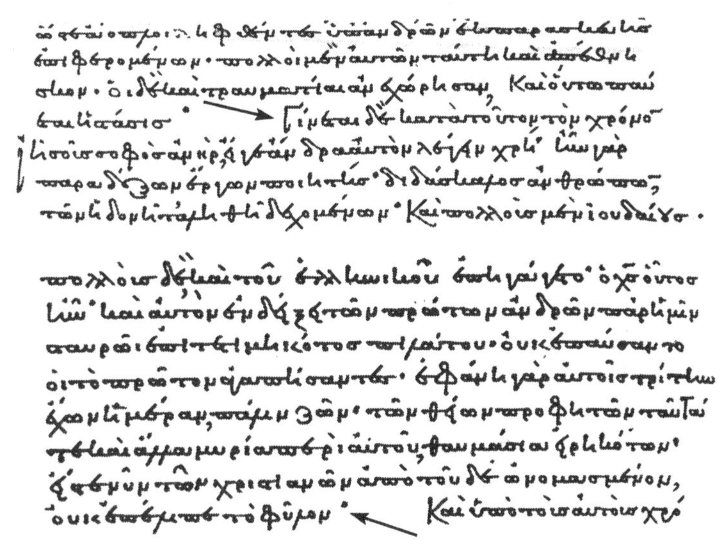

Figure 3. The oldest manuscript of the *Antiquities* of Josephus containing the *Testimonium Flavianum*, the eleventh-century *Codex Ambrosianus F128 Superior*. Arrows mark the beginning and end of the interpolation.

[From Robert Eisler, *ΙΗΣΟΥΣ ΒΑΣΙΛΕΥΣ ΟΥ ΒΑΣΙΛΕΥΣΑΣ*, Heidelberg, 1929]

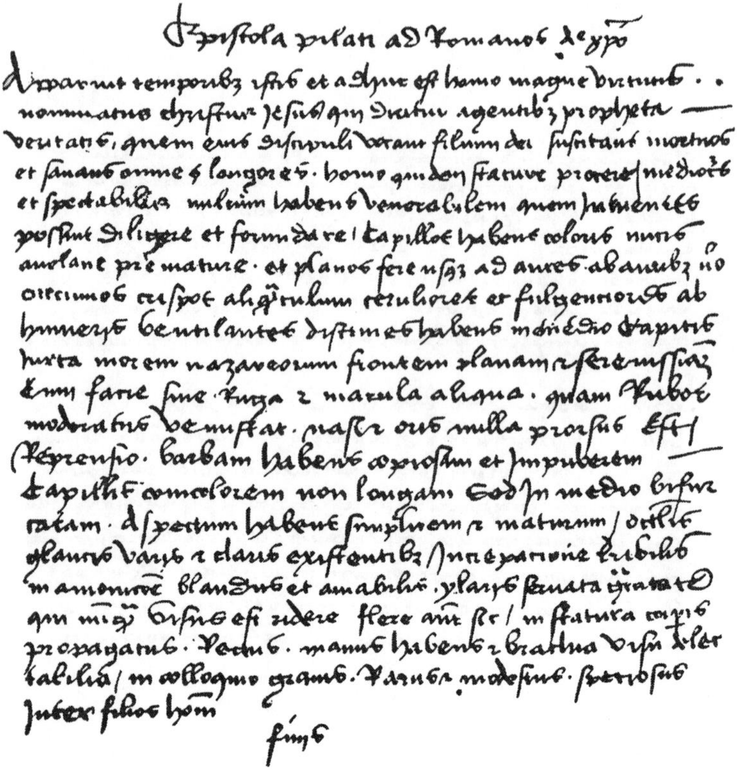

Figure 4. The Epistle of Pilate to the Romans Concerning Christ, an early Christian forgery that begins with a reflex of the *Testimonium Flavianum,* "There appeared about this time a man, if one may call him a man..." (*Cod. Paris Lat. 2962 Sæc. XV/XVI*).

[From Robert Eisler, *ΙΗΣΟΥΣ ΒΑΣΙΛΕΥΣ ΟΥ ΒΑΣΙΛΕΥΣΑΣ,* Heidelberg, 1929]

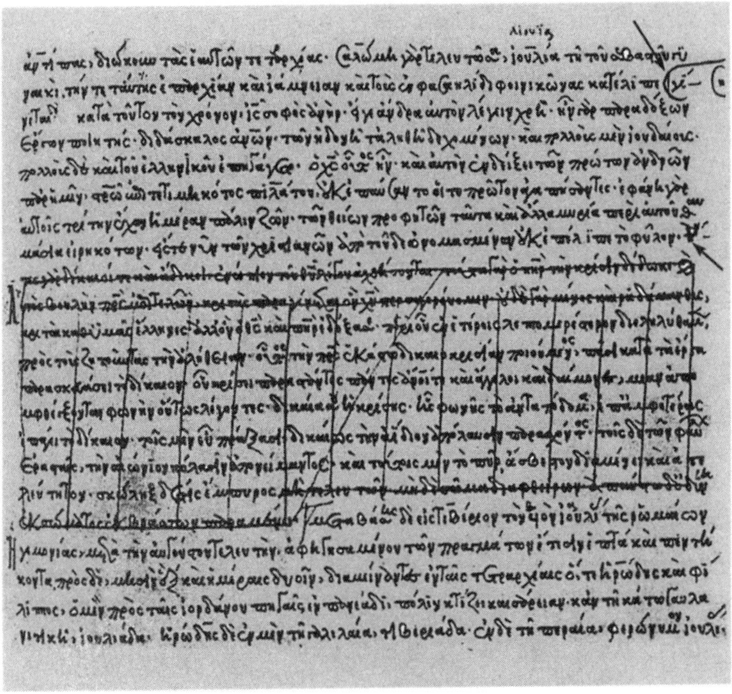

Figure 5. The absence of the *Testimonium Flavianum* from Josephus' earlier work, *The Jewish War,* was remedied by the forger of this manuscript, the *Codex Vossianus Græc. 72 Olim Petavianus,* in the University Library at Leyden. Not only did he insert the *Testimonium* from the *Antiquities* into the *War,* he further falsified the text by adding an excerpt from the writings of Bishop Hippolytus of Rome. Arrows mark the beginning and end of the *Testimonium* interpolation.

[From Robert Eisler, *ΙΗΣΟΥΣ ΒΑΣΙΛΕΥΣ ΟΥ ΒΑΣΙΛΕΥΣΑΣ,* Heidelberg, 1929]

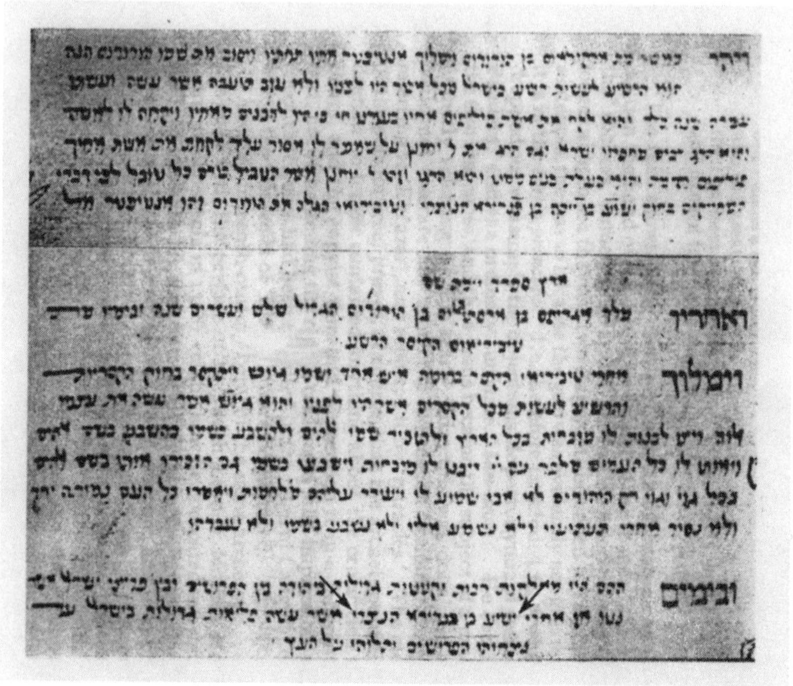

Figure 6. The Paris manuscript of Rabbi Judah Leon b.
Mosheh Mosconi's recension of the *Josippon,* a Hebrew version
of Josephus' *Jewish War* that contains passages about John
the Baptist and Jesus (*Cod. Hebr. 1280, Bibliothèque
Nationale*). Arrows mark the phrase (from right to left)
"Jeshua' ben Pandera the Nazorean." The last paragraph
reads: "In those days there was much party strife and great
disputes in Judaea between the Pharisees and the "robbers" in
Israel who followed Jeshuah ben Pandera the Naṣōraean, who
did great miracles in Israel until the Pharisees overpowered
him and hanged him upon a pole [*Alexander Haggerty Krappe
translation*].

[From Robert Eisler, *ΙΗΣΟΥΣ ΒΑΣΙΛΕΥΣ ΟΥ ΒΑΣΙΛΕΥΣΑΣ*, Heidelberg, 1929]

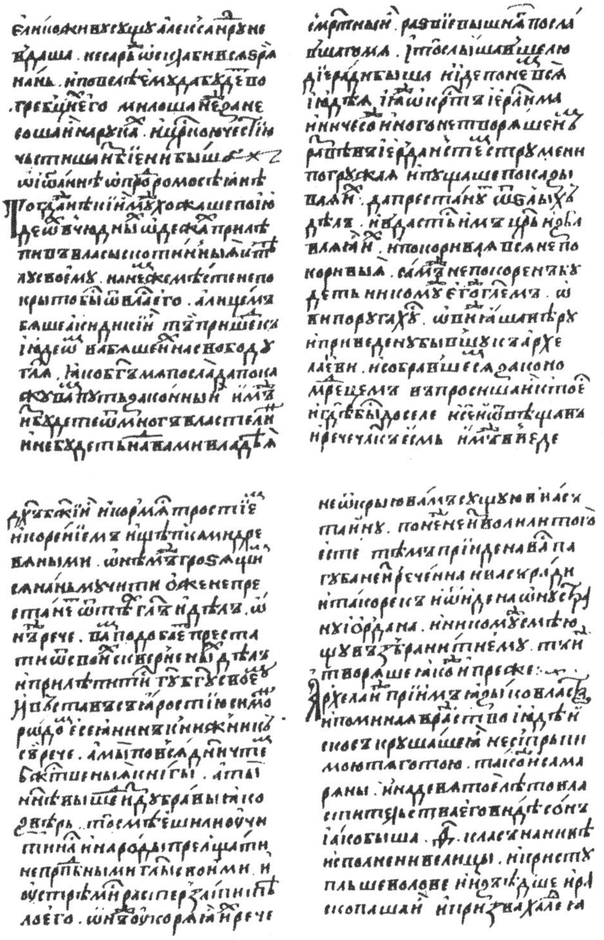

Figure 7. The most extensive interpolation of Josephus is that which occurred in the production of the Old Russian ('Slavonic') version of Josephus. These two pages of the fifteenth-century *Codex Kyrillo-Bjellos 63/1302* (St. Petersburg Public Library) tell of the appearance of a wild man – obviously John the Baptist – during the reign of Archelaus.

[From Robert Eisler, *ΙΗΣΟΥΣ ΒΑΣΙΛΕΥΣ ΟΥ ΒΑΣΙΛΕΥΣΑΣ*, Heidelberg, 1929]

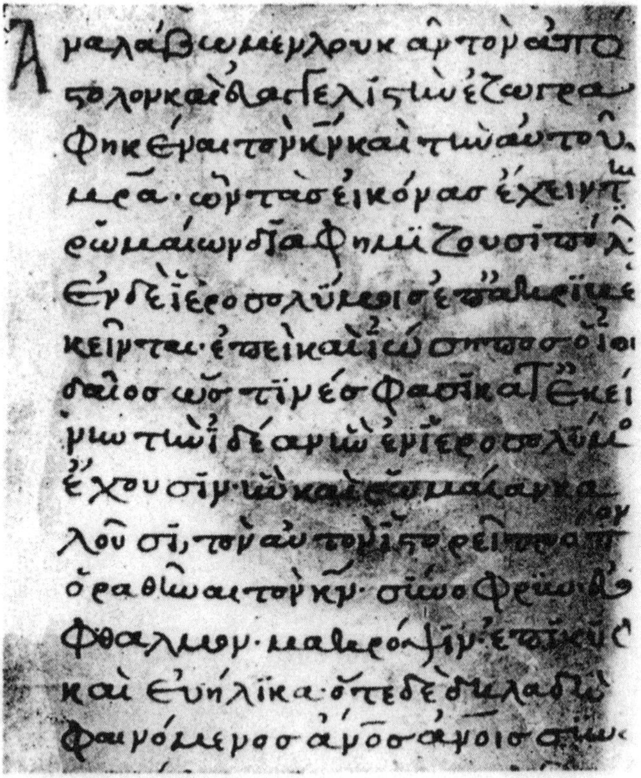

Figure 8. By the beginning of the eighth century, interpolations into Josephus went so far as to have him provide a physical description of Jesus – something the authors of the gospels seem to have overlooked. In the bottom half of this manuscript (*Andreas Cretensis, Cod. Paris, Græc. 1630*) of a work by Archbishop Andrew of Crete [b. *c*660 CE], we read: "But moreover the Jew Josephus in like manner narrates that the Lord was seen having connate eyebrows, goodly eyes, long-faced, crooked, well grown [*Alexander Haggerty Krappe translation*].

[From Robert Eisler, *ΙΗΣΟΥΣ ΒΑΣΙΛΕΥΣ ΟΥ ΒΑΣΙΛΕΥΣΑΣ*, Heidelberg, 1929]

translated into Old Russian, producing the so-called 'Slavonic Josephus.' The material corresponding to the beginning of the *Testimonium* was inserted between the third and fourth paragraphs of the ninth chapter of Book 2 of the *Wars*. As with the interpolation into the *Antiquities*, this insertion was also made in text dealing with Pontius Pilate and the disturbances associated with him. Elements from the beginning of the *Testimonium* have been greatly elaborated – although the name *Jesus* is not to be found:*

> At that time there appeared a certain man, if it is meet to call him a man. His nature and form was human, but the appearance of him more than (that) of a human (being): yet his works (were) divine. He wrought miracles wonderful and strong. Wherefore it is impossible for me to call him a human (being, simply). But on the other hand, if I look at (his) characteristic (human) nature, I will not call him an angel.
>
> And all, whatsoever he wrought through an invisible power, he wrought by a word and command. Some said of him, "our first lawgiver is risen from the dead, and hath evidenced this by many cures and prodigies." But the others thought he was (a man) sent from God. Now in many things he opposed the Law and kept not the Sabbath according to the custom of (our) forefathers. Yet again, he did nothing shameful nor underhand.
>
> And many of the multitude followed after him and hearkened to his teaching. And many souls were roused, thinking that thereby the Jewish tribes could free themselves from Roman hands. But it was his custom rather to abide without the city on the Mount of Olives. There also he granted cures to the people. And there gathered to him of helpers 150, but of the crowd a multitude.
>
> But when they saw his power, that he accomplished by a word whatsoever he would, and when they had made known to him their will, that he should enter the city and cut down the Roman troops and Pilate, and rule over them, he heeded it not. And when thereafter news of it was brought to the Jewish leaders, they assembled together with the high priest and said, "We are powerless and (too) weak to resist the Romans. Since however the bow is bent, we will go and communicate to Pilate what we have heard, and we shall be free from trouble, in order that he

---

*This and subsequent quotations from Slavonic Josephus are taken from *According to the Hebrews*, by Hugh J. Schonfield.[2-38]

may not hear (it) from others and we be robbed of (our) goods and ourselves slaughtered and (our) children dispersed."

And they went and reported (it) to Pilate. And he sent and had many of the multitude slain. And he had that wonder-worker brought up, and after he had held an inquiry concerning him, he pronounced (this) judgment: "He is (a benefactor, but not) a male-factor (nor) a rebel (nor) covetous of king(ship)." And he let him go, for he had healed his dying wife. And after he had gone to his wonted place, he did his wonted works. And when more people again gathered round him, he glorified himself by his action(s) more than all.

The scribes (therefore) being stung with envy gave Pilate thirty talents to kill him. And he took (it) and gave them liberty to carry out their will (themselves). And they took him and crucified him contrary to the law of (their) fathers.[2-39]

While expansion is in the nature of myths – the tallness of tales always grows with the passage of time – there are elements in this and its related insertions that seem to reflect very early "heresies" and documents. (As we shall see later in this book, echoes of the *Toldoth Yeshu* and the so-called *Gospel of the Hebrews* can be detected in these interpolations.) Although the forgery took place more than a millennium after the time of Josephus, the material inserted was not created new for the occasion. Hugh J. Schonfield, an expert on the ancient "Jewish Christians," has shown quite convincingly that Jewish Christian writings underlie the expansion of the text of Slavonic Josephus.

The reader may have noticed that the restoration to life of the crucified, unnamed Jesus is not to be found in the passage quoted above. Inexplicably, that part of the story is to be found replacing an *earlier* part of the Wars – text corresponding to the sixth paragraph of *chapter 2* of Book 2. The insertion is rather clumsy, referring to an "aforementioned wonder-worker" who will only be mentioned in later chapters! (Of course, it is possible that there was an interpolation into an earlier chapter that had somehow dropped out of the Greek manuscript tradition underlying the Old Russian translation.)

Claudius again sent his officers to those kingdoms, Cuspius Fadus and Tiberius Alexander, both of whom kept the people in peace, by not allowing any departure from the pure laws.

But if notwithstanding anyone did deviate from the word of the Law and information was laid out before the teachers of the Law, they punished or banished him, or sent (him) to Cæsar.

And since in the time of him (*i.e.*, Claudius) many helpers of the wonder-worker aforementioned had appeared and spoken to the people of their Master, (saying) that he was alive, although he had been dead, and "he will free you from bondage," many of the multitude hearkened to the(ir) preaching and took heed of their directions, not on account of their reputation, for they were of the humble(r) sort, some mere tailors, other sandal-makers, (or) other artisans. But wonderful were the signs which they worked, in truth what(ever) they wanted.

But when these noble governors saw the falling away of the people, they determined, together with the scribes, to seize (them) and put (them) to death, for fear lest the little might not be little, if it ended in the great. But they shrank back and were in terror at the signs, saying, "Not through drugs do such wonders come to pass; but if they do not proceed from the counsel of God, then will they quickly be exposed." And they gave them liberty to go where they would. But afterwards for the deeds done by them they sent them away, some to Cæsar, others to Antioch, for a trial of the(ir) cause, others to distant lands. [2-40]

A third major Christian interpolation into the *Wars* is found in Book 5, chapter 5, between paragraphs 4 and 5:

This curtain* (*i.e.*, of the Temple) was before this generation entire, because the people were pious; but now it was grievous to

---

*The legend of the rending of the veil (curtain) of the Temple of Yahweh can be found already in Mark, the oldest of the canonical gospels: "Then Jesus gave a loud cry and died. And the curtain of the temple was torn in two from top to bottom." [Mark 15: 37–38] Although conservative scholars have often argued that the composition of this gospel dates to before 70 CE – *i.e.*, the destruction of Jerusalem and the Temple of Yahweh by the Romans – most scholars accept the fact that Mark dates to some time after the fall of Jerusalem. To my knowledge, no one has ever sought to justify the later date on the basis of the story of the veil.

Robert Eisler, in his *The Messiah Jesus and John the Baptist, According to Flavius Josephus' Recently Rediscovered 'Capture of Jerusalem' and the Other Jewish and Christian Sources*, explains how the legend of the veil originated:

Josephus could not possibly have said that the veil in question was torn in his days and had been so ever since the death of Jesus, because the veil of the Jewish sanctuary was renewed every year. A second reserve curtain was always hung up behind it, in case it should have to be removed in the course of the year

see, for it was suddenly rent from the top to the bottom, when they through bribery delivered to death the benefactor of men and him who from his actions was no man.

And of so many other fearful signs, they tell, which happened then. And it was said that he (*i.e.*, Jesus) after being killed and laid in the grave, was not found. Some indeed hold that he

---

because of some Levitical impurity touching it by accident. Had the miracle really happened, the damaged texture would have been removed, not only in the year of the passion, but on the very day when it was rent asunder.

We know, moreover, how this particular legend originated. The last of the temple curtains was carried away to Rome by Titus with the rest of his spoils, and kept in the treasure-room of the imperial palace, where it could be seen by interested sightseers. Now, this last curtain of the temple had really been rent and was seen in this state by various Jewish visitors; small wonder, since it must have been torn from the door of the temple by the rough hands of Roman soldiery or even rescued from under the ruins. Jewish legend attributed the rending to the impatience of Titus to enter the Holy of Holies and to desecrate it. The emperor was even said to have cut his way through the curtain with his sword.

It is obvious that the Christian legend about the rent curtain must have grown up in Rome after A.D. 75, when the spoils of Jerusalem were first exhibited in public in the temple of Peace. It is, like its Jewish parallel, an ætiological myth evolved, maybe, under the influence of a pertinent prophecy in the *Testaments of the Patriarchs,* and understood afterwards in a symbolic way. [*Levi*, ch. 10: "a time will come when the wickedness of the Levites will grow to such a point that the curtain of the temple will split asunder and not hide them any more. And then you will be sent into captivity." *Benj.*, ix.: "the curtain of the temple will be split and the spirit of God descend (from the mountain of Jerusalem) to the Gentiles."][2-42]

Although this commentary is quite compelling and, I believe, essentially correct, there is a difficulty in it. If there was always a reserve curtain hanging behind the main one, why weren't *two* curtains taken to Rome? Or were two curtains taken to Rome but misinterpreted as being a single curtain torn into two parts? Whatever the case may have been with regard to a reserve curtain, the exhibition of the temple curtain in Rome in 75 CE remains as a plausible *terminus a quo* for the manufacture of the "miracle" found in the Synoptic gospels.

had risen, others that he was stolen away by his friends. But for my part I know not which speak more correctly. For one that is dead cannot rise of himself, though he may do so with the help of the prayer of another righteous man, unless he be an angel or another of the heavenly powers, or unless God himself appears as a man and accomplishes what he will and walks with men and falls and lies down and rises again as he pleases. But others said that it was impossible to steal him away, because they had set watches around his tomb, thirty Romans and a thousand Jews. Such (is the story told) of that curtain.[2-41]

2.5. B. e. Josephus the Trophy

With the insertion of a greatly inflated *Testimonium* into the *Wars of the Jews*, the history of Christian tampering with Josephus came to its climax. Even the apostles had swum into the ken of the Jewish historian! It is possible that this sacred shamming was the occupation of saintly scribes for close to a thousand years (*c*200–*c*1200 CE). Even today, there are defenders of the faith who exercise formidable casuistic skills to try to show that Josephus did indeed know of Jesus. The force of falsehood, it seems, is still needed to prop up the tottering idol of "the historical Jesus." The magical gospel Jesus cannot exist if there never was an historical Jesus. The need for external corroboration of the existence of Jesus of Nazareth has been a source of extreme discomfort for Christians ever since certain groups of them first formed the heresy that Jesus had been a man as well as a god. Josephus was the trophy pursued more than any other – despite the fact that at best he could only have reported hearsay, having been born after the time Jesus is alleged to have died.

Although objective historians are at a great disadvantage because of the mass destruction of ancient books by Christian censors over the centuries – the burning of the library at Alexandria is only the most sensational part of the story – enough material does survive to show that early Christians had definitely been challenged to show that their Messiah had been real. Justin Martyr [*c*100–*c*165], one of the earliest of the apologists, in his *Dialogue of Justin, Philosopher and Martyr, with Trypho, a Jew,* is sorely challenged by his Jewish antagonist:

> First be circumcised, then observe what ordinances have been enacted with respect to the Sabbath, and the feasts, and the new moons of God; and, in a word, do all things which have been

written in the law: and then perhaps you shall obtain mercy from God. *But Christ — if He has indeed been born, and exists anywhere — is unknown, and does not even know Himself, and has no power until Elias* [Elijah] *come to anoint Him, and make Him manifest to all. And you, having accepted a groundless report, invent a Christ for yourselves, and for his sake are inconsiderately perishing* [emphasis added].[2-43]

Whether or not Trypho was a real person or merely a rhetorical device, the survival of such an argument through all the centuries of Christian censorship comes close to being a true miracle. "Bring out your Messiah (Christ)!" Justin is taunted. "You can't do it! You can't even prove that he ever existed, let alone exists now!"

In the face of so blunt and frontal an attack, what does Justin do? Does he point out that his "Christ" is none other than a certain Jesus who used to live in Nazareth at the time of Pontius Pilate and several rulers named Herod? Of course not. It was not an option available to him, for "Nazareth" either did not yet exist in his day or it was just being settled at that very time. Had he even used the epithet "Jesus of Nazareth," he would have been challenged to produce a city as well as a savior – and it would be more than two hundred years before anyone could point with precision to the place now identified as Jesus' hometown and call it Nazareth. It is significant, I think, that Justin almost completely avoids the name Jesus itself, using titles such as *Christ* (Messiah) or *Savior* (the literal meaning of *Jesus*, the Hellenized form of the Aramaic *Yeshua*ʿ). Used as a name,* *Jesus* unavoidably conjures up images of a man of real flesh and real blood – a being existing in human time and space. *The Anointed One* (the literal meaning of the terms *Messiah* or *Christ*), however, lives easily as an ideal – as an entity beyond ordinary space and time.

---

*Of course the name *Jesus* also was a "word of power," a magical word that could be used by ancient Christians in the manner that the name *Yahweh* could be used by the initiated among the Jews. It is striking that one of the few occurrences of the name *Jesus Christ* in this dialogue finds it associated with the idea of strength, power, and even magic (miracles): "…we see and are persuaded that men approach God, leaving their idols and other unrighteousness, through the name of Him who was crucified, Jesus Christ, and abide by their confession even unto death, and maintain piety. Moreover, by the works and by the attendant miracles, it is possible for all to understand that He is the new law, and the new covenant," *etc.* [2-44]

Justin makes no attempt to answer Trypho's charges by means of historical or physical evidence of any kind. Instead, he uses the "evidence" of scripture. He triumphantly "proves" that Isaiah, Hosea, and Daniel had predicted the Christ for whom he offered his philosophical defense. While such lame argumentation cannot convince a modern skeptic, it apparently seemed convincing to Justin himself. Otherwise, he would never have left Trypho's devastating charge standing in his text as an indicator to future readers that Jesus of Nazareth was cut from the same cloth as the Wizard of Oz. Fortunately, Justin was not intelligent enough to see the inadequacy of his apology.

CHAPTER 3

James the Just, John the Baptist, and Other Perversions of Josephus

3.1. James the Just, the Brother of Jesus?

Jesus was not the only character whom early forgers sought to certify in the chronicles of Josephus. We must not suppose, however, that all the falsifiers were Christians in the ordinary sense of the word – *i.e.*, partisans of the Great Church which since fairly early times has been dubbed *Catholic* (meaning 'concerning the whole' or 'for everybody'). Indeed, the first contaminators of the Josephan text may have been Baptists – partisans of an otherwise unknown John the Baptist – or they may have been Jacobite* Jewish proto-Christians who recognized the political as well as spiritual authority of James the Just. We shall now examine some texts that bear evidence of other than ordinary Christian tampering.

As already noted, there is a second site where the received text of Josephus' *Antiquities* mentions Jesus. It is several 'books' later, in the first paragraph of the ninth chapter of Book 20. The paragraph deals with a nasty high priest named Ananus, a Sadducee, at the time that the Roman Albinus was on his way from Alexandria to Judaea to assume his post as procurator. *En passant*, it clumsily mentions the death of "the brother of Jesus,

---

*I use the term Jacobite only to signify their allegiance to James (Jacob) the Just. They should not be confused with the later Syrian sect of Monophysite Christians who refused to obey the decrees of the Council of Chalcedon of 451 CE and received the nickname Jacobites for their support of Jacob Baradaeus [490–577 CE].

who was called Christ, whose name was James." In modern times, a majority of scholars have considered this passage to be an authentic Josephan notice of Jesus. It is found in all surviving Greek editions of Josephus' *Antiquities*.

We must approach this second reference, however, with even more caution than was necessary in dealing with the *Testimonium*. This is because the name *Jesus* here is associated with the name *James* – ostensibly the character known as 'James the Just' – and we have certain proof that James was the motivation for very early tampering with the text of Josephus (probably in certain manuscript lines of his *War*, but *Antiquities* may also have been altered). Both Origen [*c*185–254 CE] and Eusebius [*c*260–*c*340 CE] refer to a Josephan passage in which the destruction of Jerusalem is attributed to the judicial murder of James the Just, a.k.a. 'James, the brother of the Lord,' a.k.a. 'James, the brother of Jesus.' This reference is not to be found in any surviving Greek manuscripts of Josephus' works, and it is obvious that although it had been interpolated into manuscripts ancestral to those owned by those fathers of the Church, it never found its way into the lines of transmission of any manuscripts that have come down to us. (The view that the passage was expunged because of Origen's dislike of it is not realistic. The Christian thing to do would have been simply to alter the passage, not delete it. Moreover, we know that the passage still existed at the time of Eusebius – indicating at least that Origen had not purged the reference from the manuscripts in the library at Caesarea.)

The fact that James the Just is known to have been cause for interpolations into the text of Josephus forces us to be even more skeptical of a passage where he is linked to Jesus. We shall examine such a passage in more detail after seeing how Origen and Eusebius provide evidence of manuscripts containing such interpolations.

3.1. A. James and Josephus in Origen

In Origen's apology *Contra Celsum* (*'Against Celsus'*), the forty-seventh chapter of Book 1 begins with an argument supporting the historicity of John the Baptist and Jesus (their historical reality appears to have been more burning a question then than now!) and then proceeds to cite an unknown passage from Josephus:

I would like to say to Celsus, who represents the Jew as accepting somehow John as a Baptist who baptized Jesus, that the existence of John the Baptist, baptizing for the remission of sins, is related by one who lived no great length of time after John and Jesus. For in the 18th book of his *Antiquities of the Jews*, Josephus bears witness to John as having been a Baptist, and as promising purification to those who underwent the rite. Now this writer, although not believing in Jesus as the Christ, in seeking after the cause of the fall of Jerusalem and the destruction of the temple, whereas he ought to have said that the conspiracy against Jesus was the cause of these calamities befalling the people, since they put to death Christ, who was a prophet, says nevertheless – being, although against his will, not far from the truth – that these disasters happened to the Jews as a punishment for the death of **James the Just, who was a brother of Jesus (called Christ)**, – the Jews having put him to death, although he was a man most distinguished for his justice. Paul, a genuine disciple of Jesus, says that he regarded this James as a brother of the Lord, not so much on account of their relationship by blood, or of their being brought up together, as because of his virtue and doctrine. If, then, he says that it was on account of James that the desolation of Jerusalem was made to overtake the Jews, how should it not be more in accordance with reason to say that it happened on account (of the death) of Jesus Christ...?[3-1] [*emphasis added*]

Even though it does not appear that Origen is quoting "Josephus" directly (although the emphasized passage may approximate the actual wording of the source), no extant manuscript of Josephus has any passage expressing the sentiment of this citation by Origen. It is instructive to compare this passage with another reference Origen makes to this lost interpolation in the seventeenth chapter of his *Commentary on Matthew*. Far from being outraged and hell-bent to purge the passage from the manuscript tradition as some apologists would have it, Origen thinks it is "a wonderful thing":

And James is he whom Paul says in the Epistle to the Galatians that he saw, "But other of the Apostles saw I none, save James the Lord's brother." [Gal. 1:19] And to so great a reputation among the people for righteousness did this James rise, that Flavius Josephus, who wrote the *Antiquities of the Jews* in twenty books, when wishing to exhibit the cause why the people suffered so great misfortunes that even the temple was razed to the ground, said, that these things happened to them in consequence of the things which they had dared to do against **James the brother of Jesus who is called Christ**. And the wonderful thing is, that, though he did not accept Jesus as Christ, he yet gave testimony that the righteousness of James was so great; and he says that the people thought that they had suffered these things because of James...[3-2] [*emphasis added*]

It may or may not be significant that in this citation, James has lost the epithet "the Just."

3.1. B. James and Josephus in Eusebius

A generation later, the same interpolation is cited by Eusebius in the twenty-third chapter of Book 2 of his *Church History* – this time, with what appears to be a direct quotation of the passage:

These things are related at length by Hegesippus, who is in agreement with Clement. James was so admirable a man and so celebrated among all for his justice, that the more sensible even of the Jews were of the opinion that this was the cause of the siege of Jerusalem, which happened to them immediately after his martyrdom* for no other reason than their daring act against him. Josephus, at least, has not hesitated to testify this in his writings, where he says, "These things happened to the Jews to avenge **James the Just, who was a brother of Jesus, that is called the Christ**. For the Jews slew him, although he was a most just man." And the same writer records his death also in the twentieth book of his *Antiquities* in the following words... [emphasis added] [*Then follows the relevant passage from Josephus quoted below.*][3-3]

Thus, both Origen and Eusebius provide unambiguous evidence that certain manuscript traditions existed in which the text of Josephus contained notices of James the Just – notices that had to have been interpolated at a very early date – which are not found in manuscripts that have survived to modern times. It seems probable they were inserted by Jewish proto-Christians for whom James was venerated as the founder of their faith. It is

---

*Implicit in the received text of Josephus quoted below is the date 62 CE for the death of James, eight years before the fall of Jerusalem!

probable that *Jesus* and *Christ* were not originally part of the interpolation but were added when the text passed from Jacobite fabricators into the falsifying factories of early Christianity.

3.1. C. James in Josephus Today

Whiston renders Josephus' lengthy first paragraph of the ninth chapter of Book 20 of the *Antiquities* as follows:

And now Cæsar, upon hearing of the death of Festus, sent Albinus into Judea as procurator; but the king deprived Joseph of the high priesthood, and bestowed the succession to that dignity on the son of Ananus, who was also himself called Ananus. Now the report goes, that this elder Ananus proved a most fortunate man; for he had five sons, who had all performed the office of a high priest to God, and he had himself enjoyed that dignity a long time formerly, which had never happened to any other of our high priests; but this younger Ananus, who, as we have told you already, took the high priesthood, was a bold man in his temper, and very insolent; he was also of the sect of the Sadducees, who were very rigid in judging offenders, above all the rest of the Jews, as we have already observed; when, therefore, Ananus was of this disposition, he thought he had now a proper opportunity [to exercise his authority.] Festus was now dead, and Albinus was but upon the road; so he assembled the Sanhedrim of the judges, **and brought before them the brother of Jesus, who was called Christ, whose name was James, and some others**, [or some of his companions;] and when he had formed an accusation against them as breakers of the law, he delivered them to be stoned: but as for those who seemed the most equitable of the citizens, and such as were the most uneasy at the breach of the laws, they disliked what was done; they also sent to the king [Agrippa] desiring him to send to Ananus that he should act so no more, for that what he had already done was not to be justified: nay, some of them went also to meet Albinus, as he was upon his journey from Alexandria, and informed him that it was not lawful for Ananus to assemble a Sanhedrim without his consent: – whereupon Albinus complied with what they had said, and wrote in anger to Ananus, and threatened that he would bring him to punishment for what he had done; on which king Agrippa took the high priesthood from him, when he had ruled but three months, and made Jesus, the son of Damneus, high priest. [*emphasis added*] 3-4

Before considering the authenticity of the James-Jesus passage quoted above, it is necessary to reexamine a previously mentioned clue about it found in the writings of the tenth-century church father Photius of Constantinople.

3.1. D. James and Josephus in Photius

It has already been noted that Photius, in his Codex 238 review of Josephus' *Antiquities*, mentions "James, the brother of the Lord" (*Ἰάκωβον τὸν ἀδελφὸν τοῦ Κυρίου*) instead of the awkward and convoluted "the brother of Jesus the so-called Messiah, James by name" (*τὸν ἀδελφὸν Ἰησοῦ τοῦ λεγομένου Χριστοῦ Ἰάκωβος ὄνομα αὐτῷ*) of the received text [20:200]. It is significant, I think, that Photius is not just using a shortened form of the received text but is referring to James in a completely different way – *without the use of the name* Jesus!

If the name *Jesus* had been present in Photius' copy of Josephus, it is hard to believe he would not have repeated it but rather have reverted to the archaic and obscure title *Brother of the Lord*. It seems extremely likely that the manuscript Photius reviewed made no mention of Jesus or the Messiah, but had instead a passage reading "And so he convened the judges of the Sanhedrin and brought before them James, the so-called Brother of the Lord, and certain others..." The book report of Photius makes it all but certain that the second alleged Josephan notice of Jesus – like the first – is inauthentic.

Unlike many of the New Testament characters, there is a small but real possibility that a certain character known as 'James the Just' – later to be titled 'Brother of the Lord' and 'Brother of Jesus' – was an historical personage. Robert Eisenman, in his unhappily titled book *James the Brother of Jesus: The Key to Unlocking the Secrets of Early Christianity and the Dead Sea Scrolls*,[3-5] makes a fairly convincing case that James the Just is to be equated with the 'Righteous Teacher' of the Dead Sea Scrolls from Qumran – thus making him an historical figure. (Unfortunately, it is not certain that the Righteous Teacher of Qumran was a real person and not a metaphor representing an ideal of the community.) Eisenman also equates James the Just with the Brother of the Lord known from Galatians 1:19 – "But I saw none of the other apostles except James the Brother of the Lord." It is striking that in Greek the title used here is *identical* to that found in Photius' review. Readers may remember also that both Origen and Eusebius quote the epithet *James the Just* as being equated to *brother of Jesus* in the "lost testimony to James" not found in surviving manuscripts of Josephus' *Antiquities*. So who – or what – was a Brother of the Lord? The answer is a bit complicated but interesting.

When the Hebrew scriptures were translated into Greek for the Hellenized Jews living in Alexandria, a peculiar problem arose relating to the secret name of the Hebrew deity Yahweh. The name *Yahweh* was a 'name of power' – a name believed to confer magical capabilities upon the priests whose job it was to guard the name's secrecy as part of the agreement ('covenant') supposed anciently to have been secured by Moses after some serious haggling with the hitherto unknown deity. Regardless of whether Moses ever existed, this is the story both Egyptian and Hebrew priests told: "Because of our contract with God, we know his secret name and can use the power of his name on your behalf. However, also because of our contract, you have to bring us your tithes and obey the following two hundred commandments."

So important was it to preserve the exclusive rights to the magic name, the priests who wrote the Torah made up a commandment forbidding "taking Yahweh's name in vain." (Notice that the English versions substitute *Lord* for *Yahweh*.) But the priestly con artists didn't stop with making one of the Ten Commandments a prohibition against unauthorized use of the name *Yahweh*. To instill a proper amount of fear and to discourage encroachment upon their priestly prerogatives, they created a commandment prescribing the death penalty for anyone guilty of misusing the secret name: "Whoever utters the name Yahweh (שֵׁם-יהוה) shall be put to death" [Lev 24:16].

The problem faced by the men engaged to translate the Hebrew scriptures into Greek (the Greek version is now known as the *Septuagint*, after the legendary seventy (or seventy-two) translators who produced it) was odd. Because Hebrew was (and still is) written with a defective alphabet – a script in which most vowels are not indicated – the secret name YHWH (יהוה) could be written without entirely giving away its pronunciation. And so, the so-called *Tetragrammaton* is to be found in many places in the Hebrew scriptures. The Greek alphabet, on the other hand, is very good at indicating vowels but is somewhat deficient in indicating consonants that are important in Hebrew. Thus, there is no separate letter for *y* in Greek, the letter *iota* serving both for the vowel *i* and the consonant *y*. The aspirate letter *h*, however, is completely absent from the Greek alphabet – the aitch sound being indicated by a mark called a 'rough breathing' placed over the vowel following the aitch sound. (The Greek letter that looks like a capital aitch is actually the letter *eta*, a long *e*.) As if this were not bad enough, there also has been no *w* in the Greek alphabet since the *digamma* (Ϝ) dropped out of use sometime before the year 500 BCE. Thus, it was impossible simply to transcribe YHWH as four consonants in Greek, and writing a phonetic equivalent of the name itself (something like *IAOΥE* or *IAOUH*) was out of the question – the translators probably would have been put to death for revealing how the name was pronounced. What to do?

The Septuagint translators solved the problem in two ways, both of them involving avoiding the word altogether. The simpler solution was to use the word *God* (ὁ Θεὸς), the word normally used to translate the Hebrew *'elohim* (אלהים), a plural word (!) which it was permissible to pronounce. While this solution often could be employed, there were numerous cases in which it could not be used, due to the frequently recurring Hebrew expression *YHWH 'ELOHIM* – which the King James translators always render as *the LORD God*. Since every word in Hebrew had to have an equivalent in the Greek text, a substitute word had to be found. Since in Hebrew usage it was already customary to substitute the word *'adonai* (אדני 'my lords' – perhaps imitating the plural *'elohim*) – the Greek translators simply rendered YHWH 'ELOHIM as *Lord the God* (Κύριος ὁ Θεος), rendering it as a singular noun, perhaps to avoid drawing attention to the polytheistic origins of the god of the Jews. And so, in both Greek and Hebrew, Yahweh was referred to as 'the Lord.' (Probably unknown to most evangelical Christians who sport bumper-stickers proclaiming "Jesus is Lord," the slogan really means 'Jesus is Yahweh.')

To return to our question concerning the nature of a 'Brother of the Lord,' it would appear that a person bearing such a title was a member of a brotherhood – a fraternity – that was in some way peculiarly committed to the service of Yahweh. It is likely that the title could have applied equally to communities of monks trying jointly to understand the mysteries of the deity, affiliations of freedom fighters seeking to purge 'the Holy Land' of pagans and pagan influence, or even brotherhoods-of-one – solitary eremites starving themselves into hypoglycemic hallucinations of 'the Lord.' It is also likely that the title 'The Brother of the Lord' was reserved for individuals who had attained a certain rank – perhaps that of leader – in such fraternities.

There is evidence that just such a fraternity was one of the sodalities involved in the ecclesiastical coalescence that became Christianity. James the Just – apparently the "brother of the Lord" referred to in Galatians 1:19 – would appear to have been its leader. That this does not refer to blood relationship – still less to a blood relationship with any Jesus – is clear from examination of the Pauline corpus and early Christian literature. Once again, Earl Doherty sums up the evidence very nicely:

> Compare also 1 Corinthians 9:5. Here is a literal translation: "Have we not the right to take along a sister (adelphēn), a wife, as do the rest of the apostles and the brothers (adelphoi) of the Lord and Cephas?" Look at the word "sister." No one would say that Paul is referring to his own or anyone else's sibling. He means a fellow-believer of the female sex, and he seems to use it in apposition to (descriptive of) the word "wife." Indeed, all translations render this "a believing wife" or "a Christian wife."
>
> This, too, should cast light on the meaning of adelphos, both here and elsewhere. It refers to a fellow-believer in the Lord. The more archaic rendering as "brethren of the Lord" conveys exactly this connotation: a community of like-minded believers, not "siblings" of each other or anyone else. Thus, a "brother of the Lord," whether referring to James or the 500, means a follower of this divine figure, and in 1 Corinthians 9:5, Paul would be referring to some of these members of the Jerusalem sect.
>
> Finally, it is not impossible that the phrase "the brother of the Lord" in Galatians 1:19 began as an interpolation or marginal gloss. Some later copyist, perhaps when a 2nd century Pauline corpus was being formed and after James' sibling relationship to the new historical Jesus had been established, may have wished to ensure that the reader would realize that Paul was referring to James the Just and not James the Gospel apostle. [3-6]

There is further evidence of the bloodless connotation of this title in Philippians 1:14, which refers to "Brothers in the Lord" (τῶν ἀδελφῶν ἐν κυρίῳ). Doherty adds:

> James was the head of a community in Jerusalem which bore witness to the spiritual Christ, and this group seems to have called itself "brethren of/in the Lord." The pre-eminent position of James as head of this group could have resulted in a special

designation for him as *the* brother of the Lord. Note, too, that such designations are always "of the Lord," never "of Jesus." We might also note that the term *"adelphos"* was common in Greek circles to refer to the initiates who belonged to the mystery cults.

But there is a further indication that early Christians knew of no sibling relationship between James and Jesus. The New Testament epistle of James opens this way: "James, a servant of God and of the Lord Jesus Christ..."

Few believe that James the Just actually wrote this letter, but if a later Christian is writing in his name, or even if only adding this ascription, common sense suggests that he would have identified James as the *brother* of the Lord Jesus if he had in fact been so, not simply as his servant. A similar void is left by the writer of the epistle of Jude. (Few likewise ascribe this letter to the actual Jude, whoever he was.) It opens "Jude, a servant of Jesus Christ, and a brother of James..."

Now if James had been Jesus' sibling, and Jude is James' brother, this would make Jude the brother of Jesus, and he appears as such in Mark 6. So now we have two Christian letters ascribed to supposed blood brothers of Jesus, yet neither one of them makes such an identification. Attempted explanations for this silence are unconvincing. They ignore the overriding fact that in the highly contentious atmosphere of most Christian correspondence, the advantage of drawing on a kinship to Jesus to make the letter's position and the writer's authority more forceful would hardly be passed up.[3-7]

Whatever Josephus may actually have written in the passage quoted above in section 1. C., it seems to me to be certain that he did not mention Jesus and – if he mentioned James at all – did not describe him as "the brother of Jesus, who was called Christ, whose name was James."

3.1. E. Evolution of James in Josephus

Despite skeptical bias occasioned by the fact that we know Josephus had been altered in other places to refer to James the Just, I think it is just possible that Josephus did actually mention him in the disputed passage in the ninth chapter of Book 20 of the *Antiquities*. If so, he would have written something like what I infer stood in the manuscript used by Photius: "And so he [Ananus] convened the judges of the Sanhedrin and brought before them James, the so-called Brother of the Lord, and certain others..."

This assumes, however, that Josephus' readers would be able to understand what a Brother of the Lord was and have some feeling for why he should have been the target of a Sadducee high priest. While the reference would have been readily understood by readers who were Jewish Christians, it is unlikely that the Roman audience for whom Josephus wrote the *Antiquities* would have made head or tail of the term. Still less, we might add, would that audience have made any sense of the received text: "[Ananus] assembled the Sanhedrim of the judges, and brought before them the brother of Jesus, who was called Christ, whose name was James, and some others...."

Nowhere does Josephus discuss Messianic movements, and the Greek word used for Messiah, *christos* (*māshīyaḥ* in Hebrew), literally means 'anointed.' Whereas the Jews anointed (oiled) their kings and priests, the Greeks anointed their wrestlers. Unexplained, the term *christos* appearing in Josephus' text would have been the occasion for considerable puzzlement (and mirth as well) amongst his readers. The discredited *Testimonium Flavianum* also makes the unwarranted assumption that readers would know who Jesus was and what messiahs were. But nowhere does Josephus tell his readers anything about christs or Jesus beyond what is contained in the two disputed passages. This is a further evidence of their spuriousness.

Both the received brother-of-Jesus text and my reconstructed "Brother of the Lord" text are implausible if attributed to Josephus himself. But whereas the received text can be ruled out by virtue of the report of Photius, my reconstructed text is not altogether impossible. More likely, however, the reconstructed text was an interpolation by a Jewish proto-Christian – a Jacobite who revered James the Just and did not know of any historical Jesus.* The received text, then, would have been the result of further doctoring by a member of the Great Church.

---

*For certain Jewish Christians, the word *Jesus* would not have been the name of an earthly person, but rather the title of a celestial being. The Greek ʹΙΗΣΟΥΣ [*Jesus*] is the equivalent of the Aramaic or Hebrew ישוע (*Yeshua*ʿ), which means *savior*. Thus, it was not Jesus of Nazareth in whom they believed, but a heavenly Savior. It is likely that Gnostic treatises such as *Dialogue of the Savior* bear witness to communities that did not interpret either the Greek *Iesous* or the Aramaic *Yeshua*ʿ as the name of a man, but rather as a title – *The Savior*.

If one looks to the larger context of the James-and-Jesus passage, there is the further possibility that the entire story about Ananus "beating Albinus to the draw" by convening the Sanhedrin and executing James and the rest likewise is a Jewish proto-Christian fabrication. There are problems in this section of Josephus' text that are difficult or impossible to solve. They could be caused by tampering, simple corruption of the text by incompetent scribes, or some combination of the two.

First of all, Ananus the son of Ananus here is said to have ruled for only three months before being deposed by King Agrippa. Josephus earlier discussed this Ananus in chapters 3–5 of Book 4 of *Wars of the Jews*. Nowhere is there a hint that he ruled only three months as high priest. To the contrary, he is high priest right up to his slaughter by the zealots and Idumeans shortly before the fall of Jerusalem. Far from being the nasty evildoer of *Antiquities* Book 20, Ananus the son of Ananus in the *Wars* is described as follows:

> I should not mistake if I said that the death of Ananus was the beginning of the destruction of the city, and that from this very day may be dated the overthrow of her wall, and the ruin of her affairs, whereon they saw their high priest, and the procurer of their preservation slain in the midst of the city. He was on other accounts a venerable, and very just man; and besides the grandeur of that nobility, and dignity, and honour, of which he was possessed, he had been a lover of a kind of parity, even with regard to the meanest of the people; he was a prodigious lover of liberty, and an admirer of democracy in government; and did ever prefer the public welfare before his own advantage, and preferred peace above all things... [*Whiston translation*][3-8]

As if this were not incompatible enough with the picture of Ananus the son of Ananus quoted above in section 1. C., there is a chronological incompatibility as well. Unless there were two different high-priest father-and-son pairs named Ananus, the Ananus who executed James has been placed (by an interpolator?) into the wrong time slot. Far from ruling at the very end of high-priest history, which ceased with the destruction of the Temple of Yahweh in 70 CE, the Ananus of our disputed passage is put in and out of office at the time that Lucceius Albinus assumed the post of procurator of Judaea – 62 CE! It is impossible to believe that Josephus could have written both accounts.

The nasty-Ananus passage has other features lacking in verisimilitude that make it sound more like a religious folktale than Josephan history. Albinus is already on the way to Jerusalem from Alexandria when Jewish envoys meet him, tell him what Ananus has done, and then instruct the new procurator as to what his rights and duties are! They tell him it was not lawful for Ananus to assemble the Sanhedrin without his consent – as if he would not himself know that. (Of course readers could not be expected to know that, and so the author of our tale needed to find a way to convey the information.) This implausible impertinence is followed by Albinus – already on the road to Jerusalem – writing an angry letter to Ananus threatening punishment unless he cease and desist. Why the letter should have gotten to Jerusalem significantly earlier than Albinus did is unexplained. Then, although the letter was allegedly sent to Ananus, King Agrippa is represented as having taken action against Ananus. Unless Albinus also sent Agrippa a pigeon-post epistle, it is hard to understand why the king should have done anything at all before the arrival of Albinus. This is another fairy-tale feature of our pericope. Finally, when Albinus does get to Jerusalem, there is no mention of his following up in the matter of Ananus:

> When Albinus reached the city of Jerusalem, he bent every effort and made every provision to ensure peace in the land by exterminating most of the *sicarii*. Now the high priest Ananias [*three manuscripts read* Ananus!] daily advanced greatly in reputation and was splendidly rewarded by the goodwill and esteem of the citizens; for he was able to supply them with money: at any rate he daily paid court with gifts to Albinus and the high priest. But Ananias had servants who were utter rascals... [*Feldman translation*]3-9

Even after allowance is made for the fact that this section of Josephus' history is confused and confusing due to the many high priests with the same or similar names (an irresistible invitation to scribal corruption) and the fact that Josephus appears always to refer to "high priest so-and-so" – never "the former high priest so-and-so" – it still seems highly likely that the entire story about Ananus and James is not authentic. As an interpolation by a Jewish proto-Christian who venerated James and had a quarrel with the establishment high priests it is entirely understandable. It does not, however, appear to have been inserted by a propagandist for the Great Church.

Was James a real person? Despite the dismal results I have obtained from examination of the Josephus forgeries, I don't think the possibility can be ruled out. The New Testament letter known as Paul's Epistle to the Galatians mentions James three times. The first notice [Gal 1:18–20] appears in 'Paul's' recounting of a business trip he made to Jerusalem: "Three years later I did go up to Jerusalem to get to know Cephas. I stayed with him for a fortnight, without seeing any other of the apostles, except James the Lord's brother. What I write is plain truth; before God I am not lying." Apart from the problem that we can't be sure if 'Paul' was a single individual or a school of theologians, there is the jarring "I am not lying" – which always makes me think, "Methinks he doth protest *too* much!" Nevertheless, the passage seems quite matter-of-fact and reasonable. It sounds like he went to meet religious leaders, one of whom was named James and held the title of "Brother of Yahweh." (Remember, in the Greek scriptures, *Yahweh* is always rendered *Lord*.) Sad to say, however, we cannot know if this is an actual reminiscence of a trip to Jerusalem or something made up to validate the writer's claims to authentic apostleship. After all, the second reference to James [Gal 1:9] advances exactly that purpose: "Recognizing, then, the favor thus bestowed upon me, those reputed pillars of our society, James, Cephas, and John, accepted Barnabas and myself as partners, and shook hands upon it, agreeing that we should go to the Gentiles while they went to the Jews." While many, if not most, of the characters in the New Testament would appear to be theological fictions, James the Just just might be real. It must not be forgotten, however, that if he was in fact an historical figure, as 'Brother of the Lord' he was not the brother of Jesus. Rather, he was the brother of another lord – Yahweh.

3.2. John the Baptist in Josephus' *Antiquities* 18:5:2 [18:116–119]

A comprehensive discussion of the question of the historicity of John the Baptist is beyond the scope and purpose of this book. However, it can simply be observed that there are problems associated with the New Testament notices of the Baptist that make them inadequate as proofs of his historicity. Similarly, the writings of the Mandaeans (*e.g.*, the *Ginza*) offer no usable data to support his historical actuality. Finally, we shall see that Josephus also does not seem to know anything reliable about the honey-and-locust-eating wild man of Christian tradition. Before examining the Josephan material, however, it is instructive to see how Jesus' 'Precursor' fits into the oldest strata of the canonical gospels and Acts – the only New Testament books that mention him.

3.2. A. The Baptist in Mark and Q

Mark, the oldest of the canonical gospels, makes mention of John the Baptist in a number of places. In my opinion, the oldest Markan mention of the Baptist – perhaps the only one to be found in the 'first edition' – is to be found in Mark 8:27–28:

> And Jesus went out, and his disciples, into the towns of Cæsarea Philippi: and by the way he asked his disciples, saying unto them, Whom do men say that I am? And they answered, John the Baptist: but some say, Elias [Elijah]; and others, One of the prophets.

This snippet of gossip makes it clear that John the Baptist could not have been a contemporary of Jesus. It treats John as though he were some ancient worthy on the level of Elijah and the prophets. For Jesus to be thought of as the reincarnation of the Baptist, either John lived a minimum of decades before the time assigned for Jesus' career, or Jesus would have had to have lived decades later than the period of Herod and Pilate. If it could be convincingly shown that John the Baptist was historical and lived at the time the disputed passage in Josephus indicates, it would be a strong argument either against the historicity of Jesus or the authenticity of the Markan passage quoted.

In the first chapter of Mark as it has come down to us, however, Jesus and John are exact contemporaries.* After the first

---

*In the Gospel of Luke, "Elizabeth" becomes pregnant with John before Mary becomes pregnant with Jesus. Astrologically, this became fixed in the church calendar with Jesus representing the winter solstice and John governing the summer solstice. Just as the winter solstice came to be adopted for the birthday of Jesus, so too the summer solstice was made the birthday of the Baptist. In astral terms, when John's 'star' was setting in the west, Jesus' 'star' would be rising in the east. "He must increase ($\alpha\dot{\upsilon}\xi\acute{\alpha}\nu\omega$) but I must decrease ($\dot{\epsilon}\lambda\alpha\tau\tau\acute{o}\omega$). He that cometh from above is above all: he that is of the earth is earthly, and speaketh of the earth: he that cometh from heaven is above all." [John 3:30–31]

verse of the gospel – actually the title, reading "The beginning of the gospel of Jesus Christ" (some manuscripts add "the Son of God") – the text begins with a Bible-study lesson exemplified by John and Jesus. Only at verse 14b does the actual gospel story begin:

> The beginning of the gospel of Jesus Christ, the Son of God;
>
> [2]As it is written in the prophets, Behold, I send my messenger before thy face, which shall prepare thy way before thee. [3]The voice of one crying in the wilderness, Prepare ye the way of the Lord, make his paths straight.
>
> [4]John did baptize in the wilderness, and preach the baptism of repentance for the remission of sins. [5]And there went out unto him all the land of Judæa, and they of Jerusalem, and were all baptized of him in the river of Jordan, confessing their sins. [6]And John was clothed with camel's hair, and with a girdle of a skin about his loins: and he did eat locusts and wild honey; [7]And preached, saying, There cometh one mightier than I after me, the latchet of whose shoes I am not worthy to stoop down and unloose. [8]I indeed have baptized you with water: but he shall baptize you with the Holy Ghost.
>
> [9]And it came to pass in those days, that Jesus came from Nazareth of Galilee, and was baptized of John in Jordan. [10]And straightway coming up out of the water, he saw the heavens opened, and the Spirit like a dove descending upon him: [11]And there came a voice from heaven, saying, Thou art my beloved Son, in whom I am well pleased. [12]And immediately the spirit driveth him into the wilderness. [13]And he was there in the wilderness forty days, tempted of Satan; and was with the wild beasts; and the angels ministered unto him.
>
> [14]Now after that John was put in prison, Jesus came into Galilee, preaching the gospel of the kingdom of God, [15]And saying, The time is fulfilled, and the kingdom of God is at hand: repent ye, and believe the gospel.

If one remove the jarring beginning of verse 14 – "Now after that John was put in prison" – the rest of verse 14 is the obvious beginning of a chapter entitled "The Beginning of the Gospel of Jesus Christ": "Jesus came into Galilee, preaching the gospel of the kingdom of God, and saying," etc. It is hard to believe that "Mark" could have assumed his readers would already know the tale of the imprisonment and execution of the Baptist. Rather, it is something a later interpolator might do, since he and his circle already were familiar with the developed story. Also, there is the further peculiarity that after we have already been told (v. 9) that "Jesus came from Nazareth of Galilee," only five verses later we are told that "Jesus came into Galilee." This has forced apologists to draw the implausible inference that "the wilderness" in which Jesus contested with Satan was not in Galilee. But this attempt to save the story only heightens the incongruity: Why doesn't the Greek text say that Jesus "came *back* into Galilee"?

Further support for the notion that verses 2–13 are not original with Mark is obtained from verse 9 – the only mention of Nazareth in the Greek text of that gospel. In that verse, contrary to the general usage of Mark, the name Jesus is 'inarticulate' in the earliest Greek manuscripts, *i.e.*, it is not preceded by the definite article. Normally, Mark refers to Jesus as ὁ Ἰησοῦς – 'the Jesus' (*i.e.*, 'the Savior'). It would appear that the verse was written by someone from a time at which it had already been forgotten that 'Jesus' was not a name, but a title.

It is a widely held opinion that John the Baptist was not present in the oldest stratum of the 'sayings gospel' generally referred to as Q (from the German *Quelle*, 'spring' or 'source').* It would appear then that after the Baptist had found his way into Q, he was inserted into Mark as well for political reasons that had developed. A rereading of the above quotation from Mark's gospel makes it clear that a major purpose of the passage was to subordinate John to Jesus – presumably at a time when there was a conflict between the early Jesus cult and a cult that revered the Baptist. By making John confess his inferiority to Jesus, the claims of the Johannine cult could be trumped. (Although this scenario is compatible with an historical John the Baptist, it is no more necessary to suppose an historical founder for the Baptist cult than for the cults of Isis or Mithra.)

The second major Markan passage retailing the tale of John the Baptist is found in chapter 6. Curiously, it takes the form of a fairy tale–like flashback – perhaps designed to obscure the fact that it too is an obvious intrusion into Mark's skimpy narrative. (In general, the very loose organization characterizing this gospel makes it hazardous to interpret every wrenching dislocation of subject as an interpolation.) The Baptist pericope occupies

---

*Q is generally accepted as having been the source for most of the Jesus sayings with which 'Matthew' and 'Luke' inflated the Greek text of Mark – which they purloined almost *in toto*.

verses 14–29 of Mark's sixth chapter, but verses both preceding and following the pericope are given here so readers may have some sense of context:

> ⁷And he [*Jesus*] called unto him the twelve, and began to send them forth by two and two; and gave them power over unclean spirits...
>
> ¹²And they [*'The Twelve'*] went out, and preached that men should repent. ¹³And they cast out many devils, and anointed with oil many that were sick, and healed them.
>
> ¹⁴And king Herod heard of him; (for his name was spread abroad:) and he said, That John the Baptist was risen from the dead, and therefore mighty works do shew forth themselves in him. ¹⁵Others said, That it is Elias [*Elijah*]. And others said, That it is a prophet, or as one of the prophets. ¹⁶But when Herod heard thereof, he said, It is John, whom I beheaded: he is risen from the dead.
>
> ¹⁷For Herod himself had sent forth and laid hold upon John, and bound him in prison for Herodias' sake, his brother Philip's wife: for he had married her. ¹⁸For John had said unto Herod, It is not lawful for thee to have thy brother's wife. ¹⁹Therefore Herodias had a quarrel against him, and would have killed him; but she could not: ²⁰For Herod feared John, knowing that he was a just man and an holy, and observed him; and when he heard him, he did many things, and heard him gladly.
>
> ²¹And when a convenient day was come, that Herod on his birthday made a supper to his lords, high captains, and chief estates of Galilee; ²²And when the daughter of the said Herodias came in, and danced, and pleased Herod and them that sat with him, the king said unto the damsel, Ask of me whatsoever thou wilt, and I will give it thee. ²³And he sware unto her, Whatsoever thou shalt ask of me, I will give it thee, unto the half of my kingdom.
>
> ²⁴And she went forth, and said unto her mother, What shall I ask? And she said, The head of John the Baptist. ²⁵And she came in straightway with haste unto the king, and asked, saying, I will that thou give me by and by in a charger the head of John the Baptist.
>
> ²⁶And the king was exceeding sorry; yet for his oath's sake, and for their sakes which sat with him, he would not reject her. ²⁷And immediately the king sent an executioner, and commanded his head to be brought: and he went and beheaded him in the prison. ²⁸And brought his head in a charger, and gave it to the damsel: and the damsel gave it to her mother.

29And when his disciples heard of it, they came and took up his corpse, and laid it in a tomb.

30And the apostles gathered themselves together unto Jesus, and told him all things, both what they had done, and what they had taught.

Perhaps because this pericope is so long and entertaining, its intrusiveness in Mark's narrative is not normally noted. But as with our previous interpolation, here again the verse preceding the story leads perfectly into the verse following it:

12And they ['the twelve'] went out, and preached that men should repent. 13And they cast out many devils, and anointed with oil many that were sick, and healed them. 30And the apostles gathered themselves together unto Jesus, and told him all things, both what they had done, and what they had taught.

Another reference to the Baptist is found in Mark's second chapter. Because of the loose organization of this chapter, the passage 2:18–20 – which recounts an encounter between Jesus and the *disciples* of John the Baptist and of the Pharisees – does not show obvious signs of insertion:

16And when the scribes and Pharisees saw him [*Jesus*] eat with publicans and sinners, they said unto his disciples, How is it that he eateth and drinketh with publicans and sinners? 17When Jesus heard it, he saith unto them, They that are whole have no need of the physician, but they that are sick: I came not to call the righteous, but sinners to repentance.

18And the disciples of John and of the Pharisees used to fast: and they come and say unto him, Why do the disciples of John and of the Pharisees fast, but thy disciples fast not? 19And Jesus said unto them, Can the children of the bridechamber fast, while the bridegroom is with them? as long as they have the bridegroom with them, they cannot fast. 20But the days will come, when the bridegroom shall be taken away from them, and then shall they fast in those days.

21No man also seweth a piece of new cloth on an old garment: else the new piece that filled it up taketh away from the old, and the rent is made worse.

22And no man putteth new wine into old bottles: else the new wine doth burst the bottles, and the wine is spilled, and the bottles will be marred: but new wine must be put into new bottles.

[Some scholars implausibly suppose verses 21–22 to be part of the answer to the question about fasting.]
23And it came to pass, that he went through the corn fields on the sabbath day; and his disciples began, as they went, to pluck the ears of corn...

It is perhaps significant that this passage recounts not an encounter between John and Jesus (*i.e.*, implying their contemporaneity), but rather between *adherents of the Baptist cult* and Jesus. It is further strange that they don't ask Jesus something like "Why do we have to fast, but your disciples don't?" Instead, they ask "Why is it that John's disciples and the disciples of the Pharisees are fasting, but yours are not?" [NEB] If this passage is not an interpolation, is it possible that 'John' (not called *the Baptist* in this passage) was inserted into an earlier saying that had nothing to do with the Baptist – the name *John* being substituted for *scribes*? If verse 18 originally had the *disciples* of the scribes and Pharisees ask *Jesus* a question, it would be the natural counterpart to verse 16 in which the *scribes and Pharisees* ask the *disciples* a question. It is interesting to note that the Gospel of Thomas (which possesses only one explicit reference to John) contains sayings [47:3–5] about wineskins and cloth patches, *with no connection to John the Baptist*:

47:3Nobody drinks aged wine and immediately wants to drink young wine. 4Young wine is not poured into old wineskins, or they might break, and aged wine is not poured into a new wineskin, or it might spoil. 5An old patch is not sewn into a new garment, since it would create a tear.3-10

The remaining Markan passage making explicit mention of John the Baptist is Mark 12:27–33:

27And they come again to Jerusalem: and as he was walking in the temple, there come to him the chief priests, and the scribes, and the elders. 28And say unto him, By what authority doest thou these things? and who gave thee this authority to do these things?
29And Jesus answered and said unto them, I will also ask of you one question, and answer me, and I will tell you by what authority I do these things. 30The baptism of John, was it from heaven, or of men? answer me.

[31]And they reasoned with themselves, saying, If we shall say, From heaven; he will say, Why then did ye not believe him? [32]But if we shall say, Of men; they feared the people: for all men counted John, that he was a prophet indeed. [33]And they answered and said unto Jesus, We cannot tell. And Jesus answering saith unto them, Neither do I tell you by what authority I do these things.

Once again, because of the loose structure of Mark's gospel, it is not possible to detect any obvious seams in the text. Nevertheless, it must be pointed out that even if this passage should prove to be authentic, it does not in any way indicate that John had been on the scene mere months before this confrontation. Furthermore, the parenthetic admission that "all held that John was in fact a prophet" [NEB] would seem to imply that John was in fact an earlier worthy of the caliber of Elijah – someone about whom all could agree. Had John been a phenomenon of then-recent months, it is unlikely that so unanimous an opinion would have confronted the priests.

Thus, a cursory examination of the oldest of the canonical gospels – with a glance at Q and the Gospel of Thomas – makes it not unreasonable to suppose that John the Baptist either was a mythical character such as Jesus and the twelve disciples, or he was a "prophet" who lived at least decades before the time assigned to him in the gospels or the passage in Josephus' *Antiquities of the Jews*.

3.2. B. The Baptist in the *Antiquities*

The fact that all known manuscripts of Josephus' *Antiquities of the Jews* contain a reference to John the Baptist and his execution by Herod Antipas, however, would seem to be strong evidence that the Baptist was an historical character. Moreover, citations of Josephus by Church Fathers would seem to indicate that Josephus did in fact write about the Baptist – or else, interpolations concerning him date to a very early period. Indeed, even the scholars of the Jesus Seminar, for the most part, have accepted the passage in the *Antiquities* as authentic.[3-11]

But is the Josephan Baptist really the product of Josephus' pen? I think not. Like the *Testimonium* and the accounts of James, it too appears to be the product of interpolators. Unlike the *Testimonium*, however, the differences between the 'Josephan'

Baptist and the Baptist of the gospels make it likely that the interpolation was not made by an adherent of what became the 'Great Church' – *i.e.*, the so-called Orthodox line of theological evolution – but rather by a Jewish Christian or an apologist for one of the myriad 'heretical' sects which are known to have existed from the earliest periods of Christian history. It might even be the work of a pre-Christian Baptist of some sort. A careful examination of the passage with respect to its context makes its likeliness as a forgery quite apparent.

The Baptist passage intrudes into a discussion in chapter 5 of *Antiquities* Book 18 where Josephus is discussing a dispute between Aretas, the king of Nabatea, and Herod Antipas, the tetrarch of Galilee and Perea. An unnamed daughter of Aretas had been married to Herod Antipas for many years. Learning that Herod had decided to marry his half-brother's wife Herodias, she fled to her father. He then declared war on Antipas, trouncing him soundly. The paragraph describing the Baptist, with some preceding and following material to provide context, is as follows:

> 1. ....So Aretas made this the first occasion of his enmity between him and Herod, who had also some quarrel with him about their limits at the country of Gamalitis. So they raised armies on both sides, and prepared for war, and sent their generals to fight instead of themselves; and, when they had joined battle, all Herod's army was destroyed by the treachery of some fugitives, though they were of the tetrarchy of Philip, joined with Aretas's army. So Herod wrote about these affairs to Tiberius; who, being very angry at the attempt made by Aretas, wrote to Vitellius, to make war upon him, and either to take him alive, and bring him to him in bonds, or to kill him, and send him his head. This was the charge that Tiberius gave to the president of Syria.
>
> 2. Now, some of the Jews thought that the destruction of Herod's army came from God, and that very justly, as a punishment of what he did against John, that was called the Baptist; for Herod slew him, who was a good man, and commanded the Jews to exercise virtue, both as to righteousness towards one another, and piety towards God, and so to come to baptism; for that the washing [with water] would be acceptable to him, if they made use of it, not in order to the putting away, [or the remission] of some sins [only,] but for the purification of the body: supposing still that the soul was thoroughly purified beforehand by righteousness. Now, when [many] others came to crowd about him, for

they were greatly moved [or pleased] by hearing his words, Herod, who feared lest the great influence John had over the people might put it into his power and inclination to raise a rebellion, (for they seemed ready to do anything he should advise,) thought it best, by putting him to death, to prevent any mischief he might cause, and not bring himself into difficulties, by sparing a man who might make him repent of it when it should be too late. Accordingly he was sent a prisoner, out of Herod's suspicious temper, to Macherus, the castle I before mentioned, and was there put to death. Now the Jews had an opinion that the destruction of this army was sent as a punishment upon Herod, and a mark of God's displeasure against him.

3. So Vitellius prepared to make war with Aretas, having with him two legions of armed men; he also took with him all those of light armature, and of the horsemen which belonged to them, and were drawn out of the kingdoms which were under the Romans, and made haste for Petra, and came to Ptolemais ... [Whiston translation][3-12]

It must be admitted that if paragraph 2 be a forgery, it is immensely more cunningly contrived than is the *Testimonium*. The fact that the picture of the Baptist is quite different from that exhibited in the gospels has led many scholars to suppose that Josephus actually wrote the words above. But such scholars have failed to realize that many non-gospel views of the Baptist existed during the first three centuries (indeed, a decidedly non-gospel type of John the Baptist holds a very prominent place in the Mandaean religion to this day), and an unknown number of them might have held the opinion now supposed to have been that of Josephus.

However this may be, it is obvious that the Baptist material intrudes into its context as roughly as does the *Testimonium*. Paragraph 3 follows paragraph 1 perfectly if paragraph 2 be taken away:

So Herod wrote about these affairs to Tiberius; who, being very angry at the attempt made by Aretas, wrote to Vitellius, to make war upon him, and either to take him alive, and bring him to him in bonds, or to kill him, and send him his head. This was the charge that Tiberius gave to the president of Syria. So Vitellius prepared to make war with Aretas, having with him two legions of armed men; he also took with him all those of light armature, and of the horsemen which belonged to them, and were drawn out of the kingdoms which were under the Romans, and made haste for Petra, and came to Ptolemais.

There are, however, four other good reasons to believe the Baptist passage to be bogus. Firstly, it is said that John was sent to the castle of Macherus to be executed. The clear implication is that the castle was Herod's to command. But the two sentences immediately preceding the above quotation of paragraph 1 show that that was not at all the case!

> [Herod's] wife having discovered the agreement he had made with Herodias, and having learned it before he had notice of her knowledge of the whole design, she desired him to send her to Macherus, which is a place on the borders of the dominions of Aretas and Herod, without informing him of any of her intentions. Accordingly Herod sent her thither, as thinking his wife had not perceived anything; now she had sent a good while before to **Macherus, which was subject to her father**, and so all things necessary for her journey were made ready for her by the general of Aretas's army, and by that means she soon came to Arabia, under the conduct of the several generals, who carried her from one to another successively; and she soon came to her father, and told him of Herod's intentions. [*emphasis added*][3-13]

While some apologists have argued that Macherus was, in fact, in Herod's domain, the point is irrelevant even if it could be shown to be true. For it is clear that *Josephus thought Macherus pertained to Aretas*, and he could not have developed amnesia for that opinion after writing just a few more sentences. It is clearly the trace of a bungling interpolator.

A second non-contextual reason for concluding paragraph 2 is an interpolation is that in it Josephus cites – without indicating he believes otherwise – the supposed Jewish view that Herod came to a bad end because of his execution of the Baptist. Elsewhere [18:7:1; 18:255], however, Josephus gives his own – differing – view of why his god punished Herodias and Herod: "And so God visited this punishment on Herodias for her envy of her brother and on Herod for listening to a woman's frivolous chatter" [*Feldman translation*]. [3-14]

A third reason for supposing this to be an interpolation is that Josephus does not mention the Baptist when discussing Herod in his earlier treatise, *The Wars of the Jews*.

A fourth reason, as we have already seen earlier, is that John the Baptist is not mentioned in the ancient Greek table of contents to Josephus' *Antiquities* but is invented for the later Latin version.

3.3. Other Christian Interpolations in Josephus

Christian interpolations into Josephus' text should not be supposed to have been limited to attempted documentation of the historicity of Jesus and the characters associated with him. They could also be made to confirm points of Christian doctrine, such as the predictive accuracy of the adopted "Old Testament" prophets. Robert Eisler[3-15] noted a late interpolation concerning the prophet Daniel in *Antiquities* 10:11:7 §276:

> And indeed it so came to pass, that our nation suffered these things under Antiochus Epiphanes, according to Daniel's vision, and what he wrote many years before they came to pass. In the very same manner Daniel also wrote concerning the Roman government, and that our country should be made desolate by them. [*Whiston translation*]

While the passage is found in all surviving Greek manuscripts, it was missing from the text used to make the second Latin translation at the time of Cassiodorus [c490–c580 CE].

A Christian interpolation concerning the prophet Jeremiah also has been demonstrated to have been made into the text of *Antiquities* 10:5:1 §79 [10:78–79]. The text now reads [*Whiston translation*]:

> Jeremiah the prophet composed an elegy to him [*Josiah*], which is extant till this time also. Moreover, this prophet denounced beforehand the sad calamities that were coming upon the city. He also left behind him in writing a description of [that destruction of our nation which has lately happened in our days, and] the taking of Babylon...

The words in square brackets are an interpolation – perhaps a Christian marginal gloss or scholion that became incorporated – something that could not have been original with Josephus. As

Eisler commented,

> The context shows that Josephus could refer the prophecy of
> Jeremiah only to the Babylonian captivity, for even in his own
> speech in *B. J.* V. 9 (§§391-3), where he had the best possible occa-
> sion to apply such prophecies to the circumstances of his own
> time, he did not dream of so doing. To the priest's son those
> prophecies had evidently been fulfilled, and he would have
> thought it absurd to expect a second fulfillment.[3-16]

Eisler noted another small-but-revealing interpolation into
Antiquities 7:3:2 (7:67) – apparently to establish a knowledge of
the Hebrews by the ancient Greeks. The full text reads as follows:

> It was David, therefore, who first cast the Jebusites out of
> Jerusalem, and called it by its own name, *The City of David*; for
> under our forefather Abraham it was called (Salem or) Solyma;
> but after that time, [some say that Homer mentions it] by that
> name of Solyma (for he named the temple Solyma, according to
> the Hebrew language, which denotes *security*). [*Whiston transla-
> tion*]

The words in square brackets were added by a Christian who
shared Eusebius' belief in the Jewish-Hellenistic theory. While
the point is of no interest or significance to modern Christians or
Atheists equally, it appears to have been of importance to ancient
Christians. Eusebius devoted the entire ninth book of his
Præparatio Evangelica to a demonstration that the early Greeks
knew of the Hebrews and that their historians agreed with the
Old Testament.

Yet another Christian interpolation is to be found in *Wars*
5:5:7 (5:236), where Josephus is describing the accoutrements of
the high priest [*Whiston translation*]:

> A mitre also of fine linen encompassed his head, which was tied
> by a blue riband, about which there was another golden crown,
> in which was engraven the sacred name (of God): [it consists of
> four vowels].

Eisler notes that

> ...the text given contains the holy name of God, and the
> priest's son Josephus would assuredly have been the last to

divulge the name to a heathen public. Furthermore, Josephus could not designate יהוה as four vowels, for the Hebrew script of his time used only three vowel characters, א, י, ו, for *a*, *i*, and *u*. There can be little doubt about the fact that the interpolation comes from a Christian hand, from some reader who was anxious to make a show of his antiquarian lore. For this there is documentary evidence. Niese's Cod. C in the Vatican and Cod. Paris Græc., No. 1428, show in the margin by the side of the words φέρων τὰ ἱερὰ γράμματα a coarse design representing the Hebrew Tetragramm. It is obvious that the bracketed words ταῦτα δ' ἐστὶ φωνήεντα τέσσαρα were originally meant to explain that marginal illustration, and were drawn into the text by a scribe's inadvertence.[3-17]

3.4. Conclusion

It would appear that religious ignorance and superstition, in addition to deliberate deception, lie behind the text of Josephus as it has come down to us. The forgeries began well before the ascendancy of the Great Church – perhaps being the work of Jewish (Ebionite, Nazorean, or even Baptist) hands. They could have been motivated by theologies whose names were forever effaced from the monuments of Christian history after Orthodoxy came to power. No information whatsoever can be extracted from the Jewish historian – whom we have studied for so many pages – that can serve as evidence of any historical Jesus. To the contrary, the silence of Josephus speaks loudly against any flesh-and-blood founder of the western world's majority faith. The very fact that he had to be falsified to give proof of the reality of 'Jesus of Nazareth' indicates that the Christians themselves had no documentable evidence of his historicity. Because they had no records or physical evidence whatsoever about the god they had recently made into a man, when challenged by Celsus or Trypho the Jew they had to manufacture both relics (to serve as physical evidence of their god-man) and would-be records – gospels and spurious insertions into the writings of credible authorities.

It is, nevertheless, rather surprising that Josephus did not appear to know anything about *Christians*, even if it is not unexpected that he knew nothing of Christ. The period in which he wrote was, after all, a period of active ferment during which Christian scribblings were being transformed into scriptures – if conventional dating of the New Testament scriptures be at all accurate. In spite of this, he is absolutely silent concerning both the alleged heaven-lowering activities of the Apostles and the hell-raising deeds of their supposed competitors. He knows nothing of any proto-Christian activities in Palestine nor anything of Christian persecution in Rome where he was writing.

If, as has long been suspected, the traditional scenario is incorrect – whereby Christianity begins in Jerusalem and then spreads to Rome and other capitals – the silence of Josephus is understandable. He focused little or no attention on Alexandria, Antioch, Ephesus, Corinth, Tarsus, or most of the other putative spawning beds whereon various scholars have inferred the larval development of Christianity must have unfolded. The presence of Christianity in Rome may not have been as early as many have supposed – a further argument against the authenticity of the story in Tacitus flamboyantly detailing the Neronian persecution of Christians.

It is, however, entirely possible that proto-Christianity was right under his nose, but Josephus didn't see it or recognize it for what it was. Who but an entomologist can see a gypsy moth in its caterpillar? But beyond this, there is strong evidence from the Pauline letters, the canonical gospels, and the Apocalypse (Revelation) that Christianity began as a mystery religion – a largely secret cult. Only after the gospel moth was out of its cocoon (sometime near the very end of the first century) would Josephus or any other historian have been able to take note of the strange cults that would merge into a Great Church which was destined one day to harness the whole Roman Empire and to goad and spur it into headlong descent into the Dark Ages of Faith.

PART II

THE RABBINICAL LITERATURE

CHAPTER 4

The Rabbis and the Mishnah

If Jesus had been an historical personage who was continually in conflict with "the scribes and Pharisees," it is only to be expected that the rabbinical descendants of his opponents would have preserved a vivid memory of his disputations and claims. It might even be expected that they would preserve details of his teachings (especially as they impinge upon the authority of 'the Law') not preserved in the canonical Christian writings. One might even expect to find an entire book in Aramaic or Hebrew in which Jesus is cited as a rabbi himself, if only to refute him in the form of the popular format "R. Yeshua said X, but R. Yehudah answered Y."

The idea that the rabbis suppressed memory of these disputes because they had always been bested in the debates is simply contrary to all that is known about the religious mind. No advocate of any religion – no matter how exotic – has ever been at a loss for words or solutions when presented with difficult arguments. One need only think of the success of amateur apologists such as Mormons and Jehovah's Witnesses to see how unlikely it would be for professional squabblers such as the rabbis to have been floored by anything any historical Jesus might have argued.

If the canonical stories about the wisdom of Jesus even as a child were true, some account of this should be found in the writings of his opponents. One would expect to find details of the family and lineage of the upstart Galilean alleged to have been born in Bethlehem in Judaea.

One might expect further that rabbinical writings would give some account of the peculiar Christian claim that even though the Jews must bear the blame for the judicial murder of their would-be Messiah, nevertheless it was the Roman government that killed him. Considering the fact that the name *Christianity* itself implies a messianic identity for our would-be Christ,* it is extremely odd to discover that not a single early rabbinical source so much as hints at messianic claims on behalf of any characters identifiable with the Jesus of Christianity.

If Jesus had *not* been an historical personage, on the other hand, one instead would expect rabbinical sources to reflect early conflicts with Christians – most likely, conflicts with Jewish Christians such as the Ebionites or the Nazoreans. (In fact, the use of the word *nōtzri* in Aramaic and Hebrew to denote Christians argues that early rabbinical Judaism had significant contact only with Nazoreans, not with Christians of the so-called 'Great Church.') In this case, nothing could be found credibly traceable to actual memories of Jesus. All would be secondhand reflections, inferences derived from Christian propaganda of one sort or another.

Apart from the question of whether or not the rabbinical writings mention Jesus of Nazareth at all, the main question to be dealt with in part 2 of this book is the question of whether the putative Jesus passages in these writings derive from interactions with Christ, interactions with Christians, or interactions with neither.

4.1. The Nature of the Rabbinical Literature

It can be argued that the main purpose of all rabbinical literature is to identify and elucidate *Torah* – the teachings believed to have been revealed to Moses by Yahweh. The major corpus of Torah, of course, is the written teaching embodied in the Pentateuch (Genesis, Exodus, Leviticus, Numbers, and Deuteronomy) – the so-called *Five Books of Moses*. But there is also an extensive oral Torah – traditions believed by Orthodox Jews to derive from information given by Yahweh to Moses separately from the material he gave him to be written down – information that was to be used to fill in those parts of the Pentateuch that were less than complete and to explain explicitly those things which were only implicit in the sacred text.

---

*The Greek word *christos*, from which both *Christ* and *Christianity* are derived, means 'anointed' and is the equivalent of the Hebrew *māshīah*, which has the same meaning. The Messiah would be the Anointed of Yahweh.

Commentary focusing on the written Torah is called *midrash*. Midrash (pl. *midrashim*) generally takes the form of a freestyle, homiletic exposition of scripture. In addition to midrash, rabbinical teachings comprise two types of material that involve the oral tradition as well: *halakhah* or *halachah,* and *haggadah.* All three types of discourse seek to make explicit the rules that are supposed to be implicit in the scriptures.

Halakhah (pl. *halakhot* or *halachoth*) comprises rules that are recognized as being valid and binding laws of religious practice. It generally takes the form of explicit commands, which may be accompanied by explanatory rationalizations. The full texts of the various sets of Ten Commandments are good examples of halakhot, except for the fact that they are part of the written 'Law' rather than part of the oral tradition.

Haggadah, on the other hand, is an illustrative type of teaching intended to build character without the aid of positive commands. It can take the form of anecdotes, parables, or stories 'with a moral.' It can involve real people such as famous rabbis, or it can be constructed completely of fictional characters. Even when it involves persons known to be historical, haggadah may still involve fictional development for the purpose of illustrating a moral principle.

The most important collections of halakhot are the two Talmuds, the Palestinian ('Jerusalem') Talmud and the Babylonian Talmud. Both Talmuds, although ostensibly collections of halakhot, contain a great deal of haggadah as well. As their names imply, the two Talmuds were published in different places: Palestine (but not in Jerusalem, despite the nickname) and Iraq. Both Talmuds share an ancient core of material, a collection of halakhot known as the *Mishnah.*

The oral traditions recorded in Hebrew in the Mishnah were collected and codified by a series of famous rabbis – including Aqiba [Akiva, *fl.* 110–135 CE] – culminating in the work of Rabbi Jehudah ha-Qadosh [Yehudah ha-Nasi], who is believed to have given final form to this collection of oral traditions around the year 220 CE. Shortly thereafter, it appears that the entire composition was committed to writing. It is important to note that until its commitment to writing, the Mishnah was a fluid and evolving creation of the rabbinical imagination. Not only did its ramshackle structure make it more subject to failures of memory than would be the case with verse epics such as the *Iliad*, in its private nature it was eminently suited for reshaping to fit the exigencies of particular political moments. When one considers how much *written* scriptures have been altered, interpolated, and otherwise compelled to serve the ends of their propagators, it is hard to take seriously historical claims based on oral traditions.*

The perplexing text history of the Mishnah and the Talmuds (see below) which contain it only heightens the need for skepticism concerning their value as historical witnesses. It can, I believe, be fairly charged that scholars of the rabbinical literature have not displayed anything close to the zeal of liberal Christian scholars in collecting ancient manuscripts of their books, collating them, and attempting to reconstruct earliest forms of the text. This is especially surprising considering the fact that Catholic censorship of Jewish writings during the Middle Ages and the early part of the age of printing effected a horrific mutilation of this literature. (Fortunately, most of the expurgated passages have been restored by scholars who have consulted the few manuscripts that have survived from the pre-print era.) According to Herbert Danby,[4-2] only three complete manuscripts of the Mishnah and only one complete manuscript of the Babylonian Talmud have survived. (Danby gives no dates for these manuscripts.) Surely, manuscripts of the Mishnah and Talmuds have survived in parts of the world not subject to the Catholic Church. Jewish scholarship generally thrived in the Islamic world, and it seems only reasonable that important manuscripts of great antiquity should be found in Iraq, Egypt, Yemen, and other parts of the non-Catholic world. Why haven't manuscript hunters worked harder to find them?

After completion of the Mishnah, the work of collecting more halakhot – the so-called *Baraitas* or *Baraithas* – continued for several centuries. These halakhot were included in elaborate commentaries that were attached to the Mishnah. Known as *Gemaras*, the Aramaic commentaries supplementing the Palestinian and Babylonian Talmuds differ in content, dialect of composition, and date of completion. The final redaction of the Palestinian Talmud (*i.e.*, the Gemara of the Palestinian Talmud) took place in 395 CE. Final redaction of the much larger Babylonian Talmud did not occur until more than a century later,

---

*A good example of how variable (and therefore, unreliable) oral transmission of stories may be can be seen in Louis Finkelstein's examination of the transmission of a Balaam story attributed to a rabbi of the fourth Tannaitic generation [110–135 CE], Eleazar of Modin.[4-1] (The *Tannaim* were scholars who compiled the Mishna.)

around the year 500 CE. (The controversial Talmud scholar Jacob Neusner dates the completion of the Babylonian Talmud even later, to around 600 CE.)

The Mishnah of Rabbi Jehudah was not the only collection of halakhot known to have existed, however. Previous Mishnas compiled by Rabbi Aqiba, R. Nathan, and R. Meir are also known to have existed, and traces of Mishnas attributable to Hillel and other Tannaitic sages can be found in the Talmuds. There is also a rival collection of halakhoth that has survived in Hebrew to modern times and is referred to as the *Tosefta* or *Tosephta* ('addition' or 'supplement'), even though part of it appears to be as ancient and authoritative as the Mishnah that forms the core of the two Talmuds. Nevertheless, substantial parts of it quote the Mishnah or are otherwise dependent upon it, and Jacob Neusner[4-3] dates the work to the third or even fourth century – after the completion of the Mishnah. The fact that all the rabbinical authorities cited in the Tosefta are also figures appearing in the Mishnah makes it appear that the Tosefta derives from the same sages who created the Mishnah – if one can believe the attributions in the Tosefta. In trying to weigh the historical value of sayings in the Tosefta, it is crucial that we be able to identify with confidence the rabbis who said them. Jacob Neusner's observations on this point are worth quoting:

> It is difficult to establish criteria for evaluating whether the Tosefta is a pseudepigraphic document, written by later figures but claiming the authority of earlier ones, or a collection of statements, external to those preserved in the Mishnah, deriving from the Mishnah's framers themselves. At this point nothing is to be taken for granted. We may assume neither the authentic, nor the pseudepigraphic, character of the Tosefta's attributions of its materials, and, with them, of the Tosefta's origin: alongside but slightly after the Mishnah, on the one side, or in the aftermath of two centuries of Mishnah exegesis among Talmudic authorities, on the other.[4-4]

In addition to the Talmuds and Tosefta, rabbinical literature also includes numerous *midrashim* commentaries, as we have already noted. The midrashim that are more halachic in nature are generally older than those that are more haggadic in nature. The halachic midrashim include *Midrash Siphra* on Leviticus, *Midrash Siphri* on Numbers and Deuteronomy, and *Midrash Mechilta*, on parts of Exodus. Although these were compiled later than the Mishnah, it is believed that some of them include some older material. The later haggadic midrashim are more numerous and include *Midrash Rabbah*, a collection of explications of the Pentateuch and the Five *Megilloth* – Ruth, Esther, Lamentations, Song of Songs, and Ecclesiastes.

The cabalistic literature, including the mystical and occult treatises *Jetzirah* and *Zohar*, since it has never been alleged to make mention of Jesus of Nazareth, will not concern us in this book.

Before we proceed to examine the rabbinical literature to see what, if anything, it has to say about Jesus of Nazareth, it is well to consider a question raised by R. Travers Herford in his *Christianity in Talmud and Midrash.* Despite his awareness of the frequent unreliability of the rabbinical literature, he was constrained by his belief in the historicity of Jesus to believe that he could sift nuggets of knowledge from the sands of sophism that fill so much of that literature. A century ago, in that seminal monograph he wrote:

> It will now be possible, as it is highly desirable, to attempt an answer to the question, What is the value, as historical evidence, of the Rabbinical literature? Can any reliance be placed upon statements found in works whose main purpose was not to impart exact knowledge of facts, but to give religious and moral teaching?
>
> Nothing is easier than to pick out from the Talmud and the Midrash statements in regard to historical events, which are palpably and even monstrously false, and that, too, when the events referred to were not very far removed from the lifetime of the author of the statements. And the conclusion is ready to hand, that if, in regard to events almost within living memory, such error was possible, reliance cannot be placed upon statements concerning events more remote. Yet that hasty conclusion is refuted by the fact that the statements referring to historical events are sometimes confirmed by external testimony, such as the writings of non-Jewish historians, and sometimes, when not directly confirmed, are still in accordance with such external testimony. No one would dream of accepting as true all the historical statements of the Talmud and Midrash; but they are certainly not all false. And it ought not to be, and I believe is not, beyond the power of a careful criticism, to distinguish with some degree of probability the historically true from the historically false. [4-5]

We can agree that not all the historical statements of the rabbinical literature are false. It remains to be seen, however, whether or not some or all of the statements *concerning Jesus* are fictional – or pertain to other persons.

4.2. Jesus in the Mishnah?

Since the Mishnah was completed in 220 CE and is the oldest part of the Talmuds, it is closest to the time at which Jesus is alleged to have lived. *A priori*, it might be expected both to have the most information on Jesus the man and to be the most reliable part of the Talmuds. Just what, then, does the Mishnah have to say about Jesus of Nazareth?

For disbelievers in the historical Jesus, it comes as no surprise to discover that the name *Jesus (Yeshu* or *Yeshuaʿ)* is nowhere to be found in the Mishnah. Moreover, the names *Ben Stada* and *Ben Pandira*, two important epithets that have been alleged as rabbinical code names for Jesus, also are missing in the Mishnah. Although both names are found in the rival Tosefta, it is not until the later Babylonian Gemara that we find mention of Yeshu ha-Notzri ('Jesus the Nazarene') as well. To be sure, the latter notices are alleged to be *Baraitas*, traditions dating from the same Tannaitic period in which the Mishnah was composed. Nevertheless, their late appearance makes them automatically suspect, and any assertion of their early nature is a thesis requiring proof.* It would appear that if Jesus is to be found in the Talmuds at all, he filled up his life backwards just as he did in the New Testament: the later the document, the more detailed the biography.

What little can be pieced together of the text history of the Mishnah indicates a degree of confusion that must be a cause for caution in considering the evidentiary value of the work. There are, it turns out, two types of Mishnah text that have existed

---

*We know from the many forged New Testament epistles ascribed to St. Paul and St. Peter how useful and irresistible it was to ascribe one's writings or sayings to earlier authorities. So too, the compilers of the rabbinical literature must frequently have yielded to the temptation to ascribe their opinions to rabbis of the early Tannaitic period. (The era of the Tannaim is considered to extend from the fourth century BCE until about 200 CE.)

side-by-side since very early times. There is the Palestinian type of text which, not surprisingly, forms the basis for commentary in the Palestinian (Jerusalem) Talmud. In addition, there is the Babylonian text-type, which is found in the Babylonian Talmud. But this is an oversimplification, because the Mishnah texts now *printed* in editions of the Babylonian Talmud are actually mixtures of the two text types. As Herbert Danby explains,

> Originally the Mishnah was not prefixed to paragraphs or chapters of the Talmuds, but was reproduced sentence by sentence (as it also is still) within the Gemara itself. It was the work of copyists of a later time to prefix a continuous text of the Mishnah in the manner now common; and the text they so prefixed was not always one which, in order and text, corresponded with the Mishnah text embedded in or assumed by the Gemara. Thus it comes about that in the Munich MS. [*dated 1342*] of the *Babylonian* Talmud ... and in the still earlier Florentine MS. [*dated 1177*], the Mishnah is of the distinctively *Palestinian* type.[4-6]

Danby gives a curious illustration of the confusion resulting from such a situation. At one point in the Babylonian Gemara there is a discussion about the 'fact' that the Mishnah omits mention of 'the eating of the Passover-offering,' yet the reading nevertheless is present in the Mishnah text. Conversely, the Palestinian Gemara includes the reading, but the reading itself is missing from the prefixed Mishnah text!

Finally, before seeing what, if anything, the Mishnah has to say about Jesus of Nazareth, it is necessary to remind readers that the Mishnah is the product of only one of several competing Jewish sects active at the turn of the era. It is only to be expected that it would be shaped by the religious issues of the time and would be biased by the value system peculiar to the Pharisees – the group from which all rabbinical Judaism derives. Josephus, describing the controversy between Sadducees and Pharisees in the time of John Hyrcanus [135–104 BCE], tells us that "the Pharisees have delivered to the people a great many observances by succession from their fathers which are not written in the law of Moses; and for that reason it is that the Sadducees reject them, and say that we are to esteem those observances to be obligatory which are in the Written Word, but are not to observe what are derived from the tradition of our forefathers."[4-7]

The tendentious nature of the Mishnah – which must always be considered in weighing its contents for their evidentiary value – is underscored by an observation of Herbert Danby:

> It is a reasonable hypothesis that a result of this controversy – a controversy which continued for two centuries – was a deliberate compilation and justification of the unwritten tradition by the Phariseean party, perhaps unsystematic and on a small scale in the earlier stages, but stimulated and fostered from time to time both by opposition from the Sadducees and by internal controversy (such as, *e.g.*, the disputes between the Schools of Hillel and Shammai) within the ranks of the Pharisees, culminating in the collections of traditional laws (*Halakoth*) from which the present Mishnah drew its material.[4-8]

We shall now consider the two passages in the Mishnah that have been considered to be references to Jesus.

4.2. A. That *Mamzer* So-and-So

The first Mishnah text we need to consider is found in the tractate *Yebamot* or *Jebamoth* (*Yevamot*, 'Sisters-in-law') at 4:13. It is repeated in the Babylonian Gemara at *Yebam.* 49[b] but is not mentioned in the Palestinian Gemara.

> **m. *Yebam.* 4:13:** Rabbi Shim'on ben 'Azzai said, "I have found a scroll of genealogies in Jerusalem; thereon was written: 'That so-and-so (איש פלוני) is a bastard (ממזר) born of an adulteress'; to confirm the words of Rabbi Yehoshua."

It is almost universally agreed by scholars that even though this passage makes no mention of Jesus by name, the reference to *so-and-so* (*pelōni*) identifies this as a coded reference to Jesus of Nazareth. Moreover, it is generally agreed that the reference to his being a *mamzer* (bastard) is an obvious reaction to late-developing (probably second-century) Christian claims of the virgin birth of their would-be savior. But was this the intent and understanding of the original author of this passage?

It cannot be doubted that from at least the Middle Ages onward, during times of persecution by Christians, *so-and-so* was used as a code word for *Jesus*. Even so, I am aware of no evidence that the word carried that signification at so early a period as that of the formation of the Mishnah – when Christianity had no power to persecute Jews. Indeed, *a priori*, unless the term *so-and-so* is a medieval retrojection into a third-century text,* we should be able safely to assume that when the term appears in documents from before the time of Constantine and the adoption of Christianity as the religion of the Roman Empire (early fourth century) it does *not* refer to Jesus.

It is a fair question to ask why this Mishnah passage is repeated in the Gemara of the Babylonian Talmud but not in the Gemara of the earlier Palestinian Talmud. Would it have been there if the Palestinian compilers had had enough time to complete their work? We know there were Christians in Palestine at the time the Palestinian Gemara was being compiled, and they must have been a thorn in the side of the rabbis. They must have been as exasperating as the Jehovah's Witnesses, Mormons, Moonies, or Jocks for Jesus of today. If the passage in question be in fact a reference to a Christian doctrine, why is it not mentioned in the Gemara written by men who actually had occasion to deal with Christians? Why is it repeated in the Gemara written by people who had far less opportunity to interact with them?

Even scholars who believe in the historicity of Jesus generally agree that even if the *so-and-so* of our passage refers to Jesus, it cannot be accepted as an actual primary witness of his historicity, for the simple fact that the *mamzer* reference would have to be a reaction to an already developed theological doctrine, *viz.*, the dogma of the virgin birth. That would put the passage as later than the edition of the Gospel of Matthew that first contained the genealogy of Jesus as traced through Joseph.† At earliest, the passage would date to the time the genealogy in Matthew

---

*Just one of many reasons for wishing we had manuscripts of the Mishnah dating from ancient times is that they would allow us to see when *so-and-so* is the original wording in a given passage or is a replacement for, say, the name of a Roman emperor.

†An early Syriac manuscript of the Gospel of Matthew, known as the *Codex Sinaiticus Syriacus,* still preserves a genealogy in which Joseph is the father of Jesus. It makes it clear that the canonical gospels went through a three-stage evolution: (1) No ancestry or birth origin given for Jesus (as in the present gospels of Mark and John); (2) Adding a genealogy of Jesus traced through Joseph back at least to David to establish his messianic potential; and (3) Adding an account of a virgin birth and altering the previously invented genealogy to be compatible with it.

was altered to allow for addition of the virgin-birth tale [Matt 1:18–25]. Furthermore, since the first rabbinical contacts almost certainly were with Jewish Christians such as the Ebionites and Nazoreans – who generally did not subscribe to the pagan notion that gods might occasionally couple with human females – and not the Hellenized Christians who used gospels such as those now found in the Greek New Testament, it must have been quite late before the rabbis would have had occasion to retort to Greek Christian idiosyncrasies. By just about anybody's reckoning, that would have been far beyond the time of any eye witnesses to Jesus himself. It would have been far too late to be of significance in establishing the historicity of Jesus.

R. Travers Herford,[4-9] whose *Christianity in Talmud and Midrash* I shall examine closely, points out that the Rabbi Shim'on ben 'Azzai mentioned in the passage under discussion was the contemporary and friend of Rabbi Aqiba* about the end of the first and beginning of the second century. Both were disciples of Rabbi Yehoshua ben Ḥananiah, who had been a singer in the Temple of Yahweh and had been the pupil of Rabbi Joḥanan ben Zaccai, who would have been old enough, Herford argues, to have seen and known Jesus.

In order to lay to rest the notion that the Mishnah *mamzer* passage in question is an allusion to Jesus, it is advisable to quote Herford's argument at length, since it is perhaps the most powerful argument in favor of the idea:

> When, therefore, Shim'on b. 'Azai reported that he had found a book of pedigrees, in which it was stated that 'a certain person' (*pelōni*) was of spurious birth, it is certainly probable that the reference is to Jesus. Unless some well-known man were intended, there would be no point in referring to him; and unless there had been some strong reason for avoiding his name, the name would have been given in order to strengthen the argument founded upon the case. For it is said that Shim'on ben 'Azai made his statement 'in order to confirm the words of R. Jehoshua.' And R. Jehoshua had laid it down that a bastard is one who is condemned to a judicial death, *i.e.*, one born of a union which was prohibited under penalty of such a death. Now Jesus undoubtedly had been condemned (though not on account of his birth) to a

---

*As we shall see later, one of two conflicting opinions represented in the Talmud has 'Jesus' be a contemporary of Aqiba – a century later than the New Testament dates.

judicial death, as the Talmud recognises... and Shim'on ben 'Azai brings the evidence of the book which he had discovered, to show that in the case of a notorious person the penalty of a judicial death had followed upon unlawful birth.

The alleged discovery of a book of pedigrees in Jerusalem may be historical; for the Jews were not prohibited from entering Jerusalem until the revolt of Bar Cocheba had been suppressed by Hadrian, A.D. 135, and ben 'Azai was dead before that time. What the book was cannot now be determined.[4-10]

Herford never prints the context of the passage in question, and so readers have no way to evaluate his claims. As soon as one looks at the material preceding the passage, however, it becomes obvious that Herford misunderstood the passage almost completely and that there is no reason at all to think that Jesus is being referred to even indirectly:

> **m. Yebam. 4:13**: Who is accounted a bastard?* [The offspring from] any [union of] near of kin which is forbidden [in the Law]. So R. Akiba. Simeon of Teman says: [The offspring of any union] for which the partakers are liable to Extirpation† at the hands of heaven. And the *Halakah* is according to his word. R. Joshua says: [The offspring of any union] for which the partakers are liable to death at the hands of the court. **R. Simeon b. Azzai said: I found a family register in Jerusalem and in it was written, 'Such-a-one is a bastard through** [a transgression of the law of] **thy neighbor's wife'‡, confirming the words of R. Joshua.** [*Herbert Danby translation*][4-11]

First of all, we may observe that Herford was wrong when he asserted that "R. Jehoshua had laid it down that a bastard is one who is condemned to a judicial death." It is not the *bastard* who is condemned to a judicial death, however, but rather his *parents*, whose actions define him. According to R. Yehoshua, a bastard is

---

*Deut 23:2. A bastard shall not enter into the congregation of the LORD; even to his tenth generation shall he not enter into the congregation of the LORD.

†Lev 18:29. For whosoever shall commit any of these abominations, even the souls that commit them shall be cut off from among their people.

‡Lev 18:20. Moreover thou shalt not lie carnally with thy neighbor's wife, to defile thyself with her.

one whose parents committed a capital sin. R. ben 'Azzai simply supports that assertion by mentioning that he had found a record which listed someone as being considered a bastard by virtue (!) of the fact that his parents had transgressed Leviticus 18:20 (the law prohibiting a man from having sex with his neighbor's wife) and Leviticus 18:29 (the law requiring death for violation of Leviticus 18:20).

Secondly, the fact that the person so classified is unnamed is completely unremarkable. The citation of a case from a genealogical register is for the simple purpose of documenting a written case of a person being classified as a bastard because his parents were capital criminals. Indeed, had the bastard in question been a person of note or notoriety he almost certainly would have been named. But it appears he was nobody of importance. He was simply *so-and-so*.

Thirdly, we need not imagine that at one time there was in Jerusalem a book of pedigrees in which Jesus of Nazareth was listed by name – even if only to be classified as a bastard instead of Son of God. Examination of the Mishnah passage in context shows that the book seen by R. ben 'Azzai, at least, had nothing to do with our would-be Messiah.

That this and many other passages in the rabbinical writings ultimately came to be understood as an allusion to Jesus is not questioned. We know that the Jews, just like the Christians, were in the habit of going back to old writings and 'discovering' new meanings and identifications in them. Just as the New Testament evangelists could go back to the Psalms and the Prophets to find hitherto unrecognized 'prophecies' of Jesus the Messiah, so too medieval Jews could go back to the writings of early rabbis and find Jesus therein as well. Just as there are not in fact any prophecies of Jesus to be found in the Psalms and the Prophets,* however, so too there are no notices of him in the earliest rabbinical literature either.

---

*The founding father Thomas Paine, in his *Examination of the Prophecies: The Age of Reason, Part Three*, investigated all the gospel claims of Old Testament prophecies of Jesus and showed that not one of them in its proper context and wording could possibly have referred to the Jesus of the gospels.[4-12]

2. B. Balaam without His Ass

The second and only other Mishnah text we need to examine is found in the tractate *Sanhedrin* ('Council,' referring to the Great Council – the Sanhedrin – which at one time dealt with capital crimes) at 10:2. As with the first alleged reference to Jesus in the Mishnah, the name *Jesus* is not to be found in this passage either. Rather, the name *Balaam* is used – allegedly as a code-word for Jesus. However, an argument presented in respect to the previous Mishnaic *so-and-so* passage bears repeating. At the time of consolidation of the Mishnah, Jews had little to fear from Christians and so had no reason to call our supposed Galilean *Balaam* instead of *Jesus*.

The passage usually is quoted in greatly abbreviated fashion, making the context unclear. To give readers a better sense of the rabbinical thinking in which the passage is imbedded, I shall quote not only the entire paragraph containing it, but the preceding paragraph and part of the following one. The translation is that of Herbert Danby:

> **m. Sanh. 10. 1:** All Israelites have a share in the world to come, for it is written, *Thy people also shall be all righteous, they shall inherit the land for ever; the branch of my planting, the work of my hands that I may be glorified* [Isa 60:21]. And these are they that have no share in the world to come: he that says that there is no resurrection of the dead prescribed in the Law, and [he that says] that the Law is not from Heaven, and an Epicurean. R. Akiba says: Also he that reads the heretical books, or that utters charms over a wound and says, *I will put none of the diseases upon thee which I have put upon the Egyptians: for I am the Lord that healeth thee* [Exod 15:26]. Abba Saul says: Also he that pronounces the Name with its proper letters.
>
> 2. **Three kings and four commoners have no share in the world to come. The three kings are Jeroboam and Ahab and Manasseh.** R. Judah says: Manasseh has a share in the world to come, for it is written, *And he prayed unto him, and he was intreated of him and heard his supplication and brought him again to Jerusalem into his kingdom* [2 Chr 33:13]. They said to him: He brought him again to his kingdom, but he did not bring him to the life of the world to come. **The four commoners are Balaam and Doeg and Ahitophel and Gehazi.**
>
> 3. The generation of the Flood have no share in the world to come, nor shall they stand in the judgment, for it is written, *My*

spirit shall not judge with man for ever [Gen 6:3]; [thus they have] neither judgment nor spirit. The generation of the Dispersion have no share in the world to come, for it is written, *So the Lord scattered them abroad from thence upon the face of all the earth* [Gen 11:8]; *So the Lord scattered them abroad*—in this world; *and the Lord scattered them from thence*—in the world to come. The men of Sodom have no share in the world to come...⁴⁻¹³

It is often argued not only that Balaam here is a reference to Jesus, but that Doeg, Ahithophel, and Gehazi are references to St. Peter, St. John (or St. James), and St. Paul, respectively. The likelihood of that argument will be considered after a detailed examination of the question of who was intended by the Mishnah's use of the name *Balaam*.

As far as I have been able to discover, the main argument in favor of the thesis that this earliest Talmudic mention of Balaam (there are later ones in the Gemaras) must be referring to Jesus is because it "clearly" cannot be referring to the character of that name in the legendary story told in Numbers 22–24. As the story now stands in its final redaction, Balaam doesn't seem to be too bad a chap – certainly not bad enough to warrant being excluded from the afterlife in the ranks of the Sodomites and the "Generation of the Flood." Their naughtiness is well known to all. But Balaam? The prophet whose ass could talk? Why should he be excluded?

The story in Numbers 22–24 has it that the Israelites, still wandering on their way out of Egypt, have encamped in the lowlands of Moab, on the side of the Jordan opposite Jericho. Balak, the king of Moab, sees the immense horde and understandably is frightened. So he sends messengers to summon Balaam the son of Beor, a soothsayer living at Pethor on the Euphrates River, for the purpose of having him lay a curse upon the Israelites so that his army can overcome them. (Apparently Balaam was especially good at cursing, having a direct line to Yahweh, by whom his curses could be made reality.)

Balaam, although not an Israelite and coming from the Euphrates River far from Palestine, turns out to be on intimate terms with the same god the novice Jews have so recently acquired. So intimate is the relationship, the deity pays a visit to Balaam to inquire who the messengers are. Balaam explains that he is being invited to curse the Israelites. Yahweh forbids him to go to Balak, so he tells the Moabites that Yahweh won't let him go.

Balak sends a second embassy to Balaam, and once again he says he will consult with Yahweh, explaining that he "cannot disobey the command of Yahweh my God in anything, small or great." Once again, Yahweh comes to Balaam during the night. This time, he tells him to go with the Moabites but orders him to do only what he (Yahweh) instructs him to do.

Balaam saddles his ass the next morning and goes with the Moabites to see Balak. Unexpectedly, since Balaam is following Yahweh's instructions exactly, the story [Num 22:22] now tells us "But God was angry because Balaam was going, and as he came riding on his ass, accompanied by his two servants [*the Moabite messengers seem to have disappeared*], the angel of Yahweh took his stand in the road to bar his way." Although the ass can see the angel, Balaam cannot. Three times, the ass balks at running into the angel; three times, she is beaten by Balaam. At this point, Yahweh causes the ass to speak and argue with Balaam about the beatings – whereupon Balaam is made to see the angel standing in his way with drawn sword. The angel repeats the same instructions Yahweh previously had given to Balaam.

When Balaam is received by Balak, he tells him [Num 22:38] "Whatever the word God puts into my mouth, that is what I will say." Three times in a row, instead of cursing the Israelites, Balaam blesses them. On the first oracular event, Balaam concludes [Num 23:10] "Let me die as men die who are righteous; grant that my end may be as theirs!" (This is not exactly the sort of thing one would expect from someone who is to be barred from the hereafter.) On the second occasion [Num 23:19], he utters the famous saying "God is not a mortal that he should lie, not a man that he should change his mind. Has he not spoken, and will he not make it good? What he has proclaimed, he will surely fulfill." After the third blessing, Balaam utters a fourth oracle which contains the famous messianic lines, "There shall come a Star out of Jacob, and a Sceptre shall rise out of Israel, and shall smite the corners of Moab, and destroy all the children of Sheth."

Balaam goes home – which now seems to be in Midian! Far from enjoying the type of death requested in his first oracle, later on he is killed by Moses and Phinehas when they are in the business of killing the five kings of Midian [Num 31:8].

Now it is indeed hard to see how the Balaam of this story could be the Balaam referred to in the Mishnah passage under consideration. But there are, in fact, good reasons to believe that there was more to the Balaam story than what we find in the

Book of Numbers as it has come down to us. Indeed, it is clear that the very chapters in which we find the story of Balaam are in fact a melding of two different versions of the story. In the first version, Balaam consults Yahweh and is forbidden [Num 22:7–14], then allowed [22:15–20] to visit Balak. In the second version [22:21–35], he does not consult with Yahweh and learns of his opposition only after being threatened by an invisible, sword-wielding angel.

It would appear from the second version of the tale that Yahweh was very displeased with something Balaam had agreed to or done. It is likely that something has been deleted by the redactor who added the whitewashing first version of the story. A clue as to what might have been left out can be found later in the Book of Numbers. Chapter 31 – the infamous chapter in which Yahweh orders a thoroughgoing genocide to be carried out among the Midianites – has Moses remonstrate with his officers: "15And Moses said unto them, Have ye saved all the women alive? 16Behold, these caused the children of Israel, *through the counsel of Balaam*, to commit trespass against the Lord in the matter of Peor, and there was a plague among the congregation of the Lord. 17Now therefore kill every male among the little ones, and kill every woman that hath known man by lying with him. 18But all the women children that have not known a man by lying with him, keep alive for yourselves." [*Emphasis added*]

Just what was it Balaam supposedly counseled? Numbers 25:1–3: "And Israel abode in Shittim, and the people began to commit whoredom with the daughters of Moab. And they called the people unto the sacrifices of their gods: and the people did eat, and bowed down to their gods. And Israel joined himself unto Baal-Peor: and the anger of the LORD was kindled against Israel."

It seems likely that there was at one time a substantial literature devoted to the Balaam character. In the Babylonian Talmud [b. *Sanh.* 106b] we read of a *"Chronicle of Balaam"* in which it supposedly was written that Balaam was thirty-three years old when Phinehas killed him. Although mainline scholars generally suppose the *Chronicle of Balaam* to be some sort of Christian gospel, it seems to me more probable that it was part of the Balaam literature of my hypothesis. It sounds like something one could expect to find some day among the moldered fragments of the Dead Sea Scrolls.*

Before examining in detail the Talmud passage mentioning the *Chronicle of Balaam* and the age of Balaam at his death according to a passage in the Babylonian Talmud, it is necessary to point out that Balaam is mentioned also in the books of Deuteronomy, Joshua, Nehemiah, and Micah in the Hebrew

---

*We know that the community of the scrolls had at least some interest in Balaam, since Numbers 24:15-17 (which mentions Balaam by name) is one of the messianic proof texts that form the so-called "4QTestimonia" 4Q175.[4-14] More tantalizing is 4Q378 Fragment 26,[4-15] a part of the mysterious *Psalms of Joshua*, which reworks words and phrases of the Numbers 24 Balaam episode into a prayer. Unfortunately, the fragment is badly damaged and we cannot know if the name Balaam itself formed part of the text.

Material from the Balaam cycle of Num 22–24 also appears in three quotations in 1QM, the so-called 'War Scroll.' In that document, written sometime around the turn of the era, the Balaam tradition has become transformed as a tool of apocalypticism, although it is not known whether Balaam's name ever occurred anywhere in the Qumran document as it does in the more famous apocalypse which forms the closing unit of the Christian New Testament. The thesis that a considerable Balaam literary tradition had come into existence by this time is supported by the following observation of John T. Greene, an expert on the Balaam traditions:

> The Balaam material quoted within 1QM has a tradition connection with the P recension [*the so-called Priestly Source hypothesized by higher critics of the Pentateuch*] of the Numbers Balaam cycle. Any entry into the *arcana mundi* of why only these three Numbers passages from the Balaam cycle were employed must be approached from the standpoint of that P trajectory. The three "footnotes" demonstrate how severely the Balaam tradition within the P trajectory had been altered by the time of the writing of the War Scroll. Balaam the figure and Balaam the type no longer served as foils against other priestly outsiders. At Qumran no nebulous outsider was held up as a paradigm, neither to be emulated, nor to be spurned. The Balaam of the recensions had all but disappeared, had become blended into the background of the Qumran P program. At Qumran the words ascribed to Balaam in... Numbers had been severed from the one who supposedly had uttered them. Balaam had been demoted: his words had been promoted.[4-16]

Bible. While not all those references are negative, they do serve to show that Balaam was a character of great interest to the biblical authors and that there was more to his story than now can be found in Numbers 22–24. Even more indicative of the existence of a Balaam literature, however, are the references to Balaam in the Christian New Testament.

In 2 Peter 2:14–16 we learn that Christians as well as Jews had nothing nice to say about Balaam:

> They have eyes for nothing but women, eyes never at rest from sin. They lure the unstable to their ruin; past masters in mercenary greed, God's curse is on them! They have abandoned the straight road and lost their way. They have followed in the steps of Balaam son of Beor, who consented to take pay for doing wrong, but had his offence brought home to him when the dumb beast spoke with a human voice and put a stop to the prophet's madness. [NEB]

In verse 11 of the epistle attributed by tradition to Jude, we find our unknown author fulminating:

> Alas for them! They have gone the way of Cain; they have plunged into Balaam's error for pay; they have rebelled like Korah, and they share his doom. [NEB]

Most illuminating of all, however, is the reference to Balaam and the Nicolaitans found in the second chapter of the Apocalypse [Rev 2:12–16]:

> "To the angel of the church at Pergamum write:
> " 'These are the words of the One who has the sharp two-edged sword: I know where you live; it is the place where Satan has his throne. And yet you are holding fast to my cause. You did not deny your faith in me even at the time when Antipas, my faithful witness, was killed in your city, the home of Satan. But I have a few matters to bring against you: you have in Pergamum some that hold to the teaching of Balaam, who taught Balak to put temptation in the way of the Israelites. He encouraged them to eat food sacrificed to idols and to commit fornication, and in the same way you also have some who hold the doctrine of the Nicolaitans. So repent! If you do not, I shall come to you soon and make war upon them with the sword that comes out of my mouth'." [NEB]

Certainly, this description of Balaam makes it reasonable to suppose that the compilers of the Mishnah would think him worthy of exclusion from paradise!

When one reflects that the fairy tale summarized above from the Book of Numbers can hardly be historical, it is immediately of interest to inquire why someone named *Balaam* was invented to play the leading role in the original fable. Although the etymology of *Balaam* (בלעם) is disputed, it would appear to have been intended as a conflation of the Hebrew words בלע (*bala'* : 'devour,' 'destroy,' 'extirpate') and עם (*'am* : 'the people'). Thus, *Balaam* would symbolize someone who leads the masses astray to their destruction. It has been suggested by G. R. S. Mead, in his book *Did Jesus Live 100 B.C.?*, that the Hebrew name is the equivalent of the Greek name *Nikolaos*, which is compounded from νικᾶν ('to conquer,' 'subdue') and λάος ('the people'). If this be correct, then the Nicolaitans mentioned in Revelation right after Balaam would be followers of Balaam. Whether the Jewish Christian redactor of the Jewish apocalypse believed to underlie the canonical Revelation intended the name to mean followers of Balaam literally or figuratively is uncertain. In any event, it appears that at the end of the first century of the common era there was an elaborate literature pertaining to Balaam and there were people who in some sense were conceived to be his followers. Whether or not they were Pauline Christians, as Mead supposes, or some other (perhaps Gnostic) group I would not hazard to guess.

While we will have more to say about Balaam later, and while it is likely that Balaam was in fact identified with Jesus at some time after the completion of the Mishnah, it seems clear enough that in this earliest occurrence *Balaam* has nothing to do with Jesus of Nazareth. That Balaam and Jesus were separate characters in rabbinical writings for a considerable period is evident from a bizarre passage in the Gemara of the Babylonian Talmud.

It will be recalled that the Gemara of the Babylonian Talmud was not completed until around the year 500 – or even 600 – of the common era. Even so, it retained a midrash concerned with the fatal war against Vespasian and Titus, allegedly reported by Rabbi Yoḥanan (200–279 CE), which clearly distinguishes Jesus from Balaam – both of whom are in Hell. It is found in the tractate *Gittin* ('Bills of Divorce') at 56ᵇ and 57ᵃ:

b. Giṭ. 56ᵇ,57ᵃ: Onqelos bar Qaloniqos, sister's son of Titus [*the conqueror of Jerusalem in 70 CE*], desired to become a proselyte.

He called up Titus by necromancy. He said to him, "Who is honoured in this world?" He replied, "Israel." "What about joining
them?" He replied, "Their words [*commandments*] are many and
thou canst not fulfill them. Go, join thyself to them in this world
and thou shalt become a leader, for it is written [Lam. i.5], *Her
adversaries have become the head.* Every oppressor of Israel is
made a head." He said to him, "What is the punishment of this
man?" [*i.e.,* "what is thy punishment"?] He replied, "That which
he determined for himself. Every day they collect his ashes and
judge him, and burn him and scatter him over seven seas."

He called up Balaam by necromancy. He said to him, "Who is
honoured in this world?" He replied, "Israel." "What about joining
them?" He replied [Deut. xxiii 6], *"Thou shalt not seek their peace
or their prosperity all [thy] days."* He said to him, "What is the
punishment of this man?" He replied, *"Per semen fervens."*
[*"Boiling in seminal fluid"*]

He called up Jesus [*The name has been restored to censored
printed versions from uncensored manuscripts*] by necromancy.
He said to him, "Who is honoured in this world?" He replied,
"Israel." "What about joining them?" He replied, "Seek their good,
seek not their harm. Every one who injures them, [it is] as if he
injured the apple of his eye." he said, "What is the punishment of
this man?" He replied, "By boiling filth." For a teacher has said,
"Every one who mocks at the words of the wise is punished by
boiling filth. Come and see the difference between the sinners of
Israel and the prophets of the peoples of the world who serve a
false religion." [*Herford translation*]4-17

As already noted, it is clear from the passage as reconstructed with the aid of uncensored manuscripts that Balaam and
Yeshu (Jesus) cannot be the same person and that at least here
the former cannot be a code word signifying the latter. Unfortunately, lacking early manuscripts of this tractate we cannot
know how authentic the *Yeshu* really is in this passage. Given the
proclivity of the rabbis to make substitutions of names in both
citations and main texts,* we cannot be certain that the earliest

---

*Examples of such substitutions are very numerous. Just a few that
are relevant to the subject of this chapter need be cited, however.

Of the main-text substitutions we have such examples as the
case of Ben Stada being said to have been hanged on the eve of
Passover in b. *Sanh.* 67a, but it is Yeshu ha-Notzri who is hung that
evening according to b. *Sanh.* 43a. In t. *Ḥul.* ii. 24, Rabbi Eliezer in
Sepphoris encounters the heretic Jacob of Chephar *Sichnin*, who is

version of this passage contained the reading *Yeshu*. In any event, there is no reason to interpret this late text as support for an historical Jesus. It does, however, appear to be related to the *Toldoth Yeshu* traditions which we shall consider in the next chapter.

There is one last argument that needs to be examined concerning the equating of Balaam with Jesus. This involves a late Babylonian Talmud haggadah that indicates that Balaam was thirty-three or thirty-four years old at death – just as has been calculated for the Jesus of the Gospels.

> **b. *Sanh.* 106b:** A certain heretic said to R. Ḥanina, "Have you ever heard how old Balaam was?" He replied, "There is nothing written about it. But from what is written (Ps. lv. 23), *Men of blood and deceit shall not live out half their days*, he must have been thirty-three or thirty-four years old." He [the heretic] said, "Thou has answered me well. I have seen the chronicle of Balaam, and therein is written "Balaam, the lame, was thirty-three years old when Pinḥas the Robber killed him'." [*Herford translation*]4-18

associated with the name Yeshu *ben Pantiri*. In b. *ʿA.bod Zar.* 16b, he encounters Jacob of Chephar *Sechanja*, who is associated with Yeshu *ha-Notzri*. In t. *Ḥul.* ii. 22,23 the heretic is Jacob of Chephar *Sama*.

Examples of differing attributions of sayings being cited include a saying concerning the unity of the deity which is attributed to R. Shimʿon ben Azai [4th Tannaitic generation, 110–135 CE] in *Sifri* §143 p. 54a and in b. *Menaḥ.* 110a, but ascribed to R. José ben Ḥalaphta [5th Tannaitic generation, 135–170 CE] in *Sifra.* 4c. In b. *Sanh.* 91a, a heretic asks a question concerning resurrection of the dead to R. Ammi [3rd Palestinian Amoraic generation, 290–320], but in b. *Sanh.* 90b, Rn. Gamliel [3rd Tannaitic generation, 80-110 CE] is asked the same question by a Caesar – presumably Hadrian [76–138 CE]! In j. *Sanh.* 27d, the simile of the arch of stone is attributed to R. Elʿazar ben Pedath [d. 279 CE], but in j. *Moʾed. Qat.* 83c it is used by R. Yoḥanan [a contemporary of Elʿazar]. In Midrash Vajiqr. r., §28, p. 40c,d, the report of the attempt to withdraw the biblical book Qoheleth (Ecclesiastes) is attributed to R. Shemuel bar Naḥmani [3rd Palestinian Amoraic generation, 290–320 CE], but it is generally believed this is a mistake and should be attributed to R. Shemuel bar Jitzḥaq [3rd Palestinian Amoraic generation, 290–320 CE].

I am certain that many more such examples can be found if one has patience. It is hazardous, therefore, to place too much faith in the historical accuracy of the rabbinical literature.

That the *Chronicle of Balaam* cannot be one of the canonical gospels is obvious, although it cannot be ruled out as a reference to a now-lost uncanonical gospel. Most likely, however, it is what it is called: a book devoted to the life, prophecies, and curses of the Midianite/Amorite prophet Balaam. Given the rather contradictory ways in which Balaam is regarded in the Bible, it is altogether reasonable to suppose there once existed a splinter group of Jews for whom Balaam was of special importance. The heretic of the passage just quoted by no means needs to have been a Jewish Christian.

The coincidence that Balaam's age at death is the same as that commonly alleged for the Jesus of the Gospels is simply that – a coincidence. It is "computed" by reasoning from a statement in one of the Psalms that deceivers live out *less than half* the normal life span (seventy years). The same sort of theological reasoning is also applied (on the same page) to Doeg and Ahitophel – two characters that we shall see have been hypothesized to be disguises for two of the Apostles:

> b. *Sanh.* 106b: [*R. Yoḥanan speaking*] "Doeg and Ahitophel did not live out half their days. It is thus taught (Ps. lv. 23), *Men of blood and deceit do not live out half their days.* All the years of Doeg were but thirty-four, and of Ahitophel only thirty-three." [*Herford translation*]4-19

Although it is widely believed that Jesus was thirty-three years old at the time of his demise, I know of no major Apostles who are believed to have been the same age at death. The New Testament gives no information whatever on the deaths of any of the Apostles, let alone their terminal ages. Even in the extensive "apocryphal" literature concerning the Apostles, I know of no traditions assigning death ages to them of thirty-three or thirty-four. Moreover, one of the earliest Christian authorities whose works survive – Irenaeus of Lyons [120–202 CE] – argued persuasively that Jesus lived past the age of fifty and died an old man!* So

---

*In the twenty-second chapter of his *Against Heresies*, Irenaeus argues against the "heretics" who taught that Jesus was in his thirties when he died. Beginning with an *a priori* theological argument, he "proves" that Jesus had to have lived through all the ages of man:

> Being a Master, therefore, He also possessed the age of a Master, not despising or evading any condition of humanity, nor

much for the "fact" that Jesus/Balaam was thirty-three years old when he died! Anticipating the findings of the following section, we may conclude not only that this page of the Babylonian Talmud is not relating Balaam to Jesus, but that it also is not relating Doeg and Ahithophel to any of his Apostles. The numbers are simply the fanciful result of "reasoning from scripture."

setting aside in Himself that law which He had appointed for the human race, but sanctifying every age, by that period corresponding to it which belonged to Himself. For He came to save all through means of Himself—all, I say, who through Him are born again to God—infants, and children, and boys, and youths, and old men. He therefore passed through every age, becoming an infant for infants, thus sanctifying infants; a child for children, thus sanctifying those who are of this age, being at the same time made to them an example of piety, righteousness, and submission; a youth for youths, becoming an example to youths, and thus sanctifying them for the Lord. So likewise He was an old man for old men, that He might be a perfect Master for all, not merely as respects the setting forth of the truth, but also as regards age, sanctifying at the same time the aged also, and becoming an example to them likewise. Then, at last, He came on to death itself... [*Roberts and Donaldson translation*]4-20

Irenaeus then proceeds to draw upon the Gospel of John and the testimony of "the elders":

Now, that the first stage of early life embraces thirty years, and that this extends onwards to the fortieth year, every one will admit; but from the fortieth and fiftieth year a man begins to decline towards old age, which our Lord possessed while He still fulfilled the office of a teacher, even as the Gospel and all the elders testify; those who were conversant in Asia with John, the disciple of the Lord, [affirming] that John conveyed to them that information. And he remained among them up to the times of Trajan [r. 98–117 CE]. Some of them, moreover, saw not only John, but the other apostles also, and heard the very same account from them, and bear testimony as to the [validity of] the statement. Whom then should we rather believe? Whether such men as these, or Ptolemæus, who never saw the apostles, and who never even in his dreams attained to the slightest trace of an apostle?

But, besides this, those very Jews who then disputed with the Lord Jesus Christ have most clearly indicated the same

In disposing of the idea that *Balaam* was intended as a code word for *Jesus* in the Mishnah, we have come to a point where we can conclude that the oldest and most authoritative body of rabbinical literature contains no information at all about any historical Jesus. The authors of the Mishnah knew him not. Before considering the passages of the Tosefta that have been alleged as references to Jesus, however, we must reexamine the Mishnah passage alleged to contain a reference to three of the Apostles.

thing. For when the Lord said to them, "Your father Abraham rejoiced to see My day; and he saw it, and was glad," they answered Him, "Thou art not yet fifty years old, and hast Thou seen Abraham?" [John 8:56–57] Now such language is fittingly applied to one who has already passed the age of forty, without having as yet reached his fiftieth year, yet is not far from this latter period. But to one who is only thirty years old it would unquestionably be said, "Thou art not yet forty years old." For those who wished to convict Him of falsehood would certainly not extend the number of His years far beyond the age which they saw He had attained; but they mentioned a period near His real age, whether they had truly ascertained this out of the entry in the public register, or simply made a conjecture from what they observed that He was above forty years old, and that He certainly was not one of only thirty years of age. For it is altogether unreasonable to suppose that they were mistaken by twenty years, when they wished to prove Him younger than the times of Abraham. [*Roberts and Donaldson translation*] 4-21

Irenaeus was not the only ancient authority who thought Jesus must have lived longer than 33 years. According to Walter Bauer,4-22 Jesus died not in the time of Tiberius but rather in the time of Claudius – as is indicated in the *Demonstrations of the Apostolic Preaching* [c74 CE] which is supported also by the *Letter of Pilate to Claudius* and by a very early interpolation in the text of Hippolytus' *Commentary on Daniel* [IV.23.3] that places his death in the first year of Claudius. Finally, a fragment surviving from Victorinus of Pettau claims Jesus was born in 9 CE, baptized in 46 CE, and died in 59 CE!

So! Jesus lived far beyond the age of thirty-three, the calculated final age of Balaam. Q.E.D.

4.2. C. Apostles in the Mishnah?

We have already seen on page 118 above that the Mishnah at Sanhedrin 10:2 mentions three kings and four commoners who have no share in the world to come: "The four commoners are Balaam and Doeg and Ahithophel and Gehazi." It has just been shown – I hope, convincingly – that the word *Balaam* does not refer to Jesus. If that be correct, it is *a priori* doubtful that the following three names would refer to his Apostles. Nevertheless, we must consider these characters separately to see if – like Balaam – they are actually the biblical characters whose names they bear.

4.2. C. a. Doeg the Edomite

Doeg (דאג or דואג 'fearful') the Edomite was not exactly a character priests and rabbis would have wanted to pass through the pearly gates. His story is found in 1 Samuel, chapters 21 and 22. He became notorious in Jewish legend as having betrayed David to Saul. Worse yet, he was believed to have massacred the priests of Yahweh at Nob, according to the tale in 1 Sam 22:16–19:

> But the king [*Saul*] said, "Ahimelech, you must die, you and all your family." He then turned to the bodyguard attending him and said, "Go and kill the priests of Yahweh; for they are in league with David, and, though they knew that he was a fugitive, they did not tell me." The king's men, however, were unwilling to raise a hand against the priests of Yahweh. The king therefore said to Doeg the Edomite, "You, Doeg, go and fall upon the priests"; so Doeg went and fell upon the priests, killing that day with his own hand eighty-five men who could carry the ephod. He put to the sword every living thing in Nob, the city of priests: men and women, children and babes in arms, oxen, asses, and sheep. [NEB]

It does not seem to me to be at all strange that a man who, without redundancy and using only a sword, could single-handedly massacre a whole city full of clergymen and asses should come to rank among the top four commoners to be excluded from the world to come. So notorious did this character become, indeed, he came to be mentioned in the superscription (title) for the 52nd Psalm: "To the chief Musician, Maschil, A Psalm of David: When Doeg the Edomite came and told Saul, and said unto him, David is come to the house of Ahimelech." In the psalm thus supposed by tradition to be aimed at Doeg, we read at verse 5: "God shall likewise destroy thee for ever; he shall take thee away and pluck thee out of thy dwelling place, and root thee out of the land of the living. Selah." This is not exactly a hymn of praise. The mention of Doeg in the title of a psalm shows that like Balaam, he too was a character vividly imprinted in the clerical consciousness. It really does not seem necessary to examine the arguments that Doeg is really a codeword for St. Peter – or for any other Apostle. If there were any independent evidence for the historicity of the Apostles, there might be some point in considering the hypotheses relating Doeg to one of them. But the historicity of the Twelve Apostles is an hypothesis in need of proof – for which absolutely none is available. It is not an hypothesis for which we have any need in order to account for the Mishnah's exclusion of Doeg from the world to come.

4.2. C. b. Ahithophel

Ahithophel (אחיתפל 'foolish brother') the Gilonite is described as a counselor of David who went over to the side of his son Absalom and then hanged himself. His story is found in 2 Samuel, chapters 15–17. Not only was Ahithophel supposed to have asked Absalom to let him go and kill David, he advised him to have sex with his father's concubines:

> 2 Sam 16:20–22. Then Absalom said to Ahithophel, "Give us your advice: how shall we act?" Ahithophel answered, "Have intercourse with your father's concubines whom he left in charge of the palace. Then all Israel will come to hear that you have given great cause of offence to your father, and this will confirm the resolution of your followers." So they set up a tent for Absalom on the roof, and he lay with his father's concubines in the sight of all Israel. [NEB]

Could anything be more abhorrent to a bunch of phobic but sex-obsessed rabbis who have spent half their lives splitting hairs over what constitutes sexual impurity? Sex on the roof – with multiple partners! Is there really any reason to suppose that Ahithophel is a code word for St. John or St. James? Again, we have no need of that hypothesis.

4.2. C. c. Gehazi

Gehazi (גיחזי 'denier,' 'diminisher') the servant of Elisha appears in chapters 4, 5, and 8 of 2 Kings. Unlike the preceding "commoners," the story of Gehazi does not seem too memorable. He is described as being a sort of secretary for the wonder-working prophet Elisha, and all but one of his appearances depict him as doing his work properly. In the fifth chapter of 2 Kings, however, he is depicted as not being all that might be desired for Yahweh's special representative in the Near East. It seems that Elisha had just cured Naaman, the commander of the army of the king of Aram, of leprosy and had refused to accept remuneration for his services. After all, it wasn't Elisha, but Yahweh and the waters of the Jordan that had cured the leper.

Whether because of avarice or because Gehazi wanted to enhance his position to secretary-treasurer, he secretly ran after Naaman, who was returning to his homeland. Deceitfully, Gehazi asked for a talent of silver and two changes of clothes, saying that Elisha wanted it for two young prophets from the hill-country of Ephraim. Naaman gave him two talents. When Gehazi arrived at home, Elisha asked him, "Where have you been, Gehazi?"

"Nowhere," said Gehazi.

"Was I not with you in spirit," Elisha replied, "when the man turned back from his chariot to meet you? Is it not true that you have the money? You may buy gardens with it, and olive-trees and vineyards, sheep and oxen, slaves and slave-girls; but the disease of Naaman will fasten on you, and on your descendants for ever."

Gehazi's skin became diseased and turned white as snow.

This is about all there is to the story of Gehazi. I must admit, it hardly seems serious enough to rank him amidst the Big Four who are to be forever excluded from the afterlife. It is difficult to suppose, however, that Gehazi is a code word for someone else, for the simple reason that the other three characters in this lineup do not seem to be symbols. Moreover, no one has ever suggested that the three kings in this pericope represent anyone other than Jeroboam, Ahab, and Manasseh. Why should the three kings be who they are, but the four commoners be other than the characters named? It seems reasonable to suppose that either all four are symbols or all four are intended to be their biblical referents.

While the Bible itself has little information about Gehazi, the rabbinical writings do deal with him in a number of places, increasing his wickedness considerably. In the Gemara to the tractate *Sotah* ('a woman suspected of adultery') of the Babylonian Talmud, on page 47a we encounter both Gehazi and Jesus the Nazarene:

b. Sotah 47a: Our Rabbis have taught: Always let the left hand repel and the right hand invite. Not like Elisha, who repulsed Gehazi with both his hands, and not like Jehoshua ben Perahjah, who repulsed Jesus the Nazarene with both his hands. What about Elisha? It is written [2 Kings v. 23], *And Naaman said, Be content, take two talents,* and it is written [*ibid.,* v. 26] *and he said to him, "Went not my heart [with thee] when the man turned from off his chariot to meet thee? Is it a time to receive silver, and to receive raiment and olive gardens and vineyards and sheep and cattle and men-servants and maid-servants?"* But had he indeed received all this? Silver and raiment was what he received. R. Jitzhaq said, "In that hour Elisha was occupied with [the law concerning] the eight [kinds of] creeping things [Lev. xi. 29, 30]. He said to him [Gehazi], "Wretch, the time has come to receive the punishment [for having partaken] of the eight creeping things, *and the leprosy of Naaman shall cleave to thee and to thy seed for ever." And there were four leprous men* [2 Kings vii. 3]. R. Johanan said these were Gehazi and his three sons. *And Elisha went to Damascus* [*ibid.,* viii. 7]. Why did he go to Damascus? R. Johanan says that he went to turn Gehazi to repentance, and he did not repent. He said to him "Repent," and he answered, "Thus have I received from thee that everyone who has sinned and caused the multitude to sin, they give him not the chance to repent." What did he do? Some say he set up a lodestone according to the sin of Jeroboam and made it stand between heaven and earth. And some say he wrote the Name upon its mouth, and it used to say "I" and "Thou shalt not have." And some say he drove our Rabbis from before him, as it is written [2 Kings vi. 1], *And the sons of the prophets said to Elisha, Behold the place where we sit is too strait for us,* whereas up till that time it had not been too small. [*Herford translation*][4-23]

A shorter variant of this story can be found in b. *Sanh.* 107b, indicating this was still an evolving tale at the time of completion of the Babylonian Gemara. Quite significantly, in that version *Jesus the Nazarene* seems not yet to have been created. He is simply *Jesus.*[4-24] Only the Munich manuscript has added *the Nazarene.* Even more relevant is the fact that in the earlier

Palestinian Gemara [j.Ḥag. 2:2] we can find a parallel story in which Patriarch Judah ben Tabbai excommunicates *an unnamed disciple* for the same reason Jehoshua ben Peraḥjah excommunicates Jesus – for "looking" at the hostess of an inn [b. *Sanh.* 107ᵇ]. As with the case of Balaam, it is likely that a folklore of sizable proportions had developed concerning Gehazi.

It will be noted that the sin of Gehazi has been altered from avarice (accepting pay for miracles) to violation of the dietary taboo against eating "creeping things" as listed in the non-Linnaean classification found in Leviticus 11:29–30: "These also shall be unclean unto you among the creeping things that creep upon the earth: the weasel, and the mouse, and the tortoise after his kind. And the ferret, and the chameleon, and the lizard, and the snail, and the mole."

Herford and other scholars have argued that the connection between Gehazi and eating taboo foods makes Gehazi a dead ringer for St. Paul, who argued so strongly against the dietary taboos of the Jews. Furthermore, the placement of Gehazi in Damascus (not explicit in the biblical text, but easily inferable from it) suggests to some St. Paul's fabled trip to Damascus – the contradictions in which we have discussed earlier, on page 17. Finally, the association – even if only by simile – with "Jesus the Nazarene" seems to clinch the identification in the minds of many scholars.

While the stories of St. Paul in the Christian New Testament do indeed indicate his opposition to Jewish rules concerning table fellowship with Gentiles and show that he was suspected by some of "being soft" on the matter of eating meat sacrificed to idols, there is not even a hint that he was eating turtle soup or *escargot*. It is simply absurd to think that St. Paul – if in fact he is one of the few historical figures in the New Testament – could have been an advocate of chameleon cuisine or mouse-and-mole pie. If in fact he had come into conflict concerning the dietary laws there can be no doubt that it would have involved the most fundamental taboo that distinguished Jew from Gentile, *viz.*, the eating of pork; but there is no hint of this in the *Soṭah* passage quoted above. Moreover, the most likely flash point in conflicts between Jews and St. Paul would have involved the issue of circumcision. But circumcision is not even hinted at in the passage under consideration. It strains probability theory to breaking to think that Paul is the referent behind Gehazi "partaking" of the eight creeping things.

The idea that Elisha's trip to Damascus is intended to symbolize Saul's supernatural adventure on his way to becoming Paul also has little to recommend it. First of all, Saul's trip probably never took place (none of the Pauline letters seem to know anything about it). Secondly, even if there were an historical kernel in the contradiction-riddled Acts accounts of Saul's conversion, it is extremely unlikely that that would be a point noted or remembered by the rabbis. (After all, even the Christians to whom all the Pauline letters had been sent would not have known the tale.) Thirdly, anyone studying only the text of 2 Kings describing the relationship between Elisha and Gehazi would infer that Gehazi was still in the employ of the prophet when he went to Damascus. There is absolutely nothing in the received text of chapters 4–8 indicating that Elisha expelled or fired Gehazi at all – let alone "with both hands." 2 Kings 8:4 still refers to Gehazi as "the servant of the man of God," even though the leprosy falls upon him at the end of chapter 5. Just three verses after identifying Gehazi thusly, 2 Kings tells us that "Elisha came to Damascus, at a time when Ben-Hadad king of Aram was ill." The natural inference is that Gehazi would have been with him. The rabbinical notion that Elisha went to Damascus to convert Gehazi contradicts the plain sense of the biblical text.

So where did the rabbis get the idea that Gehazi had been two-handedly repelled by Elisha, had been violating the law of the eight creeping things, and had gone alone to Damascus? I submit it is unlikely that this came from even a satirical life of St. Paul. More likely, as I have already indicated, these ideas derive from a lost literature about Elisha and Gehazi. We know from the New Testament that Elisha lore must have been of widespread interest during the first century, and it is hard to believe the story of his leprous secretary-treasurer would not also have been increasing in detail at this time and during the next century when so much of the rabbinical literature was taking shape.

Finally, we must consider the argument that the close association of Gehazi and Jesus the Nazarene in the simile with which our Babylonian Gemara quotation begins is a clear indication that we are dealing with someone clearly associated with Jesus – if not Paul, then some other one of his disciples. The problems with this notion are several. Let us repeat the simile to refresh our memories of its structure:

Always let the left hand repel and the right hand invite. **Not like Elisha, who repulsed Gehazi with both his hands, and not like Jehoshua ben Perahjah, who repulsed Jesus the Nazarene with both his hands**.

Logically, Elisha is to ben Perahjah as Gehazi is to Jesus. Elisha is supposed to have lived long before ben Perahjah (thought to have lived at the time of Alexander Jannaeus – 104–78 BCE!), and so Gehazi should be someone who lived *before* Jesus. The equation *Gehazi = Paul* does not square with Paul's junior relationship to Jesus. But of course, the notion that Jesus had been repulsed by ben Perahjah "does not compute" either – unless Jesus lived a century before Christ! (As we shall see a bit later, the Jesuses of the Talmud cannot possibly be the same as the character featured in the Gospels.)

This brings us to the conclusion of our examination of the two passages in the Mishnah, the oldest body of rabbinical writing extant. We have found no evidence to convince us that Yehudah ha-Nasi, the final redactor of the Mishnah, knew anything of the Jesus of Christianity. More certainly, even if he did know something about him, he made no mention of him. *A fortiori*, he knew nothing of any disciples or Apostles pertaining to the Jesus of western tradition. This seems strange even to an Atheist who does not think that Jesus was historical. Wouldn't he at least have heard the stories Christians were telling at the beginning of the third century? Wouldn't at least some of those stories have made good grist for his mill? I cannot exclude the possibility that Yehudah *does* refer to lost writings of extinct sects of Jewish Christians, but we cannot recognize them as such because all those writings were destroyed by the triumphant Pauline Christians. Since we can only imagine what those lost gospels might have been like, it is useless to speculate on this question. Unless some Nazorean or Ebionite scrolls should turn up in the Near East, we shall probably never know.

CHAPTER 5

Two Jesuses in the Tosefta?

Whereas the name *Yeshua* (Jesus) does not appear in any passage of the Mishnah that could even remotely be related to the Jesus of Christianity, the name does appear in the *Tosefta*, a somewhat later collection of halakhot and commentaries. Curiously (and significantly) the name does not appear in the form *Yeshua ha-Notzri* – 'Jesus the Nazarene' – but rather as *Yeshua ben Pandira* or *Yeshua ben Pantiri*. Both variants would be rendered in English as 'Jesus, son of Pandera' or 'Jesus, son of Panther.'

It must be admitted that the name *Panther* was associated with the Jesus of Christianity at a rather early date even by the Christians. In the year 403 CE we find the Cypriot bishop Epiphanius asserting that Panther was in fact St. Joseph's family name! In his treatise *Against the Eighty Sects,* he defends the virgin-birth story against the charge of bastardy but makes a curious statement: "Since this Joseph was himself the brother of Cleophas, he was the son of the Jacob surnamed Panther; both, I say, had that Panther as father."[5-1] It is clear that Epiphanius was driven to this astonishing invention by pressure from Jewish satirical propaganda. Whereas Epiphanius was pushed to put a Panther in the paternal lineage of Jesus, John of Damascus [c676–c754 CE] was moved to manipulate the maternal genealogy to accomodate a feline forefather. According to John [*De Fid. Orthod.* 4:14], Mary was the daughter of Joachim, who was the son of Bar Panther, who was the son of a Levi who must have been surnamed Panther. But these are far from being the oldest Christian notices of a panther in the pedigree. The name *Panther* can be traced in Jewish argumentation at least back to the time of the *True Discourse* of Celsus [c178 CE], a work which survives in part in quotations embedded in the lengthy refutation *Contra Celsum* which was attempted the better part of a century later [c248 CE] by the Christian writer Origen. In that book, Origen states the charge and attempts a refutation:

But let us now return to where the Jew is introduced, speaking of the mother of Jesus, and saying that "when she was pregnant she was turned out of doors by the carpenter to whom she had been betrothed, as having been guilty of adultery, and that she bore a child to a certain soldier [*It should be noted that a* Roman *soldier is not specified, allowing, as we shall see, for a Jesus chronology very different from that of the gospels*] named Panthera"; and let us see whether those who have blindly concocted these fables about the adultery of the Virgin with Panthera, and her rejection by the carpenter, did not invent these stories to overturn His miraculous conception by the Holy Ghost: for they could have falsified the history in a different manner, on account of its extremely miraculous character, and not have admitted, as it were against their will, that Jesus was born of no ordinary human marriage. It was to be expected, indeed, that those who would not believe the miraculous birth of Jesus would invent some falsehood. And their not doing this in a creditable manner, but (their) preserving the fact that it was not by Joseph that the Virgin conceived Jesus, rendered the falsehood very palpable to those who can understand and detect such inventions... [*Frederick Crombie translation*] 5-2

It is not likely that Origen would have realized that his attempted refutation some day would be viewed with amusement, but he must have felt it was insufficient to convince opponents. So, in the next chapter, he attacked Panthera with an argument from physiognomy – the belief that one can infer character and mental qualities by observation of facial or other bodily features:

... And if there be any truth in the doctrine of the physiognomists, whether Zopyrus, or Loxus, of Polemon, or any other who wrote on such a subject, and who profess to know in some wonderful way that all bodies are adapted to the habits of the souls, must there have been for that soul which was to dwell with miraculous power among men, and work mighty deeds, a body produced, as Celsus thinks, by an act of adultery between Panthera and the Virgin?! Why, from such unhallowed intercourse there must rather have been brought forth some fool to do injury to mankind,—a teacher of licentiousness and wickedness, and other evils; and not of temperance, and righteousness, and the other virtues! [*Frederick Crombie translation*] 5-3

Figure 9. The name *Pantera* (*i.e.*, *Panthera*) is attested by this monument which was discovered at Bingerbrück in Germany and is now in the municipal museum at Kreuznach. Tiberius Julius Abdes Pantera was born at Sidon in Phœnicia and served as an archer in a Roman cohort which was transferred to the Rhineland in the year 9 CE.

[From Robert Eisler, *ΙΗΣΟΥΣ ΒΑΣΙΛΕΥΣ ΟΥ ΒΑΣΙΛΕΥΣΑΣ*, Heidelberg, 1929]

It was a valiant effort, but Origen could not really be expected to be able to defend successfully a tale of magic against more rationalistic (even if probably equally fictitious) explanations of one of the more ridiculous dogmas of the 'Great Church'.

In addition to the *ben Pandira* passages of the Tosefta, there are passages which refer to a certain *ben Stada* that have also been believed to be references to the biblical Jesus. If we include a passage believed to refer to Jesus even though no one at all is named, we find that there are altogether five passages in the Tosefta believed by the early twentieth-century scholar R. Travers Herford to be allusions to Jesus of Nazareth. We shall examine all of them below.

5.1. The Panther's First Appearance

The first passage in the Tosefta we shall examine in which the name *Yeshua*ʿ is explicitly connected with the epithet *ben Pandira* is in reference to the treatise *Ḥullin* ('ordinary,' 'unhallowed' – referring to the non-sacrificial slaughter of animals) 2:22,23. Since the second reference to be considered is found immediately after the first [*Ḥullin* 2:24], and since the arrangement of the two pericopae within the treatise is itself a cause for suspicion, I shall quote both at once – once again in the translation of R. Travers Herford.

5.1. A. Ben Damah and Jacob of Chephar Sama (Sechanja)

> t. *Ḥul.* 2:22,23: The case of R. Elʿazar ben Damah, whom a serpent bit. There came in Jacob, a man of Chephar Sama, to cure him in the name of Jeshuaʿ ben Pandira, but R. Ishmael did not allow it. He said, "Thou are not permitted, Ben Damah." He said, "I will bring thee a proof that he may heal me." But he had not finished bringing a proof when he died. R. Ishmael said, "Happy art thou, Ben Damah, for thou hast departed in peace, and hast not broken through the ordinances of the wise; for upon every one who breaks through the fence of the wise, punishment comes at last, as it is written [Eccl. x. 8]: *Whoso breaketh a fence a serpent shall bite him.*[5-4]

5.1. B. R. Eliezer Arrested for *Minuth* [heresy]

t. Ḥul. 2:24: The case of R. Eliezer, who was arrested for Minuth (heresy), and they brought him to the tribunal (במה, βῆμα) for judgment. The governor (הגמון, ἡγεμών) said to him, "Doth an old man like thee occupy himself with such things?" He said to him, "Faithful is the judge concerning me." The governor supposed that he only said this of him, but he was not thinking of any but his Father who is in Heaven. He [the governor] said to him, "Since I am trusted concerning thyself, thus also I will be. I said, perhaps these societies err concerning these things. *Dimissus*, Behold thou art released." And when he had been released from the tribunal, he was troubled because he had been arrested for Minuth. His disciples came in to console him, but he would not take comfort. R. Aqiba came in and said to him, Rabbi, shall I say to thee why thou art perhaps grieving? He said to him, "Say on." He said to him, "Perhaps one of the Minim [*sectarians, heretics*] has said to thee a word of Minuth and it has pleased thee." He said, "By Heaven, thou hast reminded me! Once I was walking along the street of Sepphoris, and I met Jacob of Chephar Sichnin, and he said to me a word of Minuth in the name of Jeshu ben Pantiri, and it pleased me. And I was arrested for words of Minuth because I transgressed the words of Torah (Prov. v. 8), *Keep thy way far from her, and come not nigh the door of her house* (vii. 26), *for she hath cast down many wounded.*" And R. Eliezer used to say, "Ever let a man flee from what is hateful, and from that which resembles what is hateful."[5-5]

Before we consider the possible relevance of these passages to the Jesus of Christianity, we must consider their peculiar placement within the treatise *Ḥullin* in the Tosefta. As noted parenthetically above, the treatise *Ḥullin* is devoted to legal questions relating to the non-sacrificial slaughter of animals. We may ask why two anecdotes having absolutely no logical relevance to animal slaughter should have been placed in this treatise – together.

The paragraph immediately following our excerpts jolts us back to the subject of non-sacred slaughter: "He who slaughters for the sake of a burnt-offering, for the sake of peace-offerings, for the sake of a suspended guilt-offering, for the sake of Passover, or for the sake of a thank-offering, his act of slaughter is invalid." It makes our quotation look like an insertion or interpolation.

While the insertion seam marking the boundary at the end of our quotations is glaringly obvious, the boundary at the beginning of our insertion is not so stark. That is because section 2:21 immediately preceding it also has nothing to do with non-ritual slaughter. Instead, it deals with prohibitions of buying or selling anything to Gentiles, Samaritans, and *minim* (sectarians or heretics), or intermarrying with them. Nor does section 2:20, which deals with the niceties of buying or using meat from Gentiles and *minim*, from pagan temples, or meat that has been slaughtered by *minim* – the latter topic arguably being related to the subject of the treatise in question. (This section also informs us that the books of the *minim* are to be considered magical books and all their children are to be deemed *mamzerin* or bastards.) It is only upon reaching the still earlier section 2:19 that we find ourselves once more dealing with the subject of slaughter – on board ships, inside houses, or in the market place.

So what can we conclude about the placement of our Yeshua' ben Pandera (Yeshu ben Pantiri) passages? It is clear that they were inserted into the treatise *Ḥullin* either in the very final stages of completion of the Tosefta or even after it had been ostensibly completed – perhaps centuries later. Moreover, the two sections preceding our Yeshua' passages are also insertions – probably made some time before the Panther paragraphs were slipped in.

It would appear that the placement of all four sections was the result of a chain of association. The last item mentioned in 2:19 – the slaughter paragraph we must consider to mark the boundary preceding our insertions – is the problem of slaughtering animals in the market. Mysteriously, this is prohibited because one would be acting in accord with "the rules of the *minim*." The mention of heretics in connection with slaughter then probably suggested the problem of what to do with meat obtained from gentiles and *minim*, prompting the insertion of the first of our four paragraphs. This in turn would have prompted insertion of the second paragraph dealing with other problems relating to dealings with *minim*. Finally, this would have suggested the two anecdotes about Jacob of Chephar Sama (or Sichnin) – a *min* of some notoriety.

Clearly, the two pericopae mentioning Jacob and Jesus were independently circulating traditions before being lumped together in the Tosefta. Differing completely in subject matter, their only points of commonality is that they mention a *min* by the name of Jacob and the subject of heresy (*minuth*). The rabbinical *dramatis personae* are different and, although both appear to involve a character named Eleazar, in fact these are different names and persons: a certain Rabbi El'azar (אלעזר) ben Damah (supposedly the nephew of R. Ishmael) *vs.* a Rabbi Eliezer (אליעזר) who was the teacher of Rabbi Aqiba (d. 135 CE) – ostensibly R. Eliezer ben Hyrcanus (*fl.* 80–110 CE). The Rabbi Ishmael is generally identified as R. Ishmael ben Elisha (*fl.* 110–135 CE and later). Of course, we cannot know if these anecdotes are historical or manufactured with appropriate characters inserted at a time substantially later than the evident setting. (According to R. Travers Herford, Alfred Edersheim, in his nineteenth-century treatise *The Life and Times of Jesus the Messiah* [I:537], considered the tale of Eliezer and Aqiba to be plainly apocryphal. Unfortunately, the Reverend Oxford Doctor seems not to have had any scientific reason for rejecting it, other than revulsion at the thought of his Gentle Jesus discoursing about buying toilets for the high priest with the wages of a whore.)

The stories differ in their rendering of the name *Panther* – one giving us *Pandira* (פנדירא) the other *Pantiri* (פנטירי). Moreover, there are variant spellings to be found in the manuscripts. Moses Zuckermandel's edition of the Erfurt and Vienna manuscripts of the Tosefta gives us *Pantera* (פנטרא) instead of *Pandira*. (A text used by Herford[5-6] has *Pandiri* in t. *Ḥul.* 2:22–23.) If it is indeed true that both names are derived from the Greek word *panthēr* (πάνθηρ), it would seem that some substantial amount of time must have elapsed in which the forms *Pandera* and *Pantiri* could have evolved. The fact that there are variants spelled with a *tet* (ט) instead of a *tav* (ת) – the letter most often used in Hebrew to render the Greek *theta* (θ) – raises the question of whether or not there might originally have been two different Jesus characters as well as two different Jacobs that have become conflated. (The tales disagree also as to the town from which Jacob the *min* hails: one has him come from Sama (סמא), the other from Sichnin (סכנן) – some nine miles away.)

The name *Panther* (*Pantera* in Latin) is known to have been a rather common name in Syria around the turn of the era. In fact, it could be applied to persons of either sex. The name is even attested in Latin on a Roman tombstone found at Bingerbrück in Germany. Now in the museum at Kreuznach (see figure 9, p. 139), the inscription below the headless stone figure identifies it as belonging to an archer named Tiberius Julius Abdes ('Servant of Isis') Pantera, who was born at Sidon in Lebanon (Phoenicia) and served in a Roman cohort that was transferred from Syria to the Rhine in the year 9 CE. It is possible that the Hebrew spellings using a *tet* instead of a *tav* (Pantera and Pantiri) derive from the Latinized form of the name, rather than from the Greek name itself.

It is not certain, however, that the variant name *Pandera* – spelled with a *d* – derives from the same word as do the variants spelled with a *t*. Robert Eisler long ago suggested that the name *Pandera* did not come from *panther*, but rather from the Greek name *Pandaros*.[5-7] As Eisler explains, in the *Iliad* Pandaros is the person who breaks the armistice confirmed by solemn oaths and hurls a lance at Menelaus. In his punishment, he is hit in the mouth by a lance which severs his tongue. Consequently, the name *Pandaros* came to be used in the way we today use the names *Judas* or *Benedict Arnold* to symbolize traitors. (It also came to be associated with pimping, as in our English word *pander*.) Most significant, however, is the fact that Eisler was able to show that such usage had made its way from the pagans into rabbinical circles as well. The expression 'Pandar's voice' (*qala pandar*) is found in a peculiar midrash [*Gen. r.*, sect. 50, 49d] which tells us that "There were five judges in Sodom: 'Vomiter of Lies,' 'Master of Lies', 'Master of Wickedness.' 'Perverter of Justice,' and 'Pandar's Voice'." It will be noted that the midrash combines the Greek symbolism of false speaking with Sodom, the traditional symbol of sexual licentiousness and perversity. Since the name *Pandera* is associated with rape elsewhere in the rabbinical literature (including the *Toldoth Yeshu*), it could very well be the case that *Yeshua ben Pandera* is not a real name at all, but rather a satirical, made-up name.

Further uncertainty concerning this name is created by the discovery that a version of the *Toldoth Yeshu* was current in late fifteenth-century Spain in which the name is given as *Pondira* or *Pondera* (פונדיר׳א or פונדֵּירא). Consequently, the evolutionary relationship of this name is not at all clear.

Since the names *Pandera* and *Pantira* do not occur in the Mishnah, with which the Tosefta is intimately associated, it is reasonable to wonder if these names were present in the "first edition" of the Tosefta, or whether they might have been added later – when variant traditions had evolved involving one or more characters named Jesus. Did, perhaps, the first edition of the two passages quoted at the beginning of this section only read *Jesus*?

It is interesting to note that the first excerpt mentions curing "in the name of Jeshuaᶜ ben Pandira." On the face of it, this lacks verisimilitude. While it is completely plausible to suppose there were Christians running around second-century Palestine trying to heal with the well-known magical name *Jeshuaᶜ* (Jesus), the name *Panther* (or *Pandera*) is completely unattested in the many Christian spells and incantations surviving from antiquity. Healing in the name of Jeshuaᶜ ben Pandira seems highly un-likely. Names preferred by Christian magicians included *Yao Sabaoth, Jesus, Jesus Christ, Abrasax, Abraxas, Phanuel, Aablanaphanalbaa, Axeeeeeee, etc.*

The notion that both stories originally mentioned only a man or men named Jesus is supported at least weakly by the fact that in the later *Midrash on Qoheleth* the names in question are represented by our now-familiar *so-and-so*. (And Sama and Sichnin have both become Sechaniah.) While it is easy to understand why *Jesus* might be altered to *so-and-so*, it is hard to understand why *ben Pandira* would have been disguised also. It seems more likely that *Jesus ben Pandira* would have been replaced by the simple *ben Pandira*.

The suspiciousness of both passages in increased by the fact that the Palestinian Talmud does not contain the story of Rabbi Eleazar's heresy trial at all, and its parallel for the snake-bite tale simply mentions that "R. Eleazar ben Dama came to Jacob of Chafar Sama for healing." There is no Jesus ben Pandira at all.* There is, however, a clearly related story in the Palestinian Gemara which is very revealing.

The story deals with a grandson of a rabbi being healed by a magician, and is found in *Yerushalmi ᶜAbodah Zara* 2:2:

> [Joshua b. Levi] had a grandson, who swallowed [something dangerous]. Someone came along and whispered over him [and the child was healed]. When he [the magician] went out, [Joshua] said to him, "What did you say over him?"

---

*R. Travers Herford claims that a passage in j. ᶜAbod. Zar. 40ᵈ, 41ᵃ is the same as the snake-bite passage quoted from the Tosefta except that after the words "came in to cure him" is added "He said, We will speak to thee in the name of Jeshu ben Pandira." He even prints the Hebrew text for the added words. Despite diligent searching, I cannot find a Jerusalem Talmud text with the name Jesus in this pericope. Jacob Neusner's modern critical translation of *The Talmud of The Land of Israel* [1982] contains neither the name *Jesus* at this spot nor any critical note indicating its presence in other manuscripts.

He said to him such and such a word.

He said to him, "What will be [the child's fate]! If he had died but had not heard [these words], it would have been [better] for him."

[But why should the healing have worked?] It was as an error done by a ruler. [*Neusner translation*] 5-8

Please note that the magician is not identified as Jacob of Sama or anyone at all. It is hard to imagine why that name would have been suppressed. It is likely that the author of this tale didn't know who the magician was – and probably didn't care. The important point for the author was that this was a case of magical healing involving the whispering of words of power into someone's ear. While it is perfectly possible that "such and such a word" was *Jesus* or even *Jesus ben Pandira*, there is no evidence demanding it.

There is a parallel passage in *Yerushalmi Shabbat* 14:4 that is quite instructive for understanding how such stories might have evolved. Again, the translation is that of Jacob Neusner:

[Joshua b. Levi] had a grandson, who swallowed [something dangerous]. Someone came along and whispered over him in the name of [*L* contains a blank space which later was filled in: "Jesus Panteri"*] and he recovered. [*L, added between the lines: "When he [the magician] went out,"*] [Joshua] said to him, "What did you say over him?"

He said to him such and such a word.

He said to him, "It would have been better for him if he had died and thus [had not been done for him]."

It was "as an error that went out from before the ruler" (Qoh. [Eccl] 10:5).5-9

It is not clear if the writing in of *Jesus Panteri* was an act of restoring a censored passage or whether it was an act of editing an early version of a story to bring it into harmony with a later version. Regrettably, lacking ancient manuscripts of the Jerusalem Talmud and the Tosefta, we cannot choose between these alternative interpretations with certainty. It may be noted, however, that adding the name in which the healing had been done is gratuitous and creates a problem in the very next sentence. For if the magician had really whispered, Joshua could not

---

*L is the symbol for the Leiden manuscript of the Jerusalem Talmud.

have heard the name Jesus ben Pandira. On the other hand, if the whispering had been loud enough for Joshua to hear the magical name, he would not immediately have had to ask, "What did you say over him?" only to be told again "the word" he had just heard. However this all may be, it must be noted that our magician still is anonymous, and we may very well doubt the historicity of the passages in which the names *Jacob of Sama* or *Jacob of Sichnin* occur.

While it is, as admitted earlier, not impossible that the Tosefta passages under examination do refer to the Jesus of Christianity, there is no really compelling reason to believe that. The name *Jesus* was very common during the first two centuries of the common era, being by that time the equivalent of the name *Joshua* – in Greek-speaking circles at least. The fact that in later literature these names came to be associated with the Jesus of the Christians must not color our judgment concerning their significance in the earlier literature. We must no more suppose that the author of the Tosefta had Jesus Christ in mind when he wrote "Yeshua' ben Pandira" than that the first Isaiah had him in mind when he wrote "Behold, a young woman is with child and shall bear a son..." [Isa 7:14]. We must not accede to the common Christian conceit that the only major concerns of the Jews during the first two centuries were Jesus and Christianity.

The rabbis named in the two passages – if the attributions are in fact true and not of later manufacture – lived at the end of the first century and during the first half of the second century. Even if the attributions are genuine, however, it would seem almost certain that their knowledge of Jesus ben Pandira was not firsthand but rather inferred from interactions with Jewish Christians – who must by then have been a frequent annoyance to pious rabbis living in the 'Holy Land.'

5.2. Ben Stada in the Tosefta

The second character in the Tosefta generally believed to symbolize Jesus is referred to by the incomplete name *ben Stada* (בן סטדא 'son of Stada'). The expression *Yeshua ben Stada*, however, does not occur anywhere in the Tosefta. Consequently, the assertion that *ben Stada* refers to Jesus as early as the Tosefta is far less credible than the argument concerning Yeshua ben Pandira, which we examined in the preceding section. There are two references to Ben Stada in the Tosefta. The first we shall examine is in the tractate *Shabbat* ('Sabbath') 11:15:

> T. *Shabb.* 11:15: "He that cuts marks on his flesh"; R. Eliezer condemns, the wise permit. He said to them, "And did not Ben Stada learn only in this way?" They said to him, "Because of one fool are we to destroy all discerning people?" [*Herford translation*]5-10

On this our first encounter with ben Stada, we are confronted by a problem which we must discuss before we can ponder the significance of this passage from the Tosefta. Apart from the question of whom Ben Stada is supposed to represent, we have the question of whether or not the name is really *ben Stada*. Jacob Neusner's translation of this passage reads *ben Satra* (presumably representing a Hebrew/Aramaic בן סטרא) instead of *ben Stada*. Although most later compositions have the reading *ben Stada* (one passage even providing an etymology for the name!), Neusner indicates a variant *ben Sutra* (presumably reflecting a Hebrew/Aramaic בן סותרא) in the Jerusalem Talmud. Since the Tosefta contains the oldest attestation of the name, it is important to discover whether *Stada* or *Satra* is the correct, original form.

5.2. A. What's in a Name?

It is easy to see how the two readings could have come about by misreading an unfamiliar Hebrew or Aramaic word. In both languages, the letters *r* (ר) and *d* (ד) are often impossible to distinguish. The further fact that short vowels are not indicated in writing makes it possible to read the same word as *Stada* or *Satra*, depending upon one's inclination. It is as plausible to suppose that some scribe read *r* for an original *d* as that he read *d* for an original *r*. Once again, the lack of truly ancient manuscripts of the Tosefta makes it impossible to choose between *ben Stada* and *ben Satra* as the original reading of our name.

Before considering possible etymologies of the names, we may note that both possibilities are rather defective as names, being more plausible as titles. The expression *ben X* literally means 'son of X.' Normally, in Hebrew it served as the equivalent of a last name, usually being preceded by a first name – so that a complete name took the form *Y ben X*: *Yeshua ben Yonah, Shmuel ben Nathan*, and *Shimon ben Gamliel* being typical formations. The constructions *ben Stada* and *ben Satra* imply that there were men named *Stada* or *Satra*, and that they in turn were called *Stada ben-something* or *Satra ben-something*. But both names are unattested, making me conclude they are not names at all, but rather titles. (As we have already noted, complete names such as *Yeshua' ben Stada* or *Yeshua' ben Satra* are not to be found in the literature.)

Titles of the *ben Stada* form are, however, well attested both in Hebrew and Aramaic. (In Aramaic, *bar* is the equivalent of the Hebrew *ben*.) A famous case in point is that of Simon bar Kozeba who, when taking command of the rebellion against Rome [132–135 CE] changed his name to *bar Cochba*, a messianic title meaning 'Son of the Star' – referring to the Balaam prophecy [Num 24:17] "There shall come a star out of Jacob..." While many people have heard of Bar Cochba, most do not realize his actual name was Simon.

If we are dealing with a title, of course, there is a measurably increased possibility that we are dealing with a mythical character instead of an historical figure. The titles 'Prince of Peace', 'Son of Man,' and 'Wizard of Oz' leap quickly to mind. Titles, as contrasted with ordinary names, usually have a meaning suitable for the characters who bear them, whether real or fictional. So we may indulge in a bit of etymological inquiry to see whether *Stada* or *Satra* have possible meanings suitable for the character in question.

The name *ben Stada* was actually analyzed in the Babylonian Talmud, in a passage that we shall examine again later as being perhaps the culmination of the Ben Stada/Jeshua legend. Appearing in the treatise *Shabbat* [104ᵇ], the passage reads:

> **b. Shabb. 104ᵇ:** "Ben Stada was Ben Pandera. Rab. Chisda [d. 309 CE] said: The husband was Stada, the lover Pandera. (Another said): The husband was Paphos ben Jehuda; Stada was his mother; (or) his mother was Miriam, the women's hairdresser; as they would say at Pumbeditha, *Seṭath da* [Ed.– אד סטת FRZ] (*i.e.*, she was unfaithful) to her husband." [*G. R. S. Mead translation*][5-11]

We may note, first of all, that by the late date at which this Babylonian Gemara passage was written, the *ben* had been dropped and the epithet *Stada* had been applied to a woman named Miriam (Mary) and was a common expression in vogue at Pumbeditha, a Babylonian town where there was a well-known rabbinical college. Clearly, however, in Palestine before this time the word had been applied to a man. By the time of the Babylonian Gemara, however, the original significance of the word had been forgotten and, in an attempt to make order out of the welter of names and characters now so thoroughly entangled with each other, it was removed as a synonym for *ben Pandera*. On the face of it, this etymology is a response to the virgin-birth myth, which by now had developed in Christianity and would have attracted the scorn of the rabbis – who would have recognized the pagan proclivities of the dogma.

It is, of course, possible that *Stada* does not derive from Aramaic or Hebrew but is, like so much rabbinical terminology, a borrowing from Greek. If this be the case, the only reasonable candidate source for the name *Stada* is the Greek *stadaios* (σταδαῖος) 'standing erect' or 'upright.' Presumably, this would refer to the late-developing legend that Jesus had set up a brick-bat or stake and had worshiped the standing object.

If, as Herford has suggested, the name originally referred to the Egyptian charlatan mentioned in Acts 21:38, the name might derive from the Greek *anastatos* (ἀνάστατος) meaning 'seditious,' or it may come from yet some other derivative of the Greek root *sta*.

As nearly all scholars have confessed, however, there really is no convincing etymology for the title *ben Stada*. Moreover, it simply won't work as a personal name. We really don't know what it was intended to mean, but it is likely that the epithet was intended as ridicule in some now-forgotten sense.

Although there has been quite a bit of speculation on the meaning of *Stada*, I know of no speculation at all concerning the variant reading *Satra*. Interestingly, several possibilities suggest themselves which are no more far-fetched than those advanced for *Stada*.

First of all, there is a post-biblical Hebrew word *sitra* which, when written without the first vowel (סטרא) is indistinguishable from the name *Satra* as actually written in our texts. Indeed, we cannot really be sure how the name in our text was in fact vocalized by its first authors. The core meaning of the word *sitra* is 'put at the side,' 'partition,' 'separation.' One immediately thinks of such epithets as 'sectarian,' 'schismatic,' or 'heretic' – a *min*, in other words. (Then too, it might also suggest a nonstandard way to describe a women 'in her separation' – *i.e.*, a menstruating woman. Later, in the *Toldoth Yeshu*, Jesus is claimed to have been conceived of a menstruating woman!)

Secondly, there is the post-biblical Hebrew word *satar* (סטר) which has the meaning of 'he slapped' and exists in a modern Hebrew passive form *sutar* – 'he was slapped.' If, as has been claimed, *Balaam* and *Satra / Stada* actually meant *Jesus*, the story of Elisha "repelling Balaam with both hands" could conceivably give rise to an epithet meaning 'he who was slapped'. The existence of a variant reading *Sutra* in the Jerusalem Talmud slightly increases the plausibility of this etymology.

Finally – a rather long stretch, admittedly – is the possibility that both *stada* and *satra* are misreadings of the post-biblical Hebrew word *sutaf* (סטף), which means 'he was cut,' 'he was scarified.' This conceivably could be a name made up to represent the ben Stada of the Tosefta quotation at the beginning of this section – a magician who was supposed to have cut into his own flesh to hide magic writing (a tale we shall have occasion to examine shortly). While a non-final פ (*p* or *f*) is not readily confused with either ר (*r*) or ד (*d*), the final form ף (*f*) conceivably could have been mistaken for either of these letters and turned into *Sutra*, *Satra*, or even *Stada*.

5.2. B. Ben Stada Equations

Despite the fact that the rabbis later explicitly identified Ben Pandira with Ben Stada – as in the Babylonian Gemara passage quoted above – there is not the slightest reason to suppose they were the same character at the time the Mishnah and Tosefta were compiled. Indeed, *Rabbi Eliezer mentions both Yeshua ben Pandira and Ben Stada, with no indication that the two names denote one person.*

In the very Tosefta passage printed in bold at the beginning of this section [t. *Shabb.* 10:15] we have R. Eliezer referring to Ben Stada who is supposed to have cut marks upon his flesh: "And did not Ben Stada learn only in this way?" In the Babylonian Gemara [b. *Shabb.* 104ᵇ] this later is expanded to "It is tradition that Rabbi Eliezer said to the Wise, 'Did not Ben Stada bring spells from Egypt in a cut which was upon his flesh?' "

We have also already met with a Tosefta passage [t. Ḥul. 2:24] in which R. Eliezer refers to Yeshu ben Pantiri: "He [R. Eliezer] said, 'By Heaven, thou hast reminded me! Once I was walking along the street of Sepphoris, and I met Jacob of Chephar Sichnin, and he said to me a word of Minuth in the name of Jeshu ben Pantiri, and it pleased me'." Later, in the Babylonian Gemara [b. 'Abod. Zar. 16ᵇ, 17ᵃ] this story too is greatly expanded and Yeshu ben Pantiri becomes Yeshu the Nazarene.

We thus can see that at the time of the Tosefta, Ben Stada and Ben Pantiri were not the same person. At most one of them, therefore, could have been a code name for Jesus of Nazareth.

5.2. C. "That Egyptian"

As we have just noted, R. Travers Herford hypothesized that *ben Stada* originally denoted "that Egyptian" mentioned in Acts 21:38 and in Josephus' *Antiquities of the Jews* 20:8.6 and *Jewish War* 2:13.5. Apparently alluding to the Josephus story, the author of Acts creates a dialogue between Paul and the "chief captain" of the Romans: "³⁷And as Paul was to be led into the castle, he said unto the chief captain, May I speak unto thee? Who said, Canst thou speak Greek? ³⁸Art not thou that Egyptian, which before these days madest an uproar, and leddest out into the wilderness four thousand men that were murderers?"

A more fulsome account is to be found in Josephus' *Antiquities of the Jews,* Book 20, chapter 8:

5.   Now, as for the affairs of the Jews, they grew worse and worse continually; for the country was again filled with robbers and impostors, who deluded the multitude. Yet did Felix catch and put to death many of those impostors every day, together with the robbers ...
6.   These works that were done by the robbers filled the city with all sorts of impiety. And now these impostors and deceivers persuaded the multitude to follow them into the wilderness, and pretended that they would exhibit manifest wonders and signs, that should be performed by the providence of God. And many that were prevailed on by them suffered the punishment of their folly; for Felix brought them back, and then punished them. Moreover, there came out of Egypt about this time to Jerusalem, one that said he was a prophet, and advised the multitude of the

common people to go along with him to the mount of Olives, as it was called, which lay over against the city and at the distance of five furlongs. He said further, that he would shew them from hence, how, at his command, the walls of Jerusalem would fall down; and he promised them that he would procure them an entrance into the city through those walls, when they were fallen down. Now when Felix was informed of these things, he ordered his soldiers to take their weapons, and came against them with a great number of horsemen and footmen, from Jerusalem, and attacked the Egyptian and the people that were with him. He also slew four hundred of them, and took two hundred alive. But the Egyptian himself escaped out of the fight, but did not appear any more. And again the robbers stirred up the people to make war with the Romans, and said they ought not to obey them at all; and when any persons would not comply with them, they set fire to their villages, and plundered them. [*Whiston translation*]5-12

A somewhat different account of this episode is to be found in Book 2, chapter 13, of Josephus' *Wars of the Jews*, written some twenty years earlier:

4.   There was also another body of wicked men gotten together, not so impure in their actions, but more wicked in their intentions, who laid waste the happy state of the city no less than did these murderers. These were such men as deceived and deluded the people under pretence of divine inspiration, but were for procuring innovations and changes of the government; and these prevailed with the multitude to act like madmen, and went before them into the wilderness, as pretending that God would there shew them the signal of liberty; but Felix thought this procedure was to be the beginning of a revolt; so he sent some horsemen and footmen, both armed, who destroyed a great number of them.

5.   But there was an Egyptian false prophet that did the Jews more mischief than the former; for he was a cheat, and pretended to be a prophet also, and got together thirty thousand men that were deluded by him; these he led round about from the wilderness to the mount which is called the Mount of Olives, and was ready to break into Jerusalem by force from that place; and if he could but once conquer the Roman garrison and the people, he intended to domineer over them by the assistance of those guards of his who were to break into the city with him; but Felix prevented his attempt, and met him with his Roman soldiers,

while all the people assisted him in his attack upon him, insomuch that when it came to a battle, the Egyptian ran away with a few others, while the greatest part of those that were with him were either destroyed or taken alive; but the rest of the multitude were dispersed every one to their own homes, and there concealed themselves. [*Whiston translation*]5-13

Herford points out that in Josephus' story about the Egyptian false prophet the charlatan escapes. In harmony with this fact are the statements attributed to R. Eliezer, who never indicates that Ben Stada was put to death at Lydda – even though the other (unattributed) Tosefta passage concerning Ben Stada says he was:

> **t. Sanh. 10:11:** In regard to all who are worthy of death according to the Torah, they do not use concealment against them, except in the case of the deceiver. How do they deal with him? They put two disciples of the wise in the inner chamber, and he sits in the outer chamber, and they light the lamp so that they shall see him and hear his voice. And thus they did to Ben Stada in Lūd [Lydda]; two disciples of the wise were chosen for him, and they [brought him to the Beth Din] and stoned him. [*Herford translation*]5-14

Herford's opinion that Ben Stada originally referred to the Egyptian false prophet is eminently reasonable, even if nothing amounting to proof can be extracted from the rubble of history. Unlike the Jesus character of the New Testament – who escaped the notice of every ancient writer we have been able to examine – the Egyptian prophet *was* noticed by a New Testament writer as well as by a secular historian. It would be indeed surprising if he were not to be remembered also in the religious literature of the people whom he had disturbed so seriously. As we shall see in the post-Tosefta evolution of the Ben Stada character, he is strongly associated with Egypt and is considered to be a magician. This accords with Josephus' description of the Egyptian prophet, although it could also be argued that it could have been deduced from gospel accounts of Jesus' flight into Egypt and miraculous deeds as well.

It must be admitted that the anonymous Tosefta passage just quoted is not compatible with the account in Josephus, since it has Ben Stada stoned to death by Jewish authorities at Lydda, instead of escaping. Even less, however, is this compatible with claims concerning the Jesus of the New Testament – where Jesus is crucified (or hanged) by Romans in Jerusalem, 23 miles southeast of Lydda. The fact that fewer *ad hoc* assumptions are needed to transform the Egyptian of Josephus into the Ben Stada of the Tosefta than are required to derive the latter from anything remotely resembling the biblical Jesus, however, must be of at least some significance.

5.2. D. The Two Tosefta Ben Stada Passages Examined

The patience of readers expecting an explanation of the passage printed in bold at the beginning of this section by now surely has been tested beyond reason, as we have explored the etymologies of names and titles and wandered through the histories of Josephus. All but the most motivated will by now have forgotten what the passage was about. I shall, therefore, repeat it so we can consider it more closely.

> **t.** *Shabb.* **11:15:** "He that cuts marks on his flesh"; R. Eliezer condemns, the wise permit. He said to them, "And did not Ben Stada learn only in this way?" They said to him, "Because of one fool are we to destroy all discerning people?" [*Herford translation*]

The context of the quotation is a discussion of what constitutes writing when performed on the Sabbath. The terseness and lack of detail of this passage make it all but unintelligible by itself. Without exception, every scholar who has commented on this pericope has interpreted it in terms of the later elaboration in the Jerusalem Talmud – j. *Shabb.* 13d, in which 'learn' becomes 'bring magic' – and the still later Babylonian Talmud b. *Shabb.* 104b, where R. Eliezer asks "Did not Ben Stada bring spells from Egypt in a cut which was upon his flesh?" While it is obvious that Ben Stada has become a magician by the time his story is incorporated into the Gemaras of the two Talmuds, it is not at all apparent that any magical implications are to be found in the Tosefta passage being reexamined. We must underscore the fact that the context involves activities prohibited on the Sabbath – in this case, writing. Yet neither in the Tosefta nor in the Talmuds is there any hint that Ben Stada was writing on or cutting his flesh specifically on the Sabbath. Indeed, in the Babylonian version of the story, where Ben Stada brings spells from Egypt to Israel, we are dealing with an activity that could not have been completed in a single day – whether it have been a Sabbath or a Sunday. Clearly, by this stage the story has evolved way beyond whatever facts may have warranted its insertion into a Tosefta discussion of what constitutes writing on a Sabbath.

So just what *was* Ben Stada doing on the Sabbath? It could not have been writing magic spells on parchment, concealing them inside a cut in his flesh, and exporting them from Egypt. It must have been something quite simple – like tattooing himself. Tattooing was forbidden in the Torah [Lev 19:28], and the practice must have had some occult implications that caused it to be proscribed. Those vague occult connotations may have been enough to change Ben Stada into a magician. From there on, the story simply took on a life of its own.

The minimal information in this passage makes any attempt at discovering the original identity of Ben Stada hazardous if not in fact foolhardy. Certainly, in his first Tosefta appearance he bears no resemblance to the Jesus of Christianity. At the same time, he bears little resemblance to the Egyptian false-prophet of Josephus. We cannot even be sure he is an historical figure.

Proceeding now to our second Tosefta Ben Stada passage, we shall reprint it also:

> **t. Sanh.** 10:11: In regard to all who are worthy of death according to the Torah, they do not use concealment against them, except in the case of the deceiver. How do they deal with him? They put two disciples of the wise in the inner chamber, and he sits in the outer chamber, and they light the lamp so that they shall see him and hear his voice. And thus they did to Ben Stada in Lūd [Lydda]; two disciples of the wise were chosen for him, and they [brought him to the Beth Din] and stoned him. [*Herford translation*]

On the face of it, this passage shows more promise as being a possible reference to Jesus. To a Christian it is doubtless suggestive of the betrayal of Jesus by Judas. The context deals with legal processes involved in obtaining evidence against various types of offenders. Specifically, it discusses procedures for entrapment of "deceivers" – persons who would lead Jews away from the One True Faith. Certainly, from a rabbinical perspective, the Jesus of the New Testament would have been viewed as being a deceiver and one might expect that if references to Jesus were to be found anywhere at all in the Tosefta it would be here in *Sanhedrin*, a treatise dealing with capital crimes.

The impression of promise cannot be sustained, however, when one considers this pericope more closely. First of all, Christian tradition assigns but *one* betrayer to the case of Jesus; the Tosefta prescribes *two*. Secondly, Ben Stada is made to betray himself by his own words, whereas Jesus is not so depicted in the gospels. Thirdly, Ben Stada is betrayed to *Jewish authorities* and executed by them, whereas Jesus is betrayed to the *Romans* and executed by them. Fourthly, Ben Stada is *stoned* (and subsequently hung up publicly in later accounts), whereas Jesus is *crucified*. (While it is true that there are hints in the New Testament and the Church Fathers that Jesus, like the later Ben Stada, was hanged upon a tree instead of being crucified, there is no tradition of him having been stoned as required by Jewish law.) Fifthly, Ben Stada is brought before the *Beth Din*, whereas Jesus is brought before *Pilate*. As far as I can tell, Pilate is mentioned nowhere in either Tosefta or Talmuds. Quite certainly, he is not mentioned in any passages alleged to be references to Jesus. Sixthly, Ben Stada is executed in *Lydda* (modern Lod), not *Jerusalem*, which is twenty-three miles away.

We end our investigation of Ben Stada in the Tosefta by concluding that he resembles neither the Jesus of Christianity nor any likely mock-Jesus that would have been created in Jewish folklore. Who he was – if he was a real person at all – we can only hypothesize. That he was the Egyptian false prophet described by Josephus is possible, but not in any way provable from the existing data.

5.3. Crucifixion of a Nameless Twin

Probably responding to Jewish criticisms, the author of Galatians 3:13–14 – generally supposed to have been St. Paul – was moved to make an apology for the manner in which Christ was alleged to have met his death:

[13]Christ hath redeemed us from the curse of the law, being made a curse for us: for it is written, Cursed is every one that hangeth on a tree: [14]That the blessing of Abraham might come on the Gentiles through Jesus Christ: that we might receive the promise of the Spirit through faith.

This passage is considerably more understandable in the New English Bible, although its meaning is changed with respect to one important word:

[13]Christ bought us freedom from the curse of the law by becoming for our sake an accursed thing; for Scripture says, 'A curse is on everyone who is hanged on a gibbet.' [14]And the purpose of it all was that the blessing of Abraham should in Jesus Christ be extended to the Gentiles, so that we might receive the promised Spirit through faith.

Because of his use of the ambiguous Greek word *xylon*, which can mean 'wood,' 'tree,' 'club,' 'stocks,' 'gallows,' or other wooden contrivance, there is much disagreement as to just how the author of Galatians thought Christ had been executed. Although conservative apologists claim that the word here is to be rendered 'cross' – thus avoiding the appearance of a contradiction with the Gospel accounts – it is quite clear that that is *not* what the word means in the Galatians passage. The word *xylon* is being quoted from the Greek ('Septuagint,' LXX) version of the Hebrew Bible. Specifically, it is referring to LXX Deuteronomy 21:22–23:

[22]And if there be sin in any one, and the judgment of death be upon him, and he be put to death, and ye hang him on a tree: [23]his body shall not remain all night upon the tree, but ye shall by all means bury it in that day; for every one that is hanged on a tree is cursed of God; and ye shall by no means defile the land which the Lord thy God gives thee for an inheritance.

The Greek *xylon* (ξύλον) is used here to translate the Hebrew *'ēts* (עץ), a word which almost always means 'tree' in the Hebrew Bible, although it too can sometimes mean 'timber,' 'wood,' 'stick,' *etc*. Since the Hebrew word never means 'cross,' we can confidently conclude that the Galatians passage is referring to an execution carried out by some means other than crucifixion. Whether the post-execution hanging was upon a tree or a gibbet (a gallows or structure resembling a gallows upon which dead criminals were displayed for public viewing) we cannot be sure. However, the most likely type of execution that would be followed by such hanging would have been stoning – an activity apparently popular in Jewish society in those days.

St. Paul wasn't the only ancient writer who worried about Deuteronomy 21:22–23, however. The rabbis who wrote the Tosefta also had occasion to deal with it:

> **t. Sanh. 9:7:** Rabbi Meir used to say, What is the meaning of (Deut. xxi. 23), *For a curse of God is he that is hung?* [It is like the case of] two brothers, twins, who resembled each other. One ruled over the whole world, the other took to robbery. After a time the one who took to robbery was caught, and they crucified him on a cross. And every one who passed to and fro said, 'It seems that the king is crucified.' Therefore it is said, *A curse of God is he that is hung.*[5-15]

Crucifixion appears to have been a rather rare method of execution in the Jewish world, although it became a quite common practice among the Romans. About the only well-known instance of the practice was the infamous case of Alexander Jannæus [103–76 BCE] who, while feasting and publicly enjoying his concubines, crucified eight hundred Jews simultaneously and had the throats of their wives and children slit before their eyes. Perhaps because crucifixion was so unusual, many scholars have concluded that the Tosefta passage above was a reference to the crucifixion of Jesus. Herford points out that R. Meir lived in the second century and had some knowledge of the gospels. "It is hardly to be doubted," he writes, "that the above passage contains a reference to Jesus."[5-16] The phrase 'One ruled over the whole world' he understands as referring to the Christian god. 'They resembled each other' he thinks refers to 'He that hath seen me hath seen the Father.' The scornful gibe of the passersby suggests the taunts satirizing Jesus as 'King of the Jews.'

While it is not impossible for this to be a disguised reference to Jesus – especially if it is true that R. Meir had some knowledge of the written gospels – it is not at all necessary to look outside the passage itself in order to understand the meaning of at least the core fable. Since the robber was the identical twin of the king, people seeing him on the cross would think the king himself had been crucified – with no sarcasm intended. How the fable can be conceived to explain the dictum 'A curse of God is he that is hung' is, however, an inscrutable mystery even if the crucified one be Jesus. Equally inscrutable is the mystery of how anyone can see Jesus of Nazareth in a parable about identical twins – unless we are talking about the Gnostic Jesus who had a twin named Thomas Didymus.*

With this fifth quotation from the Tosefta we have completed our examination of all alleged references to Jesus in that work. We also have exhausted all the rabbinical writings old enough to be considered possible witnesses to an historical Jesus. Neither in the Mishnah nor the Tosefta have we found a single passage that is a clear and compelling allusion to Jesus, let alone contains information that could not have come from disputes with Christians. In fact, we have not found a single passage that is even plausibly a reference to Jesus. Unlike other scholars, I have tried to examine all these passages simply on the basis of what they themselves say, not allowing myself to be biased by knowledge of how later literary evolution reshaped them. That at least some of the characters whom we have met ultimately came to be associated with the Jesus of Christianity is certainly true. How this evolution occurred we shall see as we proceed to trace the growth of these characters through the Gemaras of the Palestinian and Babylonian Talmuds.

Teoma and *Didymos* are words for *twin* in Aramaic and Greek, respectively. Thus, the amusing redundancy in the Gnostic name.

CHAPTER 6

The Palestinian Talmud

When the collection of halakhot known as the Mishnah was completed in Palestine around the year 220 CE, it immediately was put to use for the purpose of establishing the authority and power of the rabbis – Pharisees who constituted the only Jewish theopolitical party left after the destruction of the Temple of Yahweh in 70 CE and the expulsion of the Jews from Jerusalem in 135 CE. Previously, power had rested with a priestly caste that tended to belong to the Sadducee party. The priests, unlike the rabbis, had been able to justify their authority with the aid of the myth of Moses and Aaron. According to that myth, Aaron had been the first priest and had passed his authority on to his descendants, right down to whomever was the current high priest. Like kings, the priests enjoyed power by virtue of heredity. With the demise of the priesthood after the cessation of the temple service, the hereditary chain of power had been broken. The rabbis, who replaced the priests as the religious leaders of Jewry, had to rework the myth of Moses and Aaron in order to make it look as though they were the proper successors to the priests. According to their revised myth, when Yahweh was telling Moses what to write down to create the written Torah – the Pentateuch – he also was giving him extra information with which to make sense of the often confusing written 'Law.' This extra information imparted to Moses – the oral law – was passed on down from Moses through Joshua to a whole bunch of later religious authorities – rabbis as it unsurprisingly turned out to be. This oral tradition of law which the rabbis claimed to have inherited from Moses became a vehicle on which the rabbis could ride to power. Unfortunately, not being available in written form, the oral law could not easily be applied to propagandizing the laity, including Jewish secular rulers. It had to be written down as the Mishnah in order to be used effectively in establishing power. So Yehudah ha-Nasi (or someone immediately after him) did just that around the year 220. So useful was the Mishnah in Palestine, it almost immediately was imported by the Babylonian Jews in Iraq. Their 'Exilarch' – a claimant to Davidic descent – made good use of the Mishnah and the rabbis who brought it to lend authority to his own secular office. (The wedding of church and state has always been of great value for mutual validation of both parties in the union, despite its disastrous effect on individual freedom.)

Not long after publication of the Mishnah, it became necessary for certain rabbinical authorities to explain more fully what it *really* was trying to say. Moreover, the Mishnah was claimed to have omitted some important halakhot. (Although it is reasonable to suppose that these halachoth were of use to some particular rabbinical party in its quest for power, I am unable to discern how in practice that might have been.) And so the Tosefta was born as a commentary and supplement to the Mishnah, sometime before the end of the fourth century.

So useful were the Mishnah and the Tosefta to the rabbis, further expansions were called for, both in Palestine and in Babylon, where by now there probably were more Jews than in the homeland. There had been one serious drawback to the Mishnah, for which compensation had to be provided: the Mishnah dealt mostly with a world that no longer existed. The Mishnah world was still that of a priesthood presiding over a functioning temple service. Something more closely related to the real world was needed. And so the two Talmuds were compiled. As I have already explained, one of these was produced in Palestine (the so-called Talmud of Jerusalem, or *Yerushalmi*) and the other in Iraq (the so-called Babylonian Talmud, or *Bavli*). Each of these contained the Mishnah and parts of the Tosefta as a sort of core surrounded by commentaries known as *Gemaras*. The Yerushalmi was completed first. Tradition places its completion about the year 395 CE – perhaps shortly after the completion of the Tosefta. Indeed, the part of the Yerushalmi which is sometimes referred to as the *Talmud of Cæsarea** is thought to have been completed around the year 350 – half a century before the rest of the Palestinian Talmud was brought to a close. The Bavli would not

---

*This earlier Talmud contained only the tractates of the civil law: *Baba Qamma* ['The First Gate'], *Baba Metzi'a* ['The Middle Gate'], and *Baba Batra* ['The Last Gate'].

be completed for another one or two centuries, depending upon which rabbinical authority one consults.

It is in the Gemara of the Babylonian Talmud that the characters we have been studying come to be identified with "Jesus the Nazarene." *The latter character is never mentioned in the Palestinian Talmud.* Only in the writings of rabbis living centuries after the era in which Jesus is alleged to have lived do we find clear-cut references to our magical messiah. The evolutionary transformation of Ben Pandera and Ben Stada into Yeshuaʿ ha-Notzri will be traced in a later chapter.

6.1. Ben Pandira in the Jerusalem Talmud

It is rather surprising to discover that the character Ben Pandira actually regresses in the Talmud of Jerusalem. I have already noted that the Tosefta story of Rabbi Eleazar's heresy trial – the story in which Jacob of Chephar Sichnin pleases R. Eleazar with a word of heresy – is not to be found in the *Yerushalmi*. Furthermore, it would appear that the mention of healing in the name of Yeshuaʿ ben Pandira also does not occur there – despite the claim of R. Travers Herford to the contrary. Jacob Neusner's translation of the *Yerushalmi ʿAbodah Zarah* ('Idolatry') 2:2 does not contain it nor indicate with a note that any textual variant contains such a thing. Neusner's rendering, with Herford's addition in bold, is as follows:

> **j. *Abod. Zar.* 2:2 IV. I:** [*It is said that*] A snake bit Eleazar b. Dama. He came to Jacob of Kefar Sama for healing. **He said, We will speak to thee in the name of Jeshu ben Pandira.** Said to [Ben Dama] R. Ishmael, "You have no right to do so, Ben Dama."
> He said to him, "I shall bring proof that it is permitted for him to heal me."
> But he did not suffice to bring proof before he dropped dead.
> Said to him R. Ishmael, "Happy are you, O Ben Dama, for you left this world in peace and did not break through the fence of the sages, and so in dying you have carried out that which has been said: 'A serpent will bite him who breaks through a wall' " (Qoh. [Eccl] 10:8])
> And did not a snake already bite him?
> But a snake will not bite him in the age to come.[6-1]

If the sentence in bold be authentic and has been removed from most manuscripts by Christian censors, the Yerushalmi version of this pericope is nearly identical to that of the Tosefta, and there has been no evolutionary development of the Pandira character at all. If, on the other hand, it has resulted from an interpolation into a single manuscript of the Yerushalmi and is properly absent in manuscripts of pre-censorship vintage, it would seem to indicate that ben Pandira had not yet been incorporated *at all* into the Tosefta at the time it was used by the compilers of the Palestinian Talmud. It thus would seem that Ben Pandira, although known to the critic Celsus* as early as *c*178 CE, did not find his way into the rabbinical literature until nearly two centuries later.

6.2. Ben Stada in the Jerusalem Talmud

It will be recalled that Ben Stada – as is also the case with Ben Pandira – is not to be found in the Mishnah, making his first appearance in two passages in the Tosefta. Unlike the case of Ben Pandira, however, both Tosefta passages reappear in the Jerusalem Talmud. Even so, Ben Stada undergoes no evolution in the Yerushalmi, since it merely repeats without comment the two Tosefta passages.

Thus, the Tosefta passage concerning writing on or cutting the skin on the Sabbath reads as follows:

> **t. *Shabb.* 11:15:** *"He that cuts marks on his flesh"; R. Eliezer condemns, the wise permit.*† He said to them, "And did not Ben Stada learn only in this way?" They said to him, "Because of

*Readers will perhaps remember that Celsus is known only through quotations used by the church father Origen in his polemic *Contra Celsum* where Origen refers to Panthera twice. According to G. R. S. Mead,[6-2] however, both places where Celsus asserts that the paramour of the mother of Jesus was a soldier named Panthera have been erased in the oldest Vatican manuscripts. He notes that they have been "bodily omitted from three codices in this country and from others." I have been unable to discover whether the other codices lack the reference to Panthera because they were copied from a manuscript in which he had been erased, or whether they reflect an authentic early tradition in which Panthera had not yet found his way into the text of Origen.

one fool are we to destroy all discerning people?" [*Herford translation*]6-3

Since the Yerushalmi leaves out the part of the Tosefta passage that was a quotation from the Mishnah (the business about cutting marks on one's flesh), it actually contains *less* of the ben Stada story than does the Tosefta [*Neusner translation*]:

> **j. Shabb. 12:4. III.**: Said R. Eliezer to them, "Now did not Ben Satra learn [Y.: bring magic] only in such wise?"
> They said to them, "Because of one fool shall we impose liability [Y: "destroy"] on all intelligent folk?" [t. *Shabb.* 11:5].6-5

I have already discussed the problem of *ben Stada* being *ben Satra* here in the Yerushalmi. It is worth reminding ourselves that this casts serious doubt upon the notion that we are dealing with a person's name rather than a title – and upon the assumption that we are dealing with an historical person rather than a contrived literary figure. At a minimum, though, we can conclude that the compilers of the Palestinian Talmud knew nothing about Ben Stada/Satra beyond what they could read in the Tosefta. Indeed, it is altogether possible that they knew nothing at all about him and uncomprehendingly were repeating the Tosefta. This conclusion is further strengthened by study of the Yerushalmi's treatment of the second Tosefta passage – the pericope about the two concealed witnesses.

Both the Tosefta and the Yerushalmi are actually commenting on Mishnah *Sanhedrin* 7:10, which Herbert Danby has translated as follows:

> **m. Sanh. 7:10**: 'He that beguiles [others to idolatry]–such is a common man that beguiles another common man. If he said to another, 'There is a god in such a place that eats this, drinks that,

---

†The italicized words are a direct quotation from the Mishnah [M. *Shabb.* 12:4]: "If during one act of forgetfulness [that it was the Sabbath] a man wrote two letters, he is culpable. Whether he wrote in ink or caustic or red dye or gum or copperas or aught that leaves a lasting mark, or on two walls forming an angle or on two tablets of an account-book so that [the two letters] could be read together, he is culpable. If a man wrote on his skin he is culpable. If he scratched [letters] on his skin, R. Eliezer declares him liable to a Sin-offering, but R. Joshua declares him not culpable." [*Danby translation*]6-4

does good in this way and does harm in that way'–they may not place witnesses in hiding against any that become liable to the death-penalties enjoined in the Law save in this case alone. If he spoke [after this fashion] to two, and they are such that can bear witness against him, they bring him to the court and stone him. If he spoke so to one only he may reply, 'I have companions that are so minded'; and if the other was crafty and would not speak before them, witnesses may be placed in hiding behind a wall. Then he says to the other, 'Say [again] what thou didst say to me in private,' and the other speaks to him [as before] and he replies, 'How shall we leave our God that is in Heaven and go and worship wood and stone?' If he retracted it shall be well with him, but if he said, 'It is our duty and it is seemly so to do', they that are behind the wall bring him to the court and stone him. If a man said, ... 'Let us go and worship it', or ... 'Let us go and sacrifice to it', or ... 'Let us go and burn incense to it', or ... 'Let us go and make a libation to it', or ... 'Let us go and bow ourselves down before it', [such a one is culpable]. 'He that leads [a whole town] astray' is he that says, 'Let us go and worship idols.'[6-6]

The Tosefta, it will perhaps be recalled, leaves out much of the Mishnah paragraph but increases in detail the entrapment procedure and introduces Ben Stada:

   t. Sanh. 10:11: In regard to all who are worthy of death according to the Torah, they do not use concealment against them, except in the case of the deceiver. How do they deal with him? They put two disciples of the wise in the inner chamber, and he sits in the outer chamber, and they light the lamp so that they shall see him and hear his voice. And thus they did to Ben Stada in Lūd [Lydda]; two disciples of the wise were chosen for him, and they [brought him to the Beth Din] and stoned him. [*Herford translation*][6-7]

In the Yerushalmi, most of the Mishnah quoted above is repeated, along with most of the Tosefta. Neusner renders the Tosefta quotation in the Yerushalmi [*Sanh.* 7:2]* as follows:

---

*Herford cites this as *j. Sanh.* vii. 16 (25c,d) and gives a variant translation: "The deceiver; this denotes a private man. Not a Sage? [*i.e.*, a rabbi]. No. From the time he deceives he is no longer a Sage. And from the time he is deceived he is no longer a Sage. How do they deal with him to work craftily against him? They conceal (in his case) two witnesses in the inner chamber and make him sit in the outer

j. Sanh. 7:12. I: [When Mishnah 7:12A refers to an ordinary fellow, does it mean to say,] "Lo, a sage is not [subject to the law]?"

[The meaning is this:] Since the person incites someone to idolatry, this is no sage.

Since one is incited to idolatry, this is no sage.

How do they get testimony against him?

They conceal against him two witnesses [Tosefta: disciples of sages], [who are put] in an inside room, and he sits in an outside room.

And they light a candle near him, so that they can see him.

And they listen to what he says.

And so did they do to Ben Stada [Sutra] in Lydda.

They appointed against him two disciples of sages, and [in consequence of what they heard and saw], they stoned him [t. Sanh. 10:11]. 6-8

Apart from further confusion as to whether our ill-fated character was the son of Stada, Satra, or Sutra, it will be observed that the Yerushalmi adds nothing to his story. Thus it appears that the compilers of the Palestinian Talmud knew nothing about this character, despite the fact that they lived in the same tiny country as the one in which he is supposed to have lived and died – a country smaller than New Jersey. As we shall see in the next section, almost all the "facts" about the life and death of Ben Stada were not "discovered" until one or two centuries later still – by men living hundreds of miles away from the scene they would describe retroactively with such authority.

6.3. Son of Man in the Jerusalem Talmud

There is a passage in the Palestinian Talmud which Herford and many other scholars have long supposed to be a reference to Jesus – or at least a reference to Christian doctrines:

---

chamber, and they light a lamp over him that they may see him and may hear his voice. Thus did they to Ben Stada in Lūd, and they concealed in his case two disciples of the wise, and they brought him to the Beth Din and stoned him."6-9

j. Taanit [Fast-days] **65ᵇ:** R. Abahu said: If a man say to thee, "I am God," he is a liar; if [he says, "I am] the son of man," in the end people will laugh at him; if [he says] "I will go up to heaven," he saith, but shall not perform it. [*Herford translation*]6-10

According to Herford, this is a dead-ringer reference to Jesus:

That it refers to Jesus there can be no possibility of doubt. R. Abahu, the speaker, was a very well-known Rabbi, who lived in Cæsarea, at the end of the third and the beginning of the fourth century; and we shall see hereafter that he had a great deal of intercourse, friendly and also polemical, with heretics, who, in some instances at all events, were certainly Christians. It is not necessary to assume an acquaintance with any of the Gospels to account for the phrases used by R. Abahu. The first and third do indeed suggest the Gospel of John, but it is enough to admit a general knowledge of what Christians alleged concerning Jesus from the Rabbi's own discussions with them.6-11

It cannot be doubted – even if the attribution of the saying to R. Abahu not be legitimate – that by the end of the third century a Palestinian rabbi could or should have been aware of Christians and their blasphemous beliefs and claims. So even if we were to accept the claim that this *Taanith* passage truly is a reference to Jesus, it would give us no independent information concerning any historical Jesus of Nazareth. But is it *really* a reference to Jesus? Or are Herford and other scholars merely responding to a religious Rorschach test – a test wherein they see Jesus instead of naked ladies?

As has so frequently been the case in our investigations, careful consideration of the context of putative Jesus allusions shows that many of them make perfect sense without any need to suppose their authors had ever heard of Jesus. So is it once again with our *Taanith* passage.

The rabbinical discussion preceding our quotation concerns the famous oracle of Balaam which we have already examined: "God is not man, that he should lie, or a son of man, that he should repent. Has he said, and will he not do it? Or has he spoken and will he not fulfill it?" [Num 23:19] In the discussion, the first sentence is split into two parts, which are discussed separately. After discussing "God is not man, that he should lie," the discussion turns to "Or a son of man, that he should repent." This leads to mention of the embarrassing contradiction in Exodus 32:14, where "the Lord repented of the evil which he had thought to do to his people."

It is at this point that R. Abahu chimes in with an inverse logical transformation of "God is not a man that he should lie": "If a man should tell you 'I am God' he is lying." The transformation of the second half of the verse, however, is not entirely parallel to the first part, and the rabbi's exercise in logic sort of falls apart: "If he says, 'I am the son of man,' in the end he will regret it." [*Neusner translation*] Perhaps significantly, where the Balaam oracle has "*a* son of man," our *Taanith* passage has "*the* son of man" – a possible apocalyptic allusion. Since Jewish speculation about the apocalyptic Son of Man figure goes back several centuries before the common era, there is no reason to fall in with the Christicentric conceit that "son of man" here can only refer to Jesus or Christian claims about him.

The third part of our *Taanith* quotation is a bit more difficult to analyze, since as it is translated by Herford it does not obviously pertain to the Balaam oracle: "If [he says] 'I will go up to heaven,' he saith, but shall not perform it." However, as Jacob Neusner translates the passage, it too refers to the oracle: " 'For I shall go up to heaven'– '*Has he said, and will he not do it?*' " [Num 23:19][6-12]

While the italicized sentence is a direct quote from the Balaam oracle, there still remains the problem of the phrase "I will go up to heaven." Where does that come from? It certainly is not part of the Numbers oracle being considered by the rabbis. Is it in fact the one phrase that ties this whole discussion to Jesus? I don't think so.

First of all, as Neusner translates the passage, it clearly is *Yahweh himself* that shall mount to the heavens. It would appear that Herford (and Mead as well) misunderstood the rhetorical nature of the negative verb – turning the exact biblical quotation "Has he not spoken, and will he not do it?" into "He saith, but shall not perform it."

Secondly, even if Herford's translation is correct and Neusner's is wrong, there are several biblical referents that could have been intended. Proverbs 30:4 asks "Who has ever gone up to heaven and come down again?" The rabbi might simply have used this as a proof text for yet another instance of a man lying.

More compelling, however, if Herford is right, is the argument that we are dealing with a reference to the oracle against the king of Babylon found in Isaiah 14:12–17:

> 14:12How art thou fallen from heaven, O Lucifer, son of the morning! how art thou cut down to the ground, which didst weaken the nations! 13For thou hast said in thine heart, *I will ascend into heaven*, I will exalt my throne above the stars of God: I will sit also upon the mount of the congregation, in the sides of the north: 14I will ascend above the heights of the clouds: I will be like the most High. 15Yet thou shalt be brought down to hell, to the sides of the pit. 16They that see thee shall narrowly look upon thee, and consider thee, saying, Is this the man that made the earth to tremble, that did shake kingdoms: 17That made the world as a wilderness, and destroyed the cities thereof; that opened not the house of his prisoners?

As Herford translates the Yerushalmi passage, Isaiah's diatribe against the king of Babylon almost certainly would have to be the referent. Exactly why this passage in Isaiah would be brought up, however, I do not know. I must confess that there is a finite possibility that this is a reference to Jesus – *if Herford's translation be correct*. I must confess also that the extreme terseness and laconic style of the Yerushalmi make his translation entirely plausible grammatically. Nevertheless, I am reasonably certain his interpretation of this text is wrong and Neusner is right. By translating the last sentence as a further direct quotation from Numbers 23:19 ("Has he not spoken, and will he not do it?"), Neusner forces the referent of 'For I shall go up to heaven' to become the god of the Jews and absolutely eliminates the possibility that Jesus could have been intended here. Neusner's translation fits much better into the context of our disputed passage, making it the expected (and necessary) continuation of the detailed commentary on Numbers 23:19.

Thus, it would seem that yet another alleged rabbinical reference to Jesus of Nazareth proves to be nothing of the kind. As late as the close of the fourth century – at least for the Palestinian rabbis involved in the discussion at hand – neither Christ nor Christianity was a serious concern. While this may be rather ego-deflating to certain Christian scholars, it seems to be an inescapable conclusion. We may well ask the reason for this profound disinterest and lack of concern, for if the vulgar model of

Christian origins be correct, a lot of explanation is in order. If, on the other hand, Christianity did not begin in Palestine and is not derivable from an historic Jesus, the silence of the rabbis is understandable and, indeed, predictable.

6.4. Balaam in the Jerusalem Talmud

Readers must, by now, have formed the impression from my frequent citations that the greatest of the early twentieth-century authorities on rabbinical allusions to the historical Jesus were R. Travers Herford, who wrote *Christianity in Talmud and Midrash,* and G. R. S. Mead, who wrote *Did Jesus Live 100 B.C.? An Enquiry into the Talmud Jesus Stories, the Toldoth Jeschu, and Some Curious Statements of Epiphanius – Being a Contribution to the Study of Christian Origins.* At least some modern authors seem to have agreed with this assessment – especially in regard to Herford – and simply have accepted their assembly of evidence, without carefully studying the primary sources for themselves.* This can be risky, as can be seen by an examination of the question of the Yerushalmi's relevance to the hypothesis that *Balaam* is a code name for *Jesus.*

If one were to judge by what these authors had to say, it could easily be supposed that the only reference to Balaam in the Yerushalmi is a curious passage explaining why the Ten Commandments and the Story of Balak and Balaam are not read daily. (I shall deal with this passage shortly.) One might suspect that Balaam – like Ben Pandira – regresses in the Yerushalmi. But that would be completely opposite to the truth.

The fact of the matter is that Balaam – like his Mishnaic associates Doeg, Ahithophel, and Gehazi – is treated in detail in the Palestinian Talmud. Moreover, definitive explanations are given for their being excluded from "the world to come." As we shall see, these explanations make it clear that the characters in question cannot possibly be code names, but do indeed represent the biblical characters we have discussed in the section on the Mishnah.

---

* Herford prints the Hebrew and Aramaic texts for only the excerpted passages he cites. No sense of context is possible without consulting the treatises themselves.

It is tempting to suppose that Herford and Mead deliberately withheld evidence in order not to weaken their theories, but such dissembling would be quite out of character for those great scholars. Rather, I think, both were so blinded by their belief in an historical Jesus that they did not perceive the significance of the data, looking only for material that they deemed novel additions to their theories. Supposing not even for a minute that Jesus was a fictional character, they were insensible to any antihistorical data encountered in their texts.

What, then, does the Yerushalmi have to say about Balaam and his associates? How does it rule out the theory that Balaam, Doeg, Ahithophel, and Gehazi are code names for Jesus and his Apostles?

6.4. A. Quoting the Mishnah

Perhaps because of its theological importance, the Palestinian Talmud quotes almost the entirety of the Mishnah's lengthy discussion of all the exceptions to the principle that "All Israelites have a share in the world to come" [m. *Sanh.* 10:1–3].

One of the early exclusions from Paradise is allotted to men who "violate the covenant" by extending the stubs of their foreskins attempting to hide the fact of their circumcision. This is followed by a lengthy digression on "four kinds of atonement," but then the main topic is restored with the declaration that "Ahaz and all of the evil kings of Israel have no portion in the world to come" – beginning commentary on the Mishnah passage with which we have already dealt on page 118, the passage mentioning three kings (Jeroboam, Ahab, and Manasseh) and four commoners (Balaam, Doeg, Ahithophel, and Gehazi) who have no share in the world to come. Detailed reasons are given for Ahaz, Hezekiah, and Manasseh being excluded.

Before finishing the discussion of all the excluded kings, however, the Yerushalmi takes up the Mishnaic exclusion of "Epicureans" from the world to come. Korah, the opponent of Moses, is taken as a prototype of the Epicurean for his wickedness in making a prayer shawl which was entirely purple – ignoring the sacred law which allows only the fringe to be purple. It was for such perversity – as well as his denial of the heavenly origin of the Torah, the prophethood of Moses, and the high priesthood of Aaron – that the earth gaped open and Korah and his minions were swallowed up into Sheol [Num 16:25–35].

People who read heretical books also are excluded, and it turns out that the books (plural) of Jesus ben Sira (Ecclesiasticus) and the books of Ben Laanah are *verboten*; but Homer is kosher. This is followed by a recounting of the rabbinical foundation myth found in the first chapter of the Mishnah's *Pirke ʾAboth* – the myth establishing the line of inheritance of 'the Law' from Moses at Sinai down to the rabbis quoted in the Mishnah.

Further digressions from the exclusion theme follow. Some, although they are irrelevant to our purpose, may be cited for amusement. We learn, for instance, that "A person should not anoint his foot with oil while it is in a shoe, or his foot when it is in a sandal." It is completely licit, however, for a man to anoint his body with oil and roll around on new leather on the Sabbath, although he should never put oil on a marble table in order to roll around on it! One can only surmise the sorts of kinky practices upon which our saintly authors had to render solemn judgments.

Shortly before resuming the discussion of the kings and commoners who are excluded from the world to come, the Yerushalmi takes up the subject of "He who whispers over a wound and says, 'I will put none of the diseases upon you which I have put on the Egyptians; for I am the Lord who heals you' [Exod 15:26]. This is only prohibited, says Rab, if the whisperer then spits. This discussion is concluded by a mention of the prohibition against pronouncing the divine name correctly – apparently because the whisperers were thought to effect their healing by means of the magical powers of the *Shem*, the secret name *Yahweh*. The god of Sinai must never be represented phonetically naked, with all his vowels showing.

We have already discussed the Tosefta passage [*Ḥul.* 2:22,23] wherein a rabbi sought to be cured of snakebite through the magic of the name *Jesus ben Pandira,* and the Palestinian Talmud passages [*ʿAbod. Zara* 2:2; *Shabb.* 14:4] wherein the grandson of Joshua b. Levi was healed by an anonymous magician who "whispered over him" and healed him – either with an unspecified 'name of power' or with the name *Jesus ben Pandira*. It would seem from the Exodus passage just quoted that all such stories are simply legalistic elaborations created to exemplify this biblical verse. The fact that this Yerushalmi *Sanhedrin* discussion is completely anonymous and theoretical is, I believe significant. At least in the beginning, the pericopae dealing with whispering and magical healings probably had nothing at all to do with Ben Pandira or with any other rogue in particular.

Finally, at the beginning of the second part of the tenth chapter of the Yerushalmi's *Sanhedrin*, we encounter the Mishnah passage for which we have been searching: "Three kings and four ordinary folk have no portion in the world to come: the three kings are Jeroboam, Ahab, and Manasseh... the four ordinary folk are Balaam, Doeg, Ahithophel, and Gehazi." Let us see what the Palestinian Talmud has to say about each of these characters and understand why they cannot be code names for Jesus and his apostles.

Readers will recall the odd fact that Jesus scholars have never suggested that the three kings of this passage represented anyone other than themselves, while nevertheless maintaining that the four commoners inexplicably had been created as codes for Jesus and other Christian luminaries. As common sense would dictate, however, the Yerushalmi's treatment of kings and commoners alike provides no grounds for so absurd an assumption.

King Jeroboam is excluded from the world to come because he made two golden calves – although there is some amount of casuistry in his defense. King Ahab, of course, is excluded because of his marriage to Jezebel and his unabashed idolatry. Manasseh, King of Judah, is excluded for his alleged murder of the prophet Isaiah:

> **j. Sanh. 10:2 VI:** When Manasseh arose, he pursued Isaiah, wanting to kill him. [Isaiah] fled from before him. He fled to a cedar, which swallowed him up, except for the show fringes [of his cloak], which revealed where he was. They came and told him. He said to them, "Go and cut the cedar down." They cut the cedar down, and blood showed [indicating that Isaiah had been sawed too].
>
> "[And also for the innocent blood that he had shed; for he filled Jerusalem with innocent blood,] and the Lord would not pardon" (2 Kings 24:4). [*Neusner translation*]6-13

Although the reasons given for excluding the first two kings are entirely derivable from the biblical text, the allegation that Manasseh had killed Isaiah derives from an extrabiblical legend and could not have been expected by scholars knowing only the biblical texts. It serves as a warning to students of the historical Jesus question that the rabbis were able to draw upon an extensive literature and tradition outside the Bible – much of which now not only is lost, it is unidentifiable. Consequently, when we encounter peculiar details or jarring dissonances in rabbinical descriptions of familiar biblical characters, we should not automatically assume the resulting image to be symbolic of someone different from the biblical character in question. While we cannot be sure of the criteria used by the rabbis to decide who should be excluded from paradise, killing a popular prophet such as Isaiah just might provide sufficient grounds. Moreover, it is hard to imagine any apostle – even allegorically – being represented as the murderer of Isaiah.*

6.4. B. The Evil Balaam

Justification in the Yerushalmi of the exclusion of Balaam from the world to come is in almost every detail predictable from the tales in the Book of Numbers and scholarly analyses and reconstructions of the evolutionary history of the biblical text:

> **j. Sanh. 10:2. VIII:** Now what did the evil Balaam do [to warrant losing his portion in the world to come]?
> It was because he gave advice to Balak son of Zippor on how to cause Israel's downfall by the sword. He said to him, "The God of this nation hates fornication. So put up your daughters for fornication, and you will rule over them." [Neusner translation]6-14

There follows an entertaining and colorful haggadic account of how the daughters – aided by little old ladies – went about achieving that noble and holy goal. In the course of this haggadah we learn that the approved method of worshipping Baal Peor was to expose one's genitals to the idol.† We also encounter a rather earthy method of theological disputation – the tale of Subetah of

---

*Far more worthy of such symbolic representation would have been the evangelist Matthew, who can fairly be said to have murdered the *text* of Isaiah by his deliberate mistranslation [Matt 1:23] of the proof text in Isa 7:14, rendering it as "Behold a virgin [instead of *young woman*] shall conceive [instead of *has conceived*] and shall bring forth a son, and they [instead of *she*] shall call his name Emmanuel..."

†It is very likely that Yahweh too at one stage in his evolution was worshipped in the same way. We learn in 2 Samuel 6:14–23 that

Ulam, who rents out his ass to a Gentile woman to take her to worship Peor. When they get to the temple, the woman instructs him to wait outside while she should go in to worship the idol. After she finishes and returns to Subetah, he in turn tells her "Wait for me here, until I go in and do just what you did." Thereupon he goes into the temple and defecates before the idol, completing his desecration by wiping himself on the nose of the idol! According to Neusner's faithful translation, "Everyone present praised him, and said to him, 'No one ever did it the way this one did it!' "[6-15]

It may be recalled that in our examination of the Balaam story in chapters 22 and 23 of Numbers, I hypothesized that there must have been an earlier version of the story in which Balaam disobeys Yahweh and goes along with Balak's messengers, thus justifying the nasty behavior of the angel in the pericope of the talking ass. Further support for this notion is found in the line the Yerushalmi gives to Phineas, who kills Balaam in the biblical account. Addressing Balaam, Phineas chides him, "You did not do what you said, for He said to you, 'You shall not go with the messengers of Balak,' but you went along with them" [*Neusner translation*].[6-16] The fact that the biblical redactors of the Balaam stories had to amalgamate at least two different versions of his career is further indication of the former existence of a voluminous literature concerning this pagan prophet.

The only possible exception to my earlier claim that the Yerushalmi's reasons for exclusion of the four commoners can all be deduced from study of the biblical text is found at the very end

---

David danced naked before the Ark – Yahweh's portable dwelling, the functional equivalent of an idol. While the text has obviously been doctored up to have David be "girded with a linen ephod," it is clear that he danced naked: "Michal the daughter of Saul came out to meet David, and said, How glorious was the king of Israel today, who uncovered himself today in the eyes of the handmaids of his servants, as one of the vain fellows shamelessly uncovereth himself." [2 Sam 6:20]

That this was actually a fertility rite, and David must have been dancing with phallus erect, is hinted at by the clinching verse of this pericope: "Therefore Michal the daughter of Saul had no child unto the day of her death." When one reflects that the main purpose of the 'Covenant' (contract) between Moses and Yahweh was to increase the fertility of the Chosen People, it is no surprise that the main sign and token of the agreement involves mutilation of the male genitalia.

of its treatment of Balaam. In a very garbled passage that may not even refer to Balaam with certainty, we read:

j. Sanh. 10:2. VIII: Another interpretation: "Among the rest of their slain"—for he hovered [in the air] over their slain, and Phineas showed him the [priestly] frontlet, and he fell down [to earth]. [*Neusner translation*]6-17

If this does indeed refer to Balaam, it is indeed something not deducible from the biblical text and would appear to derive from the now-lost Balaam literature whose existence I have postulated repeatedly. Balaam's flight and subsequent crash to earth is suggestive of the later *Toldoth Yeshu* tale of Jesus flying and being brought down to earth after being defiled in midair by Judas Iscariot. It also is suggestive of the contest between Simon Peter and Simon Magus, wherein St. Peter causes Simon Magus to crash. It is possible that this anecdote goes back to the same early pool of folk legend from which the Simon Magus tale was drawn. On the other hand, the Balaam literature which we have postulated may very well have included colorful accounts of the prophet-magician's aerobatic exploits.

Despite the enigma of a flying Balaam, the overwhelming import of the Yerushalmi's exposition is in perfect accord with the biblical character Balaam. There is absolutely nothing even remotely suggestive of Jesus. The authors of the Palestinian Talmud betray no knowledge of any historical Jesus, nor do they give us reason to suppose they have encoded information about him in stories relating to Balaam, Ben Pandira, or anyone else.

Putting it bluntly, the authors of the Palestinian Talmud did not know Jesus.

6.4. C. Doeg, Ahithophel, and Gehazi

R. Travers Herford, the early twentieth-century Christian scholar whom even Jewish scholars have cited with approbation on many issues, after a life of studying the rabbinical literature concluded that the Mishnah passage excluding Balaam alluded not only to Jesus but to his major apostles as well. It is necessary, I think, to quote him *in extenso* to understand his argument. Then we shall look at the evidence from the Yerushalmi to see how it impacts his thesis.

I return to the passage quoted above, from M. Sanh. x. 2, where it is said that Balaam, Doeg, Ahitophel and Gehazi are shut out from the world to come. Having seen that Balaam here denotes Jesus, it is natural to enquire into the meaning of the other three names. That they merely denote the three persons mentioned in the Books of Samuel and Kings is not probable; for there is nothing in the facts there recorded to show why just these three should have been so severely condemned. Following immediately after Balaam-Jesus, we can hardly avoid the conclusion that the three O.T. names denote three of the Apostles, as having shared in the work of heresy which Jesus began. Each of the three is elsewhere mentioned in the Talmud as being tainted with heresy, as will be shown hereafter... Which of the Apostles are referred to, if this hypothesis be accepted, is a question of which the answer must remain uncertain. One thinks, naturally, of Peter, James and John. But it seems to me at least highly probable that Gehazi, at all events, means Paul. It would certainly be strange if the man who more than all else except Jesus 'troubled Israel' (cf. Acts xxi. 27 fol.) would have been left out of this black list. A passage will be given presently [Sotah 47ª] where the story of Gehazi and Elisha is told in such a way as strongly to suggest Paul the renegade disciple of Gamaliel.

As for Doeg and Ahitophel, I do not know of any evidence for a particular identification. May not, however, Doeg the Edomite, who betrayed David (1 Sam. xxii. 9), possibly denote Judas Iscariot, the traitor? And the high honour in which Ahitophel was held (2 Sam. xvi. 23) suggests him as a type of Peter. These are only guesses, and as regards the proposed identification of Doeg with Judas Iscariot, I must allow that it would be more likely that the Talmud should exalt the betrayer of Jesus into a hero than condemn him to exclusion from the world to come. At the same time, I would submit that the three names which are most prominent in the list of the Apostles, the three figures which would be most likely to dwell in the memory as connected with Jesus, are Peter, Judas Iscariot, and Paul. And therefore, in spite of difficulties, I am inclined to hold that these three are denoted by Ahitophel, Doeg, and Gehazi, in the passage we have been considering. [6-18]

The modesty and undogmatic nature of the above quotation marks Herford as a man worthy of the designation 'scholar.' Nevertheless, it also demonstrates how the presupposition of an historical Jesus can seduce even great minds into failures of reality-testing and lead them to confuse their unconscious wishes with *realia.* Let us see if the Yerushalmi supports his assertion that there is nothing in the books of Samuel and Kings "to show why just these three should have been so severely condemned."

6.4. C. a. Doeg

I have already showed, in my chapter on the Mishnah, that Doeg was credited with having killed – single-handedly – all the Yahwist priests in the city of Nob. The *New English Bible* translation of 1 Samuel 22:18–19 tells us that "Doeg went and fell upon the priests, killing that day with his own hand eighty-five men who could carry the ephod. He put to the sword every living thing in Nob, the city of priests: men and women, children and babes in arms, oxen, asses, and sheep."

While there are other atrocities in the Hebrew Bible that might qualify their perpetrators for inclusion with Balaam in the ranks of the four commoners to be excluded from Paradise, most of those atrocities were carried out by biblical heroes. This considerably shrinks the field of candidates, and it would seem that Doeg qualifies nicely. Indeed, the Yerushalmi, when alluding to this passage to explain Doeg's exclusion, does not bother to quote the entire passage from 1 Samuel. It simply notes that "Doeg the Edomite turned and fell upon the priests." Doeg's notoriety was so great that the rabbis needed to say no more.

The Yerushalmi does, however, add some more details about Doeg that are not to be found in the Hebrew Bible. For example, it explains that "Doeg was a great man in learning of Torah" and implies that he was a teacher who had disciples:

> **j. *Sanh.* 10:2. IX:** "His old students got together with him, and they were studying, but he forgot [his learning]. "[This fulfills the verse which says,] 'He swallows down riches and vomits them up again; God casts them out of his belly' (Job 20:25). [That was a sign of his excommunication; and the students killed him.]" [*Neusner translation*][6-19]

While several of the Apostles might be supposed to have been learned in Torah, none are reputed to have had disciples who killed them. Once again, the existence of haggadic anecdotes not derivable from the Hebrew Bible does not justify symbolic identifications for characters. It is more parsimonious to assume that the rabbis drew upon traditions and literatures now lost.

One further explanation is given for the "setting apart" of Doeg:

> **j. Sanh. 10:2. IX:** How was he [shown ultimately] set apart? R. Haninah and R. Joshua b. Levi– One of them said, "Fire burst forth from the house of the Holy of Holies and licked round about him." [*Neusner translation*]6-20

Again, there is no biblical basis for this tale. At the same time, it would defy even a Christian imagination to see how this could refer to Peter, Paul, or any other of the named apostles. When the Yerushalmi refers to Doeg, *requiescat in pace* Mr. Herford, it is referring to Doeg.

6.4. C. b. Ahithophel

According to the Yerushalmi, Ahithophel too "was a man mighty in Torah learning." One of the reasons given for Ahithophel's exclusion from the world to come is based on the biblical account of his treason against David and his alliance with the latter's renegade son Absalom, which I have already mooted as a possible justification in my discussion of the Mishnah [p. 131]:

> **j. Sanh. 10:2. X:** This is in line with that which is written in Scripture: "Now in those days the counsel which Ahithophel gave was as if one consulted [the oracle of God; so was the counsel of Ahithophel esteemed, both by David and by Absalom]" (2 Sam. 16:23). [*Neusner translation*]6-21

The final explanation regarding Ahithophel's being "Set apart" also is a reference to the biblical text:

> **j. Sanh. 10:2. X:** When Ahithophel saw that his counsel was not followed, he saddled his ass [and went off home to his own city]. [And he set his house in order, and hanged himself; and he died, and was buried in the tomb of his father]" (2 Sam 17:23). [*Neusner translation*]6-22

While one could argue that the suicide by hanging is an allusion to the death of Judas, it must not be forgotten that only the *first* suicide of Judas was by hanging. His *second* suicide – the one recounted in the first chapter of Acts – involved explosive disembowelment. Whatever low probability one might assign to the likelihood of this passage being a reference to Judas, it would seem that Christian uncertainty as to how Judas actually died would have to reduce that probability by fifty percent! But of course, the mere fact that one feature of the Ahithophel story finds a parallel in one of the Judas stories is not adequate justification for equating Ahithophel with Judas. Moreover, the Yerushalmi's additional discussion of Ahithophel clearly are derived from a rich folk literature, the details of which have no identifiable parallel with Judas.

The first of the extrabiblical anecdotes is delightfully weird and gives us another glimpse of a wonderful literature now lost:

j. Sanh. 10:2. X: Now the ark carried the priests on high, but let them fall down; the ark carried the priests on high, but let them fall down to the ground.

David sent and brought Ahithophel. He said to him, "Will you not tell me what is with this ark, which raises the priests up high and casts them down to the ground, raises the priests on high, and casts them down to the ground?"

He said to him, "Send and ask those wise men whom you appointed!"

Said David, "One who knows how to make the ark stop and does not do so in the end is going to be put to death through strangulation."

He said to him, "Make a sacrifice before [the ark], and it will stop." [*Neusner translation*][6-23]

Now of course Ahithophel actually comes off as a good guy in this pericope. Anyone who can prevent crash landings of flying priests should be rewarded – not barred from the world to come. It would seem, however, that the reason for introducing this strange tale is to allow David to prophesy Ahithophel's death by a form of strangulation (hanging). I am at a loss to understand what this story is actually all about. It would appear that at the time of composition of both the Christian and rabbinical literatures, there existed numerous legends of flying holy men and magicians.

The second of the extrabiblical anecdotes concerning Ahithophel is one that has been preserved in Jewish folklore:

j. Sanh. 10:2. X: And so you find that when David came to dig the foundations of the Temple, he dug fifteen hundred cubits and did not reach the nethermost void. In the end he found one clay pot, and he wanted to remove it.

It said to him, "You cannot do so."

He said to it, "Why not?"

It said to him, "For I here am the cover over the great deep."

It said to him, "And how long have you been here?"

It said to him, "From the time that I heard the voice of the All-Merciful at Sinai: 'I am the Lord your God, [who brought you out of the land of Egypt, out of the house of bondage]' (Ex. 20:2), the earth shook and trembled.

"And I am set here to seal the great deep."

Even so, [David] did not listen to it.

When he removed the clay pot, the great deep surged upward to flood the world.

And Ahithophel was standing there. He said, "Thus will David be strangled [in the flood] and I shall become king."

Said David, "He who is a sage, knowing how to stop up the matter, and does not stop it, will in the end be put to death through strangulation."

[Ahithophel] said what he said and stopped up [the flood].

[Neusner translation][6-24]

This curious legend survives, as I have noted, in Jewish folklore, where it is clearly representing Ahithophel, not St. Peter or any Christian whatsoever. The folklorist Angelo S. Rappoport published a further development of this story in his book *Ancient Israel: Myths and Legends*:

Then Achitophel was compelled to tell the King what to do.

He counselled David to take a stone and engrave upon it the Ineffable Name, the Tetragrammaton, and set it in the orifice through which the waters were surging. David followed Achitophel's advice, and immediately the waters of the deep subsided, and Jerusalem and the whole world were saved from the danger that threatened them. In the end Achitophel, nevertheless, committed suicide by hanging himself. The digging proceeded, but David was not allowed to build the Temple on account of his having been a man of blood. [6-25]

Not unexpectedly, I conclude from all this that when the Yerushalmi writes about Ahithophel, it is writing about

Ahithophel. As necessary as it may be for Christian apologists to find extrabiblical evidence of the historicity of the apostles, they will not find it in the Yerushalmi.

6.4. C. c. Gehazi

Like his supposed apostolic cohorts, Gehazi too "was a man powerful in learning of Torah. But he had three bad traits: niggardliness, womanizing, and denying the resurrection of the dead" [*Neusner translation*].[6-26] To which of the holy Apostles should we compare him? The misogynist womanizer St. Paul? The gatekeeper St. Peter, who sorts out resurrected beings whose existence he denies? Before we have read past the opening sentences of the Yerushalmi's treatment of Gehazi, it becomes obvious that we are not dealing with a coded reference to any Christian apostle.

Yerushalmi proceeds then to justify the three charges by embellishment of the Elisha stories in 2 Kings. Gehazi is niggardly for having kept Elisha to himself, preventing his other disciples from entering the prophet's lecture hall. He was a womanizer according to a curious interpretation of the story of Elisha and the Shunamite woman found in 2 Kings 4:8–37. Once again, I depend upon Jacob Neusner's translation:

j. Sanh. 10:2 XI: And he was licentious: for lo, the Shunamite said to her husband, "[And she said to her husband,] 'Behold now, I perceive that this is a holy man of God, who is continuously passing our way' " (2 Kings 4:9).

Said R. Jonah, '*He* was a holy man – but his disciple was no saint'."

Said R. Abin, "The fact was that [Elisha] never in his life laid eyes on her."

And rabbis of Cæsarea say, "The reason was that he never produced a drop of semen on his garments in his entire life."

The serving girl of R. Samuel bar R. Isaac said, "I would wash the clothing of my master. In my whole life I never saw any sort of bad thing on the garments of my master."

It is written, "[And when she came to the mountain to the man of God, she caught hold of his feet.] And Gehazi came to thrust her away. [But the man of God said, 'Let her alone, for she is in bitter distress; and the Lord has hidden it from me, and has not told me]' " (2 Kings 4:27).

What is the meaning of "to thrust her away"?
Said R. Yosé b. Hanina, "He put his hand on the cleavage between her breasts."[6-27]

Readers who managed to stay awake while reading some of the more soporific parts of this book may possibly recall that when I discussed Gehazi in the chapter on the Mishnah [p. 132] I had found it necessary to fast-forward to a passage in the Babylonian Talmud – a passage representing the evolutionary end of Gehazi's character development:

> **b. Sanh. 107b:** Our Rabbis teach, Ever let the left hand repel and the right hand invite, not like Elisha who repulsed Gehazi with both hands, and not like R. Jehoshua ben Perahjah, who repulsed Jeshu (the Nazarene) with both hands. [*Herford translation*][6-28]

It is immediately obvious that the Yerushalmi tale of Elisha and the Shunamite woman is a more primitive variant of the Bavli pericope. As in the biblical story itself [2 Kings 4:27], it is Gehazi, not Elisha, who repulses; and it is the woman, not Gehazi, who is repulsed. It would appear that this allegation of sexual misconduct on the part of Gehazi led even some of the Yerushalmi's authors to feel that he himself should have been expelled by the pure and holy Elisha. The Shunamite woman was then forgotten, and Elisha "repulsed Gehazi with both hands." In fact, shortly after the Shunamite section, the Yerushalmi itself executes the first great leap forward in this evolution. After stating the opinion that Elisha went to Damascus to retrieve Gehazi and finding him to be a leper, Yerushalmi *Sanh.* 10:2 presents us with a *non sequitur*:

> **J. Sanh. 10:2. XI:** On this basis we learn that they push away [a sinner] with the left hand, but draw him near with the right hand.
> R. Yohanan said, " 'The sojourner has not lodged in the street; I have opened my doors to the wayfarer' (Job 31:32). On the basis of this verse [we learn] that they push away with the left hand and draw near with the right."
> And this is not as did Elisha, who drove away Gehazi with both hands. [*Neusner translation*][6-29]

Then, in Babylon five centuries or so *after* Jesus is supposed to have been born, the Nazarene was added to the literary company of Elisha and Gehazi, and was repulsed by Rabbi Peraḥjah – who lived about a century *before* Christ!

Finally, the third Yerushalmi reason for Gehazi's exclusion from Paradise: "Nor did he believe in the resurrection of the dead."

This allegation is derived from a strained interpretation of the biblical story of Elisha's resurrection of the son of the Shunamite woman [2 Kings 4], in which Gehazi does not follow the prophet's instructions, forcing Elisha to take care of the resurrection operation himself.

It is not necessary to exhaust all the Yerushalmi's discussion of Gehazi to see quite clearly: although he has acquired more sins than he committed in the Bible, Gehazi in the Palestinian Talmud is Gehazi.

6.4. C. d. Saved or Sacked?

On several occasions I have noted that the Yerushalmi's discussions of the three kings and four commoners who are excluded from the world to come include some amount of casuistry on their behalf. Nevertheless, it will probably come as a minor shock to learn that after all the discussion of why those sinners are to be excluded from Paradise, Yerushalmi *Sanh.* 10:2 closes with a discussion indicating that all of them will be pardoned after all! While nothing in the Talmud is ever completely clear and no conclusion can ever be drawn with certainty, nevertheless it seems about as certain as any Talmudic issue can be that our three kings and four* commoners *will* have their portion in the world to come also. After being given scriptural proofs for the rescue of most of them by name, we read in the very last sentence of the section, "It is my task to seek out for them good deeds, to make them friends once more with one another."

And they all lived happily after. After life, that is.

Would the rabbinical writers have been so generous in dispensing salvation if these characters actually had been Jesus, St. Paul, St. Peter, St. James, or St. John? I do not know, but it is worth pondering.

---

* In the Bavli, however, rescue is withheld for Balaam.

The discovery that the Talmud of the Land of Israel not only contains no mention of "Jesus the Nazarene," but contains no mention of his apostles either is of great significance to the question of the historical Jesus. Excuses can always be manufactured as to why no one noticed "Gentle Jesus"; but it is harder to explain why his apostles – under whom the Christian movement is alleged to have experienced explosive growth and influence – also slipped away undetected beneath the radar of all ancient witnesses. It becomes increasingly clear that the characters of the Gospels and Acts are, for the most part, mythical.

6.5. Knowing Christians Instead of Christ?

We complete our examination of the Palestinian Talmud with a consideration of a passage in the treatise *Berakhot* ('blessings') which mentions both *minim* (sectarians or heretics) and Balaam. I have never understood why anyone would think this passage has anything at all to do with an historical Jesus, but here it is:

> **j. *Ber.* 1:8 (3c):** For Rab Mathnah and Rab Shemuel bar Nahman says, both say, It would be proper that the Ten Words [*the Ten Commandments*] should be read every day. And why are they not read? Because of the misrepresentation of the Minim, that they might not say, "These [*i.e.*, the Ten Words] only were given to Moses on Sinai." Rab Shemuel bar Nahman in the name of Rabbi Jehudah bar Zebuda says, "It would be proper that the Parashah [*a biblical section containing the exact declarations of Balaam*] of Balak and Balaam should be read every day. And why is it not read? In order not to weary the congregation. Rab Huna says, "Because there is written in it *Lying down and rising up*" [Num. 23:24]. Rabbi Jose bar Rabbi Būn says, "Because there is written in it the going forth [out of Egypt], and the Kingdom" [Num. 23:21,22]. Rabbi El'azar says, "Because it is written in the Torah, the prophets and the Writings." [*Herford translation*][6-30]

It would seem that the recitation of the Ten Commandments had been discontinued because unspecified heretics – not necessarily Christians – were in the habit of claiming that those were the only laws given by Yahweh to Moses and that the rest of the so-called Mosaic Law was not binding. Of course, this is probably compatible with the views of certain Pauline Christian sects that rejected most Jewish Christian observances. But there may have been splinter sects within Judaism itself that had evolved away from the legalism that was becoming rabbinical Judaism. The halting of the reading of the Ten Commandments may have resulted from the pressure of early Christian *kvetching* – but then again, some other group may be due the credit and praise. By 395 CE, the year traditionally assigned to the closing of the Palestinian Talmud, everyone in the Mediterranean world should have heard of Christianity. If this passage in the Yerushalmi is in fact a reference to Christians, it is of some small interest to students of Christian history. For students of an historical Jesus, however, it has nothing to teach.

The mention that the Oracles of Balaam should also be read – but aren't because they weary the congregation – is of considerable interest, however, as it attests to the great importance ascribed to that puzzling figure. If the story of Balaam was so important in Jewish consciousness that it was felt it should be included in the synagogue service, must it not have been reinforced by extrabiblical narratives as well? Is this not further evidence of a voluminous and popular Balaam literature current during the first few centuries of the common era?

EXCURSUS

The Legend of Balaam:
The Seer Whose Ass Could Talk

Of all the alleged aliases of Jesus said to be found in the rabbinical literature, the Balaam character is the most weakly equatable to him – even in the Babylonian Talmud, where seeds first sprouted in the Mishnah so often grow into the most exotic of flowers. It would appear that the only new "evidence" for the *Balaam* = *Jesus* equation making its debut in the Bavli is a strained, interpretive translation supposedly indicating that Balaam was killed by Pontius Pilate, along with a rather straight-forward estimation that Balaam was thirty-three years old – supposedly the same age as Jesus – when he died.

This excursus will start at the end of Balaam's career – in the Babylonian Talmud. After examining the feeble claims that Balaam in the Bavli is Jesus, we will investigate the origins and evolution of the Balaam *persona* – a character of far greater significance than Jesus in ancient Jewish thought.

Ex.1. Is *Balaam* a Cipher for *Jesus* in the Bavli?

Both of the above-mentioned 'facts' supposedly proving the equivalence of Balaam and Jesus occur together in the same pericope in the Babylonian treatise *Sanhedrin*:

> **b. Sanh. 106ᵇ:** A certain heretic said to R. Ḥanina, "Have you ever heard how old Balaam was?" He replied, "There is nothing written about it. But from what is written (Ps. lv. 23), Men of blood and deceit shall not live out half their days, he must have

been thirty-three or thirty-four years old." He [the heretic] said, "Thou has answered me well. I have seen the chronicle of Balaam, and therein is written 'Balaam, the lame, was thirty-three years old when Pinḥas the Robber killed him'." [Herford translation][Ex-1]

R. Travers Herford argued nearly a century ago that "Pinḥas (Phineas) the Robber" is actually a garbled variant of *Pontius Pilate*. The argument that Phineas the Robber (פנחס ליסטאה *Pinḥas Listāāh*)* is actually Pontius Pilate is so far-fetched that it is hard to believe any scholar ever took it seriously. Nevertheless, for the sake of comprehensiveness, I shall examine Herford's argument.

"The corruption is," Herford admits, "a somewhat violent one, if the author who had written the one name was aware of the other. But he may have found a name to him unintelligible, and by the help of Num. xxxi. 8 have transformed it into Pinḥas Listāāh. Talmudic tradition did not, so far as I am aware, know the name of Pontius Pilate, or ascribe the death of Jesus to a non-Jewish tribunal. But it is certainly strange that a Jew should call Pinḥas [Phinehas] a robber, being, as he was, a highly honoured hero of tradition."[Ex-2]

For readers who are not fluent in ancient Greek and Aramaic, it should be explained that the Greek word for *robber* – *lēistēs* (λῃστής) – was borrowed into Talmudic Aramaic as *listāāh* (ליסטאה). Despite the meaning of the term in Greek, the medieval Talmud commentator Rashi explains the Aramaic word as meaning 'military general' (שׂר צבא *sar tsaba*). According to G. R. S. Mead, among the Jews the term was not a title of reproach but rather an epithet given to patriotic leaders and zealots for the Law – of whom Phineas was represented as an example *par excellence*. As Mead points out, "If *listaa* was a caricature-name, we should not find the combination 'Phineas Listaa,' but Listaa by itself."[Ex-3] Indeed, and there is no reason to suppose that *Listaa* is an abbreviation of *P'listaa* – supposedly a caricature name for Pilate.

As for "Balaam the lame," in b. *Sanh.* 105ᵃ R. Yoḥanan reports that "Balaam limped on one foot, as it is written, *And he walked haltingly* [apparently a citation of a variant reading of Num 23:3]. Samson was lame in both feet... Balaam was blind in one eye, as it is said, [*and the man*] *whose eye is open...* [Num 24:3. 'Eye' is in

---

* Herford's text incorrectly reads פנהס instead of פנחס.

the singular, implying that only one eye was open because the other was sightless.] He practised enchantment by means of his membrum [*penis*]. For here it is written, *falling, but having his eyes open*; while elsewhere is written, *And Haman was fallen on the bed whereon Esther was.*"Ex-4

On the same page of the Bavli, Mar Zuṭra agrees that "He practised enchantment by means of his penis." Mar the son of Rabina notes further that "He committed bestiality with his ass. The view that he practised enchantment by means of his penis is as was stated. The view that he committed bestiality with his ass [is because] here it is written, *He bowed, he lay down as a lion and as a great lion*; while elsewhere it is written, *At her feet.*"

It may be noted that these startling "facts" about Balaam are all derived – at least to the satisfaction of the rabbis cited – from verses in the biblical tale of Balaam, with a little help from the book of Esther. Thus, it seems clear that the lameness, unilateral blindness, and phallomancy can refer only to the biblical character in question. Certainly, they cannot refer to the Jesus of Christianity. Had he been lame and blind, his reported healings of the lameness and blindness of others would have been cause for many an ironic anecdote. As for using his penis as a substitute for a magic wand, the only indication Christians have that Jesus even had a penis is the notice in Luke 2:21 indicating that Jesus was circumcised on the eighth day. Apart from that, there is no evidence that Jesus ever used his penis for any purpose whatsoever during his lifetime. Moreover, had the Good Shepherd been overly friendly with his livestock, at least his enemies would have brayed uproariously and broadcast the fact loudly.

The fact that the rabbinical literature everywhere else knows nothing of Pontius Pilate, and never relates the death of Jesus or his alleged alter egos to Roman authorities is itself a point of interest. If the trial before Pilate never occurred, it would be expected that the Jews would not mention the idea. On the other hand, the Jews might have taken no interest in the fact even had it been historical. The fact is, however, that by the time of the Bavli the Jews *were* interested in the circumstances of Jesus' death and indicated that it was Jews, not Romans, who did him in – in two different ways. According to b. *Sanh.* 43a, "On the eve of Passover, Yeshu [*the Munich MS adds 'the Nazarene'*] was hanged. For forty days before the execution took place, a herald went forth and cried, 'He is going forth to be stoned because he practised sorcery and enticed Israel to apostacy…'"Ex-5

It would appear in this passage that we have caught a myth in the midst of formation. Only one manuscript identifies Yeshu as being *ha-Notzri* – the Nazarene. But the contradiction regarding whether Jesus was hanged or stoned is easily explained away by reference to the known tradition that after being executed, malefactors were sometimes strung up and exposed for further disgrace. Accordingly, Jesus was stoned and then hung up. Nevertheless, the text doesn't *say* that. (One is reminded of apologists who try to explain away the contradictions surrounding the deaths of Judas: He hanged himself, the rope broke, he fell forward, and he exploded!) Most important for attempts to salvage Christian traditions regarding the death of the Messiah, however, is the fact that taken in combination, these two deaths of Yeshu absolutely rule out the notion that he was crucified. While references in the New Testament and elsewhere indicating that Jesus was hanged have easily been explained by special pleaders as poetic references to crucifixion, it surely must be beyond the ability of even the most brazen expert in "Hard Sayings of the Bible" to show how Jesus could have been stoned as well as crucified.

No one knows for certain when the death of Jesus the Messiah became connected to the days of Pontius Pilate, nor does anyone know who first decided the two had been contemporaries. The earliest known mention of Pilate in the New Testament is in the Gospel of Mark, an anonymous work which most scholars believe was created shortly after the destruction of the Temple of Yahweh in the year 70 CE. What Christians believed before that concerning the death of their would-have-been savior is not known, although the several references to "hanging on a tree" found in Galatians 3:13 and even in late works such as 1 Peter [2:24] and the contrived speeches of Acts [5:30; 10:39; 13:29] may reflect some of the earliest imaginings on the subject. (The likelihood that crucifixion was a metaphor for the entry of the vernal equinoctial sun into the cross formed by the intersection of the ecliptic with the celestial equator cannot be discussed here, being far outside the subject of this book.)

Although Q, "the earliest gospel," knows nothing of Pontius Pilate, once 'Mark' had written him into the passion story, the authors of Matthew, John, and Luke followed suit, adapting the story and its characters to their own theopolitical purposes. The early second-century Acts of the Apostles,* following the Gospel of Luke by an unknown number of years, inserts Pilate into speeches

[Acts 3:13; 4:27; 13:28] concocted by the author – speeches having no historical significance whatever. There can be no doubt that the notices of Pilate in Acts of the Apostles are all derivative from the gospels and contain no first-hand information. The only other mention of Pilate in the New Testament is in 1 Timothy 6:13:

"13Now in the presence of God, who gives life to all things, and of Jesus Christ, who himself made the same noble confession and gave his testimony to it before Pontius Pilate, 14I charge you to obey your orders irreproachably and without fault until our Lord Jesus Christ appears." [NEB]

Most mainline scholars admit that the so-called Pastoral Epistles (1 & 2 Timothy and Titus) are not authentic Pauline compositions and do not reflect the earliest traditions. (The jury is still out on the question of whether or not *any* of the letters in the New Testament were actually written by the character known to Christian tradition as St. Paul.) The Gnostic Marcion [c140 CE], who assembled the first known collection of Pauline epistles, says nothing about 1 Timothy. It is not possible to say whether his silence indicates that the letter had not yet been written or that Marcion rejected it for some theological reason. In any event, Pilate is unknown to the authors of the earliest epistles, forcing us to the conclusion that the Pilate story is the invention of the author of Mark – or the author of a possible source incorporated by him.

It is sometimes argued that the Pilate story *must* be true, for if it were not true it would immediately have been challenged by persons knowing what in fact had happened – because they had been witnesses to history. The *naïveté* of this argument is obvious when one realizes that the story was created after the destruction of Jerusalem in 70 CE – in which all records were lost – and witnesses (even if in fact they had ever existed) would have been killed or dispersed. Furthermore, it presupposes that Christianity's founding documents were written in Palestine, where

---

* According to G. R. S. Mead, the church father Justin Martyr [c150 CE] "knows nothing of the Acts even when referring to Simon Magus, a reference which he could not have omitted had he known of it, and one which all subsequent heresiologists triumphantly set in the forefront of their 'refutations' of that famous heretic... There is no clear quotation from the Acts known till 177 A.D."Ex-6

witnesses to Palestinian history would be found. If, however, Christianity did not begin in Palestine, and if its foundation literature – as seems all but certain – was written elsewhere, the chance of anyone challenging successfully even the most outrageous claims would have been extremely small.

To return to the *Sanhedrin* passage that triggered all these excursions into the Christian history of Pontius Pilate: it thus becomes obvious that "Phineas the Robber" has nothing whatever to do with Pontius Pilate. The Jews can offer no support whatsoever to the late Christian legend attributing their savior's death to the Roman governor.

But what of the coincidence that Balaam is said to have been thirty-three or thirty-four years old when he was killed – just as any Sunday school pupil can tell you was the case with Jesus? Isn't that an uncanny coincidence?

Actually, it is not strange at all. On the same page as the quotation beginning this discussion, b. *Sanhedrin* applies the same calculation – derived from the same biblical verse – to Doeg and Ahitophel:

> **b. Sanh. 106ᵇ:** It is said by R. Joḥanan, "Doeg and Ahitophel did not live out half their days. It is thus taught (Ps. lv. 23), Men of blood and deceit do not live out half their days. All the years of Doeg were but thirty-four, and of Ahitophel only thirty-three." [*Herford translation*]Ex-7

Reckoning from Psalms 90:10, which says that the normal human life-span is "threescore years and ten," half a lifetime would be thirty-five years. The ages guessed for all three characters are slightly less than half the biblical quota, since if they "do not live out half their days," a number less than half of 70 is required. The approximation method used by the R. Yoḥanan seems quite obvious. As far as the rabbi is concerned, the ages for all three are mere guesses, not historical knowledge.

It is sometimes argued that the "Chronicle of Balaam" mentioned in the first quotation was actually a gospel, and that the *min* (heretic) was a Christian. If this be so, it is hard to understand why he would be quizzing a rabbi about Jesus. After all, the Christian already knew the answer and would have no reason to suppose that the rabbi would ever have bothered to learn anything about the subject. Whether or not the *min* was a Christian or some other sectarian (perhaps even a Balaamite!), he could be expected to quiz the rabbi only on subjects for which rabbis were known to be knowledgeable. Certainly, any rabbi could have been expected to have opinions on the biblical character Balaam.

While the age estimated for Balaam just happens to match the age assigned by a Christian tradition* to Jesus, the ages assigned to Doeg and Ahithophel do not match any traditions I am aware of pertaining to the major apostles. (Remember, Doeg and Ahithophel are supposed to be codes for St. Peter, St. Paul, Judas Iscariot, St. James, etc.) All this forces me to conclude that even in the Bavli – the latest of the major rabbinical treatises – Balaam has not evolved into Christ.

Even though it is now clear that the name *Balaam* had nothing to do with Jesus throughout the first five or six centuries of rabbinical literary evolution, the story of Balaam is so interesting that I wish to present a brief history of traditions about him and end with the Bavli's portrait of the sorcerer.

Ex.2. The Balaam Inscription from Deir ʿAllâ

As the Jordan River trickles its way south from the Sea of Galilee to the Dead Sea, approximately midway it is joined on the east by a tributary known as the Zerqa – the Jabbok River of biblical times. About a mile north of this tributary, in what today is the Kingdom of Jordan, is an archaeological site known as Deir ʿAllâ. There amidst the ruins of what probably was a sanctuary of some sort, on March 17, 1967, a Dutch expedition from the University of Leiden led by Henk J. Franken discovered numerous pieces of plaster with red and black writing on them. Probably datable to around 800 BCE – although dates ranging from mid-ninth century BCE to the Persian period have been suggested – the reconstructed inscription is written in a peculiar form of Aramaic, Ammonite, or a closely related, hitherto unknown language. Despite uncertainty as to language, the inscription can be read fairly well, although the many *lacunæ* make certain translation impossible. Moreover, the pieces of plaster have been assembled into two "combinations," and it is not

---

*If one follow the Markan tradition, in which Jesus seems to have had a public career of just one solar year, it would seem that Jesus must have been thirty-one, not thirty-three years old when the final curtain went down.

known for certain that the two parts really belong to a single inscription. Nevertheless, the name *Balaam, son of Beor* appears several times in the first combination – making it the oldest extrabiblical occurrence of the name. It is also older than the biblical accounts by an arguable number of centuries.

It has frequently been reported that the Deir ʿAllâ inscription proves the historicity of Balaam. But this certainly is far from being an established fact. After all, thousands of Egyptian inscriptions mentioning Osiris have been found, but few if any scholars would suggest they prove the historicity of Osiris. About all we can say is that the Deir ʿAllâ inscription is compatible with an historical Balaam and could be the source of the later accounts of him in the Book of Numbers and elsewhere in the Hebrew Bible.

It is not known why the text was written upon the plaster wall, but it is possible that it recorded divinations carried out at the site, or it could have been for instruction of seers in training. Some scholars believe the inscription to be a display copy of a much older text – sort of like the copies of the Ten Commandments one sometimes finds in courthouses in America. If Balaam was indeed an historical figure, he may have practiced his craft here rather than in Mesopotamia, as claimed in Numbers 22:5. In fact, scholars have long suspected that the Hebrew text of this verse should be emended to read "in the land of Ammon" instead of "in the land of the children of his people" [KJV] or "in the land of the Amavites" [NEB]. This reading is supported by the Samaritan Pentateuch, the Vulgate Latin Bible, the Syriac Bible, and even by several manuscripts of the Masoretic Text, according to Walter C. Kaiser, Jr.[Ex-8]

While the question of Balaam's historicity must remain open at present, it is worth noting that we do have proof here of the existence of an extrabiblical literature about him as early as perhaps 800 BCE, forcing us to conclude that the accounts of him in Numbers and other biblical books are secondary incorporations and reflections of this literature. This being the case, it should not be surprising to discover that a thousand years later, when the Mishnah and Talmuds were being compiled, they too would draw upon extrabiblical traditions pertaining to the popular sorcerer and seer.

When the authors of Numbers, Deuteronomy, Joshua, Micah, and Nehemiah took pen in hand to write about the soothsayer Balaam, just what information might they have been able to glean from their literary environment? The Deir ʿAllâ inscription gives us quite a bit of information concerning this question.

According to Jo Ann Hackett's reconstruction and translation of the inscription,[Ex-9] Balaam was the son of Beor – just as in the book of Numbers. He was a "seer of the gods," however, not a devotee of Yahweh. As in Numbers 22:20, "the gods" [*ʾilāhīn*] come to Balaam in the night – although readers of English bibles would never know it, since *ʾelohīm* ('gods') is always translated as *God*. Like the biblical Balaam, the seer of Deir ʿAllâ is an oneiromantic (a dream divinator) and he receives an oracle from El – the head god of the divine assembly and a divinity incorporated into the amalgamation of gods found in the Hebrew Bible also. The heavenly *Shaddayin* who take their place in the heavenly assembly are clearly related to the biblical *El Shaddai* – fondly rendered *God Almighty* in most English versions. The mythic milieu at Deir ʿAllâ is very similar to that of the Hebrew Bible.

Besides being a 'seer by night' and practitioner of dream divination, the Deir ʿAlla Balaam is also an ornithomantic and theromantic – one who practices divination by observing the behavior of birds and beasts, respectively. 'Combination One,' according to Hackett's reconstruction, tells how Balaam has a dream vision during the night and is frightened by its content. The gods are going to punish his people, and he weeps and fasts and explains his vision to the people. One line, which Hackett renders "and the deaf hear from afar," perhaps presages rabbinical musings of more than a thousand years later when Rabbi Elʾazar ha-Qappar claims that the voice of Balaam was so loud "that it went from one end of the world to the other" [*Jalqut Shimʿoni.* §766]. 'Combination Two,' which is very fragmentary, appears to describe events in the world of the dead. Although this suggests to me that Balaam at Deir ʿAllâ was also a necromancer – one who practices divination by calling up the dead – I do not remember any scholar ever suggesting this possibility.

Scholarly debate about Deir ʿAllâ continues quite energetically, and many fundamental questions remain in dispute or altogether unanswered. Nevertheless, it seems safe to say that the soothsayer Balaam was a significant feature in Near Eastern folklore and religion from very early times. How – and why – he came into Israelite religion I do not know, although I shall offer some speculations on this question shortly. I am certain that the answer to this question, if it could be known, would be both immensely interesting and surprising.

Ex.3. Balaam in the Hebrew Bible

Archaeologically it is now all but certain that the Israelite Exodus from Egypt never occurred and that the biblical accounts of the conquest of Canaan (Palestine) are fictions created to justify the efforts of a later Jewish state to acquire the very same territories disputed in the biblical texts. A popular account of this very contentious area of archaeology is to be found in Israel Finkelstein's *The Bible Unearthed*,[Ex-10] which argues for the creation of much of the Pentateuch's pseudohistory – especially the Deuteronomistic fantasies – in the seventh century BCE, during the reign of King Josiah. After the destruction of the northern Kingdom of Israel and the subsequent withdrawal of the Assyrians from the region, the southern Kingdom of Judah saw an opportunity to expand its territory northward. Having created the literary fiction of a United Kingdom of Israel and Judah ruled from Jerusalem by the legendary King David (whom Finkelstein thinks was historical), Josiah could claim a historical right to "reclaim" the northern territories. (The same literary fictions would be used again – several millennia later – by Zionists seeking to justify their seizure of Palestine and creation of the modern state of Israel.) Josiah took the first steps toward making the mythical Kingdom of David a reality. Although Josiah did not succeed in 'regaining' all the territories mapped out in his literary agenda – he was killed in 609 BCE at Megiddo by the forces of Pharaoh Neco II coming to help the last remnant of the Assyrian Empire against the rising threat of Babylon – the fairy tale world created by priests in his court lived on. For the better part of three millennia it would be considered history.

Ex.3. A. Balaam in Numbers 22–24

What has this to do with the biblical accounts of Balaam?

If the Exodus never occurred, Moses and his Israelite hordes did not wander in the wilderness of the Near East for forty years, sometime between 1290 and 1230 BCE – as mainline scholars suppose – or between 1450 and 1400 BCE as biblical literalists would have it. Without wandering hordes, Moses and Joshua could not have conquered Canaan. Archaeologically it appears to be a fact that they did not do so. Although it is extremely improbable that

Moses was a real person, even if he had existed, the tale in
Numbers 22 of King Balak being affrighted by Israelite hordes
led by Moses and Joshua is obviously fictional. If Balak was never
threatened by Israelite hordes, he had no need to hire a soothsayer to curse them – eliminating the cause given for Balaam's
entry into the Book of Numbers. So why was Balaam, a pagan
prophet and probable sorcerer, imported into the foundational
epic of the Jews? Why, in that epic, is Balaam portrayed both as a
wicked agent who led Israel astray "in the matter of Peor" [Num
31:15] and as the prophet who uttered what arguably is the most
important oracle ever created in support of messianic Jewish
causes – the memorable "There shall come a Star out of Jacob,
and a Sceptre shall rise out of Israel, and shall smite the corners
of Moab, and destroy all the children of Sheth" [Num 24:17] ?

As I admitted a few lines above, I do not know the answers to
these questions, but I cannot resist indulging in a few speculations. John T. Greene, in his *Balaam and His Interpreters: A
Hermeneutical History of the Balaam Traditions*[Ex-11] – despite
his belief in the historicity of David, Solomon, and the United
Kingdom of Israel and Judah – presents a very convincing theory
of the place of the Balaam stories in the theopolitical agenda of
the priests who composed most of the Pentateuch. (No, Virginia,
Moses didn't write the Pentateuch.)

Because of the degeneracy of the Hebrew Masoretic text,
there is great uncertainty as to just what "facts" need to be
explained or incorporated into an explanatory theory of the
Balaam traditions. However, Greene offers a number of suggestions that I shall try to summarize.

First of all, Greene points out that the Hebrew Bible knows
of two different men who are "the son of Beor": Bela, King of
Edom, and Balaam the soothsayer of our tale. Genesis 36:32
mentions a King Bela [*belaʿ* בלע] who is supposed to have been a
king of Edom in the twelfth or eleventh century BCE. The name
Balaam [*bilʿam* בלעם], as can be seen, in Semitic script is the
same as *Bela*, except for the final *mem*, which Greene explains
can be added to Semitic stems to form nouns when later writers
overwork a text for polemical purposes. He concludes that the biblical Balaam was actually the legendary development of a priest-
king (not a rare commodity in the Near East of those times) who
had become famous as a diviner. By the time of the Deir ʿAllâ
inscription, Balaam would have been dead for three or four centuries. (It is possible that traditional dates for the life of Balaam

might even have been the reason for setting the Exodus and Conquest in the fifteenth to thirteenth centuries BCE.)

It appears that the Book of Numbers is actually a composite confection comprised of many different individual pieces originally written for various different purposes. It is a mixture of poetry, prose, and 'lyric prose.' It was compiled some while after the 722 BCE Assyrian destruction of the northern kingdom (Israel), when priests belonging to various Yahweh-worshipping sacerdotal parties flooded into the southern kingdom, Judah, seeking asylum – and employment.

Unlike Israel Finkelstein, who dates the composition of most of these documents to the seventh century, during the reign of Josiah [d. 609 BCE], John Greene dates the Balaam cycle of Numbers 22–24 to the reign of Hezekiah [727–698 BCE]. He points out that Hezekiah's Judah was a vassal of Assyria, and that such a condition would require numerous Assyrian priests to be present in Jerusalem to direct the mandatory temple sacrifices by the vassal king on the behalf of his suzerain. It was these foreign priests, Greene believes, whom the Priestly Source hostilely satirized as Balaam – the seer who couldn't see what even an ass could see. "P was reacting to actual Assyrian agents head-quartered in Jerusalem," he writes. "He was not reacting to a phantom."[Ex-12]

I will attempt no more than a broad summary of the complicated "Documentary Hypothesis" analysis to which Greene subjects the Balaam stories in Numbers 22–24 and note that he attempts to locate the various segments, reflexes, and nuances of the Numbers text among the component documents identified by Julius Wellhausen[Ex-13] back in the nineteenth century. These documents include: J (the Yahwist Source, from Judah in the south); E (the Elohist Source, from Israel in the north); JE (a harmonized version of the first two, constructed in the south); D (the Deuteronomistic Source); and P (the so-called Priestly Source). Readers interested in knowing more details about this fascinating piece of scholarship are encouraged to read Greene's book for themselves.

Greene concludes from his analysis that there was a tenth-century BCE version of the story wherein Balaam functioned as an acceptable, non-Israelite priest who had been recruited into a Judean national priesthood and accepted as a legitimate priestly colleague. This would have constituted the J Source stratum. (There are problems in this dating, however, as Finkelstein shows fairly convincingly that there was nothing that could be considered a Judaean state in the tenth century BCE!)

Then, later than 922 but earlier than 722 BCE, a version was created that concentrated on a northern homeland for Balaam and was probably produced by the priesthood at Shiloh, a cult center approximately twenty miles north of Jerusalem. This probably cast Balaam in a negative light, as outsider mantics would not have been acceptable to this group. This would have constituted the E source stratum. E characteristically disparaged Aaron, the eponymous ancestor of the ruling Jerusalem priesthood and elevated Moses to priestly preeminence.

After 722 BCE with the destruction of Israel, a conciliation of the first two documents was effected, probably in the southern kingdom of Judah. Once again, with Israel gone, Balaam served as a model member of the priesthood in Judah. Refugee priests from the north were absorbed into the body of the southern priesthood and legitimized. This constituted the so-called JE stratum.

JE triggered a strong response from P – the Priestly Source. Written by an Aaronid priest, this reworking of the text was characterized by its hostility to outsider priests and its demonstration of the inefficacy of sacrifices offered by priests who were not certified, authorized priests of Yahweh. This P stratum specifically Greene believes was produced during the reign of King Hezekiah of Judah. In P, Aaron is superior to Moses.

Finally (apart from a few notices of the ultimate 'redaction' under Ezra in post-Exilic times), Greene detects subtle traces of the Deuteronomist's craft in certain short passages. Significantly, Numbers 23:19–20 – which we have had occasion to examine in the Yerushalmi chapter – is one of these. This is the famous "Would he [*Yahweh*] speak and not act; promise and not fulfill?"

As suggested earlier, the Balaam story is actually an amalgamation of two different stories which has been reworked by later editors with different theopolitical axes to grind. As might be expected, the biblical text contains some non-Israelite traditional materials that have been revised to suit the purposes of at least two different priestly parties. There is also at issue just exactly what sort of religious activity is licit and valid. Should priests simply perform sacrifices according to rigid rules of practice? Is divination a proper means of communicating with the deity? Should sorcery be part of a priest's practical skills? Is it all right for a priest to prophesy, or is that a form of ritual anarchy?

In addition, it is apparent that at least one of the authors of the Balaam stories wanted to demonstrate the superiority of Yahweh over all the other gods. Having the pet god of the Jews repeatedly take possession of a pagan prophet in the very midst of 'high places' acknowledged to be the haunts of other deities (especially fertility gods) was a dramatic way of showing that he was on the side of Greater Israel – whose rightful real estate included not only the lands of condemned nations but the abodes of their gods as well. As Greene puts it, "The specific mentioning of specific religious centers dedicated to specific deities was intended to neutralize them. It was a form of exorcising a site of any former religious significance and then rendering any further activity there an ignorant, empty act. This was a form of site exorcism and deity assassination."[Ex-14]

The complicated sacerdotal politics which inflames the rhetoric of our Balaam stories in the Hebrew Bible is explained rather succinctly by Greene:

> Those priests who traced their ancestry to Moses had been excluded from important urban (*i.e.*, capital city) priestly functions, and a share in any kind of power in directing the course of state Yahwism in either its Jerusalem version... or its Tirzah/Samaria/Bethel/Dan version. (Here, too, the Shilonites had assisted Jeroboam in his bid for kingship, but were then rejected in favor of another state-appointed priesthood.) These Mushite priests waged polemical warfare against rival (as they understood them) state priesthoods on two fronts. Essentially, P opposed their opposition to P's group. ...
>
> Understanding the history of the Aaronid/Zadokite priesthood within the history of Judah leads one to understand the situation of that priesthood during the reign of Hezekiah, and that in the light of the Assyrian bid for power and conquest. Priesthoods battled for power in a manner similar to corporations taking over other corporations today. One should not underestimate the urgency with which P worked and wrote. [Ex-15]

Ex.3. B. Balaam in Numbers 31

There is a strongly racist undertone throughout the Pentateuch that finds its full voice in the Book of Ezra and parts of the Talmuds. The anti-miscegenation message typically is justified by the argument that intermarriage with non-Israelites or non-Jews leads to apostasy and idolatry – capital offenses in the theocratic minds of the composers of these dreadful scriptures. In Numbers 25 we read of Israel's miscegenation with the Moabites leading to dalliance with the god Baal Peor – whom we have already learned one is to worship by genital exposure or sacramental defecation. The King James Version recounts the theologically justified lynching that ensued as follows:

25:1And Israel abode in Shittim, and the people began to commit whoredom with the daughters of Moab. 2And they called the people unto the sacrifices of their gods: and the people did eat, and bowed down to their gods. 3And Israel joined himself unto Baal-Peor: and the anger of the LORD was kindled against Israel. 4And the LORD said unto Moses, Take all the heads of the people, and hang them up before the LORD against the sun, that the fierce anger of the LORD may be turned away from Israel. 5And Moses said unto the judges of Israel, Slay ye every one his men that were joined unto Baal-Peor.

6And, behold, one of the children of Israel came and brought unto his brethren a Midianitish woman in the sight of Moses, and in the sight of all the congregation of the children of Israel, who were weeping before the door of the tabernacle of the congregation. 7And when Phinehas, the son of Eleazar, the son of Aaron the priest, saw it, he rose up from among the congregation, and took a javelin in his hand; 8And he went after the man of Israel into the tent, and thrust both of them through, the man of Israel, and the woman through her belly. So the plague was stayed from the children of Israel. 9And those that died in the plague were twenty and four thousand....

16And the LORD spake unto Moses, saying, 17Vex the Midianites and smite them: 18For they vex you with their wiles, wherewith they have beguiled you in the matter of Peor, and in the matter of Cozbi, the daughter of a prince of Midian, their sister, which was slain in the day of the plague for Peor's sake.

Readers should note that Yahweh rewards theologically motivated murder with "the covenant of an everlasting priesthood" – founding a priesthood as the engine to push forward a fundamentally racist and genocidal agenda. It should be noted also that there was no mention of Balaam in this sordid scripture.

Balaam does reenter the text of Numbers again, however, in the thirty-first chapter. Whereas chapter 25 was morally shocking, chapter 31 is downright ghastly:

31:1And the LORD spake unto Moses, saying, 2Avenge the children of Israel of the Midianites: afterward shalt thou be gathered unto thy people. 3And Moses spake unto the people, saying, Arm some of yourselves unto the war, and let them go against the Midianites, and avenge the LORD of Midian. ...

6And Moses sent them to the war, a thousand of every tribe, them and Phinehas the son of Eleazar the priest, to the war, with the holy instruments, and the trumpets to blow in his hand. 7And they warred against the Midianites, as the LORD commanded Moses; and they slew all the males. 8And they slew the kings of Midian, beside the rest of them that were slain; namely, Evi, and Rekem, and Zur, and Hur, and Reba, five kings of Midian: **Balaam also the son of Beor they slew with the sword.**

9And the children of Israel took all the women of Midian captives, and their little ones, and took the spoil of all their cattle, and all their flocks, and all their goods. 10And they burnt all their cities wherein they dwelt, and all their goodly castles, with fire. 11And they took all the spoil, and all the prey, both of men and of beasts.

12And they brought the captives, and the prey, and the spoil, unto Moses, and Eleazar the priest, and unto the congregation of the children of Israel, unto the camp at the plains of Moab, which are by Jordan near Jericho.

13And Moses, and Eleazar the priest, and all the princes of the congregation, went forth to meet them without the camp. 14And Moses was wroth with the officers of the host, with the captains over thousands, and captains over hundreds, which came from the battle. 15And Moses said unto them, Have ye saved all the women alive? 16Behold, these caused the children of Israel, **through the counsel of Balaam**, to commit trespass against the LORD in the matter of Peor, and there was a plague among the congregation of the LORD. 17Now therefore kill every male among the little ones, and kill every woman that hath known man by lying with him. 18But all the women children that have not known a man by lying with him, keep alive for yourselves....

32And the booty, being the rest of the prey which the men of war had caught, was... 35thirty and two thousand persons in all, of women that had not known man by lying with him.

According to Greene, this barbarous tale is the product of the Aaronid Priestly Source, for whom Balaam served as a code for all outsider priestly types – including prophets, wizards, magicians, and diviners – who could be considered to be in competition with the Aaronid guild of priests. Although we never knew it when reading the cycle of Balaam stories in chapters 22-24, the crime of Balaam – for which he had to suffer the penalty of death – turns out to have been advising the Midianite women to seduce the Israelite men, thus diluting their racial and religious purity. This in turn might serve as justification for executing *all* rival priests. With fewer priests to divide up the contributions required of the faithful by 'the LORD,' there would be more sheep and shekels for the authorized clergy.

Ex.3. C. Balaam in Micah 6:5

Balaam is accorded brief but favorable notice in the prophecies of Micah:

6:5O my people, remember now what Balak king of Moab consulted, and what Balaam the son of Beor answered him from Shittim unto Gilgal; that ye may know the righteousness of the LORD.

Micah supposedly wrote and prophesied during the eighth century BCE in the rural city of Moresheth, southwest of Jerusalem. Micah was opposed to a number of different priesthoods (including the Assyrian priesthood) so I am at a loss to understand why he was so lenient with Balaam. Reading behind the lines, however, we may suppose that Micah knew of more Balaam literature than just the Numbers 22–24 cycle to which he alludes. Prophets as well as priests, we may observe, took notice of the soothsayer Balaam – again an indication of widely disseminated Balaam traditions and, I submit, literature.

Ex.3. D. Balaam in Deuteronomy 23

Deuteronomy – the 'Second Law' – contains a large number of commandments in addition to the Big Ten. It is not likely that any courthouse lawn will be graced by a granite engraving of the commandment recorded in Deuteronomy 23:12–14:

23:12Thou shalt have a place also without the camp, whither thou shalt go forth abroad; 13And thou shalt have a paddle upon thy weapon: and it shall be, when thou wilt ease thyself abroad, thou shalt dig therewith, and shalt turn back and cover that which cometh from thee: 14For the LORD thy God walketh in the midst of thy camp...

Nor will church-state miscegenation advocates ever display the 'laws' ordained at the beginning of the same chapter – including the law which makes reference to Balaam:

23:1He that is wounded in the stones, or hath his privy member cut off, shall not enter unto the congregation of the LORD.

2A bastard shall not enter into the congregation of the LORD; even to his tenth generation shall he not enter into the congregation of the LORD.

3An Ammonite or Moabite shall not enter into the congregation of the LORD; even to their tenth generation shall they not enter into the congregation of the LORD for ever: 4Because they met you not with bread and with water in the way, and **because they hired against thee Balaam the son of Beor of Pethor of Mesopotamia**, to curse thee. 5Nevertheless **the LORD thy God would not hearken unto Balaam**; but the LORD thy God turned the curse into a blessing unto thee, because the LORD thy God loved thee. 6Thou shalt not seek their peace nor their prosperity all thy days for ever.

The attentive reader may have paused momentarily after reading that Yahweh "would not hearken unto Balaam" – an indication that according to the tradition followed by the Deuteronomist, Balaam originally must have intended to curse the Israelites and did not open-mindedly consult Yahweh for his ruling as depicted in the Balaam cycle in Numbers 22–24. This would, of course, give grounds for the negative view of Balaam found in the rabbinical literature and accord with his exclusion from the world to come.

Further evidence of multiple Balaam traditions even in the days of the Deuteronomist can be seen in the fact that Pethor, Balaam's home, is located in Mesopotamia, not in the land of Ammon, Amaw (land of the Amavites in NEB), or even "by the river of the land of the children of his people" (KJV) as in Numbers 22:5. The stories of Balaam certainly did get around.

Ex.3. E. Balaam in Nehemiah 13:2

The Balaam tradition found in the post-Exilic book of Nehemiah does not seem to know of the Numbers 31 tradition that the soothsayer had been guilty of counseling Moabite girls to commit whoredom with Israelite boys – even though its author advances the same racist program* as did the Priestly Source author of Numbers 31. Balaam plays the same role as he did in the fable elaborated in chapters 22–24 of that book:

> 13:1On that day they read in the book of Moses in the audience of the people; and therein was found written, that the Ammonite and the Moabite should not come into the congregation of God for ever; 2Because they met not the children of Israel with bread and with water, **but hired Balaam against them,** that he should curse them: howbeit our God turned the curse into a blessing.

---

*Nehemiah, like Ezra, sought to prevent contamination of the Jewish gene pool:

13:23In those days also saw I [*Nehemiah*] Jews that had married wives of Ashdod, of Ammon, and of Moab: 24And their children spake half in the speech of Ashdod, and could not speak in the Jews' language, but according to the language of each people. 25And I contended with them, and cursed them, and smote certain of them, and plucked off their hair, and made them swear by God, saying, Ye shall not give your daughters unto their sons, nor take their daughters unto your sons, or for yourselves. 26Did not Solomon king of Israel sin by these things? yet among many nations was there no king like him, who was beloved of his God, and God made him king over all Israel: nevertheless even him did outlandish women cause to sin. 27Shall we then hearken unto you to do all this great evil, to transgress against our God in marrying strange wives? 28And one of the sons of Joiada, the son of Eliashib the high priest, was son in law to Sanballat the Horonite: therefore I chased him from me.

29Remember them, O my God, because they have defiled the priesthood, and the covenant of the priesthood, and of the Levites. 30Thus cleansed I them from all strangers [*'ethnic cleansing'!*] and appointed the wards of the priests and the Levites, every one in his business; 31And for the wood offering, at times appointed, and for the first fruits. Remember me, O my God, for good.

As was the case with the Deuteronomy passage discussed above, Ammonites as well as Moabites bear the brunt of priestly wrath. Since Ammonites are not mentioned in the main Balaam-cycle text, we may very well wonder how they came to share the damnation of the Moabites. If Balaam came from a Pethor located in the land of Ammon (as I previously suggested emending Numbers 22:5) instead of "by the river of the land of the children of his people," and if (as Greene has suggested) Balaam was actually an ancient priest-king of Ammon, the generalized hostility to Ammonites is understandable – as is the otherwise unexplained juxtaposition cheek-by-jowl of Ammonites with Balaam in this passage. Once again, we have evidence of yet another tradition relating to Balaam.

Ex.3. F. Balaam in the Book of Joshua

Balaam's name appears three times in the book of Joshua:

13:22**Balaam also the son of Beor** the soothsayer, did the children of Israel slay with the sword among them that were slain by them.

24:9Then Balak the son of Zippor, king of Moab, arose and warred against Israel, and sent and called **Balaam the son of Beor** to curse you: 10But I would not hearken unto **Balaam**; therefore he blessed you still: so I delivered you out of his hand.

In the tradition reflected in the Joshua passages, Balaam clearly had evil intent. Not only is this shown by Yahweh's not listening to him – *i.e.*, not approving his evil designs – it is indicated by Yahweh's saving his chosen race from the sorcerer's heap-big-medicine curse. It should be noted that Balak and the Moabites here are made out to be the aggressors in the genocidal Wars of Yahweh.

Ex.4. Balaam among the Samaritans

The origins of the Samaritans is hotly contested at present and it is probably not safe to say much about their origins other than that the group presently known as Samaritans originated somewhere between the third century BCE and the beginning of the common era, precipitating out of an unstable, supersaturated suspension of mutually repellent Israelite-Judahite theopolitical parties and special-interest sodalities. Certainly by the second century BCE they had formed a community that advocated for a sanctuary on Mt. Gerizim as the proper place for sacrifice as opposed to the sanctuary in Jerusalem. The Samaritans (*shomrim*, 'observers') take their name from their strict observance of what they consider to have been a covenant between Moses and Yahweh. Like other Jews, they accept the primacy of the Pentateuch – the so-called 'Five Books of Moses' or *Torah* – as scripture. Unlike all other Jewish groups of which we have record, however, the Samaritans do not accept *any* other books as scripture – rejecting the sections of the Hebrew Bible known as the Prophets and the Writings. Believers in the inerrant transmission of the Judaeo-Christian scriptures are confronted with a nightmare when they have to consider the Samaritan edition of the first five books of the Hebrew Bible: the Samaritan version differs from the Hebrew Masoretic Text in at least six thousand ways! To be sure, the great majority of these differences are spelling differences (not all of which, however, are necessarily trivial in a language written in a defective script as is Hebrew), but there are grammatical differences as well and places indicating deliberate choices of different words. Inerrantists have to try to prove that in all six thousand places, the Masoretic Text preserves the correct reading!

Although I do not know what modern Samaritans think about Balaam, it is clear that the ancient *shomrim* viewed Balaam as a dangerous figure. In their version of his stories, by means of conscious changes in wording he is made to look like a pawn in his conversational interactions with the deity. Except for Moses, the Samaritans disavowed *all* prophets, seers, and would-be oracles claiming to make known divine desires. *A fortiori,* Balaam would feel the brunt of Samaritan polemics launched against all who have claimed to have spoken directly with Yahweh.

The Samaritan fascination with Balaam continued into medieval times. A medieval work known as the *Samaritan Chronicles*[Ex-16] incorporates a number of earlier works – parts of which are believed to go back to fairly ancient times – including a tract known as the *Samaritan Book of Joshua*. Chapters 3–5 deal with Balaam, the Moabites, and the Midianites. The third and fourth chapters retell and expand somewhat the main

Balaam cycle from Numbers 22–24. The expansion in the fourth chapter is most interesting, as it foreshadows the Talmuds' haggadic stories about how Balaam counseled the Moabites to have their daughters seduce the sons of the Israelites. (According to this Samaritan source, the Moabites sent out 24,000 girls to beguile the boys of Israel – on the Sabbath, no less!) Certainly, the Samaritans did not have Jesus in mind when they wrote about Balaam. Just as certainly, the rabbis also were not thinking about Jesus when they drew upon the same pool of folklore traditions as had the Samaritans and wrote about Balaam in the Mishnah, Tosefta, and Talmuds.

The fifth chapter of *Samaritan Book of Joshua* expands upon Numbers 31 – the shameful chapter detailing the slaughter of Balaam with the five kings of Midian and the massacre and extermination of all Midianites except for little girls. Whereas the biblical text states simply that "they [*the Israelites*] put to death also Balaam son of Beor," the Samaritan account could have served as a subject for a Händel opera. Balaam returns to the king of the Moabites in order to be rewarded for the calamity that befell the Israelites – the plague that followed the miscegenation with the Moabites. Curiously, the Moabite king (never named) just happens to be making merry with the kings of Midian. Unbeknownst to the reveling royals, twelve thousand Israelite warriors have surrounded the party room. With trumpets blaring, they breach the walls, capture the kings, and kill them with their swords. Balaam, when they find him, is in a temple carrying out his sacerdotal duties. Babbling unintelligibly, he is dragged out of the temple and brought before Joshua and Moses. Unable or unwilling to submit to the One True Faith revealed by Moses, he is killed by Israelites of the tribe of Simeon.[Ex-17]

The *Samaritan Book of Joshua* is not the only Samaritan work dealing with Balaam. The *Discourse Concerning the Angels* also mentions Balaam in order to describe the angel who stood in his way, causing his ass to object. Another work, *Asatir: The Samaritan Book of the Secrets of Moses*, also deals with Balaam. Significantly, it adds many details concerning how Balaam advised Balak to have his people "commit whoredom" and defile the Israelites. This would seem to share the same sources as do the rabbinical haggadot in the Talmuds.

John T. Greene, in his *Balaam and His Interpreters*[Ex-18] tells of an even more interesting Samaritan work, *The Birth Story of Moses*. Elaborating on Numbers 24:17 ("...a star shall come forth

out of Jacob and a scepter shall rise out of Israel...”), a birth legend is created for Moses that is a close parallel to the madcap
Star-of-Bethlehem story in the second chapter of Matthew in the
Christian Bible. Although the material unquestionably derives
from the Balaam cycle of Numbers 22–24, Balaam's name does
not appear. Rather, our Mesopotamian soothsayer is replaced by
a clone named Pilti – an Egyptian sorcerer, diviner, magician, and
prophet. Balak, the king of the Moabites, is replaced by Pharaoh.
This process of mythopoietic cloning allows Balaam to predate
Moses instead of being his approximate contemporary as in the
biblical stories.

Pilti-Balaam declares:

> For I have seen the star of Israel in the ascent, and his king-
> dom growing strong. Nigh is the apostle that is sent to them and
> the way of his star is on high, and at his hand shall be redemp-
> tion for them. [*Bowman translation*][Ex-19]

The narrative continues:

> And after nineteen days, evidence was established that the
> child from father had been begotten in the womb of his mother.
> A star showed his glory in the heavens, and the Egyptians were
> astonished at this appearance... [*Bowman translation*][Ex-20]

Looking back over what I have just written, I see to my horror
that I have succeeded in demonstrating what no Christian apologist has been able to show: an evolutionary connection between
Balaam and Jesus in early Jewish sources – assuming that the
core material in the Samaritan birth story is in fact as ancient as
experts maintain. The connecting links of the chain are as
follows: (1) The pagan prophet Balaam is caused to prophesy of a
star or comet that shall presage the military success of Israel (the
nation). (2) Balaam is transformed into Pilti, who expands the
star image into a portent of the birth of Moses. (3) Matthew, in his
conscious attempt to portray Jesus as a latter-day Moses, draws
upon the same birth-legend material as did our Samaritan
author. Balaam is made, in effect, to prophesy the birth of Christ
– as some claim he does more explicitly in the late midrash *Jalqut
Shim'oni*, where Balaam “looked forth and beheld the peoples
that bow down to the sun and moon and stars and to wood and
stone, and he looked forth and beheld that there was a man,
son of a woman, who should rise up and seek to make himself

God, and to cause the whole world to go astray." [*Herford translation*]Ex-21

I shall close this section on the Samaritans with one further observation of John Greene:

> The Samaritan materials are a gold mine of literature concerning both Balaam and the Balaam type. They demonstrate that the issues of prophecy and divination, priesthood and diviner continued to be of concern to this community. Balaam as a type was employed by them to lambaste and lampoon the "prophetic," not the "Priestly," however, regardless of the fact that they were a priestly-led group themselves who were at odds with other priestly groups. Samaritan materials outside the Samaritan Pentateuch present a program of interpretation which does not attack the exactly "priestly." Instead, it attacks every other functional type associated with mantics: prophets, gazers, diviners, wizards, seers, and magicians.Ex-22

Ex.5. Balaam and Philo Judaeus

As we have already seen, the life of Philo of Alexandria [*c*20 BCE–50 CE] encompasses the entire period allotted by historical-Jesus advocates to the earthly existence of their would-be Messiah. Although he had absolutely nothing to say about Jesus, his description of the Therapeutæ did – as I have explained earlier – throw light on a possible origin of Christianity. Beyond this, he also may illuminate the origins of the Balaam traditions in the Mishnah and Talmuds – and completely lay to rest claims that Balaam was a rabbinical code for Christ.

As for most Jewish thinkers of the first few centuries of the common era, Balaam was a figure of great importance to Philo, who discusses the soothsayer in no fewer than five different treatises: "On the Cherubim – Part 1," "On the Confusion of Tongues," "On the Migration of Abraham," "On the Changes of Names," and, most importantly, in his "On the Life of Moses – Part 1." Overall, Philo is hostile to Balaam and portrays him in such a way that it is not surprising to see rabbis two centuries later excluding him from any share in the world to come.

In typical Philonic fashion, "On the Cherubim" interprets Balaam as a negative symbol:

> Moses also represents [*portrays*] Balaam, who is the symbol of a vain people, stripped of his arms, as a runaway and deserter, well knowing the war which it becomes the soul to carry on for the sake of knowledge; for he says to his ass, who is here a symbol of the irrational designs of life which every foolish man entertains, that "If I had had a sword, I should ere now have slain thee." And great thanks are due to the Maker of all things, because he, knowing the struggles and resistance of folly, did not give to it the power of language, which would have been like giving a sword to a madman, in order that it might have no power to work great and iniquitous destruction among all whom it should meet with. But the reproaches which Balaam utters are in some degree expressed by all those who are not purified, but are always talking foolishly... [*Yonge translation*]Ex-23

It is rather surprising to learn that Moses (the supposed author of Numbers and Deuteronomy) portrays Balaam as "a runaway and deserter." Neither the Hebrew Masoretic text nor the Greek Septuagint text portrays Balaam in this way. It would seem that Philo is drawing from a larger literature about Balaam. The likelihood of this will become all but certain as we proceed through Philo's writings.

In Philo's "On the Confusion of Tongues" we see another nail being driven into Balaam's coffin lid. It may be remembered that Herford and other scholars argued that it could not have been the biblical Balaam who was being excluded from Paradise, since he had done only good things – blessing the Israelites just as Yahweh required. Here, Philo the psychoanalyst seems to argue that although Balaam *did* good things, his *intentions* were evil:

> At all events, the law says that that soothsayer and diviner who was led into folly in respect of his unstable conjectures (for the name, Balaam, being interpreted, means unstable), "cursed the people that saw"; and that, too, though as far as his words go he uttered only words of good omen and prayers. The law here looking not at the words he uttered, which, through the providence of God, did change their character, becoming good money instead of base coinage, but having regard to the *intention* in which injurious things were resolved in preference to beneficial ones. [*Yonge translation, emphasis added*]Ex-24

This sentiment is only expressed more strongly in "On the Migration of Abraham":

> Therefore, the vain Balaam, although he sang hymns of exceeding sublimity to God... is rightly judged by the wise lawgiver to have been an impious man and accursed, and to have been cursing rather than blessing; for he says that he was hired for money by the enemy, and so became an evil prophet of evil things, bearing in his soul most bitter curses against the God-loving nature, but being compelled to utter prophetically with his mouth and tongue the most exquisite and sublime prayers in their favour; for the things that he said, being very excellent, were, in fact, suggested by the God who loves virtue; but the curses which he conceived in his mind (for they were wicked) were the offspring of his mind, which hated virtue. ...
>
> Therefore, as far as blessings, and praises, and prayers, or, on the other hand, reproaches and curses are concerned, one must not so much be guided by what proceeds out of the mouth, by utterance, as by what is in the heart... [*Yonge translation*]Ex-25

Any second- or third-century rabbi reading Philo (and it is inconceivable that they did not do so) would have to conclude that Balaam was *bad* – bad enough to be excluded from the afterlife. Even without further examination of Philo's writings, it would seem that the lid of Balaam's coffin has been nailed firmly closed. It cannot be supposed that Philo had Jesus in mind when writing about Balaam, and there is no good reason to suppose that the rabbis did either. The rabbinical commentary that is not directly derivable from the biblical text is, it would seem, largely presaged in the writings of Philo and can be seen as a natural folkloric evolution developing at least in part from the Alexandrian Jewish philosopher.

Justification for the murder of Balaam is provided in "On the Changes of Names":

> Do you recollect the case of the soothsayer Balaam? He is represented as hearing the oracles of God, and as having received knowledge from the Most High, but what advantage did he reap from such hearing, and what good accrued to him from such knowledge? In his intention he endeavored to injure the most excellent eye of the soul, which alone has received such instruction as to be able to behold God, ... therefore, being overthrown by his own insane wickedness, and having received many wounds, he perished amid the heaps of wounded, because he had stamped beforehand the divinely inspired prophecies with the sophistry of the soothsayers. [*Yonge translation*]Ex-26

Philo's major exposition of the Balaam-Balak story and its *sequellae* is to be found in the forty-eighth to fifty-seventh chapters of his "On the Life of Moses: Part 1." It is somewhat startling to see how much easier to read Philo's masterful prose account is as compared to either the Hebrew Masoretic Version or the Old Greek versions. Part of the reason for this is that he expands the biblical text by imagining the thoughts of the protagonists and tries to find explanatory rationales for otherwise bizarre behavior. (To be sure, Philo cannot solve the mix-up between Midianites and Moabites in Numbers 25.*)

It must be realized that Philo was a propagandist, trying to make Judaism as sophisticated as Plato, and so we find that although the racist, indeed genocidal, philosophy informing these stories finds its counterpart in Philo, it has become much more palatable. In one exemplary case, apparently involving the genocide detailed in Numbers 31, Philo writes:

> And they led away a perfectly incalculable number of prisoners, of whom they chose to slay all of the full-grown men and women, the men because they had set the example of wicked counsels and actions, and the women because they had beguiled the youth of the Hebrews, becoming the causes to them of incontinence and impiety, and at the last of death; but they pardoned all the young male children and all the virgins, their tender age procuring them forgiveness. [*Yonge translation*]Ex-27

This may be contrasted with Num 31:17–8: "Now therefore kill every male among the little ones, and kill every woman that hath known man by lying with him. But all the women children that have not known a man by lying with him, keep alive for yourselves."

---

*Numbers 25:1 reads: "And Israel abode in Shittim, and the people began to commit whoredom with the daughters of Moab." Verses 2–5 then clearly describe the miscegenation with *Moab*. Then, in verse 6, suddenly we learn of miscegenation with a *Midianite* woman: "And behold, one of the children of Israel came and brought unto his brethren a *Midianitish* woman in the sight of Moses and in the sight of all the congregation of the children of Israel..." Although Balaam originally is from Mesopotamia in this story, in Numbers 24:5 we read that "Balaam rose up, and went and returned to his place..." (which, we learn in Numbers 31:8, was in Midian with the Midianite Kings). Then, in Numbers 26, we are back in Moab!

Yonge's clear English translation of Philo's text helps us to see how seriously the ancients took the magical acts of blessing and cursing. Nowadays, people who say "Bless you!" when someone sneezes mean nothing more than "I hope you're okay." No one any longer even thinks that saying "Bless you!" can actually improve the health or well-being of the person "blessed." Similarly, if a person says "Curse you!" (I don't think any one outside of cartoon characters actually says this any more) or "God damn you!" it means no more than "I really don't like what you've done!" or "You are really pissing me off!" People no longer believe they can actually send an annoying telemarketer to hell by simply uttering selected "bad words." (Admittedly, there are some fundamentalist preachers and prelates such as Cardinal Ratzinger who still believe in the magical powers of words, but that only shows how many thousand years behind the times those guys really are.)

So when the Moabite king Balak sought to hire the diviner Balaam, he is represented in the biblical texts and in Philo too as actually trying to get the soothsayer to use his magical skills to destroy the Israelites. In ancient times, numerous roles could be played by any particular religious practitioner. He could simultaneously be a priest (conducting sacrifices and carrying out other priestly duties), a diviner (a person who claims to be able to discover a deity's will or plans), a prophet (one who claims to be possessed by a particular deity while preaching or teaching), a magician, *etc.**

Balaam appears to have combined all these roles plus some more exotic ones as well. (In our discussion of the Deir ʿAllâ inscription we noted that he appears to have practiced divination by means of ornithomancy and theromancy.) Apparently drawing

---

* It is possible that some modern Roman Catholic priests still combine all these roles, although all of them must, at a minimum, play the role of magician in order to turn the wine into real blood and the wafer into real flesh. (Contrary to *Webster's New World Dictionary* – the quintessentially magical imperative *hocus-pocus* probably derives from *Hoc est enim Corpus meum* ['Really! This is my body!'], the words uttered at the elevation of the host, when its transubstantiation is believed to occur.) Most popes probably combine all four roles, as do many Protestant preachers. Modern religious practitioners have, of course, added a very important role not known in Balaam's day – that of chief financial officer.

upon an ample Balaam tradition existing at the turn of the era, Philo adds a stunning amount of information about Balaam:

> Now there was a man at that time very celebrated for his skill in divination, dwelling in Mesopotamia, who was initiated in every branch of the soothsayers' art. And he was celebrated and renowned above all men for his experience as a diviner and prophet, as he had in many instances foretold to many people incredible and most important events; for, on one occasion, he had predicted heavy rain to one nation at the height of summer; to another he had foretold a drought and burning heat in the middle of winter. Others he had forewarned of a dearth which should follow a season of abundance; and, on the other hand, plenty after famine. In some instances he had predicted the inundations of rivers; or, on the contrary, their falling greatly and becoming dried up; and the departure of pestilential diseases, and ten thousand other things. [*Yonge translation*][Ex-28]

It seems to me highly unlikely that Philo simply made up these specific "facts." They sound like testimonials one might expect to find in the missing sections of the plaster inscription at Deir 'Allâ. Such testimonials could have been part of an oral tradition about Balaam that survived into the days of Philo or even later.

Philo indicates in every place possible, that although Balaam ended up doing good things, his heart was evil. His words were blessings, his thoughts curses:

> But the prophet, as being even more wicked than the king, although he had always replied to the accusations which were brought against him with one true excuse, namely, that he was saying nothing out of his own head, but was only interpreting the words of another, being himself carried away and inspired, when he ought no longer to have accompanied him but to have gone away home, ran forward even more eagerly than his conductor, although in his secret thoughts he was oppressed by a heavy feeling of evil, yet still desired in his mind to curse this people, though he was forbidden to do so with his mouth. [*Yonge translation*][Ex-29]

Balaam is subjected to a withering ridicule in Philo's explanation of the story in Numbers 22, where a balking ass becomes a talking ass:

The truth is, that there was, as it seems, a divine vision,
which, as the beast, on which the diviner was seeking, saw at a
great distance as it was coming towards him, and it was frightened at it; but the man did not see it, which was a proof of his
insensibility, for he was thus shown to be inferior to a brute beast
in the power of sight, at a time when he was boasting that he
could see, not only the whole world, but also the Creator of the
world. [*Yonge translation*]. Ex-30

Most illuminating of all Philo's accounts of Balaam is a
passage that can relate both to the Jerusalem Talmud and the
Christian Apocalypse:

And Balaam replied: "All that I have hitherto uttered have
been oracles and words of God; but what I am going to say are
merely the suggestions of my own mind: and taking him [*Balak*]
by the right hand, he, while they two were alone, gave him
advice, by the adoption of which he might, as far as possible,
guard against the power of his enemies [*the Israelites*]...
As he knew that the only way by which the Hebrews could
be subdued was by leading them to violate the law, he endeav-
oured to seduce them by means of debauchery and intemperance,
that mighty evil, to the still greater crime of impiety, putting
pleasure before them as a bait; for, said he, "O king! the women
of the country surpass all other women in beauty, and there are
no means by which a man is more easily subdued than by the
beauty of a woman; therefore, if you enjoin the most beautiful of
them to grant their favours to them and to prostitute themselves
to them, they will allure and overcome the youth of your enemies.
But you must warn them not to surrender their beauty to those
who desire them with too great facility or too speedily, for resistance and coyness will stimulate the passions and excite them
more, and will kindle a more impetuous desire; and so, being
wholly subdued by their appetites, they will endure to do and to
suffer anything.
"And let any damsel who is thus prepared for the sport
resist, and say, wantonly, to a lover who is thus influenced, "It is
not fitting for you to enjoy my society till you have first abandoned your native habits, and have changed, and learnt to honour
the same practices that I do. And I must have a conspicuous
proof of your real change, which I can only have by your
consenting to join me in the same sacrifices and libations which
I use, and which we may then offer together at the same images
and statues, and other erections in honour of my gods. And the

lover being, as it were, taken in the net of her manifold and multiform snares, not being able to resist her beauty and seductive conversation, will become wholly subdued in his reason, and, like a miserable man, will obey all the commands which she lays upon him, and will be enrolled as the slave of passion. [*Yonge translation*].Ex-31

We can be sure, of course, that Balaam's speech was composed 'in character' by Philo, just as the speeches of Peter and Paul were composed by the author of Acts. Nevertheless, Philo certainly did not make up the gist of the story itself – something not to be found explicitly stated anywhere in the Hebrew Bible. Rather, that had to have come either from a widespread Balaam literature or oral tradition – or both. It was from that same pool of 'facts' that the rabbis of the Yerushalmi would drink when they wrote the entertaining account of the seduction in j. *Sanh.* 10-2:

j. *Sanh.* 10:2: Now what did the evil Balaam do [to warrant losing his portion in the world to come]?

It was because he gave advice to Balak son of Zippor on how to cause Israel's downfall by the sword. He said to him, "The God of this nation hates fornication. So put up your daughters for fornication, and you will rule over them." ...

What did they do? They built for themselves temples from Beth HaJeshimmon to the Snowy Mountain, and they set in them women selling various kinds of sweets. They put the old lady outside, and the young girl inside.

Now the Israelites would then eat and drink, and one of them would go out to walk in the marketplace, and he would buy something from a stallkeeper. The old lady then would sell him the thing for whatever it was worth, and the young girls would say, "Come on in and take it for still less." So it was on the first day, the second day, and the third day. And then, she would say to him, "From now on, you belong here. Come on in and choose whatever you like."

When he came in [he found there] a flagon of wine, Ammonite wine, which is very strong. And it serves as an aphrodisiac to the body, and its scent was enticing. ...

Now the girl would say to him, "Do you want to drink a cup of wine," and he would reply to her, "Yes." So she gave him a cup of wine, and he drank it.

When he drank it, the wine would burn in him like the venom of a snake. Then he would say to her, "Surrender yourself [sexually] to me." She would say to him, "Do you want me to 'surrender' myself to you?" And he would say "Yes." Then she took out an image of Peor from her bosom, and she said to him, "Bow down to this, and I'll surrender myself to you." And he would say to her, "Now am I going to bow down to an idol?" And she would say to him, "You don't really bow down to it, but you expose yourself to it." ...

Then he would say to her, "Surrender yourself to me."

And she would say to him, "Separate yourself from the Torah of Moses, and I shall 'surrender' myself to you." [*Neusner translation*]Ex-32

The story dissolves into rabbinical rhetorical chaos, without confirmation of the success of the seduction. Nevertheless, there is no need to doubt that anatomical complementarity was achieved by our sexual combatants.

The author of the Christian Apocalypse was much too phobic of sex to write anything as detailed as the above excerpt from the Yerushalmi. Nevertheless, it is clear that he was drawing from the same Balaamic folk tradition when he wrote [Rev 2:14]: "But I have a few things against thee, because thou hast there them that hold the doctrine of Balaam, who taught Balak to cast a stumbling block before the children of Israel, to eat things sacrificed unto idols, and to commit fornication."

If the Yerushalmi's Balaam is actually Jesus, we may fairly ask if Philo's essentially identical character also is Jesus. In that event, we would want to know why Jesus' illustrious contemporary did not call him by his correct name. If the Balaam of the Apocalypse also is Jesus...

The idea is too preposterous to pursue, but believers in application of the *Balaam = Jesus* equation in rabbinical literature should be required to explain why the equation cannot be applied in this early Jewish Christian document as well.

Ex.6. Balaam and Josephus

We have already discussed the Jewish historian Flavius Josephus [37–c95 CE] at great length with regard to the various interpolations of Jesus, John the Baptist, and James into his writings. In his *Antiquities of the Jews* [Book 4, chapter 6], he too could not resist the story of our enchanting enchanter. According to Josephus, Balaam was a prophet in addition to being a -

curse-master. Although Balaam is treated differently by Josephus than by Philo, he undergoes little significant evolution in Josephus. Balaam's counsel to the Midianites, for example, on how to seduce the Israelite swains – although differing in Josephus in most details from Philo's description of his speech – does not differ enough to allow us to tell if he has adapted Philo's account, drawn upon the same pool of folk traditions that Philo used, or had some other source. It does, however prove that there was yet one more source of grist for the mills of the Yerushalmi rabbis when they needed material with which to shape the details and features of "the wicked Balaam."

Josephus' account of Balaam's oracles against certain nations [Num 24:20–25] sounds to me almost apocalyptic – or something that could be used by an apocalyptic fraternity:

> Then fell Balaam upon his face, and foretold what calamities would befall the several kings of the nations, and the most eminent cities, some of which of old were not so much as inhabited; which events have come to pass among the several people concerned, both in the foregoing ages, and in this, till my own memory, both by sea and by land. From which completion of all these predictions that he made, one may easily guess that the rest will have their completion in time to come. [*Whiston translation*]Ex-33

It is easy to see the utility of this for a group of cultists "who hold the doctrine of Balaam" [Rev 2:14]. One may imagine Balaam's many predictions being consulted in the way certain of our smoother-brained contemporaries consult the 'prophecies' of Nostradamus. Indeed, the *Chronicle of Balaam* mentioned in Bavli *Sanh.* 106b might have been a chronological listing of dates on which specific prophecies attributed to Balaam were thought to have been fulfilled. If this be true, it would appear that both Philo and Josephus have drawn upon the *Chronicle of Balaam* in writing their accounts of the soothsayer. The *min* who refers to the *Chronicle*, then, would not be a Christian at all, but rather a member of the same cult condemned by the author of Revelation 2:14.

The most striking feature of Josephus' account of the Balak-Balaam legend (remember, the Israelite army never existed) is the way in which the confusion of Moab and Midian is resolved to produce a smoothly flowing narrative. Instead of following the confusing biblical practice of allowing the words *Moabite,*

Midianite, Moab, and *Midian* to drop where they may – no matter what the logical consequences – Josephus neatly equates the two right from the beginning: "When Balak, the king of the Moabites, who had from his ancestors a friendship and league with the Midianites, saw how great the Israelites were grown..."Ex-34

The first embassy to summon Balaam to curse the Israelites, instead of being solely from the Moabite king Balak, is a joint affair apparently initiated by the Midianites:

> Now these Midianites, knowing there was one Balaam, who lived by Euphrates, and was the greatest of the prophets at that time, and one that was in friendship with them, sent some of their honourable princes along with the ambassadors of Balak, to entreat the prophet to come to them that he might imprecate curses to the destruction of the Israelites. [*Whiston translation*]Ex-36

From here on, Josephus' account of the Balaam saga – angel, talking ass, and all – reads smoothly and no one would ever suspect the textual corruption underlying his biblical source.

Like many of the ancient rabbis, Josephus was impressed by the fact that 'Moses' – the supposed author of Numbers – wrote up Balaam's prophecies as well as his own. Josephus interprets this as a certain degree of honor being paid to the rival soothsayer:

> ...yet did he [*Moses*] also do him [*Balaam*] great honour, by setting down his prophecies in writing. And while it was in his power to claim this glory to himself, and make men believe they were his own predictions, there being no one that could be a witness against him, and accuse him for so doing, he still gave his attestation to him, and did him the honour to make mention of him on this account. But let every one think of these matters as he pleases. [*Whiston translation*]Ex-37

This seemingly generous notice of the fairness of Moses perhaps draws attention away from a problem that must have stymied many ancient biblical scholars: *Who observed the prophesying of Balaam and reported his exact words to Moses?* This is a far bigger problem than the Christian one concerning who reported the fact that all the disciples were sleeping* when Jesus was praying on the Mount of Olives [Luke 22:39–46] !

While all the negotiations between the Moabites/Midianites and Balaam was taking place, Moses and the Hebrew horde were encamped many miles away on the plains of Moab (or wherever).

There is no hint in the biblical text that an Israelite spy was present in the embassies to Balaam, nor is there notice of an Israelite spy ensconced near Balaam's home to overhear his conversations with Yahweh or the ambassadors, nor are we told there was a Jewish stenographer present on the high places where Balak and Balaam made sacrifices and Balaam gave his poetry recitals. This being the case, like the ancients, we must have to ask, "Who recorded the conversations and the prophecies?" and "How did Moses get the records?"

Even if there was a Jewish stenographer on the mountain, how did he hear all the words correctly, there being no microphones or even megaphones in those days? Wouldn't he have ended up with at least a few Monty Python–like beatitudes?[Ex-38] Why don't we have "Blessed are the cheese makers, and a star shall arise out of bacon"?

The rabbis of the time of Midrash *Jalqut Shim'oni* §766 solved the problem neatly – with magic:

> R. El'azar ha-Qappar says, God gave strength to his [Balaam's] voice, so that it went from one end of the world to the other, because he looked forth and beheld the peoples that bow

---

*Luke 22:39–46: And he came out, and went, as he was wont, to the mount of Olives; and his disciples also followed him. [40]And when he was at the place, he said unto them, Pray that ye enter not into temptation. [41]And he was withdrawn from them about a stone's cast, and kneeled down and prayed, [42]Saying, Father, if thou be willing, remove this cup from me: nevertheless not my will, but thine, be done.

[43]And there appeared an angel unto him from heaven, strengthening him. [44]And being in an agony he prayed more earnestly: and his sweat was as it were great drops of blood falling down to the ground.

[45]And when he rose up from prayer, and was come to his disciples, he found them sleeping for sorrow, [46]And said unto them, Why sleep ye? rise and pray, lest ye enter into temptation.

Modern apologists do not have as much to worry about as did the believers of several centuries ago, however. A quick check of Reuben Swanson's *New Testament Greek Manuscripts*[Ex-37] (a book that every skeptic should own) shows that all the earliest and best manuscripts of Luke do not contain the angel or the blood clots. This greatly reduces the amount of detail needing to be remembered by sleeping (dreaming?) witnesses.

down to the sun and moon and stars and to wood and stone, and he looked forth and beheld that there was a man, son of a woman, who should rise up and seek to make himself God, and to cause the whole world to go astray. Therefore God gave power to his voice that all the peoples of the world might hear, and thus he spake, 'Give heed that ye go not astray after that man, for it is written (Num. xxiii. 19) God is not man that he should lie, and if he says that he is God he is a liar, and he will deceive and say that he departeth and cometh again in the end, he saith and he shall not perform... [Herford translation][Ex-39]

So now we know. Moses was only twenty miles away at the time, and he had no trouble hearing at all. In fact, if he had had any momentary doubts about what he remembered hearing, he had only to ask anybody within fifty miles for corroboration: everyone else in the world had heard Balaam too!

Ex.7. Balaam in the Bavli: a Final Reprise

Before we can say good-bye to Balaam, it is necessary to see what the Bavli has made of him and to color in more fully the picture partially sketched out at the beginning of this lengthy excursus. We have already seen that the Balaam of the Bavli is a very naughty boy indeed. Not only is he accused of practicing divination with his penis, he is quite roundly convicted of having had carnal relations with his ass. (When he beats her with his magic wand, however, there is some uncertainty as to just which 'wand' he employed.) Allegations that Balaam, as a cipher for Jesus, was killed at the age of thirty-three by Pontius Pilate have previously been examined and found groundless. Everything we have examined closely indicates that in the Bavli, as in all earlier rabbinical literature, Balaam refers to the biblical character, not someone else.

As in the Yerushalmi, Balaam is accredited with the sexual downfall of Israel:

> **b. Sanh. 106ª.** He [Balaam] said thus to him [Balak]. 'The God of these hates lewdness, and they are very partial to linen. Come, and I will advise thee. Erect for them tents enclosed by hangings, in which place harlots, old women without, young women within, to sell them linen garments.' So he erected

curtained tents from the snowy mountain [Hermon] as far as Beth ha-Yeshimoth [*i.e.*, right from north to south], and placed harlots in them – old women without, young women within. And when an Israelite ate, drank, and was merry, and issued forth for a stroll in the market place, the old woman would say to him, 'Dost thou not desire linen garments?' The old woman offered it at its current value, but the young one for less. This happened two or three times. After that, she would say to him, 'Thou art now like one of the family; sit down and choose for thyself.' Gourds of Ammonite wine lay near her, and at that time Ammonite and heathen wine had not yet been forbidden. Said she to him, 'Wouldst thou like to drink a glass of wine?' Having drunk, [his passion] was inflamed, and he exclaimed to her, 'Yield to me!' Thereupon she brought forth an idol from her bosom and said to him, 'Worship this': 'But I am a Jew', he protested. 'What does that concern thee?' she rejoined, 'nothing is required but that thou should uncover thyself' – whilst he did not know that such was its worship. 'Nay,' [said she,] 'I will not leave thee ere thou has denied the Torah of Moses thy teacher,' as it is written, *They went in to Baal-Peor, and separated themselves unto that shame, and their abominations were according as they loved.*

And Israel abode in Shittim. R. Eliezer said: Its name was Shittim. R. Joshua said: They engaged in ways of folly, *And they called* the people unto the sacrifices of their gods.* R. Eliezer said: They met them naked; R. Joshua said: They were all excited to pollution. [*Shachter and Freedman translation*]Ex-40

There is a Balaam passage in the Bavli which R. Travers Herford believed was a reference to Jesus' mother Mary and her dalliance with a carpenter – Joseph. Out of context, the pericope is somewhat suggestive of the natal myths found in Matthew and Luke. It is necessary, therefore, to examine the preceding passage at the same time.

b. Sanh. 106ª: *And they slew the kings of Midian, beside the rest of them that were slain... Balaam also the son of Beor they slew with the sword.* What business had Balaam there? – R. Jonathan said: He went to receive his reward for the twenty-four thousand Israelites whose destruction he had encompassed. Mar Suṭra b. Ṭobiah remarked in Rab's name: This is what men say, 'When the camel went to demand horns, they cut off the ears he had.'

---

*R. Eliezer interprets the *called* of the biblical quotation as meaning "attracted the Israelites by means of their naked bodies."

> *Balaam also the son of Beor, the soothsayer, [did the children*
> *of Israel slay with the sword].* A soothsayer? But he was a
> prophet!–R. Joḥanan said: At first he was a prophet, but subse-
> quently a soothsayer. R. Papa observed: This is what men say,
> **'She who was the descendant of princes and governors,**
> **played the harlot with carpenters.'** *[Shachter and Freedman*
> *translation]*Ex-41

The opinions of Herford and Mead to the contrary notwithstanding, there is absolutely no reason to look outside the Talmud
to find the referent for *she*. Both segments commenting on the
death of Balaam develop the theme of come-down: the camel losing
his ears, the prophet decaying into a soothsayer. Attentive readers
will have noticed that the biblical quotations explicated in these
two segments are not the same. The first quotation is from
Numbers 31:8. The second one, adding the information that
Balaam was a soothsayer, is from Joshua 13:22. In order further
to characterize Balaam's come-down from prophet – a noble and
more-than-regal calling – to fortune-teller, R. Papa (head of the
rabbinical college at Sura 354–374 CE) uses the scatological
imagery of which so many rabbis were so fond to further debase
and besmirch the memory of the phallomancer. *She* is none other
than Balaam, whom I have indicated most likely was a priest-
king – and "the descendant of princes and governors." We have
seen, moreover, that Balaam was believed by the rabbis not just
to have "played the harlot," he was believed to have been an
instructor of harlotry. As for playing with carpenters [נגרי *nagari*],
there is no reason to suppose that only carpenters are intended.
Any other profession of humble and sweaty status would have
done just as well. The mistress of the manor just as easily could
have run off with a stable boy.

Earlier we had occasion to examine the lengthy passage in b.
Giṭ. 56ᵇ, 57ᵃ which describes the necromantic calling up of the
shades of the emperor Titus, Balaam, and Jesus. The obvious was
pointed out – *viz.*, that Balaam cannot be a code for Jesus if the
two are treated as entirely separate entities. We shall reprint the
passage in abbreviated form, simply to focus on the fate of
Balaam.

b. *Giṭ*. 56ᵇ, 57ᵃ: Onqelos bar Qaloniqos, sister's son of Titus
[the conqueror of Jerusalem in 70 CE], desired to become a proselyte. He called up Titus by necromancy. He said to him, "Who is

honoured in this world?" He replied, "Israel." "What about joining them?" He replied, "Their words [*commandments*] are many and thou canst not fulfill them. ...

He called up Balaam by necromancy. He said to him, "Who is honoured in this world?" He replied, "Israel." "What about joining them?" He replied [Deut. xxiii 6], *"Thou shalt not seek their peace or their prosperity all [thy] days."* He said to him, "What is the punishment of this man?" He replied, *"Per semen fervens."* [*"Boiling in seminal fluid"*]

He called up Jesus by necromancy. He said to him, "Who is honoured in this world?" He replied, "Israel." "What about joining them?" He replied, "Seek their good, seek not their harm. ...
[*Herford translation*]Ex-42

Given the sexual phobias of the rabbis, endless boiling in seminal fluid is about as horrific a punishment as can be imagined. According to Leviticus 15:16–17 [NEB], "When a man has emitted semen, he shall bathe his whole body in water and be unclean till evening. Every piece of clothing or skin on which there is any semen shall be washed and remain unclean till evening." More than being a minor inconvenience, this serves to warn men against the sudden death which would be their lot should they stumble in a state of uncleanness into the Tabernacle: "In this way you shall warn the Israelites against uncleanness, in order that they may not bring uncleanness upon the Tabernacle where I dwell among them, and so die" [Lev 15:31, NEB]. It would appear that when the rabbis – or, more accurately, their priestly predecessors – created Yahweh, they endowed him with the same sexual phobias that were their own perennial obsessions.

There is a curious passage in b. *Sanh.* 106ᵃ which Herford and others have supposed to be a clear reference to Balaam as Jesus:

b. Sanh. 106ᵃ: *And he [Balaam] took up his parable, and said, Alas, who shall live when God doeth this?* R. Shim'on ben Laqish [d. c279] said: "Woe unto him who maketh himself to live by the name of God." [*Herford translation*]Ex-43 R. Johanan said: Woe to the nation that may be found [attempting to hinder], when the Holy One, blessed be He, accomplishes the redemption of his children: who would throw his garment between a lion and a lioness when these are copulating! [*Shachter & Freedman translation*]Ex-44

R. Travers Herford, commenting on the Hebrew words translated as "when God doeth this" in the biblical quotation, allows that their meaning "is open to question." However, he argues, "by no rules of grammar or syntax could the words be made to mean, 'Who maketh himself live by the name of God.' This is a haggadic variation of the text, such as the Rabbis often permitted themselves to make ... for a homiletic purpose. And it is hard to see what purpose there could be, in the present example, other than that of making a covert allusion to Jesus, who had declared – according to the Gospels – that he should rise from the dead, of course by the power of God. The words do not apply to Balaam, at least there is nothing recorded about him that would give occasion for any such remark."Ex-45

It would appear that Herford misunderstood completely the structure and purpose of the passage in question. The rabbis are not discussing Balaam, here, but rather a line of an oracle he supposedly uttered. Specifically what they are concerned to know is perhaps impossible to determine. It would appear from the second comment that the rabbis wanted to know what kinds of behavior would warrant Yahweh's "doing this." (Despite the uncertainty as to what is meant by *this*, it is obvious that something unpleasant is understood.) If that is the case, then the first comment would be in the same logical category: Yahweh will vent his rage upon anyone who uses the magical power of the name *Yahweh* to revivify himself after death – a really neat trick even for one possessing a magic charm!

The real problem the rabbis faced, here, was the uncertain meaning of the Hebrew text with which Numbers 24:23 ends. Already at the time of the Old Greek translations (third to first centuries BCE) the passage seems to have been inscrutable. The Septuagint renders it "And he looked upon Og, and took up his parable and said, Oh, oh, who shall live, when God shall do these things?" The KJV, as noted, says "And he took up his parable, and said, Alas, who shall live when God doeth this?" The NEB, in desperation, translates the entire verse as "He uttered his oracle" – adding in a footnote "The text is obscure at every point." By contrast, the Tanakh translation is courageous and renders the unintelligible passage, "He took up his theme and said: Alas, who can survive except God has willed it!"

It is quite possible that the rabbis were just trying to figure out the meaning of a corrupt passage of scripture, and were supplying wild and colorful explanations exemplifying their unspoken interpretations. It is most unlikely – though admittedly not impossible – that Jesus was on their mind here. It is interesting to note that the medieval commentator Rashi does not seem to doubt that Balaam is intended here. In his note on this passage he writes, "Balaam, who restored himself to life by the name of God, made himself God."

If, as I have repeatedly hypothesized, there was an extensive folklore tradition devoted to Balaam – and perhaps even a group of sectarians in some peculiar way attached to him – is it too hard to imagine his magical skills had come to include use of the divine name?

Despite the exclusion of "three kings and four commoners" from a share in the world to come, the casuistry of the Bavli rabbis manages to rescue all but one of them – Balaam. "Now only Balaam will not enter [the future world], but other [heathens] will enter" [b. Sanh. 105a].Ex-46 To make sure that Balaam stays dead, he is killed four times: "Did the children of Israel slay with the sword among them that were slain by them. Rab said: They subjected him [Balaam] to four deaths: stoning, burning, decapitation, and strangulation" [b. Sanh. 106b].Ex-47

It remains only to note that in the Bavli Balaam comes to transcend a specific period of time, being identified as having lived both in the days of Jacob [d. 1689 BCE, according to traditional chronology] and in the days of the Judges [1425–1120 BCE, according to tradition]. Despite his being portrayed as an approximate contemporary of Moses [b. 1571 BCE according to tradition] in the Numbers 22–24 cycle, in the Bavli Sanh. 106a he is supposed to have connived with Pharaoh to prevent the birth or survival of Moses – exactly as does the Samaritan Pilti.

First of all, we may consider the passage b. Sanh. 105a which contains a summary of everything you ever wanted to know about Balaam but were afraid to think:

b. Sanh. 105a: FOUR COMMONERS, VIZ., BALAAM, DOEG, AHITOPHEL, AND GEHAZI. *Belo'am* [denotes without the people]. Another explanation: Balaam denotes that he corrupted a people. *The son of Beor* [denotes] that he committed bestiality. A Tanna taught: Beor, Cushan-rishathaim and Laban the Syrian are identical. Beor denotes that he committed bestiality; Cushan-rishathaim, that he perpetrated two evils upon Israel: one in the days of Jacob, and the other in the days of the Judges. But what was his real name? Laban the Syrian. [*Shachter and Freedman translation*]Ex-48

Balaam is *really* Laban the Syrian, and he lived at two different times. Somehow, Josephus' closing comment about Balaam seems appropriate here: "But let every one think of these matters as he pleases."

Finally, let us look at b. *Sanh.* 106ª, which places Balaam in the generation preceding that of Moses:

> **b. Sanh. 106ª:** *And he looked on the Kenite, and took up his parable.* Balaam said to Jethro, 'Thou Kenite, wast thou not with us in that scheme? Who then placed thee among the strong ones of the world!' And that is what R. Ḥiyya b. Abba said in R. Simai's name: Three were involved in that scheme, *viz.*, Balaam, Job, and Jethro. Balaam, who advised it, was slain; Job, who was silent, was punished through suffering; and Jethro, who fled – his descendants were privileged to sit in the Hall of Hewn Stones, as it is written, *And the families of the scribes which dwell at Jabez, the Tirathites, the Shemeathites, and Suchathites. These are the Kenites that came of Hemath, the father of the house of Rechab*, whilst elsewhere it is written, *And the children of the Kenite, Moses' father in law, went up out of the city of palm trees.* [*Shachter and Freedman translation*]Ex-49

"That scheme" was nothing less than the scheme [Exod 1:22] to drown every Israelite baby boy born in Egypt: "And Pharaoh charged all his people, saying, Every son that is born ye shall cast into the river, and every daughter ye shall save alive." Balaam now has come to be involved face-to-face with Jethro and Job! The mind stumbles to assess the dimensions of the iceberg of folk tradition that lies submerged beneath the surface of this story. By the year 500 CE, when the Bavli was completed, Balaam's *persona* had expanded in so many directions and in so many stages that he had ceased to be a single character.

Could one of those alter egos have been Jesus? I do not think so, for the simple reason that even the most divergent Balaam traditions are clearly meant to refer to the biblical character. The fact that in time Balaams were invented that chronologically were incompatible with the seer of Numbers 22–24 proves only how illogical the religious mind can be. The Babylonian Talmud is overflowing with fancy, but it is nearly empty of historical facts.

CHAPTER 7

The Babylonian Talmud

Five or even six centuries after the time at which Jesus of Nazareth is supposed to have been born in Palestine, rabbis living hundreds of miles from there in Iraq appear to have completed the literary task of creating a life for him. As had earlier been the case with the canonical and uncanonical Christian 'evangelists,' who had created a wild variety of biographies according to the different ways they imagined their Messiah to have acted, so also was it the case with the rabbis. They too ended up with more than one Jesus – if we are to believe the apologetics of certain Christians on behalf of the historicity of Jesus. Interestingly, the rabbinical Jesuses did not live at the same time as the Christian Gospel Jesuses. One of them lived nearly a century BCE, at the time of Alexander Jannaeus – a Jesus before Christ.* Another lived around two centuries after that – a Jesus after Christ! Like the Christians, the rabbis are alleged also to

---

*It would appear that this Jesus is derivable from a now-lost Jewish Christian source. Somewhat astoundingly, this same source appears to have contributed to the writings of the church father Epiphanius, Bishop of Salamis in Cyprus [c315–403 CE], who in his *Panarion Sive Arcula Adversos Octoginta Hæreses* [xxix. 3] indicates quite clearly that Jesus was born during the days of Alexander Jannæus. G. R. S. Mead, drawing upon W. Dindorf's edition of Epiphanius [Leipzig, 1859–1862] which incorporated the text of *Codex Marcianus* 125 [dated 1057 CE], presents the amazing account of Jesus' birth nearly a century before Christ:

> Now the throne and kingly seat of David is the priestly office in Holy Church; for the Lord combined the kingly and high-priestly dignities into one and the same office, and bestowed them upon His Holy Church, transferring to her the throne of

have given Jesus a father and a mother – and created a birth legend scandalously different from that in the Gospels. The Jesuses of the Babylonian Talmud were the evolutionary end-products of the characters we have already encountered in the Mishnah and Tosefta. We shall now have a look at how they all turned out.

7.1. Panther Becomes Jesus

It is only after he has reached the Bavli, the latest of the major rabbinical treatises, that Jesus of Nazareth crystallizes out of the Yeshu ben Pandira tradition. Indeed, he absorbs the Ben Stada tradition as well and acquires some surprising biographical features – not the least of which is a birth date one hundred years later than the dates implied by Matthew and Luke. All this is the work of the authors of the Babylonian Talmud and their later interpolators.

We originally encountered Ben Pandira in the Tosefta, with a report of a *min* who confided a word of heresy to Rabbi Eliezer. In order to understand what the Bavli has done to this story, it is necessary to review the earlier Tosefta version:

t. *Ḥul.* 2:24: The case of R. Eliezer, who was arrested for Minuth [*heresy*], and they brought him to the tribunal (במה,

David, which ceases not as long as the world endues. The throne of David continued by succession up to that time – namely, till Christ Himself – without any failure from the princes of Judah, until it came unto Him for whom were 'the things that are stored up,' who is Himself 'the expectation of the nations.' For with the advent of the Christ, the succession of the princes from Judah, who reigned until the Christ Himself, ceased. The order [of succession] failed and stopped at the time when **He was born in Bethlehem of Judæa, in the days of Alexander,** who was of high-priestly and royal race; and after this Alexander this lot failed, from the times of himself and Salina, who is also called Alexandra, for the times of Herod the King and Augustus Emperor of the Romans; and this Alexander, one of the anointed (or Christs) and ruling princes placed the crown on his own head... After this a foreign king, Herod, and those who were no longer of the family of David, assumed the crown.[7-1]

βῆμα) for judgment. The governor (הגמון, ἡγεμών) said to him, "Doth an old man like thee occupy himself with such things?" He said to him, "Faithful is the judge concerning me." The governor supposed that he only said this of him, but he was not thinking of any but his Father who is in Heaven. He [the governor] said to him, "Since I am trusted concerning thyself, thus also I will be. I said, perhaps these societies err concerning these things. *Dimissus*, Behold thou art released." And when he had been released from the tribunal, he was troubled because he had been arrested for Minuth. His disciples came in to console him, but he would not take comfort. R. Aqiba came in and said to him, Rabbi, shall I say to thee why thou art perhaps grieving? He said to him, "Say on." He said to him, "Perhaps one of the Minim [*sectarians, heretics*] has said to thee a word of Minuth and it has pleased thee." He said, "By Heaven, thou hast reminded me! Once I was walking along the street of Sepphoris, and I met **Jacob of Chephar Sichnin**, and he said to me a word of Minuth in the name of **Jeshu ben Pantiri**, and it pleased me. And I was arrested for words of Minuth because I transgressed the words of Torah (Prov. v. 8), *Keep thy way far from her, and come not nigh the door of her house* (vii. 26), *for she hath cast down many wounded.*" And R. Eliezer used to say, "Ever let a man flee from what is hateful, and from that which resembles what is hateful." [*Herford translation*]7-2

In what is obviously the same story in the Bavli, the heretic has been transformed from Jacob of Chephar Sichnin [יעקוב איש כפר סכנן] into Jacob of Chephar Sechanja [יעקוב איש כפר סכניא], and Yeshua‘ ben Pantiri [ישוע בן פנטירי] has become Yeshu the Nazarene [ישו הנוצרי *Yeshu ha-Notzri*]. Moreover, several centuries after the Tosefta's invention of the tale, the rabbis of the Bavli have 'remembered' exactly what Jesus had to say:

b. *Abod. Zar.* 16ᵇ, 17ᵃ: Our Rabbis teach, When R. Eliezer was arrested for Minuth they took him up to the tribunal (גרדוס, *gradus*) to be judged. The governor said to him, "Will an old man such as thou busy himself about these vain things?" He said, "Faithful is the judge concerning me." The governor supposed he said this in reference to him; but he only said it in reference to his Father in Heaven. He (the governor) said, "Since I am trusted concerning thee, *Dimissus*, thou art released." When he came to his house his disciples came in to comfort him, but he would not take comfort. R. Aqiba said to him, "Rabbi, suffer me to say something of what thou hast taught me." He said to him, "Say on." He said to him, "Rabbi, perhaps there has come Minuth into thy hand and it has pleased thee, and on account of that thou hast been arrested for Minuth." He said to him, "Aqiba, thou hast reminded me. Once I was walking in the upper street of Sepphoris, and I found a man of the disciples of **Jeshu the Nazarene**, and **Jacob of Chephar Sechanja** was his name. He said to me, "It is written in your Torah, *Thou shalt not bring the hire of a harlot,* etc. [Deut. 23:18. Thou shalt not bring the hire of a whore, or the price of a dog [*male prostitute*] into the house of the LORD thy God for any vow: for even both these are abomination unto the LORD thy God.]. What may be done with it? *Latrinæ* [*toilets*] for the high priest [may be built with it]." And I answered him nothing. He said to me, "Thus hath **Jeshu the Nazarene** taught me, *For of the hire of a harlot hath she gathered them, and unto the hire of a harlot shall they return* [Micah 1:7]. And all the graven images thereof shall be beaten to pieces, and all the hires thereof shall be burned with the fire, and all the idols therof will I lay desolate: for she gathered it of the hire of an harlot, and they shall return to the hire of an harlot.]. From the place of filth they come, and unto the place of filth they shall go." And the saying pleased me, and because of this I was arrested for Minuth; and I transgressed against what is written in the Torah [Prov. 5:8. Remove thy way far from her, and come not nigh the door of her house.], *Keep thy way far from her,* this is Minuth; *and come not nigh the door of her house,* this is the Government. [*Herford translation*][7-3]

In *Midrash Qoh. Rabb.* i. 8. (believed to have been written between 750 and 900 CE), we have essentially the same text – except for the fact that *Yeshu the Nazarene* has been replaced by *so-and-so.*

The Rabbi Eliezer of the story is believed to have lived at the end of the first century and early part of the second century of the common era. According to tradition, he belonged to the third Tannaitic generation, which was active 80–110 CE. Rabbi Aqiba, his student, belonged to the fourth Tannaitic generation, which was active 110–135 CE. If we could be confident that Eliezer and Aqiba actually said what is here reported, it would be a source of information of equal antiquity and authority (as little as that may be!) as the gospels of the New Testament. But there is no reason to accept this late effusion of rabbinical haggadah at face value. First of all, it must be noted that the story itself is not attributed to any specific authority. Rather, it is introduced by the vague "Our Rabbis teach..." It is well established that the Talmud authors were often confused in attributing who said what to whom. Moreover, they were not above fictitiously citing a famous worthy of the past to prop up their own arguments.

We must ask by what evidence, in the year 500 CE, did the Babylonian rabbis change *Sichnin* into *Sechanja*?* What source of inspiration revealed to them that Yeshua᷄ ben Pantiri was actually Yeshu ha-Notzri? And what oracle helped them to restore the lost words of Jesus' disquisition on the religious use of a prostitute's pay? Is there any reason to take any of this seriously in any historical sense?

It may be recalled that this story is absent in the Palestinian Talmud, even though it is found in the Tosefta. I have already expressed the opinion that this is evidence that this story was a late addition to the Tosefta, and that it had not yet been inserted into the edition of the Tosefta available to the Palestinian rabbis before their completion of the Yerushalmi [395 CE]. Thus, even the story about Yeshua᷄ ben Pantiri appears to be late and of doubtful historical significance.

Finally, it must be noted that this twofold mention of Jesus the Nazarene is found only in the Munich manuscript of the Babylonian Talmud. Its absence from later Talmud manuscripts is due, of course, to Catholic censorship. But why is it not found in other manuscripts believed to have eluded the censors? Is it because these manuscripts too have been censored to some extent? Or is it because Jesus the Nazarene was the invention of the scribe who penned the Munich manuscript (or one of its late ancestors)? Once again, our research is frustrated by the lack of really old Talmud manuscripts and the resultant ignorance of the text history of our document. The absence of Yeshu ha-Notzri from the Mishnah, Tosefta, and Yerushalmi, however, makes him most likely the late invention of some scribe whose work lies somewhere in the chain of manuscripts leading to the Munich text.

In any event, whether the ᷄Abodah Zarah Jesus was a late medieval European scribal invention or the creation of a fifth-century Babylonian rabbi, he is much too late to be evidence of

---

*In the ᷄Abodah Zarah translation done by Mishcon and Cohen, *Sekaniah* is identified with *Suchnin*, north of the plain of El Battauf in Galilee. Linguistically this is a highly implausible claim.[7-4]

any historical Jesus. It is not certain when Christians first became a serious enough problem for the Jews that they were forced to react to Christian claims in writing. It is curious that the Jewish reaction is documented in Christian sources – Justin Martyr's Trypho the Jew [before 165 CE] and the Jew quoted by Origen's Celsus [c178 CE] – at least several centuries before it is unequivocally documentable in the rabbinical literature. (It is impossible to prove with certainty that *any* of the *minim* discussed so frequently in the rabbinical literature are Christians rather than, say, Jewish Gnostic sectarians, Balaam partisans, or other Jewish schismatics whose existence is hinted at in ancient sources.) Nevertheless, our tomcat's son still has some evolutionary potential – as we shall see in the Bavli's treatises *Shabbat* and *Sanhedrin*.

7.2. Panther Becomes Ben Stada

In the Bavli, Ben Pandira is equated in two places with ben Stada. The passages placing alleged Jesus surrogates a hundred years after Christ appear to have been interpolated by the same hand, and indicate considerable confusion in the minds of the rabbis on this subject. Readers will have to be patient as we sort this all out. The first passage we need to consider is in the Bavli tractate *Shabbat*:

> **b. Shabb. 104^b:** "He who cuts upon his flesh." It is tradition that Rabbi Eliezer said to the Wise, "Did not Ben Stada bring spells from Egypt in a cut which was upon his flesh?" They said to him, "He was a fool, and they do not bring a proof from a fool." **Ben Stada is Ben Pandira. Rab. Hisda [217-309 CE] said, "The husband was Stada, the paramour was Pandira." The husband was Pappos ben Jehudah,* the mother was**

---

* According to Herford, Pappos ben Jehudah lived a century after the time of Jesus. A haggadah in b. *Giṭ.* 90ᵃ says that he was so distrusting of his wife that he locked her into the house whenever he had to go somewhere. He was a contemporary and friend of R. Aqiba, who was active 110–135 CE.[7-6] Believers seeking confirmation of the historicity of Jesus in the Bavli perforce must accept the 'fact' that if Ben Stada or Ben Pandira are Jesus, Jesus was born at least a century after Christ!

Stada. The mother was Miriam the dresser of women's hair, as we say in Pumbeditha, "Such a one has been false to her husband" [*S^etāth dā*]. [*Herford translation*]⁷⁻⁵

Freedman's translation gives a slightly different text sequence and 'spin' to this passage, and it may be advisable to quote this rendition before going on to the second passage equating ben Pandira with Ben Stada:

b. Shabb. 104ᵇ: *He who scratches a mark on his flesh*, [*etc.*] It was taught, R. Eliezer said to the Sages: But did not Ben Stada bring forth witchcraft from Egypt by means of scratches [*incisions*] [in the form of charms] upon his flesh? Was he then the son of Stada: surely he was the son of Pandira?—Said R. Ḥisda: The husband was Stada, the paramour was Pandira. But the husband was Pappos b. Judah?–His mother was Stada. But his mother was Miriam the hairdresser?—It is as we say in Pumbeditha: This one has been unfaithful to (lit., 'turned away from'–*satath da*) her husband. He was a fool, answered they, and proof cannot be adduced from fools.⁷⁻⁷

As already noted, the same confused argument has been inserted into a *Sanhedrin* passage dealing with a completely different subject. In *Sanh.* 67ª we find it in the context of Ben Stada's entrapment and execution:

b. Sanh. 67ª: R. Papa said: When the Mishnah states *A mesith is a hedyot* [*layman*], it is only in respect of hiding witnesses. For it has been taught: And for all others for whom the Torah decrees death, witnesses are not hidden, excepting for this one. How is it done?–A light is lit in an inner chamber, the witnesses are hidden in an outer one [which is in darkness], so that they can see and hear him, but he cannot see them. Then the person he wished to seduce says to him, 'Tell me privately what thou hast proposed to me'; and he does so. Then he remonstrates: 'But how shall we forsake our God in Heaven, and serve idols'? If he retracts, it is well. But if he answers: 'it is our duty and seemly for us', the witnesses who were listening outside bring him to the Beth din, and have him stoned. [*Then, in the Munich and Oxford manuscripts and in the older editions, there follows the material attempting to identify Ben Stada.*] **And thus they did to Ben Stada in Lydda, and they hung him on the eve of Passover. Ben Stada was Ben Padira** [*sic*]. **R. Ḥisda said: The**

> husband was Stada, the paramour Pandira. But was not
> the husband Pappos b. Judah?–His mother's name was
> Stada. But his mother was Miriam, a dresser of woman's
> hair? (נשיא מגדלא) *megaddela neshayia)*:–As they say in Pum-
> baditha, This woman has turned away (*satath da*) from her
> husband, (*i.e.*, committed adultery). [*Shechter and Freedman
> translation*][7-8]

There is a curiously parallel passage in b. *Sanh.* 43[a], in which
Yeshu (*ha-Notzri* is added in the Munich manuscript) replaces
ben Stada in the execution on the eve of Passover. (A Florentine
manuscript adds the 'fact' that it also was the eve of the Sabbath.)
As might be expected, *there is no discussion equating Pandira,
Stada, and Yeshu*. Like the preceding passage, this section relates
the execution to enticing Jews to commit idolatry:

> **b. *Sanh.* 43[a]:** *And a herald precedes him, etc.* This implies,
> only immediately before [the execution], but not previous thereto.
> [In contradiction to this] it was taught: **On the eve of the
> Passover Yeshu [the Nazarean] was hanged.** For forty days
> before the execution took place, a herald went forth and cried,
> 'He is going forth to be stoned because he has practised sorcery
> and enticed Israel to apostacy. Any one who can say anything in
> his favour, let him come forward and plead on his behalf.' But
> since nothing was brought forward in his favour **he was hanged
> on the eve of Passover [and the eve of Sabbath]!**– ʿUlla
> retorted: Do you suppose that he was one for whom a defence
> could be made? Was he not a *Mesith* [enticer], concerning whom
> Scripture says, *Neither shalt thou spare, neither shalt thou
> conceal him?* With Yeshu however it was different, for he was
> connected with the government [or royalty, *i.e.*, influential. [*This
> is followed by a discussion of the 'fact' that Jesus had five
> disciples, which we shall examine later. Shechter and Freedman
> translation*][7-9]

Now that the passages relating Ben Pandira to Ben Stada
have been examined, we can proceed to try to figure out their
meaning and significance. The reader will note, first of all, that
neither the *Shabbat* nor *Sanhedrin* passages mention Yeshu or
Yeshuaʿ at all: they deal exclusively with the names Pandira,
Stada, and Miriam. The Christians' Jesus comes to mind simply
because of the tradition that his mother too was named Miriam
(Mary) and that he was executed (but not hanged!) on the eve of

the Sabbath – which, according to John 19:31, was also the eve of Passover. It cannot be doubted, however, that the substitution of *Yeshu* – and then *Yeshu ha-Notzri* – for *Ben Stada* in *Sanh.* 43ᵃ was done by scribes who had come to believe that Ben Stada was actually the Jesus whom the Christians had elevated to godhood. (It seems to me highly unlikely that the original version of this passage made any mention of Yeshu, given its great similarity with the Ben Stada passage *Sanh.* 67ᵃ.) Of course, there is an embarrassing problem in identifying Jesus with the ben Stada of *Sanh.* 67ᵃ. Jesus is supposed to have been crucified in Jerusalem, not hanged in Lydda – a town 23 miles NW of Jerusalem!

How could rabbis writing at least as late as the fifth century* of the common era have made such a mistake? It would seem impossible that they should have been ignorant of such basic Christian 'facts' at a time when Christianity was thriving so conspicuously. The answer, I believe, lies in the likelihood that rabbis living in Babylon (Iraq) probably had little interaction with adherents of the 'Great Church' which had achieved theological and political hegemony in the core regions of the Roman Empire but had not been able to supplant early competitors still thriving in the imperial periphery. As late as the time of Mohammed [570–632 CE], holdout primitive forms of Christianity were the only sects known in Asiatic regions outside the realm of the Great Church. The New Testament gospel traditions we take for granted may have been completely unknown or at least sparsely disseminated in regions such as Iraq and Arabia. Instead, gospels now lost and differing sharply from our canonical gospels† may

---

* Even Herford admits that the passage equating Stada with Pandira cannot be earlier than the beginning of the fourth century, and cautions that it is a report of what was said in Babylonia, not Palestine.[7-10]

† In addition to the many 'apocryphal' gospel scraps one can still find in compendia such as Schneemelcher's *New Testament Apocrypha*,[7-11] I might mention the sayings gospel known as *Sufi Q*, which is discussed by Robert M. Price in his fascinating book *Deconstructing Jesus*.[7-12] Although similar in structure to the Gospel of Thomas and the reconstructed sayings gospel known as 'Q', the sayings of *Sufi Q* depict a Jesus quite different in many respects from the star actor in the canonical gospel dramas. It is possible that *Sufi Q* ultimately derives from ancient Syriac Christian sources and thus might be representative of the sort of traditions that could have diffused into Iraq and beyond.

have been the main source of Christian information available to Babylonian rabbis and Mohammed alike. (It is unlikely that they would actually have read any of these gospels, but would have learned their details from frequent discussion and disputation with local Christians who used them as scripture.)

Even though the actual interpolation of the Pandira/Stada discussion into the Talmud Gemara must have been quite late, it may nevertheless have been conditioned by traditions going back to a period even earlier than the time when the canonical gospels were concocted. Potentially, it might provide information on the process by which the Jesus biography coalesced from the rumors and tittle-tattle of the late first century, even though it can be of no use in reconstructing the biography of an actual man.

If we refer back to the bolded text in either the *Sanh.* 67a or *Shabb.* 104b passages, we see at once that material must be missing. The blunt statement that "Ben Stada is Ben Pandira" looks like a marginal note that has been inserted into the text. If that is not the case, we have the peculiar problem that in *Shabbat* the equation must be attributed to *R. Eliezer*, but in *Sanhedrin* it must be attributed to *R. Papa*! It seems clear that this equation must be viewed as an unattributable insertion into both texts. Although the next sentence ("The husband was Stada, the paramour was Pandira") is attributed to Rab. Ḥisda, whom Steinsaltz[7-13] classifies as belonging to the third-generation [290–320 CE] of Babylonian Amoraim (and thus too late to be authoritative on the subject), the statement which follows it cannot be from Ḥisda. The statement that "The husband was Pappos ben Jehudah, the mother was Stada" contradicts Ḥisda's claim that the husband was Stada and the paramour was Pandira. We are missing an attribution here. The remaining sentence – "The mother was Miriam the dresser of women's hair, as we say in Pumbeditha, 'Such a one has been false to her husband' " – is obviously an attempt to etymologize the name *Stada* as applied to a woman.

It is altogether possible that this haggadah was constructed with the Christian doctrine of the virgin birth in mind, even though the Jewish Christians of Babylonia are not likely to have believed that doctrine. It certainly seems to be grist for an anti-Christian, Jewish propaganda mill – a mill that substituted a banal bastardy for the preternatural parthenogenesis of Christian dogma.

Is it possible to draw any conclusions from this passage beyond the obvious, *viz.*, that the rabbis who wrote it were in a state of total confusion and had no knowledge of any historical Jesus? What part of this would historical Jesus apologists have us believe is true? That Stada was Pandira, or that they were two different men? Should we believe that Stada and Pandira were two men, or a man and a woman? Can any of the Ben Stada passages we have examined from the Tosefta to the Bavli support the possibility that Ben ('son of'!) Stada was a woman? (That is, after all, the conclusion to be drawn from this passage.) Are we to believe that Mary's husband was actually Pappos ben Jehudah – a man who flourished during the first third of the second century? Should we believe that St. Joseph was Ben Stada?

That at least *some* rabbis equated Ben Stada with Jesus by the time the bolded text was inserted into the Babylonian Talmud is obvious from the parallel passage in b. *Sanh.* 43ᵃ, which says that Yeshu the Nazarene, not Ben Stada, was hanged on the eve of Passover. Unfortunately, we cannot determine when the equations were inserted into the Babylonian treatises *Shabbat* and *Sanhedrin*. This is more the pity because it is precisely the *Shabbat* claim that Ben Stada brought spells from Egypt in cuts in his flesh that gave rise to a major theme of the *Sepher Toldoth Yeshu* – *viz.*, that he wrote down the secret name *Yahweh* on parchment, concealed it in cuts in his flesh, and smuggled it out of the Temple of Yahweh in order to work his magic. (This will be explored in the last part of this book.)

7.3. And Mary Is His Mother

As we have seen, the *Shabbat* and *Sanhedrin* passages we have been examining that try to equate Ben Stada with Ben Pandira have been related to Jesus of Nazareth because of the appearance therein of a woman named Miriam – the Hebrew equivalent of Mary. But it is rash to equate this particular Miriam with the mother of Jesus. After all, *Miriam* probably was the most popular Hebrew feminine name of the day, and the New Testament itself supplies us with a surfeit of Marys. It is of great interest to discover that the adulteress Miriam in question is described as being "a dresser of women's hair" – *Miriam m'gaddela nashaia*. The second word immediately suggests the name *Magdala* – the supposed hometown of one of the looser Marys of the New Testament, Mary Magdalene. It is quite possible that the rabbis were confused by all the Marys in the Christian mythology and adopted a folk etymology for *Mary Magdalene* instead of for *Mary, the Mother of God*. If Mary Magdalene is simply the result of an exercise in folk etymology, the inability of archaeologists to identify convincingly any site that ever was called Magdala* becomes understandable!

Before we consider the remaining rabbinical stories that have been fancied to refer to Mary the mother of Jesus, it is well to point out just how shaky the tradition is that posits a mother named Mary for the failed Messiah Ben Joseph. Neither the Pauline Epistles – ostensibly the oldest stratum of the New Testament – nor the later epistles know anything at all about Jesus having earthly parents. For 'Paul' at least, Jesus was a heavenly being and the possibility of him having a mother and father was never a consideration. Mary and Joseph are not to be found at the base of the Christian tradition. Astonishingly, Mary is unknown also to the authors and redactors of the Gospel of John. Surely, had they known that Jesus's mother had been named Mary, they would have noted the fact when they had the Jews of Capernaum scoff [John 6:42], "Is not this Jesus, the son of Joseph, whose father and mother we know? How is it then that he saith, I came down from heaven?"

It appears that Mary was created as the mother of Jesus by the unknown author of the Gospel of Mark – and even then her

---

* We read of a place called Magdala only in the KJV rendering of Matthew 15:39: "And he sent away the multitude, and took ship, and came into the coasts of Magdala." In most modern versions of the Bible, however, we find no trace of the place. Instead, we find the name *Magadan* – in agreement with the oldest manuscripts. Neither Magdala nor Magadan, however, is to be found in the entire Hebrew Bible nor anywhere in all of pre-Christian literature. In Mark 8:10 – the text that 'Matthew' plagiarized in producing his version of the gospel story – we find no mention of Magadan or Magdala. Instead, we read: "And straightway he entered into a ship with his disciples, and came into the parts of Dalmanutha." Of course, Dalmanutha also was completely unknown to the pre-Christian world. I formerly thought that *Magdala* was a symbolic adaptation of *Migdol*, the place where the Israelites are supposed to have encamped just before Moses parted the waters of the Red Sea. However, the promiscuous hairdresser folk etymology seems much more fitting – perhaps even convincing. It may in fact trace back to the oral traditions that shaped the formation of the New Testament gospels and gave them their cast of characters.

sole appearance in this oldest gospel is incidental. (Joseph is not found at all in Mark.) Mary in Mark, like Joseph in John, is introduced by scoffing Jews of "his own country": "Is not this the carpenter, the son of Mary, the brother of James, and Joses, and of Juda, and Simon? And are not his sisters here with us? And they were offended at him" [Mark 6:3].

In Mark, however, this verse seems to have been created simply as a pretext for stating the wise saying, "A prophet is not without honour, but in his own country, and among his own kin, and in his own house" [Mark 6:4]. It is most probable that 'Mark' got this saying (along with many others) from a Q-like sayings gospel that was actually a list of Cynic or Stoic wisdom morsels. When Mark was written, of course, the myth of the virgin birth of Jesus was still unknown. Indeed, that myth was not yet current when the oldest versions of Matthew and Luke were written – gospels that now have the greatest elaboration of that pagan syncretism. That the virgin birth stories of those two gospels were later elaborations is clear from the fact that both contain genealogies that trace the descent of Jesus through Joseph not Mary. If the virginal conception had been part of these gospels from the beginning, both would have had to create genealogies of Mary, not Joseph. (The name *Joseph* probably was chosen for the father of Jesus as a conscious melding of the two messiahs awaited in certain Jewish circles – a Messiah Ben David and a Messiah Ben Joseph.)

If the Bavli Miriam stories we are about to examine were actually intended to be references to the mother of Jesus, it is clear that they could not have been developed until well after the final editions of Matthew and Luke had been produced. Exactly when this happened is uncertain, but it is relevant to note that the oldest Syriac version of Matthew – the fourth-century *Codex Sinaiticus Syriacus*[7-14] – still says that "Jacob begat Joseph, and Joseph begat Jesus." Jesus does not acquire a Syriac virginal birth in Matthew until his appearance in the somewhat later Curetonian Syriac version and the fifth-century Peshitta. Tales of the Virgin Mary, thus, probably did not reach the Babylonian rabbis until the fifth century of the common era, and readers may judge for themselves concerning the historical value of such stories.

We encounter Miriam the women's hairdresser again in the Bavli treatise *Ḥagigah* [*'Festival Offering'*], in a pericope wildly anachronistic if Miriam is in fact "Mary, Mother of God":

b. Ḥag. 4ᵇ: When **Rab Joseph** came to this verse (Exod. 23:17) he wept. *There is that* [which] *is destroyed without justice* (Prov. 13:23). He said, Is there any who has departed before his time? None but this [told] of **Rab Bibi bar Abaji**. The Angel of Death was with him. The Angel said to his messenger, "Go, bring me **Miriam the dresser of women's hair.**" He brought him Miriam the teacher of children. He [the Angel] said, "I told thee **Miriam the dresser of women's hair.**" He said, "If so, I will take this one back." He said, "Since thou hast brought this one, let her be among the number [of the dead]." [*Herford translation*]⁷⁻¹⁵

Now Rab Joseph bar Chia was born at Stili in Babylonia in 259 CE and was the head of the rabbinical school at Pumbeditha. To increase the anachronism, the only known R. Bibi flourished in the fourth century. The Tosaphoth (medieval 12th-13th century commentators on the Talmud) attempted to resolve this anachronism, but only created a wildly antipodal one:

The Angel of Death was with him, who related what had happened to him long ago, for this story as to Miriam the women's hair-dresser took place in the time of the second temple, for she was mother of that so and so [*i.e.*, Jeschu], as is related in (treatise) *Shabbath* [104ᵇ]. [*Mead translation*]⁷⁻¹⁶

Thus, Miriam lived either in the third century CE, the fourth century CE, or before the time of Herod's remodeling of the Temple of Yahweh – probably placing her somewhere around 100 BCE! If this passage really was intended to refer to the mother of Jesus, we are forced to conclude that Christian traditions concerning the chronology of Jesus' earthly career were still fluid and inchoate at the time the *Ḥagigah* passage was compiled. Such a state of affairs would be hard to explain if there had ever been an historical Jesus. On the other hand, if this Miriam is someone else – or a literary fiction created for the purpose of splitting rabbinical hairs – there is no problem at all. Once again, to quote Josephus: "But let every one think of these matters as he pleases."

7.4. Jesus the *Mamzer*

As we shall see in our exploration of the *Sepher Toldoth Yeshu*, that anti-gospel portrays Jesus as the *mamzer* (bastard) son of Miriam, conceived while she was menstruating – a conception at least as miraculous as that accorded him in the gospels of Matthew and Luke! There is a late treatise appended to the Babylonian Talmud, called *Kallah* ['bride'],* that depicts just such a situation – anonymously:

> *Kallah* 18b: A shameless person is, according to R. Eliezer, a bastard; according to R. Joshua, a son of a woman in her separation; according to R. Akiba, a bastard *and* son of a woman in her separation. Once there sat elders at the gate when two boys passed by; one had his head covered, the other bare. Of him who had his head uncovered, R. Eliezer said, "A bastard!" R. Joshua said, "A son of a woman in her separation!" R. Akiba said "A bastard *and* son of a woman in her separation!" They said to R. Akiba, "How has thine heart impelled thee to the audacity of contradicting the words of thy colleagues?" He said to them, "I am about to prove it." Thereupon he went to the boy's mother, and found her sitting in the market and selling pulse [*selling legumes, not dressing women's hair!*]. He said to her, "My daughter, if thou tellest me the thing which I ask thee, I will bring thee to eternal life." She said to him, "Swear it to me!" Thereupon R. Akiba [*remember, Akiba died in 135 CE!*] took the oath with his lips, while he cancelled it in his heart. Then said he to her, "Of what sort is this thy son?" She said to him, "When I betook myself to the bridal chamber I was in my separation, and my husband stayed away from me. But my paranymph [*bridegroom's best man, not necessarily a soldier*] came to me, and by him I have this son." So the boy was discovered to be both a bastard and the son of a woman in her separation. Thereupon said they, "Great is R. Akiba, in that he has put to shame his teachers." In the same hour they said, "Blessed be the Lord God of Israel, who has revealed his secret to R. Akiba ben Joseph."
> [*Mead translation*]7-17

---

* There are two versions of this tractate, a short version consisting of just one chapter, and a longer version consisting of ten. The longer version was not discovered until modern times. It was first published in Vienna in 1864. Its date of composition is unknown. It is not included in Epstein's Hebrew-English edition of the Babylonian Talmud.

While the composers of the *Toldoth Yeshu* probably thought this passage (or its source) referred to Mary and Jesus, there is no reason to suppose the original author had these Christian characters in mind during its composition. Indeed, there is a strong reason to suppose he did not. The passage makes the nameless woman a contemporary of R. Akiba – who was executed in the year 135 CE! Considering the 'fact' of Roman Catholic tradition that Mary had been assumed bodily into heaven long before that date, we must conclude that this particular *mamzer*'s mom was some other wanton.

Before ending this discussion of the Bavli's *mamzer* pericopae, we need to review the most famous reference of all – the Mishnah passage *Yebam*. 4:13 which we examined in detail in the Mishnah chapter of this book:

> **m. *Yebam*. 4:13:** Rabbi Shim'on ben 'Azzai said, "I have found a scroll of genealogies in Jerusalem; thereon was written: 'That so-and-so (פלוני איש) is a bastard (ממזר) born of an adulteress'; to confirm the words of Rabbi Yehoshua."

It will perhaps be recalled that there is no elaboration of this passage in the Yerushalmi's Gemara – leaving one to wonder if it was not yet present in the Mishnah used by the compilers of the Palestinian Talmud. It is interesting to discover that although the Bavli's Gemara contains the pericope, there is no elaboration of it. In fact, not all of the Mishnah text is included:

> **b. *Yebam*. 49ᵇ:** *Said R. Simeon B. 'Azzai etc.* **[A tanna] recited: Simeon b. 'Azzai said, "I found a roll of genealogical records in Jerusalem and therein was written 'So-and-so is a bastard [having been born] from [a forbidden union with] a married woman'** and therein was also written 'The teaching of R. Eliezer b. Jacob is small in quantity but thoroughly sifted'. And in it was also written, "Manasseh slew Isaiah'." *[There follows a detailed discussion about Manasseh and Isaiah.]** [Slotki translation]* [7-18]

---

* It would appear that some sort of violence has been visited upon this passage, as the material following the bolded text has nothing whatever to do with the question being discussed for more than a page of Talmud text, *viz.*, What is a bastard? It is hard to believe that the material about Manasseh and Isaiah was intentionally inserted in order to truncate the Mishnah's discussion of bastardy. I am at a loss to explain how this material ended up at this spot.

It can be seen that the punchline of the Mishnah's argument has been omitted. As a result, readers would never know that the text in bold was actually the decisive point needed to prove the argument of R. Joshua, *viz.*, *that a bastard was defined legally as someone born to parents guilty of a capital crime*. (Since in early times the full text of the Mishnah was not printed out beside the Gemara, readers of the Gemara would have no clue as to the context of this enigmatic snippet.) Moreover, once *so-and-so* had become established as a code word for *Jesus*, it would be quite natural to understand this passage as being a veiled reference to Jesus.

Historical Jesus advocates then, if they use the simple-minded method of the rabbinical schools, might try to date this supposed Jesus reference by dating the rabbis cited in the story – gullibly accepting the dubious thesis that the rabbis named actually said what the text says they said. Although they could no longer refer to the times of the expunged R. Joshua b. Ḥananiah [3rd Tannaitic generation, 80–110 CE], they could seize with equal utility upon R. Simeon b. ʿAzzai, who was active only slightly later, in the fourth Tannaitic generation, 110–135 CE. In addition, since R. Eliezer b. Jacob also has been plopped down in the midst of an argument in which he had taken no part, why not add his dates to the enterprise? He, like the R. Joshua he supplanted, was a sage of the third Tannaitic generation. This gets us back to the period in which the canonical gospels were being composed!

After clearing all historical hurdles by leaps of faith, at this point even rationalistic believers in the historical Jesus (most rationalists disagree with my thesis of a mythical Jesus) will shift their neural-network hypothesizers into high gear and 'explain' the whole case in common-sense terms. "Because of this official record of Jesus' bastardy," we will be told, "the Christians concocted the doctrine of the virgin birth in defense. Jewish claims that Jesus was a bastard were not made up in response to the virgin-birth claims of Christians; the facts are the other way around."

As I have already shown, however, careful examination of the Mishnah itself forces us to conclude that there never was a scroll in Jerusalem in which Jesus of Nazareth was named as anybody at all, let alone as a bastard. Readers who feel even slightly seduced by this rationalistic argument are encouraged to reread chapter 4, my Mishnah chapter's discussion of this passage.

7.5. Jesus the Nazarene

Nowhere in all the rabbinical writings prior to the Bavli have we encountered the name *Jesus of Nazareth* or *Jesus the Nazarene (Yeshu ha-Notzri)*, although we have met with *Jesus ben Pandira (Yeshu ben Pantiri)*. Now, at long last, our examination of the Babylonian Talmud has brought us to the point where we can consider the only clear references to the Jesus of Christianity in all of ancient rabbinical literature. It is here that there can be no quibble as to who is meant by what is written – no nicknames or code words need bedevil this part of our study.

Unfortunately, we have no way to determine if Yeshu ha-Notzri was in the 'first edition' of the Bavli or whether he was added in later centuries. The lack of truly ancient manuscripts containing our crucial passages, once again, frustrates our study.* At best, the closing date for the compilation of the Bavli – 500 or 600 CE – may serve as a *terminus a quo* for the advent of Jesus the Nazarene into the cluttered pages of the Talmud. Although such a date is far too late for the Bavli to be of use in reconstructing biographies or histories, the stories it contains are interesting in their own right and we may be excused if we temporarily put aside our historical-critical tools and just allow ourselves to be entertained by some imaginative folklore.

---

*The oldest dated manuscript of the Mishnah goes back only to 1399–1401 CE. The oldest Tosefta manuscript is thought to have been copied in 1150. The only surviving complete manuscript of the Jerusalem Talmud was written in 1299 by Jehiel b. Jekuthiel b. Benjamin the Physician and is now at Leyden. The only complete manuscript of the Babylonian Talmud, the Munich manuscript, was copied in 1342 by Solomon b. Samson, probably in France. Manuscripts containing parts of the Bavli are dated 1176 (at Florence) and 1184 (at Hamburg). Numerous manuscripts have been retrieved from the Cairo Genizah, some of which are said to go back as far as the year 500 CE. However, I have been unable to discover what, if any, of this material pertains to the Talmuds. It is probable that much of this material has been published in Israel, but unfortunately European-language editions of the Talmuds have not made use of Genizah documents as far as I have been able to discover.

7.6. The Excommunication of Jesus

The first reference to Jesus the Nazarene that I wish to examine is one we have already encountered when we studied the Mishnah's reference to Elisha repelling Gehazi with both hands:

b. Sanh. 107ᵇ: Our Rabbis teach, Ever let the left hand repel and the right hand invite, not like Elisha who repulsed Gehazi with both hands, and not like **R. Jehoshua ben Perahjah, who repulsed Jeshu (the Nazarene) with both hands**. Gehazi, as it is written...

This continues with a quotation of 2 Kings 5:23–26, the story of Gehazi, Naaman, and Elisha. This in turn is followed by a rabbinical paraphrase of the story of Naaman being cured of leprosy and Gehazi contracting the disease. The verse 2 Kings 5:27 then provides a logical conclusion to the story:

[So] "The leprosy therefore of Naaman shall cleave unto thee, and unto thy seed for ever." And he went out from his presence a leper as white as snow [2 Kings 5:27].

In the uncensored text, this is immediately followed by a completely unrelated haggadah which tells of the excommunication of Jesus the Nazarene. It appears as though it came in on a meteorite and crash-landed on this page of the *Sanhedrin* Gemara:

b. Sanh. 107ᵇ: What of R. Jehoshua ben Perahjah? When Jannai the king [r. 104–78 BCE] killed our Rabbis, **R. Jehoshua ben Perahjah [and Jesus]** fled to Alexandria of Egypt. When there was peace, Shim'on ben Shetah sent to him, "From me [Jerusalem] the city of holiness, to thee Alexandria of Egypt [my sister]. My husband stays in thy midst and I sit forsaken." He came, and found himself at a certain inn; they showed him great honour. He said, "How beautiful is this Acsania!" [denotes both inn and innkeeper] **(Jesus) said to him, "Rabbi, she has narrow eyes."** He said, "Wretch, dost thou employ thyself thus?" He sent out four hundred trumpets and excommunicated him. He [i.e., Jesus] came before him many times and said to him, "Receive me." But he would not notice him. One day he [i.e. R. Jeh.] was reciting the Shema', he [i.e. Jesus] came before him. He was minded to receive him, and made a sign to him. He [i.e.

Jesus] thought that he repelled him. He went and hung up a tile and worshipped it. He [R. Jeh.] said to him, "Return." He replied, "Thus I have received from thee, that every one who sins and causes the multitude to sin, they give him not the chance to repent." And a teacher has said, **"Jesus the Nazarene practised magic and led astray and deceived Israel."** [Herford translation][7-19]

The beginning section – the part about repelling with both hands – is repeated verbatim in another tractate of the Bavli [b. Soṭah 47ª], as was seen back on page 133, in the discussion about Gehazi in the Mishnah. In the Soṭah version, however, this passage is not followed immediately by the story of the excommunication of Jesus in Egypt, but by the story of Elisha's trip to Damascus to bring Gehazi to repentance. Significantly, I think, in Soṭah it is Gehazi who first recites the line, "Thus I have received from thee, that every one who sins and causes the multitude to sin, they give him not the chance to repent." In Sanhedrin, of course, this line is delivered by Jesus. (Curiously, no Jesus-hunter has ever staggered out of the Talmud underbrush with this evidentiary trophy. Is this not 'proof' that Gehazi is a code name for Jesus in the Talmud?) Then, after completing the story of Gehazi and Elisha, what do we find next in Soṭah? A repetition of the Sanhedrin tale of the flight into Egypt and the excommunication of Jesus – with Jesus delivering the line just delivered by Gehazi two paragraphs before! As was the case in Sanhedrin, this passage fits the context as naturally as a meteorite in chicken soup.

In my discussion of Gehazi in the Jerusalem Talmud [pp. 183–185] I showed that the repelling-with-both-hands pericope derives from the biblical verse 2 Kings 4:27. In that story, however, it is Gehazi, not Elisha, who does the repelling in his attempt to push away the Shunamite woman who was entreating Elisha for help. This original detail is elaborated, not reversed. Gehazi tries to thrust the woman away, and R. Yosé b. Ḥanina tells us that "He put his hand on the cleavage between her breasts." With the decay of the repulsive relationship between Elisha and Gehazi, the simile with R. Jehoshua ben Peraḥjah and Yeshu ha-Notzri falls apart as well. (It will be remembered that it was the supposed contemporaneity with Jehoshua ben Peraḥjah that forced the dating of Jesus at approximately a century "before Christ.") There is no history in this part of the Bavli.

The pericope of the excommunication of Jesus also has a non-Christian ancestry. In the tractate *Ḥagigah* ['*Festival Offering*'] of the Jerusalem Talmud we have the rootstock of the Bavli's *Sanhedrin* efflorescence. In the ancestral version, however, we have an anonymous disciple instead of Jesus. Furthermore, it is not R. Jehoshua ben Peraḥjah who flees to Egypt, but rather Judah b. Tabbai – who also dates to around 100 BCE! Once again, I depend upon Jacob Neusner's rendering:

> **j. Ḥag. 2:2:** Judah b. Tabbai was nasi. Simeon b. Shatah was head of the court. Some teach it vice versa.
>
> He who says Judah b. Tabbai was nasi finds support in the incident of Alexandria.
>
> The men of Jerusalem wanted to appoint **Judah b. Tabbai** as patriarch in Jerusalem. He fled and went to Alexandria. The men of Jerusalem would write, "From Jerusalem, the great, to Alexandria, the small: How long will my betrothed dwell with you, while I am sorrowful on his account?"
>
> He departed and arrived in a boat.
>
> He said, "Do you remember what Deborah, the mistress of the house who received us, lacked?"
>
> One of his disciples said to him, "Rabbi, her eye was blinking."
>
> He said to him, "Lo, two [sins] are against you: one that you suspected *me* [of looking at her], and one that *you* looked at her. Did I say that her appearance wàs handsome of sight? I only said [handsome] in [her] deed[s]!"
>
> He was angry with him, and he went away.[7-20]

Not unexpectedly, two more supposed Talmudic testimonies to Jesus of Nazareth dissolve in the solvent of comparative text criticism.

7.7. Jesus Burns His Food

Perhaps the most inscrutable of the Bavli's references to Yeshu ha-Notzri is found in *Sanh.* 103ᵃ:

> **b. Sanh. 103ᵃ:** For Rab Ḥisda said that Rab Jeremiah bar Abba said, "What is that which is written: *There shall no evil befall thee, neither shall any plague come nigh thy dwelling* [Ps. xci. 10] ... Another explanation: *There shall no evil befall thee*, [means], "that evil dreams and evil thoughts may tempt thee not," and *neither shall any plague come nigh thy dwelling* [means] "that thou mayest not have **a son or disciple who**

burns his food in public like Jeshu the Nazarene." [*Herford translation*][7-21]

Once again, we are fortunate to have a second locus in which the enigmatic bolded text is repeated in a different context. In b. *Berakhot* ['Blessings'] 17[b] we find the following:

> **b. Ber. 17[b]:** *'There is no breaking in and no going forth, and no outcry in the streets'* [Ps. 144:14], says: *'There is no breaking in'*, that our company be not as the company of David from which Ahitophel went out, and *'there is no going forth'* that our company be not as the company of Saul, from which Doeg, the Edomite, went forth, and *'no outcry,'* that our company be not as the company of Elisha from which Gehazi went out, and *'in our streets'* that there be not to us **a son or disciple who burns his food in public like Jeshu the Nazarene.**[7-22]

It is of no small significance that in the quotation of this passage in the *Arukh** it is not Jesus who "burns his food," but Manasseh – a character much more suited for a discussion of the "Three Kings and Four Commoners" who are to be excluded from Paradise. Besides, as the wayward son of Hezekiah, Manasseh *literally* fits the context of a sentence identifying the type of son or disciple one would like to avoid having. It thus seems all but certain that *Manasseh* was the original reading, and *Yeshu ha-Notzri* appeared later on as a mutation in the text.

The discovery that the *Arukh* has Manasseh instead of Jesus burning his food is not one for which I can claim the credit. Rather, it was discovered by R. Travers Herford, the scholar whose work I have been examining throughout my discussion of the rabbinical literature. Needless to say, he did not see the significance of the fact quite in the way I do. Indeed, he argued squarely against my conclusion:

---

*The *Arukh* is a work written in Hebrew in the year 1101 CE by the Italian lexicographer and Talmudist Nathan ben Jehiel of Rome. The *Arukh* is a lexicon of the Talmud and Midrashim that contains numerous quotations of rabbinical texts cited. Since Ben Jehiel had access to much better manuscripts than survive today – manuscripts written before their texts had been embroidered by later rabbinical additions and before Catholic censorship mutilated the entire rabbinical literature – his readings of many texts are of great importance for understanding the evolution of the Talmuds and Midrashim.

The passage in b. Ber. 17^b, as quoted in the Aruch (*s.v.* קדח [Ed. *qadah*, 'to burn' FRZ]) reads thus, "burns his food in public, like Manasseh." And this has probably led the author of that work to explain the meaning of 'burns his food in public' by 'sets up idols in public,' 'establishes false worships'. But, as Rabbinowicz has shown, not "Manasseh," but "Jeshu ha-Notzri," is the original reading; and this fact is conclusive against the explanation of the author of the Aruch. It is absurd to say of Jesus that he set up idols. I conclude, therefore, that in the passage before us the reference to Jesus is intended as an example of one who inclined to heresy. [Herford]⁷⁻²³

It is of psychological interest that Herford was a Christian who, of course, believed not only in the historicity of Jesus but also was utterly convinced that the authors of the Talmuds knew a great deal about him and that, therefore, present explicit mentions of Jesus must be authentic. This bias made it impossible for him to see the real significance of the *Arukh* citation. For him, the fact that Rabbinowicz (a contemporary scholar) had shown that the Munich manuscript [1342 CE] had the reading *Yeshu ha-Notzri* overrode the fact that ben Jehiel, writing in Rome more than two centuries earlier, in 1101, would have had access to far older manuscripts whose texts could be expected to be much closer to those of the Talmud autograph – if indeed it is at all meaningful to speak of the Bavli ever having had an autograph.* It is clear that the ancient manuscripts ben Jehiel knew made no mention of Jesus. I can imagine no reason why he would have wanted to falsify this text.

---

* Hermann L. Strack, in his *Introduction to the Talmud and Midrash* comments that

> The text of the Babylonian Talmud received many additions after the compilation was completed by the Saboraim. Frequently it is quite easy to recognize these additions by the evidence from subject-matter, as when they interrupt the context of a discussion. In other instances additions betray themselves by the change of idiom, in still other cases by the fact that they are wanting in all or certain ancient witnesses. An important handle is offered by the expression *lishna 'aḥrina* 'another version'. ... Probably there never existed a uniform and universally recognized text; rather from the very beginning there must have been differences between what was taught at Sura and what at Pum Beditha. These differences persisted and, moreover, were multiplied through the circumstance that to the end of the

Much ink has been expended in scholarly attempts going back at least to Ben Jehiel to explain in several languages exactly what is meant by *burns his food in public*. I confess I do not know what it means, apart from the general sense of doing something to bring dishonor to parents or teachers. It is probably certain that the charring of toast was not what the rabbi had in mind when he wrote this passage, but a more precise understanding of the phrase is elusive. Fortunately, we do not need a more precise definition in order to see that these late passages of the Bavli cannot really pertain to the Jesus postulated by Christian – and even Atheist – historians.

7.8. Hanging Jesus

Before taking our leave of Yeshu ha-Notzri it is necessary to look one last time at the *Sanhedrin* passage describing his execution:

> **b. *Sanh.* 43ª:** And it is tradition: **On the eve of Pesaḥ they hung Jeshu [the Nazarene].** And the crier went forth before him forty days (saying), "**[Jeshu the Nazarene]** goeth forth to be stoned, because he hath practised magic and deceived and led astray Israel. Any one who knoweth aught in his favour, let him come and declare concerning him." And they found naught in his favour. **And they hung him on the eve of Pesaḥ.** Ulla says, "Would it be supposed that **[Jeshu the Nazarene] a revolutionary**, had aught in his favour?" He was a deceiver, and the Merciful hath said (Deut. 13:8), *Thou shalt not spare, neither shalt thou conceal him.* But it was different with **[Jeshu the Nazarene]**, for he was near to the kingdom. [*Herford translation*]

---

gaonic period the Talmud text was only on rare occasions read in the academies from a book, but for the most part it was recited from memory by those expert in traditional lore. As early an authority as Saadia occasionally expresses doubt concerning the correct reading. At the time of the Gaon Hai (died 1038) students in Babylonia itself were uncertain as to the authentic version in many a passage. As a matter of fact the Geonim frequently say in their answers that the questions rest upon a text which diverges from the one in vogue in Babylonia.[7-24]

That this passage originally had nothing to do with Jesus has been pointed out previously. The evidence for my claim consists of two similar passages where the person hanged on the eve of Passover is ben Stada, not Yeshu. The first passage appears farther on in the same Bavli tractate as the present citation – in b. *Sanh.* 67ª:

> **b. Sanh. 67ª:** "And they bring him to the Beth Din and stone him; and thus they did to **Ben Stada** in Lûd, and they **hung him on the eve of Pesaḥ.**"

This is more than reinforced by the more weighty, earlier notice in the Tosefta:

> **t. Sanh. 10:11:** "And thus they did to **Ben Stada** in Lûd,... and they brought him to the Beth Din and **stoned him.**"

We can be quite confident that if we could find eighth-century manuscripts of Bavli *Sanhedrin*, the equivalent of page 43ª would talk about ben Stada, not Yeshu ha-Notzri.

It is sometimes argued that the cryptic expression *he was near to the kingdom* is a reference to Jesus' claim of Davidic descent. Unfortunately, the government at the time when Jesus should have lived did not belong to the Davidic dynasty. The comment does, however, seem to presage the theme in the *Toldoth Yeshu* that Yeshu enjoyed some special relationship with Alexander Jannaeus' Queen Salome (Alexandra). This will be discussed in the last part of this book.

7.9. Disciples of Jesus (not *ha-Notzri*)

Even the Christians had a hard time getting straight just how many disciples or apostles Jesus *really* had, and even more trouble agreeing upon their names. [*See box "Disciples and Apostles: How Many and Who?", pp. 258–259*] Tradition held that there had been the astrological number twelve – one for each of the zodiacal twelve tribes of Israel. In practice, however, they named from three to thirteen of them, with only 'Matthew' specifying exactly twelve. It should not be surprising, therefore, to discover that the Talmud mentions a certain Jesus who had but five disciples. To be sure, the Talmud Jesus is not clearly identified as

Jesus the Nazarene [*Yeshu ha-Notzri*].* Nevertheless, many scholars have been unable to imagine that over the course of five centuries there could have been more than one disciple-possessing man named Jesus, and so they have supposed the Talmud is referring to none other than the putative founder of Christianity. Given the lateness of the text, of course, it is not impossible that they are right. It is quite possible that the rabbis had tapped into a folklore tradition that dated back to a period before the Christians had settled upon the astrologically necessary number of attendants for their solar surrogate deity.

The 'fact' that Jesus had five disciples – all of them executed at the same time – is found in the Bavli's tractate *Sanhedrin* immediately after the passage stating that Jesus had been hanged on the eve of Passover:

> **b. *Sanh.* 43ª: Our Rabbis have taught, Jesus had five disciples—Matthai, Neqai, Netzer, Buni, and Thodah.** They brought Matthai [before the judges]. He said, "Must Matthai be killed? For it is written [Ps. 42:2]: *Mathai* [=when] *shall* (I) *come and appear before God.*" They said to him, "Yes, Matthai must be killed, for it is written [Ps. 41:5]: *Mathai* [=when] *shall* (he) *die and his name perish.*" They brought Neqai. He said to them, "Must Neqai be killed? For it is written [Ex. 23:7]: *The Naqi* [=innocent] *and the righteous thou shalt not slay.*" They said to him, "Yes, Neqai must be killed, for it is written [Ps. 10:8]: In secret places doth he slay Naqi [=the innocent]." They brought Netzer. He said, "Must Netzer be killed? For it is written [Isa. 11:1] *Netzer* [=a branch] *shall spring up from his roots.*" They said to him, "Yes, Netzer must be killed. For it is written [Isa. 14:19]: *Thou art cast forth out of thy grave like an abominable Netzer* [=branch]." They brought Buni. He said to them, "Must Buni be killed? For it is written [Ex. 4:22]: *B'ni* [=my son], *my first born, Israel.*" They said to him, "Yes, Buni must be killed. For it is written [Ex. 4:23]: *Behold, I slay Bincha* [=thy son] *thy first born.*" They brought Thodah. He said to them,

---

*The passage in b. *Sanh.* 43ª that mentions that "Jesus had five disciples" follows immediately after the passage we have already discussed that said that "On the eve of the Passover Yeshu was hanged." Only in the Munich MS is Jesus identified as *ha-Notzri* – 'the Nazarene.' In all other texts we deal simply with *Yeshu*.

"Must Thodah be killed? For it is written [Ps. 100:1]: A Psalm for Thodah [=thanksgiving]." They said to him, "Yes, Thodah must be killed, for it is written [Ps. 50:23]: *Whoso sacrificeth Thodah* [=thanksgiving] *honoureth me*." [*Herford translation*]⁷⁻²⁵

Scholars who believe that Jesus had twelve disciples bearing any of the various names listed in the box on the next page have tried to equate the names above to those given in the Gospels. Herford reviewed these efforts and concluded that only *Matthai* bore any significant resemblance to any name in the lists of 'the Twelve'. The last, *Thodah*, superficially resembles *Thaddæus*, but that would be *Thaddai* in Hebrew, not *Thodah*. *Naqi, Netzer*, and *Buni* have no parallels among the twelve, and Herford doubted that they were real names at all – suggesting that they were made up for use in the word play of the Talmud passage. He did note, however, that there is a story in b. *Ta'an*. 19ᵇ, 20ᵃ about a certain Naqdimon b. Gorion whose real name was actually Buni. *Naqdimon* is the equivalent of *Nicodemus*, and Herford allowed this just might be an allusion to the Nicodemus "who came to Jesus by night" [John 3:1].⁷⁻²⁶

Herford admitted that a scene such as described could never have taken place, whether in a Roman or Jewish court, and concluded that it was a satire of a proceeding in a Jewish court in which five Christians ('disciples,' but not 'Disciples') were put to death.⁷⁻²⁷ He thought it possible it reflected a Jewish persecution of Christians during the Bar Kozeba revolt [132–135 CE].* This might be true, but the possibility cannot be ruled out that that these names derive from the period in the first century when the names and numbers of the Apostles/disciples were still quickening in the womb of folkloric fabrication.

Whatever may be the truth concerning this last point, I think for once Herford was probably correct – at least in his general conclusion that the event described took place long after the time implied by the New Testament stories as the period in which *the* disciples or Apostles would have been active. Hence, I would conclude that the Bavli knows nothing about any of 'the Twelve.'

---

*Justin Martyr, in chapter 31 of his first apology, claims that Christians had been persecuted by Bar Kozeba during his revolt of then-recent memory. "Barchochebas, the leader of the revolt of the Jews, gave orders that Christians alone should be led to cruel punishments, unless they would deny Jesus Christ and utter blasphemy."⁷⁻²⁸

Disciples and Apostles:

The canonical New Testament, the apocryphal New Testament, and Jewish sources give names to the followers of Jesus, and many assert that those persons constituted a group known as "the Twelve." Nevertheless, only the gospel of Matthew gives exactly twelve names. As shown below, named members of the Twelve ranged in number from three to thirteen, depending upon the source.

The Thirteen Disciples or Apostles in Mark [2:14 and 3:14*ff*]

Simon, renamed Peter	Philip
James, son of Zebedee	Bartholomew
John, son of Zebedee	Matthew
Andrew	Thomas
Simon the Canaanite	James, son of Alphæus
Judas Iscariot	

Thaddæus, or Lebbæus, or Daddæus (MSS disagree on the name)
Levi, son of Alphæus, a tax gatherer

The Thirteen Disciples-Apostles in Luke [5:27*ff* and 6:12*ff*]

Simon, given the name of Peter	Andrew
Philip	John
James	Bartholomew, or Martholomew
Matthew	Thomas, or Thomas the Twin
James, son of Alphæus	Simon, called the Zealot
Judas, son of James	Judas Iscariot

Levi, or Levi son of Alphæus, a tax gatherer

The Seven to Nine Disciples in John [1:40, 1:42, 1:44ff, 6:71, 11:16, 12:22, 20:2]

Philip	Nathanael
Thomas the Twin	Judas *not* Iscariot

Andrew (brother of Simon Peter) and an unnamed other
Simon, son of John (or Jonah), to be called Cephas (interpreted "the Rock") (MSS disagree on Simon's father)
Judas son of Simon Iscariot (or Simon from Karyot) (MSS disagree on the name)
"The other disciple, the one whom Jesus loved."

How Many and Who?

The Four or Five Disciples in Thomas [Prologue, 13:2–4, 21:1, 61:2–4]

Didymos Judas Thomas
Simon Peter
Matthew

Mary (not certainly a disciple)
Salome

The Five Disciples in the Babylonian Talmud [*Sanhedrin* 43ª]

Matthai
Naqai
Netzer

Buni
Thoda

The Twelve Apostles in Matthew [10:2]

Simon, called Peter
Andrew
James, son of Zebedee
John, son of Zebedee
Philip
Bartholomew

Thomas
Matthew, the tax gatherer
Simon the Canaanite
Judas Iscariot
·James, son of Alphæus

Lebbæus, or Lebeus, or Thaddæus, or Lebbæus surnamed Thaddæus, or Thaddæus surnamed Lebbæus (MSS disagree on the name)

The Seven Disciples in the Gospel of the Ebionites [Epiphanius *Adversus Hæreses* I 30:13]

Simon, surnamed Peter
John, son of Zebedee
James, son of Zebedee
Andrew
Thaddeus
Simon the Zealot
Judas Iscariot

Three Disciples Remaining in the Gospel of Peter [14:1–3]

Simon Peter
Andrew
Levi, son of Alphæus

I have previously expressed the opinion that if Jesus had been an historical figure who had done anything at all significant, he should have been remembered by the Jews – even if pagan writers might not have noticed him. *A fortiori*, the Jews should have preserved vivid memories of the Apostles. After all, unlike the total failure that was their supposed master, the Apostles packed more than twelve times his punch and were, according to Acts and early church traditions, resounding successes. How could their rabble-rousing have gone unnoticed? The fact that not even *one* of the twelve was noticed by the Jews is thus a more powerful argument against their historicity than is the case that has been assembled against the historicity of Jesus.

Clearly, the twelve disciples and the twelve Apostles of whom the gospels speak are theological fictions. Judas, for example, is a transparent invention of evangelists who wanted to blame the Jews for the judicial murder of their Messiah. *Judas*, after all, simply means *Jew*. It is altogether likely that there once existed an astrologically oriented proto-Christian cult that was governed by a board of twelve directors who bore the title of 'Pillar' or 'Apostle' or 'Brother of the Lord/Yahweh.' The twelve disciples then would have been made up as part of a foundation myth which, by tracing the board of directors back to Jesus himself, could be used to justify its authority and command obedience from the faithful. Deception not only advanced Christianity, it helped create it.

7.10. Conclusion

With this examination of the Babylonian Talmud, we now have completed our examination of the rabbinical literature as it has been alleged to pertain to Jesus of Nazareth. Nowhere, except in the latest literature, have we found explicit mention of Yeshu ha-Notzri – Jesus the Nazarene. Nowhere, except in the latest literature, have we found any of the alleged nicknames of Jesus equated to the alleged Galilean even by implication. By quite independent investigations, I have come to the same conclusion as did Louis Ginzberg, arguably the greatest Judaica scholar of the first quarter of the twentieth century. Coming across his essay on this subject only after I had nearly completed this book, I was delighted to read his critique of the *ben Stada* = *Jesus* equation. Even though he accepts at face value the identity and implied date of the Babylonian author of the claim, he concurs with my conclusion that Ben Stada enters the rabbinical literature as a character completely unrelated to Jesus:

> A Babylonian Amora in the second half of the third century [*I would place the actual author one or two centuries later*], who very likely never in his life saw a Christian nor knew anything about Christianity had the ingenuity to find in בן סטדא [*ben Stada*] – a sorcerer mentioned in the Tannaitic source, Tosefta Shabbat, XI, 15 – a nickname for Jesus. The identification is not only without any sound basis, but hardly possible, as has been conclusively shown by Derenbourg, *Essai*, 460 seq. and especially Chajes in the Hebrew periodical, *Ha-Goren*, IV, 33–37.[7-29]

Scoffing at the various attempts to find yet other nicknames of Jesus – or even of his disciples, such as I have criticized in my examination of the Balaam tradition – Ginzberg explains the situation with apparent amusement:

> The hunt for nicknames, however, continues merrily and soberminded scholars speak seriously of Balaam, Doeg, Ahitophel, and Gehazi as being the nicknames which the Mishnah Sanhedrin, X,1, uses for Jesus and three of his disciples. If these scholars were consistent they ought to try to identify the three kings – Jeroboam, Ahab, and Manasseh – with three Christian emperors, since the four "private persons" mentioned and the "three kings" are said in the Mishnah to form one class of grave sinners. What a pity that there were no Christian emperors at the time of the Mishnah! Numerous legends concerning these seven sinners are given in both Talmuds in connection with the statement of the Mishnah concerning them, and *these legends can by no stretch of imagination be made to apply to other persons than to those who bear these names in the Bible*. They show not only how the Amoraim understood this statement of the Mishnah, but also how much the lives of these Biblical persons occupied the fancy of the Jewish people. *One may therefore state with absolute certainty that the entire Talmudic-Midrashic literature does not know of any nicknames for Jesus or his disciples*. [*emphasis added*][7-30]

The explicit notices of Jesus the Nazarene – even if they are not late alterations of the Talmud texts – are still much too late to be evidence of any historical Jesus. This is because the Talmudic attributions of their authorship cannot be proved and thus cannot be trusted any more than the numerous sayings for which the Talmud provides multiple – that is, contradictory – attributions. When the Talmud tells us that Rabbi X said such-and-such about Jesus (or about anything at all), we cannot consult a rabbinical biochronology that says that Rabbi X died in the year 110 CE and then conclude that such-and-such was an opinion about Jesus current as early as 110 CE. Still less can we suppose that such-and-such is a *fact* about Jesus known at that time. The manuscript evidence for the Babylonian Talmud is so late that we generally have no idea at all how early – or how late – any given piece of the text came to occupy its present position. The documents of the rabbinical literature are extremely difficult, if not impossible, to date.

Jacob Neusner has criticized the traditional approach to dating these documents so convincingly that it now seems completely out of the question to rely on them for historical reconstructions of anything:

> The established protocol for dating a document rests on the premise that statements attributed to a given rabbi really were said by a historical figure, at a determinate time, and so permit us to date the document at the time of, or just after, that figure... But that date then presupposes the reliability of attributions and does not take account of pseudepigraphy in the rabbinic manner. The same sayings may be assigned to two or more authorities; the Talmud of Babylonia, moreover, presents ample evidence that people played fast and loose with attributions, changing, by reason of the requirements of logic, what a given authority is alleged to have said, for instance. Since we have ample evidence that in later times people made up sayings and put them into the mouths of earlier authorities (the Zohar is only the best-known example!), we have no reason to assign a document solely by reference to the names of the authorities found therein.[7-31]

All previous attempts to find traces of the historical Jesus in rabbinical sources have, I maintain, employed a faulty method-ology. All have retrojected the usage and interpretations of late (or even modern) documents into ancient texts. If *so-and-so* means *Jesus* in documents produced in the Warsaw Ghetto, *so-and-so* must mean *Jesus* in the sixth-century Babylonian Talmud. If that is its meaning in the Talmud, it must also mean the same thing in the third-century Mishnah. It is hard to believe that even famous scholars have practiced so illogical a method for so long, yet it seems to me that is the bald truth of the matter. In this book

I have tried hard not to commit such methodological errors. Starting with the Mishnah, I have tried to infer meanings of names and terms only from the evidence of a given text itself and not allow foreknowledge of later meanings to distort my perception of the earlier text. At each text-evolutionary stage in my progress through the literature, I have attempted to discover if any terms have undergone changes in signification.

Application of such a method has demonstrated, I think, that only the latest documents make any mention of Jesus and any information contained in those documents most certainly must have been obtained from Christians, not from Christ. The earliest document of the rabbinical tradition, the Mishnah, betrays not even a false knowledge of Jesus. It is absolutely silent in his regard. Moreover, given the generally accepted fact that the Mishnah was closed around the year 220 CE – when Christianity was a rapidly spreading nuisance – even if it did mention Jesus, its testimony would be of doubtful significance. As we proceed to progressively later works such as the Tosefta, the Yerushalmi, or the Bavli – with Christian missionaries and polemicists becoming ever more ubiquitous and persistent – the biographical value of even certifiable references to Jesus diminishes exponentially. The probability that putative biographical information was obtained from Christians approaches certainty; the probability that it was obtained from Jesus Christ approaches nullity.

A century ago, as R. Travers Herford approached the end of his *Christianity in Talmud and Midrash*, he almost lamented the sparseness of the results of his search for the historical Jesus in the rabbinical literature. Despite the Herculean labor expended and the advantage of the faulty text-historical method that he employed, he was able to turn up precious little – in fact, nothing! – pertaining to any historical Jesus. His summation of the results of his quest is almost painful to read:

> As to the historical value of the Jesus-Tradition in the Rabbinical literature, little need be said. It will have become evident, both from the consideration of the several passages in the earlier part of the book and from the analysis of them just made, that they add nothing new to the authentic history of Jesus, as contained in the Gospels. In general, though not in detail, they serve to confirm the Christian tradition, by giving independent, and indeed hostile, evidence that Jesus of Nazareth really existed, a fact which has by some been called in question. But if, beyond this, the Rabbinical Jesus-Tradition has no value

for the history of Christianity, it does throw some light upon the attitude of Judaism, as represented by the Rabbis, towards Jesus. It shows how the violent hostility directed against him during his life left only the vague and careless memory of a deceiver and an apostate. Of the great personality of Jesus not a trace remains, no sign of recognition that the 'Sinner of Israel' had been a mighty man. His birth, which Christian devotion had transfigured into a miracle, Jewish contempt blackened into a disgrace; and his death, which has been made the central point of Christian theology, was dismissed as the mere execution of a pernicious criminal. Judaism went on its way, but little troubled in mind at the thought of the man whom it had cast out.[7-32]

Of course, the true situation is even worse than Herford supposed, for even the imagined "hostile evidence that Jesus of Nazareth really existed" I trust has been shown in this book to be nothing of the kind. I hope I have been able to demonstrate convincingly that such references to Jesus as may reasonably be considered authentic are far too late to be of evidence for even the biological existence of a Nazarene Messiah.

Apologists for the historical Jesus have never been able to demonstrate convincingly that non-Christian attestations to the life of Christ are anything more than hearsay obtained from Christians. Lamentably few of them seem even to be aware of the fact that they need to do so. Worse yet, they cite Christian scriptures and the Church Fathers as though such sources can be considered serious historical evidence. One might as well have asked an ancient Egyptian if Isis and Osiris exist and have done anything significant! It is doubtful that the defenders of the historical faith would be much impressed by a Hindu's citation of the *Bhagavad-gita* as evidence of Krishna's earthly career. It is equally doubtful that the Hindu – or any other person who is not a Christian – would be impressed by a Christian's quotation of the birth legends in Matthew, Luke, or the infancy gospel. The reason historical Jesus advocates have been unable to show that non-Christian attestations are not just recycled Christian tittle-tattle seems glaringly obvious at this late date: they *are* recycled tittle-tattle. Those that are not forgeries, that is.

PART III

SEPHER TOLDOTH YESHU

CHAPTER 8

The *Toldoth Yeshu* as an Evolving Document

8.1. Introduction

After pursuing the elusive shade of Jesus through Jewish writings that are indisputably ancient, we come at last to the subject that triggered the writing of this book: the *Sepher Toldoth Yeshu*. My purpose in writing this book, as I have already explained, has been to see whether Jewish writings contain any credible evidence to show that the Jesus of Christian tradition once upon a time walked upon the soil of Palestine – breathing, sweating, metabolizing, eating, digesting, sleeping, shedding baby teeth, losing hair, and performing all bodily functions necessary to sustain a man of flesh, blood, and bones.

I hope I have been able to demonstrate to the reader's satisfaction that Jesus of Nazareth was unknown to ancient Jewish philosophers and historians, despite the Christian frauds that would make it appear that at least Josephus knew something about the failed messiah. Beyond this, I hope I have been able to show that the oldest rabbinical works – the Mishnah and Tosefta – make no veiled references to Jesus: Balaam was Balaam, not Jesus; Ben Panther and Ben Stada – whoever they might have been – originally had nothing to do with the Christ of Christianity. Only in the Babylonian Talmud, the latest of the major rabbinical writings, do we find unambiguous references to Jesus. The Bavli, alas, is much too late to be credible as historical evidence of practically anything – least of all of the historicity of the characters whose evolutionary development culminated in the sixth-century Gemara of the Babylonian Talmud.

There remains the question of whether the *Toldoth Yeshu*, a work of disputed antiquity, can bear witness to an historical Jesus. It is the purpose of this final part of my book to explore this question. Before continuing to read further in part 3, however, readers are advised first to read the two appendices that provide two different versions of the *Toldoth Yeshu* along with explanatory notes that will provide a working knowledge of the problems I shall explore in this final part of *The Jesus The Jews Never Knew*.

8.1. A. A Christian Forgery?

Madalyn Murray O'Hair, in her introduction to the 1982 American Atheist Press edition of Foote and Wheeler's 1885 publication of the *Sepher Toldoth Yeshu* [See appendix A, page 353], noted that after she had broadcast a review of the work, the American Atheist Center was flooded with angry letters and telephone calls from Jewish listeners who denied that the *Toldoth* was a Jewish work at all, insisting that it was instead a medieval Christian forgery – a scurrilous scandal sheet concocted by Christian apologists for the purpose of inciting Christian laity and rulers to violence against the Jews. With little success, she argued that details of the Toldoth had been known to ancient fathers of the Christian Church, including such luminaries as Tertullian, Origen, and Jerome. Given the fraudulent foundations of the Great Church, however, it was not at all irrational or implausible to argue that even those pillars of piety had made up the stories in order to foment hatred against the Jews. The Christian forgery argument was strengthened even further by the fact that the first known citations and printed editions of the *Toldoth* had been published by Christians – and by polemicists at that. Thus, in the thirteenth century, a Spanish Dominican by the name of Raymund Martini published his *Pugio Fidei* ('Poniard of Faith'), which contained a lengthy extract of the *Toldoth* in a section titled "*Fabula de Christi Miraculis Judaica, id est Maligna*" ('Spiteful Jewish Story About the Miracles Of Christ'). Jewish critics could well be excused for doubting the authenticity of *that* work! A century later, Martini was followed by a Portuguese Carthusian named Porchetti de Salvaticis, who quoted the *Toldoth* in his suspiciously titled "*Victoria Porcheti adversus impios Hebræos*" ('Porcheti's Victory Over the Impious Jews'), which later was published by Justiniani in Paris in 1520.[8-1] What Jew would be willing to accept *that* as an honest and unbiased report? Moreover, could any Jew be blamed for harboring doubts when learning that that infamous anti-Semite Martin Luther had published a German version in 1566 – a diatribe entitled *Vom Schem Hamphoras und vom Geschlecht Christi* ('Concerning the Ineffable Name and the Genealogy of Christ')? One hardly needs to add the 1681 edition of the *Toldoth* published by Johannes Christophorus Wagenseil bearing the decidedly unfriendly title *Tela Ignea Satanæ. Hoc est: Arcani et horribiles Judæorum adversus Christum Deum, et Christianam Religionem Libri ANEKΔOTOY* ('Satan's Fiery Web. That is, Secret and Monstrous Unpublished Books of the Jews Against Christ the God and the Christian Religion').

Despite the reasonableness of the critics' argument, however, it could not be sustained. Beginning shortly after the publication of Foote and Wheeler's edition (appendix A in this book), the discovery of more manuscripts of the *Toldoth* in Jewish contexts, the publication of those texts by Jewish scholars, and the discovery that versions of the *Toldoth* were being printed by Jews and circulated amongst them well into the nineteenth century demonstrated beyond cavil that the *Toldoth* was not a Christian canard. Rather, it was a vibrant expression of the cultural resistance of a persecuted people. It was not a single falsified document, but rather a living tradition – a tradition flourishing in the age of printing and tracing back to an antiquity of uncertain depth.

In 1902, just seventeen years after the publication of Foote and Wheeler's *Toldoth*, Samuel Krauss published *Das Leben Jesu nach jüdischen Quellen* ('The Life of Jesus According to Jewish Sources')[8-2] which described twenty-three different manuscripts of the *Toldoth* which were written in Hebrew, Yiddish, and – most importantly – Aramaic. In fact, the twenty-third 'manuscript' was actually six Aramaic fragments discovered in the Cairo Genizah.* Finding *Toldoth* manuscripts in a genizah – as well as in such out-of-the-way places as the Yemen – quite conclusively established the *Toldoth* as authentically Jewish rather than as a Christian confection.

Krauss, incorporating the work of Bischoff, classified his twenty-three manuscripts into five typological families according

---

*Pious Jews cannot simply discard worn-out prayer books, Torah scrolls, or other literature of religious importance. Instead, such books are entombed in a storage room called a genizah. According to Louis Ginzberg,[8-3] the word derives from the Hebrew verb *ganaz*, and signifies *treasure house* or *hiding place*.

to what he considered their key features.[8-4] Almost seventy years later, when William Horbury was at Cambridge University writing his doctoral dissertation *A Critical Examination of the Toledoth Jeshu*,[8-5] the number of manuscripts known had risen to well over sixty-six, and a considerable number of printed versions had come to light. Horbury had to add a sixth typological family to accommodate a *Toldoth* tradition known only from quotations in ancient and medieval works. He also revealed that the languages of *Toldoth* transmission included also Ladino (used by Iberian Sephardic Jews), Arabic (written in Hebrew characters), and Judaeo-Persian.

Horbury amassed an immense amount of information relating to the *Toldoth Yeshu* and its history. Among the more amazing discoveries he reported was the work of the Swiss scholar J. de Menasce, who showed that a Persian Zoroastrian apologist in fifth-century Armenia had made use of the Pandera story in polemic battles with Christians.[8-6] De Menasce also documented further Zoroastrian use of the story in the ninth century. Horbury also drew attention to the work of E. Stauffer, who had collected references to *Toldoth* themes and had pointed out the affinity of the *Toldoth* with the seventh-century Chinese Nestorian life of Jesus.[8-7] Horbury did not say whether the evidence indicates that the *Toldoth Yeshu* drew from the Nestorians or the Nestorians drew from the *Toldoth*.

The lesson to be learned from the profusion of manuscripts, typological families, and printed editions that have come to light is that the *Toldoth Yeshu* is not *a* book. It is not even a group of closely related books. It is a literary movement – a movement that until merely a century or so ago was still living, mutating, and blossoming in ever greater elaboration. It was a tradition exercised in secret and called by a variety of names. In addition to the title *Sepher Toldoth Yeshu* ('Book of the Generations of Jesus'), it is known as *Toldoth Yeshu ha-Notzri* ('The Generations of Jesus the Nazarene'), *Ma'ase Yeshu ha-Notzri* ('History of Jesus the Nazarene'), *Ma'ase Thola'* ('History of the Hanged', termed a 'Sloughed-off Snake Skin' (*Jüdischer Abgestreiffter Schlangenbalg*) by the early seventeenth-century converted Jew Samuel Friedrich Brenz, and *Tam u-Mu'ad* (untranslatable, but functionally equivalent to 'the *real* story'). Günter Schlichting, in his *Ein jüdisches Leben Jesu*,[8-8] analyzed a modern printed version of *Tam u-Mu'ad* into 366 elements. So great is the evolutionary variability of the texts, however, that of those 366 elements, only

154 are to be found in the Strassburg manuscript that is reprinted as Appendix B in this book.

Because of the ever-present danger of Christian persecution, *the Toldoth Yeshu* generally was circulated in secret among the Jews. Samuel Krauss, in his *Life of Jesus According to Jewish Sources,*[8-9] published a Hebrew note that he found hidden away in the middle of the text of two *Toldoth* manuscripts, that he classified as being of "Slavic type" (Σ and σ). The note poignantly describes the conditions under which the *Toldoth* struggled to survive:

> This booklet is a tradition [handed down] man to man; one may only copy it [by hand], not however have it printed. The wise at such times will see it, but keep silent, for it is an evil time. He must keep silent, a consequence of the long and bitter exile. One reads it, God forbid, not openly or before young girls and before the frivolous, still less in front of Christians who understand German, [then] will he [the reader] receive his wages and his deed precede him, for it is strongly prohibited to publish it, rather one discloses it only to the initiated, for you cannot know what the day shall bring forth, and behold, even his saints trusts he not, *etc.* I have copied it from three booklets which do not come from the same country but nevertheless agree with each other. I simply wrote it in the language of the wise [Hebrew] for he has chosen us from all the nations and has given us the language of the wise... [*my translation*]

While the *Toldoth Yeshu* in modern and late medieval times was transmitted and elaborated in a Jewish underground that had ever to be vigilant lest its discovery by Christians set loose persecutions or pogroms,* it does not appear that that was always the case. As we shall see, there is evidence that the *Toldoth Yeshu*

---

*Of course, this only was true for Jews living in territories under Christian control. It did not apply to Jews living under Islamic rule. Moses Maimonides [1135–1204], for example, was a Jewish philosopher who was born in Cordoba, Spain, under Moorish rule and settled in Cairo, where he became physician to the sultan of Egypt, Saladin. He appears to have known the *Toldoth* pericope where Jesus objects to being called a bastard (a *mamzer bar niddah*, a son of a menstruating woman) after learning of accounts that his mother had committed fornication with a Gentile – as is found in certain variant Toldoth manuscripts still extant. Writing in his *Epistle to Yemen*, Maimonides argued that Jesus was a Jew since his mother was a Jewess even though his father was a Gentile. It was mere hyperbole, he explained, to call Jesus a *mamzer*.[8-10]

– or at least its components – was known already in quite ancient times. It would seem that in these earlier periods, when Christianity did not yet wield sufficient power to persecute anyone and was instead itself the object of persecutions by the Romans, the *Toldoth Yeshu* (or at least its components) was a satirical, polemical tool employed in rabbinical Jewish controversies with messianic Jews who had adopted varieties of Christian beliefs.

8.1. B. Text Types

Whereas Krauss and Bischoff distinguished five types of Toldoth versions, and Horbury added a sixth category to accommodate materials known only from citations, the authority on ancient Jewish Christianity Hugh J. Schonfield argued in his *According to the Hebrews* that there are really only two types of text: the *Toldoth Proper*, which he conceived as a Hebrew document with some Aramaisms, and a form that he calls the *Toldoth Katon* [Hebrew *qaṭan* small], or *Toldoth Minor*, which he believed to be a shorter and later (seventh or eighth century) Aramaic document.[8-11]

The *Toldoth Proper* is represented by the sort of texts I have reprinted in appendices A and B. The *Toldoth Minor* Schonfield identifies with the fragments from the Cairo Genizah and the references in Agobard of Lyons. Both text types appear to have been known to the fourteenth-century Jewish polemicist Shemtob ibn Shaprut of Spain. In his *Eben Buchen* ('The Touchstone'), he published a Hebrew version of the Gospel of Matthew and presented a brief outline of both *Toldoth* text types. Shemtob tells us that

> Behold, ye find among them [the Jews] many books that treat of them [the miracles and wonders of Jesus]; for instance the work which was composed as a History of Jesus the Nazarene, and took place in the time of Queen Helene, and again the work composed in the Jerusalem dialect as an account of Jesus bar Pandera, which gives the time as that of Tiberius Cæsar." [*Schonfield translation*] [8-12]

The first document mentioned, which places Jesus approximately a century BCE, is the *Toldoth Proper*. The second, which adopts the chronology of the canonical gospels, is the *Toldoth Minor,* according to Schonfield's reckoning.

8.1. C. The *Toldoth Minor*

The two major witnesses to this text type are Shemtob ibn Shaprut and Agobard, Archbishop of Lyons. (The fragments from the Cairo Genizah contain too little text to be instructive.) The text according to Shemtob, as translated by Hugh J. Schonfield, reads as follows:

There came Pilate the governor, and Rabbi Joshua ben Perachiah, and Marinus the patriarch of the Jews, and Rabbi Judah Ganiba, and Rabbi Jochanan ben Mutana, and Jesus ben Pandera to Tiberias before Tiberius Cæsar. He said to them, What is your business? (Jesus) saith unto him, I am the son of God; I wound and I heal, and when one dieth, I whisper to him, and he lives; and a woman that is childless I make to conceive without a male. He (Tiberius) said unto them, In this will I prove [*test*] you. Come, I have a daughter who hath not seen a man; make it that she conceive. They say unto him, Have her brought before us. He commanded the steward to have her brought. Then they whispered to her, and she conceived.

Now when the proclamation went forth concerning Jesus, his sentence was determined that he should be crucified, and he saw the cross at the fourth hour of the day. He spake words of magic, and flew and alighted on Mount Carmel. Then said Rabbi Judah Ganiba to Rabbi Joshua ben Perachia, I will go and fetch him. To whom he answered, Go, and make mention and pronounce the name of his Lord, that is to say the Ineffable Name. So he went and flew to fetch him. When he was about to seize him, Jesus spake words of magic and went into the cave of Elijah, and shut the door. Then came Rabbi Judah Ganiba [*Krauss' text reads 'Judah the gardener'*], and said to the cave, Open, for I am the messenger of God! It opened. Jesus thereupon took the form of a cock. Rabbi Judah seized him by the border of his sindon, and came before Rabbi Joshua and his fellows. [*Schonfield translation*] [8-13]

The text according to Archbishop Agobard, as translated by G. R. S. Mead, is as follows:

For in the teachings of their elders they (the Jews) read: That Jesus was a youth held in esteem among them, who had for his teacher John the Baptist; that he had very many disciples, to one of whom he gave the name Cephas, that is Petra (Rock), because of the hardness and dullness of his understanding; that when the people were waiting for him on the feast-day, some of the youths of his company ran to meet him, crying unto him out of honour and respect, 'Hosanna, son of David;' that at last been accused on many lying charges, he was cast into prison by the decree of Tiberius, because he had made his (Tiberius') daughter (to whom he had promised the birth of a male child without [contact with] a man) conceive of a stone; that for this cause also he was hanged on a stake as an abominable sorcerer; whereon being smitten on the head with a rock and in this way slain, he was buried by a canal, and handed over to a certain Jew to guard; by night, however, he was carried away by a sudden overflowing of the canal, and though he was sought for twelve moons by the order of Pilate, he could never be found; that then Pilate made the following legal proclamation unto them: "It is manifest," said he, "that he has risen, as he promised, he who for envy was put to death by you, and neither in the grave nor in any other place is he found; for this cause, therefore, I decree that ye worship him; and he who will not do so, let him know that his lot will be in hell (*in inferno*)."

Now all these things their elders have so garbled, and they themselves read them over and over again with such foolish stubbornness, that by such fictions the whole truth of the virtue and passion of Christ is made void, as though worship should not be shown Him as truly God, but is paid Him only because of the law of Pilate. [8-14]

8.1. D. Reconstructing the Ur-text

When was the *Toldoth Yeshu* written and what were its original contents? A hint of the answer to the first part of this question might be provided by the earliest citations of elements peculiar to the *Toldoth Yeshu*, especially any that are not also found in the main rabbinical literature such as we have examined in part 2 of this book. The problem would be, of course, to see if in fact there *are* any elements of the *Toldoth* that are not found in the rabbinical literature or could not convincingly be seen as natural outgrowths of that literature. In excluding the Talmudic elements, however, should we exclude only those that are obviously quoted *verbatim* in the *Toldoth*, or all which share motifs in common with the *Toldoth*? The fact that the *Toldoth* contains motifs found also in the Talmuds does not logically entail the conclusion that it borrowed them from the Talmuds. It is entirely possible that both Talmuds and *Toldoth* derive from a common pool of folk legends that possibly are very much older than either of them. Thus, pre-Talmudic notices of elements present in both Talmuds and *Toldoth* could logically be citations of the *Toldoth* (if in fact they are found in documents much older than the Talmuds) or might merely be reflections of the folklore out of which both the Talmuds and the *Toldoth* emerged.

Regarding the question of the probable contents of the original *Toldoth Yeshu* (the so-called Ur-text), answers are not readily evincible. We could start by removing from all the extant versions all the material that is obviously incompatible with an early date – references to and citations from the Talmud, for example. The confusion of St. Peter with St. Simon Stylites [387–459 CE], as another example, could not be part of a truly early *Toldoth Yeshu*. After eliminating all obviously late material, we might then try to reconstruct an ur-text by comparing the material remaining in the various versions, selecting those motifs that are common to all, and settling on that common content as the primal plot. Unfortunately, such a procedure would beg the question of antiquity. How do we know that the whole story (or stories!) was not made up *after* Nestorius, Stylites, and the close of the Talmud? The fact that certain manuscripts of the *Toldoth* exist which lack some of these elements normally is taken as evidence that such elements are additions to certain lines of text transmission.

Unfortunately, the apparent fact that the transmission history of the Toldoth has been quite erratic – periods of written transmission (sometimes amalgamating two or more text traditions) alternating with periods of oral transmission (in which omissions and additions could produce dramatically different texts)[8-15] has discovered evidence in a number of manuscripts that the copyist's error known as *homoeoteleuton* has affected the transmission of some text families. Homoeoteleuton is an error of deletion that results when two lines of text on a manuscript page end with the same word or letters and the copyist's eye skips to the second spot to continue copying – thus leaving out all the material that was present between the two similarly terminating lines.

It seems to me that efforts to reconstruct a *Toldoth* ur-text are nearly hopeless, leaving it an open question what plot elements should be considered diagnostic of the original document. About the best we can do is scour the ancient sources to find references to any motifs now found in the various *Toldoth Yeshu* versions and consider each separate case's value as a witness to the *Toldoth Yeshu* as a connected text as distinct from a swarm of disjoint elements.

Despite my skepticism on this subject, I would be remiss if I did not mention the reconstruction of the contents of the ur-text arrived at by William Horbury, arguably the world's foremost authority on the *Toldoth Yeshu*. In his doctoral dissertation on the *Toldoth*, he listed the various topics that he felt formed a part of the *Toldoth Yeshu* as he envisaged it at the end of the third century. In Horbury's view, the Aramaic versions of the *Toldoth* now extant, despite their lack of a birth narrative, are closest to the ur-*Toldoth*.[8-16]

In the ur-*Toldoth* as thus reconstructed, Yeshu was born a *mamzer*, but whether his father was Pandera or someone else, Horbury does not indicate. A period spent as a beggar was followed by a miracle-working career – the miracles being effected either by means of Egyptian magic or by means of the *shem* (the secret name *Yahweh*). Yeshu is expelled from the community and lives as a brigand. He issues false teachings, is arrested, escapes, is recaptured, and is executed jointly with John the Baptist! (Although neither of the *Toldoth* versions printed as appendices A and B contain this double death, it is found in Aramaic manuscripts.) He is executed as a criminal by the Jews. Horbury gives three possibilities for what the *Ur-Toldoth* may have said about what happened after the execution. (Perhaps as a slip, Horbury's table of reconstructed contents[8-17] lists these as "post-crucifixion" – despite the absence of convincingly ancient Jewish attestation of Yeshu having been crucified rather than stoned or hanged.) Either he resurrected himself by magic, his disciples stole his body, or various Jews disposed of his remains. In any case, the ur-*Toldoth* as reconstructed by Horbury ended with accounts of false teachings by Yeshu's disciples.

It is a pity that it does not seem possible to reconstruct what the ur-*Toldoth* taught about the date of Yeshu's birth. That it shared the Talmud's placement of Yeshu nearly a hundred years before Christ seems likely, although if (as I argue) the *Toldoth* originated at a time before late Pauline Christianity had created the canonical historical settings for the birth and death of Jesus, it might have placed him in an even more exotic period.

8.2. Knowledge of the *Toldoth Yeshu* as a Connected Work

It is necessary now to examine the historical evidence for the existence of the *Toldoth Yeshu* both as a connected work and as swarms of disparate elements that might be evidence of a connected work. As has already been noted, the *Toldoth Yeshu* as a connected text is known from the Middle Ages, the Reformation, and the Early Modern Period. It is almost certainly the same document as the *Mar Mar Jesu* that the antipope Benedict XIII condemned in a bull of 11 May 1451.[8-18] Full texts were published by Wagenseil in 1681 (*Tela Ignea Satanæ*) and Huldreich in 1705 (*Historia Jeschua Nazareni*). Before these were Luther's 1566 German translation of a lengthy *Toldoth* extract entitled *Vom Schem Hamphoras und vom Geschlecht Christi*. In the fourteenth century was Porchetti de Salvaticis' *Victoria Porcheti adversus impios Hebræos* (printed in 1520), which was derived from the thirteenth-century Latin translation in Raymund Martini's *Pugio Fidei*.

The earliest undisputed evidence of the *Toldoth Yeshu* as a connected text is in the *Epistola... De Judaicis Superstitionibus* ('Letter... Concerning the Superstitions of the Jews') which was written around the year 826 CE by Agobard, Archbishop of Lyons.[8-19] In this letter he summarizes a certain version of the *Toldoth Yeshu* and complains, "Now all these things their elders have so garbled, and they themselves read them over and over again with such foolish stubbornness, that by such fictions the whole truth of the virtue and passion of Christ is made void."[8-20]

A different form of the *Toldoth Yeshu* is referred to shortly after Agobard (c847 CE) by his successor at Lyons, Archbishop Amulo, in his *Epistola, seu Liber contra Judæos, ad Carolum Regem* ('Letter, or Book, Against the Jews to King Charles'). Schonfield gives a translation of a passage that clearly describes the *Toldoth* story:

> The Jews, he says – blaspheme because we believe in him whom the Law of God says was hanged on a tree and cursed by God: and that later on the same day on which he was hanged they ordered that he should be buried lest, if he remained yoked (*in patibulo*) overnight, he would pollute their land... And (they say) that on the demand and order of their teacher Joshua, they took him down hastily from the tree, and thrust him into a tomb

in a certain garden full of cabbages (*caulibus pleno*) so that their
land should not be contaminated... In their own language they
call him *Ussum* (*i.e., Yasham*) *Hamizri*, which is to say in Latin
Dissipator Ægyptius (the Egyptian Destroyer)... And they say
further, that by their elders, after he was taken down from the
tree, and thrust into a tomb, that all might know that he was
truly dead and not risen, he was taken out again from the tomb,
and dragged by a rope through the whole city; and for this reason
even to-day the tomb stands empty, a stony waste, full of refuse
which they are wont to throw there.[8-21]

Apart from these ninth-century references to the *Toldoth
Yeshu*, it is quite possible that actual manuscripts of the *Toldoth*
as old or older have been retrieved from the Cairo Genizah.
Unfortunately, no radiocarbon dates have been obtained for these
fragments, and I know of no paleographic or other datings of them
that can be considered authoritative.

CHAPTER 9

Toldoth Traces amongst the Church Fathers

9.1. Justin Martyr [*c*100-114–*c*165 CE]

Justin was born around 114 CE in Samaria at Flavia Neapolis (Nablus), the ancient Shechem. After having been a Stoic and a Platonist, he converted to Christianity at Ephesus around the year 130 – becoming thereafter a peripatetic defender of the faith. In Rome, some time between 150 and 160, he wrote an *Apologia* for Christianity addressed to the philosopher-emperor Marcus Aurelius. This was followed by a *Dialogue of Justin, Philosopher and Martyr, with Trypho, a Jew*, a defense of Christianity against Judaism. Schonfield cites a number of passages in Justin's *Dialogue* that he thinks are echoes either of the *Toldoth* or its template, the *Gospel According to the Hebrews*. The authorities that Justin used included the *Memoirs of the Apostles* (which probably were not our canonical gospels), the *Gospel of Peter*, and perhaps a Greek translation of the *Gospel According to the Hebrews*.

In two places, Justin mentions that the Jews sent out countermissionaries from Jerusalem to thwart the Christians:

> After you (Jews) had crucified him (Jesus)... when you knew that he had risen from the dead and ascended to heaven, as the prophets foretold he would, you not only did not repent of the wickedness which you had committed, but at that time you selected and sent out from Jerusalem chosen men through all the land to tell that the godless heresy of the Christians had sprung up, and to publish those things which all they who knew us not speak against us. ... Accordingly, you displayed great zeal in publishing throughout all the land the bitter and dark and unjust things against the only blameless and righteous Light sent by God. [*Dial.* xvii] [*Schonfield translation*] [9-1]

As I said before, you have sent chosen and ordained men throughout all the world to proclaim that a godless and lawless heresy had sprung from one Jesus, a Galilean deceiver, whom we crucified, but his disciples stole him by night from the tomb, where he was laid when unfastened from the cross, and now deceive men by asserting that he has risen from the dead and ascended to heaven. Moreover, you accuse him of having taught those godless, lawless, and unholy doctrines which you mention to the condemnation of those who confess him to be the Messiah, and a teacher from and son of God. [Dial. cviii] [*Schonfield translation*] 9-2

Quite surprisingly, Schonfield argued that Justin was mistaken in thinking that the Jews were sending out counter-missionaries. Rather, he claimed, it was the Christians who had sent out the missionaries, and Justin got things mixed up. That Justin could have mistaken stories about his own revered apostles – after consulting scripture that he himself called *Memoirs of the Apostles* – for accounts of counter-apostles sent out by theological opponents is simply inconceivable. The only reason I can think of for Schonfield making so startling a claim is that he was Jewish and somewhat hypersensitive to anything construable as anti-Semitism. (He claimed that the refusal of nearly all New Testament scholars to accept the 'fact' that Matthew had originally been composed in Hebrew or Aramaic rather than Greek was an example of "scholarly anti-Semitism.") Schonfield argued that Justin's account of the counter-missionaries was a distorted reference to the *Toldoth's* account of Jesus' disciples dispersing three-by-three:

Then fled his (twelve) disciples and dispersed themselves among the kingdoms; three of them to Mount Ararat; three of them to Armenia; and three to Rome; and the rest to other places, and they caused the people to err... And many of our own insurgents went astray after him (Jesus), and there was strife between them and the children of Israel. [*Schonfield translation*]9-3

It seems extremely far-fetched to me that Justin was reacting to the *Toldoth Yeshu* in the two passages quoted above. The mention of the argument that the disciples had stolen Jesus from the tomb seems much more a response to the claims in canonical

Matthew.* Crucifixion, rather than stoning or hanging, and the absence of watery burial, in fact, would seem to rule out a *Toldoth* connection.

Schonfield demonstrated quite convincingly that Justin knew and used the *Gospel According to the Hebrews*, the gospel presumably parodied by the *Toldoth Yeshu*. But that Justin knew of the *Toldoth* itself remains improbable and unproved.

9.2. Tertullian [c160–c220 CE]

Tertullian – more properly, Quintus Septimus Florens Tertullianus – was born in Roman Carthage some time around the middle of the second century CE, perhaps as late as the year 160. He is believed to have lived until about the year 220. Reared as a pagan in North Africa, he went to Rome as a lawyer and became a convert to Christianity shortly before the beginning of the third century. Returning to Carthage, he wrote numerous books that became the foundation of Latin Christianity. One of the earliest formulators of the Trinitarian dogma, Tertullian earned the undying contempt and disdain of Atheists and rationalists of all denominations for his abandonment of logic and

---

*Matthew 27:62-66 claims that "Now the next day, that followed the day of the preparation, the chief priests and Pharisees came together unto Pilate, Saying, 'Sir, we remember that that deceiver said, while he was yet alive, "After three days I will rise again." Command therefore that the sepulchre be made sure until the third day, lest his disciples come by night, and steal him away, and say unto the people, "He is risen from the dead": so the last error shall be worse than the first,' Pilate said unto them, 'Ye have your watch: go your way, make it as sure as ye can.' So they went, and made the sepulchre sure, sealing the stone, and setting a watch."

This clearly is a clumsy attempt – the guard isn't posted until Jesus would have lain unguarded in the tomb for one full night! – to undercut an actual argument being used by early rabbinical Jews. Having no actual knowledge of any historical Jesus or the circumstances surrounding his life or death, and being able only to draw logical inferences from the claims being bruited about by certain Jewish Christians, they would have argued quite plausibly that if Jesus' body was missing from the tomb, his disciples must have stolen it. It is entirely probable that such Jews would have sent out emissaries to the synagogues frequented by the heretics in order to refute their preposterous claims.

reason in defense of that indefensible dogma. *"Certum est, quia impossibile est,"* was his definitive statement on the question. Literally, the Latin means "It is certain because it is impossible," but it most often has been rendered "I believe it because it is impossible" – an irrationalization zealously indulged in by defenders of the Christian faith even yet today. Rhetorically violent and sarcastic, Tertullian found the Great Church not Christian enough for his puritanical personality, and so, around the year 207, he converted to Montanism – a mad *mélange* of Pentecostalism, Puritanism, Amish plain-folkism, Quakerism, and perhaps holy-rolling.

Tertullian's *De Spectaculis* was made infamous by Edward Gibbon's *Decline and Fall of the Roman Empire*, where Enlightenment light was focused on the church father's inhuman and inhumane personality. Ostensibly a diatribe against public shows (Latin *spectāculum*), it warns true believers that "The conditions of faith… take from us also the pleasures of the public shows" [*De Spec.* I]. Culminating with his description of what even the Ringling Brothers and P. T. Barnum might concede to be "The Greatest Show on Earth" – the Last Judgment – Tertullian's book ends with a description of the joy he will experience while witnessing the torment of his rationalist enemies. It is in this final blaze of rhetoric that Tertullian taunts his opponents with a sarcasm some scholars have seen as a rejoinder to either the *Toldoth Yeshu* or the unintegrated stories from which it was compiled.

> XXX. But what a spectacle is already at hand – the return of the Lord, now no object of doubt, now exalted, now triumphant! What exultation will that be of the angels, what glory that of the saints as they rise again! What the reign of the righteous thereafter! What a city, the New Jerusalem! Yes, and there are still to come other spectacles – that last, that eternal Day of Judgement, that Day which the Gentiles never believed would come, that Day they laughed at, when this old world and all its generations shall be consumed in one fire. How vast the spectacle that day, and how wide!
>
> What sight shall wake my wonder, what my laughter, my joy and exultation? as I see those kings, those great kings, welcomed (we were told) in heaven, along with Jove, along with those who told of their ascent, groaning in the depths of darkness! And the magistrates who persecuted the name of Jesus, liquefying in fiercer flames than they kindled in their rage against the

Christians! those sages, too, the philosophers blushing before their disciples as they blaze together, the disciples whom they taught that God was concerned with nothing, that men have no souls at all, or that what souls they have shall never return to their former bodies! And, then, the poets trembling before the judgement-seat, not of Rhadamanthus, not of Minos, but of Christ whom they never looked to see! And then there will be the tragic actors to be heard, more vocal in their own tragedy; and the players to be seen, lither of limb by far in the fire; and then the charioteer to watch, red all over in the wheel of flame; and, next, the athletes to be gazed upon, not in their gymnasiums but hurled in the fire – unless it be that not even then would I wish to see them, in my desire rather to turn an insatiable gaze on them who vented their rage and fury on the Lord.

"This is he," I shall say, "**the son of the carpenter or the harlot**, the Sabbath-breaker, the Samaritan, who had a devil. This is he whom you bought from Judas; this is he, who was struck with reed and fist, defiled with spittle, given gall and vinegar to drink. This is **he whom the disciples secretly stole away**, that it might be said he had risen – **unless it was the gardener who removed him, lest his lettuces should be trampled by the throng** of visitors!"

Such sights, such exultation – what prætor, consul, quæstor, priest, will ever give you of his bounty? And yet all these, in some sort, are ours, pictured through faith in the imagination of the spirit. But what are those things which eye hath not seen nor ear heard, nor ever entered into the heart of man? [I Cor 2:9] I believe, things of greater joy than circus, theatre or amphitheatre, or any stadium. [*T. R. Glover translation*] [9-4]

Allowing my readers a moment to recoil from this repelling recital of the core of that truest of Christian's credo, I must draw attention to the third paragraph, where Tertullian sarcastically refers to our Gentle Jesus by means of epithets presumably hurled at him by early critics of Christianity. Readers with even a casual knowledge of the New Testament will recognize that almost all the points of irony are derivable from the four gospels as we now have them. There are, however, two points that seem not derivable from the canonical accounts.

The first of these is the implied charge that Jesus was "the son of the harlot." It is immediately to be noted that there is nothing in our present New Testament indicating that anyone (*i.e.*, 'the Jews') ever accused Jesus of being a bastard or son of a harlot. Moreover, this is not the charge against him to be found in the *Toldoth*, where he is a *mamzer ben ha-niddah* – the son of a menstruating woman. Quite likely, it was an informal epithet coined by Jewish critics generally who could find no easier nor more natural counterblast to fire against the nativity myths current in the early Catholic Church. It does not, therefore, imply knowledge of the *Toldoth Yeshu* in coastal North Africa at the end of the second century.

The second passage not derivable from the official gospels, however, is one that grabs our attention both due to its oddness and due to its evocation of memories of certain versions of the *Toldoth Yeshu*. "This is he whom the disciples secretly stole away, that it might be said he had risen," we imagine Tertullian sneering, "*unless it was the gardener who removed him, lest his lettuces should be trampled by the throng of visitors!*"

Lettuces makes the botanically challenged majority of readers recall the cabbage stalk upon which Yeshu was hanged when no enchanted tree could support his body. The reference to throngs of visitors suggests the *Toldoth* comment that the disciples came to mourn over Yeshu's initial burial, which is placed in a garden in a number of manuscripts. Further connection to the *Toldoth* is seen in those manuscripts in which it is a gardener who does in fact steal and rebury Yeshu's body.

In the entire Christian bible – including all the Hebrew, Aramaic, and Greek texts of which it has been compiled – the word for *gardener* occurs only once, in John 20:15. *Gardener* is almost as difficult to find in the Good Book as the word *brain* – which is not to be found anywhere at all therein. In the verse cited, it is the resurrected Jesus who speaks to Mary: "Jesus saith unto her, 'Woman, why weepest thou? whom seekest thou?' She, supposing him to be the gardener, saith unto him, 'Sir, if thou have borne him hence, tell me where thou hast laid him, and I will take him away'."

In John, as in certain manuscripts of the *Toldoth*, Jesus/Yeshu is executed in a garden and buried there as well. (It is this account in John that has given rise to the legend of the garden tomb that has been advocated so earnestly on television 'history' channels by certain 'biblical scholars' as the authentic tomb of Christ.) Tertullian's gardener, however, could not be John's gardener, since his lettuces are lacking in the officially true story. Could he be the *Toldoth*'s gardener? The answer, I believe, is "yes – but…"

A single point of agreement, no matter how striking, is usually insufficient to prove the literary dependence of one text upon another. Rather, in this case, I would argue that Tertullian is a witness to the existence in the second century of a tradition of garden execution and burial more detailed than that in John, in which a gardener is a major actor in the plot. Perhaps present in the *Gospel According to the Hebrews*, this garden burial tale would easily lead to rebuttals and parodies such as we now find in *De Spectaculis* and in the *Toldoth*, respectively. If Jesus was said to have been buried in a garden and the gardener was identified in the story as a partisan of Jesus and his disciples, what response could be more natural than the charge that he had not risen from the dead but had, like a weed, been plucked out by the gardener? Such argumentation would easily have led to charges such as those to which we may imagine Tertullian was reacting. Just as easily, it could have been numbered among the motifs incorporated a century or so later into the *Toldoth Yeshu* as its earliest versions were being compiled.

9.3. Origen [*c*185–*c*254 CE]: The *Toldoth Yeshu* and the Jew of Celsus

It is not known when the last copy of the *True Discourse* was committed to the flames as a burnt offering to the erstwhile darkling deity now worshipped in broad daylight as 'the Gentle Jesus.' Written *c*178 CE by the Roman Platonist Celsus, it appears to have been a brilliant diatribe against both Christianity and Judaism. Fortunately for our investigation, neither of those religions was powerful enough to obliterate the book for several centuries, and at least one of the church fathers – Origen of Alexandria and Caesarea – made a desperate effort around the year 248 CE to refute him. Almost all of what we know of Celsus' treatise is derived from Origen's *Eight Books Against Celsus* – better known simply by its abbreviated Latin title *Contra Celsum*. That even this much has been saved for the delectation of modern freethinkers is little short of miraculous, considering the fact that even Origen himself came under suspicion of heresy and many of his own works have not survived – themselves perhaps having passed into oblivion through the same fires of faith that consumed the works of Celsus.

It was, perhaps, inevitable that Celsus' work would be proscribed and obliterated once Christianity had grown strong enough to do it, for even Origen seemed to sense that his massive attempt at refutation was less than secure and that awareness and knowledge of Celsus would have to be suppressed:

> And if you are not impressed by the powerful arguments which succeed, then... I refer you, if you still desire an argumentative solution of the objections of Celsus, to those men who are wiser than myself, and who are able by words and treatises to overthrow the charges which he brings against us. But better is the man who, although meeting with the work of Celsus, needs no answer to it at all, but who despises all its contents, since they are contemned, and with good reason, by every believer in Christ, through the Spirit that is in him. [9-5]

Then, as now, the philosophy of the ostrich was the one most highly valued and frequently employed among Christians whenever they were tossed in the turbulent tides of critical thought.

Among the rhetorical devices employed by Celsus is a Jew who addresses Jesus directly and advances arguments presumably given to Celsus by Jewish informants at a time when the oldest of the canonical gospels was yet less than a century old. It is this 'Jew of Celsus' in whom we seek to discover any possible awareness of the *Toldoth Yeshu* or of its model, the *Gospel According to the Hebrews*.

9.3. A. The Parentage of Jesus

Our investigation begins with two passages in which the Jew addresses Jesus concerning the circumstances of his birth and lineage – his *toldoth,* if we were to think of these things in Hebrew:

> ...in imitation of a rhetorician training a pupil, he [*Celsus*] introduces a Jew, who enters into a personal discussion with Jesus... For he represents him disputing with Jesus, and confuting Him, as he thinks, on many points; and in the first place, he accuses Him of having "invented his birth from a virgin," and upbraids Him with being "born in a certain Jewish village, of a **poor woman of the country, who gained her subsistence by spinning,** and **who was turned out of doors by her**

husband, a carpenter by trade, because she was convicted of adultery; that after being driven away by her husband, and wandering about for a time, she disgracefully gave birth to **Jesus, an illegitimate child, who having hired himself out as a servant in Egypt** on account of his poverty, and **having there acquired some miraculous powers**, on which the Egyptians greatly pride themselves, returned to his own country, highly elated on account of them, and by means of these **proclaimed himself a God.**" [*Contra Celsum* I:28] [9-6]

But let us now return to where the Jew is introduced, speaking of the mother of Jesus, and saying that "when she was pregnant **she was turned out of doors by the carpenter to whom she had been betrothed, as having been guilty of adultery,** and that **she bore a child to a certain soldier named Panthera**"; and let us see whether those who have blindly concocted these fables about **the adultery of the Virgin with Panthera, and her rejection by the carpenter**, did not invent these stories to overturn His miraculous conception by the Holy Ghost... [*Contra Celsum*, I:32] [9-7]

Is there any knowledge of the *Toldoth Yeshu* in these passages? We have already examined the second passage in relation to the Tosefta back in chapter 5. It is necessary now to reconsider it and the earlier passage in the light of the *Toldoth*.

Our attention is drawn first to the Jew's accusation that Jesus had "invented his birth from a virgin." Most versions of the *Toldoth*, of course, have Yeshu lay claim to a miraculous virgin birth – even misquoting Isaiah 7:14 in the same way as the final edition of Matthew 1:23 ("Behold, a virgin shall be with child, and shall bring forth a son, and they shall call his name Emmanuel..."). On the face of it, it would appear that Celsus is replying to canonical Matthew – which almost certainly existed in his day in all its mythological splendor. But could he instead have been responding to one of the Jewish gospels? It is known, for example, that not all the Ebionites rejected the virgin birth, despite Irenaeus' complaint [*Adv. Hær.* III 21.1; V 1.3] that they had mutilated the Gospel of Matthew by removing the virgin birth pericope.[9-8] According to Eusebius [*Historia Ecclesiastica*, III 27.1-3], there existed certain Ebionites who accepted the Gentile Christian notion that the Holy Ghost had impregnated a Jewish virgin.[9-9] Thus, it would also seem possible that Celsus was twitting a Jewish Christian gospel such as the *Gospel*

*According to the Hebrews.** But could he have been taking instructions from the *Toldoth Yeshu*?

According to the Jew of Celsus, the mother of Jesus "gained her subsistence by spinning" and "was turned out of doors by her husband, a carpenter by trade, because she was convicted of adultery." Neither the *Toldoth Yeshu* nor the rabbinical literature we have studied insinuates that the mother of Jesus earned a living by spinning, and of course the notion is unknown in the New Testament. In the *Protevangelium of James* [c150 CE], however, there is a story telling how the priests needed to produce a veil for the Temple of Yahweh and recruited a twelve-year-old virgin named Mary to spin the pure purple and the scarlet for the curtain. Mary, it turns out, has already been entrusted to the 'care' of an elderly man named Joseph as a result of a dove flying out of a magic wand given to him by a priest of Yahweh.[9-10] It is possible that Celsus knew of this newly minted gospel and gained his knowledge of the spinning Mary from it. Of course, this tale may already have been part of Judeo-Christian folk legend by the middle of the second century and may have found its way into other gospels as well – including one known to Celsus.

As for Mary's betrothed being a carpenter, we may recall that Matthew 13:55 inquires, "Is this not the carpenter's son?" whereas Mark 6:3, the source from which Matthew filched his text, asks "Is not this the carpenter, the son of Mary?" I do not know what theological forces directed the evolution of Jesus from being a carpenter into becoming the son of a carpenter,[†] but it would seem that Celsus had been informed of the later stage in the development of this part of the Jesus biography. In the *Infancy Gospel of*

---

*If the *Gospel According to the Hebrews* had a virgin-birth nativity pericope in it, it would have to have been later than the Gospel of Mark and the first edition of the Gospel of Matthew. In this case, the Jewish gospel would be even less useful than the canonical gospels for establishing the historicity of Jesus.

†There may be some echo here of the Gnostic voices that contributed to the chorus that came to be known as Christianity. To the Gnostics, the Demiurge – the arrogant but rather stupid deity (Yahweh) who had created the world – was simply a carpenter (Greek τέκτων, *tektōn*) who had cobbled together the seven or eight heavens and the earth. The same Greek word *tektōn* is used in Mark and Matthew to describe the profession of Jesus and Joseph, respectively.

*Thomas** also, the father of Jesus is said to be a carpenter, a maker of plows and yokes and beds.[9-11]

In addition to the fact that the *Toldoth Yeshu* knows nothing of Miriam spinning for a living and styles her betrothed a rabbinical student rather than a carpenter,[†] its description of the circumstances of Miriam's living arrangement could not be farther removed from that alleged by the Jew of Celsus. In the *Toldoth*, as in the canonical Matthew and Luke, she is not married but merely betrothed – although one infers that more-or-less full conjugal relations were being exercised by Miriam and Yohanan.[‡] Far from being thrown out of her husband's house, she is still living in her own house (or perhaps the home of her parents). Instead of Miriam being forced to wander about until she gives birth, it is Yohanan who leaves, fleeing to Babylon. Whereas the Jew of Celsus besmirches the character of the virgin – styling her as any common adulteress – the *Toldoth* story is actually very sympathetic to Miriam, going to some length to make her the unknowing – and therefore unwilling – victim of a lecherous man. The Miriam of the *Toldoth* can hardly be the nameless mother depicted by Celsus. Far more likely, the Jew of Celsus has created a counter-character derivable from canonical Matthew. In Matthew 1:18–19 we are told,

---

*The transmission and text history of this infancy gospel appears to be very similar to that of the *Toldoth Yeshu*. Containing elements going back to the second century, it would seem not to have been fixed in writing until the fifth century. Like the *Toldoth*, it survives in a bewildering variety of manuscript types and versions. Like the *Toldoth*, it is more literary movement than book. [9-12]

†A near exception to this generalization is the *Baghdad Toledoth*, in which Miriam's *husband* is Rabbi Yohanan and Joseph Pantera is "fair in appearance and fair to look on, a man evil in his deeds; and his work that of a carpenter of wood." [9-13]

‡ In fact, the same situation can easily be understood to exist in Luke, where the virginal birth of Jesus is not as explicit as commonly supposed. To begin with, there is the circumstance of which Joseph seems to be completely unaware, that the child to come is not his own, and he is still unmarried when he takes Mary to Bethlehem: "And so Joseph went up to Judaea from the town of Nazareth in Galilee, to register at the city of David, called Bethlehem, because he was of the house of David by descent; and with him went Mary who was betrothed to him. She was expecting a child, and while they were there the time

Matt 1:18–19: Now the birth of Jesus Christ was on this wise: When as his mother Mary was espoused to Joseph, before they came together, she was found with child of the Holy Ghost. Then Joseph her husband, being a just man, and not willing to make her a public example, was minded to put her away privily.

The comment that Joseph "was minded to put her away privily" seems a natural hint for a gossip to pursue. On the other hand, we know that canonical Matthew responded to Jewish criticisms elsewhere in his text – e.g., in his defense of the resurrection story where he has a guard placed at Jesus' tomb to prevent the theft of his body – and it is altogether likely that Jewish claims of Jesus' bastardy already existed at the time when the nativity tale was added to Matthew's gospel. We must keep in mind that Jewish claims of Jesus' illegitimacy arguably may go back to a period *preceding* the invention of his parthenogenetic

came for her baby to be born..." [Luke 2:4–6, NEB].

Joseph is not at all surprised or perplexed by Mary's pregnancy, and no explanation is offered concerning the sort of relationship their "betrothal" entailed. As far as we can tell from Luke's gospel, St. Joseph and St. Mary cohabited without benefit of clergy until the ends of their lives. Unlike the case in Matthew, no angel ever clues Joseph in on the divine nature of Mary's pregnancy, and there is no indication in Luke's story as it now stands to indicate that Mary ever did explain her condition to her fiancé or even so much as tell him about the famous 'Ave Maria' episode, where the angel Gabriel warns her privately that "The Holy Ghost shall come upon thee, and the power of the Highest shall overshadow thee: therefore also that holy thing which shall be born of thee shall be called the Son of God." [Luke 1:35]

Gabriel tells her further that her cousin Elizabeth is already six months pregnant (with John the Baptist). Without asking for leave of her fiancé or offering him any reason, Mary then leaves town and visits Elizabeth for three months! When she returns "to her own house" three months pregnant (she seems not yet to have moved in with Joseph), there is no indication that she explained her pregnancy to anyone. Everyone except Elizabeth in the story could only suppose that Mary and Joseph had been having preconjugal relations and that Mary had conceived before going on vacation to the unnamed town where Elizabeth lived.

It is obvious that both the *Ave Maria* scene and the *'Magnificat'* scene (where Mary launches into a hymn of praise concerning her exalted status as Handmaiden of the Lord) are later additions to the text of Luke, since later on both Mary and Joseph are repeatedly amazed at what the shepherds and Simeon of Jerusalem have to say

parturition. If, as seems almost certain, the Matthean genealogy 'proving' the Davidic ancestry of the would-be Messiah was created before the pagan-style nativity story was added, Jews who did not accept this newly created character as 'the Christ' – *i.e.*, as the Messiah – could simply have alleged his illegitimacy in order to break the genealogical chain being used to authenticate his theopolitical office. Indeed, when Justin Martyr's Jew Trypho charges that the Christians "have invented some sort of Christ for yourselves" [chapter 8], he may be attacking not the historicity of Jesus, but rather his genealogy as a legitimate Messiah.

Considering next the charge that the illegitimate Jesus worked in Egypt, learned magic, and returned proclaiming himself to be a god, I find a great similarity to the character Simon Magus of the Clementine literature, which we shall examine shortly. "During a stay in Egypt," says the *Clement Romance*, "he acquired a large measure of Greek culture and attained to an extensive knowledge of magic and ability in it. He then came

---

about their child: "The child's *father* and mother were full of wonder at what was being said about him" [Luke 2:33 NEB]. This is quite incompatible with either Mary or Joseph knowing anything about the visitation of the angel Gabriel. The casual reference to the "father and mother" of the child appears to be left over from a pre-parthenogenesis stage in the evolution of the text. As in the case of the flood legend in Genesis and numerous other biblical compositions, the nativity and infancy sections of Luke have been cobbled together quite clumsily.

It seems to me that the stories about the births of John the Baptist and Jesus originally had nothing to do with the virgin birth dogma. After all, the genealogy inserted at Luke 3:13*ff* traces the descent of Jesus *through Joseph* – just as does the otherwise almost completely contradictory genealogy found in the first chapter of Matthew. (Interestingly, the genealogy which begins that first book of the New Testament begins with the title "The book of the generation of Jesus Christ..." If one were to translate this into Hebrew, it would read "*Sepher Toldoth Yeshu...*") Rather than these nativities being created to establish the virginity of Mary, I would argue that they were created to serve the theopolitical purpose of subjecting the cult of the Baptist to the cult of the Christ, coopting a rival religion and causing it to serve a nascent Christianity. It is of interest to note that the astral origins of both John and Jesus are reflected in the careful arithmetic that is imbedded in these stories and causes John to be born exactly six months before Jesus. To this day, the nativity of Jesus is celebrated on the date of the winter solstice (according to the Julian calendar) and John the Baptist's feast day is celebrated on the old-style date of the summer solstice!

forward claiming to be accepted as a mighty power of the very God who has created the world. On occasion he sets himself up for the Messiah and describes himself as the Standing One." Both the magician Jesus of Celsus and the Clementine Simon also closely resemble the Ben Stada of the rabbinical literature that we have already examined, at which time I noted the close similarity between *ho Stadios* ('the Standing One') and *ben Stada* (of no certain meaning in Hebrew and possibly being a misreading of *sitra*, perhaps a term at one time meaning *schismatic* or *heretic*).

There remains to be considered the sole point of the Celsus quotation under consideration that actually does accord with the *Toldoth* account, *viz.*, the use of *Panthera* as the name of Jesus' actual father. Superficially, this would seem to be a striking concordance between the Jewish source used by Celsus and the *Toldoth Yeshu*. But we must remember that the name *Panthera* (or *Pandira*) is well established in the rabbinical literature from the Tosefta onwards. Moreover, Panthera is the only putative Jesus surrogate in the early rabbinical literature who bears the praenomen *Yeshua'*. While I have shown, I hope convincingly, that there is no good reason to associate the Yeshua' ben Pandira of the Tosefta with Jesus of Nazareth, it is altogether possible that Celsus (or his Jewish source) was familiar already at that early date with the Ben Pandira legends and, noting the equivalence of the common first name *Yeshua'* with the Greek name *Iesous* (Jesus), appropriated the Panther material for his critical purposes.

If, as I consider nearly certain, Celsus did not have knowledge of the *Toldoth Yeshu*, where did he get his ideas about the Jesus of the Christians? The great similarity of his Jesus to the Simon Magus of the Clementine literature and the Ben Stada and Ben Panther characters of the Tosefta leads me to conclude that all three characters derive from a common source. It is possible that that common source is the *Gospel According to the Hebrews* as argued by Hugh Schonfield, but I doubt that a single written source can account for all the data. More likely, I suggest, all three (along with the Jesus of the Christians) derive from a common pool of interacting oral traditions tracing back perhaps as far as the time of Alexander Jannaeus – a century before the time designated by orthodox Christian tradition as the birth date of its god-man.

9.3. B. The Miracles of Jesus

There are other passages in *Contra Celsum* that Schonfield believed reflected knowledge of motifs found in the *Toldoth*, presumably known to Celsus from the putative source of the *Toldoth*, the *Gospel According to the Hebrews*. The first one I should like to examine deals with the miracles Jesus is alleged to have worked:

The old mythological fables, which attributed a divine origin to Perseus, and Amphion, and Æcus, and Minos... represented the deeds of these personages as great and wonderful, and truly beyond the power of man; but what have you [*Jesus*] done that is noble or wonderful either in deed or in word? You have made no manifestation to us, although they challenged you in the temple to exhibit some unmistakable sign that you were the son of God. (But after this, Celsus... affects to grant that those statements may be true which are made regarding his cures, or his resurrection, or the feeding of a multitude with a few loaves... and he adds): Well, let us believe that these were actually wrought by you. But what are they more than the tricks of jugglers, who profess to do even more wonderful things, or the feats performed by those who have been taught by Egyptians, who in the middle of the market-place, in return for a few obols, will impart the knowledge of their most venerated arts, and will expel demons from men, dispel diseases, invoke the souls of heroes, exhibit expensive banquets, and tables, and dishes, and dainties having no real existence, and who will put in motion, as if alive, what are not really living animals, but which have only the appearance of life. Since then, these persons can perform such feats, shall we of necessity conclude that they are sons of God, or must we admit that they are the proceedings of wicked men under the influence of an evil spirit? [*Contra Celsum*, I:67–68, Schonfield translation] 9-14

There are at least two points in this passage that remind one of elements in the *Toldoth Yeshu*. First, there is the curious comment that "they challenged you in the temple to exhibit some unmistakable sign that you were the son of God." While there is some remote resemblance here to the pericope Matthew 27:41–43,* where the

---

*__Matthew 27:41:__ Likewise also the chief priests mocking him, with the scribes and elders, said, 42He saved others; himself he cannot save. If he be the King of Israel, let him now come down from the cross, and we will believe him. 43He trusted in God; let him deliver him now, if he will have him: for he said, I am the Son of God.

priests challenged Jesus to save himself if indeed he were the Son of God, the similarity to the *Toldoth* scene where Queen Helene bids Yeshu to trot out his tricks seems slightly more similar. Nevertheless, the *Toldoth* as we know it could not have been the source for Celsus' comment. Here again, it may be that we are dealing with a morsel of folklore that found its way into both Matthew and the *Gospel According to the Hebrews*, ultimately being transformed into the *Toldoth* episode.

The second point of similarity to the *Toldoth* in this passage concerns the conjurers "who will put in motion, as if alive, what are not really living animals, but which have only the appearance of life." This calls to mind the *Toldoth* pericope where Yeshu vivifies clay birds and lets them fly away chirping. But this same legend is to be found in the *Infancy Gospel of Thomas*[9-15] and in the Qur'an [Sura III:47], where Jesus is made to declare "I have come to you, with a sign from your Lord, in that I make for you out of clay, as it were, the figure of a bird, and breathe into it, and it becomes a bird by God's leave: and I heal those born blind, and the lepers, and I quicken the dead, by God's leave..." Again, it is not likely that the *Toldoth* could have been Celsus' source for this comment.

Among the conjurer's tricks mentioned by Celsus is one that has no resemblance to anything in the versions of the *Toldoth* known to me. This is the comment about "those who have been taught by Egyptians, who in the middle of the market-place, in return for a few obols, will... exhibit expensive banquets, and tables, and dishes, and dainties having no real existence." This resembles nothing in the canonical gospels either, but does find a thematic reflex in the fifth sura of the Qur'an:

> **Sura 5:117–118:** Said Jesus the son of Mary: "O God our Lord! Send us from heaven a table set (with viands), that there may be for us – for the first and the last of us – a solemn festival and a Sign from Thee; and provide for our sustenance, for Thou art the best sustainer (of our needs).
>
> God said: "I will send it down unto you: but if any of you after that resisteth faith, I will punish him with a penalty such as I have not inflicted on any one among all the peoples."

Considering the fact that most of the Christians known to the compilers (authors?) of the Qur'an were Jewish Christians, it is conceivable that Celsus here has in mind a Judeo-Christian gospel such as the *Gospel According to the Hebrews*. However, it seems much more likely to me that Celsus is simply speaking from personal experience about the illusionist fakirs he has observed during his travels. It is difficult to decide how much of what Celsus says is his own true opinion and how much is really the slant of Origen the editor. Nevertheless, it appears that Celsus held a thoroughly skeptical opinion about 'magic' – an opinion completely different from that of Origen or the *Toldoth* compilers.

In the passage under consideration it is certainly the case that Celsus denies the reality of the prodigies mentioned. They are merely the tricks of illusionists. To both Origen and the compilers of the *Toldoth*, however, such feats of magic are real events effected through knowledge of the appropriate 'words of power.' In the case of Yeshu's magical feats in the *Toldoth*, it is the knowledge of how to pronounce the *shem* that sets in motion his miracles. Origen expounds upon the theory and praxis of such wonders in some detail:

> If, then, we shall be able to establish... the nature of powerful names, some of which are used by the learned amongst the Egyptians, or by the Magi among the Persians, and by the Indian philosophers called Brahmans, or by the Samanæans, and others in different countries; and shall be able to make out that the so-called magic is not, as the followers of Epicurus and Aristotle suppose, an uncertain thing, but is, as those skilled in it prove, a consistent system, having words which are known to exceedingly few; then we say that the name Sabaoth, and Adonai, and the other names treated with so much reverence among the Hebrews, are not applicable to any ordinary created things, but belong to a secret theology which refers to the Framer of all things. These names, accordingly, when pronounced with that attendant train of circumstances which is appropriate to their nature, are possessed of great power; and other names, again, current in the Egyptian tongue, are efficacious against certain demons who can only do certain things; and other names in the Persian language have corresponding power over other spirits; and so on in every individual nation, for different purposes. And thus it will be found that, of the various demons upon the earth, to whom different localities have been assigned, each one bears a name appropriate to the several dialects of place and country.
> [*Roberts and Donaldson translation, Contra Celsum*, I:24][9-16]

And when one is able to philosophize about the mystery of names, he will find much to say respecting the titles of the angels of God, of whom one is called Michael, and another Gabriel, and another Raphael, appropriately to the duties which they discharge in the world, according to the will of the God of all things. And a similar philosophy of names applies also to our Jesus, whose name has already been seen, in an unmistakeable manner, to have expelled myriads of evil spirits from the souls and bodies (of men), so great was the power which it exerted upon those from whom the spirits were driven out. And while still upon the subject of names, we have to mention that those who are skilled in the use of incantations, relate that the utterance of the same incantation in its proper language can accomplish what the spell professes to do; but when translated into any other tongue, it is observed to become inefficacious and feeble. And thus it is not the things signified, but the qualities and peculiarities of words, which possess a certain power for this or that purpose. [*Roberts and Donaldson translation*, *Contra Celsum*, I:25][9-17]

By such prodigious intellects was Christianity created!

Magic and sorcery figure in one other passage in *Contra Celsum* that Schonfield believed showed acquaintance with the *Gospel According to the Hebrews*:

O light and truth! Jesus with his own voice expressly declares, as you yourselves have recorded, *"There will appear among you others also, who will perform miracles like mine, but who are wicked men and sorcerers."* And he terms him who devises such things, one Satan. So that Jesus himself does not deny that these works at least are not at all divine, but are the acts of wicked men; and being compelled by the force of truth, he at the same time not only laid open the doings of others, but convicted himself of the same acts. Is it not a miserable inference, to conclude from the same works that the one is a god and the other sorcerers? [*Contra Celsum*, II:49, *Schonfield translation*][9-18]

Just as Celsus charged that Christians "have corrupted the Gospel from its original integrity, to a threefold, and fourfold, and manifold degree, and have remodeled it, so that they might be able to answer objection" [*Contra Celsum*, I:27], Origen believed that Celsus was distorting and misrepresenting Matthew

24:23–27 and Matthew 7:22–23.* Schonfield, however, argues plausibly that these are not exact parallels and that it is more likely that Celsus is citing a *logion* (saying of Jesus) from the *Gospel According to the Hebrews* that is also reflected in Justin Martyr and the Clementines [*Schonfield translations*]:

> Our Lord and Prophet, who hath sent us, declared to us that the wicked one, having disputed with him forty days, and having prevailed nothing against him, announced that he would send from among his followers apostles to deceive. [*Dial. c. Tryph.* 25]
>
> For he said, Many shall come in my name clothed outwardly in sheep's clothing, but inwardly they are ravening wolves. And there shall be schisms and heresies. [*Hom.* 11:35] [9-19]

9.3. C. The Double-Arrest Motif

After finding little or nothing in Celsus that relates convincingly to the *Toldoth*, we come finally to a pericope that looks startlingly similar to a polymorphous theme developed in all versions of the *Toldoth Yeshu*. The Jew of Celsus challenges the Christians:

> How should we deem him to be a god, who not only in other respects, as was currently reported, performed none of his promises, but who also, after we had convicted him and condemned him as deserving of punishment, was found attempting to conceal himself, and endeavouring to escape in a most disgraceful manner, and who was betrayed by those whom he called disciples? [*Contra Celsum*, II:9, *Schonfield translation*] [9-20]

---

*Matt 7:22–23: Many will say to me in that day, Lord, Lord, have we not prophesied in thy name? and in thy name have cast out devils? and in thy name done many wonderful works? And then will I profess unto them, I never knew you: depart from me, ye that work iniquity.

Matt 24:23–27: Then if any man shall say unto you, Lo, here is Christ, or there; believe it not. For there shall arise false Christs, and false prophets, and shall shew great signs and wonders; insomuch that, if it were possible, they shall deceive the very elect. Behold, I have told you before. Wherefore if they shall say unto you, Behold, he is in the desert; go not forth: behold, he is in the secret chambers; believe it not. For as the lightning cometh out of the east, and shineth even unto the west; so shall also the coming of the Son of Man be.

In the *Toldoth Yeshu*, it will be recalled, Yeshu is arrested, condemned to death, rescued by his disciples, goes into hiding, is arrested a second time, and finally is executed. This double-arrest motif is one of the more striking aspects of our satirical anti-gospel, and it is a characteristic that cannot be accounted for if the *Toldoth* be a burlesque of any one of the canonical gospels. It can, however, shed some light on the origins of the "gospels that made the cut" and were admitted into the New Testament.

While none of the canonical gospels contains explicit development of the double-arrest motif, it is implicit in the Gospel of John – which exhibits some curious features relatable to the *Toldoth* tale. In the latter, Jesus comes voluntarily before the queen, whereupon Judas defiles him and he is bereft of power. He is seized, mocked, and almost put to death when a disturbance created by his disciples allows him to escape. Perhaps significantly, he speaks of his ascension while he is before the queen. Of the official gospels, only John 8:21–23* represents Jesus as telling the Jews of his ascension. This is followed by *two* attempts by "the Jews" to stone him, and *two* escapes – outdoing the *Toldoth* as well as the synoptic gospels.

After Jesus describes his ascension in a most mysterious fashion, there is lengthy argument during which he tells his opponents "I know that ye are Abraham's seed; but ye seek to kill me, because my word hath no place in you" [John 8:37]. Shortly thereafter, he repeats the idea that the Jews want to kill him: "But now ye seek to kill me, a man that hath told you the truth, which I have heard of God: this did not Abraham" [John 8:40].

Finally, the argument ends. "Then took they up stones to cast at him; but Jesus hid himself and went out of the temple, going through the midst of them, and so passed by" [John 8:59].

Several adventures later, Jesus once again is in controversy with the Jews, who set about to stone him:

John 10:30: I and my Father are one. [31]Then the Jews took up stones again to stone him. [32]Jesus answered them, Many good works have I shewed you from my Father; for which of those works do ye stone me? [33]The Jews answered him, saying, For a

---

*__John 8:21:__ Then said Jesus again unto them, I go my way, and ye shall seek me, and shall die in your sins: whither I go, ye cannot come. [22]Then said the Jews, Will he kill himself? because he saith, Whither I go, ye cannot come. [23]And he said unto them, Ye are from beneath; I am from above: ye are of this world; I am not of this world.

good work we stone thee not; but for blasphemy; and because that thou, being a man, makest thyself God.

After a little more disputation, "they sought again to take him: but he escaped out of their hand, And went away again beyond Jordan into the place where John at first baptized; and there he abode" [John 10:39–40]. It would appear that these two attempted-execution pericopæ constitute a *doublet, i.e.,* two separate versions of a single story that had evolved into two variants in the sources used by the compilers of the Gospel of John. Not realizing they were one and the same story, they worked them both into their attempted history.

There is a hint of the double-arrest motif in the synoptic gospels, as well in the case where Pilate offers to release Jesus, but the crowd calls for the release of Barabbas instead. In Luke, this synoptic theme is exaggerated by the circumstance that Jesus is tried before Pilate, who sends him to Herod, who sends him back to Pilate! It is possible that in one of Luke's sources there were two separate arrests, with one trial before Herod and one before Pilate.

In the late apocryphal gospel *Joseph of Arimathea*, there is a curious pericope involving the temporary release of Jesus after he has been arrested:

Joseph 2:1–4: On the morrow, being Wednesday, at the ninth hour, they brought him (Jesus) into the hall of Caiaphas, and Annas and Caiaphas asked him, Why didst thou take away the law? He was silent. Why wouldst thou destroy the temple of Solomon? He was silent... Then Annas and Caiaphas privily gave gold to Judas and said, Say as you said before, that it was Jesus who stole the law. Judas agreed, but said, The people must not know that you have told me this: and you must let Jesus go, and I will persuade them. So they fraudulently let Jesus go. ... Towards evening (of Thursday) he obtained a guard of soldiers. As they went, Judas said, Whomsoever I shall kiss, take him: he it is that stole the law and the prophets. He came to Jesus and kissed him, saying, Hail, Rabbi! They took Jesus to Caiaphas and examined him, Why didst thou do this? But he answered nothing. Nicodemus and I (Joseph of Arimathea) left the seat of the pestilent, and would not consent to perish in the council of sinners. They did many evil things to Jesus that night, and on the dawn of Friday delivered him to Pilate. [*Schonfield translation,*][9-21]

Given these hints of two arrests of Jesus in the New Testament as well as in an 'apocryphal' gospel, it would seem that the *Toldoth Yeshu* preserves a motif dating to a period earlier than that of the compilation of any of the canonical gospels. Quite likely, it was still present in the *Gospel According to the Hebrews*, thus accounting for its presence in the *Toldoth Yeshu*. We can only guess at the theopolitical reasons for its removal or concealment in the gospels that now constitute the official history of Jesus.

Did the *Toldoth Yeshu* exist as a connected text in the time of Origen [*c*185–*c*254 CE]? The only evidence we have of his knowledge of documents containing thematic elements of the *Toldoth* is that he was able to quote passages from the *True Discourse* of Celsus – a document considerably older than Origen, dating to around 178 CE. But we have just seen that although Celsus was aware of a document containing at least several elements connected together as in the *Toldoth* (the components of the two-arrest plot), that document most likely was the Jewish gospel later parodied by the *Toldoth*, not the *Toldoth* itself.

Of course, many of the writings of Origen have been lost, and many have been preserved only in tampered translations. It is just possible that he knew more than we think he knew. Origen was born and educated in Alexandria. In his day, Alexandria was *the* Jewish metropolis, having a Jewish population far larger than the remnant residing in Palestine. Moreover, we know that Origen was proficient in Hebrew, having published his monumental *Hexapla* – a super-Bible comparing the Hebrew Masoretic Text with five Greek versions. If the *Toldoth* was circulating in Hebrew in Origen's day, it seems extremely likely that he would have known of it and written a full-length refutation of it, as he attempted to do in the case of Celsus. On the other hand, if the *Ur-Toldoth* was originally composed in Aramaic and circulated in that language for several centuries before being translated into Hebrew and other languages, it is possible that Origen would not have known of it. Although Origen lived, taught, and wrote for many years in Caesarea, a seaport in Palestine, I doubt that he had more than a rudimentary knowledge of Aramaic.

9.4. Arnobius of Sicca [d. 330 CE]

Latin Christianity – at least its literature – began in North Africa, not Rome, and was still almost exclusively an African enterprise during the life of Arnobius of Sicca Veneria in the North African territory of Numidia – the approximate equivalent of modern Algeria. Sicca Veneria was the seat of worship of Venus, hence the name Sicca *Veneria*. Young women often sacrificed their chastity in the temple of the goddess in order to obtain dowries that their parents were too poor to provide. This appears to have figured in the conversion of the prudish Arnobius from paganism to Christianity.

The pagans of his day apparently were complaining that the Roman Empire was in decline because of the growing Christian pestilence – anticipating the Enlightenment historian Edward Gibbon, whose *Decline and Fall of the Roman Empire* implicated Christianity as the disease that weakened that great civilization and facilitated its collapse. (Indeed, it would be the Arian Christian Goths and Vandals who would deal the death blow to the Catholic Christian Western Empire a century or so later.) In order to snuff out the growing awareness of the dangers to civilization posed by the Christians, Arnobius composed his treatise *Adversus Gentes* (also referred to as *Adversus Nationes*) – 'Against the Heathens.' Christianity had nothing to do with the calamities befalling the empire, he argued at great length. In the course of his argument, however, Arnobius revealed some interesting facts about early Christianity.

In chapter 29 of Book I, for example, he sarcastically asks his imagined pagan persecutor, "Because we approach the Head and Pillar of the Universe with worshipful service, are we to be considered... as persons to be shunned, and as godless ones?"[9-22] This worship of the "Pillar [*columen*] of the Universe" appears to be a striking confirmation of my conjecture [pp. 313–314] that Jesus was viewed as the axial pole of the universe by the author of the second-order acrostic in the *Sibylline Oracles*.

It is not known what Arnobius used for scripture, but it is clear that at least some of his sources were not in our official New Testament. He records, for example, a miracle that was not revealed to Matthew, Mark, Luke, or John:

Was He one of us, who, when He uttered a single word, was thought by nations far removed from one another and of different speech to be using well-known sounds, and the peculiar language of each? [I:46] 9-23

This rolls up into the single tongue of one man the multiple miracles of Pentecost, when the eleven apostles plus Matthias and unspecified others – as recorded in that infallible history known as the Acts of the Apostles* – became filled with a ghostly gas† and each began to prophesy in a different language. Certainly, Arnobius was not garbling the account in the second chapter of Acts: that would be impossible for a professional apologist such as he. Rather, he probably did not know of the canonical Acts and likely was referring to some now-lost gospel.

---

*Acts 2:1: And when the day of Pentecost was fully come, they were all with one accord in one place. 2And suddenly there came a sound from heaven as of a rushing mighty wind, and it filled all the house where they were sitting. 3And there appeared unto them cloven tongues like as of fire, and it sat upon each of them. 4And they were all filled with the Holy Ghost, and began to speak with other tongues, as the Spirit gave them utterance. 5And there were dwelling at Jerusalem Jews, devout men, out of every nation under heaven. 6Now when this was noised abroad, the multitude came together, and were confounded, because that every man heard them speak in his own language. 7And they were all amazed and marveled, saying one to another, Behold, are not all these which speak Galilæans? 8And how hear we every man in our own tongue, wherein we were born?

This is, of course, the pericope that provided the stimulus to create the various Pentecostal and holy roller groups that thrive even yet today. The neurophysiology of the brain disorder which affects them – glossolalia – is fairly well understood, but would take us too far from our purpose to discuss here.

† The 'Holy Ghost' of the King James Version and the 'Holy Spirit' of later versions are simply a *holy breath* (Greek ἅγιον πνεῦμα *hagion pneuma*) which, when inhaled ('inspired') can take possession of a human body. The Latin word for breath, *spiritus*, is of course the source of our English word *spirit* and betrays the primitive origins of the religious concept of souls or spirits. To the prescientific authors of the Christian Bible, breath was the vivifying principle which gave life to otherwise nonliving matter. The live man breathed, the dead

Quite likely, the glossolalia miracle of that gospel was derived from the same folk-legend tradition that inspired the glossolalia tale now enshrined as sober history in Acts.

Arnobius seems again to have been referring to a non-canonical gospel in his declarations concerning the post-resurrection appearances of Jesus:

> Was He one of us, who, after His body had been laid in the tomb, manifested Himself in open day to countless numbers of men; who spoke to them, and listened to them; who taught them, reproved and admonished them; who, lest they should imagine that they were deceived by unsubstantial fancies, showed Himself once, a second time, aye frequently, in familiar conversation; who appears even now to righteous men of unpolluted mind who love Him, not in airy dreams, but in a form of pure simplicity; whose name, when heard, puts to flight evil spirits, imposes silence on soothsayers, prevents men from consulting the augurs, causes the efforts of arrogant magicians to be frustrated, not by the dread of His name, as you allege, but by the free exercise of a greater power? [I:46]?9-23

This is much more elaborate than anything in the New Testament – including the five hundred that Paul alleges took part in a one-time mass hallucination of the risen god-man: "After that he was seen of above five hundred brethren at once; of whom the greater part remain unto this present, but some are fallen asleep" [I Cor 15:6]. Whether Arnobius was citing now-lost scriptures or simply embroidering with the resurrection yarn on his own, I do not really know. In any case, by the early fourth century the resurrection rumor had grown into a very tall tale indeed.

The passage in *Adversus Gentes* that is thought to relate directly to the problem being investigated in this book, however, is one repeating the charge that Jesus was a sorcerer who gained his magical knowledge in Egypt:

man did not. After all, when Yahweh created Adam from the dust of the earth, he had to breathe into him "the breath of life" in order to activate him. The ancients took it for granted that the gods they created in their own image would breathe just as did they themselves. The religionists of modern times have not yet found a reason for their god possessing breath, even though most of the realm he is believed to occupy consists of an oxygen-free vacuum.

My opponent will perhaps meet me with many other slanderous and childish charges which are commonly urged. Jesus was a Magian [*sorcerer*]; He effected all these things by secret arts. From the shrines of the Egyptians He stole the names of angels of might, and the religious system of a remote country. Why, O witlings, do you speak of things which you have not examined, and which are unknown to you, prating with the garrulity of a rash tongue? Were, then, those things which were done, the freaks of demons, and the tricks of magical arts? Can you specify and point out to me any one of all those magicians who have ever existed in past ages, that did anything similar, in the thousandth degree, to Christ? Who has done this without any power of incantations, without the juice of herbs and of grasses...? [I:43][9-24]

The Talmud discussion of Ben Stada learning magic in Egypt comes to mind once again: "Did not Ben Stada bring spells from Egypt in a cut which was upon his flesh?" [b. *Shabb.* 104[b]]. Arnobius does not mention the cutting of the flesh, however, and so his account seems only generally related to either the Talmud or the *Toldoth* – both of which have Yeshu conceal the magical vocables in a cut in his flesh. On the other hand, Arnobius has Jesus stealing *names* of power specifically instead of spells in general, bringing him closer to the *Toldoth* with its *shem hamphoras* than to the Talmud with its spells. Of interest also is the fact that Arnobius himself very frequently refers to the miraculous power of the *name* Jesus, which was given to his disciples and their successors to allow them to perform prodigies which Jesus performed on his own authority. "What was more sublime," Arnobius argues, "He has permitted many others to attempt them, and to perform them by the use of His name." Tricks performed in the name of Jesus, he asserts, are utterly different from feats of magic. Unfortunately, he provides no philosophical *discriminanda* that can be employed to distinguish the miraculous from the magical.

Did Arnobius know of the *Toldoth Yeshu*? Once again, I feel the answer must be "no," even though he clearly had heard some of the arguments that ultimately were incorporated into the *Toldoth*. Arnobius provides, I fear, no evidence of the *Toldoth* as a connected work extant at the beginning of the fourth century.

CHAPTER 10

The *Toldoth Yeshu* and the Clementine Literature

A mong the products of the Christian forgery industry of the second and third centuries are documents ascribed to St. Clement of Rome, who should – if one follows the internal 'evidence' contained in them – have been the second pope of Rome, the immediate successor of St. Peter. Apparently, however, other pious trumperies outweighed their testimony, pushing Clement down the line to a position after St. Linus and St. Anacletus. Although these works ostensibly deal with the adventures of Clement, they also are part of the vast Petrine literature that was concocted to advance the prestige of the Peter cult and more fully integrate it into the developing Catholic Church. Emanating originally from Elkesaite and Essene sources and then Ebionite Jewish-Christian circles in Coele-Syria,[10-1] the material contains earlier Gnostic-like sentiments (*e.g.*, the death of Jesus has no religious significance, there seem to have been anti-Pauline jibes, and the doctrine of syzygies, or pairs of opposites, is used to evolve the contests between Simon Peter and Simon Magus) that have been worked over by an orthodox Catholic. The text history of the Clementine literature is so complicated that it is not even certain what should be considered individual 'books' and what should be bunched together to form larger-scale documents. It seems to be the product of a whole factory of fabricators.

Usually, the Clementines – they now usually are referred to as 'the Pseudo-Clementines' – are divided into an older *Clementine Homilies* and a later *Clementine Recognitions*, all of which is preceded by various introductory materials. Not all of this material is relevant to our search for the origins of the *Toldoth Yeshu*, but it is very instructive for understanding the beginnings of Christianity as we think we know it.

10.1. The *Epistula Petri*

As the documents have been sorted out by Johannes Irmscher and Georg Strecker in the *New Testament Apocrypha*,[10-2] the introductory material begins with a supposed letter from St. Peter (*Epistula Petri*) to St. James in Jerusalem. Despite the rather late date of this letter, it seems to preserve the practices of the ancestral mystery cults from which Christianity evolved. In fact, as we shall see, the cult of secrecy imposed by this letter and its sequel – the so-called *Contestatio*, describing how James reacted to receipt of the letter – is reminiscent of modern cults such as the Church of Scientology.

The letter begins with a fake ascription to St. Peter and is obviously intended to be understood as having been written during the first half of the first century, rather than 150 years later:

Peter to James, the lord and bishop of the holy church: Peace be with you always from the Father of all through Jesus Christ.

Then, the secrecy of Christianity's mystery cult beginnings is reenacted:

Knowing well that you, my brother, eagerly take pains about what is for the mutual benefit of us all, I earnestly beseech you not to pass on to any one of the Gentiles the books of my preachings which I (here) forward to you, nor to any one of our own tribe before probation [*initiation*]. But if some one of them has been examined and found to be worthy, then you may hand them over to him in the same way as Moses handed over his office of a teacher to the seventy. ...

In order now that the same may also take place among us, hand over the books of my preachings in the same mysterious way to our seventy brethren that they may prepare those who are candidates for positions as teachers. For if we do not proceed in this way, our word of truth will be split into many opinions. This I do not know as a prophet, but I have already the beginning of the evil before me. For some from among the Gentiles have rejected my lawful preaching and have preferred a lawless and absurd doctrine of the man who is my enemy. And indeed some have attempted, whilst I am still alive, to distort my words by interpretations of many sorts, as if I taught the dissolution of the law...

...I earnestly beseech you not to pass on the books of my preachings which I send you to any one of our own tribe or to any foreigner before probation [*initiation*], but if some one is examined and found to be worthy, let them then be handed over in the way in which Moses handed over his office of a teacher to the seventy, in order that they may preserve the dogmas and extend farther the rule of the truth, interpreting everything in accordance with our tradition... [10-3]

In the *Contestatio* – the document designed to provide the testimony of the supposed recipients of the *Epistula Petri* and emanating either from the same pen or from the pen of another member of the theopolitical party to which the *Epistula's* forger belonged – we have further elaboration of the secrecy strictures of this hold out Christian mystery cult:

Now when James had read the epistle he called the elders together, read it to them and said: "As is necessary and proper, our Peter has called our attention to the fact that we must be cautious in the matter of the truth, that we should pass on the books of his preachings that have been forwarded to us not indiscriminately, but only to a good and religious candidate for the position of a teacher, a man who as one who has been circumcised is a believing Christian, and indeed that we should not pass on all the books to him at once, so that, if he shows indiscretion in handling the first, he may not be entrusted with the others. He ought therefore to be proved for not less than six years. ..." [10-4]

Then, after performance of some sort of water ritual, the initiate was made to take a vow of secrecy in the keeping of the secret writings. The vow is redolent of the Masons, Mormons, or Scientologists of a much later but equally primitive era:

And let him [*the initiate*] say: "As witnesses I invoke heaven, earth, and water, in which everything is comprehended, and also in addition the all-pervading air, without which I am unable to breathe, that I shall always be obedient to him who hands over to me the books of the preachings and shall not pass on to any one in any way the books which he may give to me, that I shall neither copy them nor give a copy of them nor allow them to come into the hands of a copyist, neither shall I myself do this nor shall I do it through another, and not in any other way, through cunning or tricks, through keeping them carelessly, through depositing them with another or through underhand agreement, nor in any other manner or by means of any other artifice will I pass them on to a third party. ...

"...even if I should ever come to the conviction that the books of the preachings which have been handed to me do not contain the truth, then also I shall not pass them on but shall hand them back. ... If I am sick and see death before me, I shall, if I am childless, [*consign the books to the care of my bishop*]. ... And if even I should come to believe in another god, then I swear also by him, whether he now is or is not, that I shall not proceed otherwise. ... if I am false to my word, I shall be accursed living and dead and suffer eternal punishment."[10-5]

I am unable to decide whether or not the secrecy precautions depicted in these documents reflect actual Ebionite Jewish Christian cultic practices of the middle of the third century when they were confected, or were an attempt to reconstruct – for the appearance of authenticity – the still-remembered mystery practices of the earliest church.* There is of course a third

---

*Origen, who died in the middle of the third century, felt the need to rebut the charges of the pagan philosopher Celsus that Christianity was a secret society – a mystery cult, if you will. In the first chapter of the first book of his *Contra Celsum*, Origen states the charge:

> The first point which Celsus brings forward, in his desire to throw discredit upon Christianity, is that the Christians entered into secret associations with each other contrary to law, saying, that "of associations some are public, and that these are in accordance with the laws; others, again, secret, and maintained in violation of the laws." And his wish is to bring into disrepute what are termed the "love-feasts" of the Christians, as if they had their origin in the common danger, and were more binding than any oaths. [I:1] [10-6]

In attempting to refute Celsus, Origen actually confesses that Christianity is a two-tiered system consisting of a public (exoteric) component and a secret (esoteric) part, apparently known only to initiates:

> Moreover, since he frequently calls the Christian doctrine a secret system (of belief), we must confute him on this point also, since almost the entire world is better acquainted with what Christians preach than with the favourite opinions of philosophers. For who is ignorant of the statement that Jesus was born of a virgin, and that He was crucified, and that His resurrection

possibility. The Clementine documents were composed during the golden age of Christian fraud. Numerous 'pseudepigrapha' – gospels, acts, letters, and memoirs falsely ascribed to various worthies of the Christian mythological and historical past – were being crafted; letters of Paul were being reworked to convert them from proto-Gnostic pieces into Catholic tracts; and false histories of Christianity itself were being concocted to justify and validate the claims of the various theopolitical companies contending to corner the faith-based securities market. It may simply be that the authors and redactors of the Clementines simply wanted to achieve exactly what they claimed, *i.e.*, the forestalling of competing forgers who might very well coopt the Clementine material for completely incompatible theological purposes. (In fact, this seems to have actually happened, as Essene or Gnostic material seems to have been gobbled up, partially digested, and regurgitated as a quasi-scriptural document for Catholic use.

We can skip over the *Epistula Clementis*, the Letter of Clement to James, as a forgery manufactured mostly to establish the authenticity of St. Clement as having been appointed by St. Peter himself as the second bishop of Rome – *i.e.*, the second pope – for theopolitical reasons not now discernible.

is an article of faith among many, and that a general judgment is announced to come, in which the wicked are to be punished according to their deserts, and the righteous to be duly rewarded? And yet the mystery of the resurrection, not being understood, is made a subject of ridicule among unbelievers. In these circumstances, to speak of the Christian doctrine as a *secret* system, is altogether absurd. *But that there should be certain doctrines, not made known to the multitude, which are (revealed) after the exoteric ones have been taught, is not a peculiarity of Christianity alone, but also of philosophic systems, in which certain truths are exoteric and others esoteric.* Some of the hearers of Pythagoras were content with his *ipse dixit*; while others were taught in secret those doctrines which were not deemed fit to be communicated to profane and insufficiently prepared ears. Moreover, all the mysteries that are celebrated everywhere throughout Greece and barbarous countries, although held in secret, have no discredit thrown upon them, so it is in vain that he endeavours to calumniate *the secret doctrines of Christianity*, seeing he does not correctly understand its nature. [I:7] [*Emphasis added*] [10-7]

10.2. The *Clement Romance*

Reconstructed from the *Clementine Homilies* and *Recognitions*, the novella known as the *Clement Romance* appears to be very similar to other Greco-Roman novels of the period. It describes the travels of Clement from Rome to Palestine in order to learn more about the wonder-worker reported to be operating in that territory. Clement meets the missionary Barnabas and then Simon Peter,* whom he accompanies on tours to various cities, ending up back in Rome where Peter consecrates him as bishop. (Oh, yes, Clement comes to 'recognize' and become reunited with his mother and twin brothers, from whom he became separated in childhood.)

10.2. A. Jesus in the *Clement Romance*

The *Clement Romance* is important for our study of the *Toldoth Yeshu* because of the pictures it paints of Jesus, Simon Peter, and Simon Magus, and because of the terms with which it describes those characters:

> There is a Man in Judæa who since the beginning of spring
> has been proclaiming to the Jews the kingdom of God; those, he
> states, will attain it who keep the demands of his commandments
> and of his doctrine. As proof that his speech is worthy of credit
> and is from the divine Spirit, he performs, so it is said, *by his*

---

*Although Clement becomes intimately acquainted with Barnabas and is made the traveling companion of Peter, the *Clement Romance* (as also the more nearly canonical *Acts of Peter*) makes no mention of the evangelist John Mark – the supposed author of the second Gospel. According to Acts 12:25, *etc.*, John Mark was a traveling companion of Barnabas and Saul/Paul. Early extrabiblical tradition identifies him as Peter's interpreter in Rome.

The authenticity of the Gospel of Mark is often defended by citing either an earlier tradition that Mark, at the urging of Christians in Rome, recorded what he could remember of the apostle's teachings, or a later tradition that claimed that Mark wrote his gospel during Peter's life – in fact, at the urging of the Apostle. The absence of John Mark from the Clementine literature makes it obvious that he was simply one of the many *ad hoc* inventions of a rival theopolitical movement.

mere word many signs and singularly miraculous deeds. So that, as it were in the power of God, he makes the deaf to hear and the blind to see, makes *the infirm and lame to stand erect,* expels every weakness and all demons from men, yea *even raises dead persons who are brought before him*, and besides brings *healing to lepers* whom he sees from a distance, and there is nothing at all that is impossible for him [*emphasis added*].[10-8]

While this passage superficially resembles the gospel tales, in at least some of its particulars it differs from them and is more similar to details of the *Toldoth Yeshu*. For example, although the canonical gospels depict Jesus performing miracles by means of verbal commands, there is no self-consciousness of the verbal nature of the magic. In the *Toldoth*, of course, Yeshu has stolen the *shem hamphoras*, the magical secret name of the deity, and uses it to perform most of the specific miracles enumerated in the passage just quoted. More striking, perhaps, is the fact that the Clementine account has dead bodies *brought* to Jesus for reanimation – a peculiar detail which is never seen in the canonical stories but is a striking characteristic of all the *Toldoth* variants.

10.2. B. Peter in the *Clement Romance*

Concerning Simon Peter, there is a curious dialog line in the *Romance* that reads "That is Peter, of whom I have told you that he has penetrated most deeply into the divine wisdom."[10-9] This penetrating, wise Peter certainly is not the Simon Peter of the canonical gospels! He would, however, be quite compatible with the Yeshu of the *Toldoth* (perhaps more accurately, compatible with the model satirized by the *Toldoth*) or the Yeshu or Ben Stada of the rabbinical literature we have explored in this book.

Like the Yeshu of the *Toldoth*, Simon Peter here is able to activate a small army – although instead of *allowing* the bad guys to flee, here it *causes* the bad guys to flee:

Then Simon dared, along with Appion, Annubion, Athenodorus and his other comrades, to turn against Peter in the presence of all the people: "Flee, ye people, from this man; for he is a magician – you may believe me – and has himself occasioned this earthquake and has caused these diseases to frighten you, as if he himself was a god! ... Peter with a smile and an impressive directness spoke the words: "Ye men, I admit that, God willing, I am capable of doing what these men here say and in addition am ready, if you will not hear my words, to turn your whole city upside down." Now when the multitude took alarm and readily promised to carry out his commands, Peter said: "Let no one of you associate with these magicians or in any way have intercourse with them." Scarcely had the people heard this summons when without delay they laid hold of cudgels and pursued these fellows till they had driven them completely out of the city... [10-10]

Like Yeshu, Peter also is able to heal the sick and raise the dead:

Peter, the apostle of Christ, attended many who were sick, healed those who were possessed, and through the power of the Lord Jesus Christ raised to life again numerous persons who were dead... [10-11]

10.2. C. Simon Magus in the *Clement Romance*

The description of Simon Magus appears to me to be more relevant to the Yeshu of the *Toldoth* and the supposed Jesuses of the rabbinical literature than is the description of Simon Peter, and so I shall quote a more substantial portion of the *Clement Romance*.

The father of this Simon is called Antonius, his mother Rachel. By nationality he is a Samaritan and comes from the village of Gittha, which is six miles distant from the capital. During a stay in Egypt he acquired a large measure of Greek culture and attained to an extensive knowledge of magic and ability in it. He then came forward claiming to be accepted as a mighty power of the very God who has created the world. On occasion he sets himself up for the Messiah and describes himself as the Standing One. He uses this title since he is to exist for ever and his body cannot possibly fall a victim to the germs of corruption. He also denies that the God who created the world is the highest, nor does he believe in the resurrection of the dead.[10-12]

Readers will immediately recognize the Ben Stada of the rabbinical literature in this magician who learned his tricks in Egypt. The curious epithet of Simon Magus, 'The Standing One,' (in Greek *ho Hestōs* or *ho Stadios*), is conceivably the source of the Aramaic/Hebrew *Stada*, who in later Jewish tradition came to be identified with Jesus. Conceptually, this Standing One* is equivalent to the epithet *pillar* which in Galatians 2:9† is attributed to Peter (Cephas) and John, although a different Greek word (*stúlos*)

---

*If, as seems likely, astral cults were an important component of early Christianity, such titles may have referred to the axial pole of the universe as an Atlas-like divine being. In like manner, the 'cross' (Greek *staurós*, which etymologically is related to *stúlos*, pillar) may originally have symbolized the axial pole, since the original meaning of the Greek word was simply *stake* or *pole*. Later, when the word came to connote a *cross* – i.e., two intersecting poles or stakes – it probably first came to signify the astronomical intersections of the ecliptic with the celestial equator that marked the vernal and autumnal equinoxes, where the sun appears to pass over and under the intersection points, respectively. Before it came to be represented by the familiar Latin cross (✝), it was symbolized by the Greek letter chi (χ), which more accurately reproduced the *c*23.5-degree angle of intersection of the two heavenly pathways. The chi-rho cross (☧, originally the symbol for Chronos, the god of time)[10-13] and the tropos cross (☧, originally probably the symbol for the Milky Way, the 'way' through the stars taken by the soul on its way to heavenly reward) were the earliest derivatives of the chi cross.

Jesus also may have been associated with the axial pole of the universe – the deflection of which could cause the point of the vernal equinox to move from Aries into Pisces at the start of the New Age. Support for this notion can be found in the amazing second-order acrostic found in the eighth book of *Sibylline Oracles*. Thirty-four lines long, the letters with which each line begins when read downward from line to line spell out the Greek motto ΙΗΣΟΥΣ ΧΡΕΙΣΤΟΣ ΘΕΟΥ ΥΙΟΣ ΣΩΤΗΡ ΣΤΑΥΡΟΣ – 'Jesus Chreist [*sic*] Of God The Son, Savior, Cross'.[10-14] The initials of these words, in turn (if we leave out the last word) spell out the Greek word ΙΧΘΥΣ (*ichthús*, 'fish'), which nowadays can be seen imbedded in the bowels of fish emblems attached to the rear ends of minivans, pickup trucks, and motorcycles belonging to Bikers for Christ. The *Sibylline Oracles* were among the earliest of Christian scriptures, and it is my opinion that the word *cross* with which the acrostic ends was intended to mean 'axial pole', in keeping with the astral context of the poem in which the acrostic is embedded. As axial pole of the universe, Jesus was the connection

is used. The curious charge that Simon did not believe in the resurrection of the dead calls to mind the rabbinical charge against Gehazi, who ultimately became entangled in a cast of characters that included some (such as Balaam) later identified with Jesus. It is probably relevant to remember that the Clementine literature originated in *Jewish* Christian circles.

The *Clement Romance* relates Simon Magus to John the Baptist and further underscores his character as a sorcerer:

> Simon's contact with the tenets of religion came about in the following way. There appeared a certain John the Baptist, who according to the disposition of the syzygies was at the same time the forerunner of our Lord Jesus. And as the Lord had twelve apostles according to the number of the solar months,* so also there gathered about John thirty eminent persons according to the reckoning of the lunar month. Among these was a woman Helena by name, and herewith a significant disposition

---

between earthly civilization and the 'Kingdom of the Sky' – the Kingdom of Heaven that has perplexed so many theologians and biblical exegetes.

The symbol of the fish, of course, originally was the two-fish sign representing the zodiacal constellation Pisces – the emblem of the New Age religion that was developing at the beginning of what is now referred to as the Common Era.

†**Galatians 2:9:** And when James, Cephas, and John, who seemed to be pillars, perceived the grace that was given unto me [*Paul*], they gave to me and Barnabas the right hands of fellowship, that we should go unto the heathen, and they unto the circumcision.

*The matter-of-fact admission that the twelve apostles of Jesus represented the twelve months of the year – *i.e.*, the twelve signs of the zodiac – is rather startling. Coming from a Jewish Christian source, it further reinforces the theory that Christianity was a consequence of the increasing and wide-spread solarization of Judaism that was in full swing at the turn of the era. This was a time, after all, when the vernal equinox had moved from Aries into Pisces and a new astrological age was beginning. The Kingdom of the Sky was at hand!

The lunar characterization of John the Baptist symbolizes, of course, the majoritarian form of Judaism, the form that sclerosed into rabbinism. Even today, all Jewish calendars are lunar. By the Gnostic doctrine of the syzygies (pairs of opposites), the lunar religion of John was to be superseded by the solar religion of Yeshua' – 'The Savior' in Aramaic.

prevailed. For the woman, who makes up only the half of the man, left the number 30 incomplete, precisely as in the case of the moon, the revolution of which is not altogether a month in duration. Of these thirty Simon counted with John as the first and most distinguished... John was made away with at the very time when Simon had journeyed to Egypt to study magic...

[Simon] deceives many in a plausible manner, and at the same time he performs numerous wonderful deeds, by which we would ourselves have been imposed on, had we not known that he works them by sorcery... He has also burdened himself with bloodguiltiness and has even related among his friends that he separated the soul of a boy from its body by means of secret magical invocations and keeps it in the interior of his house, where his bed is, to assist him in his performances, having in this connection drawn a likeness of the boy. This boy, he asserts, he at one time fashioned out of air by a divine transformation and then, having put his appearance on record, he returned him again to air. ... [10-15]

The charges against Simon are the same as those against Yeshu in the *Toldoth*, viz., he is a magician and a sorcerer. His creation of a living boy out of air somewhat outdoes the *Toldoth*'s tale [appendix B] of Yeshu creating living birds out of clay, but it belongs to the same category of wonders.

10.3. The *Acts of Peter*

One can hardly dispute the claim that the most distinctive – and delightful – feature of the *Toldoth Yeshu* is the aerial contest between the aerobatic Yeshu and the aeroballistic Iscariot. Whence came this episode?

Readers may recall that there existed a Jewish tradition in which Balaam, who in later times would also be associated with Jesus, seems to have been able to fly. While that tradition may in some small way have contributed to the aerobatic duel of the *Toldoth*, a much more likely source is found in the *Acts of Peter* – a work that in some degree seems to underlie the Pseudo-Clementine literature.

According to Wilhelm Schneemelcher,[10-16] reasoning from references in Tertullian's *De Baptismo* of c200 CE, the *Acts of Peter* must have originated before the year 190 CE. Like almost all early Christian literature, it was composed in Greek. It seems to have been written in Asia Minor (Turkey) or in Rome. Although it begins with some of the supposed doings of St. Paul in Rome, the main theme of the work involves the ongoing competition between St. Simon Peter and Simon Magus, ending with the famous *'Quo Vadis?'** scene and the execution of Peter.

The flight motif is introduced early in the story, as Simon prepares to enter Rome. "Tomorrow," he boasts, "you shall see me about the seventh hour flying over the city gate in the form in which you now see me speaking with you." The next day he makes good his boast. "And when the seventh hour had come, behold suddenly in the distance a cloud of dust was seen in the sky, like a smoke shining from far away with fiery rays. And when it approached the gate it suddenly vanished; and then he appeared standing among the people, while they all worshipped him and realized that it was he who had been seen by them the day before."10-18

Peter then arrives in Rome to contend with his long-time adversary. In a series of escalating contests – including an episode involving a talking dog – Peter duels with Simon and finally deals definitively with the flight-unworthy Magus. The culminating contest begins with a declaration by Simon:

> "Men of Rome, at present you think that Peter has mastered me, as having greater power, and you attend to him rather (than me). (But) you are deceived. For tomorrow I shall leave you, who are utterly profane and impious, and fly up to God, whose power I am, although enfeebled. If then you have fallen, behold I am He that Standeth. And I am going up to my Father and shall say to him, 'Even me, thy Son that Standeth, they desired to bring

---

*St. Peter is persuaded to leave Rome secretly to avoid being killed by Agrippa. "So he assented to the brethren and withdrew by himself, saying, 'Let none of you retire with me, but I shall retire by myself in disguise.' And as he went out of the gate he saw the Lord entering Rome; and when he saw him he said, 'Lord, whither goest thou [*quo vadis*] here?' And the Lord said to him, 'I am coming to Rome to be crucified.' And Peter said to him, 'Lord, art thou being crucified again?' He said to him, 'Yes, Peter, I am being crucified again.' And Peter came to himself; and he saw the Lord ascending into heaven; then he returned to Rome rejoicing and giving praise to the Lord, because he said, 'I am being crucified'; (since) this was to happen to Peter. 10-17

down; but I did not consent with them, and am returned to myself'."

And by the following day a large crowd had assembled on the Sacred Way to see him fly. And Peter, having seen a vision, came to the place, in order to convict him again this time; for when (Simon) made his entry into Rome, he astonished the crowds by flying; but Peter, who exposed him, was not yet staying in Rome, (the city) which he so carried away by his deceptions that people lost their senses through him.

So this man stood on a high place, and seeing Peter, he began to say: "Peter, now of all times, when I am making my ascent before all these onlookers, I tell you: If your god has power enough – he whom the Jews destroyed, and they stoned you who were chosen by him – let him show that faith in him is of God; let it be shown at this time whether it be worthy of God. For I by ascending will show to all this crowd what manner of being I am." And lo and behold, he was carried up into the air, and everyone saw him all over Rome, passing over its temples and its hills; while the faithful looked towards Peter. And Peter, seeing the incredible sight, cried out to the Lord Jesus Christ, "Let this man do what he undertook, and all who have believed on thee shall now be overthrown, and the signs and wonders which thou gavest them through me shall be disbelieved. Make haste, Lord, with thy grace; and let him fall down from (this) height, and be crippled, but not die; but let him be disabled and break his leg in three places!" And he fell down from that height and broke his leg in three places. Then they stoned him and went to their own homes; but from that time they all believed in Peter. [10-19]

Even though the stoning of Simon accords with the death of Yeshu in the *Toldoth*, there are, of course, significant differences between the Simon Peter–Simon Magus contest and the Yeshu–Judas Iscariot contest. In the former, most notably, there is only one flight demonstrator, whereas in the latter we are treated to a *volée à deux*. Nevertheless, it seems entirely reasonable to suppose that this Jewish Christian writing would have been known by more orthodox Jews and would have catalyzed the one-upping satirical treatment in the *Toldoth Yeshu*. That the *Toldoth* may have been modeled after the *Acts of Peter* is further suggested by the curious expression uttered by Simon: "God, whose power I am, *although enfeebled*." In the *Toldoth* – as in much other Jewish and Christian literature – the power of the deity was the unutterable divine name, the *shem hamphoras*. While this point is not made explicit in our text, it is likely that ancient readers would have understood from this passage that Simon performed his magic by means of the *shem*, although exactly why and how one in possession of the *shem* could become "enfeebled" is not immediately obvious. The question clamors to be answered. Almost certainly, something has been left out of this story. In the *Toldoth*, Yeshu becomes enfeebled after ritual defilement by Judas. What might Peter have done to enfeeble Simon? Conceivably, there may have been a contest of magical names, with *Jesus* being more potent than whatever name the Standing One was using to effect his trumpery.

If the *Acts of Peter* originated in a quasi-Gnostic setting, Simon might very well have been made to use the *shem* – the name *Yahweh* – which would have been understood to be the power of the Demiurge who created the physical world but was inferior in power to the supreme god of whom Jesus was understood to be a manifestation. That *Jesus* could trump *Yahweh* would be obvious to the intended audience of the *Acts of Peter*, but it could hardly be admitted in an orthodox Jewish satire. If the Petrine text was the model for the *Toldoth*, the magical power sources had to be made equal. The only genuinely magical name in existence, after all, was *Yahweh*. Both aerial combatants would have to burn the same fuel in their engines even if one engine was part of a missionary-positioned biplane and the other was a sodomitic ramjet.

Peter makes explicit use of the magical name *Jesus Christ* to resurrect a smoked fish that was hanging in a window. Taking the fish down and showing it to the people, he throws it into a near-by fishpond and enchants it by commanding, "In thy name, Jesus Christ, in which they still fail to believe... in the presence of all these be alive and swim like a fish!" The fish immediately is restored to life and the crowd feeds it bread for amusement.

There are many other points of similarity between the *Acts of Peter* and the *Toldoth* – as well as with other rabbinical works. Both Peter and the Magus accuse each other of sorcery and working their tricks by magic, illusion, or deception rather than by truly divine power. Both cure the halt and the lame, both restore life to the dead and movement to the paralyzed. All this applies to the Yeshu of the *Toldoth* as well.

It will be recalled that the prophet Balaam had an ass that could talk – deliver speeches, in fact – and that when Yeshu stole the *shem* from the Holy of Holies in the Temple of Yahweh he had to pass bronze dogs that barked at him and caused him to forget how to pronounce the magical word. In the *Acts of Peter* there is a wacky episode that seems to relate to both mythical motifs of the *Toldoth*. This is the sacred and sober story of the argumentative dog.

Peter pursues Simon to the home of Senator Marcellus, who is playing host to the sorcerer. Peter knocks on the door and the doorkeeper tells him that Simon has given him orders to say that Simon is not at home. The future saint spies a big dog chained up nearby and lets him loose. Thereupon the dog acquires a human voice, just as did Balaam's ass before him. "What do you bid me do, you servant of the ineffable living God?" the mutt asks the saint.[10-20] Peter answers by commanding the canine to "Go in and tell Simon in the presence of his company, 'Peter says to you, Come out in public; for on your account I have come to Rome, you wicked man and troubler of simple souls'." The obedient animal does exactly as told, repeating to Simon the exact words he was told to say. Like Yeshu who forgot the *shem* when the bronze dogs howled at him, Simon "lost the words with which he was deceiving those who stood by, and all were amazed."[10-21]

Shortly thereafter, Peter cures a demon-possessed young man who reports to Peter that "there is a huge contest between Simon and the dog which you sent; for Simon says to the dog, 'Say that I am not here' – but the dog says more to him than the message you gave; and when he has finished the mysterious work which you gave him, he shall die at your feet'."[10-22]

The drama of the talking dog is interrupted by the circumstance that the demon being driven out of the young man crashes into an important statue of Caesar, breaking it into many pieces. Marcellus fears this is going to get him into trouble, but Peter tells him that if he truly believes in Jesus he can mend the statue.

"...if you are truly repentant and believe in Christ with all your heart, take (some) running water in your hands and pray to the Lord; then sprinkle it *in his name* over the broken pieces of the statue, and it will be restored as before." And Marcellus did not doubt, but believed with his whole heart, and before taking the water in his hands he looked upwards and said, "I believe in thee, Lord Jesus Christ, for I am being tested by thine apostle Peter whether I truly believe *in thy holy name*. Therefore I take water in my hands, and *in thy name* I sprinkle those stones, that the statue may be restored as it was before. So Lord, if it be thy will that I remain in the body and suffer nothing at Cæsar's hand, let this stone be restored as it was before." And he sprinkled the water upon the stones, and the statue was restored. ... Marcellus... believed with his whole heart *in the name of Jesus Christ* the Son of God, through whom all things impossible are (made) possible.[10-23]

More testimony to the heap-big-medicine power of the Name of the Lord! But we must not forget about the talking dog.

After being told of the healing of the broken statue, we are treated to a major argument between Simon and the holy hound. Simon, it seems, has treated the dog as if he were his doorkeeper and has ordered the animal to tell Peter that Simon is not home. This enrages the canine, who launches into a major oration putting Simon in his place, stomps out of the house, seeks out Peter, reports what he has said and done, and drops dead at Peter's feet after telling him that he "shall have a great contest with Simon, the enemy of Christ."

Yeshu's use of a magical name surely must be considered one of the major concepts developed in the *Toldoth Yeshu*, and it seems significant that a 'name of power' figures prominently and repeatedly in the *Acts of Peter*. Just one more pericope need be quoted to underscore this fact:

But when night came on, Peter saw Jesus clothed in a robe of splendour, smiling and saying to him while he was still awake, "Already the great mass of the brethren have turned back to me through you and through the signs [*miracles*] which you have done *in my name*. But you shall have a trial of faith on the coming sabbath, and many more of the Gentiles and of the Jews shall be converted *in my name* to me, who was insulted, mocked and spat upon. For I will show myself to you when you ask for signs and miracles, and you shall convert many; but you will have Simon opposing you with the works of his father.* But all his (actions) shall be exposed as charms and illusions of magic. But now do not delay and you shall establish *in my name* all those whom I send you."[10-24]

*This curious expression may be connected somehow with John 8:44, where Satan is said to be the father of Jesus' opponents: "Ye are of your father the devil, and the lusts of your father ye will do. He was a murderer from the beginning and abode not in the truth, because there is no truth in him. When he speaketh a lie, he speaketh of his own: for he is a liar, and the father of it."

Satirizing a passage such as this could have led to the amusing theological problem that seems never to have been recognized by the authors of the *Toldoth*. Since the *Toldoth* authors could not admit, even in a satire, that there were two legitimate names of power, they were stuck with just *Yahweh* – creating the conundrum of how it is magic and illusion when Yeshu uses the *shem*, but legitimate miracles when the high priest or Jewish elders use it to do the same tricks.

According to the *Clement Romance*,[10-25] Simon Magus studied magic in Egypt, reminding us of the Talmudic passage [*Shabb.* 104b, *Sanh.* 67a] wherein Rabbi Eliezer asks, "Did not Ben Stada bring spells out of Egypt in a cutting in his flesh?" Surely, this Ben Stada must be the Standing One (*Stadios*) – i.e., Simon Magus, who used magical spells he learned in Egypt. That this was also attributed to Jesus at an early date can be seen from the fact that Arnobius [d. 330 CE] in North Africa complained that the critics of Christianity claimed that Jesus "was a magician; he did all his works by secret arts; from the shrines of the Egyptians he stole the names of angelic powers and hidden disciplines."[10-26] Combine this with the claim in the *Joseph Apocryphon* that Demas the robber stole the secret deposit of Solomon – a legendary king famous for his occult and magical knowledge – from the Holy of Holies in the Temple of Yahweh, and that Judas falsely blamed this on Jesus, and we have the basis for the *Toldoth* story of Yeshu's robbing of the *shem hamphoras*. Both the critics of Arnobius and the *Joseph Apocryphon* would appear to be making apologies in response to the *Toldoth Yeshu* or at least to the stories from which it was compiled. This would imply that the *Toldoth* or some of its components must be older than the time of authorship of the documents in question.[10-27]

Just one more oddity of the *Acts of Peter* may be quoted that seems related to the *Toldoth* – in this case to the *Toldoth Minor*:

> We should therefore first learn to know the will of God, or (his) goodness; for when error was in full flood and many thousands of men were plunging to destruction, the Lord in his mercy was moved to show himself in another shape and to be seen in the form of a man, on whom neither the Jews nor we were worthy to be enlightened. For each one of us saw (him) as he was able, as he had power to see. ... Our Lord wished me to see his majesty on the holy mountain; but when I with the sons of Zebedee saw the brilliance of his light, I fell as one dead, and closed my eyes

and heard his voice, such as I cannot describe... And when I stood up I saw him in such a form as I was able to take in.[10-28]

The Docetic* characteristics of this passage and the lines that follow it in the *Acts of Peter* could easily have been caricatured to produce a Yeshu who not only could appear as different images to different men, but could transform himself *à la* the *Arabian Nights* into animals or, as in the *Toldoth Minor*, a rooster. The further circumstance that the *Toldoth* transformation of Yeshu takes place on a mountain (Mt. Carmel) and the transfiguration scene recounted in the passage just quoted from the *Acts of Peter* also is set upon a mountain would seem to make a connection between these two literary creations even more probable.

Hugh Schonfield believed that the *Toldoth* was a satirical derivative of the *Gospel According to the Hebrews*, as I have already noted. It is quite possible that the *Acts of Peter* is itself a derivative of the *Acts* part of the *Gospel According to the Hebrews*. If that be true, the *Toldoth* may at least in part be a second derivative from that extinct Jewish gospel.

---

*The Docetists, who flourished in the second century and probably earlier, believed that Jesus did not have a real body, but only *seemed* (Greek δοκεῖν *dokein*) to have one. Docetism was popular among many Gnostics, who considered matter to be evil. If matter be evil, the Savior (Aramaic *Yeshuaʿ* – Jesus) could not have taken on a material body. The Gnostic Marcion employed Docetic reasoning when he denied that Jesus had been born of a woman, but rather had appeared as a grown man during the reign of Tiberius. It is my opinion that Docetism was not a Christian heresy, as traditional scholarship would have it, but rather that Catholic Christianity was a Docetic heresy. If Docetism was the more primitive form of Christianity, and if the *Acts of Peter* derives from a Docetic Christian group, then the latter 'scripture' reflects an earlier stage in the evolution of Christian tradition than that found in the canonical gospels – with the possible exception of the early strata of the Gospel of John. The *Toldoth Yeshu*, in turn, even though it be a satire, may allow more inferences about the nature of earliest Christianity than can the New Testament as we now see it. If the earliest form of Christianity was in fact Docetic, the argument that Jesus never existed as an historical figure seems fairly demonstrated.

CHAPTER 11

When Was the *Toldoth Yeshu* Composed?

In our examination of the apocryphal and patristic literature we have advanced to the early part of the fourth century without finding any convincing evidence of the *Toldoth Yeshu* as a connected work, although a number of its key motifs were well known by that time. How old, then, *is* this counter-gospel?

Obviously, the *Toldoth* must be older than the year 826 CE, when Agobard, Bishop of Lyons, quoted large sections of it. Unfortunately, as I have noted, clear and unequivocal evidence for a connected text of the *Toldoth* is lacking before that time. William Horbury, as we have already seen, attempted to reconstruct the ur-*Toldoth* text, which he placed at the end of the third century.[11-1] While I find his text reconstruction plausible, I am unable to convince myself that his dating of the text is correct. It may be, but the evidence seems insufficient to establish the fact.

Samuel Krauss, the first comprehensive scholar of the *Toldoth*, dated the ur-*Toldoth* (he created the term) to the late fourth century, at Tiberias in Galilee.[11-2] Later, Hugh J. Schonfield came to the same conclusion in his *According To The Hebrews*, and clarified somewhat the evidence for that date and *Sitz im Leben*.[11-3]

11.1. The External Evidence

In addition to the external evidence we have already examined in our search for Christian, Jewish, or pagan knowledge of the *Toldoth*, Schonfield considered several other sources he felt pointed to external knowledge of at least the genealogical aspects of the *Toldoth*. Although I am unconvinced by these data, they are of general interest and worth examining.

Schonfield cites the *Dialogue of Andronicus of Constantinople Against the Jews* [c1310 CE], in which the author 'proves' the Davidic descent of Mary from a Jewish book that he encountered in Macedonia in the home of a Jewish legal scholar named Elijah. Critical of the 'Virgin Mary,' the book asks:

> Why do Christians extol Mary so highly, calling her nobler than the Cherubim, incomparably greater than the Seraphim, raised above the heavens, purer than the very rays of the sun? For she was a woman of the race of David, daughter of Anna and Joachim who was son of Panther. Now Panther and Melchi were brothers, sons of Levi, of the stock of Matthan, whose father was David of the tribe of Judah.[11-4]

A much earlier document, the *Teaching of Jacob* [634 CE], also is cited as evidence on the same topic:

> God sent me to a certain Jew in Ptolemais (Acre), and he expounded the genealogy of Mary. I said to him mockingly, "She of Judah!" Now that Jew was a great teacher of the Law, of Tiberias. And he said, "Why do the Christians magnify Mary? She is the daughter of David and not Theotokos (*i.e.*, born of God), for Mary is a woman, daughter of Joakim, and her mother was Anna. Now Joakim is son of Panther, and Panther was brother of Melchi, as the tradition of us Jews in Tiberias has it, of the seed of Nathan, the son of David, of the seed of Judah."[11-5]

These two passages are interpreted by Schonfield as evidence that there existed Jewish documents in which the genealogy of Jesus was discussed and Panther was placed at a date approximating that of Alexander Jannaeus, around a century BCE. Schonfield situates these documents at the Jewish rabbinical college at Tiberias in the fourth century, and concludes that the genealogical data must have been obtained from Jewish Christian sources. The notion that there existed genealogical materials pertaining to Jesus at Tiberias is supported by the tenth-century Greek encyclopedia *Suidas*, whose author states, under the heading "Jesus," that a Byzantine Jew named Theodosius averred that a genealogical roll of Jesus was preserved at Tiberias.[11-6]

Believing that Jesus was an historical figure, Schonfield developed an elaborate hypothesis to account for the presence of a Syrian name in the genealogy of Jesus:

On all the evidence, then, that we have adduced above, we conclude that the name Ben Pandera, as applied to Jesus, is genuine in so far as it was an actual cognomen in use in his family, and was so recorded in his genealogical history as preserved in Jewish Christian documents. The name also entered into the genealogy of Mary through intermarriages between the several branches of the family. We suggest further that the name, which is of foreign Syrian origin, may have been acquired through the romance of Jesus' ancestress, Estha (c. 85 A.D.), who married a Syrian proselyte to Judaism, and whose son Jacob was thereupon surnamed Panthera. [11-7]

It is doubtful that a Christian apologist could have come up with a more mind-boggling defense of the historical Jesus than this. When one considers that there is no credible evidence to support *any* single component of *any* of the Jesus genealogies, Schonfield's hypothesis fairly glows in the dark as a fairy-tale fabric woven from will-o'-the-wisp flashes and *ignis fatuus* flares.

The importance of Tiberias in the genealogical references led Schonfield to focus upon that Galilean city as the place of composition of the *Toldoth*. The rabbinical college at Tiberias came into prominence in the middle of the third century, and it continued to be a renowned center of Jewish learning for almost two centuries. After that, its influence declined, and by the eighth century the city had essentially been abandoned by the Jews. Its greatest prominence was in the fourth and early fifth centuries – a period when the Nazarene Jewish Christian communities were still thriving.[11-8]

Evidence that Jewish Christian activity was rife in Tiberias at the end of the fourth century – and thus might have provided the stimulus to compose anti-Christian propaganda – is found by Schonfield in the writings of Epiphanius [c315–403 CE], who told the story of a certain Joseph of Tiberias who came from the rabbinical college of the Patriarch Judah III. Early in the fourth century, Joseph had converted to Christianity. Before his conversion, he told Epiphanius, he had become seriously ill. One of the elders whispered in his ear, "Believe that Jesus the Son of God was crucified under Pontius Pilate, and that he will come again to judge the living and the dead."[11-9] Joseph also informed Epiphanius that he had witnessed the deathbed conversion of Judah's son, Hillel II [330–365 CE]. Joseph had watched through chinks in the door as Hillel received the sacrament from the

Bishop of Tiberias – who had also been his physician. After the patriarch's death, he found Hebrew copies of Matthew, John, and Acts of the Apostles stashed away in a secret place.[11-10] 'Matthew,' Schonfield believed, was actually the *Gospel According to the Hebrews*. 'John,' he thought, was actually the Hebrew original of the canonical Apocalypse – the 'Revelation of John.' The 'Acts of the Apostles' he thought was not our canonical Acts, but rather the book referred to by Epiphanius when he noted that the Jewish Christians "have other acts which they call 'Of the Apostles'."[11-11]

Summing up the external evidence for the *Toldoth*, Schonfield concluded that "The propaganda of the Nazarenes among their non-Christian brethren, and the circulation of their Gospel with its appended Acts, provides a strong justification for the retaliatory writing of the *Toldoth* parody. Indeed, it would be difficult to imagine a time and conditions more suitable for the production of such a work than the late fourth century at Tiberias."[11-12]

11.2. The Internal Evidence

In order to assess the internal evidence relating to the time and place of composition of the *Toldoth*, Schonfield first had to strip away everything that was obviously a late addition or the likely work of one or more redactors. (Material thus eliminated for his assessment of internal evidence is marked by double square brackets in the *Toldoth* text published here as appendix B.) Then, he searched for clues in the remaining material.

A most striking clue to the *Sitz im Leben* of the compiler of the *Toldoth* Schonfield found at the end of the first section, which is titled "The Seduction" in appendix B. After the disgraced Yohanan discovered the truth about Miriam's conception, "He arose and went to Babylon." During the third and fourth centuries, there were rival rabbinical colleges in Palestine and Babylonia, and it was not uncommon for a disgruntled Palestinian student to drop out of school and switch to an academy in Babylonian Sura or Pumbeditha. Yohanan, thus, is depicted as behaving like a young rabbinical student in third- or fourth-century Palestine. If the story had been composed much later than this and at a place outside Palestine, it is not likely the author would have thought to create a peculiar detail such as this.

The story of the *Eben-Shetiyah*, the Foundation Stone of the World that is mentioned at the beginning of the section "Robbing of the *Shem*," reflects an ancient Jewish legend traceable back at least to the third century CE. It was placed immediately in front of the Ark of the Covenant in the Holy of Holies, according to the Talmud and midrashim. The *shem*, the secret name, was supposed to be found inside the Ark itself. This datum is permissive of a fourth-century dating, but of course does not require it.

At the end of the section "The Magic Contest With Judas," we read that due to the defilement of Yeshu and his fall to earth, "It is because of this that they wail on their night, and because of the thing which Juda did to him." Despite the fact that Schonfield brackets this passage as coming from the hand of a redactor, he considered it nevertheless to reflect an early date (presumably even for the first redaction), since it appears to refer to an early practice in the Eastern Church. According to the *Apostolic Constitutions* [5:15–17], Christians were enjoined on the night of Saturday before Easter "to fast and wail over the Jews, because on the day of their feast they crucified Christ."[11-13]

At the beginning of the section "The Body is Recovered," we are told that "all the Israelites followed the owner of the garden, bound cords to his [Jeschu's] feet, and dragged him round in the streets of Jerusalem..." According to the *Ecclesiastical History* of Sozomen [5:21], during the reign of the Emperor Julian the Apostate [362 CE] there was a celebrated statue of Jesus at Paneas (Caesarea Philippi, not too many miles from Tiberias) that was taken down by the pagans "and dragged round the city and mutilated."[11-14] This event probably would have been of recent memory to the compiler of the *Toldoth*, allowing its incorporation into his story.

It was because of these data and others not repeated here that Hugh Schonfield assessed the internal evidence as indicating a late fourth-century Tiberian origin for the *Toldoth Yeshu*. "The internal evidence thus endorses the external evidence," he wrote,[11-15] "and indicates a date for the ur-*Toldoth* as about the end of the fourth century, when the Nazarenes were still a force to be reckoned with by orthodox Jews, and when their peculiar traditions had not been largely obliterated by the inroads of Islam and the anti-heretical policy of the post-Nicene Church." He summed up his argument as follows:

Finally, we would stress again the unique character of the *Toldoth* as a satirical Gospel. It is more than doubtful whether Jewish opposition to Jesus at any late date would have dared to take this drastic form. If the *Toldoth* had not already been in existence, we do not believe that any mediæval apologist would have created it. In its attitude to Christianity it can only be compared to Celsus' *True Discourse* and Lucian of Samosata's *De Morte Peregrini*, pagan satires both written towards the end of the second century. In deciding on a Gospel parody as the most effective method of discrediting the Christian faith the author definitely reflects the spirit of his age; it is the early days of the Eastern Roman Empire.

This dating seems eminently reasonable, although I do not consider it to be an established fact.

It is significant, I think, that even though Schonfield believed in the reality of an historical Jesus, he did not suppose he had found actual evidence of him in his *Toldoth* research. "It now seems clear," he wrote,[11-16] "what had hitherto been suspected, that the Jews retained little if any recollection of Jesus, and consequently that their information was based on Jewish Christian tradition. We have established from early Christian remains, that specifically Jewish Christian doctrines and traditions are reflected in the *Toldoth* at every place where this can be tested." Thus, only to the extent that the *Toldoth* reliably reflects details of the *Gospel According to the Hebrews* – and only to the extent that the latter in turn preserved authentic traditions of Jesus – can we hope to find any possible evidence for an historical Jesus in *Toldoth* studies. It remains to be considered in the next chapter whether *Hebrews* was likely to have been derived from a creditable historical tradition, or whether it was merely fished out from the same ragout of folk legends and misunderstandings of mysteries from which all other gospels have been served up.

CHAPTER 12

Jewish Gospels, Jewish Christianity, and Christian Origins

Most liberal scholars – I beg forgiveness for the redundancy – take it for granted not only that Christianity is a direct off-shoot of Judaism, but also that the first Christians were Jews who had known an historical Jesus "in the flesh" and had undergone some sort of psychiatric metamorphosis that had led them to believe that Jesus had been resurrected from the dead after an actual execution by means of crucifixion.

These first Jewish Christians, then, would have held a 'low Christology' in which Jesus was not himself a god, but rather a man like the prophets who had been touched by Yahweh in some psychological sense. Low Christology, associated with an earthly biography for Jesus, is thought to mark the most primitive, earliest stage in the evolution of Christianity. 'High Christologies,' such as those of Pauline, Catholic Christianity, where Jesus Christ is Very God of Very God, are believed to be a later development. Nevertheless, despite being the opinion of the overwhelming majority of scholars, the priority of literalist, body-believing Jewish Christianity over mystical, mythical, Docetic, and Gnostic Christianity remains a mere assumption, not a proven fact.

So *were* the first Jewish Christians literalists, believing that Jesus was a mere man? Was Euhemerus [*fl. c*300 BCE] right in his theory that all the gods had first been men? Our study of the *Toldoth Yeshu* forces us to grapple with this question, since our search for the Jewish gospel satirized by the *Toldoth* requires us to consider the date of that gospel. We are compelled to see if its presumably low Christology is in fact earlier than the high Christology of, say, the Gospel of John.

Hugh J. Schonfield, the scholar who was to devote a very long lifetime to the study of Jewish forms of Christianity, had concluded already by 1937 that the *Toldoth Yeshu* was a satirical response to a long-lost gospel mentioned by Epiphanius and other church fathers – the so-called *Gospel According to the Hebrews*. But the *Toldoth* proved to be a burlesque of more than a gospel. Schonfield knew that in addition to the Jewish gospel, or life of Jesus, Epiphanius had commented that the Ebionites (a Jewish Christian group) also had their own version of an 'Acts of the Apostles':

> They (the Ebionites) have other Acts which they call "of the Apostles," among which are many things filled with their impiety, whence they have incidentally supplied themselves with arms against the truth. For they set forth certain Ascents and Instructions forsooth in the *Ascents of James*, representing him as holding forth against both temple and sacrifices, and against the fire on the altar, and many other things filled with empty talk, so that they are not ashamed in them even to denounce Paul in certain invented utterances of the malignant and deceitful work of their false apostles. [*Panarion* 30:16] 12-1

Following the suggestion of the scholar Benjamin Bacon, Schonfield argued cogently that the Hebrew Gospel-Acts combination seems to have been written as a response to the canonical Luke-Acts[12-2] – arguably the latest parts of the New Testament as it is now defined. If this be correct, it means that *Toldoth Yeshu* in its earliest recension is later than all of the New Testament and is of no more value than the latter for proving the existence of an historical Jesus. Since, however, its roots go back to the period in which the New Testament was being invented, it nevertheless may be of value in reconstructing the history of Christianity's beginnings.

If, as just indicated, the *Toldoth* is secondary to a Hebrew gospel that is itself demonstrably later than the canonical gospels, the total absence from ancient Jewish literature of credible evidence of an historical Jesus has been demonstrated. But *is* the *Gospel According to the Hebrews* demonstrably later than the canonical New Testament?

Research done after Schonfield's 1937 *According to the Hebrews* – a work to which I am immensely indebted – has complicated the question and indicates that his conclusion that there was a single Jewish gospel is probably an error. It would appear that there were at least three Jewish gospels – all of which it would seem were later than and secondary to the canonical gospels.

According to Philipp Vielhauer and Georg Strecker, who edited the Jewish-Christian gospels for the *New Testament Apocrypha*,[12-3] the problem of the Jewish-Christian gospels is "one of the most difficult which the apocryphal literature presents." Part of the difficulty, it appears, is due to the mendacity of the church father St. Jerome [c342–420] – the translator of the Vulgate Latin Bible. Jerome claimed on several occasions to have translated the *Gospel According to the Hebrews* himself:

> Also the Gospel which is called 'according to the Hebrews' and which was recently translated by me into Greek and Latin speech, which Origen also used frequently... [*De Viris Inlustribus* 2] [12-4]

Jerome claimed to have translated the gospel from a Semitic language, yet his predecessor Origen never gave any indication that the gospel had not been composed originally in Greek. Either Jerome was lying, or he wasted a great deal of effort in translating a work that was already available in Greek. Jerome's honesty is further rendered questionable by his claim that the Hebrew original of the Gospel of Matthew was still to be found in the library at Caesarea, and by the fact that he appears to consider it the equivalent of the *Gospel According to the Hebrews*:

> Matthew in Judæa was the first to compose the gospel of Christ in the Hebrew character and speech for the sake of those who came over to the faith from Judaism; who he was who later translated it into Greek is no longer known with certainty. [*Has Jerome forgotten that he himself translated it?*] Further the Hebrew text itself is still preserved in the library at Cæsarea which the martyr Pamphilus collected with great care. The Nazaræans in Berœa, a city of Syria, who use this book, also permitted me to copy it. In it it is to be noted that wherever the evangelist adduces testimonies from the Old Testament – be this done by himself or by our Lord and Saviour – he follows not the Septuagint translation but the Hebrew original text. [*Vir. Inl.* 3]

> In the Gospel which the Nazarenes and the Ebionites use, which we recently translated out of the Hebrew tongue into the Greek and which is called by most people the authentic (Gospel) of Matthew... [*Commentary on Matthew*] [12-5]

First of all, we must note that Jerome is *not* saying that Matthew was the first to write a gospel. He was merely the first to write a gospel "in the Hebrew character and speech." Secondly, we get the impression that Christianity was already a going affair outside even Hellenic Judaism, since Matthew wrote his Semitic gospel "for the sake of those who came over to the faith from Judaism." If Palestinian Jews had been the first Christians, the original gospel would have been in Hebrew or Aramaic, as indicated by church fathers such as the second-century Phrygian bishop Papias. But Jerome here gives one the distinct impression that the first gospels were in Greek (as almost all modern scholars have always maintained) and only later were rendered into Semitic tongues for the purpose of evangelizing non-Hellenic Jews.

Finally, it must be noted that Jerome could not have seen the Hebrew original of Matthew in the library at Cæsarea, for his immediate predecessor Eusebius – the owner of the library – never said he had such a treasure in his library and never identified an unknown Jewish Gospel as being the original of the Gospel of Matthew. Vielhauer and Strecker dryly comment that

> The Cœlesyrian Berœa near Aleppo was in fact a centre of the Nazaræans, *i.e.* of the Syrian Jewish Christians... Jerome can have had contact with them only during his stay in the desert of Chalcis, *i.e.* between 373 and 376... but then it is altogether inconceivable that he kept the Gospel of the Nazaræans so long to himself and was silent about it, and cited it for the first time in 386. It is equally inconceivable that the differences between the Gospel of the Nazaræans and the canonical Matthew can have struck him so little that he could consider the latter to be the translation of the former. The conclusion is inevitable that it was not the Nazaræans who communicated to him his knowledge of this gospel. [12-6]

Jerome also confuses the question of exactly what language his Nazorean gospel was composed in, and greatly obscures the problem of Jewish gospels in general by his contradictory statements and, apparently, outright lies. Nevertheless, Vielhauer and Strecker have patiently sorted out all the relevant passages in Jerome's works and compared them with the writings of Irenaeus, Clement of Alexandria, Origen, Hegesippus, Eusebius, Epiphanius, Cyril of Jerusalem, Nicephorus, and Ignatius, as well as with the *Judaikon*, readings from which are known from marginal notes in several medieval manuscripts of Matthew, and they conclude that there are in fact *three* different Jewish gospels known to the early Church Fathers, and they provide reconstructions of them based on the quotations from them that have come down to modern times.

The three Jewish gospels[12-7] are the following:

(1) **The *Gospel of the Nazaræans*.** Attested by Hegesippus [d. 180], Eusebius [c264–340], Epiphanius [c315–403], and Jerome [c342–420], this apparently was read in Aramaic or Syriac and was closely related to the canonical Matthew.

(2) **The *Gospel of the Ebionites*.** Attested by Irenaeus [c130-c200] and Epiphanius, this was composed in Greek and was perhaps the only gospel used by certain "heretical" Jewish Christians. It was closest to the Gospel of Matthew but differed from it in important details.

(3) **The *Gospel According to the Hebrews*.** Perhaps used by Papias [second century], it is attested by Eusebius, Clement of Alexandria [c150–c215], and Origen [c185–c254]. It seems to have been unlike any of the canonical gospels and was used by 'heretical' Jewish Christians.

Assuming that Vielhauer and Strecker are correct, and that the *Toldoth Yeshu* is a satire of one or all of these, we must then inquire as to the dates of authorship of these Jewish gospels. If the *Toldoth* contains evidence of an historical Jesus, to be credible it must be shown that the gospel it mocks is older than the canonical gospels that repeatedly have been shown to be of little or no historical significance. Can great antiquity be demonstrated for these three Jewish evangels?

12.1. The *Gospel of the Nazaræans*

Although it was known to Hegesippus, Eusebius, Epiphanius, and Jerome as being in Aramaic or Syriac (a dialect of Aramaic), it is not at all certain that it was composed in that language. In fact, Vielhauer and Strecker adduce persuasive evidence to

demonstrate that the Nazorean gospel was a free and expanded
Aramaic version of canonical Matthew – in effect, a targum of
Matthew.[12-8] Since canonical Matthew is in turn an expanded
reworking of Q and the Gospel of Mark, the *Gospel of the
Nazaræans* can provide no historical evidence for Jesus beyond
the unreliable material that we find in the New Testament. Of
still less significance would be a *Toldoth*ian burlesque of this
gospel. The Nazorean gospel must, therefore, be a product of the
first half of the second century – the *terminus a quo* for its
composition being the date of composition of canonical Matthew,
the *terminus ad quem* being 180 CE, when Hegesippus mentions
it.

12.2. The *Gospel of the Ebionites*

Vielhauer and Strecker show[12-9] that this edition of canonical
Matthew was originally composed in Greek. They identify it as a
'gospel harmony' combining features of all three synoptic gospels.
Epiphanius tells us that

> In the Gospel used by them, that called 'according to
> Matthew', which however is not wholly complete but falsified
> and mutilated – they call it the 'Hebrew (Gospel)' [*Hær.*
> 30.13.2][12-10]
> They have cut away the genealogy in Matthew and, as has
> already been said, have let the Gospel begin in this way: It came
> to pass, it is said, in the days of Herod, the king of Judæa, when
> Caiaphas was high priest, that there came a certain man John
> by name and baptised with the baptism of repentance in the
> river Jordan. [*Hær.* 30.14.3][12-11]

Vielhauer and Strecker agree with Epiphanius that the
Ebionite gospel (which lacked both the genealogy of Jesus and
the nativity myth) was an abridged and falsified Gospel of
Matthew, but I think they err. It is clear that 'Matthew' as we now
know it is the result of an evolution through several stages. Its
first edition may have been nothing more than a fusion of the
narrative of Mark (which contains neither genealogy nor nativity
tale) with the wise sayings of Q. The second edition probably

added a genealogy that traced Jesus' ancestry through Joseph to David, in order to demonstrate his Messianic qualifications. Then, the story of the virgin birth was added which, because it contradicted the genealogical argument, necessitated the creation of a fourth edition, which no longer stated bluntly that Joseph begat Jesus, but could not eliminate the absurdity of a genealogy – ostensibly for Jesus – which traces the ancestry of a man to which he is not related!

Rather than the Ebionite gospel being a falsification of canonical Matthew, then, I suggest it was merely a survival of the earliest edition of that gospel. Even though the Ebionite gospel, then, may witness an earlier stage of gospel evolution than that seen in the present-day edition of Matthew, by virtue of its knowing nothing of the descent, birth, and childhood of Jesus it can be seen *de facto* as another argument against his historicity. Moreover, since the *Toldoth* clearly satirizes the virgin birth myth (or, in some cases, merely the unspotted paternity and descent of Jesus), it would appear that the *Gospel of the Ebionites* was not the target of *Toldoth* ribaldry. This gospel is dated by Vielhauer and Strecker to the beginning of the second century at the earliest.

12.3. The *Gospel According to the Hebrews* (The *Gospel of the Hebrews*)

Of the three Jewish gospels here noted, this would appear most likely to have been the target for the *Toldoth* satire, as it seems to have presaged Jesus' aerobatic exploits with its verse "Even so did my mother, the Holy Spirit, take me by one of my hairs and carry me away on to the great mountain Tabor."[12-12] It seems to have been even more mythical in style than the canonical gospels and to have differed from them quite markedly.

It was large. According to the *Stichometry of Nicephorus* [Patriarch of Constantinople, 806–815 CE],[12-13] it was 2,200 lines long – just 300 lines shorter than canonical Matthew. Like the Gospel of John, it appears to have had an introduction in which the preexistence of Jesus was claimed. It seems also to have contained an account of his birth – again, a significant feature if it was to be a *Toldoth* target. A Coptic manuscript of Cyril of Jerusalem provides the following startling information:

> It is written in the *Gospel of the Hebrews*: When Christ wished to come upon the earth to men, the good Father summoned a mighty power in heaven, which was called Michael, and entrusted Christ to the care thereof. And the power came into the world and it was called Mary, and Christ was in her womb seven months. [12-14]

The primitive Gnostic mythology reflected here indicates to me at least that this gospel was written at a time of transition, when proto-Christians were trying to transform a mythical, heavenly being into a man of flesh and blood such as we find in the Gospel of Mark. It would seem to mark a stage in reification somewhat earlier than that found in the canonical Gospel of John. I would, therefore, date it to the second half of the first century. Vielhauer and Strecker, however, date it to the first half of the second century and argue convincingly that it was composed in Egypt, probably at Alexandria.

It is significant that the *Gospel According to the Hebrews* is known to have accorded special honor to James the Just, one of the few New Testament characters who may actually have been historical. If he did exist and was in fact the leader of a church in Jerusalem, there would have been need to create scriptural proofs of his authenticity as an exponent of the religion of Jesus. A passage in the *Gospel According to the Hebrews* seems tailor-made for the exaltation of James. Unfortunately for those who would seek sources in which they can have confidence, the passage in question is quoted only by an author of dubious veracity – St. Jerome:

> The Gospel called according to the Hebrews which was recently translated by me into Greek and Latin, which Origen frequently uses, records after the resurrection of the Saviour:
> And when the Lord had given the linen cloth to the servant of the priest, he went to James and appeared to him. For James had sworn that he would not eat bread from that hour in which he had drunk the cup of the Lord until he should see him risen from among them that sleep. And shortly thereafter the Lord said: Bring a table and bread! And immediately it is added: he took the bread, blessed it and brake it and gave it to James the Just and said to him: My brother, eat thy bread, for the Son of man is risen from among them that sleep. [12-15]

If my dating of the *Gospel According to the Hebrews* to the second half of the first century be correct, it would be of considerable value in reconstructing the history of the early church. Unfortunately, my dating depends upon the thesis that Christianity is a heretical form of Gnosticism, contradicting the thesis that Gnosticism was a heretical form of Christianity, as traditional scholarship has long assumed. A small book would be needed to assemble the data and arguments needed to prove that thesis, however, and I cannot attempt to do so here. Because of the blatantly mythical style of the *Gospel According to the Hebrews*, successful dating of it to the first century would provide another powerful argument against the historicity of Jesus by showing that the farther back one traces the Jesus story, the less biographical and more celestial it appears. Alas, this is a task for the future.

Despite the uncertainty in my own dating of the *Gospel According to the Hebrews* and my conclusion that it argues against an historical Jesus, it must be noted that the dating of it to the first half of the second century by Vielhauer and Strecker also would remove it as a source of evidence for an historical Jesus. Even if it did contain, somewhere in the large amount of text now lost, authentic facts of an historical Jesus, the transformation into the *Toldoth* satire has rendered them unrecognizable. Only wishful thinking, not scholarship, can descry the footprints of an historical Jesus in the Jewish gospels or their *Toldoth* transformations.

12.4. The Testimony of Sa'adia

That at least one of the Jewish gospels was later than those used by other Christian sects is indicated also by the Jewish author Sa'adia [d. 942 CE], who wrote in his *Kitab al-amānāt wa'li'tiqādāt*:

> These people [the Christians] (are divided) may God have pity upon you (into) four sects; three of them are more ancient [*aqdam*] (whereas) the fourth came out [*kharajat*] (only) recently [*qarībam*]... The fourth gives him [*i.e.*, Jesus, called a few lines above their Messiah] only the rank of a prophet, and interprets the Sonship which according to them is attributed to him just (p. 91) as we interpret (the verse): My son my first born Israel being only (an indication of) his being honoured [*tashrīf*] and preferred [*tafḍīl*] and just as others than we [*i.e.*, the Moslems] interpret the expression "Abraham, the Friend of God" [*khalīl allāh*].[12-16]

Thus, the Jewish Christians who had the most reified and literalist view of Christ and had turned him into a mere historical prophet are not the earliest of Christians but rather are among the latest to evolve. They do not have firsthand memories of an historical Jesus. They have only an imperfect grasp of the mystery of a savior who had come to earth and been given a body – by still earlier worshipers who could not deal with abstractions and had to concretize everything in order to deal with it.

The evidence, then, from the Jewish gospels shows that most, if not all of them, are later than the canonical gospels. The one possible exception, the *Gospel According to the Hebrews* (= *Gospel of the Hebrews*), appears to have been the most mythological and least 'historical.' It seems to have held a high Christology, with Jesus a preexistent being (as in the prologue of the Gospel of John).

In the Jewish gospels, as in their synoptic cousins, the later the writer, the greater the amount of biographical detail Jesus has acquired. The later an author lived after the time allotted for Jesus' terrestrial vacation, the more he knows about him! (Of course, no one has ever discovered what Jesus looked like. Was he tall or short? Fat or skinny? Handsome or ugly? Curly-haired or bald? *Basso profundo* or squeaky-voiced? Aquiline or pug-nosed? Pimple-pocked or baby-faced? The absence of such basic data from all the alleged biographies of Jesus cries out for an explanation!)

12.5. What's Wrong with the Standard Model of Christian Origins?

According to the standard model of Christian origins, a man was made into a god. Christianity began in Jerusalem after the execution of a certain messianic claimant known in his lifetime as Jesus of Nazareth. Jesus, it is alleged, had a small number of Jewish disciples who became convinced that he had been resurrected from the dead and had visited them in various theophanies. Joined by another Jewish seer and visionary named Saul of Tarsus, who came from a Mithraic stronghold now part of modern Turkey, these individuals, along with hundreds of helpers recently converted to the cause of Jesus the Messiah, went out to all the parts of the Roman Empire as apostles of the new faith now being formed. Some of these, however, such as John, James, and Peter (Cephas) are supposed to have stayed at home in Jerusalem for at least a while to rule over a church that had been formed at the epicenter of Yahweh's seismic intrusion into human affairs. Within a shockingly short period of time, churchly outposts of the new religion had been established at the uttermost reaches of the Roman Empire. No sooner had the religion undergone its miraculous expansion than it was wracked by dissension and a proliferation of heresies – some of which, surprisingly enough, appear to be at least as old as orthodoxy itself.

It is generally supposed that non-Hellenic Jewish Christianity is the oldest and most authentic form of Christianity – the Christianity that existed before the Hellenized Saul/Paul introduced Greco-Roman mystery elements into the faith and turned the mortal man Jesus into the immortal god Christ.

I believe the standard model is wrong: a man did not become a god. Rather, a god was changed into a man. Jesus (Aramaic *Yeshua*ʿ, meaning 'Savior') was originally a god in a mystery religion that formed at the turn of the era when the vernal equinox moved from the zodiacal sign of Aries (the ram or lamb) into Pisces (the fishes). Like Mithras before him, Jesus was a *chronocrat* or time-lord modeled after Chronos* the time-god of the mysteries. Jesus was to rule in the new celestial kingdom that was initiated astronomically and astrologically sometime early in the first century of the common era. Just as the chief symbol of Mithraism was the depiction of the *taurobolium* – the sacrifice of a bull, marking the movement of the equinox from Taurus (the bull) into Aries, so too the passage from Aries into Pisces was associated with the image of the sacrificial lamb, the two fishes that were (and still are) the astrological symbol for Pisces, and the chi-rho cross – which actually was the Greek abbreviation for Chronos, as we know from a copy of Aristotle's *Constitution of Athens* which was found in the ruins of Pompeii.[12-17]

---

*The connection between Chronos and Christianity received some unexpected support not too many years ago when Shlomo Pines published "The Jewish Christians of the Early Centuries of Christianity According to a New Source"[12-18] and made known the text of an Arabic manuscript that contains a work by the tenth-century Muʿtazilite author ʿAbd al-Jabbār al-Hamadānī entitled *Tathbīt Dalāʾil Nubuwwat Sayyidinā Muḥammad* – 'The Establishment of Proofs for the Prophethood of Our Master Mohammed.' Ostensibly a

I do not think that Christianity began in a single place at a specific time. Rather, I think it started to develop around the time of the Roman poet Virgil [d. 19 BCE] in the eastern half of the Mediterranean, involving places from Rome to Alexandria. Its earliest inventors included Hellenized Jews who seem to have been aware of sun-god roots of Yahwism[12-23] and were increasingly "solarizing" their various brands of non-rabbinic Judaism and had become aware of Hipparchus' discovery [c128 BCE][12-24] of the precession of the equinoxes, pagan "God-fearers" who were deeply impressed by Jewish mysticism and claims of immense antiquity, astrologically savvy Jewish sectarians such as those at Qumran on the Dead Sea, the Therapeutae of whom Philo wrote, Essene splinter groups, and early Gnostics who had not yet evolved the flamboyancies now associated with Gnosticism. According to my view, Christianity is not a plant with a taproot going down to a single specific depth, but rather it is a braid in time, comprised of numerous strands of tradition, some going

piece of Muslim anti-Christian polemic, the work in fact incorporates much material derived from ancient Jewish Christian sources.

One of the materials incorporated into al-Jabbar's work tells us that "The Romans and the Greeks had a feast, called the Nativity of Time [i.e., Chronos], which celebrated the return of the sun in January. They introduced into it various modifications and called it the Nativity of Christ or the Nativity."[12-19] According to Pines, this must refer to the January 5 Feast of Epiphany, which up to the end of the fourth century was widely celebrated in the East as the birthday of Jesus and is still celebrated as such by the Armenian Church. According to Epiphanius [Panarion, II 51, 22, 8-11],[12-20] the Feast of Epiphany coincided with that of the birth of Aion as celebrated in Alexandria.

Aion (Æon or Eon), it may further be noted, was the son of Chronos.[12-21] He was an advisor of Zeus, who rolled the wheel of time. He was prominent in the Orphic mysteries, and a festival for him celebrated on January 3 is also known. He could signify both Mithras and Chronos – as well as Jesus, as we now learn from Shlomo Pines. Even more striking relationships between Aion and Christian concepts were noted long ago by Robert Eisler,[12-22] who demonstrated that Aion was the World-Soul of Anaximines just as Chronos was the World-Soul for Pythagoras. Aion was, it would seem, the prototype for both the divine *Logos* ('Word') and the *Hagion Pneuma* ('Holy Breath' or 'Holy Spirit') of Christian mythology, as he is identified as both Logos and *pneuma* in the pagan literature associated with the mysteries.

farther, some less remotely into the indefinite past. At various places, certain strands diverge from the braid, fray out, and disappear into oblivion, while other strands are taken up into the braid from diverse sources. In short, Christianity was no different in its beginnings than were the religions of Greece and Rome.

Originally a god pure and simple, Jesus at first was the property of mystery cults. Whether due to lapses in security or otherwise, it appears that the mystery of Jesus leaked out to *hoi polloi*, who did not understand the symbolism of the mysteries. A religion that once contained exoteric elements that it published in order to propagandize potential recruits, as well as esoteric elements understood only by initiates, it ultimately lost its esoteric components and became a literalist religion that even the most intellectually challenged could understand. It became the religion of Right to Lifers, creation scientists, holy rollers, and snake-handlers. A celestial being became reified, was given a physical existence, and then acquired a biography – a biography that grew in detail for several centuries. It would appear that Docetism was the connecting link between the mysteries and orthodox beliefs. The Docetists believed that Jesus only *seemed* (Greek δοκεῖν *dokein*, 'seem') to have a physical body.

It is regrettable that I have neither space nor time to demonstrate the truth of my thesis in this book. I can do no more here than to show that a careful analysis of ancient Jewish writings is consistent with the hypothesis. If I can elude the Reaper long enough, I hope to finish my book *Inventing Jesus*, which will, it is my hope, adduce sufficient evidence to convince impartial scholars that Christianity began without a physical Christ.

12.6. Did the Jews Know Jesus?

The search for the historical Jesus in Jewish sources now has reached its end. Nowhere have we been able to find a mention of him that was not derivable from Christian sources, whether they relate to the canonical gospels, the apocryphal gospels, or to what may reasonably be reconstructed as the propaganda of early Christians. The greatest *Toldoth* scholar of the first half of the twentieth century, Hugh J. Schonfield, agreed with this conclusion – at least as it pertains to the *Toldoth Yeshu*. "We think that it will be admitted," he wrote, "that the case for the *Toldoth* depending on Christian tradition as well for its canonical as for its uncanonical details is now established beyond a peradventure."[12-25] Nowhere

– neither in the *Toldoth* nor in the certainly ancient literature of the Jews – have we found any compelling evidence to make us believe that the Jews of antiquity had any firsthand knowledge of a man named Jesus of Nazareth. The Jews were reacting to Christianity, not to Christ.

Nearly a century ago, a scholar named M. Freimann came to essentially the same conclusion. Freimann went even further, however, and cited evidence from an early source that he claimed indicated that the ancient Jews themselves had admitted that they possessed no tradition concerning the Nazarene in question.[12-26,27] Freimann believed that the early fifth-century dialogue *Altercatio Simonis et Theophili* ('The Cross-Examination of Simon and Theophilus') explicitly contained an admission by the Jewish character (Simon) that the Jews had no tradition concerning Jesus. Moreover, he believed the *Altercatio* to have been a reworking of the lost second-century *Dialogue of Jason and Papiscus*, which would place this admission in an historically crucial period. William Horbury, the *Toldoth* expert whose work I have had several occasions to discuss, denies this, however, and claims the *Altercatio* should simply be considered an early fifth-century piece of propaganda. Moreover, he does not interpret the Latin text in the same way that Freimann did, thinking that *Christus* should be translated as *Messiah* rather than *Christ*. Even so, I think Freimann's understanding of the Latin makes more sense than does Horbury's, and so I shall summon the temerity to disagree with the world's greatest living authority on the *Toldoth Yeshu*.

12.7. The *Altercatio Simonis et Theophili*

"If what you are telling me is indeed true," Simon begins, "that our forefathers crucified him, I am thrown into consternation to understand how Christ could have undergone sufferings which are both accursed and ridiculous." Holding the opinion that so unusual an event would have been recorded in Jewish writings or traditions, he then adduces two examples of supposed crucifixions from scripture and Jewish tradition: "We know perfectly well the accursed Haman, who tried to do away with our race and was justly crucified by our forefathers [*hanged, not crucified, in Esther 7:10*], and we celebrate his death according to the tradition we have received from them. And we read of Absalom, the parricide, who was hung on a tree" [*2 Sam 18:9-15, also not a crucifixion*].

Then comes the crucial sentence: "But if Christ [*or the Messiah, in Horbury's view*] actually suffered this penalty, why have we not received it as a tradition from our forefathers, why have we not found it in our written records, so that, if he had been an enemy of our people, we might rejoice?" Then Simon adds an *ad hominem* fillip: "You ought to blush with shame, Theophilus, if you agree with this in the slightest degree. For it is written in Deuteronomy 21:23, 'Accursed are all who hang on a tree'."*

If *Christus* really means 'Christ' rather than 'the Messiah,' this is an extremely important indication that as late as the fifth century, at least one Jewish community had no memory of Jesus of its own and was entirely dependent on what Christians were telling them about him. My reading of *Christus* as 'Christ' follows not only Freimann, but the great historian of dogma Adolf von Harnack as well. To be candid, *pace* William Horbury, the reading 'Christ' should be a no-brainer, since the whole dialogue ostensibly is concerned with Christ, not messiahs. Furthermore, by the fifth century it is unlikely that Latin-speaking Jews would even know that *Christus* came from the Greek *Christos* which was the equivalent of the Hebrew *māshīaḥ* and meant 'the anointed one'. Already in New Testament times, for many people *Christ* was a name, no longer a title. *Christ* had become Jesus' last name – his cognomen. (His first name, it will be remembered, also began as a title – *Yeshua* meaning 'the Savior' in Aramaic and Hebrew.)

---

*Aestuo vehementer cogitatione, potuisse Christum tam maledictum et ludibriosam sustinere passionem, si tamen vera sunt, quæ dicitis, a patribus nostris crucis patibulo eum esse suffixum. Scimus plane Aman maledictum a patribus nostris pro merito suo esse crucifixum, qui genus nostrum petierat in perditionem, in cuius mortem perevoluto anno gratulamur et sollemnia votorum facta celebramus, quæ a patribus tradita accepimus, et Abessalon, qui ad cædem patris patricida fuit, pependisse illum in arbore legimus. Christus autem, si patibulum mortis huius sustinuit et in cruce pependit, cur non hoc ipsum a patribus accepimus nec passum in scripturis nostris invenimus, ut si inimicus genti nostræ esset, gauderemus? Erubescere poteris, Theophile, si hoc dictum minime comprobaveris. Nam scriptum est in Deuteronomio: maledictus omnis, qui pendet in ligno.[12-28]

Envoi

The fact that the Jews of antiquity had no firsthand knowledge of Jesus of Nazareth – and could only react to the claims of Christian polemics by taking them at face value – is of enormous importance to students of the history of religions. It undermines the last bulwark of 'evidence' for the existence of the quondam Galilean Cynic sage, prophet, bandit, armed revolutionary, pacifist, ascetic, free lover, New Ager, or apocalypse herald that has been created by so many would-be biographers of the historical Jesus. I have not dealt with the non-Jewish 'evidence' – the New Testament and the pagan historians – for the simple reason that it has been known at least since the 1790s that that material is of no significance in establishing the historicity of Jesus. Starting with the colossal 1795 thirteen-volume œuvre of Charles François Dupuis [1742–1809] – *Origine De Tous Les Cultes* – in which the astrological origins of Christianity and other religions was first elucidated, many scholars have contributed to the debunking of the New Testament as being an historically significant source of information concerning Jesus. Noteworthy modern scholars writing in this vein are G. A. Wells (*The Historical Evidence for Jesus*) and Earl Doherty (*The Jesus Puzzle*).

The historical Jesus has always been made to stand on two legs: the New Testament and Jewish literature. The New Testament leg I consider to have been sawed off long ago. Amputation of the Jewish leg has been, I hope, the achievement of this book. With both his legs missing, the figure of Jesus must now either hover in the air – like the god he started out as in the Christian mysteries or like the Yeshu he became in the *Toldoth* – or he must fall to earth like a deflated balloon. I think the latter fate is the one that must now befall him, for in truth the historical Jesus has never stood firmly on the ground. He has always hovered ever so slightly above it, breathing a gas that since the beginning has been lighter than air. The gases that first filled the Jesus balloon, I think, were the effluvia that emanated from tumid brains that first assayed to understand the motional details of the starry sky that moved in majesty above their awe-filled heads. The apparent movement of the sun through the starry houses of the zodiac and the very real progression of the earthly seasons were, until the age of science, mysteries that must have spawned countless religions during the long prehistory and history of humankind.

As with the Mithras balloon that preceded it with such success, inflation of the Jesus balloon was a byproduct of the discovery of the precession of the vernal equinox – the apparent backwards movement through the zodiacal houses of the point in the sky where the sun in spring seems to ascend above the celestial equator. At that time, the sun god staged his annual resurrection from astronomical death and ascended toward the highest heaven, now in regions of the spangled sky that differed from his former haunts. A phenomenon so difficult for pre-scientific minds to perceive let alone to understand, it seemed as though the very dome of heaven had been knocked out of kilter. Only a god pushing on the axial pole of the universe could do that. A new god for a new age was needed, a chronocrat to succeed Mithras – a sun god who still would be born on the winter solstice and could also be worshiped on Sunday.

And they called his name Jesus. And they plucked him from the skies and laid him in a manger – in a stable no longer located between Orion and Andromeda, a stable now situated in a dry and dusty region of the planet we call Earth. And they bestowed upon him flesh and blood, breath and bones – and even a foreskin. And then they crucified him, but could not allow his body to undergo corruption. And so, they raised him from his literary tomb and launched him back into the night sky – into the same mysterious realm wherein they first had found him. Very God of Very God, Coeternal with the Father, the *Logos* that had existed from the beginning, the Alpha and the Omega – Jesus became an infinite being who could no longer be comprehended by human minds. Once again, the infinite had to be made finite for mortal minds to understand. A biography, not a theography, was needed. Anonymous writers and editors who later would be christened Matthew, Mark, Luke, and John satisfied the need. And all the rest is theology, not history.

APPENDIX A

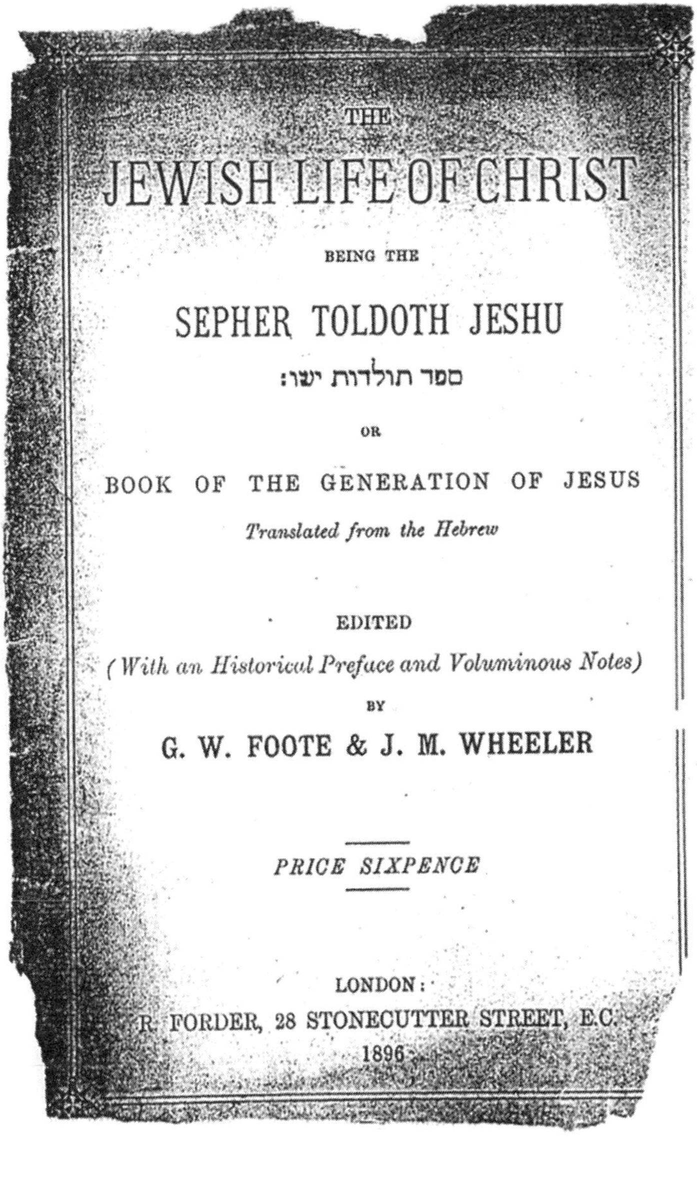

THE

JEWISH LIFE OF CHRIST

BEING THE

SEPHER TOLDOTH JESHU

ספר תולדות ישו:

OR

BOOK OF THE GENERATION OF JESUS

Translated from the Hebrew

EDITED

(With an Historical Preface and Voluminous Notes)

BY

G. W. FOOTE & J. M. WHEELER

PRICE SIXPENCE

LONDON:

R. FORDER, 28 STONECUTTER STREET, E.C.

1896

Figure 10. A nineteenth-century edition of Foote & Wheeler's *Sepher Toldoth Jeshu.*

THE

JEWISH LIFE OF CHRIST

Being the

SEPHER TOLDOTH JESHU

ספר תולדות ישו:

BOOK of the GENERATION of JESUS

Translated from the Hebrew

(*With an Historical Preface and Voluminous Notes*)

by G(eorge) W(illiam) Foote & J(oseph) M(azzini)
Wheeler

(Originally published by Progressive Pub. Co, London,
1885)

With an Introduction by

Madalyn Murray O'Hair

Copyright © 1982 American Atheist Press

ISBN: 0-910309-02-7

INTRODUCTION

Most Atheist Bible scholars have known about the *Sepher Toldoth Jeshu* (*The Jewish Life of Christ*) for over a hundred years. Yet no one researching the life of the mythological Jesus Christ can find references to it in any of the standard works. At the time that it was first reviewed in the American Atheist Radio Series in June 1973, the American Atheist Center received highly critical letters, telephone calls, and ultimately threats from Jewish organizations in the United States denouncing the broadcasts as anti-Semitic. This was followed by 'critiques' put together by several Jewish 'scholars' to support that charge, accompanied by demands that apologies be issued for broadcasting the *Sepher Toldoth Jeshu*. Those demands were ignored.

Indeed, the Jews — attacked by the Christians, in the Middle Ages particularly, with their Talmud often destroyed — continue to hold an unreasonable fear of disclosure that at any time in their history they could have composed any piece of literature in derogation of Jesus Christ. The position of the Jews, currently, is that this piece of literature was written by Christian clerics in the 1500s in order to place an onus on the Jews, the better to persecute them, since it would incite against the Jews the ordinary Christian reading it.

All of their protestations are of naught since it is obvious that Quintus Septimus Florens Tertullianus, a Christian apologist often called "the greatest of the ancient church writers," who lived 160 to 220, knew of certain of these elements, then preserved in great elaboration. Writing his *Adversus Judæos* about 197–198, the bishop of Carthage (Tertullian) rhetorically addressed the Jews with "This is your harlot's son." In the *Clementine Recognitions* (i. 42), generally ascribed to the third century, but which contains far older material, we read, "For some of them, watching the place with care, when they could

not prevent His rising again, said that He was a magician."
Also, Origen, who lived 185 to 253, one of the church's most
prolific writers, undertook to refute a Jew named Celsus. In
doing so, he demonstrated in his book *Contra Celsum* that he
was well aware of the story of Panthera and Mary.

The converted philosopher Arnobius, who wrote his
treatise *Against the Nations* somewhere about 303–313, states
that the commonest argument against the Christians
concerning Jesus was, "He was a Magus; he did all these
things by secret arts; from the shrines of the Egyptians he
stole the names of angels of might and hidden disciplines."

In his *Letter to Heliodorus*, which was written in 374,
Jerome writes, "He is that son of a workman and of a harlot;
He it is who ... fled into Egypt; He the clothed with a scarlet
robe; He the crowned with thorns; He a Magus demon-
possessed, and a Samaritan!" And in 375, we find Epiphanius
stating in the genealogy of Jesus (*Hær.* lxxvii. 7) that Joseph
was the son of a certain Jacob whose surname was Panther.
The writer John Chrysostom, in his *Homilies on the Psalms,*
written toward the close of the fourth century (*Ps.* viii. no. 3.
c.v.), remarks: "And if you ask them [the Jews], 'Why did ye
crucify the Christ?' — they reply, 'Because he was a deceiver
and a sorcerer'." Gregontius, Bishop of Taphar in Arabia,
writing in the second half of the fifth century, in his *Disputatio
cum Herbano Judæo* states that the Jews declared that Jesus
had been put to death because he was a magician. John of
Damascus in the genealogy of Mary, in the eighth century,
(*De Fid. Orthod.,* iv. 14) recognizes Bar Panther and Panther
(Pandera).

Generally speaking, in all ages Atheist scholarship has
been good. It seeks merely to uncover. There is no attempt to
place any onus on any group. This interesting Jewish life of
Jesus has had a long, long history. It is no less and no more
absurd than the history of Jesus put together by the
Christians. Each should equally blush at their own credulity.
Atheists here give you as good a history of this story as you
will find anywhere. Read it and decide for yourself what you
think about it.

—Madalyn Murray O'Hair

PREFACE

When we first announced our intention of publishing a translation of this work, we were unaware that it had ever appeared in English before it was inserted in the New York *Truth Seeker* by "Scholasticus." This able and learned writer, who has since published his translation, with other highly interesting matter, under the title of *Revelations of Antichrist Concerning Christ and Christianity* (Boston: J. P. Mendum; New York: D. M. Bennett; 1879) supposed that he was the first who introduced it to the English-speaking world. He was, however, mistaken. We have quite recently lighted on a translation published by Richard Carlile in 1823. It was done by a Jew, who stated that it had "never before been *wholly* translated into any modern language." He appears to have been right in this statement, as the earliest continental translation we can trace is in German, and was published at Stuttgart in 1850, in a volume together with the apocryphal gospels, by Dr. R. Clemens. No copy of the Richard Carlile edition (the Hebrew translator does not give his name) is to be found in the British Museum. It is a sixteen-page octavo pamphlet with an editor's preface, probably by Carlile himself, and a dedication by the translator, "To the clergy of the Church of England." His English text is substantially the same as that now published. Some of its phrases are rough and racy, possibly owing to his strict adherence to the original; and instead of veiling in Latin the amours of Pandera and Miriam, he relates them in plain English, with biblical naïveté.

The *Sepher Toldoth Jeshu* was first published in Latin, with the Hebrew text in parallel columns, by J. C. Wagenseil in his *Tela Ignea Satanae,* a collection of Jewish anti-Christian tracts, all translated into Latin, with attempted refutations. To collect these valuable tracts, Wagenseil traveled widely through Spain and into Africa, where the chief centers of Jewish learning then existed. His work was published at Altdorf in 1681.

A later and widely different version, the *Sepher Toldoth Jeshu Ha Notzri*, was published by J. J. Huldrich at Leyden in 1705. It is certainly a more modern version of the Jeshu story. Interpolations are found referring to Worms and the people of Germany, and the narrative abounds with capricious fantasies that belong to the superstition of a later age.

A shorter and earlier version of the Jeshu story was probably used by Luther and condensed in his *Schem Hamphoras,* although Mr. Gould[1] considers that "the only *Toldoth Jeshu* he was acquainted with was that afterwards published by Wagenseil." Luther was stung by it into a characteristic fit of vituperation, as the following passage will show:

> The haughty evil spirit jests in the book with a threefold mockery. First, he mocks God, creator of heaven and earth, with his son, Jesus Christ, as you may see for yourself if you believe, as a Christian, that Christ is the son of God. Secondly, he mocks all Christendom, because we believe in such a son of God. Thirdly, he mocks his own Jews by giving them such a scandalous, foolish, doltish thing about brazen dogs and cabbage-stalks, *etc.,* which would make all dogs bark to death, if they could understand it, at such raving ranting, senseless, foaming mad fools. Is not this a master of mocking, who can effect three such great mockeries? The fourth mockery is that herewith he has mocked himself, as we shall one day to our joy see, thank God!
>
> — *Werke,* Wittemberg, 1566, volume 5, page 515.

Long before the *Sepher Toldoth Jeshu* was published, in our modern sense, it was known to the learned. The work came to light in the dawning after the Dark Ages, but, says Mr. Gould, "it was kept secret, lest the sight of it should excite tumults, spoliation, and massacre." Those who know how flamingly the evidences of Christianity have been written on the tear-washed and bloodstained pages of Jewish history will appreciate this cautious reserve.

---

[1] *The Lost and Hostile Gospels,* by Rev. S. Baring Gould, M.A.; 1874.

It was doubtless the Jeshu story which was denounced and prohibited by Pope Valentine in his bull of May 11, 1514, under the title of *Mar Mar Jesu.*[2] Dr. G. B. de Rossi, in his *Dizionario Storico degli Autori Ebrei,* catalogues a book entitled ישו מעשה which he considers the same as the *Toldoth Jeshu,* and which may also be the same as the proscribed work.

In the thirteenth century, Raymond Martini, a Dominican friar, composed a work against the Jews and Mohammedans, with the suggestive title of *Pugione fidei (The Dagger of Faith).* Without naming the *Toldoth Jeshu,* he gave long extracts from it, or at least a good summary. A Latin rendering of Martini's Jeshu story appears in a folio volume by Porcheti de Salvaticis, published at Paris in 1520, and entitled *Porcheti victoria adversus impios Hebreos (Porcheti's Victory over the Impious Hebrews).* As the Inquisition took part with Porcheti, the impious Hebrews did not venture to dispute the victory.

The author of *Revelations of Antichrist* gives a complete translation of Porcheti's Latin narrative. It is substantially the same as the one now published, although much shorter. It ends with the hanging of Jeshu, and makes no allusion to any of the matters in our fourth chapter.

The learned Rossi, in his work already cited, after referring to Wagenseil and Huldrich, says that besides their editions, several manuscript copies are to be found in various libraries. Some, he says, bear the different title of *Maasi Jesu,* or that of *Storia di Gesù o del Crocifisso (The History of Jesus the Crucified).* Rossi goes on to say that the most pronounced deists, who have drawn from the Hebrew writings, and from the *Chissuk Emuna* of Rabbi Isaac ben Abraham, arguments against Christianity and its founder, agree that *this* book is a mass of rabbinical sophisms and revolting false inventions; the celebrated Mendelssohn, whom he places among these deists, protesting [sic] that it is one of those books which no sensible Hebrew reads or knows. It may be remarked, however, in opposition to Rossi, that the anonymous Jew who translated Carlile's edition of our work says "it is considered of authority by the wise men of our nation." Even Mr. Gould

2 Rodriguez de Castro, *Biblia Espana,* Book 1, page 223.

throws no doubt upon its having been widely and honestly accepted by the 'chosen race.'

Perhaps the deist whom Rossi had principally in his mind was Voltaire. The heresiarch of Ferney, in his *Lettres sur les juifs,* says that:

> Le *Toledos jesu* est le plus ancien écrit Juif qui nous ait été transmis contre notre réligion. C'est une vie de Jésus-Christ, toute contraire à nos saints evangiles; elle parait être du premiér siècle, et même écrite avant les évangiles. ("The *Toldoth Jeshu* is the most ancient Jewish writing that has descended to us against our religion. It is a life of Jesus Christ, altogether different from our holy gospels. It appears to be of the first century, and even to have been written before the gospels.")

Voltaire's error seems to have arisen from his supposing that Celsus "cited" the work, whereas he merely cites the story of Pandera, which forms its nucleus. In his *Philosophical Dictionary* article *Messiah,* Voltaire writes on the *Toldoth Jeshu* in a delicious vein of grave irony, which appears to have deceived the author of *Antichrist* himself, who is certainly no fool, nor devoid of humor.

Mr. Gould devotes a chapter to "the Jew of Celsus." Celsus wrote, about A.D. 170, a work called *The True Word* (*Logos*), of which, as well as of the author, Mr. J. A. Froude gives a very interesting account in his fourth volume of *Short Studies on Great Subjects.* The writings of this early opponent of Christianity, like those of others, such as Porphyry, who would not bow to the Nazarene, were ruthlessly suppressed, so that nothing remains of them except the extracts given by Origen in his refutation. In a passage which will be found among our footnotes, Celsus describes Jesus as a bastard, born of a Jewish countrywoman and a soldier named Panthera. The genealogy of Jesus, given by Epiphanius, induces Mr. Gould to say that "it shows that in the fourth century the Jewish stories of Panthera had made such an impression on the Christians that his name was forced into the pedigree of Jesus." Basnage, in his *History of the Jews* (Taylor's translation) has an extremely interesting passage on this subject:

Celsus is excusable in having upbraided Christians with the virgin being forced by a soldier called Pandera, but how can Epiphanius (A.D. 367) be excused, who assures us that Jesus was the son of Jacob surnamed Panthera? Or how can John of Damascus (A.D. 760) be justified, who is indeed of another opinion, but for all that makes him come into the genealogy of J. Christ? For he maintains that Panthera was great-grandfather to Mary, and Barpanther her grandfather. Raban Maur (A.D. 874) doth also speak of these two men; and the learned Grotius (A.D. 1640) made an advantage of this tradition, as if it had been well grounded, that so the romance invented about the virgin might appear more probable. And indeed the name given here to the soldier, Panther, is a Greek one; how then can it be introduced into the genealogy of J. Christ as the surname of a family? There is good reason to believe that it was invented only to make the birth of the Messiah more odious. The panther, or male of the panther, is a savage and cruel beast that couples with a lioness, and from thence proceeds the leopard. ... The manuscript of a rabbi is also quoted, wherein it is said that as the leopard is produced by the mixture of different species, so J. Christ sprung from a Greek soldier and a Jewish woman. Those who reckon Panthera among Christ's ancestors fall into the snare which the most inveterate enemies of the Christian religion have laid for them. Emmanuel de Tesauro is one of these, for he blesses the fate of Marham and Panther because Jesus Christ came from them (Book 4, chapter 27).

The learned Basnage rather hobbles than walks out of the difficulty. We leave it to the Christians to explain satisfactorily why Panthera crept into the ancestry of their savior.

Mr. Gould's treatment of Celsus we should be obliged to consider disingenuous if we did not think it confused. Mr. Gould, in fact, is far from being an accurate writer. He sometimes forgets on one page what he has written on another; his chronology is often full of gross and obvious blunders; and his proofs have been read with remarkable carelessness. For instance, through thirty-six successive headlines he has allowed *Jewish ante-gospels* to stand for *anti-gospels*, which is exactly what he is laboring to disprove. In short, with a great appearance of scholarship, Mr. Gould is a very untrustworthy guide.

With respect to Celsus, Mr. Gould says it is "remarkable" that "living in the middle of the second century and able to make inquiries of aged Jews, whose lives had extended to the first century, he should have been able to find out next to nothing about Jesus and his disciples except what he read in the gospels." Now there is no proof that Celsus ever saw our gospels, and his account of Jesus is very unlike theirs. And is the story of Christ's birth, which involves the central doctrine of the incarnation "next to nothing"? Besides, Mr. Gould had staring him in the face the declaration of Celsus, as quoted by Origen, that he "could relate many things more concerning Jesus, all of which are true, but which have quite a different character from what his disciples relate touching him." To this Origen replies, in short, You cannot. But as Celsus had no opportunity of rejoining, having incontinently died a century before his opponent took the field, it is hardly fair to assume that he was lying.

Celsus' contemporary, Justin Martyr, one of the early fathers, in his dialogue with Trypho the Jew, bitterly complains that the Jews had sent persons into all parts of the world to publish blasphemies against Jesus. Of what value, then, is Origen's denial of these things a century later?

In the Babylonian Gemara of the Talmud, which, although not completed until about A.D. 500, represents the authoritative traditions of the Jews, the name of Pandera is given to the father of Jeshu; and the same parentage is given in the Jerusalem Gemara, which was compiled independently a century earlier. Amidst a great deal of confusion, by Mr. Gould worse confounded, this one fact shines out incontestable and unquestioned.

Mr. Gould's theory of the origin and development of the Jeshu story supposes on the part of the Jews a flagrant ignorance of their own language, traditions, and history; and what, except the necessity of supporting a theory, could lead him to state that "The Jew of Celsus had already fused Jesus of Nazareth with the other two Jehoshuas" of the Talmud? The Jew of Celsus relates nothing of Jesus at all resembling the later Talmudic confusions of the two Jehoshuas; and those confusions probably arose through the discordant opinions of different rabbis of various ages being cited indifferently. In his anxiety to prove that the *Sepher Toldoth Jeshu* is entirely a production of the Middle Ages, Mr. Gould maintains that "the Jews in A.D. 500, when the Babylonian Gemara was completed, had no traditions whatever concerning Jesus of Nazareth." But his contention may be opposed by the weightier opinion of Lardner and Lightfoot, that the Talmudic references to Jeshu clearly point to Jesus Christ.

In discussing the date of the *Sepher Toldoth Jeshu,* Mr. Gould says (page 69) that neither Wagenseil's nor Huldrich's version "can boast of a greater antiquity than, at the outside, the twelfth century. It is difficult to say with certainty which is the earlier of the two. Probably both came into use about the same time." But with his usual laxity he advances a very different opinion later on page 115, where he says "That this second version of the life of Jeshu is later than the first one, I think there can be little doubt." He even goes to the length of suggesting that the Huldrich version may have "been composed after the Reformation."

The center of Mr. Gould's theory, around which his orbit is extremely eccentric, may be found in the following passage:

> The persecution to which the Jews were subjected in the Middle Ages from the bigotry of the rabble or the cupidity of princes, fanned their dislike for Christianity into a flame of intense mortal abhorrence of the founder of that religion whose votaries were their deadliest foes. The *Toledoth Jeschu* is the utterance of this deep-seated hatred, the voice of an oppressed people execrating him who had sprung from the holy race, and whose blood was weighing on their heads.

This appears to us a very lame theory. In our opinion the *Sepher Toldoth Jeshu* betrays no vehement malignity; it narrates everything with an air of candor; and we confidently leave the reader to judge for himself. We perceive in this work many marks of antiquity, and evidences of a far closer acquaintance with the manners, customs, and opinions of the Jews in Palestine than is betrayed in our Greek gospels.

If we except the fourth chapter, which forms no part of the life of Jeshu, but is related to it very much as the Acts of the Apostles is related to the gospels, the only indication of a late authorship is the reference to the Talmud. But that may have been originally a marginal gloss, afterwards incorporated with the text, like so many "interpolations" in the New Testament. Even, however, if the date of the work was slightly subsequent to the compilation of the Talmud, we are still within measurable distance of the earliest Christian manuscripts.

If, as Mr. Gould maintains, the *Sepher Toldoth Jeshu* is a "counter-gospel," written to asperse the character of Jesus Christ, it is a singular thing that the authors did not keep closer to the gospel story. How, for instance, came they to place the birth of Jeshu in the reign of Jannæus, at least ninety years before the alleged birth of Christ? How came they to make him contemporary with Rabbi Simeon ben Shetach, who flourished about 90 B.C.? Satire is futile unless it adheres to familiar features, and we can scarcely imagine sane men so stupid as the satirists of the *Sepher Toldoth Jeshu* must have been if Mr. Gould's theory be true.

The reader perhaps may say "But, if Jesus Christ was born in the first year of our era, and Jeshu was born ninety years before, how can they have been one and the same person?" To which we reply, that there is no proof of Jesus Christ having been born in the first year of our era, and many indications to the contrary. Christian chronology has been arbitrarily established. There was great uncertainty among the early Christians, who reckoned like all Roman subjects from the reign of the Caesars, not only as to the birth, but also as to the age of their savior. Irenæus, the first Christian father who mentions the four gospels, maintains that Jesus was fifty years old at his death, and the chronology of Luke is absolutely inconsistent with Roman history, as well as being at variance with that of Matthew. It might likewise be effectively argued from the only chronological reference in Paul's epistles (2 Corinthians 11:32, "In Damascus the governor under Aretas the king kept the city of the Damascenes with a garrison, desirous to apprehend me") that the great apostle himself flourished at least sixty-two years before our era. According to his own statement, he escaped arrest at Damascus while the city was "under Aretas the king," who must have ruled there before the city was captured by Pompey (62 B.C.) and made a part of the Roman Empire.*

We would not dogmatize, but we venture to think that the Christian legend of Jesus may have originated in the Jewish story of Jeshu. This theory at any rate accounts for the hero's introduction to the world. The two Hebrew versions of a career similar to that of Jesus, as well as the Talmud, agree in making Jeshu the illegitimate son of Pandera and a Jewish maiden; and Celsus flung the same charge at the Christians before our present gospels can be proved to have existed. That both the Jewish and the Christian story are largely fabulous, we cheerfully concede, but no advantage can be derived to either from that fact. We now leave the question with the reader. It is for him to decide whether it is more probable that the father of Jesus was a human being or the intangible third person of a hypothetical trinity.

G. W. Foote
J. M. Wheeler

March, 1885

---

*Ed.– The Nabatean king Aretas II was an ally of Gaza against Alexander Jannæus of Judea in 96 BCE. Aretas III (87?–62 BCE) was the first Nabatean to rule over Damascus. After the death of Queen Alexandra of Judaea (our Queen Helene?) in 68 BCE, he took the side of her son Hyrcanus II. Pompey's envoy Scaurus entered the fray, however, producing an agreement that sent Aretas back to Nabatea, gave Syria (including, of course, Damascus) to Rome, and gave Jerusalem to Alexandra's younger son Aristobulus II. It is Aretas IV (9 BCE–40 CE) that tradition credits with threatening the life of St. Paul. I am unaware of any evidence that he exercised power in Damascus at that time, however. FRZ

THE JEWISH LIFE OF CHRIST

CHAPTER 1

1. In the year 671, of the fourth millenary[1] (of the world), in the days of Jannæus, the king, a great misfortune happened to the enemies of Israel.

2. There was a certain idle and worthless debauchee named Joseph Pandera,[2] of the fallen tribe of Judah.

---

[1] "In the year 671 of the fourth millenary." The Rev. S. Baring Gould translates it "in the year 4671," which, he says, would be 910 B.C. We cannot understand this computation; it agrees with no chronology known to us, neither the Samaritan, the Septuagint, Josephus, nor Usher. According to the established Jewish chronology, the world was 3,761 years old at the beginning of the era of the Christ myth. The year 3671 would therefore be 90 B.C. This fairly harmonizes with what Gibbon says of "the anachronism of the Jews, who place the birth of Christ near a century sooner." It also agrees with the date of Jannæus, the Sadducee king of Judaea, who reigned from 106 B.C. to 79 B.C. If we suppose, with the author of *Revelations of Antichrist*, that the Olympiad of Iphitus is meant in the text, the year 671 of that era, which began 884 B.C., would be 106 B.C. This brings the birth of Jeshu barely within the reign of Jannæus. On the whole we prefer to regard the Jewish chronology as the one the writer employed. He wrote for Jews and would naturally use it.

[2] Pandera, according to the Jewish Gemara (compiled between the fourth and sixth centuries of our era, but containing ancient traditions orally transmitted), was the paramour of a wanton who went astray from her husband. The Talmudic references to Miriam and Pandera may be found fully cited in the works of Lightfoot and

3. He was a man of fine figure and rare beauty, but spent his time in robbery and licentiousness. He lived at Bethlehem of Judea.[3]

Lardner. These scattered accounts of Jesus, when brought together, give us the following: In the time of Janneus the Sadducee, one Mary, a plaiter of woman's hair, was false to her husband, and had, by a person named Pandera, a son called Jesus. This son was taken in tutorship by Rabbi Joshua ben Perachiah, president of the Sanhedrim, and, at the time when the rabbis were persecuted by Jannæus, accompanied him to Alexandria in Egypt, where he learnt how to charm diseases, and other magic arts. On his return with his master they fell out because Jesus praised a woman's beauty. Jesus then taught new doctrines, defamed the rabbis, and gave himself up to magical practices. He had five chief disciples, Mathai (Matthew?), Nakai, Nezer, Boni, and Thodah (Thaddeus?). They were put to death and Jesus himself was stoned at Lud or Lydda, twenty-two miles northwest of Jerusalem, and then hanged on the evening before the Passover.

Celsus, writing in the second century, as quoted by Origen who "refuted" him a hundred years later, says that Jesus was born of a countrywoman, and that "when she was pregnant she was turned out of doors by the carpenter to whom she had been betrothed, as having been guilty of adultery, and that she bore a child to a certain soldier named Panthera." (*Origen against Celsus*, Book 1, chapter 32, page 431 — *Ante-Nicene Christian Library*). This calumny the Christian father easily confuted by such powerful arguments as that God would not make a teacher of a bastard, and that some animals — for instance vultures — conceived without any connection with a male.

Celsus, speaking on behalf of the Jews, further says, as reported by his opponent, "that he [Jesus] having been brought up as an illegitimate child, and having served for hire in Egypt, and then coming to the knowledge of certain miraculous powers, returned from thence to his own country, and by means of those powers proclaimed himself to be God" (Book 1, chapter 38, page 438).

[3] Pandera's living at Bethlehem might account for the gospel tradition of Jesus being born there. According to the apocryphal *Gospel of Mary*, she lived at Jerusalem before Joseph married her, and Bethlehem is not far from the holy city. Actually, it is more probable that Jesus was born at Nazareth, where Joseph lived. The rabbinical writers refer to him as *ha notzri,* a native of Nazareth; his disciples were called Nazarenes before they received the name of Christians; and a Nazarene is still the designation for a Christian throughout the East. [Ed. —As explained in the footnote on the first page of the

4. Nearby there lived a widow, who had a daughter named Miriam,[4] of whom mention is several times made in the Talmud as a dresser of women's hair.

5. This daughter was betrothed by her mother to a very chaste, gentle, and pious youth named Jochanan.

6. Now it happened that Joseph occasionally passed by Miriam's door and saw her. Then he began to have an unholy affection for her.

7. So he went to and fro about the place, and at length the mother said to him, "What maketh thee so thin?" He replied, "I am madly in love with Miriam."

8. Then, said the mother, "I would not deny thee the favor; see if she is willing, and do with her as thou pleasest."

9. Obeying her counsel, Joseph Pandera went frequently by the house, but did not find a suitable time until one sabbath evening, when he happened to find her sitting before the door.

10. Then he went into the house with her, and both sat down in a dormitory near the door, for she thought he was her betrothed, Jochanan.

11. *Tum ea homine ait: Ne me attingio; in menstruis sum. Sed is morem illi non gerebat, cumque circa eam voluntati suæ obsequutus fuisset in domum suam abit.*

---

introduction to this book, it is almost certain there was no place called Nazareth in the first centuries BCE and CE. Thus, the epithet *notzri* cannot refer to a native of a town called Nazareth. It is, rather, a reference to "the Branch" (*netzer*) of Isaiah 11:1. FRZ]

4 Miriam is the Hebrew word for Mary, and signifies *bitterness*. Lardner says, "In several other places of these Talmudical writers, Mary is called a 'plaiter of woman's hair,' as may be seen in Lightfoot p. 270. And from some things alleged just now it seems that thereby they denote a transgressor of the laws of purity. And we are led to think that by this description they intended to represent not her outward condition, but her moral character." ("Jewish Testimonies," *Works*, 1838, volume 6, page 524).

12. *Circa medium noctis iterum in eo exardescere desiderium malum. Ergo somno levatus ad domum Miriamis viam affectans, ad cellam se confert, factumque repetit.*

13. *Valde autem exhorruit puella, et quid hoc, ait, tibi vult, Domine, quod eadem nocte bis me convenisti? Idque non passa sum ab eo inde tempore quo sponsam me tibi elegisti.*

14. *Verum in silens repetit, nec verbum nullum proloquitur. Ergo Miriam queri: Quousque tu pecato scelus addis? annon pridem tibi dixi esse me menstruatam?*

15. *Verum ille non attendebat ad ejus verba, sed desiderio satisfaciebat, ac tum postea iter pergebat suum.*[5]

---

[5] We are obliged to keep these passages veiled in Latin. There are worse things in the Bible, but we do not feel at liberty to emulate the indecency of the inspired writers. A reference to Leviticus 20:18 [Ed. —"And if a man shall lie with a woman having her sickness, and shall uncover her nakedness; he hath discovered her fountain, and she hath uncovered the fountain of her blood: and both of them shall be cut off from among their people" MMOH] will give a fair idea of the meaning of Miriam's exclamation in the first sentence.

[Ed.—After having served twelve months in prison for committing the 'crime' of blasphemy, G. W. Foote could not risk publishing this passage in clear and understandable English. Considering the innocuousness of the passage as we shall present it below, it is hard to appreciate the hardships endured by Atheists living in Victorian England. A free rendering of the somewhat eccentric Latin is as follows:

11. *Then she says to the man: "Do not touch me; I am menstruating." But he paid no attention to her wishes at all. After subjecting her to his will, he went home. 12. Around midnight, an evil desire inflamed him once again. So, rising from sleep and making his way to Miriam's house, he betakes himself to her chamber and repeats the deed. 13. However, the girl was exceedingly horrified, and she says: "Why, my Lord, do you want to do this? You have come to me twice this night. Never have I experienced such a thing since that time when you became betrothed to me." 14. Notwithstanding, in silence he repeats the deed without uttering a single word. Whereupon Miriam began to complain: "How far will you go to pile crime upon sin? Did I not just tell you I am menstruating?" 15. Nevertheless, he paid no attention to her words. He satisfied his desire and afterwards continued again on his way.* FRZ]

16. After three months, Jochanan was told that his betrothed was with child.

17. In great agitation, he went to his preceptor, Simon ben Shetach,[6] and, telling him about the matter, asked him what he ought to do.

18. The preceptor inquired, "Dost thou suspect anyone?" Jochanan said, "Nobody, except Joseph Pandera, who is a great debauchee, and liveth near her house."

19. The preceptor said, "My son, take my advice, and keep silent; for if he hath been there he will surely go there again. Therefore be wise, and get a witness, so that thou mayest bring him before the great Sanhedrim."

20. The young man went home and was sorely troubled during the night. He thought to himself, "When this thing becometh known the people will say it was my doing."

21. Therefore, to avoid the shame and disgrace, he ran away to Babylon[7] and there took up his abode.

22. In due time Miriam brought forth a son and named him Jehoshua, after her mother's brother.

---

6 This rabbi is undoubtedly an historical character. He flourished about 90 B.C., and is mentioned in the Talmud. It was customary for rabbis, like the Greek sophists, to take pupils, who generally became their disciples. Paul tells us (Acts 22:3) that he was "brought up ... at the feet of Gamaliel." [Ed. —"I am verily a man which am a Jew, born in Tarsus, a city in Cilicia, yet brought up in this city at the feet of Gamaliel, and taught according to the perfect manner of the law of the fathers, and was zealous toward God, as ye all are this day." MMOH]

7 Ever since the captivity there had been an extensive Jewish colony at Babylon, where the chief part of the Gemara was compiled, and whither many Hebrews repaired after the fall of Jerusalem. This reference to Babylon seems an unmistakable touch of authentic history.

23. She sent the boy to a teacher named Elchanan, with whom he made progress in learning, for his mind was very bright.[8]

24. And it came to pass by and by that he met the senators of Sanhedrim at Jerusalem.

25. It was then the custom that whoever met those senators should cover his head and bow down.

26. But this boy as he walked past them bared his head, and touching his forehead saluted the principal only.

27. Then all began to say, "What impudence! Probably he is a bastard." And one of them said, "Indeed he is a bastard, and the son of an adulteress."[9]

---

[8] The apocryphal *Gospel of the Infancy* and the *History of Joseph* both give Jesus a schoolmaster, and both praise his bright parts. Luke 2:40 also says "And the child grew, and waxed strong in spirit, filled with wisdom, and the grace of God was upon him." The only indication, however, that Jesus could write is furnished by the passage in John 8:8 ("And again he stooped down, and wrote on the ground"), but this story of his writing on the ground is wanting in the earliest manuscripts.

[9] Jesus in our gospels argues with the rabbis, and bestows all his impertinence on his mother; but Jeshu offers it all to the doctors. The same story is thus told in the Talmud: "As once the elders sat at the gate there passed two boys before them. One uncovered his head, the other did not. Then said Rabbi Elieser, 'The latter is certainly a bastard'; but Rabbi Jehoshua said, 'He is the son of an adulteress. Akiba said, 'He is both a bastard and a son of an adulteress. [Ed.– Many of the Toldoth manuscripts style him as the bastard son of a *menstruating woman* – something almost as miraculous as a virgin birth. FRZ] They said to him, 'How canst thou oppose the opinion of thy companions?' He answered, 'I will prove what I have said.' Then he went to the boy's mother, who was sitting in the market selling fruit, and said to her, 'My daughter, if you will tell me the truth I will promise you eternal life.' She said to him, 'Swear to me.' And he swore with his lips, but in his heart he did not ratify the oath." Lardner notes that "though no person is here named, there can be no doubt who is intended." [Ed.—Rabbi Elieser would appear to be R. Eliezer b. Hyrcanus (*fl.* 80–110 CE; Rabbi Jehoshua must be R. Yehoshua b. Peraḥyah (Perachiah, *fl.* 2nd century BCE; and R. Akiba (Akiva) seems to be R. Aqiba (*fl.* 110–135 CE) according to dates given by Rabbi Adin Steinsaltz (*The Talmud: The Steinsaltz Edition, A Reference Guide*) FRZ]

28. Presently Simeon ben Shetach said, "I remember now that not many years ago my pupil Jochanan came to me and said,

29 " 'Alas! what a shame and disgrace has happened to me! for Miriam my betrothed is with child, not by me, but by someone else.' This is the son of that Miriam.

30. "And when I inquired if he suspected anyone, he said, 'Joseph Pandera,'[10] who was a near neighbor of hers."

31. "And soon afterwards Jochanan went in shame to Babylon, where he dwelleth even now."

---

[10] R. von der Alm conjectures that the Christian story kept the first name of Pandera – Joseph – as that of the father of Jesus. According to Luke 4:22, the Jews inquired of Jesus, "Is not this Joseph's son?" [Ed. —"And all bare him witness, and wondered at the gracious words which proceeded out of his mouth. And they said, 'Is not this Joseph's son?' " MMOH] They obviously knew or suspected nothing of his divine parentage. The passage in brackets in Luke's genealogy, 3:23 [Ed. — "And Jesus himself began to be about thirty years of age, being (as was supposed) the son of Joseph, which was the son of Heli," MMOH] representing Jesus as the "supposed" son of Joseph, is the language of the evangelist himself, who was not a contemporary. The friends and countrymen of Jesus allude to him as a man, a carpenter, and the son of a carpenter. See Mark 6:3 [Ed. —"And many hearing him were astonished, saying, 'Is not this the carpenter, the son of Mary, the brother of James and Joses, and of Judah, and Simon? and are not his sisters here with us?' And they were offended at him" MMOH]; Matthew 13:55 [Ed. —"They were astonished, and said ... 'Is not this the carpenter's son? is not his mother called Mary? and his brethren, James, and Joses, and Simon, and Judas?' " MMOH]. In the face of these texts, it is astonishing that Origen, in reply to Celsus, should assert that "in none of the gospels current in the churches is Jesus himself ever described as being a carpenter." This sweeping denial can only be explained on one of three hypotheses: Origen's unscrupulous audacity, his ignorance of our gospels, or the subsequent interpolation of the passage he contradicts. [Ed. —In later manuscripts of Mark 6:3, Jesus is not himself described as a carpenter, but as "the son of the carpenter and Mary" — an obvious harmonization with Matt 13:55. It would seem that already at the time of Origen manuscripts of Mark 6:3 existed which, by simple alteration of the Greek text, transformed Jesus from a carpenter into a non-practicing son of a carpenter. FRZ]

32. Then they all said, "If these things are so, this boy is indeed a bastard and the son of an adulteress."[11]

33. Then they published him as such by the blowing of three hundred trumpets,[12] declaring him not fit to come into the congregation, and called his name Jeshu, signifying that his name and memory deserved to perish.[13]

34. When it became known that he was declared unworthy to be admitted into the congregation, Jeshu with a sad heart fled to Upper Galilee, where he dwelt many years.[14]

---

[11] Bastard is a strong word, but it is accurate of Jesus as well as of Jeshu. There was a Jewish law against bastards entering the congregation until the tenth generation. (Deuteronomy 23:2 — "A bastard shall not enter into the congregation of the Lord, even to his tenth generation shall he not enter into the congregation of the Lord.")

[12] Proclamations among the Jews were made by the sound of trumpets. See many places in the Old Testament. The same ceremony has been performed in more modern times. The blowing of rams' horns was a conspicuous feature in the excommunication of Spinoza. [Ed.—In the Babylonian Talmud, Yeshu is heralded by *four* hundred trumpets. FRZ]

[13] Jehoshua, which we shorten into Joshua, is a common Jewish name, of which Jesus is the Greek form. It means 'Jehovah is his salvation.' Rabbi Abraham Farrisol, in his אברהם מגן (*Megan Abraham*), chapter 59, says "His name was Jeshua, but as Rabbi Moses Maimonides has written it, and as we find it throughout the Talmud, it is written *Jeshu*. They have carefully left out the *ain*, because he was not able to save himself." So Elias in *Tish Bi*, under the word *Jeshu*, says "Because the Jews will not acknowledge him (Jesus) to be the savior, they do not call him Jeshua, but reject the *ain* and call him Jeshu." By omitting this letter, a peculiar significance was given to the name. In the curtailed form it is composed of the letters *jod, shin, vau,* which are taken to stand for: וזכרונו שמו ימח — 'his name and remembrance shall be extinguished,' the meaning which is given in the text.

[14] Jesus also returned from Jerusalem and dwelt in Galilee, from which district all his disciples were chosen. It was just the place for prophets and demagogues. Renan remarks very justly that "Palestine was one of the countries most in arrear in the science of the day; the Galileans were the most ignorant of all the inhabitants of Palestine, and the disciples of Jesus might be reckoned among the most stupid Galileans."

35. In those days there was a stone in the temple on which was inscribed the inexpressible name of God.[15]

36. For when David laid the foundation[16] he found a certain stone at the mouth of an abyss on which the name was engraved, and taking it up he deposited it in the holy of holies.

37. But when the wise men feared that perchance studious youths might learn this name and bring destruction upon the world (which calamity may God forbid), they made by magic

---

[15] This was the *shem hamphoras* — שם המפרש, the sacred ineffable name, by which expression the Jews name Jehovah or Jahveh, the correct pronunciation of which is lost, the word *adonai* (Lord) being substituted. The rabbis affirm that the decadence of Israel is due to the loss of this sacred name, and that if anyone were able to pronounce it, he might thereby create or destroy worlds. Numerous wonders are ascribed to it. By its aid Moses slew the Egyptian, and it was engraved on Solomon's seal. The great prophet must, however, have forgotten it during his residence with Jethro; for according to the kabbalists, he spent forty days on Mount Sinai, learning it afresh from the angel Saxaël.

[16] Mr. Gould considers that this verse shows the writer's "amazing ignorance" of Jewish history, which represents Solomon as the builder of the temple. But the remark rather shows Mr. Gould's amazing ignorance; for, according to rabbinical tradition, although Solomon erected the temple, its foundation was laid by David: and this tradition is corroborated by 1 Chronicles 22:1–4 [Ed. —"Then David said, 'This is the house of the Lord God, and this is the altar of the burnt offering for Israel. And David commanded to gather together the strangers that were in the land of Israel; and he set masons to hew wrought stones to build the house of God. And David prepared iron in abundance for the nails for the doors of the gates, and for the joinings; and brass in abundance without weight; Also cedar trees in abundance: for the Zidonians and they of Tyre brought much cedar wood to David." MMOH] The foundation stone of the temple is said to have been the same block that Jacob reposed on (Genesis 28:22 — "And this stone, which I have set for a pillar, shall be God's house: and of all that thou shalt give me I will surely give the tenth unto thee,") and which he prophesied "shall be God's house."

two brazen lions,[17] and placed them at the entrance of the holy of holies, one on the right and the other on the left.

38. If, therefore, anyone drew near and learned the hidden name, as he went away the lions would roar, so that in his fright he would forget the name forever.

39. Now when the report that Jeshu was a bastard had spread abroad, he left upper Galilee and, coming secretly to Jerusalem, he went into the temple and there learned the sacred letters.

40. And when he had written the hidden name on a piece of parchment, and spoken it, that he might feel no pain, he cut open his flesh and enclosed therein the mysterious parchment. Then, having again pronounced the name, he closed up the flesh.[18]

41. But to enter the temple it was necessary to use magic and incantations, otherwise how could the most holy priests, the descendants of Aaron, have allowed him to go therein.

---

[17] The Talmud calls them "brazen *dogs*," and Luther appears to have thought them of this species. Alm refers to Ezekiel 1:10 ("As for the likeness of their faces, they four had the face of a man, and the face of a lion, on the right side: and they four had the face of an ox on the left side; they four also had the face of an eagle,") containing a description of the cherubim, Jehovah's four-faced bodyguard, one aspect being leonine. Madame Blavatsky thinks the text refers unmistakably to these Hebrew chimeras, or, to use her own phrase, "symbolical monstrosities" (*Isis Unveiled*, 1877, volume 2, page 201).

[18] The Talmud refers to a similar performance in the query "Did not ben Stada bring enchantment out of Egypt in the cutting which was in his flesh?" Ben Stada (the son of Stada), of course, is Jesus, who according to our gospels went into Egypt. It is curious that Revelation 19:12,16 ascribes to Jesus "a name written, that no man knew but he himself" and this, or an equivalent name, was "on his thigh" but whether tattooed or sewn in we are not informed. [Ed. —"His eyes were as a flame of fire, and on his head were many crowns; and he had a name written, that no man knew, but he himself . . . And he hath on his vesture and on his thigh a name written, 'king of kings, and lord of lords'." MMOH]

42. Therefore it is manifest that Jeshu did all this by the art of magic and the power of an impure name.[19]

43. As he was coming out of the door the lions roared and he forgot the name.

44. So he went outside the city, and, having reopened his flesh, drew forth the writing, examined well the characters, and got full retention of the name.

45. Then he went to the place of his nativity, and with loud voice cried out,

---

[19] According to several passages in our gospels, the Pharisees charged Jesus with casting out devils through Beelzebub, the prince of devils. There are many illustrations in the Bible of the superstition of using the divine name as a spell. When Jacob wrestled with the angel he demanded his name (Genesis 32:29—"Tell me, I pray thee, thy name.") Manoah made the same request to the angel who predicted the birth of Samson (Judges 13:17—"And Manoah said unto the angel of the Lord, 'What is thy name, that when thy sayings come to pass we may do thee honor?") The third commandment prohibits the taking of God's name in vain (Exodus 20:7—"Thou shalt not take the name of the Lord thy God in vain; for the Lord will not hold him guiltless that taketh his name in vain." See also Lev. 24:16 —"And he that blasphemeth the name of the Lord, he shall surely be put to death, and all the congregation shall certainly stone him: as well the stranger, as he that is born in the land, when he blasphemeth the name of the Lord, shall be put to death.") Jesus (Mark 16:17—"And these signs shall follow them that believe; In my name shall they cast out devils; they shall speak with new tongues") says of his disciples "in my name they shall cast out devils." According to Acts 3:16 [Ed.—"And his name through faith in his name hath made this man strong, whom ye see and know: yea, the faith which is by him hath given him this perfect soundness in the presence of you all" MMOH], his name made a lame man strong; and Peter in answer to the question "By what power or by what name have ye done this?" replies (Acts 4:12) that, "Neither is there salvation in any other: for there is none other name under heaven given whereby we must be saved." Paul also (Philippians 2:9) says, "Wherefore God also hath highly exalted him, and given him a name which is above every other name: that at the name of Jesus every knee should bow, of things in heaven, and things in earth, and things under the earth."

46. "Who are these bad men who report me to be a bastard and of impure birth? They are themselves bastards and impure.

47. "Did not a virgin bear me? Did not my mother conceive me in the top of her head?[20]

48. "Indeed I am the son of God, and concerning me the prophet Esaias spoke, saying, 'Behold, a virgin[21] shall conceive, *etc.*'

49. "Did I not form myself, and the heaven, earth, sea and all things contained therein?"

50. Then they all answered and said, "Make known by some sign, and show by a miracle that thou art God."

51. He, answering, said, "Bring hither to me a dead man, and I will restore him to life."

52. The people made haste, and having dug into a certain sepulchre, found there nothing but dry bones.

53. And when they told him that they had found only bones, he said, "Bring them hither."

---

[20] Jeshu boasts of his virgin mother; the Christians claim the same glory for Jesus, and probably with equal truth. Mary did not, however, conceive at the top of her head, although according to Ambrose, she was impregnated through the ear – "*Maria per aurem impregnata est.*" Dr. Clemens mentions an early Christian belief that Jesus was born from his mother's head. Both these notions are plagiarisms from the Greek mythology, which represents Minerva as springing full-armed from the brain of Jove. Justin Martyr, indeed, in his *First Apology* (chapter 21) places the miraculous births of Jesus and the offspring of Jove in the same category. In the legends of the birth of Buddha, the Indian savior is born from the side of his mother Maya.

[21] The claims of Jeshu and Jesus are equally founded on a false interpretation of Isaiah. The word *almah* (7:14 — "Therefore the Lord himself shall give you a sign; Behold, a virgin [*almah*] shall conceive, and bear a son") means any young woman, whether single or wedded. Besides, Isaiah took care to fulfill his own prediction by the aid of a female colleague, leaving nothing to be added by the labor of his successors (8:3 — "And I went unto the prophetess; and she conceived, and bare a son. Then said the Lord to me, 'Call his name Mahershalalhashbaz'.")

54. And when they were brought, he put all the bones together and covered them with skin, flesh, and nerves, so he that had been a dead man stood up on his feet alive.

55. The people seeing this, marveled. Then he said, "Do ye wonder at this? Bring hither a leper and I will cure him."[22]

56. And when they had brought a leper he restored him to health in like manner through the *shem hamphoras*.

57. When the people saw this, they fell down and worshipped him, saying, "Verily thou art the son of God."[23]

58. And it came to pass, after the fifth day, that the dismal tidings were brought to Jerusalem, the most holy city, and there all the things were told which Jeshu had done.

59. Then the profligates rejoiced greatly; but the old men, the devout, and the wise wept bitterly; and in the greater and the lesser Sanhedrim there was sore lamentation.

60. At length they all resolved to send messengers to Jeshu, saying among themselves, "It may be that by the help of the Lord we shall capture him, bring him to judgment, and condemn him to death."

61. Therefore they sent Ananias and Achasias, most honorable men of the lesser Sanhedrim, who went and fell down before Jeshu in adoration, thereby augmenting his wickedness.

62. Therefore, thinking that they were sincere, he received them with a smiling face and appointed them leaders of his wicked flock.

---

[22] Jeshu's readiness to work a miracle is in striking contrast to the reluctance of Jesus. Instead of calling people evil, wicked, and adulterous for seeking a sign, he promptly acquiesces in their request and at once calls for a good subject.

[23] Matthew puts a similar exclamation into the mouth of the centurion at the crucifixion.

63. Then they thus began to appeal to him: "Lo, the leading citizens of Jerusalem have sent us ambassadors to thee, praying that thou wouldst deign to come to them, for they have heard that thou art the son of God."

64. Then said Jeshu, "What they have heard is true, and lo, I will do all that ye ask, but upon this condition:

65. "That all the senators of the greater and lesser Sanhedrim, and those also who have defamed my nativity, shall come forth and worship me, receiving me even as servants receive their lords."

66. The messengers, returning to Jerusalem, reported all that had been said.

67. The elders and devout men answered, "We will do all that he asketh."

68. Therefore the men went again to Jeshu and declared that they would do whatever he desired. Then Jeshu said, "I will go with you at once."

CHAPTER 2

1. And it came to pass that when Jeshu came to Nob,[1] which is near Jerusalem, he said to them "Have ye here a good and comely ass?"

2. And when they replied that one was at hand, he said, "Bring him hither."

3. And a beautiful ass being brought, he mounted upon him and went to Jerusalem.

4. As he entered the city all the people sallied out to meet him.

5. And raising his voice he said to them, "Concerning me the prophet Zacharias testified, saying, 'Behold thy king cometh to

---

[1] The story here is marvelously like that of Matthew 21:1–9 [Ed.— "And when they drew nigh unto Jerusalem, and were come to Bethphage, unto the mount of Olives, then sent Jesus two disciples, Saying unto them, 'Go into the village over against you, and straightway ye shall find an ass tied, and a colt with her: loose them, and bring them unto me. And if any man say aught unto you, ye shall say, "The Lord hath need of them" and straightway he will send them.' All this was done, that it might be fulfilled which was spoken by the prophet, saying, 'Tell ye the daughter of Zion, behold, thy king cometh unto thee, meek, and sitting upon an ass, and a colt the foal of an ass.' And the disciples went, and did as Jesus commanded them. And brought the ass, and the colt, and put on them their clothes, and they set him thereon. And a very great multitude spread their garments in the way; others cut down branches from the trees, and strewed them in the way. And the multitudes that went before, and that followed, cried, saying, 'Hosanna to the son of David: blessed is he that cometh in the name of the Lord; hosanna in the highest'." MMOH] No one has been able to determine the position of Bethphage, where Jesus obtained his asses; but the situation of Nob is well known. It lies near Jerusalem, and is mentioned in the Old Testament and in Josephus.

thee, just and having salvation, lowly and sitting upon an ass, and a colt the foal of an ass'."[2]

6. These things being known, there was great weeping and rending of garments, and the devout men went and complained to the queen.

7. (She was Queen Helena, the wife of king Jannaeus mentioned above; she reigned after the death of (her) husband. She is otherwise called Oleina, and had a son Nunbasus, the king, otherwise called Hyrcanus, who was slain by his subordinate Herod).[3]

---

[2] Zechariah's prophecy (9:9 — "Rejoice greatly, O daughter of Zion; shout, O daughter of Jerusalem: behold, thy king cometh unto thee: he is just, and having salvation; lowly, and riding upon an ass, and upon a colt the foal of an ass") is understood by this writer, but misunderstood by Matthew, who was evidently unacquainted with Jewish idioms. Hebrew authors often gained emphasis by iteration; witness especially the song of Deborah on Jael and Sisera. Zechariah, therefore, intended only one donkey; but Matthew stupidly puts him on two. Jeshu's biography, with better Hebrew and better taste, puts him on one.

[3] This parenthesis is probably an interpolation. The widow of Alexander Jannaeus is called Alexandra by Josephus (*Antiquities*, Book 13, chapter 16): She reigned nine years after the death of her husband, leaving two sons, Hyrcanus and Aristobulus, both of whom reigned after her. Hyrcanus was killed by Herod (*Antiquities*, Book 25, chapter 2). The interpolator has possibly confounded Queen Alexandra with Helena, queen of Adiabene, noted among the Jews as a gentile proselyte who visited Jerusalem (*Antiquities*, Book 20, chapter 2). Mr. Gould thinks that the Helena referred to in the text 'is probably the mother of Constantine, who went to Jerusalem in A.D. 326 to see the holy sites, and, according to an early legend, discovered the three crosses on Calvary.' This supposition, however, is gratuitous and absurd. Constantine's mother was a proselyte to Christianity. It was the more ancient queen Helena, who was a famous proselyte to Judaism, that a Hebrew writer would probably bear in mind.
[Ed.—G. R. S. Mead argues that Jannæus' wife Alexandra is indeed the Helena of our story. It seems that Alexandra's Semitic name was Salome, which further became distorted to Salina which, with the normal mutation of *s* > *h* in Greek, became the Helena of our tale. Mead quotes [pp. 392–3] from a 1057 CE manuscript of

8. The devout men said to the queen, "This fellow deserveth the worst punishment, for he is a seducer of the people. Prithee, grant us the power, and we will take him by subtlety."

9. The queen answering, said, "Call him hither that I may understand the accusation."

10. But she thought to save him from their hands, because she was related to him by blood.

11. Now the wise men, perceiving her design, said to her, "Do not, O royal mistress, undertake to do this lest thou shouldest become his abettor; for by his sorceries he leadeth men into error and crime."

12. At the same time they explained to her the whole matter of the *shem hamphoras*, and then added, "It is for thee to impose punishment, for he deserveth the worst."

13. Then they narrated the history of Joseph Pandera.

14. Wherefore the queen said, "I have heard you and will consent to this. Bring him to me and let me hear what he saith, and see what he doeth; for everybody telleth me of the great miracles he performeth."

15. The wise men replied, "We will do as thou sayest."

Epiphanius (c315–403) which indicates that the church father also placed Jesus in the time of Alexander Jannæus: "For with the advent of the Christ, the succession of the princes from Judah, who reigned until the Christ Himself, ceased. The order [of succession] failed and stopped at the time when He was born in Bethlehem of Judæa, in the days of Alexander, who was of high-priestly and royal race; and after this Alexander this lot failed, from the times of himself and Salina, who is also called Alexandra, for the times of Herod the King and Augustus Emperor of the Romans; and this Alexander, one of the anointed (or Christs) and ruling princes placed the crown on his own head... After this a foreign king, Herod, and those who were no longer of the family of David, assumed the crown." Elsewhere, Epiphanius carefully dates the birth of Jesus to 2 BCE — two years after the death of Herod! It is somewhat startling to learn that Epiphanius — in further agreement with the Toldoth tale — managed to work Panther (Pandera) into his genealogy of Jesus. FRZ]

16. Therefore they sent for Jeshu and placed him before the queen.

17. Then thus the queen spoke, "I have heard that thou performest many wonderful miracles. Now do one in my presence."

18. Jeshu replied, "Whatever thou commandest, I will do. Meanwhile I pray this one thing: that thou wilt not give me into the hands of these wicked men who have pronounced me a bastard."

19. The queen replied, "Fear nothing."

20. Then Jeshu said, "Bring hither a leper and I will heal him."

21. And when a leper was brought he laid his hand upon him, and invoking the almighty name restored him to health, so that the flesh of his face became like that of a boy.[4]

22. Furthermore Jeshu said, "Bring hither a dead body."

23. And a dead body being brought, he straightway put his hand upon it, and pronounced the name, and it revived and stood upon its feet.

24. Then said Jeshu, "Esaias[5] prophesied concerning me, 'Then shall the lame man leap as a hart, *etc*'."

25. Then the queen turning to the wise men said, "How can ye affirm that this man is a sorcerer? Have I not seen him with

---

[4] Jesus healed lepers as well as Jeshu; see Luke 7:22 [Ed.— "Then Jesus answering said unto them, 'Go your way, and tell John what things ye have seen and heard; how that the blind see, the lame walk, the lepers are cleansed, the deaf hear, the dead are raised, to the poor the gospel is preached'." MMOH] and many other passages. Leprosy appears to have been a prevalent disease among the chosen people, and Jehovah spent a great deal of his time in legislating for its treatment. Compare 2 Kings 5:14, where Naaman's flesh "became again like unto the flesh of a little child."

[5] See Isaiah 35:6 [Ed.—"Then shall the lame man leap as an hart, and the tongue of the dumb sing: for in the wilderness shall waters break out, and streams in the desert." MMOH]

mine own eyes performing miracles as if he were the son of God?"

26. But the wise men answering, said, "Let not the queen speak thus, for most certainly this man is a sorcerer."

27. But the queen said, "Get ye hence from my sight, and never again bring a like accusation before me."[6]

28. Therefore the wise men left the presence of the queen, sad at heart, and conferring one with another they said, "Let us show ourselves crafty, so that this fellow may fall into our hands."[7]

29. Moreover a certain one of them said, "If it seemeth good to you, let one of us also learn the name, as he did, and perform the miracles, and perchance we may take him."

30. The wise men approved of this device, and said, "Whoever shall learn the name and shall secure this fellow, to him shall be given a double reward in the world to come."

31. Forthwith a certain one of the wise men named Judas[8] arose and said, "If ye will answer for the blame of the offense by which I shall speak the almighty name, I will learn it.

32. "And peradventure God in his mercy and great goodness will bless me, and bring into my hands this bastard and son of an adulteress."

---

6 Queen Helena's reluctance to meddle with Jeshu is very similar to the legend of Pilate's wife in Matthew 27:19: "Have thou nothing to do with that just man," says the wife of the Roman governor.

7 Compare Matthew 26:3,4 — "Then assembled together the chief priests ... and consulted that they might take Jesus by subtlety, and kill him." It may be remarked that while our narrative allows ample time for the capture of Jeshu, the gospel narratives huddle up that of Jesus in the crudest manner; the plot, the betrayal, the seizure all happening in one evening, or in an incredibly short space of time.

8 Judas is here one of the "wise men" or rabbis. It is remarkable that the opponent of Jeshu and the betrayer of Jesus bore the same name, and the presumption is that both characters are founded on a common legend.

33. Then all with one voice cried out, "On us be the guilt.[9] Do as thou hast proposed, and may thy work prosper."

34. Therefore he also went into the holy of holies, and did the same that Jeshu had done.

35. Then going through the city he cried out, "Where are they who report that this bastard is the son of God? Am not I, who am only flesh and blood, able to do all the things which Jeshu hath done?"

36. The queen and her ministers having heard of this, Judas was brought before her, accompanied by the elders and wise men of Jerusalem.

37. But the queen summoned Jeshu and said to him, "Show us what thou hast lately done." And he began to perform his miracles before the people.

38. Then Judas spoke these words to the queen and all the people: "Nothing that this fellow doeth is wonderful to us. Let him nestle among the stars and I will hurl him down."[10]

39. Then Jeshu thus addressed the whole people. "Have ye not been from the beginning, from the time when I first knew you, a stiffnecked people?"[11]

40. Judas answered, "Is it not true that thou dost practice wickedness, thou bastard and son of an adulteress?

---

[9] Compare Matthew 27:25 — "Then answered all the people, and said, 'His blood be on us, and on our children'."

[10] This phrase, like many in our gospels, is misappropriated and spoiled from the Old Testament. Obadiah 4 says, "Though thou exalt thyself as the eagle, and though thou set thy nest among the stars, thence will I bring thee down, saith the Lord." The author, like our gospel writers, could misquote the Old Testament and blaspheme at the same time.

[11] Compare Matthew 13:15 [Ed. —"For this people's heart is waxed gross, and their ears are dull of hearing, and their eyes they have closed." MMOH] See also Exodus 32:9 [Ed.—"And the Lord said unto Moses, 'I have seen this people, and, behold, it is a stiffnecked people'." MMOH]

41. "Did not our master Moses say concerning thee, 'If thy brother, the son of thy mother, entice thee, saying, "Let us, *etc.*," thou shalt bring the man out, and stone him with stones that he die,'[12] *etc.*?"

42. But the bastard answering, said, "Did not Esaias prophesy concerning me?

43. "And are not these the words of my great forefather (David) concerning me: 'The Lord said unto me, "Thou art my son; this day have I begotten thee?'" '[13]

44. "And in like manner in another place he said, 'The Lord said unto my lord, sit thou at my right hand.'[14]

---

12 See Deuteronomy 13:6–10, containing the malignant law of heresy, with which the Jews justify the death of Jesus. [Ed. —"If thy brother, the son of thy mother, or thy son, or thy daughter, or the wife of thy bosom, or thy friend, which is as thine own soul, entice thee secretly, saying, 'Let us go and serve other gods, which thou hast not known, thou, nor thy fathers'; Namely, of the gods of the people which are round about you, nigh unto thee, or far off from thee, from the one end of the earth even unto the other end of the earth; Thou shalt not consent unto him, nor hearken unto him; neither shall thine eye pity him, neither shalt thou spare, neither shalt thou conceal him: But thou shalt surely kill him; thine hand shall be first upon him to put him to death, and afterwards the hand of all the people. And thou shalt stone him with stones, that he die; because he hath sought to thrust thee away from the Lord thy God which brought thee out of the land of Egypt, from the house of bondage." MMOH] If the hero of our gospels was indeed the son of Jehovah, his fate was a remarkable instance of poetical justice.

13 Psalms 2:7 [Ed.—"I will declare the decree: the Lord hath said unto me, 'Thou art my son, this day have I begotten thee'." MMOH] — "My beloved son" was said of Jesus by the holy dove at his baptism, and "this day have I begotten thee" is added in the ancient gospel according to the Hebrews. This latter clause would, of course, be inconsistent with the story of Matthew, who represents Jesus as having been miraculously conceived thirty years earlier.

14 Psalms 110:1. [Ed. —"The Lord said unto my lord, 'Sit thou at my right hand, until I make thine enemies thy footstool.' " MMOH) It is likewise quoted by Jesus. See Matthew 22:44. [Ed. — *Ibid.*]

45. "And now I will ascend to my heavenly father and will sit at his right hand, and ye shall behold it with your eyes.[15] But thou, Judas, shall not attain to this."

46. And now Jeshu uttered the almighty name, and there came a wind and lifted him up between heaven and earth.

47. Forthwith Judas invoked the same name, and the wind also suspended him between heaven and earth; and thus both soared round about through the air.[16]

48. At the sight of these things all were astonished. But Judas again recited the name, and seizing the wretch sought to hurl him down to the earth.

49. Then Jeshu also invoked the name for the purpose of bringing Judas down, and thus they wrestled together.

50. But Judas seeing that his strength was not equal to that of Jeshu, moistened him with the sweat of his body.*

---

[15] Compare John 20:17 — "But go to my brethren, and say unto them I ascend unto my father..." and especially Mark 14:62 — "And Jesus said, 'I am: and ye shall see the son of man sitting on the right hand of power, and coming in the clouds of heaven" and Mark 16:19 — "So then after the Lord had spoken unto them he was received up into heaven, and sat on the right hand of God."

[16] Acts narrates a similar contest between Peter and Simon Magus, under which designation Paul is clearly aimed at in the *Clementine Recognitions*. Simon Magus, by the power of sorcery, flew through the air, and seemed to be going to heaven; and straightway Peter (of course *not* by sorcery) invoked the name of Jesus Christ, when down fell Simon in quarters (*Ante-Nicene Christian Library*, Volume 26, page 273). Mr. Gould, after a slight reference to this legend, adds that "it reminds one of the contest in the *Arabian Nights* between the queen of beauty and the djin in the story of the Second Calendar."

*Ed.–This is a euphemism of the translator. Various manuscripts and versions of the *Toldoth* have Judas befoul Jeshu by urinating or ejaculating semen upon him. A very late Yiddish version (the so-called Oxford Manuscript of Erich Bischoff [*Ein jüdisch-deutsches Leben Jesu*, Leipzig, Verlag Wilhelm Friedrich, 1895]) has Judas sodomize Jeshu in midair in order to bring him down unclean to earth! To add indignity to disgrace, the sixteenth-century *Ma'ase*

51. Wherefore being rendered impure, they were both deprived of the use of the *shem hamphoras* until they were washed.[17]

52. Then a death sentence was brought against Jeshu, and they said to him, "If thou wouldst be free, do the things which thou hast been wont to do hitherto."[18]

53. But Jeshu, when he found himself unable to do them raised his voice in lamentation saying,

54. "David, my forefather, prophesied concerning me, saying, 'Yea, for thy sake we are killed all the day long,[19] *etc.*'"

55. When his disciples and the wicked crowd that adhered to him saw these things, being exposed to the danger of death, they fought with the elders and the wise men of Jerusalem, and enabled Jeshu to escape from the city.[20]

56. So Jeshu went speedily to Jordan;[21] and when he had washed and purified himself, he declared again the name and repeated his former miracles.

Thola manuscript described by S. F. Brenz [Horbury, p. 413] has the defiled Yeshu fall into a cesspit or privy after the aerial duel. FRZ

[17] The sacred name could only be pronounced in a state of perfect purity, which may account for its being lost among the Jews.

[18] Compare Matthew 27:40 [Ed. —"And saying, 'Thou that destroyest the temple, and buildest it in three days, save thyself. If thou be the son of God, come down from the cross'" MMOH], where Jesus is invited to work a miracle in his own favor by descending from the cross, but Jesus, like Jeshu, was unable to respond.

[19] Psalms 44:22. [Ed.—"Yea, for thy sake are we killed all the day long; we are counted as sheep for slaughter." MMOH] Quoted also in Romans 8:36. [Ed.— *Ibid.*]

[20] Jeshu's disciples stick by him, and he escapes. The disciples of Jesus "all forsook him and fled." Jeshu appears to have made a better selection.

[21] The Jordan, where Jesus was baptized, was a sacred river, a miniature Ganges. Naaman washed in it to remove his leprosy, and Jeshu purifies himself in its waters.

57. Moreover, he went and took two millstones, and made them float upon the water, and seating himself on them he caught fishes[22] before the multitude, which they then did eat.

58. When the report of this thing reached Jerusalem, all the wise and devout men began to weep, and to say,

59. "Who will dare to risk death by going and taking away from this bastard the almighty name? Lo, we pledge ourselves that he shall enjoy eternal happiness."

60. Then Judas offered himself to go; to whom the wise men said, "Go in peace."

61. Therefore Judas went in disguise, and mingled among the wicked fellows.

---

[22] Readers will remember the miraculous draught of fishes in our gospels, and the walking on water, which may be considered equivalent to floating the millstones. In miraculously feeding the multitude, Jeshu took the precaution to furnish himself with fish.

CHAPTER 3

1. About the middle of the night God put the bastard into a deep sleep, and Judas enchanted him in his sleep.

2. Then Judas entered into Jeshu's tent, and with a knife cut his flesh and took out therefrom the sacred parchment.

3. Jeshu awoke out of sleep affrighted by a great and horrid demon.

4. Wherefore he said to his disciples, "Ye shall know now that my heavenly father hath commanded me to come to him; I go because he seeth that I have no honor among men."[1]

5. Then his disciples said, "What is to become of us?"

6. He answered, "O blessed ones, great will be your reward if ye keep my words, for ye shall sit at my right hand with my heavenly father."[2]

7. Then they all lifted up their voices and wept.

8. But Jeshu said, "Do not weep, for a great reward is in store for your piety; only beware lest ye transgress my words."

9. To which all responded, "Whatsoever thou commandest we will do, and whosoever proveth disobedient to thy commands, let him die."

10. Then said Jeshu, "If ye listen to my words and obey my commands ye will treat me with favor and justice. As ye go to

---

[1] Compare John 5:41—"I receive not honor from men."

[2] Jesus equals and exceeds this presumption. See Matthew 19:28— "Verily I say unto you, That ye which have followed me, in the regeneration when the Son of man shall sit in the throne of his glory, he also shall sit upon twelve thrones, judging the twelve tribes of Israel."

fight for me at Jerusalem I will hide myself by mingling with you so that the citizens of Jerusalem may not know me."³

11. These things Jeshu spoke deceitfully, that he might go to Jerusalem and enter the temple and again obtain the knowledge of the name.

12. Not in the least suspecting his evil intent, they all responded, "All things that thou commandest we will do, nor will we depart therefrom a finger's breadth, either to the right or to the left."

13. Again he said, "Make oath to me." So they all from the least to the greatest, bound themselves by an oath.

14. And they did not know that Judas was among them, because he was not recognized.

15. Afterwards Judas said to the attendants, "Let us provide for ourselves uniform garments, so that no one may be able to know our master."*

16. This device pleased them, and they carried it out.

---

³ A remarkably similar passage occurs in John 7:8–10. According to this gospel, although it is not mentioned by either of the others, Jesus sends his brethren up to Jerusalem, and remains behind in Galilee himself because his "time was not yet come." But as soon as they are gone, he follows them "not openly, but, as it were, in secret." [Ed. — "Go ye up unto this feast: I go not up yet unto this feast; for my time is not yet full come. When he had said these words unto them, he abode still in Galilee. But when his brethren were gone up, then went he also up unto the feast, not openly, but, as it were, in secret." MMOH]

*Ed.—The accounts in the synoptic gospels of Judas' betrayal of Jesus have never made much sense. Why would the authorities need to have the sign of a traitor's kiss to identify a man who supposedly had been haranguing crowds and was known to all — especially when he was in a small group of thirteen men? If, however, he was in a group of hundreds (as frequently is alleged in various *Toldoth* versions) and all were dressed alike, a special sign would indeed be needed. It is very likely that this version more authentically preserves the pre-gospel story from which 'Mark' and the other evangelists drew than do the canonical accounts of the betrayal. It is not implausible to suppose this story was truncated and distorted to serve the political

17. Then they journeyed to Jerusalem, there to celebrate the feast of unleavened bread.[4]

18. Now when the devout men saw Judas they rejoiced with great joy, and said to him, "Point out to us we pray thee, what remaineth to be done."

19. (For he had secretly withdrawn himself and come to the elders and wise men of the city.)

20. Then Judas related all that had happened, and how he had obtained the name from the bastard.

21. Wherefore they rejoiced, and Judas said to them, "If ye will obey my orders, tomorrow I will deliver this fellow into your hands."

22. Then said the wise men, "Hast thou enough knowledge of his going and coming?"

23. Judas replied, "Everything is known to me. Lo, he goeth to the temple to attend the sacrifice of the paschal victim, but I have sworn to him by the Ten Commandments not to deliver him into your hands.

24. "And he hath with him two thousand men.[5] Be ye prepared therefore tomorrow, and know that the man before whom I bow down in adoration, he is the bastard. Act bravely, attack his followers, and seize him."

25. Simeon ben Shetach and all the rest of the wise men danced for joy, and they promised Judas to obey his orders.

and theological agendas of the New Testament authors. (Pursuing a different agenda, the gospel of 'John' leaves out the betrayal kiss altogether, and there is no mention of Judas committing suicide.) FRZ

4 See Luke 22:1 — "Now the feast of unleavened bread drew nigh, which is called the Passover."

5 Jesus also must have had a large following, probably consisting for the most part of fanatical Galileans. They doubtless assisted him in clearing the precincts of the temple, and they were dreaded by the high priests who seized him suddenly by night, "for they feared the people."

26. The next day came Jeshu with all his crowd, but Judas went out to meet him, and falling down before him he worshipped him.

27. Then all the citizens of Jerusalem, being well armed and mailed, captured Jeshu.

28. And when his disciples saw him held captive, and that it was vain to fight, they took to their legs[6] hither and thither, and gave themselves up to bitter weeping.

29. Meanwhile the citizens of Jerusalem, waxing stronger, conquered the bastard and his crowd, killing many of them, while the rest fled to the mountains.

30. Then the elders of Jerusalem brought Jeshu into the city, and bound him to a marble pillar, and scourged him, saying, "Where now are all the miracles thou hast wrought?"

31. Then they took thorn branches, and weaving a crown out of them, put it on his head.

32. Then the bastard becoming thirsty, said, "Give me some water to drink."

33. So they offered him vinegar. Having tasted it, he cried out with a loud voice,

34. "My forefather David prophesied concerning me, saying, 'And they gave me gall for meat, and in my thirst they gave me vinegar to drink'."

35. They answering, said, "If thou art God, why didst thou not make known before thou didst drink that vinegar (that) was offered to thee?"*

---

[6] Jeshu's disciples only leave him when they see that further resistance to the authorities is useless.

*Ed.—Again, the *Toldoth* story makes more sense than do the canonical accounts of the vinegar and gall. The purpose of the vinegar is completely lost in the Markan account – the oldest of the canonical gospels: Mark 15:36 "And one [of the bystanders] ran and filled a sponge full of vinegar, and put it on a reed, and gave him to drink, saying, Let alone; let us see whether Elias will come to take him

36. Then they added, "Thou dost stand now upon the verge of the grave, nor wilt thou at last convert gall into good fruit."

37. But Jeshu, weeping bitterly, said, "My God, my God, why hast thou forsaken me?"[7]

down." The vinegar is related neither to mockery nor to Elijah. 'Matthew' does no better, even after mixing the vinegar with gall: Matthew 27:34 "They gave him vinegar to drink mingled with gall: and when he had tasted thereof, he would not drink." Nor can 'Luke' make the vinegar any more explicable: Luke 23:36 "And the soldiers also mocked him, coming to him, and offering him vinegar. 37 And saying, If thou be the king of the Jews, save thyself." The vinegar is completely gratuitous, having no obvious relation to the theme of mockery. 'John,' on the other hand, gives up all pretense of associating the vinegar with mockery and makes it into an incongruous fulfillment of prophecy: John 19:28 "After this, Jesus knowing that all things were now accomplished, that the scripture might be fulfilled, saith, I thirst. 29 Now there was set a vessel full of vinegar: and they filled a sponge with vinegar, and put it upon hyssop [*a plant whose twigs were used for sprinkling in certain ancient Jewish rites*], and put it to his mouth. 30 When Jesus therefore had received the vinegar, he said, It is finished: and he bowed his head and gave up the ghost."

If the passion source used by the four evangelists (perhaps the script of a mystery play) had a mockery story like that of the Toldoth tale, it is not hard to understand why they would not want to use it. It so simply proves the non-divinity of Jesus that it is hard to imagine a way to get around it if the whole story were told. Other elements of the mockery, however, could be turned to good account. The mocking taunt "Save thyself, and come down from the cross" [Mark 15:30] is easily seen as 'proof' that Jesus was a willing sacrifice for the salvation of mankind. This toothless mockery could be kept; the full story about the vinegar could not.

Once again, it appears the Toldoth account more faithfully preserves an extremely early tradition than do the canonical gospels. FRZ

[7] The scourging, the crown of thorns, the mocking, and the vinegar for drink are such familiar features of our gospel story that it is unnecessary to cite particular texts. Jeshu's exclamation is also exactly the same as that of Jesus. It is the first verse of the twenty-second Psalm — "*Eloi, Eloi, lama sabacthani*" — "My God, my God, why hast thou forsaken me?"

38. Then the elders said, "If thou art the son of God, why dost thou not deliver thyself out of our hands?"

39. Jeshu replied, "My blood is shed for mortals, for thus Esaias prophesied, 'And from his wounds we are healed'."[8]

40. Afterwards they brought Jeshu before the greater and lesser Sanhedrim, where sentence was pronounced that he should be stoned and hanged.[9]

41. The same day was the preparation for the Sabbath and also the preparation for the Passover.[10]

---

[8] Isaiah 53:5. [Ed.—"But he was wounded for our transgressions, he was bruised for our iniquities: the chastisement of our peace was upon him, and with his stripes we are healed." MMOH] This misinterpreted prophecy of the suffering messiah has largely contributed to the Christian doctrine of the atonement. Matthew 26:28 makes Jesus say at the Last Supper, "This is my blood of the new testament, which is shed for many for the remission of sins."

[9] Jeshu's trial and sentence are strictly according to Jewish law and practice, while that of Jesus outrages it in every particular. Rabbi Wise, in his *Martyrdom of Jesus of Nazareth*, page 66, has the following trenchant remarks on this subject: "The whole trial, from the beginning to the end, is contrary to Jewish law and custom as in force at the time of Jesus. No court of justice with jurisdiction in penal cases could or ever did hold its session in the place of the high priest. There were three legal bodies in Jerusalem to decide penal cases: the great Sanhedrim of seventy-one members, and the two minor Sanhedrim, each of twenty-three members. The court of priests had no penal jurisdiction except in the affairs of the temple service, and then over priests and Levites only."

[10] This agrees with John, but not with Matthew, Mark, and Luke, who all represent Jesus as having already eaten of the Passover. The fourth gospel is a later production, and its author had an opportunity to correct silently some of his predecessors' mistakes. Rabbi Wise, in his *Origin of Christianity,* page 30, writes: "In the first place the Jews did no public business on that day; had no court sessions, no trials, and certainly no executions on any sabbath or feast day. And in the second place, the first day of the Passover never was on a Friday, and never can be, according to the established principles of the Jewish calendar." These statements, which could be amply justified by biblical and Talmudic references, put Matthew, Mark, and Luke out

42. Thence taking him out to the place of punishment they stoned him to death.[11]

43. Then the wise men commanded him to be hanged on a tree, but no tree was found that would support him for all, being frail, were broken.

44. His disciples seeing this, wailed and cried out, "Behold the goodness of our master Jeshu, whom no tree will sustain."

of court, for they clearly assert that Jesus was crucified on the first day of the Passover. Rabbi Wise sensibly concludes that they "adopted the first day of the Passover because they taught the dogma that Jesus died to redeem all sinners. The fact concerning the day was shaped to suit the dogma. Israel was redeemed from Egyptian bondage on the day celebrated ever after that event as the feast of the Passover; therefore the death of Jesus, the second redemption, must have taken place on the self same day. ... But this is impossible."

[11] The punishment for blasphemy is prescribed in Leviticus 24:16 [Ed.—"And he that blasphemeth the day of the Lord, he shall surely be put to death, and all the congregation shall certainly stone him: as well the stranger, as he that is born in the land, when he blasphemeth the name of the Lord, shall be put to death," MMOH] and that for perverting to the worship of false gods in Deuteronomy 13:10 [Ed.— "And thou shalt stone him with stones, that he die; because he hath sought to thrust thee away from the Lord thy God, which brought thee out of the land of Egypt, from the house of bondage. MMOH]. Stoning was the method of execution in both cases. Jeshu therefore died according to the Jewish law. The subsequent hanging was perhaps equivalent to the exposure of traitors' heads on temple bar. Jesus, according to our gospels, was crucified: but there was a diversity of opinion on this point among the early Christians. Paul preached "Christ and him crucified," but his great rival Peter, in Acts 5:30, speaks of "Jesus, whom ye slew and hanged on a tree" [Ed.— "Then Peter and the other apostles answered and said, "We ought to obey God rather than men. The God of our fathers raised up Jesus, whom ye slew and hanged on a tree" MMOH], and again in Acts 10:39 ("And we are witnesses of all things which he did both in the land of the Jews, and in Jerusalem; whom they slew and hanged on a tree"). Peter further says (13:29) "And when they had fulfilled all that was written of him, they took him down from the tree, and laid him in a sepulchre"; and again in his first epistle (1 Peter 2:24, "Who in his own self bare our sins in his own body on the tree, that we, being dead to sins, should live unto righteousness: by whose stripes ye are

45. But they knew not that he had enchanted all wood when he was in possession of the name.[12]

46. But he knew that he would surely suffer the penalty of hanging, as it is written, "When any man shall be judged to death for an offense and shall be put to death, then thou shalt hang him, *etc.*"

47. Then Judas, when he saw that no wood would hold him up, said to the wise men, "Behold the subtlety of this fellow, for he hath enchanted the wood that it might not sustain him.

48. "But there is in my garden a great stem of a cabbage;[13] I will go and bring it hither; perhaps it will hold the body."

49. To whom the wise men said, "Go and do so." So Judas went at once and brought the stalk, and on it Jeshu was hanged.

50. Toward night the wise men said, "It is not lawful for us to break one letter of the divine law in regard to this fellow; we must do to him what the law demands, even though he did seduce men."

---

healed"). When Peter and Paul differ as to the execution of Jesus, it is not difficult to decide which should be believed. Peter had, as Paul had not, the advantage of being present. Peter does indeed refer twice in Acts 2 to Jesus as crucified [Ed.—2:23 "Him, being delivered by the determinate counsel and foreknowledge of God, ye have taken, and by wicked hands have crucified and slain... 36 Therefore let all the house of Israel know assuredly, that God hath made that same Jesus, whom ye have crucified, both Lord and Christ" MMOH], but it is in a long speech which was probably composed for him by the author. In any case, these references do not destroy the force of his frequent allusions to hanging. Paul himself, too, in Galatians 3:13, appears to side for once with Peter. "Christ," he says, "hath redeemed us from the curse of the law, being made a curse for us for it is written, 'Cursed is everyone that hangeth on a tree'." On the whole it is not improbable that Jeshu and Jesus died the same death.

[13] It must have been an immense cabbage. Perhaps it was a Jerusalem artichoke. The anonymous Jew who translated the *Sepher Toldoth Jeshu* for Richard Carlile says the plant was a small species of palm tree. [Ed.— The Jewish scholar Hugh J. Schonfield (*According to the Hebrews*, p. 50) interprets this as a carob tree. FRZ]

51. Therefore they buried him where he was stoned.

52. Now about the middle of the night his disciples came and sat down by the grave and wept and mourned for him.

53. Judas seeing this, took away the body and hid it in his garden under a brook. Diverting the water elsewhere, he buried the body in the channel and then brought the water back.

54. On the morrow, when the disciples came again and sat down to weep, Judas said to them, "Why do ye weep? Look and see if the buried man is there."

55. And when they looked and found he was not there, the miserable crowd cried out, "He is not in the grave but hath ascended to heaven."[14]

56. For he foretold this himself when alive, and as if concerning himself the saying was interpreted, "But God will redeem my soul from the power of the grave; for he shall receive me; Selah."

57. Meanwhile, the queen finding out what had been done, commanded the wise men of Israel to appear; and when they came she said to them,

58. "What have ye done with this man whom ye have accused of being a sorcerer and a seducer of men?"

59. They answered, "We have buried him according to the requirement of our law."

60. Then she said, "Bring him hither to me."

61. And they went and sought for him in the grave, but did not find him.

62. Then returning to the queen, they said, "We know not who hath taken him from the grave."

---

[14] Compare Matthew 28:6 —"He is not here, for he is risen, as he said. Come, see the place where the Lord lay."

63. The queen answered and said, "He is the son of God and hath ascended to his father in heaven; for thus it is prophesied of him, 'For he shall receive me; Selah'."

64. Then the wise men said, "Do not allow these thoughts to come into thy mind, for verily he was a sorcerer"; and they gave proof by their own testimony that he was a bastard and the son of an adulteress.

65. The queen replied, "Why do I exchange words with you in vain? For if ye bring him hither, ye shall be found innocent, but if not, none of you shall survive."

66. They all responded in these words: "Give us time that we may discover the upshot of this affair. Peradventure we may find him there, but if we do not succeed, do unto us whatever pleaseth thee."

67. She allowed them three days' time, and they departed grieved at heart lamenting, and not knowing what to do.

68. Therefore they ordered a fast, and when the appointed time came and they had not found the body, many left Jerusalem to escape the sight of the queen.

69. Among the rest went a certain old man named Rabbi Tanchuma.* He in great sorrow wandering through the fields, saw Judas sitting in his own garden, eating.

70. Coming up to him, Rabbi Tanchuma said, "How is this? Why dost thou take food when all the Jews fast and are in sore distress?"

71. Judas, greatly astonished, inquired wherefore they fasted.

72. Rabbi Tanchuma replied, "It is because of this bastard who hath been hanged and buried near the place of stoning; he hath been taken away from the grave, and none of us know who hath taken him.

---

*Ed.— According to Rabbi Adin Steinsaltz, there was a R. Tanḥuma b. Abba who lived in Palestine and was active in Talmud work around 350–375 CE. [*The Talmud: The Steinsaltz Edition. A Reference Guide*]
FRZ

73. "But his worthless disciples declare that he hath gone up to heaven, and the queen threateneth all of us Israelites with death unless we find him."

74. Then Judas asked, "If this fellow shall be found, will it bring safety to the Israelites?"

75. Rabbi Tanchuma said. "Indeed it will."

76. Then said Judas, "Come, and I will show thee the man, for I took him away from the grave because I feared less perchance his impious followers might steal him from the tomb,[15] and I hid him in my garden, and made the brook run over him."

77 Then Rabbi Tanchuma hastened to the wise men of Israel and related the matter.

78. Therefore they all assembled, and tying the body to a horse's tail, brought it and threw it down before the queen, saying, "Behold the man of whom thou hast said, 'He hath gone up to heaven'."

79. When the queen saw him, she was overwhelmed with shame and unable to speak.

---

[15] An analogous story is found in Matthew 28:11-15 [Ed. —"Now when they were going, behold, some of the watch came into the city, and showed unto the chief priests all the things that were done. And when they were assembled with the elders, and had taken counsel, they gave large money unto the soldiers, Saying, 'Say ye, "His disciples came by night, and stole him away while we slept." And if this come to the governor's ears, we will persuade him, and secure you.' So they took the money, and did as they were taught: and this saying is commonly reported among the Jews until this day." MMOH] But Matthew's story is incredibly absurd. [Ed.—It is clear that the unknown author of the Gospel of Matthew has invented this story for the purpose of disarming Jewish propaganda of the exact sort seen here in the Toldoth. While it does not seem likely that 'Matthew' was reacting to the Toldoth itself, it is highly probable that the Toldoth traces its own descent to the propaganda pool against which our evangelist was reacting. FRZ]

80. Moreover, while the body was thus dragged about for some time, the hair of the head was pulled out.

81. And this is the reason why now the hair of a monk is shaved off in the middle of the head; it is done in remembrance of what happened to Jeshu.[16]

---

[16] This is perhaps a later addition. It is no part of the story, but merely a speculation of the author. As a matter of fact, he was mistaken; for the tonsure was in use among Buddhist monks before the Christian era; Gautama himself being represented as performing the ceremony on his son Rahula.

CHAPTER 4

1. After these things the strife between the Nazarenes and Judæans grew so great that it caused a division between them, and a Nazarene meeting a Judæan would kill him.[1]

2. The trouble increased more and more for thirty years, when the Nazarenes, having increased to thousands and myriads, prohibited the Israelites from coming to the greater festivals in Jerusalem.[2]

3. Then there was great distress among the Israelites, like what it was in the day when the (golden) calf was forged, so that no one knew what to do.

4. The pernicious faith increased and spread abroad, and there came forth twelve men[3] (bad offspring of foul ravens), who wandered through twelve kingdoms and spread false doctrines among mankind.

5. Some of the Israelites followed them, and these being of high authority, strengthened the Jeshuitic faith; and because they gave themselves out to be apostles of him who was hanged, the great body of the Israelites followed them.

---

[1] The later and more voluminous *Sepher Toldoth Jeshu*, edited by Huldrich, makes Joseph Pandera a Nazarene, and represents him as settling at Nazareth with Miriam and Jeshu after their return from Egypt, whither they had gone on account of a famine in Palestine.

[2] Probably an anachronism. It perhaps alludes to an actual occurrence in the early part of the second century of the era of the Christ myth. Archdeacon Farrar says that "in A.D. 120, Ælia Capitolina was built by Hadrian on the ruins of Jerusalem, and Christians were allowed free access to it, while no Jew was suffered to approach it." (*Early Days of Christianity*, page 491.)

[3] Christian legends likewise represent the twelve apostles as going to various countries.

6. The wise men seeing this desperate state of things were sorely distressed, for wickedness abounded among the Israelites.

7. Therefore everyone turning to his companion said, "Woe unto us; what sins have we committed that in our time so shameful a thing should happen in Israel, such as neither we nor our ancestors ever before heard of?"

8. There with great sadness and weeping they sat down, and with their eyes turned towards heaven said:

9. We pray thee, "O Lord, God of heaven, to give us counsel what to do, for we are entirely ignorant as to what ought to be done. We lift our eyes to thee.

10. "In the midst of the people of Israel innocent blood is shed on account of this bastard and son of an adulteress.

11. "Wherefore are we stretched on tenterhooks while the hand of the Nazarene prevaileth against us and great numbers of us are killed?[4]

12. "But few of us are left, and on account of sins in which the house of Israel is implicated these things have happened.

13. "Do thou indeed for thy name's sake give us counsel what to do that we may be delivered from the wicked crowd of Nazarenes."

14. When they had thus prayed, a certain aged man from among the elders whose name was Simeon Kepha (Simon Cephas)[5] who frequented the holy of holies, said to the rest,

---

[4] Another anachronism, probably referring to the same period as verse 2. The Christians enjoyed immunity from persecution, but there is no doubt that the Jews suffered dreadfully from pagan and Christian after the fall of Jerusalem.

[5] The whole of this chapter, which is no part of the life of Jeshu but merely an addendum, is terribly confused; and Mr. Gould's attempted elucidations only leave it in greater obscurity. He seeks to explain it by events that occurred many centuries later. But a more obvious and satisfactory explanation may be given. Simeon Kepha is probably Peter, whose Judaising proclivities are well known; and Elias

15. "My brethren and people, hear me: If ye approve my counsel I will root out these wicked men from the society of Israel, and they shall have no more any part or heritage with the Israelites.

16. "But is it necessary that ye shall take upon you the guilt of an offense?"

17. All responded saying, "The sin be upon us; carry out thy purpose."

18. Therefore Simeon ben Kepha went into the sanctuary and wrote out the almighty name, and cut his flesh with a knife and placed it therein.

19. Then going from the temple he drew forth the writing, and when he had learned the name he went away to the chief city of the Nazarenes.

20. And raising his voice he cried out, "Whosoever believeth in Jeshu let him come unto me, for I am sent by him."

21. Soon a great multitude drew near to him, as many as the sands of the sea, and said to him, "Show us something to confirm to us that thou art sent by him."

22. And when he asked what sign they required of him, they replied, "The miracles which Jeshu when alive performed do thou also exhibit to us."

23. Therefore he commanded them to bring hither a leper; and when they had brought him, he laid his hand upon him and he was healed.

(verse 46) is perhaps Paul, who withstood him, and preached the gospel to the Gentiles. Christianity was originally nothing but a Jewish sect, and there were greater differences between the Sadducees and the Pharisees than between the Pharisees and the Christians. The Book of Revelation shows how intensely Jewish was the spirit of the early church, and at the same time it indicates the intrusion of foreign elements. Peter and Paul represented respectively these opposing tendencies. It may be added that the miracles here ascribed to Simeon Kepha are somewhat similar to those recorded of Peter in the Acts. [Ed.—For more information on Simeon Kepha, see footnotes on pages 447 and 449 of Appendix B. FRZ]

24. Again he asked them to bring to him a dead man, and when one was brought he laid his hand upon him and he revived and stood upon his feet.

25. The wicked men seeing this fell down to the ground, before him, saying, "Without doubt thou art sent by Jeshu, for when he was alive he did these things for us."

26. Simeon Kepha then said, "I am sent by Jeshu, and he hath commanded me to come to you. Give me an oath that ye will do all things that I command."

27. So at once they all exclaimed, "We will do all that thou commandest."

28. Then Simeon Kepha said, "Know ye that he who was hanged was the enemy of the Israelites and their law, because of the prophecy of Esaias, saying, 'Your new moons and appointed holidays my soul hateth'.

29. "Moreover, be it known to you, that he did not delight in the Israelites, even as Hosea prophesied, 'Ye are not my people'.

30. "And although it be in his power to sweep them from the earth in one moment, nevertheless he did not wish to utterly destroy them, but desired that there should ever be in your midst witnesses of his hanging and stoning.

31. "Moreover, he underwent those great sufferings and sorrows that he might redeem us from hell.

32. "And now he exhorteth and commandeth you no longer to ill-treat any of the Judæans; but if a Judæan saith to a Nazarene, 'Go with me one mile,' let him go with him two miles.

33. "And if a Judæan striketh a Nazarene on his left cheek, let him turn to him the right also; that in this world they may have their reward, but in the world to come may be punished in hell.

34. "If ye do these things, ye shall be worthy to sit with him in his seats.[6]

35. "Lo this also he requireth of you, that ye do not celebrate the feast of the Passover, but that ye hold sacred the day on which he died.

36. "And that instead of the feast of Pentecost ye keep holy the fortieth day after the stoning, in which he ascended to heaven.

37. "Instead of the feast of Tabernacles let the day of the nativity be made holy; and on the eighth day afterwards observe the memory of his circumcision."[7]

38. All responded to these words, "Whatsoever thou sayest, we will do; remain with us now."

39. To which he said, "I will abide with you if ye will allow me to abstain from all food according to his precept, and only eat the bread of misery and drink the water of sorrow.

40. "But ye must build me a tower in the midst of the city on which I may sit even till the day of my death."

41. The people answered, "We will do as thou sayest."

42. Therefore they built a tower and put him thereon; and every day they brought him his allowance of miserable bread and scanty water, even up to the hour of his death, he staying there all the time.*

---

[6] Compare Matthew 19:28 — "And Jesus said unto them, 'Verily I say unto you, That ye which have followed me, in the regeneration when the Son of man shall sit in the throne of his glory, ye also shall sit upon twelve thrones, judging the twelve tribes of Israel'."

[7] Verses 36–37. The Christian festivals of Good Friday, Ascension Day, Christmas, and the circumcision are here plainly described. Peter was "of the circumcision," and it is natural to represent Simeon Kepha as enjoining its observance on the Nazarenes. The inclusion of the festival of the circumcision in this list also points to the antiquity of the text; for it was commemorated in the early church until its suppression by Pope Gelasius (A.D. 492–496).

*Ed.— Simon Peter here is being confused with St. Simeon Stylites. See footnote on page 449. FRZ

43. For truly he served the God of our fathers Abraham, Isaac, and Jacob, and composed many beautiful hymns, which he published through all the region of Israel, that they might be a perpetual monument to him; and he repeated all the hymns of his masters.

44. This Simeon lived on that tower six years, and when he came to die he commanded that he should be buried within it; and that request they obeyed.

45. Afterwards they devised a most abominable fraud, and at this very time that tower is to be seen at Rome, and they call it Peter – that is, the name of a stone, because he sat on a stone even to the day of his death.

46. After the death of Rabbi Simeon Kepha there arose a man named Elias,[8] a wise man but of corrupt mind who went to Rome and publicly said:

47. "Know ye that Simeon Kepha hath deceived you, for your Jeshu gave to me his commands, saying, 'Go and tell them:

48. " 'Let no one believe that I despise the law; for whoever wishes to be initiated by circumcision I will allow him'.

49. "But he who refuses to observe this, let him be plunged in foul water; nor indeed if he abstains from this shall he incur danger'."

50. "This also he requireth: that not on the seventh day but the first on which the heavens and the earth were created ye shall worship."

51. And he added many other bad instructions.

52. But the people said, "Confirm to us by a miracle that Jeshu hath sent thee."

Note 8. Rabbi Wise (*Origin of Christianity*) considers Paul to be the *acher* (Elias) of the Talmud, who was also called Elisha ben Abuah. He was an apostate disciple of Gamaliel, and was alleged to have visited paradise, as Paul was lifted into "seventh heaven." The views of Elias on the unimportance of ceremonies agree with those expressed by Paul in his epistles; and Paul, like Elias, is supposed to have met a violent death at Rome.

53. And he said, "What miracle do ye expect?"

54. Scarcely had he spoken when a stone fell from a huge wall and crushed his head.

55. So perish all thine enemies, O Lord; but let those who love thee be even as the sun when it shineth in its strength.

Selah, selah, selah.

APPENDIX

JESUS IN THE TALMUD

The references to Jesus in the Talmud being binding on every orthodox Jew, we think it well to transcribe from Lightfoot's *Hebrew and Talmudical Exercitations* (Oxford, 1859) the following passages upon Matthew 2:14 ("When he arose, he took the young child and his mother by night, and departed into Egypt"):

There are some footsteps in the Talmudists of this journey of our savior into Egypt, but so corrupted with venomous malice and blasphemy (as all their writings are), that they seem only to have confessed the truth, that they might have matter the more liberally to reproach him; for as they speak: "When Jannia (*Bab. Sanedr.*, folio 107, 2), the king, slew the rabbins, R. Joses ben Perahiah and Jesus went away into Alexandria, in Egypt. Simeon ben Shetah sent thither, speaking thus: 'From me, Jerusalem, the holy city, to thee, O Alexandria in Egypt, my sister, health. My husband dwells with thee, while I, in the meantime, sit alone.' Therefore he rose up and went." And, a little after, "He brought forth four hundred trumpets, and anathematized" (Jesus). And, a little before that, "Elisæus turned away Gehazi with both his hands." And R. Joshua ben Perachiah thrust away Jesus with both his hands.

Did (*Schabb.*, folio 164, 2) not ben Stada* bring enchantments out of Egypt in the cutting which was in his flesh?

Under the name of ben Stada they wound our Jesus with their reproaches, although the Glosser upon the place, from the

---

*Ed.— While Yeshu is called ben Pandera in the *Toldoth* versions, some scholars believe that in the Talmud he often is referred to as ben Stada or ben Satda. According to G. R. S. Mead [p. 171], the Gemara of the Babylonian Talmud [b. *Shabb.* 104[b] and b. *Sanh.* 67[a]] gives an attempted etymology of this name:

"Ben Stada was Ben Pandera. Rab Chisda said: The husband was Stada, the lover Pandera. (Another said): The husband was Paphos ben Jehuda; Stada was his mother; (or) his mother was Miriam the

authority of R. Tam, denies it: for thus he, R. Tam saith, "This was not Jesus of Nazareth, because they say here, ben Stada was in the days of Paphus, the son of Judah, who was in the days of R. Akiba: but Jesus was in the days of R. Josua, the son of Perachiah, *etc.*"

Wagenseil continues the story from the Gemara. While Jesus and Joshua ben Perachiah were at Alexandria, they were hospitably treated by a rich and learned lady who, in Madame Blavatsky's opinion, personifies Egypt. Joshua praised her hospitality, and Jesus found her beautiful, notwithstanding a "defect in her eyes." Upon declaring so to his master, Joshua cursed and drove him away, it being forbidden by the rabbis to look with admiration on female beauty.

Lightfoot, upon Matthew 27:31 ("And after that they had mocked him, they took the robe off from him, and put his own raiment on him, and led him away to crucify him"), says:

> These things are delivered in *Sanhedrim* (Cap. 6, hal. 4) of one that is guilty of stoning. If there be no defence found for him, they led him out to be stoned, and a crier went before, saying aloud thus: "N., the son of N., comes out to be stoned, because he hath done so and so. The witnesses against him are N. and N.; whosoever can bring anything in his defence, let him come forth and produce it." On which the Gemara of Babylon: "The tradition is, that on the evening of the Passover Jesus was hanged, and that a crier went before him for forty days, making this proclamation: 'This man comes forth to be stoned, because he dealt in sorceries, and persuaded and seduced Israel; whosoever knows of any defence for him, let him come forth and produce it.' But no defence could be found, therefore they hanged him on the evening of the Passover. Ulla saith, "His case seemed not to admit of any defence, since he was a seducer, and of such God hath said, 'Neither shalt thou spare him, neither shalt thou conceal him.' (Deut. 13:8)"

---

women's hairdresser; as they would say at Pumbedith, S*e*ṭath da (*i.e.*, she was unfaithful) to her husband."

Hugh J. Schonfield [p. 120], on the other hand, noting the obvious confusion of the Yeshu stories with the traditions concerning Simon Magus (Simon the magician rival of St. Peter), derives *stada* from the Greek *stadios* ('the standing one') – a common epithet of Simon Magus. Schonfield believes ben Pandera and ben Stada were not confused with each other until the end of the second century CE. FRZ

On Matthew 27:56, which speaks of Mary Magdalene and Mary the mother of James and Joses, Lightfoot notes that the name מגדלא Magdalene, which is several times applied in the Talmud to Miriam, the mother of Jeshu, means a plaiting or curling of the hair, a profession which it appears was resorted to by harlots, so that the word, like *stada,* was used as an euphemism for a coarser term. *Bab. Sanh.*, folio 67, 1: "They stoned the son of Stada in Lydda, and they hanged him up on the evening of the Passover. Now this son of Stada was son of Pandira. . . . As they say in Pombadetha, she departed from her husband."

In the Jerusalem Talmud, the following occurs: "A child of a son of Rabbi Joses, son of Levi, swallowed something poisonous. There came a man who pronounced some words to him in the name of Jesus, son of Pandera, and he was healed. When he was going away Rabbi Joses said to him: 'What word did you use?' He answered, such a word. Rabbi Joses said to him: 'Better had it been for him to die, than to hear such a word.' And so it happened that he instantly died." Upon which Lardner remarks: "Another proof this of the power of miracles inherent in the disciples of Jesus, and at the same time a mark of the malignity of the Jewish rabbins."

In another place the Jerusalem Gemara *Avoda Sara,* folio 27, says: "A son of Dama was bitten by a serpent. There came to him James of Sechania to cure him in the name of Jesus, son of Pandera, but the rabbi Ismael would not suffer it."

The Gemara tract *Sanhedrim,* folio 43, mentions that Jeshu had five disciples, Matthai, Nakai, Nezer, Boni, and Thoda.

Mr. Gould remarks:

> That there really lived such a person as Jeschu ben Pandira, and that he was a disciple of the rabbi Jehoshua ben Perachia, I see no reason to doubt. That he escaped from Alexander Janneus with his master into Egypt, and there studied magical arts; that he returned after awhile to Judea, and practiced his necromantic arts in his own country, is also not improbable. Somewhat later the Jews were famous, or infamous, throughout the Roman world as conjurors and exorcists. Egypt was the headquarters of magical studies. That Jeschu, son of Pandira, was stoned to death in accordance with the law, for having practiced magic, is also

probable. The passages quoted are unanimous in stating that he was stoned for this offence. The law decreed this as the death sorcerers were to undergo.

WAS JESUS HANGED?

Lightfoot and Lardner, our two great English authorities, translating from the Talmud, say that Jeshu was hanged. We have ourselves, in a footnote (see page 395, note 11, chapter 3, v. 42), shown that stoning was the Jewish method of execution, and that numerous passages in the New Testament refer to Jesus as having been hung on a tree, and therefore accursed. Mr. Gould arbitrarily changes "hung" into "crucified," in order to bolster up his theory that the Jews confused their Jeshu with the Christian Jesus. Far more probable theories of the origin of the crucifixion legend may be ventured. Rabbi Wise considers that it may have arisen from the story of Antigonus. He writes, "Dion Cassius says, 'Antony now gave the Kingdom to a certain Herod, and having stretched Antigonus on the cross and scourged him, which had never been done before to a king by the Romans, he put him to death.' The sympathies of the masses for the crucified king of Judea, the heroic son of so many heroic ancestors, and the legends growing, in time, out of this historical nucleus, became, perhaps, the source from which Paul and the evangelists preached Jesus as the crucified king of Judea." (*History of the Hebrew's Second Commonwealth*, 1880, Cincinnati, page 206.)

The Roman cross was not, as Christian painters have universally represented it, shaped thus †. Its real form was a T, the upright portion being a fixture in the place of execution, and the crosspiece, or *patibulum*, being carried from the court or prison by the culprit, less as a burden than as a mark of ignominy. The true cross was an ancient phallic symbol, and it was used in Egyptian hieroglyphics as the sign of life. Derived from immemorial ages before Christianity, its extensive use in religious symbolism would naturally prompt the founders and propagators of new creeds and sects to adopt it in their systems. The early Christians, beginning with Paul, deserted the story of Jesus being hung, and transferred the rope to Judas. Then by developing the story of the crucifixion, and slightly varying the form of the Roman cross, they elevated their savior to a position whence he radiated the mysticism of all religions.

LARDNER ON THE *TOLDOTH JESHU*

Dr. Lardner, in his *Jewish Testimonies* (*Works*, 1838, Volume 6, chapter 7, page 558), after citing from the Talmud, says in a note, "Some learned men have of late appealed to a work entitled *Toldoth Jeshu*. I am of opinion that Christianity does not need such a testimony nor witnesses. I have looked over it several times, with an intention to give some account of it; but, after all, I could not persuade myself to attempt it; for it is a modern work, written in the fourteenth or fifteenth century, and is throughout, from the beginning to the end burlesque and falsehood; nor does the shameless writer acknowledge anything that has so much as a resemblance to the truth, except in the way of ridicule."

We have shown in our preface that the Jeshu story is very ancient, and in substance was quoted by a Christian author in the thirteenth century, and even then without being referred to as a recent composition. As for "ridicule," the miracles of the New Testament are fully as absurd as those of the *Sepher Toldoth Jeshu*, only we are accustomed to them, and this is one of those instances in which familiarity does *not* breed contempt. How Dr. Lardner would have laughed at finding in the Jeshu story a lively narrative of devils' adventures in men and pigs, or of the hero's being lugged through the air by the devil and perched on a pinnacle. Such fables are "burlesque," "false," and "shameless" to every man who finds them in another's faith.

CELSUS

We have already in our preface referred to Mr. Froude's essay on Celsus. The famous 'infidel's' reflections on the birth of Jesus have also been dealt with in one of our footnotes. The title of his work was *Logos Alethes*, which Dr. Donaldson translates as *The True Discourse* and Mr. Froude as *The True Account*. "The book is now lost to us," says Professor Luthardt, "having been destroyed by the Christian zeal of the following centuries."

Mr. Froude says of it:

> The book was powerful and popular, and it proved a real obstacle to the spread of Christianity among the educated classes. Origen's answer decided the controversy in the church's favor; but in the reconsideration of the theological position which has been forced upon the modern world, what Celsus had to say has become of peculiar interest to us, and I have endeavored to reconstruct, in outline, his principal positions. His arguments lie under every disadvantage; the order is disarranged, the objections are presented sometimes in his own words, sometimes in paraphrases and epitomes, and are brought forward in the attitude in which they could be most easily overthrown. Often we are left to discover what he must have said from details of the rejoinder.

Mr. Froude likewise gives a summary of the charge against Jesus which Celsus puts into the mouth of a Jewish adversary of Christianity. Apostrophising Jesus, he says:

> You were born in a small Jewish village. Your mother was a poor woman who earned her bread by spinning. Her husband divorced her for adultery. You were born in secret, and were afterwards carried to Egypt, and were bred up among Egyptian conjurors. The arts which you there learnt you practiced when you returned to your own people, and you thus persuaded them that you were God. It was given out that you were born of a virgin. Your real father was a soldier, named Panther.

It may be added that from his reference to Epiphanius, John of Damascus, and the Talmud, Mr. Froude appears to attach some weight to these taunts of Celsus.

Celsus was a man of learning, acuteness, and wit, and writing in the second century, he was in a much better position than any modern apologist of Christianity to judge of its originality and its miraculous pretensions. He knew that it was primarily an offshoot of Judaism, afterwards strengthened and improved by large derivations from Greek theosophy; and he pointed out what the early fathers never denied, that the Christian miracles were intellectually on a level with the prodigies of paganism, the only dispute being as to the character of the supernatural power they manifested. Unfortunately, nothing of this great skeptic's work survives, except the extracts preserved in Origen's refutation; and however honest this celebrated father may have been, it is impossible, especially in view of Mr. Froude's objections, to take his reply as a complete statement of his opponent's positions.

Mr. Gould starts an original argument on this subject. "Had," he says, any of the stories found in the *Toldoth Jeschu* existed in the second century, we should certainly have found them in the book of Celsus." Our answer to this is threefold. First, Christian bigotry has left us no copy of "the book of Celsus," which is therefore an unappealable authority. Second, Celsus *does* twit the Christians with worshipping as God a bastard Jew, born of Pandera and a Jewish woman, and who worked miracles by magic, which is the very nucleus of the Jeshu story.

Third, where the Christian father distinctly challenges another "calumny" as to Jesus being a carpenter, Celsus is right and Origen clearly wrong. Had the Skeptic himself been able to peruse the father's answer, it is probable that, instead of being converted, he would have found fresh food for mirth, and been convinced of the hopelessness of attempting to turn Christians from their favorite superstition.

JESUS AND MAGIC

Strange as the charge of magic may sound to us, it was common to both sides in the early controversy between Christianity and its opponents. That was not an age in which miracles were denied. The modern habit of criticism, resulting from long acquaintance with the methods of physical science, scarcely existed then. Miraculous stories were not investigated, but accepted or rejected as they favored or opposed existing beliefs. Gibbon satirically remarks that an Athanasian is obdurate to the force of an Arian miracle; and neither the Christians, the Jews, nor the pagans could succeed in convincing each other by the greatest display of miraculous power. When Tertullian, in the name of the Trinity, challenged the deities of paganism to a public contest, he was only attesting the universal belief in magic. Jesus himself, as we read in the gospels, was accused by the Jews of casting out devils by the power of Beelzebub; and in reply, he simply retorted the charge on his adversaries.

From this time until Christianity was victorious and paganism finally suppressed, the charge of magic was constantly preferred against Jesus. According to the apocryphal *Gospel of Nicodemus*, the Jews "said to Pilate, 'Did we not say unto thee, he is a conjuror?'" Justin Martyr, in the middle of the second century, says the Jews of his time still asserted that the miracles of Jesus were performed by magical arts. This charge he also, like his master, retorted on his opponents. He even appeals to "necromancy divination by immaculate children, dream-senders, and assistant spirits" in proof of another life. We may safely assert that all the Christian fathers, as well as Justin Martyr, believed in magic and necromancy. The *Clementine Recognitions* allude to the same charge against Jesus; and Arnobius, writing at the end of the third century or the beginning of the fourth, says: "My opponents will perhaps meet me with many other slanderous and childish charges which are commonly urged. Jesus was a magician (sorcerer); he effected all these things by secret arts. From the shrines of the Egyptians he stole names of angels of might, and the religious system of a remote century." (*Ante-Nicene Christian Library*, Volume 19, page 34.)

JESHU'S CONTEMPORARIES

King Jannæus, in whose reign Jeshu is placed, was a Sadducee. He persecuted the rabbis, and Joshua ben Perachiah, the president of the Sanhedrim, fled to Egypt, leaving Simeon ben Shetach as his deputy. With respect to this persecution, Rabbi Wise writes:

> The Pharisees being persecuted in the days of Alexander Jannai, the number of Nazarites increased. Three hundred of them came at one time to Jerusalem to fulfill their vows. Simon (ben Shetach) was enabled so to construe the law that it was unnecessary for one half of them to make the prescribed sacrifices."

Can these Nazarites have been the Nazarenes referred to in the Jeshu story? Such a confusion of names is more than possible, for the author of our first gospel has actually perpetrated it. He sends Jesus home to Nazareth to fulfill the prophecy "He shall be called a Nazarene." But the only prophecy of that kind in the Old Testament is in the angel's prediction of the birth of Samson, who was neither to shave nor to drink strong drink, but to be "a Nazarite from the womb." The Nazarite was an ancient teetotaller, and had no connection whatever with Nazareth.

On the death of Jannæus, his wife succeeded him on the throne. Josephus gives her name as Alexandra. She may, however, have had the second name of Helena. She was perhaps the queen Helena of the Jeshu story; for the Martini version represents this personage as "governing all Israel," a function which was never performed by Helena of Adiabene nor by Helena the mother of Constantine. It is, however, quite possible, as we have said in a footnote (see page 380, chapter 2, note 3), that the tradition confused her name with that of the celebrated proselyte.

Simeon ben Shetach was of great repute among the Jews, being called a second Ezra. He restored the traditional law, and made attendance at public schools compulsory. He is said to have refused to save his own son, condemned on the testimony of false witnesses, because it had been done according to the letter of the law.

APPENDIX B

A JEWISH LIFE OF JESUS

Reprinted from *Did Jesus Live 100 B.C.? An Enquiry into the Talmud Jesus Stories, the Toldoth Jeschu, and Some Curious Statements of Epiphanius—Being a Contribution to the Study of Christian Origins*, by George Robert Stow Mead (Theosophical Publishing Society, London & Benares, 1903). The English text is a translation from the German of *Das Leben Jesu nach jüdischen Quellen*, by Samuel Krauss (S. Calvary & Co., Berlin, 1902). The German text, in turn, is a translation from the Hebrew of the famous Strassburg manuscript transcribed in the same book. It appears to represent the text from which Raymund Martini quoted during the thirteenth century and is in substantial agreement with the so-called Persian text from nineteenth-century Bokhara. It is closely allied in type to the text published by Wagenseil in 1681. The ellipses (...) represent lacunæ in the Hebrew text.

A JEWISH LIFE OF JESUS

The Seduction

1. The beginning of the birth of Jeschu. His mother was Miriam [a daughter] of Israel. She had a betrothed of the royal race of the House of David, whose name was Jochanan.* He was learned in the law and feared heaven greatly. Near the door of her house, just opposite, dwelt a handsome [fellow]; Joseph† ben Pandera cast his eye upon her.

---

*Ed.–Rabbi Adin Steinsaltz lists a number of rabbis named Yohanan (Jochanan) which we may consider in attempting to place, chronologically, Jochanan, the cuckold of our tale. The earliest known rabbi of this name was Yohanan ben Zakkai, who flourished during the second Tannaitic generation (40–80 CE). He was followed by two like-named rabbis in the fourth Tannaitic generation (110–135 CE), Yohanan ben Berokah and Yohanan ben Nuri. After the expulsion of the Jews from Jerusalem in 135 CE, there were two more: Yohanan HaSandlar ('the cobbler') of the fifth Tannaitic generation (135-170 CE) and Yohanan ben Nappaha, of the second Amoraic generation (250–290 CE).

The general confusion as to when exactly Jesus was supposed to have interacted with human history is, of course, reflected in the canonical gospels as well as in Jewish sources. Matthew 2:1 has him be born during the reign of Herod the Great [d. 4 BCE], whereas Luke 2:2 places the birth of Jesus during the census of Quirinius [6 CE]. The prologue of the Gospel of John asserts Jesus the Word to have existed "In the beginning," before the beginning of the world itself. The Pauline letters make no effort at historical placement of Jesus at all.

An early Jewish Christian source translated from the Arabic by Shlomo Pines ["The Jewish Christians of the Early Centuries of Christianity According to a New Source"] places Jesus even earlier than the *Toldoth* variant reproduced in appendix A. Whereas that text places Jesus at the time of Alexander Jannaeus [90 BCE], the Jewish Christian source places him approximately five hundred years before the Council of Nicaea – which was held in 325 CE! The

It was at night, on the eve of the Sabbath, when drunken he crossed over to her door and entered in to her. But she thought in her heart that it was her betrothed Jochanan; she hid her face and was ashamed. ... He embraced her; but she said to him: Touch me not, for I am in my separation. He took no heed thereat, nor regarded her words, but persisted. She conceived by him. ...*

---

fact that Jewish Christians, of all people, should have placed Jesus 175 years before Christ only reinforces my opinion that Semitic language–speaking Jews were not the first Christians, but rather among the latest – having adopted him as a prophet only after he had been divested of divinity completely and had acquired a human history.

This is further supported by the Jewish author Sa'adia [d. 942 CE] – also cited by Pines [p. 276] – who indicates that the Christians who reject the divinity of Jesus are the latest of "the four sects":

"...the Christians are divided, may God have pity on you, into four sects. Three of them are more ancient, whereas the fourth came out only recently... The fourth gives him [i.e. Jesus, called a few lines above their Messiah] only the rank of a prophet, and interprets the Sonship, which according to them is attributed to him, just as we [i.e., Jews, FRZ] interpret [the verse]: My son, my first born, Israel being only [an indication of] his being honored and preferred, and just as others than we [i.e., the Moslems] interpret the expression 'Abraham, the Friend of God'."
FRZ

†Ed.–To most Bible scholars, that Jesus' father was named Joseph is a simple given. After all, both Matthew and Luke trace the lineage of Jesus through a man named Joseph. (The evangelists disagree as to whether his grandfather was named Jacob or Heli (Eli), however.) Some scholars, however, believe the Messiah's father *had* to be named Joseph because of the pre-Christian belief in a Messiah ben Joseph ('Christ, son of Joseph'). In the *Toldoth* tradition, the father of Jesus is simply Joseph, the son of Panther. (The equivalence of *Pandera* and *Panther* is more easily seen when it is realized that in some Greek dialects, the pronunciation of the letter theta (θ, *th*) survived as simply an aspirated *t* (like the *t* in English *bat*, not like the *th* in *think*) until late antiquity, and that voiceless consonants following an *n* easily become voiced – turning *t* or *th* to *d* or *dh*.) FRZ

* Ed.–It is natural to suppose that the story of Jesus' bastardy was composed as a Jewish response to Christian claims of a virgin birth

At midnight came her betrothed Rabbi Jochanan. She said to him: What meaneth this? Never hath it been thy custom, since thou wast betrothed to me, twice in a night to come to me.

He answered her and said: It is but once I come to thee this night.

She said to him: Thou camest to me, and I said to thee I was in my separation, yet heeded'st thou not, but did'st thy will and wentest forth. When he heard this, forthwith he perceived that Joseph ben Pandera had cast an eye upon her and done the deed. He left her; in the morning he arose and went to Rabbi Simeon ben Shetach.*

He said to him: Know then what hath befallen me this night with my betrothed. I went in to her after the manner of men...; before I touched her she said: Thou hast already this night come once to me, and I said to thee I was in my separation, and thou gavest no ear to me, [didst] thy will and wentest forth. When I heard such words from her, I left her and [went forth].

Rabbi Simeon ben Shetach said to him: Who came into thy mind?

He answered: Ben Pandera, for he dwelleth near her house and is a libertine.

He said to him: I understand that thou hast no witness for this thing, therefore keep silence; I counsel thee, if he have come once, then can he not fail to come a second time; act wisely; at that time set witnesses against him.

Some time after the rumor went abroad that Miriam was with child. Then said her betrothed Jochanan: She is not with

of the sort in vogue in pagan mythology and politics. Certainly, the later developments of the *Toldoth* bastardy theme clearly have Christian claims in mind. However, Yeshu the Bastard could be pre-Christian in origin. He could have been a real person or a made-up character designed to focus debate on the legal question of what to do with a woman who is impregnated by deception. It is very well suited for rabbinical debating contests – the menstrual issue appearing to be forensically as irresistible as it is biologically ridiculous. FRZ

*According to Mead [pp. 163–4], R. Simeon ben Shetach could be inferred to be contemporary with R. Joshua ben Perachiah. He is also known as the Rabbinic president of the golden age of Pharisæan prestige in the days of Queen Salome (Alexandra) [d. 68 BCE]. FRZ

child by me; shall I abide here and hear my shame every day from the people?

He arose and went to Babylon. After some [time she bore] a son, and they called his name Joshua after his mother's brother; ⟦but when his corrupt birth was made public they called him Jeschu.⟧*

How the Bastardy of Jeschu Was Made Public

2.His mother gave him to a teacher, so that he might become wise in the Halacha, and learned in the Torah and the Talmud.† ⟦ Now it was the custom of the teachers of the law that no disciple and no boy should pass on his way by them without his head being covered and his eyes cast to the ground, from reverence of the pupils towards their teachers.

One day that rogue passed by, and all the wise were seated together at the door of the synagogue — that is, they called the school-house synagogue; that rogue then passed by the Rabbis, head on high and with uncovered pate, saluting no one, nay, rather, in shameless fashion showing irreverence to his teacher.

After he had passed by them, one of them began and said: He is a bastard (mamzer). The second began and said: He is a bastard and son of a woman in her separation (mamzer ben ha-niddah).⟧

Another day the Rabbis stopped in tractate Nezikin‡; then began that one to speak Halachoth§ before them.

---

*Passages marked with double square brackets are adjudged by Hugh J. Schonfield (*According to the Hebrews*) to be late additions to the text.

†Ed.–Mention of the Talmud makes it obvious that this passage, at least, is quite late and cannot be part of any putative pre-Christian story. FRZ

‡The fourth Talmud order, "Damages," dealing with civil and criminal law.

§Decisions or rules of law.

Thereupon one of them began and said to him: Hast thou then not learned: He who giveth forth a Halacha in the presence of his teacher, is guilty of death?

That one answered and said to the wise ones: Who is the teacher and who the disciple? Who of the twain is wiser, Moses or Jethro? Was it not Moses, father of the prophets and head of the wise? And the Torah, moreover, beareth witness of him: And from henceforth there ariseth no prophet in Israel like unto Moses. Withal Jethro was an alien, ... yet taught he Moses worldly wisdom, as it is written: Set thou over them rulers of thousands, and rulers of hundreds. But if ye say that Jethro is greater than Moses, then would there be an end to the greatness of Moses.

When the wise heard this, they said: As he is so very shameless, let us enquire after him. They sent to his mother, [saying] thus: Tell us, pray, who is the father of this boy?

She answered and said: ..., ⟦but they say of him, that he is a bastard and son of a woman in her separation.⟧

Then began Rabbi Simeon ben Shetach: To-day is it thirty years since Rabbi Jochanan her betrothed came to me; at that time he said to me: That and that hath befallen me.

He related all that is told above, ...how Rabbi Simeon answered Rabbi Jochanan, and how when she was with child, he [R. J.] for great shame went to Babylon and did not return; but this Miriam gave birth to this Jeschu, and no death penalty awaits her, for she hath not done this of her own will,* for Joseph ben Pandera laid in wait for her ... the whole day.†

When she heard from Rabbi Simeon that no death penalty awaited her, she also began and said: Thus was the story;

---

*Ed.—This exculpation of Mary is inexplicable if this were merely an anti-Christian polemic or satire. Rather, it has the air of a haggadah resulting from rabbinical debates on the subject of what constitutes true adultery. If this be the true nature of this pericope, it is entirely possible that Mary and Joseph are not historical but are merely characters invented to give form to a thesis for rabbinical debate. FRZ

†Ed.—Schonfield renders this problematic passage "but Joseph the son of Pandera sought occasion for fornication every day." FRZ

and she confessed. But when it went abroad concerning Jeschu, ⟦that he was called a bastard and son of a woman in her separation,⟧ he went away and fled to Jerusalem.*

The Robbing of the *Shem*

3.Now the rule of all Israel was in the hand of a woman who was called Helene.† And there was in the sanctuary a foundation-stone—and this is its interpretation: God founded it and this is the stone on which Jacob poured oil—and on it were written the letters of the Shem,‡ and whosoever learned it, could do whatsoever he would. But as the wise feared that the disciples of Israel might learn them and therewith destroy the world, they took measures that no one should do so.

---

*Bischoff's recension states that this enquiry took place at Tiberias in Galilee.

†Ed.–Mead supposes that this Helene is actually Salome, the wife of Alexander Jannaeus. There is some evidence that Salome was called Selene in Greek. Invoking the well-known phonological shift of *s* > *h* in Greek, *Selene* becomes *Helene*. This verse is the beginning of the lengthy quotation by Raymund Martini in the theirteenth century. FRZ

‡ Krauss: "*Des erklärtcn Gottesnamens.*" But *shem hamphoras* (*hamephoresch*) would perhaps be better rendered by the "ineffable name," that is, the name that ought not to be pronounced, the name of which only the consonants Y. H. V. H. are given, which are not pronounceable, but only indicate the pronunciation as known to the initiated. I use *shem* throughout for the longer form *shem hamphoras*.

Ed.–As noted by Mead above, the *shem* refers to the divine name *YHWH*, mere pronunciation of which required the death penalty [Lev 24:16]. It was the name the third commandment (according to Protestant numbering) says we must not "take in vain." Probably pronounced *Yahweh*, the name actually was the *secret* name of the Israelite deity. The ancient Hebrews, like the Egyptians and other neighboring peoples, believed in the magical power of names – especially secret names. If one knew someone else's secret name, he or she held magical power over that person. Priesthoods everywhere were able to hoodwink laymen into believing that they (the priests) knew the secret names of the deities they 'served.' For a fee, the

Brazen dogs were bound to two iron pillars at the entrance of the place of burnt offerings,* and whosoever entered in and learned these letters—as soon as he went forth again, the dogs bayed at him; if he then looked at them, the letters vanished from his memory.

This Jeschu came, learned them, wrote them on parchment, cut into his hip and laid the parchment with the letters

---

priests could bend their gods to the will of their clients by secret use of the secret names of the deities.

It was no different among the Hebrews. The entire 'covenant' between Moses and Yahweh is nothing less than a lengthy contract stipulating what must be done in exchange for revelation of the secret name. As described in the third and fourth chapters of the book of Exodus, Moses haggles with 'the Lord' to learn his secret name.[In reading aloud the Hebrew Bible, Jews must pronounce the word *YHWH* as *Adonai* ('my Lord'). In the Greek translation of the Hebrew scriptures (the Septuagint), the name *YHWH* does not appear. Instead, the word *Kurios* ('Lord') is substituted. A similar practice is followed in the King James Version, where the Hebrew *YHWH* is rendered 'LORD'.]

When asked what his name is [Exod 3:14], Yahweh replies "I AM THAT I AM." This is clarified by the redactor of Exodus in the next verse, where the secret name Yahweh slips out as "the Lord [*Yahweh*, in the Hebrew text] God of your fathers." As soon as Moses learns the secret name, he starts to do magic tricks – the leprosy trick being found in the *Toldoth* story as well.

Since the slogan *Jesus is Lord* means 'Jesus is Yahweh,' it should not be surprising to learn that early Christians also practiced magic. Instead of the *shem*, however, they could substitute the name Jesus, as well as numerous other 'words of power' [*Ancient Christian Magic: Coptic Texts of Ritual Power,* edited by Marvin Meyer and Richard Smith].

The magical heritage of Christianity is still apparent today – as can be seen in the quintessentially magical centerpiece of the Roman Catholic mass where, it is believed, the priest literally 'transubstantiates' bread and wine into flesh and blood. But even in Protestantism, the belief in the magical power of the name *Jesus* is ubiquitously apparent. "All hail the power of Jesus' name!" is sung everywhere. Everywhere, to make sure prayers will be efficacious, prayers are concluded with the magical "In Jesus' name, we pray. Amen." FRZ

---

* Or rather, the door by which the burnt offerings were brought in.

therein—so that the cutting of his flesh did not hurt him—then he restored the skin to its place. When he went forth the brazen dogs bayed at him, and the letters vanished from his memory. He went home, cut open his flesh with his knife, took out the writing, learned the letters, went and gathered together three hundred and ten of the young men of Israel.

Jeschu Claims to be Messiah and Works Miracles With the *Shem*

4. He said to them: Behold then these who say of me ⟦I am a bastard and son of a woman in her separation;⟧ they desire power for themselves and seek to exercise lordship in Israel. But see ye, all the prophets prophesied concerning the Messiah of God, and I am the Messiah. Isaiah prophesied concerning me: Behold the virgin shall conceive, bear a son, and he shall be called Emmanuel. Moreover, my forefather David prophesied concerning me and spake: The Eternal [Y.H.V.H.] said to me: Thou art my son; this day have I begotten thee. He begat me without male congress with my mother; yet they call me a bastard! He further prophesied: Why do the heathen rage, *etc.*, the kings in the country rise up, *etc.*, against His anointed.* I am the Messiah, and they, so to rise up against me, are children of whores, for so it is written in the Scripture: For they are the children of whores.†

---

*Ed.–This and following verses not only betray familiarity with developed Christian tradition, they show familiarity with the Book of Acts [Acts 13:33, 4:25–26]. Perhaps significantly, chapters 3 and 4 of Acts deal with magical healing involving the name of Jesus itself as a 'word of power.' Peter and John enchant a man lame from birth, "In the name of Jesus Christ the Nazarene, rise up and walk!" [Acts 3:6] In verse 4:7 – after these magicians are arrested – they are asked, "By what power, or by what name, have ye done this?" To this they reply, "By the name of Jesus Christ the Nazarene... doth this man stand here before you whole." It also seems significant that this quote is followed in the *Toldoth* also by the healing of a man lame from birth, followed by the arrest of the magician. FRZ

† A.V.: "children of whoredoms."

The young men answered him: If thou art the Messiah, show unto us a sign. He answered them: What sign do ye require that I should do for you? Forthwith they brought unto him a lame man, who had never yet stood upon his feet. He pronounced over him the letters, and he stood upon his feet. In the same hour they all made obeisance to him and said: This is the Messiah. He gave them another sign. They brought to him a leper; he pronounced over him the letters, and he was healed. There joined themselves to him apostates from the children of his people.[*]

Jeschu and Queen Helene

When the wise saw that so very many believed on him they seized him and brought him before Queen Helene, in whose hand the land of Israel was. They said to her: This man uses sorcery and seduces the world.

Jeschu answered to her as follows: Already of old the prophets prophesied concerning me: And there shall come forth a rod out of the stem of Isai (Jesse),[†] and I am he. Of him

[*]Ed.–In the Wagenseil text, at this point there is a lengthy passage telling how the news of Yeshu reaches Jerusalem and the Sanhedrin plots his capture. The Sanhedrin sends Annani and Ahaziah, who pretend to be followers of Jesus, to invite him to come to Jerusalem. Jesus agrees, provided that the Sanhedrin come out to receive him and acknowledge his lordship. The elders humor him and Jesus starts off for Jerusalem. Upon coming to Nob, he asks for an ass and rides into Jerusalem in fulfilment of Zechariah 9:9. The elders accuse him before the queen, who is related to him and asks to see him so that she can save him. To dissuade her, the elders reveal his shameful birth and how he stole the *shem* to acquire his magical powers. FRZ

[†]Ed.–That this might reflect a very early tradition is seen by the fact that according to Epiphanius, the Christians were called Jessaeans before they were called Christians. This doubtless is of relevance for understanding the appelation *Notzri* given to them by the Jews. Isaiah 11:1 refers to "a rod out of the stem of Jesse, and a Branch (*netzer*) shall grow out of his roots." The title *Yeshua' Netzer* – 'The Savior, The Branch' – became "Jesus the Nazarene." Further misunderstanding of the term Nazarene let to the creation of a place that never existed before the second century CE – Nazareth. FRZ *Cf*. note 1 to general introduction, page 1.

saith the Scripture: Blessed is the man who walketh not in the counsel of the ungodly.

She said to them: Is this truly in your law, what he saith?

They answered: It is in our law; but it hath not been said concerning him, for it is said therein: And that prophet [etc.], put the evil away from the midst of thee. But the Messiah for whom we hope, with him are [other] signs, and it is said of him: He shall smite the earth with the rod of his mouth. With this bastard these signs are not present.

Jesus said: Lady, I am he, and I raise the dead.

In the same hour the queen was affrightened and said: That is a great sign.

Apostates still joined themselves to him, were with him, and there arose a great schism in Israel.

Jeschu's Miracles in Galilee

5. Jeschu went to Upper Galilee. The wise assembled together, went before the queen and said to her: Lady, he practiseth sorcery and leadeth men astray therewith.

Therefore sent she forth horsemen concerning him, and they came upon him as he was seducing the people of Upper Galilee and saying to them: I am the Son of God, who hath been promised in your law. The horsemen rose up to take him away, but the people of Upper Galilee suffered it not and began to fight.

Jeschu said unto them: Fight not, have trust in the power of my Father in heaven.

The people of Galilee made birds out of clay; he uttered the letters of the Shem, and the birds flew away.* At the same hour they fell down before him.

---

*Ed.—It appears that this passage draws from the same mythical traditions that inspired ancient Christians to compose infancy gospels such as the second-century *Infancy Gospel of Thomas*. In that tale, the five-year-old Jesus fashions twelve sparrows out of clay on the sabbath, claps his hands, and shouts "Off with you!" Thereupon the sparrows fly away chirping. [*New Testament Apocrypha*, Vol. I. *Gospels and Related Writings*, rev. ed., edited by Wilhelm Schneemelcher, p. 444.] The author of the Qur'an also seems to have

He said to them: Bring unto me a millstone. They rolled it to the sea-shore; he spake the letters, set it upon the surface of the sea, sat himself thereon, as one sits in a boat, went and floated on the water.

They who had been sent, saw it and wondered; And Jeschu said to the horsemen: Go to your lady, tell her what ye have seen! Thereupon the wind raised him from the water and carried him onto the dry land.

The horsemen came and told the queen all these things; the queen was affrighted, was greatly amazed, sent and gathered together the elders of Israel and spake unto them: Ye say he is a sorcerer, nevertheless every day he doeth great wonders.

They answered her: Surely his tricks* should not trouble thee! Send messengers, that they may bring him hither, and his shame shall be made plain.

At the same hour she sent messengers, and his wicked company also joined itself onto him, and they came with him before the queen.

---

been familiar with this legend – and accepted it as historical. In section 5 of Sura 3, the story of Mary's virginal parturition is retailed as an example of words having magical power – not only to produce a child without the agency of a physical father, but also to vivify birds of clay: "III:47. She [Mary] said: 'O my Lord! How shall I have a son when no man hath touched me?' He said: 'Even so: God createth what He willeth: When He hath decreed a plan, He but saith to it, "Be," and it is! 48. And God will teach him the Book and Wisdom, the Law and the Gospel, 49. And (appoint him) as apostle to the Children Of Israel, (with this message): "I have come to you, with a Sign from your Lord, in that I make for you out of clay, as it were, the figure of a bird, and breathe into it, and it becomes a bird by God's leave: and I heal those born blind, and the lepers, and I quicken the dead, by God's leave..." ' " [*The Holy Qur-an: Text, Translation and Commentary*, by Abdullah Yusuf Ali] FRZ

* "*Sachen.*"

The Magic Contest with Judas

Then the wise men of Israel took a man by name Juda Ischariota, brought him into the Holy of Holies, where he learned the letters of the Shem, which were engraved on the foundation-stone, wrote them on a small [piece of] parchment, cut open his hip, spake the Shem, so that it did not hurt, as Jeschu had done before.

As soon as Jeschu with his company had returned to the queen, and she sent for the wise men, Jeschu began and spake: For dogs encompassed me. And concerning me he [David] said: Tremble not before them.

As soon as the wise men entered and Juda Ischariota with them, they brought forward their pleas against him, until he said to the queen: Of me it hath been said: I will ascend to heaven.* Further it is written: If He take me, Sela! He raised his hands like unto the wings of an eagle and flew, and the people were amazed because of him: How is he able to fly twixt heaven and earth!

Then spake the wise men of Israel to Juda Ischariota:
Do thou also utter the letters and ascend after him. Forthwith he did so, flew in the air, and the people marveled: How can they fly like eagles!

Ischariota acted cleverly,† flew in the air, but neither could overpower the other, so as to make him fall by means of the Shem, because the Shem was equally with both of them. When Juda perceived this he had recourse to a low trick; he befouled‡ Jeschu, so that he was made unclean and fell to the earth, and with him also Juda.

---

*Ed.–The aerobatic contest between Jeschu and Judas appears to be an evolution of the same tradition that is found in the apocryphal *Acts of Peter*, where the magician Simon Magus flies above the city of Rome and is brought to earth by Simon Peter, without the latter himself being launched into flight. [*The New Testament Apocrypha*. Vol. II., rev. ed., edited by Wilhelm Schneemelcher, pp. 312-313.] FRZ

†Text uncertain.

‡Ed.—The Hebrew text actually says Ischariota urinated upon Jeschu. A closely related manuscript says he ejaculated on Jeschu to render him ritually unclean! FRZ

⟦It is because of this that they wail on their night,* and because of the thing which Juda did to him.⟧

Jeschu is Condemned to Death.

At the same hour they seized him and said to Helene: Let him be put to death! ...† Let him tell us who smote him.‡ So they covered his head with a garment and smote him with a pomegranate staff. As he did not know,§ it was clear that the Shem had abandoned him, and he was now fast taken in their hands.

He began and spake to his companions before the queen: Of me it was said: Who will rise up for me against the evil

---

* Christmas. *Weihnachten* = *Weinennachten*, comments Krauss. But if this wordplay were intended, then the original of such a gloss in this recension was composed in German, and the Hebrew would be a translation from the German and not from Aramaic. But as the Hebrew text existed already in the thirteenth century, this does not seem probable. [Ed.—According to Schonfield (p. 223), this in fact refers to a practice in the early Eastern Church. In the Apostolic Constitutions (Bk. V, 15–17), on Saturday night before Easter Sunday Christians are instructed "to fast and wail over the Jews, because on the day of their feast they crucified Christ." FRZ]

†Evidently a *lacuna* occurs here in the text. The text of Martini adds: "If he be the Son of God."

‡Ed.—This seems more authentic than the gratuitous and seemingly purposeless "smote him on the head with a reed" of the Markan passion account [Mark 15:19] – the oldest of the Synoptic versions. Matthew reworks the reed into a new story that presents no challenge to his supernatural claims concerning Jesus. One easily can understand why the evangelists would not want to recount the details of a mockery that demonstrated so simply that Jesus had no supernatural powers – almost certainly the reason Luke and John leave out the story altogether! It would appear that the *Toldoth* story here is earlier than the gospel version. FRZ

§Ed.—In another recension it is said that seventy elders with seventy staves of different woods smite him, and he is asked to say by whom and with what kind of staff he has been smitten, but he can tell neither the name of the smiter nor the wood of the staff. FRZ

doers? But of them he said: The proud waters. And of them he said: Stronger than rocks make they their countenance.

When the queen heard this she reproved the apostates, and said to the wise men of Israel: He is in your hand.*

---

*Ed.—In the Wagenseil version there follows a long section in which the disciples fight with the elders and help Yeshu to escape. He bathes in the Jordan to purify himself and recover the power of the *shem*. He repeats his former miracles, causing a millstone to float and catching fish to feed the crowd. Judas agrees with the sages to bring him back to face judgment. In disguise, he infiltrates the Yeshu adherents. God makes Yeshu fall into a deep sleep so Judas can enter his tent and extract the parchment recording the *shem* from beneath Yeshu's skin. Yeshu awakens, realizing his loss. This is followed by a passage which Hugh Schonfield [p. 46] translates as follows:

> Wherefore he said to his disciples, Know that my heavenly Father desireth to receive me because he seeth that I have no honour among men. Then say his disciples unto him, and what is to become of us? He saith unto them, Blessed are ye and blessed is your portion if ye hearken to my voice, for ye shall sit at my right hand with my heavenly Father. Then they all lifted up their voices and wept. But Jesus saith unto them, Weep not, for there is a reward for your deeds; only beware lest ye transgress my words. Then answered they, and said, Whatsoever thou commandest we will do, and whosoever shall be disobedient to thy words, let him die.
>
> Then said Jesus unto them, If ye will indeed hearken to my voice, ye will show me favour and truth. As ye go with me to Jerusalem, I will disguise myself and go among you that the men of Jerusalem may not know me. These things spake Jesus deceitfully, that he might go to Jerusalem in secret and enter into the temple and learn the Name. But they knew not that his thought was of evil, and they all answered and said, All that thou commandest we will do, neither will we turn to the right hand or to the left. And he said, Swear unto me. So they swear unto him from the least to the greatest.
>
> Now they knew not that Judas was among them, for he was not recognized. After this Judas said to the disciples, Let us provide for ourselves similar garments, that no one will know who is our master. And the saying was good in their eyes; and they did so. And they took their way to come to Jerusalem for the feast day, being the feast of unleavend bread.
>
> Now when the wise men saw Judas they rejoiced exceedingly, and they said to him, Tell us, we pray thee, all that we should do;

Jeschu Is Rescued by His Disciples

6.They departed from the queen and brought him to the synagogue of Tiberias and bound him to the pillars of the ark. Then there gathered together the band of simpletons and dupes, who believed on his words and desired to deliver him out of the hand of the elders; but they could not do so, and there arose great fighting between them.

When he saw that he had no power to escape, he said: Give me some water. They gave him vinegar in a copper vessel. He began and spake with a loud voice: Of me David prophesied and said: When I was thirsty they gave me vinegar to drink.

On his head they set a crown of thorns. The apostates lamented sore, and there was fighting between them, brother

for he had withdrawn secretly from them to come to the elders of the city and the wise men. Then Judas related to them all that had taken place, and how he had obtained the Name from that bastard. Wherefore they rejoiced exceedingly. Then Judas said to them, If ye will obey my voice, on the morrow I will deliver this bastard into your hands. Then said the wise men, Dost thou know his going and coming? And he said, Of a surety I know it, and, behold, on the morrow he goeth to the temple to sacrifice the sacrifice of the Passover; but I have sworn unto him by the ten commandments that I will not deliver him into your hands: moreover, he hath with him two thousand men all of them dressed in like garments. Be ye therefore ready on the morrow, and that man before whom I bow down and prostrate myself, that is the bastard. And Simeon the son of Shetach and all the wise men and elders rejoiced with great joy and they agreed to do according to the words of Judas.

And it came to pass on the morrow that Jesus came with all his multitude, and Judas came forth before him and bowed down and prostrated himself unto him with his face to the ground. Then all the men of Jerusalem being well-armed and mailed captured Jesus. And when his disciples saw that he was captive in their hands, and that it was in vain to fight, they took to their legs, and lifted up their voices and wept bitterly. And the men of Jerusalem waxed stronger, and conquered the bastard, the son of a woman in her separation, with his multitude, slaying many of them, while the rest fled to the mountains. FRZ

with brother, father with son; but the wise men brought the apostates low.

He began and spake: Of me he prophesied and said: My back I gave to the smiters, *etc*. Further of these the Scripture saith: Draw hither, sons of the sorceress. And of me hath been said: But we held him, *etc*. And of me he said: The Messiah shall be cut off and he is not.

When the apostates heard this, they began to stone them with stones, and there was great hatred among them.

The Betrayal of Jeschu

Then were the elders afraid, and the apostates bore him off from them, and his three hundred and ten disciples brought him to the city of Antioch, where he sojourned till the rest-day of Passover.* Now in that year Passover fell on the Sabbath and he and his sons [*sic*] came to Jerusalem, on the rest-day of Passover, that is on the Friday, he riding on an ass and saying to his disciples: Of me it was said: Rejoice greatly, Daughter of Zion, *etc*.

In the same hour they all cried aloud, bowed themselves before him, and he with his three hundred and ten disciples went into the sanctuary.

Then came one of them, who was called Gaisa [that is, Gardener]†, and said to the wise men: Do you want the rogue?

---

*Ed.–In the Wagenseil text, this is followed by "then Yeshu hastened to Jordan and bathed and purified himself and pronounced the *shem* once again clearly and performed miracles again just as before." FRZ

†Ed.–According to Schonfield, *ga'isa* means *thief* or *robber* in Aramaic. I have been unable to verify neither *gardener* nor *thief* as the proper meaning of this word. Both meanings resonate with hints found in the Gospel of John. *Gardener* recalls the 'fact' that Jesus was entombed in a garden [John 19:41–42] and was mistaken for the gardener by Mary [John 20:15. "Thinking it was the gardener, she said, 'If it is you, sir, who removed him, tell me where you have laid him, and I will take him away'."]. *Thief,* on the other hand, recalls the peculiar pericope in John 12:4–6, where Judas Iscariot is called a thief: "At this, Judas Iscariot, a disciple of his – the one who was to betray him – said, 'Why was this perfume not sold for thirty pounds and given to the poor?' He said this, not out of any care for the poor,

They said: Where is he to be found? He answered: He is in the sanctuary,—that is to say, in the school-house. They said to him: Show him unto us. He answered them: We, his three hundred and ten disciples, have already sworn by the commandments, that we will not say of him who he is; but if ye come in the morning, give me the greeting,* and I will go and make an obeisance before him, and before whom I make obeisance, he is the rogue. And they did so.

The disciples of Jeschu gathered together, went and gave their fellows the greeting, for they were come from all places to pray on the Mount of Olives on the Feast of Unleavened Bread.

Then the wise men went into the sanctuary, where those were who had come from Antioch, and there was also the rogue among them. Thereupon Gaisa entered with them, left the rest of the company, made an obeisance before the rogue Jeschu. Whereupon the wise men saw it, arose against him and seized him.

Proofs from Scripture

¶ 7. They said to him: What is thy name? He answered: Mathai. They said to him: Whence hast thou a proof from the Scripture ? He answered them: When *(mathai)* shall I come and see the face of God? They said to him: When *(mathai)* shall he die and his name perish?

Further they said to him: What is thy name? He answered: Naki. They said to him: Whence hast thou a proof from the Scripture? He answered: with pure *(naki)* hands and a clean heart. They said to him: He remaineth not unpunished.

Further they said to him: What is thy name? He answered: Boni. They said: Whence hast thou a proof from the Scripture?

---

but because he was a thief; he used to pilfer the money put into the common purse, which was in his charge." FRZ

*That is the customary form of greeting (probably the kiss of peace) used among the followers of Jeschu, as we learn from Bischoff's recension.

He answered: My first-born son *(imeni)* is Israel. They said: Of thee it was said: Behold, I will slay thy first-born son.

Further they said: What is thy name? He answered: Netzer. They said: Whence hast thou a proof from the Scripture ? He answered them: A branch *(netzer)* shall spring up out of his roots. They said to him: Thou art cast forth from thy sepulchre, like an abominable branch *(netzer)*. And thus still more, as he gave himself many names.*⟧

Jeschu Is Hanged on a Cabbage Stalk

Forthwith they seized him, and his disciples could not deliver him. When he saw himself brought to death he began and spake: Verily hath David prophesied of me and said: For Thy sake are we smitten every day. And of you said Isaiah: Your hands are full of blood. And of you said the prophet before God: They slew Thy prophets with the sword.

The apostates began to lament and could not deliver him. At the same hour was he put to death. And it was on Friday on the rest-day of Passover and of the Sabbath. When they would hang him on a tree *(Holz)*, it brake, for there was with him the Shem.†

But when the simpletons saw that the trees brake under him,‡ they supposed that this was because of his great godliness, until they brought him a cabbage-stalk. For while he was yet alive he knew the custom of the Israelites, that they would hang him; he knew his death, the manner of his being put to death, and that they would hang him on a tree. At that time he brought it to pass by means of the Shem, that no tree should bear him; but over the cabbage-stalk he did not utter

---

*Ed.– In the Talmud [*Sanhedrin* 43ᵃ], Jesus is said to have five disciples: Matthai, Naki, Boni, Netzer, and Thoda. The Bodlean MS of the *Toldoth* omits this entire section, which is in fact an interpolation from the Talmud [*Sanh.* 43ᵃ]. FRZ

† This is in contradiction with c. 7.

‡ Another recension tells us that they tried every tree (there being seventy kinds).

the pronounced name, for it is not tree but green-stuff, and so*
[in special years there are] in Jerusalem cabbages with more
than a hundred pounds [of seed] unto this day.

When they had let him hang until the time of afternoon
prayer,† they took him down from the tree, for so it is written:
His body shall not remain all night upon the tree, *etc*. They
buried him ... on Sunday, and the apostates of his people wept
over his grave.

The Body Is Stolen from the Grave

8.Some of the young men of Israel passed by them. They
spake to them in the Aramaic tongue: Why do the foolish ones
sit by the grave? Let us look! The foolish ones said in their
heart, that they [the young men] would see him in the grave,
but they found him not.

Thereupon the foolish ones sent to Queen Helene, saying:
He whom they put to death was a Messiah, and very many
wonders did he show while living, but now after his death they
buried him, but he is not in the grave, for he is already ascended to heaven, and it is written: For He taketh me, *Sela!* Thus
did he prophesy concerning himself.

She sent to the wise men and said: What have ye done
with him? They answered her: We have put him to death, for
that was the judgment concerning him.

She said to them: If ye have already put him to death,
what have ye done then? They answered her: We have buried
him. Forthwith they sought him in the grave and found him
not.

Thereupon she said to them: In this grave ye buried him;
where is he therefore?

Then were the wise men affrighted and wist not what to
answer her, for a certain one had taken him from the grave,
borne him to his garden, and stopped the water which flowed
into his garden; then digged he in the sand and buried him,
and let the water flow again over his grave.

---

*Text defective. Krauss supplies the lacuna with the words in brack-
ets, but this is by no means a satisfactory conjecture, as we shall see
from the reading preserved by Raymund Martini.

†About three o'clock.

The Proclamation of the Queen

The queen said: If ye show me not Jeschu, I will give you no peace and no escape. They answered her: Give us an appointed time and terms.

When she had granted them an appointed time, all Israel remained lamenting in fasting and prayer, and the apostates found occasion to say: Ye have slain God's anointed!

And all Israel was in great anguish, and the wise men and all the land of Israel hurried from place to place because of the great fear.

Then went forth an elder from them, whose name was Rabbi Tanchuma;* he went forth lamenting in a garden in the fields.

When the owner of the garden saw him, he said to him: Wherefore lamentest thou? He answered: For this and this; because of that rogue who is not to be found; and lo, already is it the appointed time which the queen granted, and we are all in lamentation and fasting.

As soon as he heard his words, that all Israel is as them who mourn, and that the rogues say: He is gone up into heaven, the owner of the garden said: Today shall joy and gladness reign in Israel, for I have stolen him away because of the apostates, so that they should not take him and have the opportunity for all time.†

---

*Ed.– According to Rabbi Adin Steinsaltz [*The Talmud: The Steinsaltz Edition, A Reference Guide*], Rabbi Tanḥuma b. Abba flourished 350-375 CE. FRZ

†Bischoff's recension reads: "And thereafter make trouble for the Israelites."

The Body Is Recovered

Forthwith they went to Jerusalem, told them the good tidings, and all the Israelites followed the owner of the garden, bound cords to his [Jeschu's] feet, and dragged him round in the streets of Jerusalem, till they brought him to the queen and said: There is he who is ascended to heaven!

They departed from her in joy, and she mocked the apostates and praised the wise men.

The Disciples of Jeschu Make Strife in Israel

9. His disciples fled and scattered themselves in the kingdom; three of them [went] to Mount Ararat, three of them to Armenia, three to Rome, the others to other places, and misled the peoples, but everywhere where they took refuge, God sent his judgment upon them, and they were slain.

But many among the apostates of our people went astray after him; there was strife between them and the Israelites, ...* confusion of prayers and much loss of money.†

Everywhere where the apostates caught sight of the Israelites they said to the Israelites: Ye have slain God's anointed! But the Israelites answered them: Ye are children of death, because ye have believed on a false prophet!

Nevertheless they went not forth from the community of Israel, and there was strife and contention among them, so that Israel had no peace.

When the wise men of Israel saw this they said: [It is now] thirty years since that rogue was put to death, [and] till now we have no peace with these misguided ones, and this hath befallen us because of the number of our sins, for it is written:

---

*This word in the text is uncertain.

†Bischoff's recension reads: "And they made Israel lose much money, which went into the hands of non-Jews."

They have moved me to wrath with their not-God*; they have provoked me to anger with their vanities, *etc.*; ⟦—that is the Christians, who are not [?naught]†;⟧ with a base people will I provoke them; ⟦—that is, the Ishmaelites.‡⟧

The wise said: How long shall the apostates profane Sabbath ... and feasts, and slay one another? Let us rather seek for a wise man who may take these erring ones out of the community of Israel. It is now thirty years that we have admonished them, but they have not returned to God, because they have taken it into their heads that Jeschu is the Messiah, and so may they go to destruction and peace be with us.

How Elijahu Removed Them from Israel

10. The wise men agreed on a man whose name was Elijahu [Ed.—*Elijah* FRZ], and he was very learned in the Scripture and they said to him: ... We have agreed, that we will pray for thee, that thou shalt be counted as a good Israelite in the other world. Go, and do good for Israel, and remove the apostates from us, that they may go to destruction!

Elijahu went to the Sanhedrin at Tiberias to Antioch,§ and made proclamation throughout the whole land of Israel: Whoso believeth on Jeschu, let him join himself to me! Then said he to them: I am the messenger (apostle) of Jeschu, who sent me to you, and I will show you a marvel, as Jeschu did.

They brought unto him a leper, and he laid his hand upon him, so that he was healed. They brought unto him a lame man, he uttered the Shem, laid his hand on him, and he was healed and stood upon his feet.

Forthwith they fell down before him and said: Truly thou art the messenger of Jeschu, for thou hast shown us marvels as he did.

---

*A.V: " They have moved me to jealousy with *that which is* not God."

†Krauss adds in a note: "Who worship a not-God."

‡That is, the Mohammedans.

§This seems to be a gloss.

He said to them: Jeschu sendeth you his greeting and saith: I am with my Father in heaven at His right hand, until He shall take vengeance on the Jews, as David said: Sit thou on my right hand, *etc.*

At the same hour they all lamented and added foolishness to their foolishness.

Elijahu said to them: Jeschu saith to you: Whosoever will be with me in the other world, let him remove himself from the community of Israel and join himself not to them; for my Father in heaven hath already rejected them and from henceforth requireth not their service, for so said He through Isaiah: Your new-moons and feasts my soul hateth, *etc.*

The Commandments of Jeschu

But Jeschu saith to you: Whosoever will follow me, let him profane the Sabbath, for God hateth it but instead of it He keepeth the Sunday, for on it God gave light to His world. And for Passover which the Israelites solemnize, keep yet it on the Feast of the Resurrection, for he is risen from his grave; for the Feast of Weeks, Ascension, for on it he is ascended to heaven; for New Year, Finding of the Cross; for the Great Fast Day [Day of Atonement], the Feast of the Circumcision: for Chanuka (the Feast of Lights], Calendæ [New Year].

The foreskin is naught, circumcision is naught; whosoever will circumcise himself, let him be circumcised; whosoever will not circumcise himself, let him be not circumcised. Moreover, whatsoever God created in the world, from the smallest gnat to the mightiest elephant, pour forth its blood upon the ground and eat it, for so it is written: As the green grass have I given you all. If one of them compel you to go a mile, go with him twain; if a Jew smite you on the left side turn to him the right also; if a Jew revile you, endure it and return it not again, as Jeschu endured it; in meekness he showed himself, therewith he showed you also meekness as he practised it, that ye might endure all that any should do to you. At the last judgment Jeschu will punish them, but do ye have hope according to your meekness, for so it is written: Seek ye the Lord, all ye meek of the earth, *etc.* Until he separated them from Israel.

But Elijahu who gave them these laws, the not-good ones, did it for the welfare of Israel, and the Christians [Ed.–*notzri*, 'Nazarenes' FRZ] call him Paul. After he had introduced these laws and commandments, the erring ones separated themselves from Israel, and the strife ceased.*

The Heresy of Nestorius

¶ 11. A long time after, the Persian power arose; then a Christian departed from them, made a mock of them, just as the heretics had laughed at the wise men [of Israel].

He said to them: Paul was in error in his scripture when he said to you: Circumcise yourselves not—for Jeschu was circumcised. Further hath Jeschu said:

I am not come to destroy even one jot from the law of Moses, but to fulfill all his words. And that is your shame, which Paul laid upon you, when he said: Circumcise yourselves not.

But Nestorius† said to them: Circumcise yourselves, for Jeschu was circumcised.

Further said Nestorius: Ye heretics! Ye say Jeschu is God, though he was born of a woman. Only the Holy Spirit rested on him as on the prophets.

Nestorius who began to argue with the Christians, persuaded their women; he said to them: I will enact that no Christian take two wives.

But as Nestorius became detestable in their eyes, there arose a strife between them, so much that no Christian would pray to the abomination of Nestorius, or the followers of Nestorius to the abomination of the Christians.

Then Nestorius went to Babylon to another place, the name of which was Chazāzā, and all fled before him, because Nestorius was a violent man.

---

*Ed.–Schonfield argues that the *Toldoth* originally ended at this point – as does the Bodlean MS. FRZ

†Ed.–The historical Nestorius was a monk from Antioch who became patriarch of Constantinople (428–431 CE). He objected to calling Mary the Mother of God. Condemned by several church councils, Nestorius was exiled. His followers dispersed into Persia, India, China, and even Mongolia. FRZ

The women said to him: What requirest thou of us? He answered them: I require only that ye receive from me the bread-and-wine offering.

Now it was the custom of the woman of Chazāzā, that they carried large keys in their hands.

He gave one of them the offering; she cast it to the ground. Whereupon the women cast the keys in their hands upon him; smote him, so that he died, and there was for long strife between them.

Shimeon Kepha

¶ 12. Now the chief of the Sanhedrin, his name was Shimeon Kepha—and why was he called Kepha?* Because he stood on the stone on which Ezekiel had prophesied at the river Kebar,† and on that stone it was that Shimeon heard a voice from heaven.‡ When the Christians heard that Shimeon Kepha was one of those who heard a voice from heaven, and that stores of wisdom were in him, they envied the Israelites,

---

*Ed.–*Kepha* (Cephas in the KJV and other Christian translations of the New Testament) is Aramaic for 'rock' – *petros* in Greek. Thus, *Shimeon Kepha* is the Aramaic equivalent of Simon Peter. In Christian mythology, Simon receives the nickname Peter not because of Ezekiel's rock, but because he is the metaphorical rock on which Jesus plans to build his church. This is punningly presented in the Catholic interpolation Matthew 16:18–19: "And I say also unto thee, That thou art Peter, and upon this rock I will build my church; and the gates of hell shall not prevail against it. And I will give unto thee the keys of the kingdom of heaven: and whatsoever thou shalt bind on earth shall be bound in heaven: and whatsoever thou shalt loose on earth shall be loosed in heaven." Quite significantly, this proof text for Roman Catholic primacy is absent from an Arabic quotation from "the Gospels" made by the tenth-century author ʿAbd al-Jabbār, who wrote that "The Christians say in the Gospels that this Jesus said to his disciples: "What do people say about me?" They said: "Some say that you are Elijah, others say you are John the Baptist." And he said: "And you, my companions, what do you say about me?" And they said: "In our opinion, you are Christ." And he said: "Do not say this." [Pines, "Jewish Christians," pp. 281–282] FRZ

†This is transliterated in the A.V. as *Chebar*, presumably following the Septuagint *Chobar*. This Babylonian stream, near which Ezekiel

that so great a man was found in Israel, ... God brought it into Shimeon's mind to go to Jerusalem ... on the Feast of Tabernacles. And there were gathered together all the bishops and the great ancient* of the Christians. They came to Shimeon Kepha to the Mount of Olives on the day of the great Feast of Willow-twigs.† When they saw his wisdom, that [there was] not one in Israel like unto him, ... to turn him to the religion of the Christians, and they constrained him, saying: If thou dost not profess our religion, we will put thee to death, and not leave even one remaining in Israel to go into the sanctuary.

When the Israelites perceived this, they besought him: Humour them, act according to thy wisdom; so shall neither sin nor guilt be on thee.

Thereupon when he perceived the hard fate for Israel, he betook himself to the Christians, and said to them: On this condition do I become a convert to your religion, that ye put no Jew to death, that ye smite him not and suffer him to go in and out in the sanctuary.

The ancient§ and the Christians accepted his words and all these his conditions. He made a condition with them, that they

---

had his prophetic visions, is now identified with one of the canals (Bab. *nārāti*) of Babylonia, Hilprecht having twice found mention of a certain *nāru* called Kabaru. (See art., "Chebar," in *Encyclopædia Biblica*)

‡*Bath-kol,* lit., "daughter of a voice," that is, a "small voice," an inner voice.

*Presumably the pope.

†The sixth, or rather seventh, day of the Feast of Tabernacles.

§Ed.–Simon Peter's submission to the Roman pope curiously parallels the subordination of Peter to Jesus in the gospels where, despite repeated proofs of his inferiority *vis-à-vis* Jesus, he becomes the foundation stone for Roman Christianity. Early in the evolution of Catholicism it seems to have been necessary to assimilate at least two rival religions – religions having John the Baptist and Simon Peter as their figureheads. The canonical gospels' stories of these two characters are mythical reflections of theopolitical history. FRZ

would build him a lofty tower;* he would go into it, would eat no flesh, nor aught save bread and water, letting down a box by a cord, for them to supply him with only bread and water, and he would remain in the tower until his death.

All this he did with respect to God, that he might not be stained and sullied by them and that he might not mix with them; but to the Christians he spake in their sense as though he would mourn for Jeschu and eat no flesh or aught else, but bread and water only.

They built him a tower, and he dwelt therein; he sullied himself not with eating, and prayed not to the Cross.

The Scriptures of Shimeon

Afterwards he composed in the tower Keroboth, Jotzroth, and Zulthoth† in his name, like Eliezer ben Kalir.‡ He sent and gathered together the elders of Israel, and handed over to their care all that he had found in his mind, and charged them that they should teach it to the leaders in prayer§ and use it for prayers, so that they might make mention of him for good.

---

*Ed.–Here Simon Peter has become confused with Simeon Stylites (c390–459), a northern Syrian hermit who spent approximately the second half of his life atop a 60–70-foot pillar near Antioch. Clearly, this part of the story has to be later than the time of Simeon Stylites. FRZ

†Various kinds of synagogue poetry.

‡ A famous synagogue poet, whose probable date is about 900 AD.

§*Vorimetern* = precentors.

They, moreover, sent it* to Babylon to Rabbi Nathan,† the Prince of the Exile, and they showed it to the heads of the schools, to the Sanhedrin, and they said: It is good, and they taught it to the headers in prayer of all Israel, and they used it for prayers. Whosoever would mention the name of Shimeon in his chanting did so. May his memory endure to the life of the other world. But God in his mercy ... him as a good defender. Amen! *Sela!*]

---

* That is, the book of prayers.

†Can this be meant for R. Nathan ha-Babli, who came from Babylonia in the days of R. Shimeon ben Gamaliel II, and settled in Palestine? The recension of the Sayings of the Fathers attributed to Rabbi Nathan, included in the *Pirke Aboth* tractate of the Talmud, is probably to be attributed to him. He belonged to the fourth generation of Tannaim, that is to say, he flourished about 160–220 AD.

REFERENCE NOTES

Introduction

In-1 Bellarmino Bagatti, *Excavations in Nazareth. Vol. I. From the Beginning Till the XII Century* (Jerusalem: Franciscan Printing Press, 1969).

In-2 M. Avi-Yonah, "A List of Priestly Courses from Caesarea." *Israel Exploration Journal* 12 (1962):137-9.

In-3 Jack Finegan, *The Archeology of the New Testament* (Princeton: Princeton University Press, 1992), 46.

In-4 Julius Africanus. *In* Vol. 9 of *Ante-Nicene Christian Library: Translations of the Writings of the Fathers Down to A.D. 325*. Edited by Alexander Roberts and James Donaldson. Edinburgh: T. and T. Clark, 1867–1872.

In-5 Origen, *Contra Celsum. In* Vol. 23 of *Ante-Nicene Christian Library: Translations of the Writings of the Fathers Down to A.D. 325*. Edited by Alexander Roberts and James Donaldson (Edinburgh: T. and T. Clark, 1867–1872).

In-6 J. W. Jack, *The Historic Christ* (London: James Clarke, 1933), 39.

In-7 Finegan, *Archeology*, 362.

In-8 John E. Remsburg, *The Christ: A Critical Review and Analysis of the Evidences of His Existence* (New York: The Truth Seeker Company, 1909), 40–42.

In-9 Earl Doherty, *The Jesus Puzzle* (Ottawa: Canadian Humanist Publications, 1999), 222.

In-10 Georg Voigt, *Die Wiederbelebung Des Classischen Altertums, oder Das Erste Jahrhundert Des Humanismus*, 4th ed., 1895, 2 vols. (reprinted Berlin: Walter de Gruyter, 1960) I:249–256.

Chapter 1. Philo Judaeus and Others Who Never Knew Jesus

1-1 Remsburg, *The Christ*, 24–25.

1-2 Photius of Constantinople. *Myriobiblon Sive Bibliotheca. In* Vol. 103, cols. 65–66 of *Patrologia Græca*. Edited by J.-P. Migne (Paris, 1857–1886).

1-3 Eusebius, *Church History. In* Vol. 1 of *A Select Library of Nicene and Post-Nicene Fathers of the Christian Church*. Second series. Edited by Philip Schaff and Henry Wace (New York: The Christian Literature Company, 1890–1900).

1-4 Robert Taylor, *The Diegesis* (Boston: Abner Kneeland, 1834), 70.

1-5 Taylor, *The Diegesis*, 72.

1-6 Burton Mack, *A Myth of Innocence: Mark and Christian Origins* (Philadelphia: Fortress Press, 1988).

1-7 Jerome, *Saint Jerome on Illustrious Men*, translated from the Latin by Thomas P. Halton. *In* Vol. 100 of *The Fathers of the Church: A New Translation* (Washington, D.C.: The Catholic University of America Press, 1999), 18.

1-8 *Saint Jerome on Illustrious Men*, 23.

1-9 N. G. Wilson, *Photius, The Bibliotheca. A Selection*, translated with notes (London: Duckworth, 1994), 122.

1-10 Remsburg, *The Christ*, 25–26.

1-11 Taylor, *The Diegesis*, 83–84.

Chapter 2. Faking Flavius

2-1 Joseph Wheless, *Forgery in Christianity: A Documented Record of the Foundations of the Christian Religion* (Moscow, Idaho: Psychiana, 1930), xxi.

2-2 Wheless, *Forgery in Christianity*, xviii–xix.

2-3 Augustine, *On Lying* (*Nicene and Post-Nicene Fathers*, Series 1, 3:466).

2-4 Wheless, *Forgery in Christianity*, xxvi–xxvii.

2-5 Taylor, *The Diegesis*, 271.

2-6 *Newman's Apologia Pro Vita Sua. The Two Versions of 1864 & 1865 Preceded by Newman's and Kingsley's Pamphlets*. With an introduction by Wilfrid Ward (London: Oxford University Press, 1913), 439–440.

2-7 Origen, *Commentary On Matthew*, Book X, §17 in Vol. 25 of *Ante-Nicene Christian Library. Translations of the Writings of the Fathers Down to A.D. 325*, additional volume, containing early Christian works discovered since the completion of the series, and selections from the Commentaries of Origen; ed. by A. Menzies (Edinburgh, 1897).

2-8 St. John Chrysostom, *Homilies on St. John* (Nicene and Post-Nicene Fathers, Series 1. 14:44).

2-9 Robert Eisenman, *James the Brother of Jesus: The Key to Unlocking the Secrets of Early Christianity and the Dead Sea Scrolls* (New York: Viking, 1996), 4.

2-10 Earl Doherty, *The Jesus Puzzle: Did Christianity Begin with a Mythical Christ?* (Ottawa: Canadian Humanist Publications, 1999), 222.

2-11 William Whiston, *Josephus: Complete Works* (Grand Rapids: Kregel Publications, 1981), *Antiquities*, XVIII, 3.

2-12 Origen, *Commentary on Matthew*, Book X, §17.

2-13 Whiston, *Josephus, Antiquities*, XX, 9.

2-14 Remsburg, *The Christ*, 30–31.

2-15 St. John Chrysostom, *Homilies on the Gospel of St. Matthew* (*Nicene and Post-Nicene Fathers*, Series 1. 10:457).

2-16 St. John Chrysostom, *Homilies on the Acts of the Apostles and the Epistle to the Romans* (Nicene and Post-Nicene Fathers, Series 1. 11:32).

2-17 St. John Chrysostom, *Homilies on Galatians, Ephesians, Philippians, Colossians, Thessalonians, Timothy, Titus, and Philemon* (*Nicene and Post-Nicene Fathers*, Series 1. 13:358).

2-18 St. John Chrysostom, *Homilies on St. John*, 14:44.

2-19 René Henry, *Photius Bibliothèque*, Vol. V, codices 230–241 (Paris: Société d'Édition «Les Belles Lettres» 1967), 152 *et passim*.

2-20 Cited by René Henry, *Photius Bibliothéque*, Vol. 5, 143, note 1.

2-21 Photius, *Myriobiblon Sive Bibliotheca* (*Patrologia Græca* 104: 1187–1188c).

2-22 Henry, *Photius Bibliothèque*, Vol. 5, 149.

2-23 Henry, *Photius Bibliothèque*, Vol. 5, 149–50.

2-24 Henry, *Photius Bibliothèque*, Vol. 5, 151.

2-25 Henry, *Photius Bibliothèque*, Vol. 5, 152.

2-26 Josephus, *Antiquities* (Loeb Classical Library. Cambridge: Harvard University Press, 1926–1965) 4:636–637.

2-27 Josephus, *Antiquities* (Loeb Classical Library. Cambridge: Harvard University Press, 1926–1965) 9:394.

2-28 John P. Meier, "Jesus in Josephus: A Modest Proposal," *The Catholic Biblical Quarterly*, 52 (1990):76–103.

2-29 Abelard Reuchlin, *The True Authorship of the New Testament*, 1979, 1986. Published by the Abelard Reuchlin Foundation, P.O. Box 5652, Kent WA 98064. ISBN 0-930808-02-9. Distributed by Vector Associates, P.O. Box 6215, Bellevue, WA 98008.

2-30 Doherty, *The Jesus Puzzle*, 209.

2-31 Shlomo Pines, *An Arabic Version of the Testimonium Flavianum and its Implications* (Jerusalem: Israel Academy of Sciences and Humanities, 1971).

2-32 Pines, *An Arabic Version of the Testimonium Flavianum*, 8–11.

2-33 Pines, *An Arabic Version of the Testimonium Flavianum*, 26.

2-34 Jerome, *De Viris Illustribus*, Vol. 23, cols. 663–664 in *Patrologia Latina*. Edited by J.-P. Migne (Paris, 1844–1886).

2-35 O. von Gebhardt, *Hieronymus — De Viris Inlustribus in griechischer Über-setzung, Texte und Untersuchungen*, XIV (Leipzig, 1896).

2-36 Hugo Gressmann, *Studien zu Eusebs Theophanie* (Leipzig: J. C. Hinrichs'sche Buchhandlung, 1903), 39.

2-37 Hugo Gressmann, *Die Theophanie. Die Griechischen Bruchstücke Und Übersetzung Der Syrischen Überlieferung.* 2nd rev. ed. edited by Adolf Laminski. *Eusebius Werke.* Vol. 3, part II (Berlin: Akademie Verlag, 1992), 250.

2-38 Hugh J. Schonfield, *According to the Hebrews* (London: Duckworth, 1937) 160–164.

2-39 Schonfield, *According to the Hebrews*, 161–162.

2-40 Schonfield, *According to the Hebrews*, 163.

2-41 Schonfield, *According to the Hebrews*, 164.

2-42 Robert Eisler, *The Messiah Jesus and John the Baptist, According to Flavius Josephus' Recently Rediscovered 'Capture of Jerusalem' and the Other Jewish and Christian Sources* (London: Methuen, 1931) 146–147.

2-43 Justin Martyr, *Dialogue of Justin, Philosopher and Martyr, with Trypho, a Jew. In* Vol. 2 of *Ante-Nicene Christian Library* (Edinburgh: T. and T. Clark, 1870), chap. 8.

2-44 Justin Martyr, *Dialogue of Justin, Philosopher and Martyr, with Trypho, a Jew, In* Vol. 2 of *Ante-Nicene Christian Library* (Edinburgh: T. and T. Clark, 1870), chap. 11.

Chapter 3. James the Just, John the Baptist, and Other Perversions of Josephus

3-1 Origen, *Contra Celsum. In* Vol. 23 of *Ante-Nicene Christian Library* (Edinburgh: T. and T. Clark, 1872), Book I, chap. 47.

3-2 Origen, *Commentary on Matthew. In* Vol. 25 of *Ante-Nicene Christian Library* (Edinburgh: T. and T. Clark, 1897), chap. 17.

3-3 Eusebius, *Church History. In* Vol. 1 of *A Select Library of Nicene and Post-Nicene Fathers of the Christian Church*, second series (New York: The Christian Literature Company, 1890–1900) Book II, chap. 23.

3-4 Whiston, *Josephus, Antiquities*, XX, 9:423–424.

3-5 Robert Eisenman, *James the Brother of Jesus: The Key to Unlocking the Secrets of Early Christianity and the Dead Sea Scrolls* (New York: Viking, 1997).

3-6 Doherty, *The Jesus Puzzle*, 335, n. 26.

3-7 Doherty, *The Jesus Puzzle*, 57–58.

3-8 Whiston, *Josephus, Antiquities*, XX, chap. 4, §5.2.

3-9 Josephus, *Jewish Antiquities, Book XX, General Index*, with an English translation by Louis H. Feldman. Loeb Classical Library Vol. 456 (Cambridge: Harvard University Press, 1965) 109–111.

3-10 W. Barnes Tatum, *John the Baptist and Jesus. A Report of the Jesus Seminar* (Sonoma, California: Polebridge Press, 1994), 86.

3-11 Tatum, *John the Baptist and Jesus*, 1994.

3-12 Whiston, *Josephus, Antiquities*, 18:5:1–3.

3-13 Whiston, *Josephus, Antiquities*, 18:5:1.

3-14 Josephus, *Antiquities* (Loeb Classical Library. Cambridge: Harvard University Press, 1926–1965), 18:255.

3-15 Robert Eisler, *The Messiah Jesus and John the Baptist, According to Flavius Josephus' Recently Rediscovered 'Capture of Jerusalem' and the Other Jewish and Christian Sources*, edited and translated from the German by Alexander Haggerty Krappe (London: Methuen, 1931), 609.

3-16 Eisler, *The Messiah Jesus*, 609.

3-17 Eisler, *The Messiah Jesus*, 610.

Chapter 4. The Rabbis and the Mishnah

4-1 Louis Finkelstein, "The Transmission of the Early Rabbinic Traditions," *Hebrew Union College Annual* 16 (1941) 115–35.

4-2 Herbert Danby, *The Mishnah: Translated from the Hebrew With Introduction and Brief Explanatory Notes* (Oxford: Oxford University Press, 1933, 1987), *xxx–xxxi*.

4-3 Jacob Neusner, *The Tosefta: An Introduction* (Atlanta, Georgia: Scholars Press, 1992).

4-4 Neusner, *The Tosefta: An Introduction, xxii*.

4-5 R. Travers Herford, *Christianity in Talmud and Midrash* (London: Williams & Norgate, 1903) 25–26.

4-6 Danby, *The Mishnah, xxxi*.

4-7 Whiston, *Josephus, Antiquities*, XIII, 10:6.

4-8 Danby, *The Mishnah, xviii–xix*.

4-9 Herford, *Christianity in Talmud and Midrash, 43ff*.

4-10 Herford, *Christianity in Talmud and Midrash*, 44–45.

4-11 Danby, *The Mishnah*, 225.

4-12 Thomas Paine, *The Age of Reason. Part Three. Examination of the Prophecies.* Edited and annotated by Frank Zindler (Austin, Texas: American Atheist Press, 1993)

4-13 Danby, *The Mishnah*, 397.

4-14 Michael Wise, Martin Abegg, Jr., and Edward Cook, *The Dead Sea Scrolls: A New Translation* (San Francisco: Harper, 1996), 230.

4-15 Wise, *The Dead Sea Scrolls*, 340.

4-16 John T. Greene, *Balaam and His Interpreters: A Hermeneutical History of the Balaam Traditions* (Atlanta, Georgia: Scholars Press, 1992) 99.

4-17 Herford, *Christianity in Talmud and Midrash*, 67-68.

4-18 Herford, *Christianity in Talmud and Midrash*, 72.

4-19 Herford, *Christianity in Talmud and Midrash*, 75.

4-20 Irenaeus, *Against Heresies*, Book II, chap. 22. *In* Vol. 5 of *Ante-Nicene Christian Library: Translations of the Writings of the Fathers Down to A.D. 325.* Edited by Alexander Roberts and James Donaldson (Edinburgh: T. and T. Clark, 1867–1872).

4-21 Irenaeus, *Against Heresies*, Book II, chap. 22. *In* vol. 5 of *Ante-Nicene Christian Library.*

4-22 Walter Bauer, "The work and sufferings of Jesus," in Vol. I of *New Testament Apocrypha*, by Edgar Hennecke, ed. Wilhelm Schneemelcher, 1st English edition translated by R. McL. Wilson. (Philadelphia: Westminster Press, 1965) 433–436.

4-23 Herford, *Christianity in Talmud and Midrash*, 97.

4-24 Mead, *Did Jesus Live 100 B.C.?* (London: Theosophical Publishing Society, 1903), 137.

Chapter 5. Two Jesuses in the Tosefta?

5-1 Epiphanius, *Panarium Sive Arcula Adversus Octoginta Hæreses. In* Vol. 42 of *Patrologia Græca.* Book III, Vol. 2, 78:7 (cols. 707–708).

5-2 Origen, *Contra Celsum. In* Vol. 23 of *Ante-Nicene Christian Library*, book I, chap. 32.

5-3 Origen, *Contra Celsum. In* Vol. 23 of *Ante-Nicene Christian Library*, book I, chap. 33.

5-4 Herford, *Christianity in Talmud and Midrash*, 103.

5-5 Herford, *Christianity in Talmud and Midrash*, 137.

5-6 Herford, *Christianity in Talmud and Midrash*, 345.

5-7 Eisler, *The Messiah Jesus and John the Baptist,* 408.

5-8 Neusner, Jacob, *et al. The Talmud of the Land of Israel* (Chicago: University of Chicago Press, 1982), 33:63–64.

5-9 Neusner *et al. The Talmud of the Land of Israel* (Chicago: University of Chicago Press, 1982), 11:395.

5-10 Herford, *Christianity in Talmud and Midrash*, 54-55.

5-11 Mead, *Did Jesus Live 100 B.C.?*, 171.

5-12 Whiston, *Josephus, Antiquities*, XX, 8.

5-13 Whiston, *Josephus, Wars of the Jews*, II, 13.

5-14 Herford, *Christianity in Talmud and Midrash*, 78–79.

5-15 Herford, *Christianity in Talmud and Midrash*, 86–87.

5-16 Herford, *Christianity in Talmud and Midrash*, 87.

Chapter 6. The Palestinian Talmud

6-1 Neusner, *The Talmud of the Land of Israel*, Vol. 33, *Abodah Zarah* (Chicago: University of Chicago Press, 1982), 66–67.

6-2 Mead, *Did Jesus Live 100 B.C.?*, 129–130.

6-3 Herford, *Christianity in Talmud and Midrash*, 54–55.

6-4 Danby, *The Mishnah*, 111.

6-5 Neusner, *The Talmud of the Land of Israel*, Vol. 11, *Shabbat* (Chicago: University of Chicago Press, 1982), 364.

6-6 Danby, *The Mishnah*, 393.

6-7 Herford, *Christianity in Talmud and Midrash*, 78–79.

6-8 Neusner, *The Talmud of the Land of Israel*, Vol. 31, *Sanhedrin and Makkot* (Chicago: University of Chicago Press, 1982), 255–256.

6-9 Herford, *Christianity in Talmud and Midrash*, 79.

6-10 Herford, *Christianity in Talmud and Midrash*, 62.

6-11 Herford, *Christianity in Talmud and Midrash*, 62–63.

6-12 Neusner, *The Talmud of the Land of Israel*, Vol. 8, *Taanit* (Chicago: University of Chicago Press, 1982), 183.

6-13 Neusner, *The Talmud of the Land of Israel*, Vol. 31, *Sanhedrin and Makkot*, 334.

6-14 Neusner, *The Talmud of the Land of Israel*, Vol. 31, *Sanhedrin and Makkot*, 337.

6-15 Neusner, *The Talmud of the Land of Israel*, Vol. 31, *Sanhedrin and Makkot*, 339.

6-16 Neusner, *The Talmud of the Land of Israel*, Vol. 31, *Sanhedrin and Makkot*, 341.

6-17 Neusner, *The Talmud of the Land of Israel*, Vol. 31, *Sanhedrin and Makkot*, 342.

6-18 Herford, *Christianity in Talmud and Midrash*, 70-71.

6-19 Neusner, *The Talmud of the Land of Israel*, Vol. 31, *Sanhedrin and Makkot*, 343.

6-20 Neusner, *The Talmud of the Land of Israel*, Vol. 31, *Sanhedrin and Makkot*, 343.

6-21 Neusner, *The Talmud of the Land of Israel*, Vol. 31, *Sanhedrin and Makkot*, 346.

6-22 Neusner, *The Talmud of the Land of Israel*, Vol. 31, *Sanhedrin and Makkot*, 346.

6-23 Neusner, *The Talmud of the Land of Israel*, Vol. 31, *Sanhedrin and Makkot*, 344.

6-24 Neusner, *The Talmud of the Land of Israel*, Vol. 31, *Sanhedrin and Makkot*, 345.

6-25 Angelo S. Rappoport, *Ancient Israel: Myths and Legends* (New York: Bonanza Books, 1987) 116–117.

6-26 Neusner, *The Talmud of the Land of Israel*, Vol. 31, *Sanhedrin and Makkot*, 347.

6-27 Neusner, *The Talmud of the Land of Israel*, Vol. 31, *Sanhedrin and Makkot*, 347.

6-28 Herford, *Christianity in Talmud and Midrash*, 50.

6-29 Neusner, *The Talmud of the Land of Israel*, Vol. 31, *Sanhedrin and Makkot*, 349.

6-30 Herford, *Christianity in Talmud and Midrash*, 77.

Excursus: The Legend of Balaam:
The Seer Whose Ass Could Talk

Ex-1 Herford, *Christianity in Talmud and Midrash*, 72.

Ex-2 Herford, *Christianity in Talmud and Midrash*, 73–74.

Ex-3 Mead, *Did Jesus Live 100 B.C.?*, 201.

Ex-4 Epstein, ed., *Hebrew-English Edition of the Babylonian Talmud. Seder Neziḳin, Sanhedrin*, translated by Jacob Shachter and H. Freedman (New York: Traditional Press, 1979), 131a.

Ex-5 Epstein, ed., *Hebrew-English Edition of the Babylonian Talmud. Seder Nezikin, Sanhedrin*, 122ª.

Ex-6 Mead, *Did Jesus Live 100 B.C.?*, 41.

Ex-7 Herford, *Christianity in Talmud and Midrash*, 75.

Ex-8 W. C. Kaiser, Jr., "Balaam Son of Beor in Light of Deir Alla and Scripture: Saint or Soothsayer?" In *"Go to the Land I Will Show You": Studies in Honor of Dwight W. Young*. (Winona Lake, Indiana: Eisenbrauns, 1996), 97.

Ex-9 Jo Ann Hackett, *The Balaam Text from Deir 'Allâ* (Chico, California: Scholars Press, 1984), 29–30.

Ex-10 Israel Finkelstein and Neil Asher Silberman, *The Bible Unearthed: Archæology's New Vision of Ancient Israel and the Origin of Its Sacred Texts* (New York: The Free Press, 2001).

Ex-11 John T. Greene, *Balaam and His Interpreters: A Hermeneutical History of the Balaam Traditions* (Atlanta: Scholars Press, 1992).

Ex-12 Greene, *Balaam and His Interpreters*, 62.

Ex-13 Julius Wellhausen, *Prolegomena to the History of Ancient Israel*, with preface by W. Robertson Smith (New York: The Meridian Library, 1957).

Ex-14 Greene, *Balaam and His Interpreters*, 45.

Ex-15 Greene, *Balaam and His Interpreters*, 184.

Ex-16 Th. Guil. Joh. Juynboll, *Chronicon Samaritanum, Arabice Conscriptum, Cui Titulus Est Liber Josuae* (Leiden: S. & J. Luchtmans, 1848). Also, John Bowman, *Samaritan Documents*. Pittsburgh Original Texts and Translation Series (Pittsburgh: The Pickwick Press, 1977).

Ex-17 Juynboll, *Chronicon Samaritanum*, 137.

Ex-18 Greene, *Balaam and His Interpreters*, 125*ff.*

Ex-19 John Bowman, *Samaritan Documents*, 286.

Ex-20 Bowman, *Samaritan Documents*, 287.

Ex-21 Herford, *Christianity in Talmud and Midrash*, 63–64.

Ex-22 Greene, *Balaam and His Interpreters*, 134.

Ex-23 Philo Judæus, *The Works of Philo, Complete and Unabridged*. Rev. ed. Translated from the Greek by C. D. Yonge (Peabody, Massachusetts: Hendrickson) X:32–34, 83.

Ex-24 Philo Judaeus, *The Works of Philo*, XXXI:159, 248.

Ex-25 Philo Judaeus, *The Works of Philo*, XX:113-117, 264.

Ex-26 Philo Judaeus, *The Works of Philo*, XXXVII:202-203, 358.

Ex-27 Philo Judaeus, *The Works of Philo*, LXVII:311, 488.

Ex-28 Philo Judaeus, *The Works of Philo*, XLVIII:264, 484.

Ex-29 Philo Judaeus, *The Works of Philo,* LII:286, 486.

Ex-30 Philo Judaaeus, *The Works of Philo,* XLVI:272, 484.

Ex-31 Philo Judaeus, *The Works of Philo,* LIII:294–LIV:299, 486–487.

Ex-32 Neusner, *The Talmud of the Land of Israel,* Vol. 31, *Sanhedrin and Makkot,* 337-338.

Ex-33 Whiston, *Josephus, Antiquities,* IV, 6:5, 91.

Ex-34 Whiston, *Josephus, Antiquities,* IV, 6:2, 90.

Ex-35 Whiston, *Josephus, Antiquities,* IV, 6:2, 90.

Ex-36 Whiston, *Josephus, Antiquities,* IV, 6:13, 93.

Ex-37 Reuben Swanson, ed., *New Testament Greek Manuscripts: Luke* (Sheffield: Sheffield Academic Press, 1995), 375.

Ex-38 *Monty Python's Life of Brian,* Prod. John Goldstone, dir. Terry Jones (London: Handmade Films, 1979).

Ex-39 Herford, *Christianity in Talmud and Midrash,* 63–64.

Ex-40 Epstein, *Hebrew-English Edition of the Babylonian Talmud. Seder Nezikin, Sanhedrin,* 106ᵃ.

Ex-41 Epstein, *Hebrew-English Edition of the Babylonian Talmud. Seder Nezikin, Sanhedrin,* 131ᵇ.

Ex-42 Herford, *Christianity in Talmud and Midrash,* 67–68.

Ex-43 Herford, *Christianity in Talmud and Midrash,* 75.

Ex-44 Epstein, *Hebrew-English Edition of the Babylonian Talmud. Seder Nezikin, Sanhedrin,* 106ᵃ.

Ex-45 Herford, *Christianity in Talmud and Midrash,* 76.

Ex-46 Epstein, *Hebrew-English Edition of the Babylonian Talmud. Seder Nezikin, Sanhedrin,* 105ᵃ.

Ex-47 Epstein, *Hebrew-English Edition of the Babylonian Talmud. Seder Nezikin, Sanhedrin,* 106ᵇ.

Ex-48 Epstein, *Hebrew-English Edition of the Babylonian Talmud. Seder Nezikin, Sanhedrin,* 105ᵃ.

Ex-49 Epstein, *Hebrew-English Edition of the Babylonian Talmud. Seder Nezikin, Sanhedrin,* 106ᵃ.

Chapter 7. The Babylonian Talmud

7-1 Mead, *Did Jesus Live 100 B.C.?,* 392–393.

7-2 Herford, *Christianity in Talmud and Midrash,* 137–138

7-3 Herford, *Christianity in Talmud and Midrash,* 138–139.

7-4 Epstein, ed. *Hebrew-English Edition of the Babylonian Talmud. Seder Nezikin, 'Abodah Zarah.* Translated into English with notes and glossary by A. Mishcon and A. Cohen (New York: Traditional Press, 1979), 17ª.

7-5 Herford, *Christianity in Talmud and Midrash,* 35.

7-6 Herford, *Christianity in Talmud and Midrash,* 40.

7-7 Epstein, ed. *Hebrew-English Edition of the Babylonian Talmud. Seder Mo'ed, Shabbath,* translated into English with notes and glossary by H. Freedman (New York: Traditional Press, 1979), 104ᵇ.

7-8 Epstein, *Hebrew-English Edition of the Babylonian Talmud. Seder Nezikin, Sanhedrin,* 67ª.

7-9 Epstein, *Hebrew-English Edition of the Babylonian Talmud. Seder Nezikin, Sanhedrin,* 122ª.

7-10 Herford, *Christianity in Talmud and Midrash,* 41.

7-11 Wilhelm Schneemelcher, *New Testament Apocrypha.* Rev. ed. English translation by R. McL.Wilson (Louisville: Westminster/John Knox Press. 1989–1990), 2 vols.

7-12 Robert M. Price, *Deconstructing Jesus* (Amherst, New York: Prometheus Books, 2000), 116*ff.*

7-13 Adin Steinsaltz, *The Talmud: The Steinsaltz Edition. A Reference Guide* (New York: Random House, 1989), 34.

7-14 Robert L. Bensly, J. Rendel Harris, and F. Crawford Burkitt, *The Four Gospels in Syriac Transcribed from the Sinaitic Palimpsest,* with an introduction by Agnes Smith Lewis (Cambridge: Cambridge University Press, 1894), 2.

7-15 Herford, *Christianity in Talmud and Midrash,* 41.

7-16 Mead, *Did Jesus Live 100 B.C.?,* 162.

7-17 Mead, *Did Jesus Live 100 B.C.?,* 156–157.

7-18 Epstein, ed. *Hebrew-English Edition of the Babylonian Talmud. Seder Nashim, Yebamoth,* translated into English with notes and glossary by Israel W. Slotki (New York: Traditional Press, 1979), 49ᵇ.

7-19 Herford, *Christianity in Talmud and Midrash,* 50–51.

7-20 Neusner, *The Talmud of the Land of Israel,* vol. 11, *Ḥagigah,* 56.

7-21 Herford, *Christianity in Talmud and Midrash,* 56–57.

7-22 Herford, *Christianity in Talmud and Midrash,* 60.

7-23 Herford, *Christianity in Talmud and Midrash,* 61.

7-24 Hermann L. Strack, *Introduction to the Talmud and Midrash* (Philadelphia: The Jewish Publication Society of America, 1931), 77.

7-25 Herford, *Christianity in Talmud and Midrash,* 90-91.

7-26 Herford, *Christianity in Talmud and Midrash,* 92-93.

7-27 Herford, *Christianity in Talmud and Midrash*, 93.

7-28 Justin Martyr, *Dialogue of Justin, Philosopher and Martyr, with Trypho, a Jew. In Vol. 2 of Ante-Nicene Christian Library* (Edinburgh: T. and T. Clark, 1867–1872).

7-29 Louis Ginzberg, "Some Observations on the Attitude of the Synagogue Towards the Apocalyptic-Eschatological Writings," *Journal of Biblical Literature* 41 (1922): 121.

7-30 Ginzberg, "Some Observations on the Attitude of the Synagogue," 121–122.

7-31 Neusner, *Introduction to Rabbinic Literature*. The Anchor Bible Reference Library (New York: Doubleday, 1994), 654.

7-32 Herford, *Christianity in Talmud and Midrash*, 359–360.

Chapter 8. The *Toldoth Yeshu* as
an Evolving Document

8-1 Hugh J. Schonfield, *According to the Hebrews* (London: Duckworth, 1937), 30.

8-2 Samuel Krauss, *Das Leben Jesu nach jüdischen Quellen* (Berlin: S. Calvary, 1902).

8-3 Louis Ginzberg, *Genizah Studies in Memory of Doctor Solomon Schechter*. I. *Midrash and Haggadah* (New York: Hermon Press, 1928), vii.

8-4 Krauss, *Das Leben Jesu nach jüdischen Quellen*, 27–37.

8-5 William Horbury, *A Critical Examination of the Toledoth Jeshu*. Diss. (microfilm) (Cambridge: Cambridge University, 1970)

8-6 Horbury, *A Critical Examination of the Toledoth Jeshu*, 365.

8-7 Horbury, *A Critical Examination of the Toledoth Jeshu*, 368.

8-8 Günter Schlichting, *Ein jüdisches Leben Jesu: Die verschollene Toledot-Jeschu-Fassung Tam û-mû'âd. Einleitung, Text, Übersetzung, Kommentar, Motivsynopse, Bibliographie* (Tübingen: J. C. B. Mohr (Paul Siebeck), 1982), 229–266.

8-9 Krauss, *Das Leben Jesu nach jüdischen Quellen*, 11.

8-10 A. S. Halkin, *Moses Maimonides' Epistle to Yemen* (New York, 1952, 12) cited in Horbury, *A Critical Examination of the Toledoth Jeshu*, 234.

8-11 Schonfield, *According to the Hebrews*, 32.

8-12 Schonfield, *According to the Hebrews*, 33.

8-13 Schonfield, *According to the Hebrews*, 209.

8-14 Mead, *Did Jesus Live 100 B.C.?*, 290–291.

8-15 Horbury, *A Critical Examination of the Toledoth Jeshu*, 223, 272.

8-16 Horbury, *A Critical Examination of the Toledoth Jeshu*, 433–435.

8-17 Horbury, *A Critical Examination of the Toledoth Jeshu*, 434.

8-18 Schonfield, *According to the Hebrews*, 29.

8-19 Schonfield, *According to the Hebrews*, 29.

8-20 Schonfield, *According to the Hebrews*, 29–30.

8-21 Schonfield, *According to the Hebrews*, 128–129.

Chapter 9. *Toldoth* Traces amongst the Church Fathers

9-1 Schonfield, *According to the Hebrews*, 107.

9-2 Schonfield, *According to the Hebrews*, 107–108.

9-3 Schonfield, *According to the Hebrews*, 109–110.

9-4 Tertullian. *Apology – De Spectaculis*. Translated with an introduction by T. R. Glover. Loeb Classical Library (Cambridge: Harvard University Press, 1984), 297–301.

9-5 Origen, *Contra Celsum*. In Vol. 23 of *Ante-Nicene Christian Library: Translations of the Writings of the Fathers Down to A.D. 325*. Edited by Alexander Roberts and James Donaldson (Edinburgh: T. and T. Clark, 1867–1872), preface.

9-6 Origen, *Contra Celsum*. *Ante-Nicene Christian Library*, Book I, chap. 28.

9-7 Origen, *Contra Celsum*. *Ante-Nicene Christian Library*, Book I, chap. 32.

9-8 Philipp Vielhauer and Georg Strecker, in vol. 1 of *New Testament Apocrypha*, by Wilhelm Schneemelcher. Revised edition. English translation by R. McL. Wilson (Louisville, Kentucky: Westminster/John Knox Press. 1989–1990), 136.

9-9 Philipp Vielhauer and Georg Strecker, in *New Testament Apocrypha*, 137.

9-10 Oscar Cullmann. *In* Vol. 1 of *New Testament Apocrypha*, by Wilhelm Schneemelcher. Revised edition. English translation by R. McL. Wilson (Louisville, Kentucky: Westminster/John Knox Press. 1989–1990) 429–430.

9-11 Oscar Cullmann, in *New Testament Apocrypha*, 447.

9-12 Oscar Cullmann, in *New Testament Apocrypha*, 439–443.

9-13 Horbury, *A Critical Examination of the Toledoth Jeshu*, 283.

9-14 Schonfield, *According to the Hebrews*, 135.

9-15 Oscar Cullmann, in *New Testament Apocrypha*, 444.

9-16 Origen, *Contra Celsum. Ante-Nicene Christian Library*, Book I, chap. 24.

9-17 Origen, *Contra Celsum. Ante-Nicene Christian Library*, Book I, chap. 25.

9-18 Schonfield, *According to the Hebrews*, 136–137.

9-19 Schonfield, *According to the Hebrews*, 137.

9-20 Schonfield, *According to the Hebrews*, 137.

9-21 Schonfield, *According to the Hebrews*, 96.

9-22 Arnobius. *The Seven Books of Arnobius Against the Heathen (Adversus Gentes). In* Vol. VI of *The Ante-Nicene Fathers.* Edited by Alexander Roberts and James Donaldson. 1861. (Repr. Grand Rapids: Eerdmans, 1982), Book I, chap. 29, 420.

9-23 Arnobius, *Adversus Gentes*, Book I, chap. 46, 426.

9-24 Arnobius, *Adversus Gentes*, Book I, chap. 43, 425.

Chapter 10. The *Toldoth Yeshu* and the Clementine Literature

10-1 Johannes Irmscher and Georg Strecker, 2nd edition, "The Pseudo-Clementines." *In* Vol. II of *New Testament Apocrypha*, by Wilhelm Schneemelcher. Rev. ed. English translation by R. McL. Wilson (Louisville, Kentucky: Westminster/ John Knox Press. 1989–1992), 483–493.

10-2 Johannes Irmscher and Georg Strecker, "The Pseudo-Clementines," 493–494.

10-3 Johannes Irmscher and Georg Strecker, "The Pseudo-Clementines," 493–494.

10-4 Johannes Irmscher and Georg Strecker, "The Pseudo-Clementines," 494–495.

10-5 Johannes Irmscher and Georg Strecker, "The Pseudo-Clementines," 495–496.

10-6 Origen, *Contra Celsum. Ante-Nicene Christian Library*, book I, chap. 1.

10-7 Origen, *Contra Celsum. Ante-Nicene Christian Library*, book I, chap. 7.

10-8 Johannes Irmscher and Georg Strecker, "The Pseudo-Clementines," 505.

10-9 Johannes Irmscher and Georg Strecker, "The Pseudo-Clementines," 508.

10-10 Johannes Irmscher and Georg Strecker, "The Pseudo-Clementines," 524.

10-11 Johannes Irmscher and Georg Strecker, "The Pseudo-Clementines," 529.

10-12 Johannes Irmscher and Georg Strecker, "The Pseudo-Clementines," 512.

10-13 Among the manuscripts retrieved from the libraries of Pompeii-Herculaneum, which were destroyed in the year 79 CE, is a copy of Aristotle's *Constitution of the City of Athens*. In that document, the name *Chronos* is abbreviated in the form of a chi-rho cross. Edward Maunde Thompson, *An Introduction to Greek and Latin Palaeography* (Oxford: At the Clarendon Press, 1912), 78, 79, 81; M. Edmond Saglio, *Dictionnaire Des Antiquités Grecques Et Romaines d'Après Les Textes Et Les Monuments*. Vol. 4. (Paris: Librairie Hachette Et Cie, 1918) 1133–1134.

10-14 Fridericus Adolphus Heinichen in his *Eusebii Pamphili Vita Constantini et Panegyricus atque Constantini ad Sanctorum Coetum Oratio* (*Eusebii Pamphili Scripta Historica*, Vol. II) (Leipzig: Hermann Mendelssohn, 1869), 225–226.

10-15 Johannes Irmscher and Georg Strecker, "The Pseudo-Clementines," 512–514.

10-16 Schneemelcher, "The Acts of Peter," 283.

10-17 Schneemelcher, "The Acts of Peter," 314.

10-18 Schneemelcher, "The Acts of Peter," 290.

10-19 Schneemelcher, "The Acts of Peter," 312-313.

10-20 Schneemelcher, "The Acts of Peter," 296.

10-21 Schneemelcher, "The Acts of Peter," 296.

10-22 Schneemelcher, "The Acts of Peter," 297.

10-23 Schneemelcher, "The Acts of Peter," 297-298.

10-24 Wilhelm Schneemelcher, "The Acts of Peter," 300.

10-25 Johannes Irmscher and Georg Strecker, "The Pseudo-Clementines," 512.

10-26 Schonfield, *According to the Hebrews*, 120; Arnobius, *Adversus Gentes*, book I, chap. 43, 425.

10-27 Schonfield, *According to the Hebrews*, 120–121.

10-28 Schneemelcher, "The Acts of Peter," 303.

Chapter 11. When Was the *Toldoth Yeshu* Composed?

11-1 Horbury, *A Critical Examination of the Toledoth Jeshu*, 443–445.

11-2 Samuel Krauss, *Das Leben Jesu nach jüdischen Quellen* (Berlin: S. Calvary, 1902), 245–248.

11-3 Schonfield, *According to the Hebrews*, 214–227.

11-4 Schonfield, *According to the Hebrews*, 147.

[11-5] Schonfield, *According to the Hebrews,* 146–147.

[11-6] Schonfield, *According to the Hebrews,* 147.

[11-7] Schonfield, *According to the Hebrews,* 149.

[11-8] Schonfield, *According to the Hebrews,* 216.

[11-9] Schonfield, *According to the Hebrews,* 217.

[11-10] Schonfield, *According to the Hebrews,* 217.

[11-11] Schonfield, *According to the Hebrews,* 218.

[11-12] Schonfield, *According to the Hebrews,* 219.

[11-13] Schonfield, *According to the Hebrews,* 223.

[11-14] Schonfield, *According to the Hebrews,* 225.

[11-15] Schonfield, *According to the Hebrews,* 227.

[11-16] Schonfield, *According to the Hebrews,* 226.

Chapter 12. Jewish Gospels, Jewish Christianity, and Christian Origins

[12-1] Schonfield, *According to the Hebrews,* 175–176.

[12-2] Schonfield, *According to the Hebrews,* 175.

[12-3] Philipp Vielhauer and Georg Strecker, "Jewish-Christian Gospels." *In* Wilhelm Schneemelcher (ed.), *New Testament Apocrypha*, Vol. 1 (Louisville: Westminster/John Knox Press, 1990) 134–178.

[12-4] Vielhauer and Strecker, "Jewish-Christian Gospels," 142.

[12-5] Vielhauer and Strecker, "Jewish-Christian Gospels," 145.

[12-6] Vielhauer and Strecker, "Jewish-Christian Gospels," 146.

[12-7] Philipp Vielhauer and Strecker, "Jewish-Christian Gospels," 152.

[12-8] Vielhauer and Strecker, "Jewish-Christian Gospels," 157.

[12-9] Vielhauer and Strecker, "Jewish-Christian Gospels," 167.

[12-10] Vielhauer and Strecker, "Jewish-Christian Gospels," 140.

[12-11] Vielhauer and Strecker, "Jewish-Christian Gospels," 141.

[12-12] Vielhauer and Strecker, "Jewish-Christian Gospels," 177.

[12-13] Schneemelcher, "The Stichometry of Nicephorus." *In* Vol. I of *New Testament Apocrypha*, 41.

[12-14] Vielhauer and Strecker, "Jewish-Christian Gospels," 177.

[12-15] Vielhauer and Strecker, "Jewish-Christian Gospels," 178.

12-16 Shlomo Pines, "The Jewish Christians of the Early Centuries of Christianity According to a New Source," *Proceedings of the Israel Academy of Sciences and Humanities* 2 (1968):276.

12-17 Edward Maunde Thompson, *An Introduction to Greek and Latin Palaeography* (Oxford: At the Clarendon Press, 1912), 78, 79, 81.

12-18 Pines, "The Jewish Christians of the Early Centuries of Christianity According to a New Source," 237–310.

12-19 Pines, "The Jewish Christians of the Early Centuries of Christianity According to a New Source," 268.

12-20 Pines, "The Jewish Christians of the Early Centuries of Christianity According to a New Source," 268.

12-21 Georg Wissowa, "Aion," in *Paulys Real-Encyclopädie der Classischen Altertumswissenschaft.* Rev. ed. (Stuttgart: J. B. Metzlerscher Verlag, 1894).

12-22 Robert Eisler, *Weltenmantel Und Himmelszelt: Religionsgeschichtliche Untersuchungen Zur Urgeschichte Des Antiken Weltbildes* (Munich: C. H. Beck'sche Verlagsbuchhandlung Oskar Beck, 1910), II 421–423, 666–667, 674–675, 707.

12-23 J. Glen Taylor, *Yahweh and the Sun: Biblical and Archaeological Evidence for Sun Worship in Ancient Israel* (Sheffield: JSOT Press, 1993).

12-24 David Ulansey, *The Origins of the Mithraic Mysteries: Cosmology and Salvation in the Ancient World* (New York: Oxford University Press, 1989).

12-25 Schonfield, *According to the Hebrews,* 130–131.

12-26 Horbury, *A Critical Examination of the Toledoth Jeshu,* 312.

12-27 M. Freimann, "Wie verhielt sich das Judentum zu Jesus und dem entstehenden Christentum?" *Monatsschrift für Geschichte und Wissenschaft des Judentums,* 54 (1910):697–712.

12-28 Horbury, *A Critical Examination of the Toledoth Jeshu,* 318–319.

BIBLIOGRAPHY

Africanus, Julius. *In* Vol. 9 of *Ante-Nicene Christian Library: Translations of the Writings of the Fathers Down to A.D. 325.* Edited by Alexander Roberts and James Donaldson. Edinburgh: T. and T. Clark, 1867–1872.

Ali, Abdullah Yusuf. *The Holy Qur-an: Text, Translation and Commentary.* Washington: The Islamic Center, 1978.

Ante-Nicene Christian Library: Translations of the Writings of the Fathers Down to A.D. 325. Edited by Alexander Roberts and James Donaldson. Edinburgh: T. and T. Clark, 1867–1872. 24 vols. plus additional volume, containing early Christian works discovered since the completion of the series, and selections from the Commentaries of Origen; ed. by A. Menzies. Edinburgh, 1897.

Arnobius. *The Seven Books of Arnobius Against the Heathen (Adversus Gentes).* *In* Vol. 6 of *The Ante-Nicene Fathers.* Edited by Alexander Roberts and James Donaldson. 1861. Repr. Grand Rapids: Eerdmans, 1982.

Augustine. *On Lying. In* Vol. 3 of *The Nicene and Post-Nicene Fathers.* Series 1. Edited by Philip Schaff. 1886–1889. 14 vols. Repr. Grand Rapids: Eerdmans, 1980.

Avi-Yonah, M. "A List of Priestly Courses from Caesarea." *Israel Exploration Journal* 12 (1962):137–9.

Bagatti, Bellarmino. *Excavations in Nazareth.* Vol. I. *From the Beginning Till the XII Century.* Translated from the Italian by Fr. E. Hoade. Jerusalem: Franciscan Printing Press, 1969.

Bammel, Ernst, ed. *The Trial of Jesus: Cambridge Studies in Honour Of C F D Moule. London:* SCM Press Ltd, 1970.

Bensly, Robert L., J. Rendel Harris, and F. Crawford Burkitt. *The Four Gospels in Syriac Transcribed from the Sinaitic Palimpsest,* with an introduction by Agnes Smith Lewis. Cambridge: Cambridge University Press, 1894.

Bowman, John. *Samaritan Documents.* Pittsburgh Original Texts and Translation Series. Pittsburgh: The Pickwick Press, 1977.

Brandon, S. G. F. *The Trial of Jesus of Nazareth.* New York: Dorset Press, 1968.

Chrysostom, St. John. *In* Vols. 9–14 of *The Nicene and Post-Nicene Fathers,* Series 1. Edited by Philip Schaff. 1886–1889. 14 vols. Repr. Grand Rapids: Eerdmans, 1983.

Dalman, Gustaf H. *Aramäish-Neuhebräisches Handwörterbuch zu Targum, Talmud, und Midrasch.* Second edition. Frankfurt a. Main: J. Kauffmann Verlag, 1922.

Danby, Herbert. *The Mishnah. Translated from the Hebrew with Introduction and Brief Explanatory Notes,* Oxford: Oxford University Press, 1987.

Doherty, Earl. *The Jesus Puzzle: Did Christianity Begin with a Mythical Christ?* Ottawa: Canadian Humanist Publications, 1999.

Drews, Arthur. *The Legend of Saint Peter: A Contribution to the Mythology of Christianity.* Translated, with foreword and appendix of selected reference texts by Frank R. Zindler. Austin: American Atheist Press, 1997.

Edersheim, Alfred. *The Life and Times of Jesus the Messiah.* Eighth ed. revised. New York: Longmans, Green, and Co. 1905. 2 vols.

Eisenman, Robert. *James the Brother of Jesus: The Key to Unlocking the Secrets of Early Christianity and the Dead Sea Scrolls.* New York: Viking, 1997.

Eisler, Robert. *Weltenmantel Und Himmelszelt: Religionsgeschichtliche Untersuchungen Zur Urgeschichte Des Antiken Weltbildes.* Munich: C. H. Beck'sche Verlagsbuchhandlung Oskar Beck, 1910. 2 vols.

Eisler, Robert. *ΙΗΣΟΥΣ ΒΑΣΙΛΕΥΣ ΟΥ ΒΑΣΙΛΕΥΣΑΣ: Die Messianische Unabhängigkeitsbewegung Vom Auftreten Johannes Des Taufers Bis Zum Untergang Jakobs Des Gerechten Nach Der Neuerschlossenen Eroberung Von Jerusalem Des Flavius Josephus Und Den Christlichen Quellen.* Heidelberg: Carl Winters Universitätsbuchhandlung, 1929. 2 vols.

Eisler, Robert. *The Messiah Jesus and John the Baptist, According to Flavius Josephus' Recently Rediscovered 'Capture of Jerusalem' and the Other Jewish and Christian Sources,* edited and translated from the German by Alexander Haggerty Krappe, London: Methuen, 1931.

Ellegård, Alvar. *Myten om Jesus: Den tidigaste kristendomen i nytt ljus.* Göteborg: Bonnier Fakta Bokförlag, 1992.

Epiphanius. *Panarium Sive Arcula Adversus Octoginta Hæreses. In* Vols. 41–42 of *Patrologia Græca.* Edited by J.-P. Migne, Paris, 1863.

Epstein, I., ed. *Hebrew-English Edition of the Babylonian Talmud. Seder Nezikin, 'Abodah Zarah.* Translated into English with notes and glossary by A. Mishcon and A. Cohen. New York: Traditional Press, 1979.

Epstein, I., ed. *Hebrew-English Edition Of The Babylonian Talmud. Seder Mo'ed, Hagigah.* Translated into English with notes and glossary by M. Ginsberg. New York: Traditional Press, 1979.

Epstein, I., ed. *Hebrew-English Edition of the Babylonian Talmud. Seder Mo'ed, Shabbath.* Translated into English with notes and Glossary by H. Freedman. New York: Traditional Press, 1979.

Epstein, I., ed. *Hebrew-English Edition of the Babylonian Talmud. Seder Nashim, Yebamoth.* Translated into English with notes and glossary by Israel W. Slotki. New York: Traditional Press, 1979.

Epstein, I., ed. *Hebrew-English Edition of the Babylonian Talmud. Seder Nezikin, Sanhedrin.* Translated into English with notes and glossary by Jacob Shachter and H. Freedman. New York: Traditional Press, 1979.

Epstein, I., ed. *Hebrew-English Edition of the Babylonian Talmud. Soṭah.* Translated into English with notes and glossary by A. C. Hen. New York: Traditional Press, 1979.

Eusebius. *Church History, Life of Constantine the Great, and Oration in Praise of Constantine. In* Vol. 1 of *A Select Library of Nicene and Post-Nicene Fathers of the Christian Church.* Second series. Translated into English with prolegomena and explanatory notes. Edited by Philip Schaff and Henry Wace. New York: The Christian Literature Company, 1890–1900.

Eusebius. *Ecclesiastical History.* Translated by Kirsopp Lake and J. E. L. Oulton. 2 vols. Loeb Classical Library. Cambridge: Harvard University Press, 1926-1932.

Eusebius. *The History of the Church from Christ to Constantine.* Translated with an introduction by G. A. Williamson. New York: Dorset Press, 1965.

Falk, Gerhard. *The Jew in Christian Theology: Martin Luther's Anti-Jewish Vom Schem Hamphoras, Previously Unpublished in English, and Other Milestones in Church Doctrine Concerning Judaism.* Jefferson, North Carolina: McFarland, 1992.

Finegan, Jack. *The Archeology of the New Testament. The Life of Jesus and the Beginning of the Early Church.* Rev. ed. Princeton: Princeton University Press, 1992.

Finegan, Jack. *Handbook of Biblical Chronology.* Rev. ed. Peabody, Massachusetts: Hendrickson, 1998.

Finkelstein, Israel, and Neil Asher Silberman. *The Bible Unearthed: Archæology's New Vision of Ancient Israel and the Origin of Its Sacred Texts.* New York: The Free Press, 2001.

Finkelstein, Louis. "The Transmission of the Early Rabbinic Tradition," *Hebrew Union College Annual,* 16 (1941):115–35.

Franken, Henk. "Balaam at Deir 'Alla and the Cult of Baal." Pp. 183–202 in *Archaeology, History and Culture in Palestine and the Near East: Essays in Memory of Albert E. Glock.* Edited by Tomis Kapitan. Atlanta: Scholars Press, 1999.

Freimann, M. *"Wie verhielt sich das Judentum zu Jesus und dem entstehenden Christentum?" Monatsschrift für Geschichte und Wissenschaft des Judentums,* 54 (1910):697–712.

Freimann, M. *"Die Wortführer des Judentums in den ältesten Kontroversen zwischen Juden und Christen," Monatsschrift für Geschichte und Wissenschaft des Judentums,* 55 (1911):555–585.

García Martínez, Florentino. *The Dead Sea Scrolls Translated. The Qumran Texts in English.* Translated from the Spanish by Wilfred G. E. Watson. Leiden: E. J. Brill, 1994.

Gebhardt, O. von. *Hieronymus – De Viris Inlustribus in griechischer Übersetzung: Texte und Untersuchungen,* XIV, Leipzig, 1896.

Ginzberg, Louis. "Some Observations on the Attitude of the Synagogue Towards the Apocalyptic-Eschatological Writings," *Journal of Biblical Literature.* 41 (1922): 115–136.

Ginzberg, Louis. *Genizah Studies in Memory of Doctor Solomon Schechter.* Vol. I: *Midrash and Haggadah*; Vol. II: *Geonic and Early Karaitic Halakah*; Vol. III (by Israel Davidson): *Liturgical and Secular Poetry.* Reprint, New York: Hermon Press, 1969.

Greene, John T. *Balaam and His Interpreters: A Hermeneutical History of the Balaam Traditions.* Atlanta, Georgia: Scholars Press, 1992.

Gressmann, Hugo. *Studien zu Eusebs Theophanie*, Leipzig: J. C. Hinrichs'sche Buchhandlung, 1903.

Gressmann, Hugo. *Die Theophanie. Die Griechischen Bruchstücke Und Übersetzung Der Syrischen Überlieferung.* 2nd rev. ed. edited by Adolf Laminski. *Eusebius Werke.* Vol. 3, part II. Berlin: Akademie Verlag, 1992.

Hackett, Jo Ann. *The Balaam Text from Deir ʿAlla.* Chico, California: Scholars Press, 1984.

Hadas-Lebel, Mireille. *Flavius Josephus: Eyewitness to Rome's First-Century Conquest of Judea.* Translated by Richard Miller. New York: Maxwell Macmillan International, 1993.

Hayward, C. T. R. "Balaam's Prophecies as Interpreted by Philo and the Aramaic Targums of the Pentateuch." Pages 19–36 in *New Heaven and New Earth: Prophecy and the Millennium. Essays in Honour of Anthony Gelston.* Edited by P.J. Harland and C.T.R. Hayward. Leiden: Brill, 1999.

Heinichen, Fridericus Adolphus. *Eusebii Pamphili Vita Constantini et Panegyricus atque Constantini ad Sanctorum Coetum Oratio (Eusebii Pamphili Scripta Historica*, Vol. II), Leipzig: Hermann Mendelssohn, 1869.

Henry, René. *Photius Bibliothèque.* Paris: Société d'Édition «Les Belles Lettres,» 1967. 7 vols.

Herford, R. Travers. *Christianity in Talmud and Midrash.* London: Williams & Norgate, 1903. Repr. 1966 by Reference Book Publishers, Clifton, New Jersey.

Hoftijzer, Jacob, and G. van der Kooij, eds. *The Balaam Text from Deir ʿAllâ Re-evaluated. Proceedings of the International Symposium held at Leiden 21–24 August 1989.* Leiden: E. J. Brill, 1991.

Horbury, William. *A Critical Examination of the Toledoth Jeshu.* Dissertation (microfilm), Cambridge University, 1970.

Horbury, William. *Jews and Christians in Contact and Controversy.* Edinburgh: T. & T. Clark 1998.

Hruby, Kurt. *Die Stellung der jüdischen Gesetzeslehrer zur werdenden Kirche.* Zürich: Theologischer Verlag Zürich, 1971.

Irenaeus of Lyons. *Against Heresies. In* Vol. 9 of *Ante-Nicene Christian Library: Translations of the Writings of the Fathers Down to A.D. 325.* Edited by Alexander Roberts and James Donaldson. Edinburgh: T. and T. Clark, 1867–1872.

Jack, J. W. *The Historic Christ. An Examination of Dr. Robert Eisler's Theory According to the Slavonic Version of Josephus and the Other Sources.* London: James Clarke, 1933.

Jerome. *De Viris Illustribus,* Vol. 23 in *Patrologia Latina.* Edited by J.-P. Migne. Paris, 1844–1886.

Jerome. *Saint Jerome on Illustrious Men.* Translated from the Latin by Thomas P. Halton. *In* Vol. 100 of *The Fathers Of The Church: A New Translation.* Washington, D.C.: The Catholic University of America Press, 1999.

Josephus, Flavius. *Josephus, Complete Works.* Translated by William Whiston, Foreword by William Sanford LaSor. Grand Rapids, Michigan: Kregel Publications, 1981.

Josephus. Translated by H. St. J. Thackeray, Ralph Marcus, and Louis H. Feldman. Loeb Classical Library. Cambridge: Harvard University Press, 1926–1965. 10 vols.

Justin Martyr. *Dialogue of Justin, Philosopher and Martyr, with Trypho, a Jew. In* Vol. 2 of *Ante-Nicene Christian Library: Translations of the writings of the Fathers Down to A.D. 325.* Edited by Alexander Roberts and James Donaldson. Edinburgh: T. and T. Clark, 1867–1872.

Juynboll, Th. Guil. Joh. *Chronicon Samaritanum, Arabice Conscriptum, Cui Titulus Est Liber Josuae.* Leiden: S. & J. Luchtmans, 1848.

Kaiser, W. C., Jr. "Balaam Son of Beor in Light of Deir Alla and Scripture: Saint or Soothsayer?" Pages 95–106 in *"Go to the Land I Will Show You": Studies in Honor of Dwight W. Young.* Edited by Joseph E. Coleson and Victor H. Matthews. Winona Lake, Indiana: Eisenbrauns, 1996.

Klausner, Joseph. *From Jesus to Paul,* translated from the Hebrew by William F. Stinespring. New York: Macmillan, 1944.

Krauss, Samuel. *Das Leben Jesu nach jüdischen Quellen.* Berlin: S. Calvary, 1902.

Lauterbach, Jacob. Z. *Rabbinic Essays.* Cincinnati: Hebrew Union College Press, 1951.

Leisegang, Hans. *Der Heilige Geist. Das Wesen und Werden der mystisch-intuitiven Erkenntnis in der Philosophie und Religion der Griechen.* Vol. 1, part 1. *Die vorchristlichen Anschauungen und Lehren vom ΠΝΕΥΜΑ und der mystisch-intuitiven Erkenntnis.* Leipzig, 1919. Reprinted 1967 by Wissenschaftliche Buchgesellschaft, Darmstadt.

Lightfoot, John. *Horæ Hebraicæ Et Talmudicæ.* Oxford: Oxford University Press. Reprinted as *A Commentary on the New Testament from the Talmud and Hebraica,* with introduction by R. Laird Harris, Peabody, Massachusetts: Hendrickson Publishers, 1989. 4 vols.

Mack, Burton. *A Myth of Innocence: Mark and Christian Origins.* Philadelphia: Fortress Press, 1988.

Mead, G. R. S. *Did Jesus Live 100 B.C.? An Enquiry into the Talmud Jesus Stories, the Toldoth Jeschu, and Some Curious Statements of Epiphanius—Being a Contribution to the Study of Christian Origins*. London: Theosophical Publishing Society, 1903.

Mead, G. R. S. *The Gnostic John the Baptizer. Selections from the Mandæan John-Book*. London: John M. Watkins, 1924.

Meier, John P. "Jesus in Josephus: A Modest Proposal" *The Catholic Biblical Quarterly*, 52 (1990):76–103.

Мешерский, Н. А. История Иудейской Войны Иосифа Флавия в Древнерусском Переводе. Москва-Ленинградъ Издательство Академии Наук СССР, 1958.

Meyer, Marvin, and Richard Smith, eds. *Ancient Christian Magic: Coptic Texts of Ritual Power*. San Francisco, HarperSanFrancisco, 1994.

Moberly, R.W.L. "On Learning to be a True Prophet: the Story of Balaam and his Ass." Pages 1–17 in *New Heaven and New Earth: Prophecy and the Millennium. Essays in Honour of Anthony Gelston*. Edited by P. J. Harland and C. T. R. Hayward. Leiden: Brill, 1999.

Monty Python's Life of Brian. Prod. John Goldstone. Dir. Terry Jones. London: Handmade Films, 1979.

Moore, Michael S. *The Balaam Traditions: Their Character and Development*. Atlanta, Georgia: Scholars Press, 1990.

Mras, Karl. *Eusebius Werke. Achter Band. Die Praeparatio Evangelica. Zweiter Teil, Die Bücher XI bis XV, Register*. Berlin: Akademie-Verlag, 1956.

Neubauer, Adolphe. *La Géographie du Talmud*. Amsterdam: Meridian Publishing Co., 1965.

Neusner, Jacob. *Politics and Theology in Talmudic Babylonia*. Syracuse, New York: Syracuse University Press, 1969.

Neusner, Jacob, *et al*. *The Talmud of the Land of Israel*. Chicago: University of Chicago Press, 1982. 35 vols.

Neusner, Jacob. *The Tosefta: An Introduction*. Atlanta, Georgia: Scholars Press, 1992.

Neusner, Jacob. *The Tosefta. Translated from the Hebrew*. New York, Hoboken: Ktav Publishing House, 1977–1986. 6 vols.

Neusner, Jacob. *Introduction to Rabbinic Literature*. The Anchor Bible Reference Library. New York: Doubleday, 1994.

Newman's Apologia Pro Vita Sua. The Two Versions of 1864 & 1865 Preceded by Newman's and Kingsley's Pamphlets. With an introduction by Wilfrid Ward. Oxford University Press, London: 1913, reprinted 1931.

Nicene and Post-Nicene Fathers, The. Edited by Philip Schaff. 1886–1889. 14 vols. Repr. Grand Rapids: Eerdmans, 1980.

Origen. *Contra Celsum*. Vol. 23 in *Ante-Nicene Christian Library: Translations of the Writings of the Fathers Down to A.D. 325*. Edited by Alexander Roberts and James Donaldson. Edinburgh: T. and T. Clark, 1867–1872.

Origen. *Commentary on John and Commentary on Matthew.* Vol. 25 in *Ante-Nicene Christian Library. Translations of the Writings of the Fathers Down to A.D. 325.* Edited by Allan Menzies. Edinburgh: T. and T. Clark, 1897.

Paine, Thomas. *The Age of Reason. Part Three. Examination of the Prophecies.* Edited and annotated by Frank Zindler. Austin, Texas: American Atheist Press, 1993.

Papias. *Fragments. In* Vol. 9 of *Ante-Nicene Christian Library: Translations of the Writings of the Fathers Down to A.D. 325.* Edited by Alexander Roberts and James Donaldson. Edinburgh: T. and T. Clark, 1867–1872.

Pardo, David Samuel ben Jacob. *Sefer Hasde David.* (in Hebrew) 10 vols. Jerusalem: H. Vagshal, 1994.

Patrologia Græca. Edited by J.-P. Migne. 162 vols. Paris. 1857–1886.

Patrologia Latina. Edited by J.-P. Migne. 217 vols. Paris, 1844–1864.

Philo Judaeus. *The Works of Philo, Complete and Unabridged.* rev. ed. Translated from the Greek by C. D. Yonge. Peabody, Massachusetts: Hendrickson.

Photius of Constantinople. *Myriobiblon Sive Bibliotheca.* Vols. 103–104 in *Patrologia Græca.* Edited by J.-P. Migne. Paris, 1857–1886.

Pines, Shlomo. *An Arabic Version of the Testimonium Flavianum and its Implications.* The Israel Academy of Sciences and Humanities. Jerusalem, 1971.

Pines, Shlomo. "The Jewish Christians of the Early Centuries of Christianity According to a New Source," *Proceedings of the Israel Academy of Sciences and Humanities* 2 (1968):237–310.

Porter, Stanley E. *The Criteria for Authenticity in Historical-Jesus Research: Previous Discussion and New Proposals,* Journal for the Study of the New Testament Supplement Series 181, Sheffield: Sheffield Academic Press, 2000.

Price, Robert M. *Deconstructing Jesus.* Amherst, New York: Prometheus Books, 2000.

Rappoport, Angelo S. *Ancient Israel: Myths and Legends.* New York: Bonanza Books, 1987. 3 vols.

Remsburg, John E(leazer). *The Christ: A Critical Review and Analysis of the Evidences of His Existence.* New York: The Truth Seeker Company, 1909.

Reuchlin, Abelard. The True Authorship of the New Testament. Kent, Washington: Abelard Reuchlin Foundation, 1979, 1986.

Saglio, M. Edmond. *Dictionnaire Des Antiquités Grecques Et Romaines d'Après Les Textes Et Les Monuments.* Vol. 4. Paris: Librairie Hachette Et Cie, 1918.

Salomonsen, Børge. *Die Tosefta. Seder IV: Nezikin. 3: Sanhedrin–Makkot.* Stuttgart: Verlag W. Kohlhammer, 1976.

Schaff, Philip. Saint Chrysostom: *Homilies on the Gospel of St. John and The Epistle To The Hebrews.* A Select Library of the Nicene and Post-Nicene Fathers of the Christian Church. Vol. 14. Reprinted Grand Rapids, Michigan: Wm. B. Eerdmans, 1983.

Schlichting, Günter. *Ein jüdisches Leben Jesu: Die verschollene Toledot-Jeschu-Fassung Tam û-mû'âd. Einleitung, Text, Übersetzung, Kommentar, Motivsynopse, Bibliographie.* Tübingen: J. C. B. Mohr (Paul Siebeck), 1982.

Schneemelcher, Wilhelm. *New Testament Apocrypha.* Rev. ed. English translation by R. McL. Wilson. Louisville, Kentucky: Westminster/John Knox Press. 1989–1990. 2 vols.

Schonfield, Hugh J. *According to the Hebrews.* London: Duckworth, 1937.

Schwab, Moïse. *Le Talmud De Jérusalem.* Paris: Editions G.-P. Maisonneuve, 1960. 6 vols.

A Select Library of Nicene and Post-Nicene Fathers of the Christian Church. Second series. Translated into English with prolegomena and explanatory notes. Edited by Philip Schaff and Henry Wace. New York: The Christian Literature Company, 1890–1900. 14 vols.

Smith, Morton. *Jesus the Magician.* San Francisco: Harper & Row, 1978.

Steinsaltz, Adin. *The Talmud: The Steinsaltz Edition. A Reference Guide.* New York: Random House, 1989.

Strack, Hermann L. *Introduction to the Talmud and Midrash.* Philadelphia: The Jewish Publication Society of America, 1931.

Suetonius, Gaius. *The Lives of the Cæsars* and *The Lives of Illustrious Men.* Translated by J. C. Rolfe. Loeb Classical Library. Cambridge: Harvard University Press, 1920. 2 vols.

Swanson, Reuben, ed. *New Testament Greek Manuscripts: Variant Readings Arranged in Horizontal Lines Against Codex Vaticanus. Luke.* Foreword by Bruce Metzger. Sheffield: Scheffield Academic Press, 1995.

Tacitus, Publius Cornelius. *The Histories* and *The Annals.* Translated by C. H. Moore and John Jackson. Loeb Classical Library. Cambridge: Harvard University Press, 1937–1981. 5 vols.

Tatum, W. Barnes. *John the Baptist and Jesus. A Report of the Jesus Seminar.* Sonoma, California: Polebridge Press, 1994.

Taylor, J. Glen. *Yahweh and the Sun: Biblical and Archaeological Evidence for Sun Worship in Ancient Israel.* Sheffield: JSOT Press, 1993.

Taylor, Robert. *The Diegesis; Being a Discovery of the Origin, Evidences, and Early History of Christianity, Never Yet Before or Elsewhere So Fully and Faithfully Set Forth.* Boston: Abner Kneeland, 1834.

Tertullian. *Apology – De Spectaculis.* Translated with an introduction by T. R. Glover. Loeb Classical Library. Cambridge: Harvard University Press, 1984.

Tertullian. *In* Vols. 7, 11, 15, and 18 of *Ante-Nicene Christian Library: Translations of the Writings of the Fathers Down to A.D. 325.* Edited by Alexander Roberts and James Donaldson. Edinburgh: T. and T. Clark, 1867–1872.

Thompson, Edward Maunde. *An Introduction to Greek and Latin Palaeography.* Oxford: Clarendon Press, 1912.

Ulansey, David. *The Origins of the Mithraic Mysteries: Cosmology and Salvation in the Ancient World.* New York: Oxford University Press, 1989.

Vogler, Werner. *Jüdische Jesusinterpretationen in christlicher Sicht.* Weimar: Hermann Böhlaus Nachfolger, 1988.

Voigt, Georg. *Die Wiederbelebung Des Classischen Altertums, oder Das Erste Jahrhundert Des Humanismus,* 4th ed., 1895, 2 vols. (reprinted Berlin: Walter de Gruyter, 1960).

Wellhausen, Julius. *Prolegomena to the History of Ancient Israel,* with preface by W. Robertson Smith. New York: The Meridian Library, 1957.

Wellhausen, Julius. "Der arabische Josippus," *Abhandlungen der Königlichen Gesellschaft der Wissenschaften zu Göttingen. Philologisch-Historische Klasse.* Neue Folge. Band I. No. 4. Aus den Jahren 1896–1897. Berlin: Weidmannsche Buchhandlung, 1897.

Wells, G. A. *The Historical Evidence for Jesus.* Buffalo, New York: Prometheus Books, 1982.

Wheless, Joseph. *Forgery in Christianity: A Documented Record of the Foundations of the Christian Religion.* Moscow, Idaho: Psychiana, 1930. Reprinted 1999, Montana: Kessinger Publishing Co.

Whiston, William. *Josephus: Complete Works.* Grand Rapids: Kregel Publications, 1981.

Wilson, N. G. *Photius, The Bibliotheca. A Selection.* Translated with notes. London: Duckworth, 1994.

Wise, Michael, Martin Abegg, Jr., and Edward Cook. *The Dead Sea Scrolls: A New Translation.* HarperSanFrancisco, 1996.

Wissowa, Georg. "Aion," in: *Paulys Real-Encyclopädie der Classischen Altertumswissenschaft.* Rev. ed., Stuttgart: J.B. Metzlerscher Verlag, 1894.

Wünsche, August. *Der Midrasch Kohelet. In* Vol. 1 of *Bibliotheca Rabbinica: Eine Sammlung Alter Midraschim.* Hildesheim: Georg Olms Verlagsbuchhandlung, 1967. 4 vols.

Zeitlin, Irving M. *Jesus and the Judaism of His Time.* Cambridge: Polity Press, 1988.

Zuckermandel, Moses Samuel. *Tosefta ʿal pi kitve yad Erfurt u-Vinah.* (In Hebrew.) Jerusalem: Sifre Vahrman, 1963.

SCRIPTURE INDEX

New Testament

Palestinian Talmud

Babylonian Talmud

Midrash

Qur'an

SUBJECT INDEX

A

'Abd al-Jabbar, Catholic proof-text absent from Matthew quotation by, 447; note on Christian Nativity of Time festival, 339*f*

Aaron, disparaged by Pentateuchal E source, 201; Moses inferior to in P source, 201; myth of Moses and, 161

Aaronid priesthood, as source of genocide story in Num 31, 205

Abahu, Rabbi, on claims of going to heaven, 168*f*

Abin, Rabbi, on Elisha and Gehazi, 183

Absalom, Ahithophel's advice to, 131; alliance with Ahithophel, 180

According to the Hebrews, of Hugh J. Schonfield, 330

Acrostic, second-order, in *Sibylline Oracles*, 301, 313

Acts of Peter, 315*ff*; Docetism in, 322; magical flight of Simon Magus in, 434; quasi-Gnostic origins of, 318; *Quo Vadis?* in, 316; *Toldoth Minor* similarities to, 321; William Schneemelcher dating of, 315

Acts of the Apostles, contradictory stories of Paul's conversion, 17*f*; mentions Bernice, niece-in-law of Philo, 16; Nazarene version of, 326; speeches in not authentic, 17*f*; St. Paul's conversion, 135; unknown to Arnobius, 302

Acts of the Apostles (Ebionite), Epiphanius on, 330

Adiabene, Queen Helena of, Queen Alexandra confused with, 380

Adonai, as name of power, 295

Adulteress, so-and-so born to, 246

Adultery, of Miriam, 238; of mother of Yeshu, 288

Aelia Capitolina, Jews expelled from, 401

Aerial contest. *See* Contest, aerial.

Africa, North, knowledge of *Toldoth Yeshu* in, 284; Latin Christianity beginning in, 301

Against Celsus (Origen), 4

Against Celsus. See also *Contra Celsum.*

Agobard, Archbishop of Lyons, *Epistola... de Judaicis Superstitionibus* of, 277; G. R. S. Mead's translation of, 273; quotes *Toldoth Yeshu*, 323; *Toldoth* text of, 273

Agrippa, St. Peter flees Rome because of, 316

Ahab, 132; excluded from world to come, 172; not identified with Christian emperor, 261

Ahaz, excluded from world to come, 172, 174

Ahithophel, 127, 131; alliance with Absalom, 180; an apostle in Mishnah?, 130; as code for Jesus, 172, 174; as code for Peter, 178; barred from world to come, 229; David asks him to stop priests from flying, 181; etymology of name, 131; in Palestinian Talmud, 177; mighty in Torah learning, 180; not an apostle, 128; not a nickname for Jesus, 261; stops up waters of the deep, 182; suicide by hanging of, 180; treason against David, 180

E

Goths, in fall of Rome, 301

Gould, Rev. S. Baring, *The Lost and Hostile Gospels*, 356

Governor, Roman title, 18

Great Church, Babylonian rabbis had little contact with, 239

Greene, John T., *Balaam and His Interpreters*, 199*ff*, 210; on evolution of Balaam story, 122; on genocide story in Num 31, 205; on priesthoods battling for power, 202

Gregontius, cited by Madalyn Murray O'Hair, 354

Guards, for tomb of Jesus, 281

H

h, no such letter in Greek, 81-82

Hackett, Jo Ann, on Balaam inscription, 197

Hadrian, builds Aelia Capitolina on ruins of Jerusalem, 401

Haggadah, 107

Hairdresser, Miriam as, 149, 237*f*, 240*f*, 243*f*

Halakhah, 107

Halton, Thomas P., translation of Jerome, 24

Haman, crucifixion of, 342; tried to exterminate the Jews, 342

Hananiah, Yehoshua ben, Rabbi, 115

Hanging, Ahithophel's suicide by, 180; of Jesus and Ben Stada, 157; of Jesus, 158, 192, 254*f*, 412*ff*; of Jesus on a tree, 277; of Judas, explosive disembowelment vs., 180*f*; of Yeshu, 238*f*; of Yeshu on cabbage stalk, 284, 440*f*

Hanina, Rabbi, 180; and age of Balaam, 126, 189

Harlot, hire of, 234; son of, Tertullian comments on, 283

Harlots, for seduction of Israelites, 225

Harnack, Adolf von, on translating the *Altercatio Simonis*, 343

Healing, in name of Yeshua' ben Pandira, not in Palestinian Talmud, 163; magical, 145*f*

Heaven, going up to, 168

Hebrew Bible, no mention of Nazareth, 2

Hegesippus, mentioned, 78

Helena, disciple of John the Baptist, 314

Helena, etymology of name, 380

Helena, Queen, identity of, 417; of Adiabene, Queen Alexandra confused with, 380; wife of King Jannaeus, 380*f*

Helene, Queen, Queen Alexandra as, 363; Queen Salome (Alexandra) as, 428; bids Yeshu to perform miracles, 294

Hell, Jesus in, 124

Herald, announces stoning of Yeshu, 191; precedes Yeshu, 238

Heresy, R. Eliezer arrested for, 141

Heretic, a certain, on age of Balaam, 189

Herford, R. Travers, *Christianity in Talmud and Midrash*, 263-264; claimed Phineas the Robber was variant of Pontius Pilate, 190; on 'bastard,' 116-117; on Alfred Edersheim, 143; on analysis of ancient rabbinical writings, 100; on covert allusion to Jesus in b. Sanh. 106a, 228; on Gehazi as St. Paul, 134; on going to heaven passage in Palestinian Talmud, 168; on Jesus and Apostles in Mishnah and Palestinian Talmud, 177*ff*; on Pappos ben Jehudah as contemporary of R. Aqiba, 236; on Rabbi Meir, 159; on Rabbi Shim'on ben 'Azzai, 115; on snake-bite story, 145; on the Egyptian false prophet, 154; on Tosefta, 140; on trial of five disciples, 257; scholarly

Lord, meaning of term, 82

Lost and Hostile Gospels, The, by Rev. S. Baring Gould, 356

Lucanus, would likely have commented on "The Christ," 13*f*

Lucian of Samosata, *De Morte Peregrini* of, in dating *Toldoth Yeshu*, 328

Lucian, would likely have commented on "The Christ," 13*f*

Lucifer, ascending to heaven claim of, 170

Lucius, says parts of Philo actually written 3rd century CE, 22

Luke, Gospel of, virgin birth not completely explicit in, 289

Luke-Acts, Hebrew Gospel-Acts a response to canonical, according to Benjamin Bacon, 330

Lunar religion, rabbinism as, 314

Luther, Martin, anti-Semitism of, 269; *Vom Schem Hamphoras und vom Geschlecht Christi* of, 269, 277

Lydda, as site of death of Ben Stada, 154; Ben Stada at, 166*f*; Ben Stada hanged at, 237*f*; tricking and stoning of Ben Stada at, 156, 157

Lying, Lies. *See* **Forgery or Fraud.**

M

Ma'ase Thola', 270; Samuel Friedrich Brenz on, 270; Yeshu falls into cesspit in, 387

Ma'ase Yeshu, equated with *Toldoth* by G.B. de Rossi, 357

Ma'ase Yeshu ha-Notzri, 270

Mack, Burton, early church similar to fraternal supper-club, 23

Madalyn Murray O'Hair, introduction to *Sepher Toldoth Yeshu*, 268

Magadan, not Magdala, 242

Magdala, fictional New Testament site, 242

Magdalene, etymology of name, 411; Mary, and Miriam the hairdresser, 241

Magi, claimed by Origen to have words of power, 295

Magic, bringing from Egypt, 321; Celsus' opinion on, 295; Jesus said to practice it, 250; Justin Martyr's belief in, 416; learned in Egypt, 291; practiced by Jesus, 415*f*; practiced by Jesus, *Clementine Recognitions* allusion to, 416; Simon Magus learns in Egypt, 315; usage in prayer, 429

Magic. *See also* **Miracles.**

Magician, Ben Stada as, 155; healing by, 145

Magus, Simon. *See* **Simon Magus.**

Maimonides, Moses [1135–1204], *Epistle to Yemen* of, 271; *mamzer bar niddah* reading known to, 271

Male prostitute, price of, 234

Mamzer (bastard), 113–117; Jesus as, 245*ff*; Jesus called a, 271

Mamzer ben ha-niddah, Yeshu as, 284

Mamzerin, children of *minim* as, 142

Man, Son of, *See* **Son of Man.**

Man of Sin, The, (Dead Sea Scrolls), not a reference to Paul, 9

Manasseh, 132; burns his food according to the *Aruch*, 252; excluded from world to come, 172; not identified with Christian emperor, 261; pursues Isaiah, 174; slays Isaiah, 246

Mandaean religion, has a different John the Baptist, 97

Mandaeans, writings of don't prove reality of John the Baptist, 88

Mantics, 212